S0-BZG-284

Cape Cod, Nantucket & Martha's Vineyard

2004

by Laura M. Reckford

WILEY

Wiley Publishing, Inc.

About the Author

Laura M. Reckford is a writer and editor living on Cape Cod. Formerly the managing editor of *Cape Cod Life Magazine,* she has also been on the editorial staff of *Good Housekeeping* magazine and *Entertainment Weekly.* She is currently a reporter for the *Falmouth Enterprise* newspaper. She is also co-author of *France For Dummies* (published by Wiley Publishing, Inc).

Published by:

Wiley Publishing, Inc.

111 River St.
Hoboken, NJ 07030-5744

ISBN 0-7645-4281-8

Editor: Christina Summers
Production Editor: Donna Wright
Cartographer: John Decamillis
Photo Editor: Richard Fox
Production by Wiley Indianapolis Composition Services

For information on our other products and services or to obtain technical support, please contact our Customer Care Department within the U.S. at 800/762-2974, outside the U.S. at 317/572-3993 or fax 317/572-4002.

Wiley also publishes its books in a variety of electronic formats. Some content that appears in print may not be available in electronic formats.

Manufactured in the United States of America

5 4 3 2 1

Contents

List of Maps

An Invitation to the Reader

In researching this book, we discovered many wonderful places—hotels, restaurants, shops, and more. We're sure you'll find others. Please tell us about them, so we can share the information with your fellow travelers in upcoming editions. If you were disappointed with a recommendation, we'd love to know that, too. Please write to:

Frommer's Cape Cod, Nantucket & Martha's Vineyard 2004
Wiley Publishing, Inc. • 111 River St. • Hoboken, NJ 07030-5744

An Additional Note

Please be advised that travel information is subject to change at any time—and this is especially true of prices. We therefore suggest that you write or call ahead for confirmation when making your travel plans. The authors, editors, and publisher cannot be held responsible for the experiences of readers while traveling. Your safety is important to us, however, so we encourage you to stay alert and be aware of your surroundings. Keep a close eye on cameras, purses, and wallets, all favorite targets of thieves and pickpockets.

Other Great Guides for Your Trip:

Frommer's Portable Nantucket & Martha's Vineyard
Frommer's New England
Frommer's USA

Frommer's Star Ratings, Icons & Abbreviations

Every hotel, restaurant, and attraction listing in this guide has been ranked for quality, value, service, amenities, and special features using a **star-rating system.** In country, state, and regional guides, we also rate towns and regions to help you narrow down your choices and budget your time accordingly. Hotels and restaurants are rated on a scale of zero (recommended) to three stars (exceptional). Attractions, shopping, nightlife, towns, and regions are rated according to the following scale: zero stars (recommended), one star (highly recommended), two stars (very highly recommended), and three stars (must-see).

In addition to the star-rating system, we also use **seven feature icons** that point you to the great deals, in-the-know advice, and unique experiences that separate travelers from tourists. Throughout the book, look for:

Finds	Special finds—those places only insiders know about
Fun Fact	Fun facts—details that make travelers more informed and their trips more fun
Kids	Best bets for kids and advice for the whole family
Moments	Special moments—those experiences that memories are made of
Overrated	Places or experiences not worth your time or money
Tips	Insider tips—great ways to save time and money
Value	Great values—where to get the best deals

The following **abbreviations** are used for credit cards:

AE	American Express	DISC	Discover	V	Visa
DC	Diners Club	MC	MasterCard		

Frommers.com

Now that you have the guidebook to a great trip, visit our website at **www.frommers.com** for travel information on more than 3,000 destinations. With features updated regularly, we give you instant access to the most current trip-planning information available. At Frommers.com, you'll also find the best prices on airfares, accommodations, and car rentals—and you can even book travel online through our travel booking partners. At Frommers.com, you'll also find the following:

- Online updates to our most popular guidebooks
- Vacation sweepstakes and contest giveaways
- Newsletter highlighting the hottest travel trends
- Online travel message boards with featured travel discussions

What's New in Cape Cod, Nantucket & Martha's Vineyard

The following are highlights of what's new in the Cape and Islands.

GETTING AROUND For those going to **Martha's Vineyard**, there is one and possibly two new options. New in 2003, the fast ferry from Rhode Island to Oak Bluffs makes the trip in 90 minutes and avoids Cape Cod traffic jams. The **Vineyard Fast Ferry Company** (© 401/295-4040; www.vineyardfastferry.com) runs a seasonal high-speed catamaran called *Millennium* that leaves from Quonset Point in North Kingston. The round-trip cost is $48 for adults and $36 for children.

Another new option for Vineyard vacationers is a high-speed ferry from New Bedford to the island. Schedule and fare details had not yet been worked out as of press time, but you can contact the **Steamship Authority** (© 508/477-8600 or www.steamship authority.com) for information.

Also new this year for the **Steamship Authority,** passengers can now buy their tickets online at the company's new updated website. No more waiting on hold for an eternity for ferry tickets if you log onto **www.steamship authority.com**. See p. 35.

THE UPPER CAPE Falmouth has several new restaurants on the scene, and one is surely one of the best on the Cape. **Phusion Grille** (Woods Hole; © 508/457-3100) overlooking Eel Pond on Water Street, offers exquisite, creative fare and some of the best service in town. This is New American cuisine with decidedly Asian influences.

Whether you opt for the pan-seared scallop and lobster cakes or the steak au poivre with wasabi horseradish cream sauce, you'll be overwhelmed with satisfaction. Also new in recent years are **RooBar** (© 508/548-8600) and **La Cucina Sul Mar** (© 508/548-5600), both on Main Street, making Falmouth's central district a destination for dinner. Also new on the restaurant scene is a new location for **Pesci's** (100 Davis Straits, a few blocks east of Main Street; © 508/495-5553), a perfect little Italian restaurant that is one of Falmouth's best kept secrets. See "Where to Dine" under "Falmouth" in chapter 4.

The **Heritage Museum and Gardens** in Sandwich (© 508/888-3300) is now a year-round attraction. The museum is open Friday through Wednesday in season and Tuesday through Sunday in off season. Attractions here include the antique car collection, Native American exhibits, antique carousel (available for unlimited rides), and new this year, an exhibit about the history of the Cape Cod Baseball League.

THE MID CAPE Bill Putman has added more red sports cars to his collection at the **Simmons Homestead Inn** in Hyannisport (© 800/637-1649 or 508/778-4999) and has turned the collection into a "museum." There are more than 55 cars now. Curious tourists who want to ogle the cars pay $5 admission. Those who stay at the inn also get to revel in the good company of the innkeeper. See p. 109.

THE LOWER CAPE The Cape Cod Museum of Natural History (© **508/896-3867**) in Brewster, as a way to deal with the downturn in the economy, has decided to stay open seasonally only. The museum will close October through April.

THE OUTER CAPE Major renovation work on the **Salt Pond Visitor Center** (© **508/255-3421**) in Eastham is expected to be completed in the late spring of 2004. The visitor center will be closed during the renovation, but visitors will still be able to walk the trails and obtain maps at a temporary visitor booth. They can also travel up to Provincetown to the Province Lands Visitors Center (© **508/487-1256**), which has similar displays and programs.

Provincetown's Summer Shuttle service through town and to the beaches is the most popular way to get around this small but congested community. The frequency of the buses has been increased for 2004. Visitors coming from Boston can take the ferry to Provincetown and easily get around the area without a car. For more information call © **508/432-3400.**

The 40-room **Crowne Pointe Historic Inn** (© **877/CROWNE1** or 508/487-6767) at 82 Bradford St. is a newly restored property perched high on Bradford Street and the latest entry in Provincetown's high-end lodging sweepstakes. The inn and grounds are exquisitely maintained with deluxe common areas and attractive gardens. Rooms are spacious, and some of the deluxe rooms and suites have fireplaces, wet bars, and whirlpool spas. There is also a heated outdoor pool and a 10-person outdoor spa. See p. 208.

NANTUCKET The **Whaling Museum** (13 Broad St., Nantucket; © **508/228-1894**), one of the region's top attractions, is undergoing a major renovation this year. The renovation should be completed by the fall of 2004. Some exhibits will be displayed at the Friends Meeting House (© **508/228-1894**), an 1838 historic property at 7 Fair St., during the renovation. See p. 230.

The newest Nantucket inn, **The Veranda House** on 3 Step Lane (© **508/228-0695;** www.theveranda house.com) is an example of a superb renovation of a historic building. The owners have made this 20-room inn into a stylish version of a classic guesthouse. The inn is located in a quiet neighborhood, a short walk from the center of town. It is perched on a hill, so rooms on the third floor have distant harbor views. Three wrap-around verandas surround the inn on its three floors. The inn's entire property is covered by a wireless Internet service. Rates through the year are $100 to $250 for standard rooms and $250 to $350 for suites.

MARTHA'S VINEYARD After a fire destroyed the 200-year-old Tisbury Inn in Vineyard Haven in 2001, the fate of the property was uncertain. It reopened this year as the **Mansion House Inn** (9 Main St., Vineyard Haven; © **800/332-4112** or 508/693-2200), a luxury 32-room inn in the center of Vineyard Haven. The three-story building is once again a community hub, with a restaurant, health club, and shops. Many of the rooms have kitchenettes, plasma-screen televisions, and extra-large bathtubs. Some have harbor views. All the rooms are equipped with high-speed Internet service. One of the most unique features of the inn is the 75-foot mineral spring (no chlorine) swimming pool in the health club in the inn's basement. **Zephrus** (© **508/693-3416**), the hotel's restaurant, is open to the public for lunch and dinner, and also supplies room service for guests until late in the evening. See p. 288.

The Best of Cape Cod, Nantucket & Martha's Vineyard

Only 70 miles long, Cape Cod is a curling peninsula that encompasses hundreds of miles of beaches and more freshwater ponds than there are days in the year. The ocean's many moods rule this thin spit of land, and in summer, it has a very sunny disposition indeed. And little wonder. The "arm" of the Cape has beckoned wayfarers since precolonial days. More than 17 million visitors flock from around the world to enjoy nature's non-stop carnival, a combination of torrid sun and cool, salty air.

On the Cape, days have a way of unfurling aimlessly but pleasantly, with a round of inviolable rituals. First and foremost is a long, restful stint at the beach (you can opt for either the warmer, gently lapping waters of the bay or the pounding Atlantic surf). The beach is generally followed by a stroll through the shops of the nearest town and an obligatory ice-cream stop. After a desalinating shower and perhaps a nap (the pristine air has a way of inspiring impromptu snoozes), it's time for a fabulous dinner. There are few experiences quite so blissful as sitting at a picnic table overlooking a bustling harbor and feasting on a just-caught, butter-dripping, boiled lobster.

Be forewarned, however, that the Cape can be a bit too popular at full swing. Although it's hard to fathom why the settlers waited nearly 3 centuries to go splashing in the surf, ever since the Victorians donned their bathing costumes there's been no stopping the waves of sun-, sand-, and sea-worshippers who religiously pour onto this peninsula and the Islands beyond every summer.

Experienced travelers are beginning to discover the subtler appeal of the off season, when the population—and prices—plummet. For some, the prospect of sunbathing with the midsummer crowds on sizzling sand can't hold a candle to the chance to take long, solitary strolls on a windswept beach, with only the gulls as company. Come Labor Day (or Columbus Day, for stragglers) the crowds clear out, and the whole place hibernates until Memorial Day weekend, the official start of "the season." It's in this downtime that you're most likely to experience the "real" Cape. For some, it may take a little resourcefulness to see the beauty in the wintry, shuttered landscape (even the Pilgrims, who forsook this spot for Plymouth, didn't have quite the necessary mettle), but the people who do stick around are an interesting, independent-minded lot worth getting to know.

As alluring as it is on the surface, the region becomes all the more so the more you learn about it. One visit is likely to prompt a follow-up. Although you can see all of the Cape, and the Islands as well, in a matter of days, you could spend a lifetime exploring its many facets and still just begin to take it all in. Early Pilgrims saw in this isolated spot the opportunity for religious freedom, whaling merchants the watery road to riches, and artists the path to capturing the brilliance of nature's palette. Whatever the incursions of commercialism and overdevelopment, the land is suffused with spirit, and it attracts seekers still.

Narrowing down possible "bests" is a tough call, even for a native of the region. The selections in this chapter are intended merely as an introduction to some of the highlights. They're listed from closest to farthest along the Cape, followed by the Islands. A great many other outstanding resorts, hotels, inns, attractions, and destinations are described in the pages of this book. Once you start wandering, you're sure to discover bests of your own.

Basic contact information is given for the enterprises listed below. You'll find more information by referring to the appropriate chapters of the book.

1 The Best Beaches

It is difficult to identify the best beaches without specifying for whom: fearless surfers or timid toddlers, party types or incurable recluses? The bayside and sound beaches, for instance, tend to be much more placid than those on the ocean, and thus preferable for little ones who only plan to splash and muck about.

- **Sandy Neck:** This relatively unpopulated, 6-mile barrier beach, extending from the eastern edge of Sandwich to shelter Barnstable Harbor, features pretty little dunes seldom seen on the bayside. Hike in far enough (but avoid the nests of piping plovers), and you're sure to find a secluded spot. Adventurous types can even camp overnight with permission (© **508/362-8300**). See "Beaches & Recreational Pursuits" under "Sandwich" in chapter 4.

- **Falmouth Heights:** On a clear day, you can see Martha's Vineyard from this hip beach in Falmouth's most picturesque neighborhood. Grand turn-of-the-20th-century homes compete for the view with newer motels, and the beach fills up with families throughout the day. Off season, this beach is virtually deserted, perfect for romantic arm-in-arm strolling. See "Falmouth" in chapter 4.

- **Nauset:** Located along the outer "elbow" of the Cape, this barrier beach descends all the way from East Orleans to a point parallel to Chatham—about 9 miles in all, each mile increasingly deserted. The entry point, however, is a body squeeze: It's here that the young crowd convenes to strut their stuff. Administered by the town of Orleans, but still considered part of the Cape Cod National Seashore, Nauset Beach has paid parking, restrooms, and a snack bar. See "Beaches & Recreational Pursuits," under "Orleans," in chapter 6.

- **Cahoon Hollow:** Spectacular Cahoon Hollow Beach on the rough, frigid Atlantic Ocean is a winding trek down a 75-foot dune. See "Beaches & Recreational Pursuits" under "Wellfleet" in chapter 7. One Wellfleet favorite, which boasts a most unusual music club housed in an 1897 lifesaving station is called **The Beachcomber**—referred to fondly as the 'Comber, or better yet, 'Coma (© **508/349-6055**). Twenty-somethings are the primary patrons, but lingering families also enjoy the reggae and rock that starts to leak out late in the afternoon on summer weekends. See p. 192.

- **Race Point:** Free of the sexual politics that predominate the beaches closer to Provincetown (certain sections of Herring Cove Beach are tacitly reserved for gays or for lesbians), Race Point—another

Cape Cod National Seashore (CCNS) beach-cum–visitor center (☎ **508/487-1256**) at the northernmost tip of the Cape—is strictly nondenominational. Even whales are welcome—they can often be spotted with the bare eye, surging toward Stellwagen Bank. See "Beaches & Recreational Pursuits," under "Provincetown," in chapter 7.

- **Jetties Beach:** Nantucket's beaches as a rule have the best amenities of any beaches in the region; most have restrooms, showers, lifeguards, and food concessions. For families and active types, Jetties Beach (just a half mile from the center of town) can't be beat. There are boat and windsurfing rentals,

tennis courts, volleyball nets, a playground, and great fishing (off the eponymous jetties). It's also scenic (those jetties again) with calm, warm water. See "Beaches & Recreational Pursuits" in chapter 8.

- **Aquinnah Beach** (formerly **Gay Head**) (Martha's Vineyard): These landmark bluffs on the western extremity of Martha's Vineyard (call the **chamber of commerce** at ☎ 508/693-0085 for directions) are threatened with erosion, so it's no longer politically correct to engage in multicolored mud baths, as hippies once did. Still, it's an incredibly scenic place to swim—come early to beat the crowds. See "Beaches & Recreational Pursuits" in chapter 9.

2 The Best Bike Routes

Blessed with many gently rolling hills, the Cape and Islands are custom-made for a bike trek—whether as a way to get to the beach or as an outing unto itself.

- **Cape Cod Canal:** On this 14-mile loop maintained by the **U.S. Army Corps of Engineers** (☎ **508/ 759-5991**), you can race alongside the varied craft taking shortcuts through the world's widest sea-level canal. See "Beaches & Recreational Pursuits" under "Sandwich" in chapter 4.

- **Shining Sea Bicycle Path** (☎ **508/548-8500**): Connecting Falmouth to Woods Hole by way of the shore and the picturesque Nobska Lighthouse, this 3½-mile path lets you dash to the ferry or dally at the beach of your choice. See "Beaches & Recreational Pursuits" under "Falmouth" in chapter 4.

- **Cape Cod Rail Trail** (☎ **508/ 896-3491**): Reclaimed by the Rails-to-Trails Conservancy, this paved railroad bed currently stretches some 25 miles from South Dennis all the way to Wellfleet,

with innumerable detours that beckon en route. See chapters 5 through 7.

- **Province Lands Trail** (☎ **508/ 487-1256**): Offering by far the most rigorous workout, this 7-mile network swoops among the parabolic dunes and stunted forests at the very tip of the Cape. Take your time enjoying this somewhat spooky moonscape. Be sure to stop off at Race Point Beach for a bracing dip, and at the **Province Lands Visitor Center** (☎ **508/ 487-1256**) as well. See "Beaches & Recreational Pursuits" under "Provincetown" in chapter 7.

- **Nantucket Town to Madaket** (☎ **508/228-1700**): Only 3 miles wide and 14 miles long, Nantucket is a snap to cover by bike. The 6-mile Madaket path crosses undulating moors to reach a beach with boisterous surf. See "Beaches & Recreational Pursuits" in chapter 8.

- **Nantucket Town to Surfside** (☎ **508/228-1700**): An easy, flat few miles from town, Surfside Beach is a perfect mini-excursion

Cape Cod

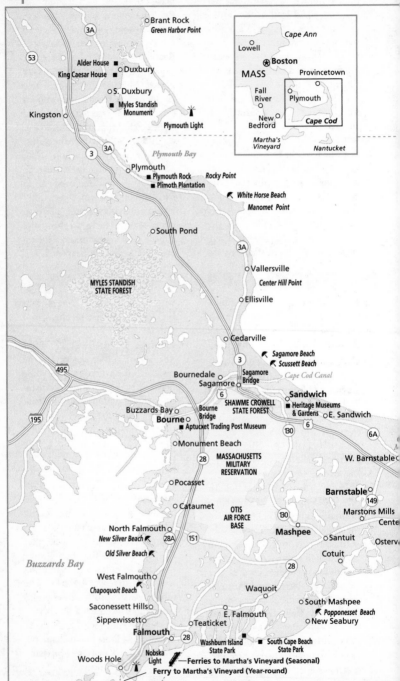

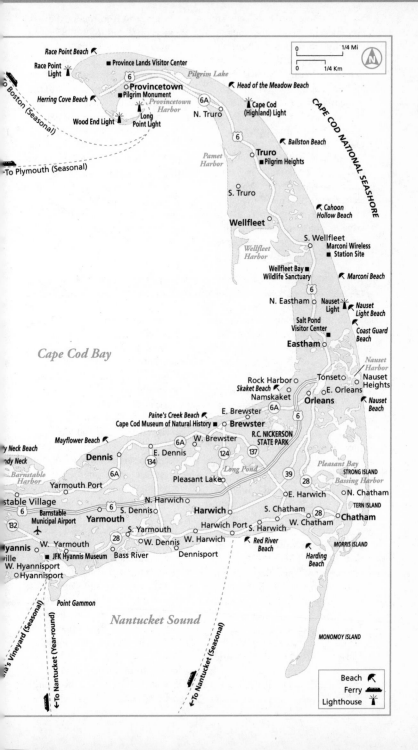

To Boston (Seasonal)

Race Point Beach ☈

Race Point Light ☼

■ Province Lands Visitor Center

Pilgrim Lake

☈ Head of the Meadow Beach

Herring Cove Beach ☈

Provincetown
■ Pilgrim Monument

Provincetown Harbor

6A

N. Truro

☼ Cape Cod (Highland) Light

CAPE COD NATIONAL SEASHORE

Wood End Light ☼

Long Point Light ☼

To Plymouth (Seasonal)

6

Pamet Harbor

Truro
■ Pilgrim Heights

☈ Ballston Beach

S. Truro

Wellfleet ○

☈ Cahoon Hollow Beach

S. Wellfleet
Marconi Wireless ■ Station Site

Wellfleet Harbor

Wellfleet Bay ■ Wildlife Sanctuary

☈ Marconi Beach

6

N. Eastham ○ Nauset ☼ Light

☈ Nauset Light Beach

Salt Pond Visitor Center ■

☈ Coast Guard Beach

Eastham ○

Cape Cod Bay

Nauset Harbor

Rock Harbor ○ Tonset ○

Nauset Heights

Skaket Beach ☈ ○ E. Orleans

Namskaket

Orleans ○

☈ Nauset Beach

6A

Paine's Creek Beach ☈
Cape Cod Museum of Natural History ■ E. Brewster ○

Brewster ○

6

Mayflower Beach ☈

W. Brewster ○

R.C. NICKERSON STATE PARK

y Neck Beach

6A

ndy Neck

Dennis ○ E. Dennis ○

Pleasant Bay

STRONG ISLAND

Bassing Harbor

Barnstable Harbor

6A

134

124

Long Pond

137

Yarmouth Port ○

Pleasant Lake ○

39

28

E. Harwich ○ ○ N. Chatham

stable Village

6

Barnstable Municipal Airport

6

N. Harwich ○

S. Dennis ○

Harwich ○

S. Chatham ○

TERN ISLAND

28

○ Chatham

Yarmouth

S. Yarmouth ○

Harwich Port ○ S. Harwich ○ W. Chatham ○

132

yannis

28

W. Yarmouth ○ ○ W. Dennis W. Harwich ○

MORRIS ISLAND

■ JFK Hyannis Museum

Bass River

Dennisport

☈ Red River Beach

ville

W. Hyannisport ○

○ Hyannisport

Harding Beach ☈

Point Gammon

Nantucket Sound

MONOMOY ISLAND

a's Vineyard (Seasonal)

To Nantucket (Year-round)

To Nantucket (Seasonal)

0 ——— 1/4 Mi
0 ——— 1/4 Km

N

Beach ☈
Ferry ⛴
Lighthouse ☼

for the whole family. There are even benches along the route if you'd like to stop and admire the scrub pine and beach plums. When you return to town, pause at Brant Point to watch the yachts maneuver in and out of Nantucket Harbor. See "Beaches & Recreational Pursuits" in chapter 8.

- **Oak Bluffs to Edgartown** (Martha's Vineyard; © **508/693-0085**): All of Martha's Vineyard is easily accessible for two-wheel recreationalists. This 6-mile path hugs the water almost all the way, so you're never far from a refreshing dip. See "Beaches & Recreational Pursuits" in chapter 9.

- **Chilmark to Aquinnah** (Martha's Vineyard; © **508/693-0085**): The Vineyard's awe-inspiring vistas of ponds, inlets, and ocean greet you at every turn as you bike along State Road and then turn onto the Moshup Trail, a road that takes you along the coast up to Aquinnah, formerly known as Gay Head. It's a strenuous ride with perhaps the best scenic views in the region. On the way back, treat yourself to a bike-ferry ride to the fishing village of Menemsha. See "Beaches & Recreational Pursuits" in chapter 9.

3 The Best Small Towns & Villages

The prettier towns of the Cape and Islands combine the austere traditionalism of New England—well-tended historic houses punctuated by modest white steeples—with a whiff of their own salty history.

- **Sandwich:** For a "gateway" town, Sandwich is remarkably composed and peaceful. Not-too-fussy preservation efforts have ensured the survival of many of this first settlement's attractions, such as the pond that feeds the 17th-century **Dexter Grist Mill** (© **508/888-4910**). Generous endowments fund an assortment of fascinating museums including the multifaceted **Heritage Museums and Gardens** (© **508/888-3300**), which is famous for its splendid rhododendrons but has many other exhibits that should interest all members of the family. See p. 65.

- **Woods Hole:** Besides being the Cape's main gateway to Martha's Vineyard, Woods Hole is a world-renowned science community, a charming fishing village, and a bohemian mecca. A proper tour of Woods Hole should include visits to the aquarium and the Woods Hole Oceanographic Institution, a stroll along the bustling harbor, and a drink at the Cap'n Kidd, the Cape's top tavern. See "Falmouth" in chapter 4.

- **Yarmouth Port:** It may look somewhat staid on the surface (Hallet's, the local soda fountain, hasn't changed much since 1889, except to start renting videos), but there are a number of quirky attractions here. A museum features the works of author/illustrator Edward Gorey, a Yarmouth Port resident who died several years ago. The wholly original restaurant **Jack's Out Back,** run by restaurateur Jack Braginton-Smith, serves up the Cape's most reasonably priced fare with a sense of humor. There's also the gloriously jumbled **Parnassus Books** owned by vintage bookseller Ben Muse. Stop at Inaho, all but hidden within an ordinary frame house, for the Cape's best sushi. See "Yarmouth" in chapter 5.

- **Chatham:** Only Provincetown offers better strolling-and-shopping options, and Chatham's versions are G-rated. In summer, Friday-night band concerts draw multigenerational crowds by the thousands. This is perhaps the Cape's quaintest town. For a fun natural history lesson, take a boat ride to see the hordes of seals on uninhabited Monomoy Island. See "Chatham" in chapter 6.

- **Wellfleet:** A magnet for creative artists (literary as well as visual), this otherwise classic New England town is a haven of good taste—from its dozens of shops and galleries to its premier restaurant, Aesop's Tables. All is not prissy, however: certainly not the iconoclastic offerings at the **Wellfleet Harbor Actors' Theatre** (*C* **508/349-6835**) or the goings-on at the 'Comber. See "Wellfleet" in chapter 7.

- **Provincetown:** At the far tip of the Cape's curl, in intensely beautiful surroundings, is Provincetown. Provincetown's history goes back nearly 400 years, and in the last century, it's been a veritable headquarters of bohemia—more writers and artists have holed up here than you could shake a stick at. It's also, of course, among the world's great gay and lesbian resort areas—people come here for the pleasure of being "out" together in great numbers. If you're uncomfortable with same-sex public displays of affection, this stop might be best left off your itinerary. More open-minded straights will have a great time—Provincetown has savory food, fun shopping, terrific company, and fascinating people-watching. See "Provincetown" in chapter 7.

- **Nantucket Town:** It looks as though the whalers just left their grand houses, cobblestone streets, and a gamut of enticing shops offering luxury goods from around the world. Tourism may be rampant but without the tackier side effects, thanks to stringent preservation measures. Time has not so much stood still here as vanished. So relax and shift into island time, dictated purely by your desires. See chapter 8.

- **Oak Bluffs, Martha's Vineyard:** This harbor town on Martha's Vineyard evolved from a Methodist campground that sprang up in the mid–19th century. Pleased with the scenic and refreshing oceanside setting (and who wouldn't be?), the faithful started replacing their canvas tents with hundreds of tiny, elaborately decorated and gaudily painted "gingerbread" cottages. Still operated primarily as a religious community, the revivalist village is flanked by a commercial zone known for its rocking nightlife. See chapter 9.

- **Edgartown, Martha's Vineyard:** For many visitors, Edgartown *is* Martha's Vineyard. Its regal captains' houses and manicured lawns are symbols of a more refined way of life. Roses climb white picket fences, and the tolling of the Whaling Church bell signals dinnertime. By July, gleaming pleasure boats fill the harbor passing Edgartown Lighthouse, and shops overflow with luxury goods and fine art. Edgartown's old-fashioned Fourth of July parade harkens back to small-town America, as hundreds line Main Street cheering the loudest for the floats with the most heart. It's a picture-perfect little town, a slice of homemade apple pie to go with nearby Oak Bluff's hot-fudge sundae. See chapter 9.

4 The Best Luxury Hotels & Inns

• **Chatham Bars Inn** (Chatham; ℂ **800/527-4884** or 508/945-0096): The last of the grand old oceanfront hotels, this is hands-down the most elegant place to stay on Cape Cod. A 5-year, multimillion-dollar renovation has only added to the splendor of this resort. While the luxury suites go for $1,500 a night, regular rooms can be had for less than a third of that. Lunch at the Beach House Grill, with sand underfoot, is a delight. And by all means, have an evening cocktail on the majestic porch overlooking the Atlantic Ocean. The service throughout the hotel is impeccable, and the best part is that this is a family-friendly place—bring the kids and treat yourself. You only live once. See p. 158.

• **Wequassett Inn Resort and Golf Club** (Chatham; ℂ **800/225-7125** or 508/432-5400): This Chatham institution occupies its own little peninsula on Pleasant Bay and offers excellent sailing and tennis clinics. It is also next to the Cape's newest premier golf course and guests have members' privileges. You'll be tempted to just relax, though—especially if you score one of the clapboard cottages, done in an upscale country mode, right on the water. The refurbished restaurant, **28 Atlantic,** is now one of the Cape's best. See p. 158.

• **Captain's House Inn** (Chatham; ℂ **508/945-0127**): An elegant country inn that positively drips with good taste, this is among the best small inns in the region. Most rooms have fireplaces, elegant paneling, and antiques throughout; the rooms are sumptuous yet cozy. This may be the ultimate spot to enjoy Chatham's Christmas Stroll festivities, but you may need to book your room a couple of years in advance. See p. 159.

• **Brass Key Guesthouse** (Provincetown; ℂ **800/842-9858** or 508/487-9005): What do you get when you take a charming inn and add a couple of million dollars plus a lot of good taste? The Brass Key Guesthouse, now a compound consisting of five historic buildings, has been transformed into *the* place to stay in Provincetown. With Ritz-Carlton–style amenities in mind, Michael MacIntyre and Bob Anderson have created a paean to luxury. These are the kind of innkeepers who think of everything: Pillows are goose down, showers have wall jets, and gratis iced tea is delivered poolside. See p. 208.

• **Cliffside Beach Club** (Nantucket; ℂ **800/932-9645** or 508/228-0618): Right on the beach and within walking distance (about 1 mile) of town, this is the premier lodging on the island. It may not be as fancy as some, but there's a sublime beachy-ness to the whole setup with the simply decorated rooms; the cheerful, youthful staff; the sea of antique wicker in the clubhouse; and of course, the blue, yellow, and green umbrellas lined up on the beach. Lucky guests on the Fourth of July get a front-row seat for the fireworks staged at Jetties Beach nearby. See p. 235.

• **Charlotte Inn** (Edgartown, Martha's Vineyard; ℂ **508/627-4751**): Edgartown tends to be the most formal enclave on Martha's Vineyard, and this Anglicized compound of exquisite buildings is by far the fanciest address in town. The rooms are distinctively decorated: One boasts a baby grand piano, and another, its own thematic dressing room. The conservatory restaurant, **L'étoile** (© **508/627-5187**), is among the finest you'll find on this side of the Atlantic. See p. 274.

5 The Best Hotel Deals

- **Simmons Homestead Inn** (Hyannisport; © **800/637-1649** or 508/778-4999): Bill Putman may be the most personable and hospitable innkeeper on Cape Cod. He is determined that his guests have an excellent vacation, a factor that may make the Simmons Homestead Inn one of the best deals around. A former race-car driver/ad exec, Putman has filled his inn with a merry mishmash of animals (stuffed, sculpted, or painted). But his passion is cars, and you'll enjoy touring his "museum" of more than 55 red sports cars. See p. 109.

- **Lamb and Lion Inn** (Barnstable; © **800/909-6923** or 508/362-6823): Part B&B, part motel, this historic Cape cottage has been turned into a comfortable lodging with a pool. Hallways have murals, and rooms are creatively decorated. You'll be charmed by innkeeper Alice Pitcher and her three tiny Yorkies. See p. 111.

- **Isaiah Hall B&B Inn** (Dennis; © **800/736-0160** or 508/385-9928): Fancy enough for the Broadway luminaries who star in summer stock at the nearby Cape Cod Playhouse, this former farmhouse in Dennis is the antithesis of glitz. The great room doubles as a green room—an actors' hangout—and breakfast is celebrated communally in the country kitchen. The plainer rooms will set you back less than a pair of orchestra tix. See p. 130.

- **The Orleans Inn** (Orleans; © **508/255-2222**): Don't miss this inn, perched right on the edge of Town Cove. I recommend a room facing the water. Built in 1875, the inn was recently restored to its former grandeur. The water view and great location make this a terrific value. See p. 171.

- **The Inn at Duck Creeke** (Wellfleet; © **508/349-9333**): In one of the Cape's most charming towns, this humble and historic complex offers no-frills rooms, some with shared bathrooms, for bargain prices. With grandmotherly touches like chenille bedspreads, it will make you feel right at home. A good restaurant and a tavern are also on the property. See p. 190.

- **White Horse Inn** (Provincetown; © **508/487-1790**): Look for the blue-shuttered sea captain's house with the bright-yellow door with the intriguing oval window. The very embodiment of Provincetown funkiness, this inn has hosted such celebrities as cult filmmaker John Waters and poet laureate Robert Pinsky. Rooms are short on amenities (no cable TV here) but long on artfulness. Innkeeper Frank Schaefer has been in Provincetown for 35 years and can give you a quick history of art by pointing out the original works that grace the walls of the inn. See p. 213.

- **Cliff Lodge** (Nantucket; © **508/228-9480**): A freshened-up 1771 captain's house about a block from the center of town, this cheerful inn has knowledgeable, friendly innkeepers. Rooms range in size, but all are spotless with colorful quilts and splatter-painted floors. This is a well-run establishment with reasonable prices, a rarity on Nantucket. See p. 239.

- **Edgartown Inn** (Martha's Vineyard; ✆ **508/627-4794**): This quirky, old-fashioned inn is located in the heart of Edgartown. Smells of freshly baked goodies fill the air,

and the staff is friendly and helpful. Most important, prices have stayed reasonable, a rarity on the Vineyard. See p. 277.

6 The Best Restaurants

It wasn't long ago that "fancy" food in these parts began and ended with classic French. Several spots still uphold the old standards, but the New American Revolution has sparked evermore inventive ways to highlight local delicacies. The best luxury hotels (see above) all maintain superlative restaurants, and soaring on par with them are the following choices, some chef-owned and all truly memorable.

- **Phusion Grille** (Falmouth; ✆ **508/457-3100**): This is Falmouth's best restaurant, combining excellent food, professional service, and a terrific location on Eel Pond in Woods Hole. The interior is all blond wood and Asian screens, but nothing blocks the views through the wraparound floor-to-ceiling windows. The chef/owner Bin Phu combines his classical training with imaginative innovations nightly. See p. 90.

- **The Regatta of Cotuit at the Crocker House** (Cotuit; ✆ **508/428-5715**): What most distinguishes the Regatta from its competition is the sensational service, far exceeding most local establishments. In addition, the Regatta of Cotuit has a quintessential old Cape Cod setting—the building was once a stagecoach inn, and the decor is formal Federal style. Food here is consistently excellent, with fresh ingredients, generous portions, and creative preparations. See p. 114.

- **Ristorante Barolo** (Hyannis; ✆ **508/778-2878**): This wonderful Italian restaurant is tucked away in an office complex on North

Street. The authentic Northern Italian cuisine is carefully prepared and served with style and exuberance. It's a romantic spot for a special dinner but also a good choice for a large group. See p. 112.

- **abbicci** (Yarmouth Port; ✆ **508/362-3501**): It's a bit of a shock to find this sophisticated Northern Italian restaurant tucked into an antique Cape on the Old King's Highway. Those in the know have discovered abbicci, though, and it can be tough to get a reservation here on a summer weekend. Instead, go during the week when the skilled staff is a little more relaxed, and you can linger over the delicate cuisine and the fine wine that should accompany it. See p. 123.

- **28 Atlantic** (Chatham; ✆ **508/432-5400**): This restaurant at the Wequassett Inn and Resort in Chatham has recently undergone a multimillion-dollar makeover, and the results are impressive. Floor-to-ceiling plate-glass windows give diners a panoramic view of Pleasant Bay as they dine in this elegant setting. The menu is loaded with delicacies from around the world. Professional waiters will see to your comfort and thorough satisfaction. See p. 162.

- **The Bramble Inn Restaurant** (Brewster; ✆ **508/896-7644**): An elegantly established entry in the Lower Cape dining scene, this is a favorite for those who don't mind a rather steeply priced, four-course, fixed-price dinner. The five intimate dining rooms are decorated with antique china and fresh flowers. Chef Ruth Manchester is a local favorite for her extraordinary, evolving cuisine. See p. 143.

- **Martin House** (Provincetown; ℂ **508/487-1327**): Easily one of the most charming restaurants on the Cape, this snuggery of rustic rooms happens to contain one of the Cape's most forward-thinking kitchens. The team favors regional delicacies. The peaceful, softly lit rooms make an optimal setting for exploring new tastes. See p. 214.

- **Òran Mór** (Nantucket; ℂ **508/228-8655**): Chef/owner Peter Wallace has worked his magic on this humble space, transforming it into an elegant and very romantic setting for his unusual and creative cuisine. His eclectic style ranges from very spicy, hot fusion to simple international dishes, with many grilled items on the menu. An excellent sommelier is on hand to assist wine lovers. See p. 244.

- **L'étoile** (Edgartown, Martha's Vineyard; ℂ **508/627-5187**): This exquisite conservatory at the elegant Charlotte Inn has long been the best restaurant on the Vineyard, if not the entire region. The fixed-price dinner, a triumph of French cuisine, may be a tad extravagant, but . . . for a special occasion, you can't do any better than this. See p. 282.

7 The Best Clam Shacks

- **The Clam Shack** (Falmouth Harbor; ℂ **508/540-7758**): The ultimate clam shack sits on the edge of the harbor and serves up reasonably priced fried seafood with all the fixings. Order the fried clams (with bellies, please!), and squeeze into the picnic tables beside the counter to await your feast. See p. 93.

- **Mill Way** (Barnstable Harbor; ℂ **508/362-2760**): Sort of a gourmet clam shack, Mill Way offers succulent specialties beyond the usual picnic-table fare. This is a seasonal joint (open May to mid-Oct), and when it's open, it's packed, so go early and hungry. See p. 115.

- **Cap't Cass Rock Harbor Seafood** (Orleans; no phone): Take a photo of the family in front of this shack covered with colorful buoys, then go inside and chow down. Hearty portions of simply prepared fresh fish keep diners coming back year after year. See p. 173.

- **Moby Dick's Restaurant** (Wellfleet; ℂ **508/349-9795**): Unfortunately, word has spread about this terrific restaurant, and it can get pretty mobbed here around suppertime. Still, it's a terrific place to bring the family, screaming kids and all. The clambake special is a 1¼-pound lobster, native Monomoy steamed clams, and corn on the cob. Perfect. See p. 191.

- **Sayle's Seafood** (Nantucket; ℂ **508/228-4599**): Take a 10-minute walk from town on Washington Street Extension, and you'll arrive at this fish store–cum–clam shack. Charlie Sayles is a local fisherman, and everything here is deliciously fresh. Get your fried clams to go, and eat them picnic-style at the beach. See chapter 8.

- **The Bite** (Menemsha, Martha's Vineyard; ℂ **508/645-9239**): A travel writer once called it the best restaurant on Martha's Vineyard, perhaps in retaliation for a high-priced meal in Edgartown. Nevertheless, this is a top-shelf clam shack, tucked away in a picturesque fishing village. Order your meal to go and stroll over to the beach, which has the best sunset views on the island. The fried clams are delicious; some say the secret is the batter. Of course, the fish, unloaded just steps away, couldn't be fresher. What more could you want? See p. 289.

8 The Best Shopping

No matter how spectacular the scenery or splendid the weather, certain towns have so many intriguing shops that you'll be lured away from the beach, at least temporarily. The inventory is so carefully culled or created that just browsing can be sufficient entertainment, but slip a credit card into your cutoffs just in case.

- **Chatham:** Old-fashioned, tree-shaded Main Street is packed with inviting storefronts, including the **Chatham Glass Company** (© **508/945-5547**), where you can literally look over their shoulders as glass treasures take shape, and **Mark, Fore & Strike** for classic and sporty Cape Cod clothes (© **508/945-0568**). See p. 156 and 157.
- **Wellfleet:** The commercial district is 2 blocks long; the art zone is twice that. Pick up a walking map to locate the galleries in town: **Cherrystone Gallery** (© **508/349-3026**) tops the don't-miss list. Seekers of low-key chic will want to check out two designers, **Hannah** (© **508/349-9884**) and **Karol Richardson** (© **508/349-6378**). See p. 188 and 189. For designer produce and impeccable seafood, peruse the array at the homey **Hatch's Fish & Produce Market** (© **508/349-2810** for fish, or 508/349-6734 for produce) behind Town Hall. See p. 192.
- **Provincetown:** Overlooking the import junk that floods the center of town, the 3-mile gamut of Commercial Street is a shopo-holic's dream. It's all here, seemingly direct from SoHo: sensual, cutting-edge clothing (for every sex and permutation thereof), art, jewelry, antiques, and more. And whatever you really need but didn't know you needed can be found at **Marine Specialties** (© **508/487-1730**), a warehouse packed with surplus essentials. See p. 207.
- **Nantucket:** Imagine Martha Stewart cloned a hundredfold, and you'll have some idea of the tenor of shops in this well-preserved 19th-century town. Centre Street—known as "Petticoat Row" in whaling days—still caters to feminine tastes, and the town's many esteemed antiques stores would never deign to present anything less than the genuine article. See p. 233.
- **Edgartown:** Though it's the dowdiest of Martha's Vineyard's towns, this ferry port boasts the best shops, from **Bramhall & Dunn** for housewares (© **508/693-6437**) to **The Great Put On** for designer and contemporary women's wear (© **508/627-5495**); and, of course, Carly Simon's **Midnight Farm** (© **508/693-1997**) for country home and personal furnishings. You might want to save some cash, though, for the multi-ethnic boutiques of Oak Bluffs or the pricey preppy redoubts of Edgartown. See p. 273.

9 The Best Bars & Clubs

- **Roadhouse Café** (Hyannis; © **508/775-2386**): Most consider this the best bar in town and, even better, it's for grown-ups. There is live music nightly in the new "Back Door Bistro" and a sizzling Monday-night Jazz Series popular with locals and those in the know. See p. 112.

- **The Beachcomber** (Wellfleet; ℂ **508/349-6055**): Perched atop the towering dunes of Cahoon Hollow Beach, this bar and dance club is one of the most scenic watering holes on Cape Cod. Although the crowd tends to be on the young and rowdy side, the young at heart are also welcome. You *will* end up on the dance floor, so wear comfortable shoes. See p. 192.

- **Crown & Anchor** (Provincetown; ℂ **508/487-1430**): The specialty bars at this large complex span leather, disco, comedy, drag shows, and cabaret. See p. 219.

- **The Chicken Box** (Nantucket; ℂ **508/228-9717**): The Box is the rocking spot for the 20-something crowd, but depending on the band or theme (reggae, disco, and so on), sometimes it seems like the whole island is shoving their way in here. Jimmy Buffett has been known to make an appearance late at night at least once every summer to jam with the band. See p. 249.

- **Offshore Ale Company** (Oak Bluffs, Martha's Vineyard; ℂ **508/ 693-2626**): The Vineyard's first and only brewpub features eight locally made beers on tap and entertainment 6 nights a week in season. See p. 290.

2

Planning Your Trip to Cape Cod & the Islands

Once you've made it over one of the bridges guarding the Cape Cod Canal, getting around is relatively easy—and you can bypass the bridges, of course, by flying or boating in. The Cape is really many capes: tony in spots, tacky in others; sometimes it's a nature lover's dream, sometimes a living historical treasure, sometimes a hotbed of creativity. This chapter will introduce you to the Cape's top spots and should steer you there smoothly; the town-by-town chapters should help you zone in on the area that will suit you best.

1 The Lay of the Land

Newcomers—known locally as "wash-ashores"—invariably struggle with the terms "Upper" and "Lower," used to describe, respectively, the westernmost and easternmost sections of the Cape. The distinction is thought to allude to the longitude, which decreases as you head east. Many find it helpful to use the analogy of the "arm" of Cape Cod, with the upper cape towns of Sandwich, Falmouth, Bourne, and Mashpee forming the upper arm; Chatham the elbow of the lower arm; and Provincetown the "fist." On Martha's Vineyard, similar confusion reigns over what's meant by "up-island" and "down-island." Down-island consists of the touristy port towns of Vineyard Haven, Oak Bluffs, and Edgartown. In the summer months, locals try to stay up-island, avoiding down-island at all costs.

Even the term "land" may be a bit misleading; the Cape and Islands are actually just heaps of sand, sans bedrock. Described geologically as "terminal moraine," they're what remains of the grit heaved and dumped by the motion of massive glaciers that finally receded some 12,000

years ago, leaving a legacy of "kettle ponds"—steep-sided freshwater pools formed when sharp fragments of the glacier were left to melt in place. Under the relentless onslaught of storms and tides, the landmass's outlines are still subject to constant change and eventual erasure.

The modern landscape is vastly different than what was visible a century ago. Virtually all the trees represent new growth. The settlers, in their rush to build both houses and ships and to fuel both hearths and factories, plundered all the lumber. Were it not for the recession during the late 19th century, you'd be looking at turnip fields and "poverty grass"—so called because it will grow anywhere, needing next to nothing to survive. Instead, the Lower Cape and Mid Cape are now lushly forested, and if the tree cover gets spindly along the Outer Cape, it's the result of battery by salt winds rather than human depredation. The Islands also show the effects of the ocean winds—predominantly those out of the southwest. Harbor towns and down-island areas enjoy a canopy of trees, while the more exposed portions

Cape Cod & the Islands

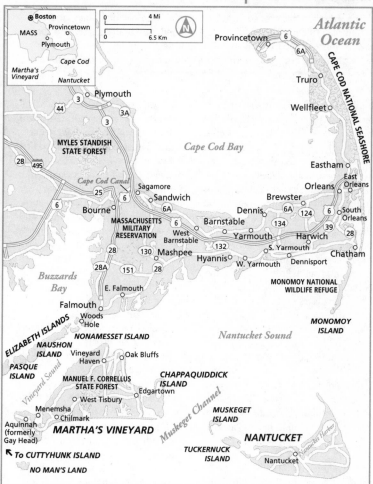

consist primarily of grassy sand plains and moors.

The 15 towns on Cape Cod represent many different capes, with often quite distinct personalities to match the varied landscape. Few similarities exist, for instance, among rural Truro, rowdy Hyannis, and historic Sandwich Village. Most frequent vacationers to Cape Cod return to the same village every year, rarely venturing beyond town lines. But the resourceful visitor who explores the region, perhaps driving the Old King's Highway (Rte. 6A), shopping in Chatham, beaching it at the National Seashore, and checking out an island or two, will have a good idea of the area's diversity.

Visitors may be confused by the similarity of place names on the Cape, particularly in the mid-cape area. When you book a room, it may be helpful to understand these distinctions. Barnstable County consists of the 15 towns on Cape Cod, all of which are made up of individual villages. The largest town on

---

Fun Fact **Here Today, Gone Tomorrow**

The shoreline has eroded about a full mile since colonial times, and current scientific predictions give the Cape and Islands a projected life span of as much as 5,000 more years—or as little as 500. Not to make light of the situation, but this is all the more reason to enjoy them while you can!

Cape Cod is called Barnstable, and it is made up of the following eight villages: Cotuit, Osterville, Marstons Mills, Centerville, Hyannis, Hyannisport, West Barnstable, and (is there an echo in here?) Barnstable Village.

Despite the similar names, towns and even villages on the Cape retain their distinct characters. For instance, charming and historic Barnstable Village along Route 6A (the historic Old King's Hwy.) couldn't be more different from Hyannis (off Rte. 28; transportation hub and home of the mall). Both are villages in the town of Barnstable. In the same vein, the village of West Barnstable (off Rte. 6A; sleepy, rural, and historic) doesn't have much in common with Osterville (off Rte. 28 on the coast; wealthy and preppy). Other notable villages in Barnstable include Cotuit (off Rte. 28; historic and charming), Marstons Mills (off Rte. 28 but inland; mainly residential), Centerville (off Rte. 28; beachy, yet with some commercial sprawl), and Hyannisport (off Rte. 28 on the coast; a residential neighborhood made famous by the Kennedys).

A number of other villages and towns are notable for their unique characteristics. Woods Hole—where bohemians and scientists coexist in a bustling ferry port—is a village in the town of Falmouth, a historic but not musty town with a pleasant Main Street and picturesque town green. Chatham and Osterville both have main streets that are destinations for shoppers seeking expensive, quality wares. Gay-friendly Provincetown has a colorful main street with great people-watching opportunities. Sandwich may well be the quaintest town; Wellfleet, the most artsy. West Barnstable, Barnstable, Yarmouth Port, Dennis, and Brewster are all prototypical New England villages along the historic Old King's Highway. Of these, Dennis Village has the most going on, with museum, cinema, and playhouse all in one historic complex. The Outer Cape towns (Eastham, Wellfleet, Truro, and Provincetown) have the National Seashore beaches, but many families prefer the accessibility of villages like West Dennis and Harwich Port on Nantucket Sound, which offer pretty beaches with calm surf and warmer waters.

On the Islands, location is also an important factor. Most visitors to Nantucket will want to choose lodging in town, where everything is within walking distance. On Martha's Vineyard, down-island towns (Vineyard Haven, Oak Bluffs, and Edgartown) host the majority of the action—shops, restaurants, and fellow tourists. If a serene escape from the grind is what you seek, you may want to be up-island (West Tisbury; Chilmark, including the village of Menemsha; or Aquinnah), but you'll need a car—or a passion for biking—to enjoy these locations.

Socially, a parallel could be drawn between the slightly more conservative types that populate the older, more protected communities, and the renegades who gravitate to the wilder extremes. Towns like Sandwich, Falmouth, and Edgartown will suit conventional visitors, while 20-somethings and adventurous types of all ages will probably feel more at home in an open-minded, forward-thinking setting such as Wellfleet or Provincetown. Families are sure to have a fabulous time at whatever spot they choose because all it takes to keep most kids happily absorbed is some splashing surf and an expanse of sand.

Route 28 east of Hyannis, an eyesore of tacky strip-mall development, represents a warning of what the future holds unless residents continue to clamp down on zoning. Though the pressures of development are unrelenting, Cape lovers have done a pretty good job, so far, of fending off more egregious offenders. The Cape Cod National Seashore—though hotly protested when it was instituted in 1961—serves as a living reminder of the beauty that otherwise would have almost inevitably been lost or reserved solely for the enjoyment of the ultra-rich.

Today, it is the unspoiled natural beauty and historical charm of the area that attracts visitors. Cape Cod's yearly haul of 17 million visitors infuses the region with more than $700 million in revenues. Tourism has been the leading business sector since the late 19th century and is likely to remain so for centuries to come.

2 Visitor Information

For the free *Getaway Guide,* which covers the whole state, contact the **Massachusetts Office of Travel and Tourism,** 100 Cambridge St., 13th Floor, Boston, MA 02202 (✆ **800/ 447-MASS,** ext. 454, or 617/727-3201; www.massvacation.com).

The **Cape Cod Chamber of Commerce,** routes 6 and 132, Hyannis, MA 02601 (✆ **888/332-2732** or 508/862-0700; fax 508/362-2156; www.capecodchamber.org); **Martha's Vineyard Chamber of Commerce,** Beach Road, Vineyard Haven, MA 02568 (✆ **508/693-0085;** fax 508/ 693-7589; www.mvy.com); and **Nantucket Island Chamber of Commerce,** 48 Main St., Nantucket, MA 02554 (✆ **508/228-1700;** fax 508/ 325-4925; www.nantucketchamber. org), can provide location-specific information and answer any questions that may arise. In addition, most towns on the Cape have their own chambers of commerce, which are listed in the relevant chapters that follow.

If you're a member of the **American Automobile Association (AAA;** ✆ 800/222-8252), they'll provide a complimentary map and guide covering the area.

HOSTEL INFORMATION Hostelling International/American Youth Hostels (✆ 202/783-6161) offers low-cost dorm accommodations at five sites on the Cape and Islands. Rates vary but average around $15 per person per night for nonmembers; members (membership $25 a year for adults, $15 for adults over 54, $10 for children under 18) pay somewhat less. Note that there's a "lockout" period (typically 10am–5pm daily), and, likely, a limit on the length of stay. HI/AYH properties are located in Eastham, just off the bike trail; in a former Coast Guard station overlooking Ballston Beach in Truro; adjoining the 4,000-acre Manuel F. Correllus State Forest in West Tisbury on Martha's Vineyard; and in an 1874 lifesaving station on Surfside Beach on Nantucket. For details, see "Where to Stay" in the relevant chapters.

SPORTS INFORMATION Cape Cod Chamber of Commerce (✆ 508/ 862-0700; fax 508/362-2156; www. capecodchamber.org) offers a brochure outlining fishing and hunting options. Those interested in outdoor activities will find reams of info through the **Great Outdoor Recreation Pages**

(www.gorp.com). Birders should call the **Cape Cod Museum of Natural History** (✆ 508/896-3867) for info about the Cape Cod Bird Club, or call the **Birdwatchers General Store** in Orleans (✆ 508/255-6974) for top spots and the latest sightings. Many of the Cape's golf clubs are open to the public; for an annotated listing and advice, call ✆ **800/TEE-BALL,** or www.teeballgolf.com, "the chamber of golf."

3 Money

Though the Cape and Islands— especially the Islands—might seem pricey compared to nontourist areas, visitors used to city prices will find costs quite reasonable. Basically, you can get by on very little if your comfort needs are minimal (rooms in older motels go for as little as $50 a night). Then again, you could spend $1,000 or more on a room—per night. Most of the nicer rooms fall between $150 and $250 a night.

Restaurant prices offer as wide a range. You could dine on clam rolls, for instance, at less than $10 a head, or blow that much or more on a mere appetizer. With such a great variety of dining styles available everywhere, the choice is yours.

TRAVELER'S CHECKS   Traveler's checks are accepted at hotels, motels, restaurants, and most stores, as are credit cards. They are something of an anachronism these days, but since many banks now impose a fee every time you use your card to withdraw money from an ATM in a different city or bank, you may be better off with traveler's checks. You can get traveler's checks at almost any bank; American Express cardholders can charge them over the phone and avoid the 1% fee by calling ✆ **800/221-7282.** If you opt to carry traveler's checks, make sure to record their serial numbers and keep them separate from the checks themselves.

ATMs   ATMs are available throughout the area, at banks and supermarkets, so you can get cash as you travel. Call one of the major networks, such as **Cirrus** (✆ 800/424-7787; www.mastercard.com) or **PLUS** (✆ 800/843-7587; www.visa.com), to find the nearest location. Be sure to check your bank's daily withdrawal limit before you leave. Foreign travelers should check with their banks beforehand to make sure their PINs (personal identification numbers) will work abroad.

Should you require personal service, the banks with the greatest number of branches include **Fleet** (✆ 800/841-4000; www.fleet.com) and the 25-odd branches of **Cape Cod Bank & Trust Company** (✆ 800/458-5100; www.ccbt.com). Both banks will exchange all foreign currencies, although you might want to stop at the exchange booth at Logan Airport in Boston.

CREDIT CARDS   Credit cards are invaluable when traveling. They are a safe way to carry money and provide a convenient record of all your expenses. You can also withdraw cash advances from your credit cards at any bank (though you'll start paying hefty interest on the advance the moment you receive the cash, and you won't receive frequent-flier miles on an airline credit card). At most banks, you don't even need to go to a teller; you can get a cash advance at the ATM if you know your PIN. If you've forgotten your PIN or didn't even know you had one, call the phone number on the back of your credit card and ask the bank to send it to you. It usually takes 5 to 7 business days, though some banks will provide the number over the phone if you pass some security clearance such as telling them your mother's maiden name.

THEFT Almost every credit card company has an emergency 800-number that you can call if your wallet or purse is stolen. They may be able to wire you a cash advance off your credit card immediately, and in many places, they can deliver an emergency credit card in a day or two. The issuing bank's 800-number is usually on the back of the credit card—though, of course, that won't help you very much if the card has been stolen. The toll-free information directory will provide the number if you dial © **800/555-1212.** Citicorp Visa's U.S. emergency number is © **800/336-8472.** American Express cardholders and traveler's check holders should call © **800/221-7282** for all money emergencies. MasterCard holders should call © **800/307-7309.**

Odds are that if your wallet is gone, it won't be recovered. However, after you realize that it's gone and you cancel your credit cards, it is still worthwhile to inform the police. Your credit card company or insurer may require a police report number.

4 When to Go: Climate & Events

Once strictly a seasonal destination, opening with a splash on Memorial Day weekend and shuttering up come Labor Day, the Cape and Islands now welcome more and more tourists to witness the tender blossoms of spring and the fiery foliage of autumn. During these shoulder seasons, lodging tends to cost less, and a fair number of restaurants and attractions remain open. Most important, traffic is manageable. In addition, the natives tend to be far more accommodating in the off season, and shopping bargains abound.

August is by far the most popular month, followed by July (especially the July 4th weekend). You are virtually guaranteed good beach weather in July and August. September and October, though, are splendid, too: The ocean retains enough heat to make for bearable swimming during the sunny days of Indian summer, and the subtly varied hues of the trees and moors are always changing, always lovely. The Atlantic Ocean will be bone-chillingly cold, but May and June are also enticing as gardening goes way beyond hobby in this gentle climate, and blooms are profuse from May right through the summer. Unless your idea of the perfect vacation requires a swim in the ocean, you'll be better off (for example, fewer people and better deals) if you visit the Cape slightly off season: May, June, September, or October.

OFF SEASON In the last few years, a number of entertaining town festivals and events have attracted crowds in the spring and fall. Provincetown has the **Arts Festival** in late September and October. Truro's town festival, **Truro Treasures,** is also held in September. Of course, the **cranberry festivals** all take place in the fall. Harwich has the largest event, usually spanning two weekends in September. Some say the most crowded time on Nantucket is during the Christmas Stroll in early December; the entire month before Christmas is known as **Nantucket Noel,** with lots of holiday events. Martha's Vineyard also rolls out the red carpet in December with events in Edgartown and Vineyard Haven, including Santa arriving on the ferry. Many towns on the Cape, including Sandwich, Osterville, Falmouth, and Chatham, also have big holiday festivals. Spring brings **daffodil festivals** in Brewster and Osterville and on Nantucket (book your ferry reservations way in advance for this one).

Some establishments persist straight through the truly quiet season—January through March—and it's a rare treat to enjoy these historic towns and pristine landscapes with almost no one but natives stirring about. To avoid disappointment in the off season, however, always be sure to call ahead to check schedules.

WILDLIFE The wetlands of the Cape and Islands are part of one of the country's greatest annual wildlife spectacles: the passage of thousands of migratory sea-, shore-, and songbirds in spring and fall. Warblers, herons, terns, and oystercatchers; shorebirds like avocets and the endangered piping plover; dozens of species of ducks; huge flocks of snow geese, owls, and hawks—these are just a few of the birds that take a rest stop on the Cape as they pass along the Atlantic Flyway, which for some birds extends from winter homes in South America to breeding grounds in the vast, marshy tundra within the Arctic Circle. March, April, October, and November are all good months to see migrating waterfowl. August is the month to observe migrating shorebirds, with thousands stopping to feed at places like Monomoy Island, Nauset Marsh, and Sandwich's Great Marsh. Fewer shorebirds stop at the Cape in spring, but those that do will be decked out in the bird equivalent of a tux—their breeding plumage. Songbirds pass through in May, in their brightest plumage and in full-throated song (both color and voice are muted in the fall migration). If you're birding on the Cape during the height of the summer season, you'll find plenty of herons, egrets, terns, and osprey wherever you find sand and wetlands.

The other great wildlife-watching opportunity this region is known for is **whale-watching.** The humpbacks, huge finbacks, and small minkes all cluster to feed around the Stellwagen Bank north of Provincetown from April all the way through November.

Monomoy Island is worth a special trip in late winter, when thousands of **harbor seals** take their version of a holiday in the sun, retreating to Monomoy from Maine and points north. At that time of year, they share the island with many thousands of wintering sea ducks. For info call the **Cape Cod Museum of Natural History** (© 508/896-3867).

CLIMATE

The Gulf Stream renders the Cape and Islands generally about 10° warmer in winter than the mainland, and offshore winds keep them about 10° cooler in summer (you'll probably need a sweater most evenings). The only downside of being surrounded by water is the tendency toward fog; typically, it's sunny about 2 days out of 3—not bad odds. And the foggy days can be rather romantic. Pack some good books for when it pours.

THE SEASONS

SUMMER The official beginning of summer on Cape Cod is heralded by the **Figawi sailboat race** from Hyannis to Nantucket on Memorial Day weekend. Traffic all over the Cape

---

Tips **Shopping Bargains**

Provincetown's October sales are to die for. Discounts often range from 50% to 70% off as merchants clear the shelves before closing for the winter. And remember, Provincetown is not just tacky T-shirt stores. There are excellent men's and women's clothing stores, as well as a surfeit of fancy home-accessories stores that have opened in the past few years. See p. 205.

is horrendous, and ferries are booked solid. It's a rowdy party weekend, but then, strangely, things slow down for a few weeks until late June. The first few weeks of June can be a perfect time to visit the region, but be forewarned: You may need to request a room with a fireplace. Weather this time of year, particularly in the Outer Cape, can be unpredictable at best. At worst, it's cold and rainy. Don't count on swimming in the ocean unless you're a member of the Polar Bear Club. Late June weather is usually lovely. July 4th is another major mob scene weekend to be avoided. July and August can be perfect—sunny and breezy—or damp, foggy, and humid. Usually it's a combination of the two. Heavily trafficked Labor Day is another weekend you'll probably want to avoid.

AUTUMN It usually starts feeling like fall around mid-September on Cape Cod. Leaves start to change color, roads start to unclog, and everyone seems happier. Day temperatures are perfect for long hikes along the seashore. By October, you'll need a sweater during the day, and evenings can be downright chilly. But this is a lovely time of year on the Cape and Islands.

WINTER It's not supposed to snow on Cape Cod, but it does. A few years ago, some towns got close to 100 inches. During another recent winter, the Cape received virtually no snow until a surprise blizzard on April 1. The holidays are quite popular for family gatherings on the Cape and Islands. January through March are on the bleak side. This is when a lot of locals head south to sunnier climes.

SPRING April is a cheerful time on the Cape and Islands. Daffodil festivals abound. Folks are gearing up for the summer season. It's a time for last-minute fix-up jobs: painting and repairing. In May and June, the entire Cape blossoms, but the weather can be rainy this time of year.

Hyannis's Average Monthly Temperatures

	Jan	Feb	Mar	Apr	May	June	July	Aug	Sept	Oct	Nov	Dec
High Temps. (°F)	40	41	42	53	62	71	78	76	70	59	49	40
(°C)	4	5	6	12	17	22	26	24	21	15	9	4
Low Temps. (°F)	25	26	28	40	48	56	63	61	56	47	37	26
(°C)	-4	-3	-2	4	9	13	17	16	13	8.3	3	-3

CAPE COD & THE ISLANDS CALENDAR OF EVENTS

April

Brewster in Bloom, Brewster. You'll find open houses, a crafts fair and flea market, a parade, and hot-air balloons. The Old King's Highway (Rte. 6A) is lined with thousands of daffodils. Call ✆ **508/896-3500.** Late April.

Daffodil Festival, Nantucket. Spring's arrival is heralded with masses of yellow blooms adorning everything in sight, including a cavalcade of antique cars. Call ✆ **508/228-1700.** Late April.

May

Herb Festival, Sandwich. Activities include exhibits, talks, and garden walks at the Green Briar Nature Center. Call ✆ **508/888-6870.** Mid-May.

Cape Maritime Week, Cape-wide. A multitude of cultural organizations mount special events, such as lighthouse tours, highlighting the region's nautical history. Activities include Coast Guard open houses, lectures, walking tours, and more. The week is sponsored by the Cape Cod

Commission. Call ✆ **508/362-3828.** Mid-May.

Chatham Maritime Festival, Chatham. A festival to raise awareness of Chatham's fishing industry with food and events at the Chatham Fish Pier and on Main Street. Call ✆ **508/945-5199.** Early May.

Nantucket Wine Festival, Nantucket. Vintners from all over converge on Nantucket for wine tastings and cuisine provided by some of the island's top chefs. The Grand Cru is the main event. Call ✆ **508/228-1128.** Late May.

Figawi Sailboat Race, Hyannis to Nantucket. This is the largest—and wildest—race on the East Coast. Intense partying in Hyannis and on Nantucket surrounds this popular event. Call ✆ **508/362-5230.** Late May.

Dexter Rhododendron Festival, Sandwich. Heritage Museums and Gardens—at the peak of bloom—sells offshoots of its incomparable botanical collection. Call ✆ **508/888-3300.** Late May.

June

Brewster Historical Society Antiques Fair, Brewster. This outdoor extravaganza features 80 top dealers. Call ✆ **508/896-3500.** Early June.

A Taste of the Vineyard, Martha's Vineyard. Island restaurateurs offer samplings of their specialties at Edgartown's Whaling Church to benefit the Martha's Vineyard Preservation Trust. Call ✆ **508/627-8017.** Mid-June.

Harborfest Celebration, Nantucket. It's a chance to sample competing chowders and board tall ships. Call ✆ **508/228-1700.** Mid-June.

Provincetown Film Festival, Provincetown. Focusing on alternative film, this fete has brought out celebrities like John Waters and Lily Tomlin. Call ✆ **508/487-FILM.** Mid-June.

Nantucket Film Festival, Nantucket. This annual event focuses on storytelling through film and includes showings of short- and feature-length films, documentaries, staged readings, panel discussions, and screenplay competitions. Sponsors include *Vanity Fair* magazine, so you may see a celebrity or two. Call ✆ **508/228-1700.** Mid-June.

St. Barnabus Strawberry Festival, Falmouth. Pick your own strawberries at Tony Andrews Farm in Hatchville and indulge in strawberry shortcake on the town green. Call ✆ **508/548-8500.** Mid-June.

Aptucxet Strawberry Festival, Bourne. The Aptucxet Trading Post Museum, a replica of the country's first store, hosts crafts demonstrations, accompanied by fresh strawberry shortcake. Call ✆ **508/759-9487.** Late June.

Provincetown Portuguese Festival, Provincetown. This cultural event celebrates Provincetown's Portuguese heritage with music, dancing, exhibits, food, a parade, fireworks, and the traditional Blessing of the Fleet. Call ✆ **508/487-3424.** Late June.

Rock & Roll Ramble, Sandwich. Vintage cars from the '50s and '60s converge on Heritage Museums and Gardens for a concert and mutual admiration. Call ✆ **508/888-3300.** Late June.

July

Edgartown Regatta, Martha's Vineyard. A highly social sailing event. Call ✆ **508/627-4364.** Early July.

Wampanoag Pow Wow, Mashpee. Native American tribes from around the country converge to enjoy traditional dances and games.

Call ✆ **508/477-0208.** July 4th weekend.

Independence Day, Falmouth. Festivities include a Blessing of the Fleet and fireworks at Falmouth Heights Beach. Your best bet is to park in town earlier in the evening and walk over to the Heights. Call ✆ **508/548-8500.** July 4th weekend.

Independence Day, Nantucket. The highlight of the island's busiest weekend is fireworks on Jetties Beach. Call ✆ **508/548-8500.** July 4th weekend.

Independence Day, Edgartown. An old-fashioned, small town parade and fireworks over Edgartown Harbor are the highlights of this beloved event. Call ✆ **508/548-8500.** July 4th weekend.

Independence Day, Provincetown. Festivities include a spirited parade, entertainment, and fireworks over the harbor. Call ✆ **508/487-3424.** July 4th weekend.

Independence Day, Barnstable. A spectacular fireworks display over either Barnstable Harbor or Hyannis Harbor (depending on the nesting of the piping plovers). Call ✆ **800/4-HYNNIS.** July 4th weekend.

Barnstable County Fair, East Falmouth. This old-fashioned, 6-day agricultural extravaganza is complete with prize produce and livestock. Call ✆ **508/563-3200.** Mid-July.

August

Jazz by the Sea and Pops by the Sea, Hyannis. Celebrity "conductors"—such as Julia Child wielding a wooden spoon—enliven these two outdoor concerts. Call ✆ **800/4-HYNNIS.** Early August.

Possible Dreams Auction, Martha's Vineyard. Resident celebrities give—and bid—their all to support the endeavors of Martha's Vineyard Community Services. Call ✆ **508/693-7900.** Early August.

In the Spirit Arts Festival, Martha's Vineyard. Oak Bluffs celebrates its cultural diversity with food, music, and children's fun. Call ✆ **508/693-0085.** Early August.

Mashpee Night at the Pops, Mashpee Commons. A concert by the Cape Cod Symphony Orchestra followed by fireworks. This event attracts about 15,000 pops fans. Call ✆ **508/477-0792.** Early August.

Falmouth Road Race, Falmouth. Joggers and world-class runners turn out in droves—9,500 strong— for this annual sprint race cover just over 7 miles. Entry registration is by lottery and ends in May. No unregistered runners are allowed to participate. Call ✆ **508/540-7000 or** check out their website, **www.falmouthroadrace.com**. Mid-August.

Carnival Week, Provincetown. The gay community's annual blowout features performers, parties, and an outrageous costume parade. Call ✆ **508/487-2313.** Mid-August.

Agricultural Society Livestock Show and Fair, Martha's Vineyard. In West Tisbury, you'll find a classic country carnival and a great leveler. Call ✆ **508/693-9549.** Mid-August.

Sandcastle and Sculpture Day, Nantucket. This fairly serious but fun contest is categorized by age group, which ups the odds of winning. Call ✆ **508/228-1700.** Mid-August.

Festival Days, Dennis. Six days of events, including fun-for-the-family activities, includes a kite-flying contest, canoe race, crafts fair, and more. Call ✆ **800/243-9920** or 508/398-3568. Late August.

Illumination Night, Martha's Vineyard. The Oak Bluffs campground is lit with hundreds of Japanese lanterns. Campground officials keep this event a secret until the last minute, so it's hard to plan ahead. Call ✆ **508/693-0085.** Late August.

New England Jazz Festival, Mashpee. This event, sponsored by the Boch Center for the Performing Arts, is a weekend of big-name performers. Call ✆ **508/477-2580** or check their website, **www.boch centerarts.com**. Late August.

Oak Bluffs Fireworks and Band Concert, Martha's Vineyard. It's the summer's last blast. Call ✆ **508/ 693-0085.** Late August.

Pops Goes the Summer, Barnstable County Fairgrounds, Falmouth. Experience a Cape Cod Symphony Orchestra Concert followed by fireworks. Call ✆ **508/548-8500.** Late August.

September

Bourne Scallop Festival, Bourne. This annual weekend event features food, crafts, rides, musical entertainment, and more. Call ✆ **508/ 759-6000.** Early September.

Windmill Weekend, Eastham. This jolly community festival includes a sand-art competition, road races, band concerts, an arts-and-crafts show, a tricycle race, and professional entertainment. The highlight of this weekend is the square dance held under the historic windmill. Call ✆ **508/255-3444.** Early September.

Cranberry Festival, Harwich. This is a chance to observe and celebrate the colorful harvest, with 9 days of events ranging from pancake breakfasts to fireworks. Call ✆ **800/441-3199** or 508/432-1600. Mid-September.

Martha's Vineyard Striped Bass and Bluefish Derby, Martha's Vineyard. In its 56th year, the region's premier fishing derby and one of the country's oldest is a month-long classic contest. Call

✆ **508/693-0085.** Mid-September to mid-October.

Sandwich Boardwalk Celebration, Sandwich. This community did some serious bonding years ago when their boardwalk was damaged by a storm, and everyone pitched in to build a new one. This festival, with professional kite flying and entertainment for families, has become an annual tradition. Call ✆ **508/888-1233.** Late September.

Provincetown Arts Festival, Provincetown. Building up to the Provincetown Art Association and Museum Annual Consignment Auction (✆ 508/487-1750), this festival, which takes place over four weekends, is an extraordinary opportunity to collect works spanning the past century. Local artists hold open studios, actors stage readings of Eugene O'Neill, and galleries hold special exhibits. Call ✆ **508/487-3424.** Late September to mid-October.

Harbor Swim for Life, Provincetown. Stalwart swimmers participate in this event to raise money for local AIDS organizations. The race is followed by a festive Mermaid Brunch and a sunset "Festival of Happiness" on Herring Cove Beach. Call ✆ **508/487-3684.** Late September.

October

Trash Fish Banquet, Provincetown. Unsung, or perhaps undersung, species are creatively cooked to benefit the Center for Coastal Studies. Call ✆ **508/487-3622.** Mid-October.

Women's Week, Provincetown. This is a gathering of artists, entertainers, and educators, as well as women who just want to have fun. Call ✆ **508/487-2313.** Mid-October.

Walking Weekend, Cape-wide. Over 45 guided walks (averaging

2 hr. in length) are sponsored by an organization called Cape Pathways to foster appreciation for the Cape's unique ecology and cultural accomplishments. Call ℭ **508/862-0700.** Mid-October.

Nantucket Harvest Festival, Nantucket. This festival features inn tours and a big chowder contest, just when the foliage is at its burnished prime. Call ℭ **508/228-1700.** Mid-October.

Nantucket Arts Festival, Nantucket. This week-long event includes a wet-paint sale, mini–film festival, writers and their works, gallery exhibitions, artist demonstrations, theater, concerts, photography, and more. Call ℭ **508/228-1700.** Mid-October.

Yarmouth Seaside Festival, Yarmouth. Enjoy a parade, fireworks, arts and crafts, contests, and sporting events. Call ℭ **508/778-1008.** Mid-October.

November

Chatham's Christmas by the Sea, Chatham. A month of townwide events include historic-inn tours, carolers, hayrides, open houses, a dinner dance, and Santa. Call ℭ **508/945-5199.** Late November through December.

Lighting of the Pilgrim Monument, Provincetown. The Italianate tower turns into a monumental holiday ornament, as carolers convene below. Call ℭ **508/487-1310.** Thanksgiving Eve (late Nov).

Harbor Lighting, Hyannis. The boats parade by, a-twinkle with lights, and Santa arrives via lobster boat. Call ℭ **508/362-5230.** Late November.

Fall Festival, Edgartown. Family activities at the Felix Neck Wildlife Sanctuary include a treasure hunt, wildlife walks, and wreath making.

Call ℭ **508/627-4850.** Late November.

December

Christmas Stroll, Nantucket. The island briefly stirs from its winter slumber for one last shopping/feasting spree, attended by costumed carolers, Santa in a horse-drawn carriage, and a "talking" Christmas tree. This event is the pinnacle of **Nantucket Noel,** a month of festivities starting in late November. Ferries and lodging establishments book up months before this event, so you'll need to plan ahead. Call ℭ **508/228-1700.** Early December.

Falmouth Christmas by the Sea, Falmouth. A weekend of caroling, tree lighting, Santa, entertainment, and a parade that centers on the historic and lavishly decorated Falmouth Village Green. Call ℭ **508/548-8500.** Early December.

Christmas in Sandwich, Sandwich. Seasonal open houses, exhibits, community caroling, and merchant promotions take place throughout the town. Call ℭ **508/759-6000.** Early December.

Holly Folly, Provincetown. The 2nd Annual Gay and Lesbian Holiday Festival has events open to all, including guest house tours, holiday parties, the Reindeer Run, concerts, and more. Call ℭ **508/487-2313.** Early December.

Yarmouth Port Christmas Stroll, Yarmouth Port. Stroll along the Old King's Highway for open houses, visits with Santa, and caroling. Call ℭ **508/778-1008.** Early December.

Christmas Weekend in the Harwiches, Harwich. This townwide celebration features entertainment, merchant promotions, hayrides, visits with Santa, and more. Call ℭ **508/432-1600.** Mid-December.

First Night, Chatham. Following Boston's lead, Chatham puts on a festive evening featuring local performers. Call ✆ **508/945-5199.** New Year's Eve.

5 Health & Insurance

STAYING HEALTHY

Even in this northerly clime, sunburn is a real hazard—as is, increasingly, **sun exposure,** whatever the latitude. For most skin types, it's safest to start with a lotion with a high SPF and work your way down. Be sure to reapply often, according to the directions; and no matter how thoroughly you slather on lotion, try to stay in the shade during prime frying time—11am to 2pm. Kids should always wear sunscreen with a high SPF number, or a coverup such as a T-shirt, if they're going to be playing outside for long periods of time (and just try to stop them!). Sunglasses with UVP (Ultra Violet Protection) lenses will help shield your eyes.

The sea breezes keep most **mosquitoes** on the move, but not always (said Thoreau: "I have never been so much troubled by mosquitoes as in such localities"), so pack some bug spray. The most dangerous insect you're likely to encounter may not be so easily dissuaded.

Unfortunately, pinhead-size **deer ticks,** which transmit Lyme disease (named for the Connecticut community where the malady was diagnosed), are widespread along the Massachusetts coast, and they're especially active just when you're apt to be there: April through October. Nantucket has the dubious distinction of having the highest concentration of Lyme disease in the country. A vaccine tested there is now on the market. Ask your doctor if you should consider the vaccine. If caught in its early stages—symptoms include a ring-shaped rash and flu-like achiness—the disease is easily countered with antibiotics; if it's left untreated, however, the effects could eventually prove fatal.

The best protection, so far, is prevention. Avoid walking in brush or high grass—it's bad for the dunes, anyway. If you insist on bushwhacking, cover up in light-colored clothing (the better to spot any clinging ticks), consisting of a long-sleeved shirt and long pants tucked into high white socks. Camping stores such as EMS sell bush pants that are perfect for this purpose—they're actually comfortable in warm weather. For double protection, spray your clothes and hands (but not face) with a DEET-based insect repellent. Check your clothes before removing them, and then check your body; it helps to use a mirror, or call upon a significant other. Showering after such an outing is a good safeguard. If, despite your best precautions, you find you've brought home a parasite, remove it with tweezers by pulling directly outward, if you can manage to do so without squeezing the body (that would only serve to inject more bacteria into your bloodstream). Dab the bite with alcohol to help disinfect it, and save the tick in a closed jar. If you're within a few minutes of a medical facility, have a doctor deal with the extraction; if you do it yourself, go for testing and treatment as soon as you can and take the tick with you.

The **Lyme Disease Foundation** (✆ 860/525-2000) distributes brochures to tourist areas and is also able to field questions. Other good sources of information are the **Centers for Disease Control** (✆ 888/232-3228 or 404/332-4555) and the **Massachusetts Department of Public Health** (✆ 508/947-1231).

There's one other very good reason not to go in for splendor in the grass:

poison ivy. The shiny, purplish, three-leafed clusters are ubiquitous and potent; if you so much as brush past a frond, the plant's oil is likely to raise an itchy welt. Clothing that has been in contact with the plant can spread the harmless but irritating toxin to your skin; it's even transmitted by smoke. If you think you've been exposed, your best bet is to wash with soap immediately (otherwise the oil may spread elsewhere on your body). Calamine lotion—available without prescription at all drugstores—should help soothe the itching. You won't spread the rash by scratching, since it's the oil that does the spreading, but scratches could get infected, so resist the temptation.

There's one key health precaution you can take if you plan to do any bicycling while on the Cape and Islands: **a helmet.** In Massachusetts, children 12 and under are required to wear one. All the good bike shops rent helmets as well, and those few extra bucks could save your life.

Pack an adequate supply of any **prescription drugs** you'll need in your carry-on luggage, and also bring copies of your prescriptions. If you wear contact lenses, pack an extra pair in case you lose one. If you have a serious medical condition or allergy, wear a **Medic Alert Identification Tag** (✆ **800/825-3785;** www.medicalert. org), which will immediately alert doctors to your condition and give them access to your records through Medic Alert's 24-hour hot line. Membership is $35, plus a $15 annual fee. If you have dental problems, a nationwide referral service known as **1-800-DENTIST** (✆ **800/336-8478**) will provide the name of a nearby dentist or clinic.

INSURANCE

There are three kinds of travel insurance: trip cancellation, medical, and lost luggage coverage. **Trip-cancellation insurance** is a good idea if you have paid a large portion of your vacation expenses upfront. The other two types of insurance, however, don't make sense for most travelers. Rule number one: Check your existing policies before you buy any additional coverage.

Your existing health insurance should cover you if you get sick while on vacation (though if you belong to an HMO, you should check to see whether you are fully covered when away from home). For independent travel health-insurance providers, see below. Your homeowner's insurance should cover stolen luggage. The airlines are responsible for $1,250 on domestic flights if they lose your luggage; if you plan to carry anything more valuable than that, keep it in your carry-on bag.

The differences between travel assistance and insurance are often blurred, but in general, the former offers on-the-spot assistance and 24-hour hot lines (mostly oriented toward medical problems), while the latter reimburses you for travel problems (medical, travel, or otherwise) after you have filed the paperwork. The coverage you should consider will depend on how much protection is already contained in your existing health insurance or other policies. Some credit and charge card companies may insure you against travel accidents if you buy plane, train, or bus tickets with their cards. Before purchasing additional insurance, read your policies and agreements carefully. Call your insurers or credit/charge card companies if you have any questions.

If you do require additional insurance, try one of the companies listed below. But don't pay for more than you need. For example, if you need only trip-cancellation insurance, don't purchase coverage for lost or stolen property. Trip-cancellation insurance costs approximately 6% to 8% of the total value of your vacation.

Among the reputable issuers of travel insurance are:

- **Access America,** 6600 W. Broad St., Richmond, VA 23230 (© **866/807-3982;** www.access america.com).
- **Travel Guard International,** 1145 Clark St., Stevens Point, WI 54481 (© **800/826-4919;** www. travelguard.com).
- **Travel Insured International, Inc.,** P.O. Box 280568, East Hartford, CT 06128 (© **800/243-3174;** wwwtravelinsured.com).
- **Travelex Insurance Services,** P.O. Box 9408, Garden City, NY 11530-9408 (© **888/457-4602;** www.travelex-insurance.com).

6 Tips for Travelers with Special Needs

FOR TRAVELERS WITH DISABILITIES

A disability shouldn't stop anyone from traveling. The free *Getaway Guide* offered by the **Massachusetts Office of Travel and Tourism** (© **800/447-MASS** or 617/727-3201) is keyed for accessibility. Though the larger, more popular establishments, as well as newer (1990s) constructions, are generally up to code, a great many of the Cape's older, historic buildings are difficult to retrofit, and the task is prohibitively expensive for many small-business owners, much as they might like to upgrade. Your best bet is to check accessibility when calling ahead to confirm hours or make reservations. You'll find most places eager to do whatever they can to ease the way; but if you run into problems, you might want to contact the **Cape Organization for Rights of the Disabled** (© **800/541-0282** or 508/775-8300). For information on services available in the state, call the **Massachusetts Network of Information Providers** (© **800/642-0249** or 800/764-0200) during business hours.

A World of Options, a 658-page book of resources for disabled travelers, costs $35 ($30 for members) and is available from **Mobility International USA,** P.O. Box 10767, Eugene, OR 97440 (© **541/343-1284** voice and TDD; www.miusa.org). Annual membership for Mobility International is $35, which includes their quarterly newsletter, *Over the Rainbow.* In addition, **Twin Peaks Press,** P.O. Box 129, Vancouver, WA 98666 (© **360/694-2462**), publishes travel-related books for people with disabilities.

You can join the **Society for Accessible Travel & Hospitality (SATH),** 347 Fifth Ave., Suite 610, New York, NY 10016 (© **212/447-7284;** fax 212/725-8253; www.sath.org), for $45 annually, $30 for seniors and students, to gain access to their vast network of connections in the travel industry. They provide information sheets on travel destinations and referrals to tour operators that specialize in travel for people with disabilities. Their quarterly magazine, *Open World for Disability and Mature Travel,* is full of good information and resources. A year's subscription is $13 ($21 outside the U.S.).

The **Moss Rehab Hospital** (© **215/456-9600**) has been providing friendly and helpful phone advice and referrals to travelers with disabilities for years through its Travel Information Service (© **215/456-9603;** www.mossresource net.org).

Travelers with disabilities may also want to consider joining a tour that caters specifically to them. Reputable specialized tour operators include **Accessible Journeys** (© **800/TINGLES** or 610/521-0339), for slow walkers and wheelchair travelers; **The Guided Tour, Inc.** (© **215/782-1370**); **Wilderness Inquiry** (© **800/728-0719** or 612/379-3858); and **Directions Unlimited** (© **800/533-5343**).

Hertz and **Avis** both provide hand-controlled cars with up to 3 days of advance notice (see "Getting Around," later in this chapter), and both **Amtrak** (℗ **800/USA-RAIL**) and **Greyhound** (℗ **800/752-4841**), which serves Boston, offer special fares and services for travelers with disabilities; call at least a week in advance for details.

You can obtain a copy of *Air Transportation of Handicapped Persons* by writing to Free Advisory Circular No. AC12032, Distribution Unit, U.S. Department of Transportation, Publications Division, M-4332, Washington, DC 20590.

The **National Park Service** issues free "Golden Access Passports," which entitle people with disabilities and a guest of their choice to free admission into national parks, forests, and wildlife refuges. (You will have to provide proof of disability.) The passport can be obtained at park entrances.

Vision-impaired travelers should contact the **American Foundation for the Blind,** 11 Penn Plaza, Suite 300, New York, NY 10001 (℗ **800/ 232-5463**), for information on traveling with Seeing Eye dogs.

FOR SENIORS

With relatively mild winters and splendid summers, Cape Cod and the Islands are popular retirement spots. In fact, as of the 2000 U.S. Census, more than a third of the population was 55 or older. Businesses from museums to B&Bs cater to this clientele with attractive discounts, and many restaurants offer early-bird specials (smaller portions at lower prices, offered before the ordinary dinner hour). Mention that you're a senior when you first call to make your travel reservations, and be sure to carry some form of identification that establishes your birth date, such as a driver's license or passport.

Both **Amtrak** (℗ **800/USA-RAIL**) and **Greyhound** (℗ **800/752-4841**), which serves Boston, offer discounted fares to persons over 62.

You should also inquire about the resources of **Elder Services of Cape Cod and the Islands** (℗ **800/244-4630** or 508/394-4630).

Members of **AARP**, 601 E St. NW, Washington, DC 20049 (℗ **800/ 424-3410** or 202/434-2277; www. aarp.com), get discounts not only on hotels but on airfares and car rentals, too. AARP offers members a wide range of special benefits, including *AARP: The Magazine* and a monthly newsletter.

The Mature Traveler, a monthly 12-page newsletter on senior travel, is a valuable resource. It is available by subscription ($30 a year) from GEM Publishing Group, Box 50400, Reno, NV 89513-0400. GEM also publishes *The Book of Deals,* a collection of more than 1,000 senior discounts on airlines, lodging, tours, and attractions around the country; it's available for $9.95 by calling ℗ **800/460-6676.** Another helpful publication is *101 Tips for the Mature Traveler,* available from Grand Circle Travel, 347 Congress St., Suite 3A, Boston, MA 02210 (℗ **800/221-2610** or 617/350-7500; fax 617/346-6700).

Elderhostel is a national organization that offers affordably priced educational programs for people over 55. Programs generally last a week, and prices average about $350 per person, including classes, room, and board. For information on programs held on the Cape and Islands, contact the main office at 75 Federal St., Boston, MA 02110-1941 (℗ **617/426-7788;** www.elderhostel.org), and request a free catalog.

FOR GAY & LESBIAN TRAVELERS

Gay and lesbian travelers, singly or in pairs, will feel right at home in Provincetown, a world-renowned gay vacation capital. They should also feel comfortable wandering farther afield. This is a sophisticated, semi-urban population, and you'll rarely encounter an overtly bigoted innkeeper, shopkeeper, or restaurateur. If you do, report them to the **Massachusetts Commission Against Discrimination,** 1 Ashburton Place, Room 601, Boston, MA 02108 (© **617/727-3990**). To avoid unpleasant situations, read between the lines of promotional literature ("fun for the whole family" may mean rampant bedlam and not much fun for you), or be blunt in stating your expectations (for example, "It will be for myself and my partner [name goes here], and we'd like a queen bed, if possible"). The descriptions of each establishment listed in this book should give some idea of their suitability and compatibility.

The **International Gay & Lesbian Travel Association (IGLTA)** (© **800/448-8550** or 954/776-2626; fax 954/776-3303; www.iglta.org) links travelers with the appropriate gay-friendly service organization or tour specialist. With around 1,200 members, it offers quarterly newsletters, marketing mailings, and a membership directory that's updated quarterly. Membership often includes gay or lesbian businesses but is open to individuals for $150 yearly, plus a $100 administration fee for new members. Members are kept informed of gay and gay-friendly hoteliers, tour operators, and airline and cruise-line representatives. Contact the IGLTA for a list of its member agencies, who will be tied into IGLTA's information resources.

General gay and lesbian travel agencies include **Above and Beyond Tours** (© **800/397-2681;** mainly gay men), and **Yellowbrick Road** (© **800/642-2488;** gay and lesbian).

Out and About, 8 W. 19th St., no. 401, New York, NY 10011 (© **800/929-2268** or 212/645-6922; www.outandabout.com), offers guidebooks and a monthly newsletter packed with good information on the global gay and lesbian scene.

FOR FAMILIES

Basically a giant sandbox with a fringe of waves, the Cape and Islands are ideal family vacation spots. A number of the larger hotels and motels offer deals whereby kids can share their parent's room for free. But beware of the fancier B&Bs: Although it's illegal for them to do so, some actively discriminate against children (see "Tips on Accommodations," later in this chapter). The kind that do are apt to be the kind that children dislike, so it's no great loss. For the most part, the local tourism industry is big on serving family needs, so there's not much you'll need to do by way of advance preparation.

Family Travel Times is published six times a year by TWYCH (Travel with Your Children; © **888/822-4388** or 212/477-5524; familytraveltimes.com) and includes a weekly call-in service for subscribers. Subscriptions are $40 a year for quarterly editions. Call the number above for a free publication list and a sample issue.

FOR SINGLE TRAVELERS

Many people prefer to travel alone—except for the relatively steep cost of booking a single room, which usually costs the same price as a double.

Several tour organizers cater to solo travelers. **Experience Plus** (© **800/685-4565;** fax 907/484-8489) offers an interesting selection of singles-only trips. **Travel Buddies** (© **800/998-9099** or 604/533-2483) runs single-friendly tours with no singles supplement.

You may also want to research the **Outdoor Singles Network** (P.O. Box 781, Haines, AK 99827). An established quarterly newsletter (since 1989) for outdoor-loving singles ages 19 to 90, the network will help you find a travel companion, pen pal, or soul mate within its pages. A 1-year subscription costs $45, and your own personal ad is printed free in the next issue. Current issues are $15. Write for free information or check out the group's website at www.kcd.com/bearstar/osn.html.

7 Getting There

BY CAR

Visitors from the south (New York, for example) will approach the Cape Cod Canal via Route I-95 to Route 195 to Route 25 and the Bourne Bridge. Those coming from Boston can either come that way (reaching Rte. 25 via I-93 to Rte. 24 and I-495) or head directly south from Boston on I-93 to Route 3, leading to the Sagamore Bridge.

The bridges are only 3 miles apart, with connecting roads on both sides of the canal, so either will do. The one you choose will most likely depend on where you're going. If you're planning to head south to Falmouth or taking a ferry to Martha's Vineyard, you'll want to take the Bourne Bridge and follow Route 28 about ten miles to Falmouth.

If you're heading farther east of the Sagamore Bridge to any of the other 14 towns on the Cape, you'll want to travel over the Sagamore Bridge and take Route 6 or its scenic sidekick, Route 6A, which merges with Route 28 in Orleans. From Orleans, the main road is Route 6 all the way to Provincetown.

Those traveling to Nantucket should take the Sagamore Bridge and drive down Route 6 until reaching exit 7. From there you can follow signs to the ferry terminal in Hyannis.

The big challenge, actually, is getting over either bridge, especially on summer weekends, when upwards of 100,000 cars all try to cross at once. Savvy residents avoid at all costs driving onto the Cape on Friday afternoon or joining the mass exodus on Sunday (or Mon, in the case of a holiday weekend), and you'd be wise to follow suit. Call SmarTraveler (© 617/374-1234 or cellular *1) for up-to-the-minute news on congestion and alternate routes, as well as parking availability in the pay-per-night parking lots that serve the island ferries.

Traffic can throw a major monkey wrench into these projections, but on average, driving time to Hyannis is about 7 hours from New York and 2 hours from Boston. It'll take about 1 to 1½ hours more to drive all the way to Provincetown.

Traffic can truly be a nightmare on peak weekends. Cars are enough of a bother on the Cape itself: If you're not planning to cover much ground, forego the "convenience" and rent a bike instead (some B&Bs offer "loaners"). On the Islands, cars are truly superfluous. Expensive to ferry back and forth ($158 one-way to Nantucket in season, and that's if you manage to make a reservation months, even a year, in advance or are willing to sit in "standby" for many hours), a car will only prove a nuisance in the crowded port towns, where urban-style gridlock is not uncommon. Should you change your mind and want to go motoring once you arrive, you can always rent a car on the Islands (see "Getting Around," below), usually for *less than the cost of bringing your own vehicle over.*

If you do come by car, have a mechanic check it out beforehand. If you're a member of the **American Automobile Association (AAA;** © 800/222-4357) or another national auto club, call beforehand to ask about travel insurance, towing services, free trip planning, and other services that may be available.

BY BOAT

Arriving by water gives you a chance to decompress from city worries, while taking in glorious views both coming and going. All the ferries are equipped to carry bikes, for about $10 round-trip.

Tips A Word About Traffic

Cape Cod traffic is nothing if not predictable. You do not want to be driving over the Bourne or Sagamore bridges to come onto the Cape on a summer Friday between 4 and 8pm. Saturday between 10am and 3pm is also not a good time to arrive. Most of all, you do not want to try to get off the Cape on a Sunday or holiday Monday between 2 and 8pm. If you find yourself in one of the infamous Cape Cod traffic jams (on Memorial Day in 2000, traffic was backed up 18 miles east from the Sagamore Bridge), there are options. Here are my personal traffic-beating tips. Don't tell anyone.

1. Always take the Bourne Bridge. It is almost always a less-crowded route. You can connect to Route 6 from the canal road, or see number 3 below.

2. When heading off the Cape on Route 6, turn off at exit 5. Take Route 149 south to Route 28. At the Mashpee Rotary, take Route 151 to Route 28 in North Falmouth. Take Route 28 to the Bourne Bridge.

3. To get on the Cape to points east of Yarmouth, follow the above in reverse.

4. If you are traveling to Nantucket and plan to park your car in Hyannis, watch the signs on Route 6 to see if the parking lot at Cape Cod Community College is open. If it is, take exit 6 and make a right turn onto Route 132. Cape Cod Community College is about a half mile on the right. A free shuttle will take you to the ferry.

5. If you are heading to Martha's Vineyard, consider taking a passenger ferry from New London or New Bedford (see chapter 9). Otherwise, be alert to the signs on Route 28 about parking lots. These signs are accurate. If they say the lot is full in Woods Hole, then you will not be allowed to park there, so don't bother driving down to check it out. Follow the signs to the open parking lots, and a free shuttle bus will take you to the ferry.

Bay State Cruise Company (© 617/748-1428 or 508/487-9284 [seasonal]; www.baystatecruises.com) runs a fast ferry to Provincetown from Boston, in addition to a daily round-trip conventional ferry, both from Commonwealth Pier at Boston's World Trade Center. The fast ferry makes several trips a day in season. The trip, which takes under 2 hours, costs $35 one-way, $55 round-trip adults; $20 one-way, $45 round-trip for children; and $30 one-way, $50 round-trip for seniors. The conventional ferry leaves daily late June through Labor Day, and on weekends late May to late June and mid- to late September. The voyage ($18 one-way, $29 round-trip for adults; $14 one-way, $19 round-trip for children 4–11; $15 one-way, $23 round-trip for seniors) takes about 3 hours each way.

You can also ferry directly to Provincetown from Plymouth, in season, with **Captain John Boats** (© 508/747-2400); the trip takes 1½ hours and costs $30 round-trip for adults, $25 for seniors, $20 for children 12 and under. Bikes cost an extra $3. In July and August, only round-trip tickets are sold, and trips run daily. In mid- to late June and September, trips leave Tuesday, Wednesday, Saturday and Sunday. From late May to mid-June, trips run weekends only.

For detailed information on ferries to the Islands, see the "Getting There" sections in chapters 8 and 9. The three "down-island" ports of Martha's Vineyard are hooked up to the Cape and mainland in various ways. Oak Bluffs has the busiest harbor in season. It's served by the **Hy-Line** from Hyannis or Nantucket (© **508/778-2600;** www.hy-linecruises.com), the *Island Queen* from Falmouth Harbor (© **508/548-4800;** www.islandqueen. com), and the state-run **Steamship Authority** car ferry from Woods Hole (© **508/477-8600;** www.islandferry. com, where you can buy tickets online). Edgartown is serviced by the **Falmouth Ferry Service,** a passengers-only ferry called the *Pied Piper* (© **508/548-9400;** www.falmouth ferry.com), which leaves from the west side of Falmouth Harbor and makes a 1-hour crossing (six crossings a day in season). Vineyard Haven welcomes Steamship Authority car and passenger ferries from Woods Hole year-round (over 30 crossings a day on weekends in season). If you want to bring your car, you'll need a reservation (© **508/477-8600** or online at **www.steamship authority.com**), although there's limited standby space available for those willing to wait around, except during certain peak-demand stretches in summer. Passengers not planning to bring a car do not need a reservation. The **Steamship Authority** (in New Bedford; © **508/997-1688;** www. steamshipauthority.com) also runs a passenger ferry, called *Schamonchi,* from New Bedford daily in summer. There are four trips a day on weekends in season. The *Schamonchi* ride takes about 1½ hours but spares travelers coming from New York the long drive onto the Cape. The New Bedford service may be replaced with fast ferry

service in 2004. The *Island Queen* makes the quickest crossing, at about 35 minutes. Round-trip fares on all ferry choices to Martha's Vineyard range from about $11 to $30, depending on the distance, and the round-trip rate for cars in season is $110. Parking averages $10 per day. Including all of the ferry services, there are dozens of crossings a day in summer.

Nantucket is linked in season to Harwich Port by the **Freedom Cruise Line** (© **508/432-8999;** www.nantucket islandferry.com), which makes three trips a day in season and one trip a day in spring and fall. Nantucket is also linked to Hyannis and Oak Bluffs by Hy-Line (© **508/778-2600;** www. hy-linecruises.com). When taking the Hy-Line ferry, you'll need to reserve a parking spot in advance. The **Steamship Authority** passenger/car ferry from Hyannis to Nantucket (© **508/477-8600;** www.steamshipauthority. com) operates year-round, making six crossings each day in season.

There are competing high-speed ferries to Nantucket. It used to take over 2 hours to get to Nantucket by ferry, but the passengers-only **MV** *Grey Lady* (© **800/492-8082**), Hy-Line's high-speed catamaran, cuts the time in half, for more than twice the slow-boat price ($58 round-trip versus $27). It's a smooth, comfortable trip. The Steamship Authority runs its own high-speed catamaran, the *Flying Cloud,* which also makes the trip in 1 hour. Fares are $52 round-trip for adults and $39 round-trip for children.

Both the Steamship Authority and Hy-line also run slow ferries (2¼ hr.) to Nantucket. The Steamship Authority charges $13 each way, and Hy-Line charges $13.50 each way. Hy-Line's passenger ferry, the **MV** *Great Point,* which makes the trip in under 2 hours, offers a first-class lounge for $46 round-trip, $23 one-way. Incidentally, transporting a car costs an astronomical $330 round-trip in season—which makes it pretty silly to bring a car when you consider that the island is only 3 miles wide and 15 miles end to end. A bike ($10 round-trip) will more than suffice.

A certain frenzy usually accompanies the ferry departures, but if you arrive about an hour early, you should have plenty of time to drop off your luggage at the pier beforehand, so you won't have to lug it around. Call **SmarTraveler** (see "By Car," above) or listen to radio station 1610 AM to find out what's up and whether traffic is clogged. The Steamship Authority boats offer a luggage trolley, which often fills to capacity half an hour or more before departure, so it pays to get there early. The Hy-Line staff cheerfully attends to all the loading of luggage and bikes. It's a lot less hassle.

Note: See the note on bus–ferry connections under "By Bus," below. The same holds true for return journeys: Ferry arrival times tend to be more reliable, but give yourself plenty of time, and don't take a chance on the last bus of the day.

BY PLANE

Most major carriers offer service to **Boston's Logan Airport,** and from there, it's a quick half-hour commuter flight to Hyannis (about $100 round-trip), Provincetown (about $160 round-trip), or the Islands (to the Vineyard, about $100 round-trip; to Nantucket, about $125 round-trip). It's also easy to shuttle in from New York (from La Guardia to Hyannis, about $500 round-trip; from La Guardia to Martha's Vineyard, about $210 round-trip; from La Guardia to Nantucket, about $315 round-trip). Non-stop flights from either La Guardia or Newark to Hyannis, Martha's Vineyard, or Nantucket take about 1 hour and 15 minutes. Connections are also available between these airports and to New Bedford, and private charters are easy to arrange. Comparison shopping by phone (or computer) can pay off, since preliminary research will help you find the best deal. For example, Continental offers service to Hyannis from La Guardia Airport and a seasonal service from Newark Airport to Martha's Vineyard and Nantucket. US Airways services Hyannis from La Guardia; they also service Martha's Vineyard and Nantucket from both Logan and La Guardia. Cape Air is the only airline currently offering service from Logan Airport to Provincetown.

Among the larger airlines serving Logan Airport are **American** (✆ 800/433-7300; www.aa.com), **Continental** (✆ 800/525-0280; www.continental.com), **Delta** (✆ 800/221-1212; www.delta.com), **Northwest** (✆ 800/225-2525; www.nwa.com), **United** (✆ 800/241-6522; www.ual.com), and **US Airways** (✆ 800/428-4322; www.usairways.com).

Carriers to the Cape and Islands include all of the above, plus **Cape Air/Nantucket Airlines** (✆ 800/352-0714 or 508/771-6944; www.flycapeair.com), **US Airways/Colgan Air** (✆ 800/272-5488 or 508/775-7077; www.colganair.com), **Island Airlines** (✆ 800/248-7779 or 508/775-6606; www.nantucket.net/trans/islandair), and **Nantucket Airlines** (✆ 800/635-8787 or 508/790-0300; www.nantucketairlines.com). Flying over to Nantucket from Hyannis takes about 12 to 20 minutes, depending on the weather, costs about $79 round-trip, and is a great way to avoid the hectic ferry scene. Island Air and Cape Air make the most frequent trips from Hyannis to Nantucket, and between these two air carriers alone, there are over 50 flights per day. Charter flights are offered by Island Air and Nantucket Airlines (see above), as well as by **Westchester Air** (✆ 800/759-2929).

The commuter flights have their own little fare wars, so it's worth calling around. And though flights may lessen in frequency during the off season, fares descend as well.

From Logan Airport in Boston, the Cape is about a 1½- to 2½-hour drive, depending on traffic and how far along it you intend to go. Hyannis, the Cape's transportation hub, is about a 2-hour drive, or 2½ hours via the Plymouth & Brockton bus line (℡ **508/771-6191**); from there, you can take a ferry ride to either island.

BY BUS

Greyhound (℡ **800/231-2222**) connects Boston with the rest of the country, and **Bonanza Bus Lines** (℡ **800/ 556-3815** or 508/548-7588) covers a good portion of southern New England. Logan Airport to Falmouth costs about $17 each way. Bonanza links Boston's Logan Airport and South Station with Bourne, Falmouth, and Woods Hole; its buses from New York reach the same destinations, plus Hyannis. From New York to Hyannis or Woods Hole, the 6-hour ride costs about $45 each way. **Plymouth & Brockton** (℡ **508/771-6191; www. p-b.com**) offers service from Logan and South Station to Hyannis by way of Sagamore and Barnstable, and offers connections from there to the towns of Yarmouth, Dennis, Brewster, Orleans, Eastham, Wellfleet, Truro, and Provincetown.

Note: If you plan to catch a ferry, don't count on the bus arriving on time (there's no telling what the traffic may do). Plan to take the second-to-last ferry of the day, so you have a backup; and even so, schedule your arrival with an hour to spare.

8 Getting Around

BY CAR

Traveling by car does offer the greatest degree of flexibility, although you'll probably wish no one else knew that. While traffic can often be frustrating, parking is another problem. In densely packed towns like Provincetown, finding a free, legal space is like winning the lottery. Parking is also problematic at many beaches. Some are closed to all but residents, and visitors will almost always have to pay a day rate of about $10. Renters staying a week or longer can arrange for a discounted week-long or month-long sticker through the local town hall (you'll probably need to show your lease, as well as your car registration). You can usually squeeze into the Cape Cod National Seashore lots if you show up early (by 9am); here the fee is only $10 a day, or $30 per season.

Further complicating the heavy car traffic on the Cape is the seemingly disproportionate number of bad drivers. A few key traffic rules: A right turn is allowed at a red light after stopping, unless otherwise posted. In a rotary (think traffic circle with Boston drivers), cars within the circle have the right of way until they manage to get out. Four-way stops call for extreme caution or extreme courtesy, and sometimes both.

Rental cars are available at the Hyannis Airport and at branch offices of major chains in several towns. The usual maze of rental offers prevails. Almost every rental firm tries to pad its profits by selling Loss-Damage Waiver (LDW) insurance at a cost of $8 to $15 extra per day. Before succumbing to the hard sell, check with your insurance carrier and credit card companies; chances are, you're already covered. If not, the LDW may prove a wise investment. Exorbitant charges for gasoline are another ploy to look out for; be sure to top off the tank just before bringing the car in.

Certain car-rental agencies have also set maximum ages or may refuse to rent to those with bad driving records. If such restrictions might

Travel Times to Cape Cod & the Islands

New York to Hyannis	5 to 7 hours, depending on traffic
Boston to Hyannis	1½ hours with no traffic
Sagamore Bridge to Orleans	1 hour; with high-season traffic, 2 to 3 hours
Sagamore Bridge to Provincetown	1½ hours with little traffic
Hyannis to Sagamore Bridge	½ hour; on Sunday afternoons in season, 3 hours
Bourne Bridge to Woods Hole	45 minutes; Friday afternoons in season, 1¾ hours
Hyannis to Nantucket by plane	12 minutes
Hyannis to Nantucket by Steamship Authority ferries	2¼ hours
Hyannis to Nantucket by Hy-Line ferries	1¾ hours
Hyannis to Nantucket by Steamship Authority or Hy-Line high-speed catamaran	1 hour
Woods Hole to Martha's Vineyard aboard the Steamship Authority ferries	45 minutes
Falmouth to Edgartown, Martha's Vineyard, aboard the *Pied Piper*	1 hour
Falmouth to Oak Bluffs, Martha's Vineyard, aboard the *Island Queen*	35 minutes

affect you, ask about requirements when you book to avoid problems later.

It's worthwhile to call around to the various rental companies to compare prices and to inquire about any discounts available (members of AAA or AARP, for instance, may be eligible for reduced rates). The national companies represented on the Cape and Islands include **Avis** (© 800/331-1212), **Budget** (© 800/527-0700), **Hertz** (© 800/654-3131), **National** (© 800/227-7368), and **Thrifty** (© 800/367-2277).

Internet resources can make comparison-shopping easier. **Travelocity** (www.travelocity.com) and **Microsoft Expedia** (www.expedia.com) help you compare prices and locate car-rental bargains from various companies nationwide. They will even make your reservation for you once you've found the best deal.

BY BOAT
For ferries linking the Cape and Islands, see "Getting There" in chapters 8 and 9. Other local water-taxi services and cruise opportunities are listed by town in the appropriate chapters.

BY BIKE
The bicycle is the perfect conveyance for the Cape and Islands, for distances great and small. The Cape has some extremely scenic bike paths, including the glorious Cape Cod Rail Trail, which meanders through seven towns for over 25 miles. Two wheels are the best way to explore Nantucket's flat terrain, and there are scenic bike routes through all six towns on Martha's Vineyard. You'll find a rental shop in just about every town (see the listings

under "Bicycling" in subsequent chapters), or better yet, bring your own.

BY MOPED

They're legal on the Islands and can be rented at many bicycle-rental shops, but locals loathe them: They're noisy, polluting, traffic-clogging, and a menace both to their riders and to innocent bystanders. In other words, *caveat renter,* and expect some dirty looks.

BY TAXI

You'll find taxi stands at most airports and ferry terminals. The Islands also offer jitney services with set rates, such as **Adam Cab** on Martha's Vineyard (*©* **800/281-4462** or 508/693-3332) and **A-1 Taxi** on Nantucket (*©* **508/228-3330**). Several offer bike racks or can arrange for bike transportation with advance notice—call around until you find what you need. Some companies offer sightseeing tours. Among the larger taxi fleets on the Cape are **Falmouth Taxi** (*©* **800/618-8294** or 508/548-4100), **Hyannis Taxi Service** (*©* **800/773-0600** or 508/775-0400), and Provincetown's **Mercedes Cab** (*©* **508/487-3333**), which delivers elegance at no extra charge. Other cab companies are listed in the Yellow Pages, as are limousine liveries.

BY BUS

To discourage congestion and provide a pleasant experience, a growing number of towns offer free or low-cost in-town shuttles in season. You'll find such services in Falmouth, Woods Hole, Mashpee, Hyannis, Dennis, Yarmouth, Harwich, Martha's Vineyard, and Nantucket. Each town's chamber of commerce can fill you in, or call the **Cape Cod Regional Transit Authority** (*©* **800/352-7155** or 508/385-8326). For commercial bus service between towns, see "Getting There," earlier in this chapter.

TRAVEL TIMES Please note that traffic is very heavy driving over the bridges onto the Cape on Friday afternoons and going over the bridges off the Cape on Sunday afternoons. Saturdays can also have heavy traffic because it is the start and end of most rental units. The Bourne Bridge is usually less crowded than the Sagamore Bridge, but unless you are going to Falmouth, you'll have to merge with the Sagamore Bridge traffic on Route 6 anyway. If you are trying to catch a ferry, particularly in Hyannis, always leave plenty of extra time.

9 Tips on Accommodations

The listings in this book feature a range of summer rates for a double room. Keep in mind that this figure does not take into account the sales tax, which can go as high as 9.7%, depending on the town. Prices off season are typically discounted by about 20% to 30%, sometimes more.

Virtually every town on the Cape has lodgings to suit every taste and budget. The essential trick is to secure reservations months—possibly as much as a year—in advance for the peak season of July through August (June and Sept are getting crowded, too). You can't count on luck; in fact, unless you're just planning a day trip,

you probably shouldn't even visit at the height of summer unless you've prearranged a place to stay.

Accommodations range from sprawling, full-facility resorts to cozy little B&Bs with room for only a handful of guests. The price differential, surprisingly enough, may not be that great. A room at a particularly exquisite inn might run more than a modern hotel room with every imaginable amenity.

Because there are hundreds of lodging establishments of every stripe throughout the Cape and Islands, I've focused only on those with special qualities: superb facilities, for example, or especially friendly and helpful hosts. I've personally visited every place listed in this guide, but worthy new inns—as well as resurrected old ones—are constantly popping up.

RESERVATIONS SERVICES   Several reservations services cover the region, but the only one I can personally vouch for—their standards being as exacting as mine—is **Destinations** (© **800/333-4667** or 508/790-0566). Representing hundreds of top inns throughout New England, Destinnations can also design custom tours that cater to special interests, such as golf or antiquing.

Otherwise, it's buyer beware when it comes to such promotional terms as "water view" or "beachfront" (Provincetown's in-town beach, for instance, is quite scenic for strolls, but a bit too close to an active harbor to make for pleasant swimming). To spare yourself disappointment, always call ahead to request a brochure. Some inns and hotels offer special packages, which they may or may not list, so always inquire. Most require a 2-night minimum on weekends, 3 or even 5 if it's a holiday weekend. All provide free parking, although in a congested area such as Provincetown, you may have to play musical spaces.

FAMILY-FRIENDLY   Although all lodgings in the state are prohibited by law from discriminating on the basis of age, a lot of the fancier, fussier B&Bs will be none too happy if you show up with a young child or infant in tow. You might not be too happy either, spending your entire vacation attending to damage control. It can't hurt to inquire—perhaps anonymously, before calling to book—about an establishment's attitude toward children and its suitability for their needs. If you get the impression that your child won't be welcome, there's no point in pushing it: The child, sensing correctly that he/she is not wanted, is likely to exceed your worst expectations. If, on the other hand, you know your child to be a reliable model of "company behavior," you might want to risk an unannounced arrival.

It's probably easier from the outset, though, to seek out places that like having kids around. Motels are always a safe bet (it's what they're designed for), and the descriptions provided here should indicate other likely spots.

A popular family option—but again, you must make plans as much as a year in advance—is to rent a cottage or house by the week, or even month (see below).

RENTING A COTTAGE OR HOUSE   Families planning a Cape Cod vacation, especially families with young children, should consider renting a cottage or house rather than choosing an inn or hotel. The trick to finding a great rental can be summed up in two words: *Book early.* Start calling realtors in January and February (if not sooner—some vacationers who return every summer book a year in advance). If you can visit earlier in the year to check out a few places, that helps, but if not, you may be able to view choices on a realtor's website or see photos that the realtor can mail to you.

⌈Tips⌋ Hit the Pavement

Sometimes the best way to find a good rental is to drive around the area you want to rent in and look for handwritten signs advertising rentals by owners. These rentals tend to be cheaper (no realtor commission), and you'll know just what you are getting into before you sign on the dotted line.

Believe it or not, there are parts of Cape Cod that are not close to a beach. When talking to a realtor, ask specifically for rentals on the water, with views of the water, or within a half mile of a beach. You'll have a better Cape Cod vacation if you are within walking distance of a beach.

Prices on rentals vary, but they are always much lower off season. Depending on the rental, off season could mean late June or even late August, so ask what the cut-off dates are for high-season prices. Location is the single biggest factor in determining price: A two-bedroom cottage could cost $800 a week in Dennis or $8,000 a week on Nantucket. Tell your realtor your price range and what you are looking for, and he or she will select appropriate listings for you to choose from.

Each town's chamber of commerce can put you in touch with local realtors. You can also call the **Cape Cod and the Islands Association of Realtors** (© 508/957-4300; www.cciaor. com) for a complete list of realtors in the area.

Here is a list of good realtors with rentals in different regions of the Cape and on the Islands: **Real Estate Associates** in North Falmouth (© 508/ 563-7173), **Kinlin/Grover Realtors** in Sandwich (© 508/888-1555), **Bay Village Realty** in Brewster (© 800/ 833-4958), **Duarte/Downey Real Estate** in Truro (© 508/349-7588),

Linda R. Bassett Vacation Rentals on Martha's Vineyard (© 800/338-9201), and **Nantucket Real Estate Co.** on Nantucket (© 508/228-3131).

CAMPING INFORMATION A number of state parks and recreation areas maintain campgrounds; for a full listing for the state, contact the **Department of Conservation and Recreation,** Division of Forests and Parks (© 617/727-3180).

The largest such area on the Cape is the 2,000-acre **Nickerson State Park** (© 508/896-3491), offering over 400 campsites. The Massachusetts Audubon Society offers limited tenting at its 1,000-acre **Wellfleet Bay Wildlife Sanctuary** (© 508/349-2615).

Note: Camping is expressly forbidden within the Cape Cod National Seashore (with the exception of a few "grandfathered" commercial campgrounds) and on Nantucket. Seashore camping is not allowed on Martha's Vineyard either. The Vineyard has one campground, called **Martha's Vineyard Family Campground** on Vineyard Haven–Edgartown Road (© 508/ 693-3772), which is in the middle of the island and not near a beach.

A partial list of private campgrounds that belong to the **Massachusetts Association of Campground Owners** appears in the Massachusetts Office of Travel and Tourism's free *Getaway Guide* (© 800/447-6277, ext.454).

10 Planning Your Trip Online

Researching and booking your trip online can save time and money. Then again, it may not. It is simply not true that you always get the best deal online. Most booking engines do not include schedules and prices for budget airlines, and from time to time you'll get a better last-minute price by calling the airline directly, so it's best to call the airline to see if you can do better before booking online.

On the plus side, Internet users today can tap into the same travel-planning databases once accessible only to travel agents—and do it at the same speed. Sites such as **Frommers. com, Travelocity.com, Expedia.com,** and **Orbitz.com** allow consumers to comparison shop for airfares, access special bargains, book flights, and reserve hotel rooms and rental cars.

But don't fire your travel agent just yet. Although online booking sites offer tips and hard data to help you bargain-shop, they cannot endow you with the hard-earned experience that makes a seasoned, reliable travel agent an invaluable resource, even in the Internet age. And for consumers with a complex itinerary, a trusty travel agent is still the best way to arrange the most direct flights to and from the best airports.

Still, there's no denying the Internet's emergence as a powerful tool in researching and plotting travel time. The benefits of researching your trip online can be well worth the effort.

Last-minute specials, such as weekend deals or Internet-only fares, are offered by airlines to fill empty seats. Most of these are announced on Tuesday or Wednesday and must be purchased online. They are only valid for travel that weekend, but some can be booked weeks or months in advance. Sign up for weekly e-mail alerts at airline websites or check mega-sites that compile comprehensive lists of last-minute specials, such as **Smarter Living** (www.smarterliving.com) or **WebFlyer** (www.webflyer.com).

Some sites, such as Expedia.com, will send you **e-mail notification** when a cheap fare becomes available to your favorite destination. Some will also tell you when fares to a particular destination are lowest.

TRAVEL PLANNING & BOOKING SITES

Keep in mind that because several airlines are no longer willing to pay commissions on tickets sold by online travel agencies, these agencies may either add a $10 surcharge to your bill if you book on that carrier—or neglect to offer those carriers' schedules.

The list of sites below is selective, not comprehensive. Some sites will have evolved or disappeared by the time you read this.

- **Travelocity** (www.travelocity.com or www.frommers.travelocity.com) and **Expedia** (www.expedia.com) are among the most popular sites, each offering an excellent range of options. Travelers search by destination, dates, and cost.
- **Orbitz** (www.orbitz.com) is a popular site launched by United, Delta, Northwest, American, and Continental Airlines. With this site, you're granted access to the largest database of low rates, airline tickets, rental cars, hotels, vacation packages, and other travel products. You get, among other offerings, available fares from more than 450 airlines.
- **Qixo** (www.qixo.com) is another powerful search engine that allows you to search for flights and accommodations from some 20 airline and travel-planning sites (such as Travelocity) at once. Qixo sorts results by price.
- **Priceline** (www.priceline.com) lets you "name your price" for airline tickets, hotel rooms, and rental cars. For airline tickets, you can't say what time you want to fly—you have to accept any flight between 6am and 10pm on the dates you've selected, and you may have to make one or more stopovers. Tickets are nonrefundable, and no frequent-flier miles are awarded.

SMART E-SHOPPING

The savvy traveler is armed with insider information. Here are a few tips to help you navigate the Internet successfully and safely.

- **Know when sales start.** Last-minute deals may vanish in minutes. If you have a favorite booking site or airline, find out when last-minute deals are released to the public. (For example, Southwest's specials are posted every Tues at 12:01am central time.)

- **Shop around.** If you're looking for bargains, compare prices on different sites and airlines—and against a travel agent's best fare. Try a range of times and alternative airports before you make a purchase.
- **Stay secure.** Book only through secure sites (some airline sites are not secure). Look for a key icon (Netscape) or a padlock (Internet Explorer) at the bottom of your Web browser before you enter credit card information or other personal data.
- **Avoid online auctions.** Sites that auction airline tickets and frequent-flier miles are the number-one perpetrators of Internet fraud, according to the National Consumers League.
- **Maintain a paper trail.** If you book an E-ticket, print out a confirmation, or write down your confirmation number, and keep it safe and accessible—or your trip could be a virtual one!

ONLINE TRAVELER'S TOOLBOX

Veteran travelers usually carry some essential items to make their trips easier. Following is a selection of online tools to bookmark and use.

- **Visa ATM Locator** (www.visa.com), for locations of PLUS ATMs worldwide; or **MasterCard ATM Locator** (www.mastercard.com), for locations of Cirrus ATMs worldwide.
- **Foreign Languages for Travelers** (www.travlang.com). Learn basic terms in more than 70 languages and click on any underlined phrase to hear what it sounds like. *Note:* Free audio software and speakers are required.
- **Intellicast** (www.intellicast.com) and **Weather.com** (www.weather.com). Weather forecasts for all 50 states and for cities around the world.
- **Mapquest** (www.mapquest.com). This best of the mapping sites lets you choose a specific address or destination, and in seconds, it will return a map and detailed directions.
- **Cybercafes.com** (www.cybercafes.com) or **Net Café Guide** (www.netcafeguide.com/mapindex.htm). Locate Internet cafes at hundreds of locations around the globe. Catch up on your e-mail and log onto the Web for a few dollars per hour.
- **Universal Currency Converter** (www.xe.net/currency). See what your dollar or pound is worth in more than 100 other countries.
- **U.S. State Department Travel Warnings** (www.travel.state.gov/travel_warnings.html). Reports on places where health concerns or unrest might threaten U.S. travelers. The site also lists the locations of U.S. embassies around the world.

FAST FACTS: The Cape & Islands

American Express The **American Express Travel Service** office is at 1600 Falmouth Rd. in Centerville (© **800/937-1255** or 508/778-2310) and is open Monday to Friday from 9am to 5:30pm.

Area Code The telephone area code for the Cape and Islands is **508.** You must always dial 1 and this area code first, even if you are making a call within the same town.

Business Hours Business hours in public and private offices are usually Monday to Friday from 8 or 9am to 5pm. Most stores are open Monday to Saturday from 9:30 or 10am to 5:30 or 6pm; many are also open on Sunday from noon to 5pm or earlier. Virtually every town has some kind of convenience store carrying food, beverages, newspapers, and household basics; and the larger communities have supermarkets, which generally stay open as late as 10 or 11pm.

Currency Exchange See chapter 3.

Dentists Dentists are listed in the Yellow Pages; among those serving emergencies is **Dr. William J. Scheier** of Orleans (© **508/255-2511**). Most hospitals will gladly provide referrals, or call © **800/DENTIST.**

Doctors For a referral, contact **Cape Medsource** at the Falmouth Hospital (© **800/243-7963** or 508/457-7963), **Ask-a-Nurse** at Cape Cod Hospital (© **800/544-2424**), or the **Physician Referral Service** at Massachusetts General Hospital in Boston (© **617/726-5800**). Physicians and surgeons are also listed by specialty in the Yellow Pages.

Drugstores All the larger towns have pharmacies that are open daily. The ones with the longest hours are likely to be located within a supermarket. A **24-hour CVS drugstore** is located at 176 North St. in Hyannis (© **508/775-8346** pharmacy, or 508/775-8977 store).

Emergencies Phone © **911** for fire, police, emergency, or ambulance; be prepared to give your number, address, name, and a quick report. If you get into desperate straits—if, for example, your money is stolen and you need assistance arranging to get home—contact the **Travelers Aid** office in Boston (© **617/542-7286**).

Fishing Licenses Contact the local town hall of the area in which you want to fish (see individual chapters under "Fishing" for addresses). Massachusetts residents pay $13.50 for a 3-day pass or $28.50 for a season pass; nonresidents pay $24.50 for a 3-day pass or $38.50 for a season pass.

Hospitals The **Cape Cod Hospital** at 27 Park St., Hyannis (© **508/771-1800,** ext. 5235), offers 24-hour emergency medical service and consultation, as does the **Falmouth Hospital** at 100 Ter Heun Dr. (© **508/457-3524**). On the Islands, contact the **Martha's Vineyard Hospital** on Linton Lane in Oak Bluffs (© **508/693-0410**) or **Nantucket Cottage Hospital** on South Prospect Street (© **508/228-1200**).

Information See "Visitor Information," earlier in this chapter and specific chapters for local information offices.

Liquor Laws The legal drinking age in Massachusetts is 21. Bars are allowed to stay open until 1am every day, with "last call" at 12:30am. Beer and wine are sold at grocery as well as package stores; hard liquor, at package stores only. No liquor can be sold on Sunday, though bars can serve drinks. A few towns on Martha's Vineyard are "dry" by choice or tradition (no alcohol can be sold or served), but at most establishments lacking a liquor license, you're welcome to bring your own wine or beer; if in doubt, call ahead.

Maps Maps of the Cape and Islands are available from the **Cape Cod Chamber of Commerce,** routes 6 and 132, Hyannis, MA 02601 (© **888/332-2732** or 508/362-3225); the **Martha's Vineyard Chamber of Commerce,** P.O. Box 1698, Beach Rd., Vineyard Haven, MA 02568 (© **508/693-0085;** fax 508/696-0433; www.mvy.com); and the **Nantucket Island**

Chamber of Commerce, 48 Main St., Nantucket, MA 02554 (© **508/228-1700**). For maps of Massachusetts, contact the **Massachusetts Office of Travel and Tourism,** 100 Cambridge St., 13th Floor, Boston, MA 02202 (© **617/727-3201;** fax 617/727-6525).

Newspapers/Magazines The Cape Cod Times is published daily and runs regular supplements on arts and antiques, events and entertainment, and restaurants. In addition, almost every town has its own weekly or bi-weekly local paper. Martha's Vineyard has two weekly papers, *The Martha's Vineyard Times* and the *Vineyard Gazette,* each offering insight into regional issues. *Cape Cod Life* is a glossy bimonthly with beautiful photography of the area. Each island has its own glossy. *Provincetown Arts,* published yearly, is a must for those interested in local arts and letters. In addition, a great many summer-guide magazines are available (don't expect much novel information), and free booklets with discount coupons are ubiquitous; the nicest of these, with a friendly tone and a lot of useful information, is the *Cape Cod Guide.*

Overnight Delivery For the location of the nearest **Federal Express** drop-off box, or to arrange a pickup, call © **800/238-5355.**

Police For police emergencies, call © **911.**

Radio Out of about a score of local AM and FM radio stations, two can be counted on for local color (in the "alternative album" mode): WOMR (91.9 FM) out of Provincetown and WMVY (92.7 FM) from Martha's Vineyard. The classical choice is WFCC (107.5 FM), which also features twice-daily birding reports. All three stations come in clearly on the Cape and Islands.

Safety A great many people on the Cape and Islands still don't lock their houses, let alone their cars. However, the idyll may not last long: Real crime, from petty theft to rape, has made inroads everywhere, even on isolated Nantucket. So, all your city smarts should apply. Do lock up, keep a close hold on purses and cameras (especially in restaurants: don't just sling them over a chair), and don't frequent deserted areas alone, even in broad daylight. For the most part, the natives' good faith is warranted.

Smoking In the past few years, 14 out of 15 Cape Cod towns have gone "smoke-free" to some extent. The towns of Falmouth, Barnstable, Yarmouth, Dennis, Brewster, Chatham, Orleans, Eastham, Wellfleet, Truro, and Provincetown, and the islands of Martha's Vineyard and Nantucket, have all passed some variation on laws forbidding smoking in public places as a way to protect nonsmokers from secondhand smoke. This means that in the majority of restaurants and even bars in these towns, you cannot light up. A few bars have installed a ventilation system and/or a separate area where smoking is allowed, but these are few and far between. While some large hotels set aside rooms for smokers, the vast majority of lodging establishments on Cape Cod are nonsmoking. There is one establishment in Barnstable where smoking is currently allowed. At **Puff the Magic,** 649 Main St., Hyannis (© **508/771-9090**), a cigar bar where no food is served, you can puff to your heart's discontent.

On Martha's Vineyard, all restaurants are smoke-free except those in Oak Bluffs and Edgartown that have separately enclosed and ventilated bar areas. Since the other four towns on the Vineyard are "dry," meaning no alcohol can be sold, there are no bar areas in those towns and therefore no smoking at all in restaurants. There is also no smoking allowed in the common areas of inns on the Vineyard. There may be some inns where certain rooms are designated for smokers, and visitors wishing to smoke should inquire when they book their rooms.

Taxes In Massachusetts, the state sales tax is 5%. This tax applies to restaurant meals (but not food bought in stores) and all goods, with the exception of clothing items priced lower than $175. The hotel tax varies from town to town; the maximum, including state tax, is 9.7%.

Taxis See "Getting Around," earlier in this chapter.

Telephone Local pay-phone calls cost 35¢, and "local" typically means a small radius; a call to the next town over could cost a dollar or more. Beware of "slamming" (the usurpation of phone services by a small, over-priced carrier): Whatever the label on the phone, use the 800 number on your calling card. Smaller inns and B&Bs may not have phones in the rooms, but they generally provide a communal courtesy phone on which you can make local calls and charge long-distance calls. If you do have an in-room phone, check whether there's a per-call surcharge—they can quickly add up.

Tides If you have any question about the effect of the tides on beaches you plan to hike (they differ dramatically from town to town and could leave you stranded), check the tide chart in a local newspaper before heading out.

Transit Information An ever-growing number of towns are providing free or low-cost shuttle services to reduce congestion. To find out if there's one that serves the place where you plan to stay, contact the **Cape Cod Regional Transit Authority** (© 800/352-7155). On the Islands, the phone number for **Martha's Vineyard Transit Authority** is © 508/693-440; and for **Nantucket Regional Transit Authority**, it's © 508/228-7025. The respective chambers of commerce—for **Martha's Vineyard** (© 508/693-0085) and **Nantucket** (© 508/228-1700)—can also provide maps and schedules for public transportation.

Weather For the latest reports and forecasts, call the **WQRC** (99.9 FM) **Forecast Phone** (© 508/771-5522), available around the clock.

3

For International Visitors

The pervasiveness of American culture around the world may make you feel that you know the States pretty well, but leaving your own country requires an additional degree of planning. This chapter will help prepare you for the more common problems visitors may encounter and illuminate some of the more puzzling aspects of daily life in the U.S.

1 Preparing for Your Trip

ENTRY REQUIREMENTS

Immigration laws are a hot political issue in the United States these days, and the following requirements may have changed somewhat by the time you plan your trip. Check at any U.S. embassy or consulate for current information and requirements. You can also plug into the **U.S. State Department's** website at www.state.gov.

VISAS The U.S. State Department has a **Visa Waiver Pilot Program** allowing citizens of certain countries to enter the United States without a visa for stays of up to 90 days. At press time these included Andorra, Argentina, Australia, Austria, Belgium, Brunei, Denmark, Finland, France, Germany, Iceland, Ireland, Italy, Japan, Liechtenstein, Luxembourg, Monaco, the Netherlands, New Zealand, Norway, San Marino, Slovenia, Spain, Sweden, Switzerland, and the United Kingdom. Citizens of these countries need only a valid passport and a round-trip air or cruise ticket in their possession upon arrival. If you first enter the United States, you may also visit Mexico, Canada, Bermuda, and/or the Caribbean islands and return to the United States without a visa. Further information is available from any U.S. embassy or consulate. Canadian citizens may enter the United States without visas; they need only proof of residence.

Citizens of all other countries must have: (1) a valid passport that expires at least 6 months later than the scheduled end of their visit to the United States; and (2) a tourist visa, which may be obtained without charge from any U.S. consulate.

OBTAINING A VISA To obtain a visa, the traveler must submit a completed application form (either in person or by mail) with a 1½-inch square photo and must demonstrate binding ties to a residence abroad. Usually you can obtain a visa at once or within 24 hours, but it may take longer during the summer rush from June through August. If you cannot go in person, contact the nearest U.S. embassy or consulate for directions on applying by mail. Your travel agent or airline office may also be able to provide you with visa applications and instructions. The U.S. consulate or embassy that issues your visa will determine whether you will be issued a multiple- or single-entry visa and any restrictions regarding the length of your stay.

British subjects can obtain up-to-date passport and visa information by calling the **U.S. Embassy Visa Information Line (© 0891/200-290)** or the **London Passport Office** (© **0990/ 210-410**) for recorded information.

IMMIGRATION QUESTIONS Telephone operators will answer your inquiries regarding U.S. immigration policies or laws at the **Immigration and Naturalization Service's Customer Information Center** (© **800/375-5283**). Representatives are available from 9am to 3pm, Monday through Friday.

MEDICAL REQUIREMENTS Unless you're arriving from an area known to be suffering from an epidemic (particularly cholera or yellow fever), inoculations or vaccinations are not required for entry into the United States. If you have a disease that requires treatment with narcotics or syringe-administered medications, carry a valid, signed prescription from your physician to allay any suspicions that you may be smuggling narcotics (a serious offense that carries severe penalties in the U.S.).

For HIV-positive visitors, requirements for entering the United States are somewhat vague and change frequently. According to the latest publication of *HIV and Immigrants: A Manual for AIDS Service Providers,* although INS doesn't require a medical exam for everyone trying to come into the United States, INS officials may keep out people whom they suspect are HIV positive. INS may stop people because they look sick or because they are carrying AIDS/HIV medicine.

If an HIV-positive noncitizen applying for a nonimmigrant visa knows that HIV is a communicable disease of public health significance but checks "no" on the question about communicable diseases, INS may deny the visa because it thinks the applicant committed fraud. If a nonimmigrant visa applicant checks "yes," or if INS suspects the person is HIV positive, it will deny the visa unless the applicant asks for a special waiver for visitors. This waiver is for people visiting the United States for a short time, for instance, to attend a conference, to visit close relatives, or to receive medical treatment. It can be a confusing situation, so for up-to-the-minute information concerning HIV-positive travelers, contact the Centers for Disease Control's **National Center for HIV** (© **404/332-4559**; www.hivatis. org) or the **Gay Men's Health Crisis** (© **212/367-1000**; www.gmhc.org).

DRIVER'S LICENSES Foreign driver's licenses are mostly recognized in the U.S., although you may want to get an international driver's license if your home license is not written in English.

PASSPORT INFORMATION

Safeguard your passport in an inconspicuous, inaccessible place like a money belt. If you lose it, visit the nearest consulate of your native country as soon as possible for a replacement. Passport applications are downloadable from the Internet sites listed below.

FOR RESIDENTS OF CANADA

You can pick up a passport application at one of 28 regional passport offices or most travel agencies. The passport is valid for 5 years and costs $60. Children under 16 may be included on a parent's passport but need their own to travel unaccompanied by the parent. Applications, which must be accompanied by two identical passport-size photographs and proof of Canadian citizenship, are available at travel agencies throughout Canada or from the central **Passport Office, Department of Foreign Affairs and International Trade,** Ottawa, ON K1A 0G3 (© **800/567-6868**; www. dfait-maeci.gc.ca/passport). Processing takes 5 to 10 days if you apply in person, or about 3 weeks by mail.

FOR RESIDENTS OF THE UNITED KINGDOM

If you already possess a passport, it's always useful to carry it. To pick up an application for a regular 10-year passport (the Visitor's Passport has been abolished), visit your nearest passport office, major post office, or travel agency. You can also contact the London Passport Office at ✆ 0171/271-3000 or search its website at www.open.gov.uk/ukpass/ukpass.htm. Passports are £21 for adults and £11 for children under 16.

FOR RESIDENTS OF IRELAND

You can apply for a 10-year passport, costing 57€, at the Passport Office, Setanta Centre, Molesworth Street, Dublin 2 (✆ 01/671-1633; www.gov.ie/iveagh). Those under age 18 and over 65 must apply for a 12€ 3-year passport. You can also apply at 1A South Mall, Cork (✆ 021/272-525), or over the counter at most main post offices.

FOR RESIDENTS OF AUSTRALIA

Apply at your local post office or passport office or search the government website at www.dfat.gov.au/passports. Passports are A$126 for adults and A$63 for those under 18.

FOR RESIDENTS OF NEW ZEALAND

You can pick up a passport application at any travel agency or Link Centre. For more info, contact the Passport Office, P.O. Box 805, Wellington (✆ 0800/225-050). Passports are NZ$80 for adults and NZ$40 for those under 16.

CUSTOMS
WHAT YOU CAN BRING IN

Every visitor over 21 years of age may bring in, free of duty, the following: (1) 1 liter of wine or hard liquor; (2) 200 cigarettes, 100 cigars (but not from Cuba), or 3 pounds of smoking tobacco; and (3) $100 worth of gifts. These exemptions are offered to travelers who spend at least 72 hours in the United States and who have not claimed them within the preceding 6 months. It is altogether forbidden to bring into the country foodstuffs (particularly fruit, cooked meats, and canned goods) and plants (vegetables, seeds, tropical plants, and the like). Foreign tourists may bring in or take out up to $10,000 in U.S. or foreign currency with no formalities; larger sums must be declared to U.S. Customs on entering or leaving, which includes filing form CM 4790. For more specific information regarding U.S. Customs, call your nearest U.S. embassy or consulate, or the **U.S. Customs** office at ✆ 202/927-1770; www.customs.ustreas.gov.

WHAT YOU CAN BRING HOME

U.K. citizens returning from a non-EC country have a Customs allowance of: 200 cigarettes; 50 cigars; 250 grams of smoking tobacco; 2 liters of still table wine; 1 liter of spirits or strong liqueurs (over 22% volume); 2 liters of fortified wine, sparkling wine, or other liqueurs; 60cc (ml) perfume; 250cc (ml) of toilet water; and £145 worth of all other goods, including gifts and souvenirs. People under 17 cannot have the tobacco or alcohol allowance. For more information, contact HM Customs & Excise, Passenger Enquiry Point, 2nd Floor Wayfarer House, Great South West Road, Feltham, Middlesex, TW14 8NP (✆ 0181/910-3744; 44/181-910-3744 from outside the U.K.), or consult their website at www.open.gov.uk.

For a clear summary of **Canadian** rules, write for the booklet *I Declare,* issued by **Revenue Canada,** 2265 St. Laurent Blvd., Ottawa, ON K1G 4KE (✆ 613/993-0534). Canada allows its citizens a $500 exemption, and you're allowed to bring back duty-free 200 cigarettes, 2.2 pounds of tobacco, 40 imperial ounces of liquor, and 50 cigars. In addition, you're allowed to mail gifts to Canada from abroad at the rate of C$60 a day, provided they're unsolicited and don't contain alcohol or tobacco (write on the package "Unsolicited gift, under $60 value"). All valuables should be declared on the Y-38 form before departure from Canada, including serial numbers of valuables you already own, such as expensive foreign cameras. *Note:* The $500 exemption can be used only once a year, and only after an absence of 7 days.

The duty-free allowance in **Australia** is A$400 or, for those under 18, A$200. Personal property mailed back from the United States should be marked "Australian goods returned" to avoid payment of duty. Upon returning to Australia, citizens can bring in 250 cigarettes or 250 grams of loose tobacco, and 1,125ml of alcohol. If you're returning with valuable goods you already own, such as foreign-made cameras, you should file form B263. A helpful brochure, available from Australian consulates or Customs offices, is *Know Before You Go.* For more information, contact **Australian Customs Services,** GPO Box 8, Sydney, NSW 2001 (℡ **02/9213-2000**).

The duty-free allowance for **New Zealand** is NZ$700. Citizens over 17 can bring in 200 cigarettes, or 50 cigars, or 250 grams of tobacco (or a mixture of all three if their combined weight doesn't exceed 250g); plus 4.5 liters of wine and beer, or 1.125 liters of liquor. New Zealand currency does not carry import or export restrictions. Fill out a certificate of export, listing the valuables you are taking out of the country; that way, you can bring them back without paying duty. Most questions are answered in a free pamphlet available at New Zealand consulates and Customs offices: New *Zealand Customs Guide for Travellers, Notice no. 4.* For more information, contact New Zealand Customs, 50 Anzac Ave., P.O. Box 29, Auckland (℡ **09/359-6655**).

INSURANCE

Although it's not required of travelers, health insurance is highly recommended. Unlike many European countries, the United States does not usually offer free or low-cost medical care to its citizens or visitors. Doctors and hospitals are expensive and in most cases will require advance payment or proof of coverage before they render their services. Policies can cover everything from the loss or theft of your baggage and trip cancellation to the guarantee of bail in case you're arrested. Good policies will also cover the costs of an accident, repatriation, or death. See "Health & Insurance" in chapter 2 for more information. Packages such as **Europ Assistance** in Europe are sold by automobile clubs and travel agencies at attractive rates. **Travel Assistance International** (℡ **800/821-2828**) is the agent for Europ Assistance in the United States.

Though lack of health insurance may prevent you from being admitted to a hospital in nonemergencies, don't worry about being left on a street corner to die: The American way is to fix you now and bill the living daylights out of you later.

INSURANCE FOR BRITISH TRAVELERS   Most big travel agents offer their own insurance and will probably try to sell you their package when you book a holiday. Think before you sign. **Britain's Consumers' Association** recommends that you insist on seeing the policy and reading the fine print before buying travel insurance. **The Association of British Insurers** (℡ **0171/600-3333**) gives advice by phone and publishes the free *Holiday Insurance,* a guide to policy provisions and prices. You might also shop around for better deals: Try **Columbus Travel Insurance Ltd.** (© 0171/375-0011) or, for students, **Campus Travel** (© 0171/730-2101).

INSURANCE FOR CANADIAN TRAVELERS Canadians should check with their provincial health plan offices or call **HealthCanada** (© 613/957-2991) to find out the extent of your coverage and what documentation and receipts you must take home in case you are treated in the United States.

MONEY

CURRENCY The U.S. monetary system is painfully simple: The most common bills (all ugly, all green) are the $1, $5, $10, and $20 denominations. There are also $2 bills (seldom encountered), $50 bills, and $100 bills (the last two are usually not welcome as payment for small purchases). Note that a newly redesigned $100 and $50 bill were introduced in 1996, a redesigned $20 bill was introduced in 2003 and redesigned $10 and $5 bills were introduced in 2000. Despite rumors to the contrary, the old-style bills are still legal tender.

There are six denominations of coins: 1¢ (1 cent, or a penny); 5¢ (5 cents, or a nickel); 10¢ (10 cents, or a dime); 25¢ (25 cents, or a quarter); 50¢ (50 cents, or a half dollar); and, prized by collectors, the rare $1 piece (the older, large silver dollar and the newer, small Susan B. Anthony coin). A new gold $1 piece was introduced in 2000.

Note: The "foreign-exchange bureaus" so common in Europe are rare even at airports in the United States and non-existent outside major cities. It's best not to change foreign money (or traveler's checks denominated in a currency other than U.S. dollars) at a small-town bank, or even a branch in a big city; in fact, leave any currency other than U.S. dollars at home—it may prove a greater nuisance to you than it's worth.

TRAVELER'S CHECKS Though traveler's checks are widely accepted, make sure that they're denominated in U.S. dollars, as foreign-currency checks are often difficult to exchange. The three traveler's checks that are most widely recognized—and least likely to be denied—are **Visa, American Express,** and **Thomas Cook.** Be sure to record the numbers of the checks, and keep that information separately in case they get lost or stolen. Most businesses are pretty good about taking traveler's checks, but you're better off cashing them in at a bank (in small amounts, of course) and paying in cash. Remember: You'll need identification, such as a driver's license or passport, to change a traveler's check.

CREDIT CARDS & ATMs Credit cards are the most widely used form of payment in the United States: **Visa** (BarclayCard in Britain), **MasterCard** (EuroCard in Europe, Access in Britain, Chargex in Canada), **American Express, Diners Club, Discover,** and **Carte Blanche.** You must have a credit or charge card to rent a car. There are, however, a handful of stores and restaurants that do not take credit cards, so be sure to ask in advance. Most businesses display a sticker near their entrance to let you know which cards they accept. (*Note:* Often businesses require a minimum purchase price, usually around $10, to use a credit card.)

It is strongly recommended that you bring at least one major credit card. Hotels, car-rental companies, and airlines usually require a credit-card imprint as a deposit against expenses, and in an emergency, a credit card can be priceless.

You'll find automated teller machines (ATMs) on just about every block—at least in almost every town—across the country. Some ATMs will allow you to draw U.S. currency against your bank and credit

Travel Tip

Be sure to keep copies of all your travel papers separate from your wallet or purse, and leave copies with someone at home should you need them faxed in an emergency.

cards. Check with your bank before leaving home, and remember that you will need your personal identification number (PIN) to do so. Most accept Visa, MasterCard, and American Express, as well as ATM cards from other U.S. banks. Expect to be charged up to $3 per transaction, however, if you're not using your own bank's ATM.

One way around these fees is to ask for cash back at grocery stores that accept ATM cards and don't charge usage fees. Of course, you'll have to purchase something first.

SAFETY

GENERAL   Tourist areas in the United States are generally safe, and the Cape and Islands are safer than most. Although a number of towns, particularly the larger ones, suffer their share of crime (much of it drug- and alcohol-related), there's no such thing as a "bad neighborhood" here, per se. However, with crime on the increase everywhere, you need to stay alert and take the usual precautions. Avoid carrying valuables with you on the street or at the beach, and be discreet with expensive cameras and electronic equipment. When milling in crowds (in Hyannis or Provincetown, for example), place your billfold in an inside pocket, and hang onto your purse; anything kept in a backpack should be buried beyond reach. In closely packed places, such as restaurants, theaters, and ferries, keep your possessions in sight, and never sling a bag over the back of your chair: It's too easy a target. Alas, anything left visible in a car, locked or unlocked, is an open invitation, even in secluded Nantucket.

It would be rare in this region to find security staff screening all those who enter a hotel, especially if there's a restaurant on the premises, so don't relax your guard until your door is securely locked. Many areas are still so countrified that homeowners don't even lock their doors, and you'll find that most B&Bs are fairly laissez-faire; a few lack bedroom door locks altogether. If you're traveling light, it shouldn't matter, but if you're the cautious type, inquire about security measures before setting out.

Women, unfortunately, are no safer here than anywhere else, so avoid visiting deserted areas alone, even during the day. Hyannis can get a bit rowdy when its dance clubs are in full swing, and even more so when they let out. For the most part, though, this is a peaceful place, more like the 1950s, and as long as you keep your wits about you, you should be able to relax, relatively speaking.

DRIVING SAFETY   Though Massachusetts is quite strict, drunk driving is a definite hazard: The police logs are full of offenses, from foolish to fatal. The best tactic is to avoid the offenders as much as possible, primarily by staying off the roads late at night. It's probably not a good idea to cover long distances at night, in any case, since there are no 24-hour gas stations to help out in case of emergency. In the event of a breakdown, drivers are usually advised to stay in the car with the doors locked until the police arrive. This is a small and friendly enough place, though, that it would probably be all right to take a chance on the kindness of strangers. Use your judgment, and err, if at all, on the side of caution.

Carjacking has yet to make an appearance on the Cape, but car theft runs high in Massachusetts as a whole, so lock your doors even if the natives never bother.

2 Getting to the Cape & Islands

The idea of traveling abroad on a budget is something of an oxymoron, but travelers can reduce the price of a plane ticket by several hundred dollars if they take the time to shop around. Overseas visitors can take advantage of the **APEX** (advance-purchase excursion) fares offered by all the major U.S. and European carriers. Aside from these, attractive values are offered by Virgin Atlantic from London to Boston and New York. For the best rates, compare fares and be flexible with the dates and times of travel.

A number of U.S. airlines offer service from Europe to the United States. If they do not have direct flights from Europe to Boston's Logan Airport (the closest international airport to the Cape and Islands), they can book you straight through on a connecting flight. You can make reservations by calling one of the following numbers in London: **American Airlines** (✆ 0181/ 572-5555), **Continental** (✆ 4412/ 9377-6464), **Delta** (✆ 0800/414- 767), or **United** (✆ 0181/990-9900).

Logan Airport is served by more than 40 carriers, including **British Airways** (✆ 081/897-4000 in the U.K.) and **Air Canada** (✆ 800/776- 3000). Any airline not served by this airport—the 15th busiest in the world—is likely to fly into New York, only a 30-minute commuter flight away.

IMMIGRATION & CUSTOMS

The visitor arriving by air, no matter what the port of entry, should cultivate patience and resignation before setting foot on U.S. soil. Getting through **immigration control** may take as long as 2 hours on some days, especially summer weekends, so have this guidebook or something else to read handy. Add the time it takes to clear Customs, and you will see that you should make a very generous allowance for delay in planning connections between international and domestic flights—figure on 2 to 3 hours at least.

In contrast, for the traveler arriving by car or by rail from Canada, the border-crossing formalities have been streamlined to the vanishing point. And for the traveler by air from Canada, Bermuda, and some places in the Caribbean, you can sometimes go through Customs and Immigration at the point of departure, which is much quicker.

3 Getting Around the United States

BY PLANE On transatlantic or transpacific flights, some large U.S. airlines (for example, Northwest and Delta) offer **special discount tickets** for any of their U.S. destinations under the name **Visit USA.** The tickets or coupons are not on sale in the United States and must be purchased before you leave your point of departure. This system is the best, easiest, and fastest way to see the United States at low cost. You should obtain information well in advance from your travel agent or the office of the airline concerned, since the conditions attached to these discount tickets can be changed without advance notice.

BY TRAIN International visitors can also buy a **USA Railpass,** good for 15 or 30 days of unlimited travel on Amtrak (✆ 800/USA-RAIL; www. amtrak.com). The pass is available through many foreign travel agents. At press time, a 15-day pass costs $295 off-peak, $440 peak; a 30-day pass costs $385 off-peak, $550 peak. With a foreign passport, you can also buy passes at some Amtrak offices in the United States, including locations in San Francisco, Los Angeles, Chicago, New York, Miami, Boston, and Washington, D.C. Reservations are generally required and should be made for each part of your trip as early as possible. Amtrak also offers an **Air/Rail Travel Plan** that allows you to travel by both train and plane; for information call ✆ **800/440-8202.**

BY BUS Although bus travel is often the most economical form of public transit for short hops between U.S. cities, it can also be slow and uncomfortable—certainly not for everyone. **Greyhound/Trailways** (✆ **800/231-2222;** www.greyhound. com), the sole nationwide bus line, offers an **Ameripass** for unlimited travel for 7 days at $209, 10 days at $259, 15 days at $319, 30 days at $429, 45 days at $469, and 60 days at $599. Special rates are available for senior citizens, children, and students. Passes can be purchased at a Greyhound terminal or on the Greyhound website. (If you plan to purchase your ticket on the website, please do so well in advance.)

See the "Getting There" and "Getting Around" sections in chapter 2 for more information on getting from Logan Airport to the Cape and Islands and other transportation questions.

FAST FACTS: For the International Traveler

Automobile Organizations Auto clubs will supply maps, suggested routes, guidebooks, accident and bail-bond insurance, and emergency road service. The major auto club in the United States, with roughly 1,000 offices nationwide, is the **American Automobile Association (AAA).** Members of some foreign auto clubs have reciprocal arrangements with the AAA and enjoy its services at no charge. If you belong to an auto club in your home country, inquire about AAA reciprocity before you leave. You may be able to join the AAA even if you're not a member of a reciprocal club; to inquire, call the AAA (✆ **800/222-8252**).

In addition, some automobile-rental agencies now provide many of these same services. Inquire about their availability when you rent your car.

Automobile Rentals To rent a car, you need a major credit card and a valid driver's license. Sometimes a passport or an international driver's license is also required if your driver's license is in a language other than English. You usually need to be at least 25 years of age, although some companies do rent to younger people (they may add a daily surcharge). Most of the major car-rental companies are represented on the Cape and Islands (see "Getting Around" in chapter 2).

Business Hours Banks are typically open weekdays from 9am to 3 or 4pm, and there's 24-hour access to the automated teller machines (ATMs) at most banks and other outlets. Generally, offices are open weekdays from 9am to 5pm. Most stores are open 7 days a week and late into the evening in season. See "Business Hours" in "Fast Facts: The Cape & Islands," in chapter 2.

Climate See "When to Go: Climate & Events," in chapter 2.

Currency Exchange With many extensive banking chains, such as **Fleet** (℃ **800/841-4000**; www.fleet.com) and **Cape Cod Bank & Trust** (℃ **800/458-5100**; www.ccbt.com), now offering exchange services for virtually all foreign currencies, you can wander without fear of running out of cash. To get started, you might want to get some pocket money at the currency-exchange booths at Logan Airport.

Drinking Laws See "Liquor Laws" in "Fast Facts: The Cape & Islands," in chapter 2.

Electricity The United States uses 110 to 120 volts AC, 60 cycles, compared to 220 to 240 volts AC, 50 cycles, as in most of Europe. In addition to a 100-volt transformer, small appliances of non-American manufacture, such as hair dryers and shavers, will require a plug adapter, with two flat parallel pins.

Embassies & Consulates All embassies are located in Washington, D.C.; some consulates are located in major U.S. cities, and most nations have a mission to the United Nations in New York City. There are no consulates on the Cape or Islands; however, Boston boasts three dozen. There is no consular representation in Massachusetts for **New Zealand,** but there are **British** and **Canadian** consulates in Boston (see below).

The **embassy of Australia** is at 1601 Massachusetts Ave. NW, Washington, DC 20036 (℃ **202/797-3000**). There is a consulate at 20 Beacon St., Boston, MA 02108 (℃ **617/542-8655**).

The **embassy of Canada** is at 501 Pennsylvania Ave. NW, Washington, DC 20001 (℃ **202/682-1740**). There's a consulate at Copley Place, Boston, MA 02116 (℃ **617/262-3760**).

The **embassy of Great Britain** is at 3100 Massachusetts Ave. NW, Washington, DC 20008 (℃ **202/462-1340**). There's a consulate at 600 Atlantic Ave., Boston, MA 02110 (℃ **617/245-4500**).

The **embassy of Ireland** is at 2234 Massachusetts Ave. NW, Washington, DC 20008 (℃ **202/462-3939**). There's a consulate at 535 Boylston St., Boston, MA 02116 (℃ **617/267-9330**).

The **embassy of New Zealand** is at 37 Observatory Circle NW, Washington, DC 20008 (℃ **202/328-4800**).

For information on other consulates, call **information** (℃ **411,** or consult the blue pages of the Boston phone book.

Emergencies Call ℃ **911** to report a fire, contact the police, or get an ambulance. This is a toll-free call (no coins are required at a public telephone).

If you encounter serious problems while traveling, call the **Travelers Aid Society of Boston** (℃ **617/542-7286**), part of a nationwide, non-profit, social-service organization dedicated to helping travelers in difficult straits. Services might include reuniting families inadvertently separated while traveling; providing food and/or shelter to people temporarily stranded without cash; and even emotional counseling. The society maintains offices at terminals A and E at Logan Airport and an information booth at South Station. Though there are no offices on the Cape, give them a call if you need help.

Gasoline (Petrol) One U.S. gallon equals 3.8 liters or 0.85 imperial gallons. Several grades (and price levels) of gasoline are usually available at most gas stations, and the names change from company to company. The unleaded ones with the highest octane rating are among the most expensive and probably unnecessary (most rental cars take the least expensive regular unleaded gas).

Holidays On the following legal national holidays, banks, government offices, and post offices are closed (stores, restaurants, and museums may be as well): January 1 (New Year's Day), the third Monday in January (Martin Luther King, Jr., Day), the third Monday in February (Presidents' Day), the last Monday in May (Memorial Day), July 4 (Independence Day), the first Monday in September (Labor Day), the second Monday in October (Columbus Day), November 11 (Veterans Day), the fourth Thursday in November (Thanksgiving), and December 25 (Christmas). Massachusetts institutions also observe Patriots' Day on the third Monday in April, and Boston's municipal offices may be closed for Evacuation Day (March 17) and Bunker Hill Day (June 17). Also, in presidential election years (2004, 2008, and so on), the Tuesday following the first Monday in November is Election Day, a national legal holiday.

Legal Aid The foreign tourist will probably never become involved with the American legal system. If you are "pulled over" for a minor infraction (such as driving over the speed limit), never attempt to pay the fine directly to the police officer; this could be construed as attempted bribery, a much more serious crime. Pay fines by mail or directly to the local clerk of the court. If accused of a more serious offense, say and do nothing before consulting a lawyer. Here the burden is on the state to prove a person's guilt beyond reasonable doubt, and everyone has the right to remain silent, whether he or she is suspected of a crime or actually arrested. Once arrested, a person can make a telephone call to a party of his or her choice: Call your consulate or embassy.

In less urgent situations, you may wish to consult the **Legal Aid hot line** (℡ 800/742-4107).

Mail If you'd like your mail to follow you on your vacation but aren't sure what your address will be, arrange to have it sent in your name c/o General Delivery at the post office of a town you expect to stay in or pass through (call ℡ **800/275-8777** for information on the nearest post office); be sure to include the five-digit ZIP (postal) code after the state abbreviation (MA). You'll have to pick up your mail in person and provide an ID, preferably with a photo (a driver's license or passport, for example). There is no charge for this service.

Mailboxes are not as ubiquitous on the Cape and Islands as they are in the city, so you may have to go to the post office in any case to send your own mail—or give it to your innkeeper for inclusion with theirs. The domestic postage rates are currently 23¢ for a postcard and 37¢ for a letter; again, be sure to include the ZIP code to speed delivery. Overseas rates vary, so ask your innkeeper or inquire at the post office.

The post office offers express mail, or you might use a commercial service such as **Federal Express** (call ℡ **800/238-5355** to arrange for a pickup, at a slight surcharge, or to find out the location of the nearest drop-off box). Credit cards can be used as payment. To be delivered to you, FedEx packages must be labeled with your full address, including ZIP code and telephone number.

Measurements The United States, with rare exception, does not operate on the metric system. For a detailed chart explaining U.S. measurements, see the inside front cover.

Newspapers & Magazines Distributed throughout New England, the *Boston Globe* (owned by the *New York Times*) does an excellent job of reporting international as well as domestic news. For local periodicals offering events listings and coverage of regional issues, see "Newspapers/Magazines" in "Fast Facts: The Cape & Islands," in chapter 2.

Radio & Television Audiovisual media, with four coast-to-coast networks (ABC, CBS, NBC, and Fox), joined by the Public Broadcasting System (PBS) and local channels on UHF, offer a choice of about a dozen channels, and cable ups the choice to dozens more. Because broadcast reception tends to be poor on the Cape and non-existent on the Islands, most establishments subscribe to cable, including, quite often, "premium channels" such as HBO. Only the more luxurious smaller inns provide TVs in the rooms; most have a set in the sitting room. Many hotels and motels provide in-room cable, both basic and premium, as well as the option of pay-per-view movies. Most lodgings come with a clock radio. You'll find a wide choice of national and local radio stations offering various kinds of talk shows and music, from classical and country to jazz and rock. News and weather updates are usually broadcast on the hour, and all but certain educational stations are punctuated by frequent commercials. For local favorites, see "Radio" in "Fast Facts: The Cape & Islands," in chapter 2.

Safety See "Safety" under "Preparing for Your Trip," earlier in this chapter.

Taxes In the United States there is no VAT (value-added tax) or other indirect tax at a national level. Every state, and each city in it, has the right to levy its own local tax on all purchases, and none of it is refundable to foreign visitors. In Massachusetts, the statewide sales tax, with certain exceptions, is 5%. For further details, see "Taxes" in "Fast Facts: The Cape & Islands," in chapter 2.

Telephone, Telegraph, Telex, Fax & E-Mail On Cape Cod, you have to dial one **(1)** plus the area code **(508)** before every phone number, even when you are calling a number within the same town where you are making the call.

The telephone system in the United States is run by private corporations, so rates, especially for long-distance service and operator-assisted calls, can vary widely—even on calls made from public telephones. Local calls in Massachusetts usually cost 35¢. Pay phones do not accept pennies, and few will take anything larger than a quarter.

Hotel surcharges on long-distance and even local calls can be steep (often $1 per call); they should be posted on the phone, and if not, ask the hotel operator before calling around. You're usually better off using a public pay telephone: There should be one in your hotel's lobby, and you'll find them in most restaurants and gas stations as well. Outdoor pay phones usually are found in a glass booth or a waist-level console.

Most long-distance and **international calls** can be dialed directly from any phone. For calls to Canada and other parts of the United States, dial 1 followed by the area code and the seven-digit number. For international calls, dial **011** followed by the country code, city code, and telephone number.

Note that all calls to area codes **800**, **788**, or **888** are **toll-free**. However, calls to numbers with the area codes **700** and **900**—commercial lines that reverse the charges—can be very expensive (several dollars or more per min.), and they may exact a minimum charge of $15 or more.

For **reversed-charge or collect calls**, and for **person-to-person** calls, dial **0** (zero, not the letter *O*) followed by the area code and number; an operator will come on the line to assist you, and you should specify the particular type(s) of service you want. To make an international call, ask for an overseas operator.

For local or long distance **directory assistance** ("Information"), dial ☏ **411**.

Like the telephone system, **telegraph and telex services** are provided primarily by **Western Union**. You can dictate your message over the phone (☏ **800/325-6000**) or inquire about local offices where you can both send and receive messages as well as money (note, however, that the service charges for wiring money may run as high as 15%–20% of the total). There are 15 Western Union offices on the Cape and two on each of the Islands.

Most of the larger hotels offer **fax service**, but the fee is usually quite high. Copy shops often offer fax service, as do packing services such as Mail Boxes Etc., which has four offices on the Cape. (Look in the Yellow Pages under "Packing Services.")

Of course, if you have a laptop with a modem and phone jack, you can send and receive your own faxes, or access the Internet to send e-mail. The largest online service in the U.S. is **America Online** (☏ **800/827-3338**), which now also owns **CompuServe** (☏ **800/848-8990**).

Telephone directories for the Cape and Islands combine several types of listings. Usually, emergency numbers are listed inside the front cover, followed by community service listings, dialing instructions, and information on rates. The **White Pages**, which list subscribers in alphabetical order, are in some cases divided between private and business users (the latter appear grouped at the end, with a dark border). At the back of the book, the **Yellow Pages** list businesses by categories, such as automobile repairs, drugstores (pharmacies), restaurants, bookstores, and places of worship. In addition, the telephone directories that cover this region include a supplement offering useful tourist information and discount coupons.

Time   The United States (with the exception of Alaska and Hawaii) falls into **four time zones:** Eastern Standard Time (EST), Central Standard Time (CST), Mountain Standard Time (MST), and Pacific Standard Time (PST). All of Massachusetts (like New England as a whole) observes Eastern Standard Time, which runs, for example, 5 hours behind London time, or 3 hours ahead of Los Angeles. Daylight saving time, when clocks are set forward an hour, remains in effect from the first Sunday in April to the last Sunday in October.

Tipping Except in cases of exceptionally neglectful or downright rude service, tipping restaurant servers is not so much an option as an expectation (some would say, obligation). The waitstaff, as a rule, receives less than the minimum hourly wage, with the assumption that tips will make up the difference. In a seasonal economy such as that prevailing on the Cape and Islands, workers may need to make enough in 3 or 4 months to get through the winter, when the job market all but disappears. Only a handful of restaurants and hotels applies an across-the-board gratuity of 15%. That amount is standard, however, for adequate service, and if you have substantial complaints, it would be far better to take it up with the management than take it out on the servers. For especially friendly or helpful service, go to 20% or more of the pre-tax total, including beverages. A bartender should be tipped at the same rate. As a rule, maitre d's and sommeliers do not expect a separate tip; they'll usually get a share of the total. A tip of $1 per vehicle for valet parking, or $1 per garment for coat-checking (a rarity here), is appreciated. No tipping is expected in self-service or fast-food restaurants, though college-bound employees may leave a cup beside the cash register to collect contributions.

In hotels, tip the bellhops $1 per piece (the same goes for skycaps at airports and railroad stations) and leave the housekeeping staff $1 to $2 per night. Cab drivers typically receive 15% of the fare; hairdressers and barbers, 15% to 20% of the bill. Tipping movie and theater ushers or gas-station attendants is not expected.

Toilets You won't find public toilets or "restrooms" on the streets in most U.S. cities, but they can be found in hotel lobbies, bars, restaurants, museums, department stores, railway and bus stations, or service stations. Note, however, that restaurants and bars in resorts or heavily visited areas may reserve their restrooms for the use of their patrons. Some establishments display a notice that toilets are for the use of patrons only. You can ignore this sign or, better yet, avoid arguments by paying for a cup of coffee or a soft drink, which will qualify you as a patron. Large hotels and fast-food restaurants are probably the best bets for good, clean facilities. If possible, avoid the toilets at parks and beaches, which tend to be dirty.

4

The Upper Cape: Sandwich, Bourne, Falmouth & Mashpee

Just over an hour from Boston by car, the Upper Cape towns have become bedroom as well as summer communities. They may not have the let-the-good-times-roll feel of towns farther east, but then again they're spared the transient qualities that come with seasonal flows. Shops and restaurants—many catering to an older, affluent crowd—tend to stay open year-round.

The four Upper Cape towns are all quite different. Bourne straddles the Cape Cod Canal; a couple of its villages (Bournedale and Buzzards Bay) are on the mainland side, and the others (Cataumet, Pocasset, Monument Beach, and Sagamore) are on the Cape side. The Canal provides this area with most of its recreational opportunities: biking, fishing, canal cruises, and the herring run. Cataumet is perhaps the prettiest village in Bourne, while many of Bourne's businesses, including popular factory outlets, are located on the mainland side of the bridge in Buzzards Bay.

Sandwich is the Cape's oldest town. At its core sits a lovely historic village, offering lots of unique shops and charming inns. Still, the town is primarily a pastoral place, with several working farms. In East Sandwich, miles of conservation land lead out to Sandy Neck, a barrier beach extending into Barnstable. The Old King's Highway (Rte. 6A) winds its way through Sandwich past a number of fine gift shops, galleries, and specialty stores.

Falmouth, the site of Cape Cod's first summer colony, is one of the larger towns on the Cape; it has a sizable year-round population of 32,000. Main Street—with a number of high-end boutiques and galleries, in addition to the usual touristy T-shirt shops—offers prime strolling and shopping. Falmouth's village green is quintessential New England, with two imposing historic churches: St. Barnabas, a sturdy reddish stone; and the First Congregational, a white-clapboard, steepled church boasting a Paul Revere bell. Just north of Falmouth center, along Route 28A, lies West Falmouth, perhaps the most attractive of Falmouth's eight villages; it has several good antiques stores, a fine general store, and a picture-perfect little harbor.

The most scenic drive in Falmouth leads to the beach at Falmouth Heights, a bluff covered with grand, shingled Victorians built during the first wave of tourist fever in the late 1800s. Falmouth's southernmost village is Woods Hole, which is the main ferry port for Martha's Vineyard. Home at any given time to several thousand research scientists, it has a certain neo-bohemian panache, lively bars, and an air of vigorous intellectual inquiry. It's also a working fishing village and one of the most picturesque spots on the Cape.

Mashpee is the ancestral home of the Cape's Native American tribe, the Wampanoags. Much of the town's coastline is occupied by a huge resort called New Seabury, while inland, the Mashpee National Wildlife Refuge sponsors frequent walking tours through its thousands of woodland acres.

1 Sandwich ★★★

3 miles E of Sagamore; 16 miles NW of Hyannis

Sandwich is both the oldest town on the Cape and, arguably, the most quaint. Towering oak trees and historic houses line its winding Main Street. Two early-19th-century churches and the columned Greek Revival Town Hall, in service since 1834, surround the town square. A 1640 gristmill still grinds corn beside bucolic Shawme Pond, which is frequented by swans, geese, ducks, and canoeists. To the north, villagers have built a boardwalk over the extensive salt marsh. Farther east, Sandy Neck, one of the Cape's most beautiful beaches, reaches into Cape Cod Bay.

Sandwich was founded in 1637 by a contingent of Puritans looking for a quiet place to worship. There is still an element of peacefulness in this little town located just a few miles from the Sagamore Bridge.

Sandwich's claim to fame is its prominence as the home to the nation's first glass factories in the early to mid–19th centuries. The famous Boston and Sandwich Glass Company and others employed over 500 craftspeople in town. In fact, the town still supports a number of highly skilled glassmakers. Sandwich is fortunate to have two very well-endowed museums—the **Heritage Plantation** ★★★ and the **Sandwich Glass Museum** ★—as well as several quirkier sites, like the **Green Briar Nature Center & Jam Kitchen** ★.

Many historic homesteads have been converted into charming bed-and-breakfasts that welcome guests year-round. There are also many excellent antiques shops in the area. The town is a convenient base for exploring other parts of the Cape that may offer more lively activities, like the nightlife of Hyannis or the ocean beaches of Wellfleet.

ESSENTIALS

GETTING THERE   If you're driving, turn east on Route 6A toward Sandwich after crossing either the Bourne or Sagamore bridge. The Sagamore Bridge will get you closer to your destination. You can also fly into Hyannis (see "Getting There" in chapter 2).

VISITOR INFORMATION   Contact the **Cape Cod Chamber of Commerce,** routes 6 and 132, Hyannis, MA 02601 (© **888/332-2732** or 508/862-0700; fax 508/362-2156; www.capecodchamber.org), open year-round, mid-April to mid-November daily 9am to 5pm; mid-November to mid-April Monday to Saturday 10am to 4pm. Stop in at the **Route 25 Visitor's Center** (© **508/759-3814;** fax 508/759-2146), open daily, year-round, Sunday to Wednesday 9am to 5pm, Thursday 9am to 8pm, Friday 9am to 9pm, and Saturday 9am to 7pm. The **Cape Cod Canal Region Chamber of Commerce,** 70 Main St., Buzzards Bay (© **508/759-6000;** fax 508/759-6965; www.capecodcanalchamber.org), open year-round, daily 9am to 5pm, can provide literature on both Sandwich and Bourne. A consortium of Sandwich businesses has put together an excellent walking guide (with map) available at most inns in town.

A GET-ACQUAINTED STROLL

This walk starts at the Sandwich Glass Museum, ends at the Dunbar Tea Shop, and takes 2 to 4 hours, depending on the number of stops you make; you'll cover about 1¼ miles. Your best bet is to explore the village on any midsummer day between 10am and 4pm, except Sunday, when some spots are closed.

You may park (free with admission) at the **Sandwich Glass Museum,** 129 Main St. (© **508/888-0251**), a well-curated collection tracing the town's history with an emphasis on glass made in Sandwich from 1825 to 1888.

Farther down Grove Street is **Old Cemetery Point,** overlooking peaceful Shawme Pond, about ⅓ mile down the road. Read the historic headstones and keep an eye out for box turtles. Head back through the center of town and observe the exterior of **Old Town Hall,** on Main Street—a magnificent Greek Revival edifice, complete with Doric columns. It still houses some town offices. Continue down Main Street, past the **First Church of Christ,** which is topped by an impressive spire. Built by a colleague of renowned Boston architect Charles Bulfinch in 1847, it was reportedly modeled on Sir Christopher Wren's St. Mary-le-Bow, in London. The next church you'll pass, to your left, is an 1833 meetinghouse, which recently had been used as a doll museum but is currently vacant.

Farther down Main Street, across the street from the popular Dan'l Webster Inn, you'll find **The Weather Store** at 146 Main St. (© **508/888-1200**). This unique shop stocks weather vanes, globes, sundials, and more and is devoted to the observation and understanding of New England's famously quirky weather.

Continue down Main Street and take a left on Jarves Street to admire the **Belfry Inn and Bistro** (© **800/844-4542** or 508/888-8550), a church and rectory converted into a very smart inn and restaurant. The restaurant, with its soaring ceilings and stained glass, is one of the prettiest and most unique dining spaces on Cape Cod.

Retracing your steps along Jarves Street, make a left-right zigzag along Main and School streets to reach Water Street, which skirts the eastern edge of Shawme Pond. Directly opposite, on the shore side of Water Street, you'll spot the **Hoxie House** 🏛 at 18 Water St. (© **508/888-1173**), one of the oldest houses on the Cape. The interior is spare—not out of any aesthetic ideal but because resources were so hard to come by in colonial New England. The settlers didn't even have closets because they were taxed as an additional room, windows were tiny to avoid the tax on glass, and pockets were considered a waste of good material. Entertaining docents explain all the details in frequent tours.

After the Hoxie House tour, head northward along Water Street, passing (on the same side) the **Thornton W. Burgess Museum,** 4 Water St. (© **508/888-4668**), which celebrates the life and work of native son Burgess (1874–1965). He was a highly successful author of children's books and creator of such still-beloved characters as Jimmy Skunk and Grandfather Frog. Just past the Burgess Museum is the **Dexter Grist Mill** 🏛 (© **508/888-4910**), a lovingly restored water mill (ca. 1640). The millstones still grind corn; buy a bag of meal to go, but only if you'll have a chance to whip up something later in the day (it doesn't keep well). Now that you're back at the center of town, this is a good time to pause for a spot of tea. The **Dunbar Tea Shop,** 1 Water St. (© **508/833-2485**), serves hearty lunches, teas, and breakfasts. The attached shop features British imports and antiques, including vintage books. It's a pleasant place to while away a good portion of the afternoon.

BEACHES & RECREATIONAL PURSUITS

BEACHES   For the Sandwich beaches listed below, nonresident parking stickers—$40 for the length of your stay—are available at **Sandwich Town Hall**

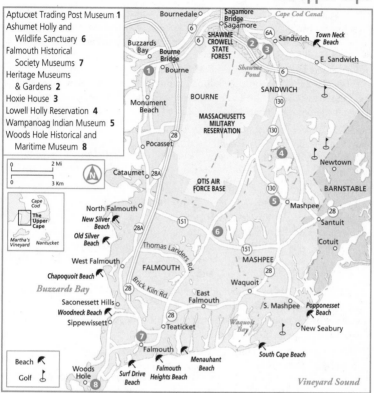

Aptucxet Trading Post Museum **1**
Ashumet Holly and
    Wildlife Sanctuary **6**
Falmouth Historical
    Society Museums **7**
Heritage Museums
    & Gardens **2**
Hoxie House **3**
Lowell Holly Reservation **4**
Wampanoag Indian Museum **5**
Woods Hole Historical and
    Maritime Museum **8**

Annex, 145 Main St. (© **508/833-8012**). *Note:* No swimming is allowed within the Cape Cod Canal, as the currents are much too swift and dangerous.

- **Sandy Neck Beach** 🏖🏖🏖, off Sandy Neck Road in East Sandwich: This 6-mile stretch of silken barrier beach with low, rounded dunes is popular with endangered piping plovers—and their nemesis, off-road vehicles (ORV). That means that the ORV trails are closed for most, if not all, of the summer while the piping plover chicks hatch. ORV permits ($100 per season for nonresidents) can be purchased at the gatehouse (© **508/362-8300**). ORV drivers must be equipped with supplies like a spare tire, jack, shovel, and tire-pressure gauge. Parking costs $10 per day in season. Up to 3 days of camping in self-contained vehicles is permitted at $10 to $12 per night.
- **Town Neck Beach,** off Town Neck Road in Sandwich: A bit rocky but ruggedly pretty, this narrow beach offers a busy view of passing ships, plus restrooms and a snack bar. Parking costs $10 per day, or you could hike from town (about 1½ miles) via the community-built boardwalk spanning the salt marsh.
- **Wakeby Pond,** Ryder Conservation Area, John Ewer Road (off South Sandwich Rd. on the Mashpee border): The beach, on the Cape's largest freshwater pond, has lifeguards, restrooms, and parking ($10 per day).

BICYCLING The **U.S. Army Corps of Engineers** (recreation hot line: © **508/ 759-5991**) maintains a flat, 14-mile loop along the **Cape Cod Canal** 🏖🏖🏖, equally suited to bicyclists, skaters, runners, and strollers. The most convenient place to park (free) is at the Bourne Recreation Area, north of the Bourne Bridge, on the Cape side. You can also park at the Sandcatcher Recreation Area at the end of Freezer Road in Sandwich.

The closest bike-rental shop is **P&M Cycles** at 29 Main St. in Buzzards Bay (© **508/759-2830**), opposite the railroad station. The shop also offers free parking. On the Cape side of the Canal, access is at the Bourne Recreation Area, just north of the Bourne Bridge, along Canal Road.

BOATING   If you want to explore by canoe, you can rent one in Falmouth and paddle around Old Sandwich Harbor, Sandy Neck, or the salt-marsh maze of Scorton Creek, which leads out to Talbot Point, a wooded spit of conservation land.

FISHING   Sandwich has eight fishable ponds; for details and a license, inquire at **Town Hall** in the center of town (© **508/888-0340**). Permits cost nonresidents $38.50 for the season, $24.50 for a 3-day pass. Children, seniors, and Massachusetts residents receive discounts. No permit is required to fish from the banks of the Cape Cod Canal. Here your catch might include striped bass, bluefish, cod, pollock, flounder, or fluke. Call the **U.S. Army Corps of Engineers** (© **508/759-5991**) for Canal tide and fishing information.

FITNESS   The local fitness center is the **Sportsite Health Club** at 315 Cotuit Rd. in Sandwich (© **508/888-7900**). It offers 15,000 square feet of Nautilus and other fitness equipment, along with steam baths, saunas, classes, and free child care. A 1-day pass costs $12.

GOLF   The **Sandwich Hollows Golf Club,** on Service Road in East Sandwich (© **508/888-3384**), is a 6,200-yard, par-71 town-owned course. In season, a round costs $30 to $60. The 18-hole, par-3 **Holly Ridge Golf Course,** on Country Club Road in South Sandwich (© **508/428-5577**), is, at 2,900 yards, shorter and easier. A round costs $29 in season.

NATURE & WILDLIFE AREAS   The **Shawme–Crowell State Forest,** off Route 130 in Sandwich (© **508/888-0351**), offers 285 campsites and 742 acres to roam. Entrance is free; parking costs $2. The **Sandwich Boardwalk,** which the community rebuilt in 1991 after Hurricane Bob blew away the 1874 original, links the town and Town Neck Beach by way of salt marshes that attract many birds, including great blue herons.

As if to signify how oddly enchanted this little corner of the world is, there's a sweet little (57-acre) nature center here—and within it is an even sweeter kitchen, where local ladies have been cooking up jams and jellies since 1903. The **Green Briar Nature Center & Jam Kitchen** ☆ is at 6 Discovery Hill (off Rte. 6A, about 1½ miles east of town center; © **508/888-6870**); once you've caught a whiff of the jam, you'll want to take some home. (Try the local delicacy, beach-plum jelly.) Children will be intrigued by the expansive kitchen, as well as some old-fashioned nature exhibits on such animals as rabbits, turtles, iguanas, and snakes. The center is open mid-April to December, Monday through Saturday 10am to 4pm, Sunday 1 to 4pm; January to mid-April Tuesday through Saturday 10am to 4pm. Admission by donation. Summer story time is at 10:30am on Monday, Wednesday, and Saturday, costing $1 per person.

TENNIS   Sandwich has public courts at the Wing School, Oak Ridge School, Forestdale School, and Sandwich High School. Contact the **Sandwich Recreation Department** (© **508/888-4361**) for details.

SANDWICH HISTORICAL SIGHTS

Dexter Grist Mill 🎐 (Kids)   This charmingly weathered building has survived some 3½ centuries and at least as many lives. At present, it serves its original purpose, grinding corn with turbine power; you can watch the wooden gears in action and buy a bag to take home and cook up into colonial "jonnycakes" (short for "cakes for the journey") or trendy polenta. Fresh corn meal costs $3.50 for a 2-lb bag, $9 for three bags. During the glassmaking boom of the 1800s, this venerable mill was but one of many pressed into service to keep the factory workers well fed. When the laborers dispersed, the mill sat useless until a local entrepreneur thought to convert it into a tearoom to serve the new tide of tourists arriving by motorcar. The mill was fully restored in 1961 and will probably be good for a few more centuries of stalwart service.

Water St. (on Shawme Pond, behind Town Hall). 📞 508/888-4910. Admission $3 adults, $1.50 children 6–12; combination ticket for Dexter Mill and Hoxie House ($4 adults, $2 children) available from the Hoxie House (see below). Mid-June to mid-Oct Mon–Sat 10am–4:45pm. Closed mid-Oct to mid-June.

Heritage Museums and Gardens ⭐⭐⭐ (Finds) (Kids)   This is one of those rare museums that appeals equally to adults and the children they drag along: The latter will leave clamoring for another visit. All ages have the run of 76 beautifully landscaped acres, crisscrossed with walking paths and riotous with color in late spring, when the towering rhododendrons burst forth in blooms that range from soft pink to gaudy orange. Scattered buildings house a wide variety of collections, from Native American artifacts to Cape Cod Baseball League memorabilia. The art holdings, especially the primitive portraits, are outstanding. The high point for most children will be a ride on the 1912 carousel (safely preserved indoors). Also sure to dazzle is the replica Shaker round barn packed with gleaming antique automobiles, including some once owned by celebrities (don't miss Gary Cooper's Duesenberg). Next door is the Carousel Cafe, good for a restorative snack, including soups, sandwiches, and salads. The gift shop at the gatehouse is also worth checking out. Call ahead for a schedule of the outdoor summer concerts usually held Sundays around 2pm, free with admission.

Grove and Pine sts. (about ½ mile southwest of the town center). 📞 508/888-3300. Admission $12 adults, $10 seniors, $6 children 6–16, free for children under 5. AE, DISC, MC, V. May–Oct Fri–Wed 9am–6pm, Thurs 9am–8pm; Nov–April Wed–Sun 10am–4pm. Closed Mon. No tickets sold after 4:15pm.

Hoxie House 🎐   Once a contender for the title of the Cape's oldest house (a couple of privately owned Provincetown houses appear to have a stronger claim), this saltbox (ca. 1680) is nonetheless a noteworthy beauty, with its diamond-pane windows and broad interior planking—made of "king's wood," so called because England's king had, under pain of severe penalty, reserved the larger trees for his warships. The house was occupied, pretty much as is, with neither electricity nor plumbing, into the 1950s, which explains how it remained so remarkably intact. Even so, it had to be taken apart and reassembled to serve as the model colonial home you see today. Fortunately, restorers opted not for the cluttered colonial revival look but a stark austerity that's much more historically accurate and shows off to advantage a handful of antiques on semi-permanent loan from Boston's Museum of Fine Arts.

18 Water St. (on Shawme Pond, about ¼ mile south of the town center). 📞 508/888-1173. Admission $3 adults, $1.50 children 12–16, free for children under 12; combination ticket ($3 adults, $1.50 children) available here for Dexter Grist Mill (see above). Mid-June to mid-Oct Mon–Sat 10am–4:45pm. Closed mid-Oct to mid-June.

Sandwich Glass Museum ⭐⭐ (Finds)   Even if you don't consider yourself a glass fan, make an exception for this fascinating museum, which captures the history of the town above and beyond its legendary industry. A brief video introduces Deming Jarves's brilliant endeavor, which flourished from 1828 to 1888, bringing glassware—a hitherto rare commodity available only to the rich—within reach of the middle classes. Jarves picked the perfect spot, surrounded by old-growth forest, to fuel the furnaces, with a harbor handy for shipping in fine sand from farther up the coast and salt-marsh hay with which to pack outgoing orders. All went well until Midwestern factories started using coal; unable to keep up with their level of mass production, he switched back to hand-blown techniques just as his workforce was ready to revolt.

None of this turmoil is evident in the dainty artifacts displayed in a series of sunny rooms; and, of course, the fact that the factory's output was finite makes surviving examples all the more valuable. Since the museum is run by the Sandwich Historical Society, one room is given over to changing exhibits highlighting other eras in the town's history, such as its stellar seafaring days. An excellent little gift shop stocks Sandwich-glass replicas, as well as original glassworks by area artisans. The museum completed a major expansion in 2002. Highlights include a furnace where glass-blowing demonstrations are featured and a multimedia theater.

129 Main St. (in the center of town). © 508/888-0251. www.sandwichglassmuseum.org. Admission $3.75 adults, $1 children 6–14, free for children under 6. Apr–Dec daily 9:30am–5pm; Feb–Mar Wed–Sun 9:30am–4pm. Closed Jan, Thanksgiving, and Christmas.

Thornton W. Burgess Museum ★ *Kids*   Prominent in the early half of the 20th century, this prolific and locally bred children's book author racked up 170 tomes to his credit, as well as 15,000 stories. His somewhat simple texts, featuring anthropomorphic animals prone to preaching, may seem a bit dated, but they still go over big with little listeners, especially at the summer-afternoon story hours (call for details). The gift shop carries reissues of his work, should they desire a memento. It's also worth a peek inside to see Harrison Cady's spirited illustrations and exhibits attesting to Burgess's other life work, conservation. He may have inherited this interest from his aunt (the original inhabitant of this 1756 cottage), who gained a certain notoriety for claiming that she could communicate directly with the animal and plant worlds. The museum offers walking tours of Victorian Sandwich on Thursday mornings in June, July, and August. Tours start on the museum grounds at 10:30am. Animal story times take place Monday, Thursday, and Saturday mornings at 10:30am in July and August, weather permitting.

4 Water St. (on Shawme Pond, near the center of town). © 508/888-4668. www.thorntonburgess.org. Suggested donation $2 adults, $1 children. Mid-Apr to Oct Mon–Sat 10am–4pm, Sun 1–4pm. Closed Nov to mid-Apr.

KID STUFF

The venerable 18-hole **Sandwich Minigolf** (© 508/833-1905), at the corner of Main Street and Route 6A, is a grassy 1950s classic that encapsulates Cape Cod history. Built on a former cranberry bog, it boasts an unusual floating green. Admission is $6 for adults, $4.50 for children.

SHOPPING

Small as it is, Sandwich has a handful of appealing shops—some with items you're unlikely to find anywhere else. Most of the shops are concentrated in the center of town. Several of the museums listed above (see "Sandwich Historical Sights," above) also have worthwhile gift shops.

ANTIQUES & COLLECTIBLES The **Sandwich Antiques Center,** 131 Rte. 6A, at Jarves Street (℗ **508/833-3600**), showcases wares from over 100 dealers in 6,000 square feet of rooms. It's headed by a congenial auctioneer and offers virtual one-stop shopping for the likes of Sandwich glass, primitives, country furnishings—you name it. The center is open daily year-round.

ARTS & CRAFTS The **Giving Tree Gallery,** 550 Rte. 6A, East Sandwich, about 4 miles east of the town center (℗ **508/888-5446**), is an art and fine-craft gallery with something extra: a nature walk through the woods. Intriguing sculptures are placed strategically around the property. The path through a bamboo forest is for those who appreciate a Far Eastern aesthetic. In fact, there's something very Zen about the whole Giving Tree experience. It's closed January to late May.

For the finest in art glass and the perfect souvenir of your Sandwich vacation, visit **The Glass Studio,** 470 Rte. 6A, East Sandwich (℗ **508/888-6681**), where master glass blower Michael Magyar crafts one-of-a-kind pieces like his "sea bubbles" series and Venetian-style goblets.

BOOKS **Titcomb's Book Shop,** 432 Rte. 6A, East Sandwich, about 4 miles east of the town center (℗ **508/888-2331**), has a terrific selection of books (both new and used) relating to Cape Cod and much more. Look for the life-size statue of Ben Franklin out front.

FOOD & WINE **Crow Farm,** 192 Rte. 6A, ¼ mile east of the town center (℗ **508/888-0690**), is a picture-perfect farm stand harboring superb local produce like sweet corn, tomatoes, peaches, and apples, as well as flowers. It's closed Sunday in summer but open daily in spring and fall. It's closed late December through April.

GIFTS/HOME DECOR The **Weather Store,** 146 Main St. (℗ **508/888-1200**), has a fascinating collection of meteorological paraphernalia, old and new, ranging from antique instruments to coffee-table books. While technically open year-round, from January through April, it's open by chance or appointment.

SEAFOOD **Joe's Lobster & Fish Market,** off Coast Guard Road, near Sandwich Marina (℗ **800/491-2971** or 508/888-2971), is where to go for the freshest fish and shellfish to prepare at your cottage rental.

WHERE TO STAY

Sandwich has a number of motels along Route 6A, but the one with the best location is **Sandy Neck Motel** at 669 Rte. 6A, East Sandwich (℗ **800/564-3992** or 508/362-3992; www.sandyneck.com), which sits at the entrance to the road leading to Sandy Neck, the best beach in these parts. Rates are $89 to $99 double and $125 to $225 for one- and two-room efficiencies. It's closed November to mid-April.

EXPENSIVE

Bay Beach ★★   Each of the three rooms in this luxurious beachfront home, overlooking Town Neck Beach with a view of the Sagamore Bridge and the boat traffic along the Canal, has amenities to add to a romantic interlude, like a fireplace, double Jacuzzi, and CD player. As Sandwich's only on-beach lodging option, Bay Beach offers immaculate, modern rooms perfect for couples seeking privacy and comfort.

3 Bay Beach Lane (on Town Beach), Sandwich, MA 02563. ℗ **800/475-6398** or 508/888-8813. Fax 508/888-5416. www.baybeach.com. 3 units. Summer $245–$325 double. Rates include full breakfast. MC, V. Closed Nov–Apr. No children under 16. *In room:* A/C, TV/VCR w/pay movies, fridge, hair dryer, iron.

The Dan'l Webster Inn ★★   This large and popular lodging and dining spot in the center of Sandwich village is a dependable bet for a comfortable stay or a hearty meal. The inn encompasses a modern main building, designed to look historic, as well as several historic homes nearby that have been outfitted with modern amenities. The main building sits on the site of a colonial tavern favored by Daniel Webster, the famous orator and prominent Boston lawyer, who enjoyed fishing on the Cape. The inn is operated by the Catania family (owners of the Hearth 'N Kettle restaurants dotting the Cape) with professionalism and style. All the rooms are ample and nicely furnished with reproductions. The suites located in nearby historic houses are especially appealing; they feature fireplaces and canopy beds. There are also eight deluxe one-room suites in the main building with amenities like balconies, gas fireplaces, oversize whirlpool baths, and heated tile floors in the bathrooms. The inn's common spaces are convivial, if bustling; sometimes tour buses stop here. The restaurant, which turns out surprisingly sophisticated fare, is quite good, especially considering the high volume of customers (see "Where to Dine," below).

149 Main St. (in the center of town), Sandwich, MA 02563. ⓒ 800/444-3566 or 508/888-3622. Fax 508/888-5156. www.danlwebsterinn.com. 54 units. Summer $159–$229 double, $219–$359 suite. Rates include full breakfast off season only. AE, DC, DISC, MC, V. **Amenities:** Restaurant and tavern/bar; small outdoor heated pool; access to nearby health club; room service (8am–9pm in season, 11am–9pm off season). *In room:* A/C, TV, dataport, hair dryer, iron.

MODERATE

The Belfry Inne ★★ *Finds*   This church-turned-inn right in the center of Sandwich Village is about the most creative renovation on Cape Cod. The turreted 1879 rectory is the gaudiest "painted lady" in town. The rooms are creatively decorated and romantic, with queen-size retrofitted antique beds, a claw-foot tub (or Jacuzzi) for every room, and a scattering of fireplaces and private balconies. The third floor, with its single attic rooms and its delightful *Alice in Wonderland* mural leading up to the belfry, is perfect for families with children. Next door is the Abbey, a former church that owner Chris Wilson has converted into six fun and deluxe guest rooms, and a very fine restaurant (see below). The Abbey rooms are painted vivid colors and tucked cleverly into sections of this old church. One room features a stained-glass window; another has angel windows. All of the Abbey rooms have Jacuzzis. Mr. Wilson recently purchased the Village Inn (see below), just down the road, with 8 rooms decorated in a French country style.

8 Jarves St. (in the center of town), Sandwich, MA 02563. ⓒ 800/844-4542 or 508/888-8550. Fax 508/888-3922. www.belfryinn.com. 22 units. Summer $95–$195 double. Rates include continental breakfast. AE, MC, V. **Amenities:** Restaurant.

Isaiah Jones Homestead ★ *Value*   Of the many B&Bs in Sandwich Center, this one is a particularly good value, though the fancier rooms tend to be more expensive (and more elegant) than those at other small B&Bs in town. Innkeepers Jan and Doug Klapper have carefully appointed this courtly 1849 Victorian with fine antiques and reproductions. Many rooms have additional romantic touches like fireplaces and whirlpool baths. Two mini-suites in the Carriage House have sitting alcoves. The room named for industrial magnate Deming Jarves boasts an inviting floral-curtained half-canopy bed and an oversize whirlpool tub. The gentility that prevails at the candlelight breakfast, served with fine china and crystal, completes the picture.

165 Main St. (in the center of town), Sandwich, MA 02563. ⓒ 800/526-1625 or 508/888-9115. Fax 508/888-9648. www.isaiahjones.com. 7 units. Summer $115–$175 double. Rates include full breakfast. AE, DISC, DC, MC, V. Children under 12 cannot be accommodated. *In room:* AC, hair dryer, no phone.

Wingscorton Farm Inn ★★ *Kids* *Finds*   This 7-acre farmhouse inn will delight youngsters and animal lovers of all ages. It's been a working farm since 1758 and still houses a cheerful brood of sheep, goats, dogs, cats, chickens, a pet turkey, and a potbellied pig on its tree-shaded grounds. The main house is a classic colonial with a "keeping room" boasting a 9-foot-long hearth. Upstairs are two paneled bedrooms with canopy beds, working fireplaces, braided rugs, and antiques. Modernists might prefer the carriage house, with its skylight-suffused loft bedroom, kitchen (with woodstove), and private deck and patio; it doesn't cost appreciably more. There is also a cottage on the grounds. Guests staying in the main inn and carriage house can enjoy a hearty multi-course breakfast at the long farmhouse table in the kitchen. A private bay beach is a short walk down a country lane.

11 Wing Blvd. (off Rte. 6A, about 5 miles east of the town center), East Sandwich, MA 02537. © 508/888-0534. Fax 508/888-0545. 3 units, carriage house, cottage. Summer $175 suite, $200 carriage house; $1,100 weekly cottage. Rates for suites and carriage house include full breakfast. AE, MC, V. Pets welcome. *In room:* A/C, TV, fridge, no phone.

INEXPENSIVE

Captain Ezra Nye B&B ★ *Value*   This handsome 1829 Federal manse with its fanlight and twin chimneys is set in the center of the village, within walking distance of many historic sites. Rooms, if not ultra-luxurious, are nicely appointed with eclectic antiques. Rates are a bargain, and breakfast tends to be substantial, along the lines of goat cheese soufflé or upside-down apple French toast.

152 Main St. (in the center of town), Sandwich, MA 02563. © 800/388-2278 or 508/888-6142. Fax 508/833-2897. www.captainezranyehouse.com. 6 units (5 shower; 1 tub/shower). Summer $120–$135 double, $175 suite. Rates include full breakfast. AE, DISC, MC, V. Children under 10 cannot be accommodated. *In room:* A/C, no phone.

The Inn at Sandwich Center *Value*   This historic B&B started out as a plain 1750s saltbox and got a fancy Federal makeover a century later. Rooms are spacious and tastefully decorated with reproductions. Amenities include robes, bottled water, and handmade chocolates. A full breakfast, featuring homemade

---

Kids **Family-Friendly Hotels & Restaurants**

Betsy's Diner in Falmouth (p. 92)   This classic 1950s diner offers all the old faves, plus home-baked pastries.

The Clam Shack in Falmouth (p. 93)   Children will love the size of this place (it's Lilliputian), the plain fare, and all the activity on the harbor.

The Silver Lounge Restaurant in North Falmouth (p. 92)   This is the favorite restaurant of generations of kids because of the little red caboose attached to the side. There are just nine booths in the caboose, so you'll need to get there early if you want to snag one.

Spring Garden Inn in East Sandwich (p. 70)   With its spacious tree-shaded backyard and pool, this well-maintained motel is understandably popular with families.

Wingscorton Farm Inn in East Sandwich (see above)   What could beat a working farm—with a beach within walking distance—for both education and fun?

specialties like pecan maple French toast, is served in the keeping room, with its original fireplace and beehive oven. Owners Ann and Charlie Prevs, who bring a touch of southern hospitality to the inn, are working to upgrade this charming B&B to the quality of a small luxury hotel by having extras like high-quality linens and bath products. The Sandwich Glass Museum is directly across the street. Loaner bikes are available.

118 Tupper Rd. (in the center of town), Sandwich, MA 02563. © **800/249-6949** or 508/888-6958. Fax 508/888-2746. www.innatsandwich.com. 5 units. Summer $130–$170 double. Rates include full breakfast in season, continental off season. AE, MC, V. Children under 12 cannot be accommodated. **Amenities:** Loaner bikes. *In room:* A/C, hair dryer, no phone.

Seth Pope House 1699 Bed & Breakfast (Value)

Perhaps not everyone would be comfortable sleeping in a 300-year-old home, but traditionalists will be delighted with these gracious accommodations provided by innkeepers John and Beverly Dobel. Each room in this lovingly maintained 1699 saltbox has a distinctive decor. The Colonial Room features exposed beams, a pencil-post bed, and a cherry bonnet chest. The Victorian Room is pink-accented with plenty of marble. Also pleasant is the Pineapple Room, with twin pineapple-post beds and a salt-marsh view. Breakfast in the old keeping room features a parfait of fruit, granola, and yogurt followed by a baked omelet or stuffed French toast.

110 Tupper Rd. (in the center of town), Sandwich, MA 02563. © **888/996-7384** or 508/888-5916. 3 units (shower only). Summer $90–$95 double. Rates include full breakfast. MC, V. Closed Nov–Apr. *In room:* A/C, no phone.

Spring Garden Inn ★ (Kids) (Value)

This well-maintained, beautifully landscaped motel overlooks acres of conservation land known as the Great Sandwich Salt Marsh. Every room comes with a south-oriented patio or porch that takes in the lush view. Barbecue grills and picnic tables are available outside on the mahogany deck. With its spacious, tree-shaded backyard and pool, the reasonably priced motel is understandably popular with families. Guests will also appreciate the complimentary homemade continental breakfasts.

578 Rte. 6A (P.O. Box 867; about 5 miles east of the town center), East Sandwich, MA 02537. © **800/303-1751** or 508/888-0710. Fax 508/833-2849. www.springgarden.com. 11 units (9 tub/shower; 2 shower only). Summer $109 double, $124 efficiency. Rates include continental breakfast. DISC, MC, V. Closed Dec–Mar. **Amenities:** Outdoor pool. *In room:* A/C, TV/VCR, fax, fridge, coffeemaker, iron.

Spring Hill Motor Lodge ★

This motel boasts all sorts of amenities, and the owners keep it in top condition. The interiors are cheerfully contemporary, the grounds verdant. In addition to the motel rooms, there are four cottages that are light, airy, and comfortable. The cottages have full kitchens (microwave ovens instead of standard ovens) as well as two televisions and a VCR.

351 Rte. 6A (about 2½ miles east of the town center), East Sandwich, MA 02537. © **800/647-2514** or 508/888-1456. Fax 508/833-1556. www.sunsol.com/springhill. 24 units (20 tub/shower), 4 cottages (shower only). Summer $95–$150 double, $155–$225 efficiency, $185–$250 or $1,100 weekly for 1-bedroom cottage, $225–$325 or $1,400 weekly for 2-bedroom cottage. AE, DC, DISC, MC, V. **Amenities:** Elegantly landscaped heated outdoor pool; oversize night-lit tennis court. *In room:* A/C, TV, fridge, coffeemaker.

The Village Inn at Sandwich ★★ (Finds)

Why envy the guests relaxing in rockers on the wraparound porch of this gracious 1860 Federal house when you could be among them? Better yet, you'll have recourse to surprisingly light and airy sleeping quarters, with gleaming bleached floors, California-ish splashes of colorful fabric, and enveloping duvets. From the French country–style dining room to the cozy dormer attic, the mood is one of carefree comfort. This inn is now owned by Chris Wilson (see Belfry Inn, above), known for his high-quality inn properties.

4 Jarves St. (in the center of town), Sandwich, MA 02563. © **800/922-9989** or 508/833-0363. Fax 508/833-2063. www.capecodinn.com. 8 units, 2 with shared bathroom (showers only). Summer $110 shared bathroom, $125–$130 double. Rates include continental breakfast. AE, DISC, MC, V. *In room:* No phone.

WHERE TO DINE
MODERATE

Aquagrille ✦ SEAFOOD   Overlooking Sandwich's picturesque marina and not-so-picturesque power plant, this dining spot, owned by the respected Zartarian family of The Paddock Restaurant in Hyannis, is trying hard to be the premier place for fish in Sandwich. All the elements are in place: a spacious, attractive dining room decorated in pleasing aqua shades, a glass-enclosed harbor-view deck; and a long, curving bar. The food is delicious and plentiful, with fish (grilled or fried) the obvious choice, plus lots of pasta dishes. The towering lobster salad with haricot vert, tomato, avocado, chives, and crème fraîche is the perfect antidote to a steamy summer night. Those with larger appetites may want to try the baby back pork spareribs with peach barbecue sauce, which comes with—what else?—potato salad and Boston baked beans. Other favorites are the seafood paella and the filet with fried lobster tail, a very satisfying surf and turf. Try to get a table that doesn't face the power plant.

14 Gallo Rd. (next to Sandwich Marina). © **508/888-8889**. www.aquagrille.com. Reservations recommended. Main courses $8–$20. AE, DC, MC, V. Apr–Oct Mon–Fri 11:30am–2:30pm and 5–9pm, Sat–Sun noon–9pm; call for off-season hours.

The Belfry Bistro ✦✦ *Finds* NEW AMERICAN   Sandwich's most romantic dining option is located in a renovated abbey, formerly a Catholic church. The Gothic space is quite spectacular, with flying buttresses supporting the ceiling's high arches. Once seated, guests can concentrate on the snowy, dense linens, intimate lighting, and pleasing menu. Portions are generous and elegantly presented. The menu changes seasonally, but among the appetizers you might find a lobster, scallop, and leek "bundle" wrapped in phyllo dough, baked golden brown, and served on a bed of sautéed leeks and scallions with a chardonnay cream sauce. The entrees run the gamut from the delicate shrimp scampi with artichoke hearts to the hearty grilled filet mignon served with garlic and leek mashed potatoes on a white bean ragout. Desserts here are clearly a specialty; especially good is the old-fashioned Victorian gingerbread with fresh berries. An early bird menu served Tuesday to Friday features three-course dinners from $17 to $19. There is a piano bar Friday and Saturday nights. Because this restaurant hosts many weddings and other events, it is sometimes closed to the public, so be sure to call ahead.

8 Jarves St. (in the center of town). © **508/888-8550**. Reservations recommended. Main courses $19–$29. AE, MC, V. Feb–Dec Tues–Sat 5–10pm; call for off-season hours. Closed Jan.

The Dan'l Webster Inn ✦✦ AMERICAN   You have a choice of four main dining rooms—from a casual, colonial-motif tavern to a skylight-topped conservatory fronting a splendid garden. The atmospheric Tavern at the Inn, with its own pub-style menu, is perhaps the most popular. All of the dining rooms are served by the same kitchen, under the masterful hand of chef/co-owner Robert Catania. A restaurant on this scale could probably get away with ho-hum, middle-of-the-road food, but his output is on a par with that of the Cape's best boutique restaurants. Try a classic dish like the *fruits de mer* (seafood) in white wine, or try a seasonal highlight (the specials menu changes monthly). For lighter appetites, half portions are available. There is also a children's menu.

149 Main St. (in the center of town). ℰ 508/888-3622. Reservations recommended. Main courses $18–$29, Tavern menu $7–$14. AE, DC, DISC, MC, V. Daily 8am–9pm; call for off-season hours.

INEXPENSIVE

The Bee-Hive Tavern ⭐ INTERNATIONAL   A cut above the rather characterless restaurants clustered along this stretch of road, this modern-day tavern employs atmospheric old-time touches without going overboard. Green-shaded banker's lamps, for example, illuminate the dark wooden booths, and vintage prints and paintings convey a clubby feel. The food is good if not spectacular, and well priced for what it is. The menu features straightforward steaks, chops, and fresh-caught fish among the pricier choices, while burgers, sandwiches, and salads cater to lighter appetites (and wallets). This is a great option for lunch, when you should try one of the Cape's best lobster rolls.

406 Rte. 6A (about ½ mile east of the town center), East Sandwich. ℰ 508/833-1184. Main courses $7–$16. MC, V. Mon–Sat 11:30am–3pm and 5–9pm; Sun 8–11:30am, noon–3pm, and 5–9pm.

The Dunbar Tea Shop BRITISH   Whether you choose the cozy confines of the Tea Room on a crisp autumn day or the shady outside grove in summer, you'll enjoy the hearty English classics served here. Lunch beginning at 11am features homemade soups, salads, and sandwiches like the Farmer's Lunch (crusty warm bread, roast beef, horseradish sauce, and English mustard). The Tea Room also serves tea, of course, with all the traditional fixings and accompaniments you'd expect. A tea-themed gift shop is attached.

1 Water St. (in the center of town). ℰ 508/833-2485. www.dunbarteashop.com. Main courses under $10. DISC, MC, V. June–Oct daily 11am–5pm; Oct–May 11am–4:30pm.

Marshland Restaurant (Value) DINER   Locals have been digging this diner for two decades. This is home-cooked grub, slung fast and cheap. You'll gobble up the hearty breakfast and be back in time for dinner, when fried seafood plates are a specialty.

109 Rte. 6A. ℰ 508/888-9824. Most items under $10. No credit cards. Mon 6am–2pm; Tues–Sat 6am–8pm. Open year-round.

SWEETS

Sweet tooth acting up? Stop by Sandwich's appropriately named **Ice Cream Sandwich** ⭐ at 66 Rte. 6A, across from the Stop & Shop (ℰ 508/888-7237), for a couple of scoops of the best local ice cream. Try the Cape Cod chocolate chunk. Closed November through March.

SANDWICH AFTER DARK

Horizons on Cape Cod Bay   On summer weekends, a light bar menu is served until midnight at this beachside party spot with decks overlooking the town beach. On Friday and Saturday nights in season, there's live music, like acoustic guitar. There's also a large bar area, pool table, and large-screen TV. Closed November to March. 98 Town Neck Rd. ℰ 508/888-6166. No cover.

Sandwich Auction House   Do you have the guts—not to mention the funds—to be a player? You'll find out soon enough as the bidding grows heated over an ever-changing parade of antique goods, from chests to portraits to spinning wheels. Antique-rug auctions take place once a month. The record set here so far was for an antique toy pedal car that fetched $77,000. Sit on your hands if you must. Auctions are held the first and third Saturday of every month, year-round; previews start at 2pm the same day. MasterCard and Visa are accepted.

15 Tupper Rd. (at Rte. 6A). ℰ 508/888-1926. Fax 508/888-0716. Free admission.

2 Bourne

4 miles W of Sagamore; 16 miles NW of Hyannis

Bourne, a primarily residential community with seven villages, hugs Buzzards Bay on both sides of the Cape Cod Canal. But for the maddening traffic and sundry other evidence of encroaching modernization, this bucolic community is probably not all that different from what President Grover Cleveland encountered when, evidently attracted by the trout, he decided to set up his summer White House at Monument Beach in the 1890s. That house is long gone, but one vestige—his personal train station—is on view at the Aptucxet Trading Post Museum, a reconstructed version of this country's first place of commerce, where Pilgrims traded with Native Americans and the Dutch. Also visible from here—and from the Cape Cod Canal bike path, which runs right past the post—is the intriguing **Vertical Lift Railroad Bridge** (built in 1935); its track moves up or down to permit the passage, respectively, of ships or trains. Cataumet, with its winding roads, is the most upscale village in Bourne. Though a tad run-down, Buzzards Bay with its Main Street paralleling the Canal has most of the shops. A developer recently unveiled plans to build a 1-million-square-foot mall next to the Bourne Bridge rotary—a controversial topic, to say the least, in this unassuming town.

Somewhat introverted and intent on its own old-fashioned pleasures, Bourne is best savored by those seeking the very, very quiet life.

ESSENTIALS

GETTING THERE   To get to Buzzards Bay, take Exit 1 off Route 25 before crossing the Bourne Bridge. To get to Cataumet, Monument Beach, and other Bourne villages, cross either the Bourne or Sagamore bridge, and turn west on Route 6A toward Bourne. You can also fly into Hyannis (see "Getting There" in chapter 2).

VISITOR INFORMATION   Contact the **Cape Cod Chamber of Commerce** (see "Visitor Information" in the "Sandwich" section, earlier in this chapter) or stop at the **Route 25 Visitor's Center.** The **Cape Cod Canal Region Chamber of Commerce,** 70 Main St., Buzzards Bay (© **508/759-6000**), can provide literature on both Sandwich and Bourne.

BEACHES & RECREATIONAL PURSUITS

BEACHES   Bourne has only one public beach: **Monument Beach** ✭, off Shore Road. Half the parking lot is free (this fills up fast), and the other half requires a sticker from **Bourne Town Hall** at 24 Perry Ave. in Buzzards Bay (© **508/759-0623**). Though the beach is small and pebbly, it's picturesque. Full public-beach facilities accompany the relatively warm waters of Buzzards Bay.

BICYCLING   See "Bicycling" under "Sandwich," earlier in this chapter. The **Cape Cod Canal bike path** ✭✭✭, 14 miles on both sides of the Canal, is one of the best on the Cape. On the mainland side of the Canal, on Main Street in Buzzards Bay, access is at the far end of Buzzards Bay Park. The closest bike-rental shop is **P&M Cycles** at 29 Main St. in Buzzards Bay (© **508/759-2830**), opposite the railroad station. Rentals are $6 an hour, $25 for the full day. The shop also offers free parking. On the Cape side of the Canal, access is at the Bourne Recreation Area, just north of the Bourne Bridge, along Canal Road.

BOATING   If you have your own canoe or kayak or want to rent one in Falmouth, you'll enjoy exploring Back River and Phinney's Harbor at Monument

Kids Ocean Quest

No visit to the Cape would be complete without some type of seafaring excursion on the Atlantic. If you're not a sailor or if you don't have the time or budget for an all-day boat trip, consider a unique, hands-on discovery cruise with **Ocean Quest** ★★, Water Street (in the center of town), Woods Hole (© **800/376-2326** or 508/385-7656; www.ocean questonline.org). Departing from Woods Hole, these 1½-hour harbor cruises are perfect for families, as real marine research is conducted with passengers serving as bona fide data collectors.

Here's how it works. Participants are split into two teams. Up in the bow, company founder Kathy Mullin, or a scientist borrowed from one of the revered local institutes, trains the new crew in the niceties of reading water temperature, assessing turbidity, and taking other key measurements. In the stern, passengers get to examine the specimens hauled up by the dredger. Midway into the trip, the teams switch stations, so that everyone gets to contemplate topics such as the sex life of a spider crab or why the water looks a particular shade of blue or green. Kids get a real kick out of being addressed as "Doctor," and even adults who think they know it all will probably come away much better informed.

The 90-minute cruise costs $20 for adults and $15 for children 3 to 12; boats shove off four times a day Monday through Friday from mid-June to early September. Trips depart at 10am, noon, 2pm, and 4pm. Reservations are strongly recommended.

Beach. **Cape Cod Kayak** (© **508/563-9377;** www.capecodkayak.com) rents kayaks (free delivery) by the day or week and offers lessons and Ecotours on local waterways. Canoe and kayak rentals are $25 to $35 for a half day, $35 to $45 for a full day. Lessons are $30 per hour. Four-hour trips are $50.

FISHING   So plentiful are the herring making their spring migration up the **Bournedale Herring Run** ★★ (© **508/759-5991,** Route 6 in Bournedale, about 1 mile southwest of the Sagamore Bridge rotary), that you can net them once they've reached their destination, Great Herring Pond. You can obtain a shellfish permit from **Bourne Town Hall** at 24 Perry Ave., Buzzards Bay (© **508/ 759-0613**). Also plentiful here are pickerel, white perch, walleye, and bass. For freshwater fishing at Flax Pond and Red Brook Pond in Pocasset, you'll need a license from the **Bourne Town Hall** (see above). You can also obtain a license at **Red Top Sporting Goods** at 265 Main St. in Buzzards Bay (© **508/759-3371**). Surf-casting along the Cape Cod Canal requires no permit.

ICE-SKATING   The **John Gallo Ice Arena,** 231 Sandwich Rd. in Bourne (© **508/759-8904**), is open to the public daily from September to March and reduced hours in the summer. Rates are $2 for adults, $1 for children.

NATURE & WILDLIFE AREAS   The Bourne Conservation Trust has managed to get hold of a handful of small plots; for information, contact the town **Conservation Commission** (© **508/759-0625**). The largest tract is the **Four Ponds Conservation Area/Town Forest,** which consists of 280 acres off

Barlows Landing Road in Pocasset. The 40-acre **Nivling–Alexander Reserve** (off Shore Rd. at Thaxter Rd.) has three walking trails and flanks Red Brook Pond, where fishing is permitted (see above); it offers a half-mile wooded walk past several cranberry bogs. The **U.S. Army Corps of Engineers** (© 508/ 759-5991), which is in charge of the **Cape Cod Canal,** gives free naturalist-guided nature walks and slide shows about the Canal.

TENNIS   In the Bourne area, public courts are located near the old schoolhouse on County Road in Cataumet, and in Chester Park, opposite the railroad station in Monument Beach. For information, call the **Bourne Memorial Community Center** on Main Street in Buzzards Bay (© 508/759-0650), which also has courts.

VISIT A MUSEUM

Aptucxet Trading Post Museum   Long before the Canal was a twinkle in Myles Standish's (and later, George Washington's) eye, Native Americans had been portaging goods between two rivers, the Manomet and Scusset, that once almost met at this site; its name in Algonquian means "little trap in the river." The Pilgrims were quick to notice that Aptucxet made an ideal trading spot, especially since, as Gov. William Bradford pointed out, it would allow them to trade with the Dutch to the south without "the compassing of Cape-Codd and those dangerous shoulds [shoals]." In 1627, the Pilgrims built an outpost here, hoping to cash in as conduits for native-caught pelts. The present building is a replica, built after a pair of local archaeologists, using ancient maps, uncovered the original foundation in 1926. The other detritus they dug up (arrowheads, pottery shards, and so on) is displayed in a roomful of rather dim, crowded display cases. Also be sure to have a look at the **Bournedale Stone,** which was discovered serving as a threshold for a Native American church built in the late 17th century. Overturned, it revealed strange, runelike inscriptions—fueling the legend (unsubstantiated as yet) that Vikings roamed the Cape around A.D. 1000.

Even though the building is not authentic, the curator does a very good job of conjuring up the hard, lonely life led by the pair of sentinels assigned here. Several other odd artifacts are scattered about the grounds, such as **President Grover Cleveland's personal train station** from his estate at Gray Gables, and a **windmill** used as an art studio by his good friend and fishing companion, the hugely successful actor Joseph Jefferson. Driven out of Sandwich for his scandalous profession (he was a Democrat to boot!), Jefferson was avenged when he was buried there with a tart epitaph: "We are but tenants; let us assure ourselves of this, and then it will not be so hard to make room for the new administration, for shortly the Great Landlord will give us notice that our lease has expired."

A new exhibit focuses on the making of salt, once a booming industry on Cape Cod. Replica saltworks have been constructed, and the knowledgeable docent will walk you through the process. You might even get a sample of gourmet salt to take home.

The **Cape Cod Canal bike path** ★★★ runs right behind the museum. This is a good spot from which to observe the **Vertical Lift Railroad Bridge** ★, which represented state-of-the-art technology for its time (1935, when it cost $1.5 million). Rush hour, between 5 and 6pm, is your best chance to catch the bridge lowering its trestle (for the garbage cars headed off-Cape). In the off season, you might get a colorful sunset thrown in for good measure.

24 Aptucxet Rd., off Perry Ave. (about ½ mile west of the town center), Bourne Village. © 508/759-9487. Admission $3.50 adults, $1.50 children 6–18. July–Aug Mon–Sat 10am–4pm, Sun 2–4pm; Apr–June and Sept to mid-Oct Tues–Sat 10am–5pm. Closed mid-Oct to Mar.

TAKE A CRUISE

Cape Cod Canal Cruises ⭐ *Kids* . Get an underbelly view of the Cape's two swooping car bridges and its unusual railroad bridge as you wend your way among a wide array of interesting craft, and a narrator fills you in on the Canal's history. Basically, it was the brainchild of New York financial wizard Augustus Perry Belmont, who completed it in 1914 at a cost of $16 million and never saw a penny of profit. Found to be too narrow and perilous (the current reverses with the tides, roughly every 6 hr.), the ambitious waterway was handed over to the U.S. Army Corps of Engineers for expansion in 1928 at the discount price of $11.5 million. It continues to serve as a vital shortcut, sparing some 30,000 boats yearly the long, dangerous circuit of the Outer Cape.

The 4pm **family cruise,** offered Monday to Saturday, is a real bargain, at $10 per adult and free for children 12 and under. The Sunday afternoon trip is accompanied by New Orleans–style jazz, and the sunset entertainment cruises on Friday and Saturday (adults over 21 only) feature live bands.

Onset Bay Town Pier (on the northern side of the Canal, about 2 miles west of the Bourne Bridge), Onset. ℂ 508/295-3883. www.hy-linecruises.com. Tickets $10–$14 adults, free–$8 children 12 and under. AE, DISC, MC, V. Mid-June to Sept departures daily 10am and 1:30pm; Mon–Sat 4pm, Tues–Thurs 7pm, Fri–Sat 8pm. Call for off-season schedule. Closed mid-Oct to Apr.

TAKE YOURSELF OUT TO A BALL GAME

Sports fans of all ages will enjoy taking in nine innings of the Grand Old Game. Part of the elite-amateur **Cape Cod Baseball League** (ℂ 508/432-6909; www.capecodbaseball.org), the Braves play at Coady School Field, in Buzzards Bay, in July and August. Call the **Cape Cod Canal Region Chamber of Commerce** (ℂ 508/759-6000) to check the schedule.

KID STUFF

Stuck with a gray day? Pack the family off to **Adventure Isle** on Route 28, about 2 miles south of the Bourne Bridge (ℂ 800/535-2787 or 508/759-2636). Older kids can tackle the laser-tag arena, go-carts, bumper boats, bumper cars, minibikes, batting cages, and video games, among other juvenile delights. Little kids have their own little amusement park, complete with mini-Ferris wheel, giant slides, mini-golf, and a train with clanging bell. Prices are reasonable ($1.75–$4 per ride), but they're sure to add up quickly. Buy an unlimited-rides pass for $9.95 to $12 to save money. The **Miniature Golf** course, at the intersection of County Road and Route 28A in Cataumet (ℂ 508/563-7450), offers 18 holes of Astroturf with a gold-rush theme. This is cheap fun: $5 adults, $4 children gets you two rounds if it's not too crowded. *Be forewarned:* There's an **ice-cream parlor** ⭐ next door, and you can't expect to escape without a lick.

SHOPPING

Instead of the usual cutesy Cape Cod shops, Bourne is known for its factory outlets. **Tanger Outlet Center,** located at the Bourne rotary on the mainland side of the Bourne Bridge (ℂ 800/482-6437), has the following outlets: Liz Claiborne, Levis, Nine West, and Izod. **Cape Cod Factory Outlet Mall,** just off Route 6, Exit 1, Sagamore (ℂ 508/888-8417), has 20 stores including Van Heusen, L'Eggs/Hanes/Playtex/Bali, Osh Kosh B'Gosh, Bass Shoe, and Samsonite. Here are a few other notable stops:

GIFTS You can observe artisans continuing the tradition of the Boston & Sandwich Glass Company at **Pairpoint Glass Works,** 851 Sandwich Rd. (Rte. 6A, at the foot of the Sagamore Bridge), Sagamore (ℂ 800/899-0953 or

508/888-2344). Thomas J. Pairpoint was a leading designer in the 1880s. The output is on the conservative side and includes skillful replicas. Glass blowing takes place Monday to Friday from 9am to 4pm. Bargain-lovers flock to the **Christmas Tree Shops** at the Sagamore Bridge, Sagamore (✆ **508/888-7010**). The stock here is not just holiday-related. Housed in an oversize thatch-roofed Tudor cottage, complete with spinning windmill (you can't miss it), the array is Woolworthian in scope, but of much higher quality. There are six more outlets elsewhere on the Cape.

SEAFOOD You couldn't hope for a fresher catch than what you'll find at **Cataumet Fish,** 1360 Rte. 28A, Cataumet (✆ **508/564-5956**). Buy a whole fish or cart home a couple of lobsters.

WHERE TO STAY

The Beachmoor ⭐ (Value) Quite a bit off the beaten track, this sleepy property located right at the mouth of the Cape Cod Canal next to the Massachusetts Military Academy offers bargain rates and a pleasant ambience. There is a tiny private beach in front of the hotel. Views (particularly sunsets) from one of the bedrooms, the commons room, and the superb casual restaurant on the first floor (see "Where to Dine," below) are memorable. Rooms are decorated individually and with flair, and there's loving attention to detail throughout. For instance, iron bedsteads are romantically draped with gauzy fabric, and curtains are handmade with lacy netting. Out front is a private beach perfect for sunning.

11 Buttermilk Way, Buzzards Bay, MA 02532. ✆ 508/759-7522. www.beachmoor.com. 6 units. Summer $85–$95 double, $125 suite. Rates include continental breakfast. AE, DC, DISC, MC, V. **Amenities:** Restaurant (see below). *In room:* TV/VCR, no phone.

WHERE TO DINE

The Beachmoor ⭐⭐ NEW AMERICAN If you happen to be anywhere near the Bourne Bridge and in need of dinner, you'll want to head over to the Beachmoor in Buzzards Bay. They serve up terrific food along with a wonderful view of the Cape Cod Canal. Specialties at dinner include Beachmoor Stew (shrimp, clams, scallops, lobster, and fish in a saffron broth) and the daily trilogy, which might include poached salmon with béarnaise sauce, grilled swordfish with basil butter, and broiled scallops in lemon butter. Save room for dessert, and if baked pear is on the menu, don't hesitate. It's a heavenly concoction with crisp-on-the-outside, doughy-on-the-inside squares surrounding the delicate baked pears, served with vanilla ice cream and raspberry sauce. Evening entertainment is offered on Fridays (Nick Lombardo sing-along) and Saturdays (Al "Fingers" Russo at the piano bar). On Sundays, there's a brunch buffet for $15.

11 Buttermilk Way, Buzzards Bay. ✆ 508/759-7522. Reservations recommended. Main courses $13–$28. AE, DC, DISC, MC, V. Apr–Sept Wed–Sat 5–10pm, Sun 11:30am–8pm; call for off-season hours. Closed Jan–Mar.

The Chart Room ⭐⭐ SEAFOOD Great sunset views over Red Brook Harbor and fresh fish are reason enough to visit this dockside restaurant, housed in a former railroad barge at a busy marina. A piano bar lends a bit of elegance, as does the well-heeled clientele.

1 Shipyard Lane (in the Kingman Yacht Center, off Shore Rd.), Cataumet. ✆ 508/563-5350. Dinner reservations required. Main courses $12–$25. AE, MC, V. Mid-June to early Sept daily 11:30am–10pm; mid-May to mid-June and early Sept to mid-Oct Thurs–Sun 11:30am–10pm. Closed mid-Oct to mid-May.

The Parrot Bar and Grill NEW AMERICAN For years, the Blue Parrot, a gritty bar with a sour reputation, occupied this crossroads in Cataumet. A new owner has cleaned the place up and resuscitated it as an upbeat casual family restaurant specializing in seafood and pasta. Try the lobster pie or the blackened swordfish with Southwestern salsa. Thursday to Saturday, live local bands entertain.

1356 Rte. 28A, Cataumet. © **508/563-6464**. Reservations not accepted. Main courses $10–$15. MC, V. Daily 11am–10pm.

AN INTERNET CAFE

The best web cafe on the Cape is **The Daily Brew Coffee Bar and Cafe,** Cataumet Square, Cataumet (1370 Rte. 28A, Cataumet; © **508/564-4755**), where you can get awesome espressos, cappuccinos, and baked goods, as well as soups, salads, and sandwiches. There are several computers upstairs if you want to log on. There is outside seating on a covered patio in back. The cafe is open 6:30am to 6pm Monday through Thursday and until 7pm on Friday and Saturday.

BOURNE AFTER DARK

On weekends, local bands draw a crowd of young adults to the **Courtyard Restaurant and Bar,** Cataumet Square, Cataumet (© **508/563-1818**). There's no cover charge. From here you can barhop next door to **The Parrot Bar and Grill,** 1356 Rte. 28A (see "Where to Dine," above), which has live music Thursday to Saturday in season. No cover.

3 Falmouth ★★★

18 miles S of Sagamore; 20 miles SW of Hyannis

Falmouth is a classic New England town, complete with church steeples encircling the town green and a walkable and bustling Main Street. It offers a variety of activities and summer events for vacationers, from beautiful beaches and bike paths to weekly outdoor band concerts and summer theater. Founded in 1660 by Quaker sympathizers from Sandwich (where Congregationalists considered theirs the one true path), Falmouth proved remarkably arable territory: By the 19th century, it reigned as the strawberry capital of the world. Today, with over 32,000 year-round residents, it's the second largest town on the Cape, after Barnstable.

After more than a century of catering to summertime guests (it was the first "fashionable" Cape resort, served by trains from Boston starting in the 1870s), Falmouth residents have hospitality down to an art—a business, too, but people are so genuinely welcoming, you'll tend to forget that. The area around the historic **Village Green** ★★ (given over to military exercises in the pre-Revolutionary days) is a veritable hotbed of B&Bs, with each vying to provide the most elaborate breakfasts and solicitous advice. Put yourself in the hands of your hosts, and you'll soon feel like a native.

Officially a village within Falmouth (one of eight), tiny **Woods Hole** ★★★ has been a world-renowned oceanic research center since 1871, when the U.S. Commission of Fish and Fisheries set up a primitive seasonal collection station. Today the various scientific institutes crowded around the harbor—principally, the National Marine Fisheries Service, the Marine Biological Laboratory (founded in 1888), and the Woods Hole Oceanographic Institute (a newcomer as of 1930)—have research budgets in the tens of millions of dollars and employ thousands of scientists. Woods Hole's scientific institutions offer a unique opportunity to get in-depth—and often hands-on—exposure to marine biology.

Belying the stereotype of the nerdy scientist, the Woods Hole community is far from uptight; in fact, it's one of the hipper communities on the Cape. In the past few decades, a number of agreeable restaurants and shops have cropped up,

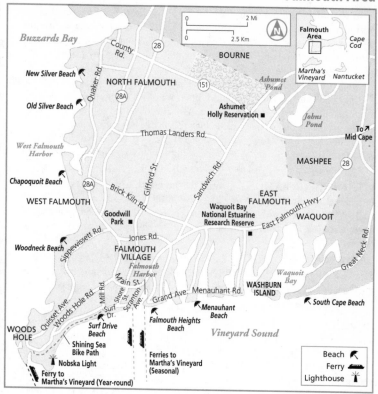

Buzzards Bay

County Rd.

28

BOURNE

New Silver Beach

NORTH FALMOUTH

151

Ashumet Pond

To Mid Cape

Quaker Rd.

28A

Old Silver Beach

Ashumet Holly Reservation

Johns Pond

Thomas Landers Rd.

West Falmouth Harbor

MASHPEE

28

Chapoquoit Beach

28A

Brick Kiln Rd.

Gifford St.

Sandwich Rd.

EAST FALMOUTH

WEST FALMOUTH

Goodwill Park

Waquoit Bay National Estuarine Research Reserve

East Falmouth Hwy.

WAQUOIT

Sippewissett Rd.

Jones Rd.

Great Neck Rd.

Woodneck Beach

FALMOUTH VILLAGE

Falmouth Harbor

Waquoit Bay

WASHBURN ISLAND

South Cape Beach

Main St.

Shore St.

Scranton Ave.

Grand Ave.

Menauhant Rd.

Menauhant Beach

Mill Rd.

Surf Dr.

Falmouth Heights Beach

Quisset Ave.

Woods Hole Rd.

Surf Drive Beach

WOODS HOLE

Shining Sea Bike Path

Nobska Light

Vineyard Sound

Ferries to Martha's Vineyard (Seasonal)

Ferry to Martha's Vineyard (Year-round)

Beach
Ferry
Lighthouse

Falmouth Area
Cape Cod
Martha's Vineyard
Nantucket

0   2 Mi
0   2.5 Km

making the small, crowded gauntlet of Water Street (don't even think of parking here in summer) a very pleasant place to stroll.

West Falmouth (which is really more north of town, stretched alongside Buzzards Bay) has held on to its bucolic character and makes a lovely drive, with perhaps an occasional stop for the more alluring antiques stores. **Falmouth Heights**, a cluster of shingled Victorian summerhouses on a bluff east of Falmouth's harbor, is as popular as it is picturesque; its narrow ribbon of beach is a magnet for all, especially families. The **Waquoit Bay** area, a few miles east of town, has thus far eluded the over-commercialization that blights most of Route 28, and with luck and foresight will continue to do so. Several thousand acres of this vital estuarine ecosystem are now under federal custody.

ESSENTIALS
GETTING THERE   After crossing either the Bourne or Sagamore bridge, take Route 28 or 28A south. Crossing the Bourne Bridge will get you closer to your destination. Or fly into Hyannis (see "Getting There" in chapter 2).

Falmouth's bus station near the center of town is serviced by Bonanza Bus Lines (59 Depot Ave.; © **508/548-7588;** www.bonanzabus.com). Daily express buses run to and from Boston's Logan Airport, as well as Boston's South Station train and bus terminal ($29, round-trip). There are also daily buses to Providence, Rhode Island ($39 round-trip); T. F. Green Airport in Providence; and New York City ($93 round-trip).

To get around Falmouth and Woods Hole (where parking in summer is a mathematical impossibility due to ferry traffic to Martha's Vineyard), use the **Whoosh Trolley,** which makes a circuit every 20 minutes down Falmouth's Main Street to Woods Hole from 9:30am to 7:10pm Monday to Friday and until 10:30pm on weekends from late May to late September. You can pick up the trolley at the Falmouth Mall on Route 28, where there is plenty of parking.

Tip: The **Whoosh Trolley**'s extended hours (until 10:30pm Fri–Sat in the summer) means you can use it to go down to Woods Hole in the summer for dinner. Otherwise, parking in Woods Hole in high season can be a major challenge.

The **Sea Line Shuttle** (✆ **800/352-7155**) connects Woods Hole, Falmouth, and Mashpee with Hyannis year-round (except holidays). The fare ranges from $1 to $3.50, depending on distance; children under 5 ride free.

VISITOR INFORMATION   Contact the **Falmouth Chamber of Commerce,** Academy Lane, Falmouth, MA 02541 (✆ **800/526-8532** or 508/548-8500; fax 508/548-8521; www.falmouth-capecod.com), or the **Cape Cod Chamber of Commerce** (see "Visitor Information" in the "Sandwich" section, earlier in this chapter).

WINDING DOWN   For a well-earned pick-me-up, take a biscotti break at **The Coffee Obsession** 👍 (✆ **508/540-2233**), a hip and friendly coffee bar in the Queens Buyway at the corner of North Main and Palmer Avenue.

BEACHES & RECREATIONAL PURSUITS

BEACHES   While Old Silver Beach, Surf Drive Beach, and Menauhant Beach will sell a 1-day pass, most other Falmouth public beaches require a parking sticker. Passes to Old Silver are $15 and passes to Surf Drive and Menauhant are $10. Renters can obtain temporary beach parking stickers, for $50 per week or $80 per month, at **Falmouth Town Hall,** 59 Town Hall Sq. (✆ **508/548-7611**), or at the **Surf Drive Beach Bathhouse** in season (✆ **508/548-8623**). The town beaches for which a parking fee is charged all have lifeguards, restrooms, and concession stands. Here is a list of some of Falmouth's public shores:

- **Falmouth Heights Beach** 👍👍👍, off Grand Avenue in Falmouth Heights: Once a rowdy spot, this is primarily a family beach these days. Parking is sticker-only. This neighborhood supported the Cape's first summer colony; the grand Victorian mansions still overlook the beach, though now they are joined by a bevy of motels.

- **Grew's Pond** 👍👍, in Goodwill Park off Palmer Avenue in Falmouth: This freshwater pond in a large town forest stays fairly uncrowded, even in the middle of summer. While everyone else is experiencing beach rage, trying to find parking at Falmouth's popular saltwater beaches, here you park for free and can wander shady paths around the pond. There are picnic tables, a playground, barbecue grills, a lifeguard, and restrooms.

- **Menauhant Beach** 👍, off Central Avenue in East Falmouth: A bit off the beaten track, Menauhant is a little less mobbed than Falmouth Heights Beach and better protected from the winds. A 1-day pass costs $10.

- **Old Silver Beach** 👍👍👍, off Route 28A in North Falmouth: Western-facing (great for sunsets) and relatively calm, this warm Buzzards Bay beach is a popular, often crowded, choice. This is the chosen spot for the college crowd and other rowdy young folk. Mothers and their charges cluster on the opposite side of the street where a shallow pool formed by a sandbar is perfect for toddlers. There is a bathhouse with showers. Windsurfers are available to rent in season. A 1-day pass costs $10.

• **Surf Drive Beach** ✪✪✪, off Shore Street in Falmouth: About a half mile from downtown, and appealing to families, this is an easy-to-get-to choice with limited parking. The tidal beach between the jetties is a shallow, calm area called "the kiddie pool." There is an outdoor shower. A 1-day pass costs $10.

BICYCLING   The **Shining Sea Bicycle Path** ✪✪✪ (✆ 508/548-8500) is a 3.3-mile beauty skirting Vineyard Sound from Falmouth to Woods Hole; it connects with a 23-mile scenic-road loop through pretty Sippewissett. This is one of the Cape's most scenic bike paths and one of the few that travels alongside the shoreline. You can park at the trail head on Locust Street in Falmouth or at any spot in town (parking in Woods Hole is scarce). The closest bike shop—convenient to the main cluster of B&Bs, some of which offer "loaners"—is **Corner Cycle** at Palmer Avenue and North Main Street (✆ 508/540-4195). A half-day bike rental is $14, a 24-hour rental $18. For a broad selection of vehicles—from six-speed cruisers to six-passenger "surreys"—and good advice on routes, visit **Holiday Cycles** at 465 Grand Ave. in Falmouth Heights (✆ 508/540-3549), where a half-day bike rental is $15, a 24-hour rental $25, a week's rental $75. The surreys rent for $20 to $30 an hour.

The Falmouth Chamber of Commerce offers a map and brochure about the Shining Sea Bicycle Path. Biking along this former railroad track that follows prehistoric Wampanoag Indian trails, the bike path passes 21 acres of woodlands, marsh, swamp, salt ponds and seascape.

The path's name is a nod to Falmouth's own Katharine Lee Bates, who wrote the lyrics to "America the Beautiful" with its verse, "And crown thy good with brotherhood, from sea to shining sea!"

BIRD-WATCHING   The **Shining Sea Bicycle Path** (see above) is a great spot to bird-watch. Keep an eye out for yellow-breasted chats and orange-crowned warblers, as well as waterfowl like mallards and buffleheads. You may also see majestic herons, egrets, and osprey.

Massachusetts Audubon (✆ 508/362-1426) offers day-long trips to **Cuttyhunk** out of Falmouth Harbor most Sundays from late August through September. The 50-foot boat can take 45 people and has an enclosed cabin. The trips feature naturalist-led guided walks, and participants have a choice of taking short, medium, or long walks on the island. Boats leave Falmouth Harbor at 9am and return at 5pm. The cost is $50 for adults, $45 for seniors, and $40 for ages 16 and under. There are discounts for Audubon members.

BOATING   **Patriot Party Boats,** 227 Clinton Ave. (at Scranton Ave. on the harbor), Falmouth (✆ 800/734-0088 or 508/548-2626; www.patriotpartyboats.com, www.TheLiberte.com), offers one-stop shopping for would-be boaters. The Patriot fleet includes a poky fishing/sightseeing vessel, the *Patriot Too;* and a 74-foot, three-masted schooner, the **Liberte** ✪✪ (2-hr. sails; $20–$25 adults, $15–$18 children 12 and under). While wending among the Elizabeth Islands, some privately owned by the Forbes family, *Patriot Too* owner Jim Tieje can give you the scoop on local gossip and lore. Two-hour sunset cruises on the *Patriot Too,* which are BYOB, take place in July and August and cost $15 for adults, $10 for kids 12 and under. The boat, which can take 49 people, departs at 6pm. On the *Liberte,* Jim's brother Chris Tieje hauls up the sails and regales passengers about his custom-made schooner, while the impressive vessel cruises the sound. For info on fishing trips, see below.

Cape Cod Kayak (✆ 508/563-9377; www.capecodkayak.com) rents kayaks (free delivery) by the day or week, and offers lessons and eco-tours on local waterways. Canoe and kayak rentals are $25 to $35 for a half day, $35 to $45 for a full day. Lessons are $30 per hour. Four-hour trips are $50.

If you want to explore on your own, **Waquoit Kayak Company** at **Edward's Boat Yard,** 1209 E. Falmouth Hwy., East Falmouth (© **508/548-9722**), rents out canoes ($45 half day, $59 full day) and kayaks ($35 half day, $49 full day) for exploring Waquoit Bay (see "Nature & Wildlife Areas," below). **Washburn Island** ✮✮✮, a protected reserve with wooded trails and pristine beaches, is about a 1-hour paddle via canoe.

FISHING   Falmouth has six fishable ponds. A complimentary fishing map and guide are available from the Falmouth Chamber of Commerce. Freshwater fishing and shellfishing licenses can be obtained at **Falmouth Town Hall,** 59 Town Hall Sq. (© **508/548-7611,** ext. 219). Freshwater fishing licenses can also be obtained at **Eastman's Sport & Tackle,** 150 Main St. (© **508/ 548-6900**).

Surf Drive Beach is a great spot for surf-casting, once the crowds have dispersed. Other good locations are the jetties off Nobska Point in Woods Hole and Bristol Beach on Menauhant Road in East Falmouth.

To go after bigger prey, head out with a group on one of the **Patriot Party Boats** based in Falmouth's Inner Harbor (© **800/734-0088** or 508/548-2626). Boats leave twice daily in season. The clunky *Patriot Too,* with an enclosed deck, is ideal for family-style "bottom fishing" (4-hr. sails $30 adults, $20 children under 12; equipment provided).

For sportfishing out of Falmouth Inner Harbor, call Capt. Bob MacGregor of the **Hop-Tuit** (© **508/540-7642**), who trolls for striped bass, bluefish, bonito, and school tuna on half-day, full-day, and night trips. A half-day trip costs $500 for six people; a full day costs $700. Captain Dan Junker of **Cool Running Charters** (© **508/457-9445**) takes his boat *Relentless* out of Falmouth Harbor and around Nantucket Sound, Vineyard Sound, and the Elizabeth Islands for bass, blues, tuna, and shark.

FITNESS   If you're jonesing for time in the gym, the **Falmouth Sports Center** at 33 Highfield Dr. (© **508/548-7433**) offers weight-training facilities for $8 per day. Racquet sports cost an extra $13 to $21 per person, per hour.

GOLF   Falmouth abounds in golf courses—six public ones at last count. Among the more notable is the challenging 18-hole championship course at **Ballymeade Country Club,** 125 Falmouth Woods Rd. (© **508/540-4005**). Greens fees are $58 (weekdays) and $76 (weekends) and include carts.

ICE-SKATING   Public skating ($4 per person) is offered year-round at the **Falmouth Ice Arena,** 9 Skating Lane off Palmer Avenue (© **508/548-7080**), the home rink of Colleen Coyne, who was part of the gold medal 1998 Olympic hockey team; call for information and hours.

NATURE & WILDLIFE AREAS   **Ashumet Holly and Wildlife Sanctuary** ✮✮, operated by the Massachusetts Audubon Society at 186 Ashumet Rd., off Route 151 (© **508/362-1426**), is an intriguing 49-acre collection of more than 1,000 holly trees spanning 65 species and culled worldwide. Preserved by the state's first commissioner of agriculture, who was concerned that commercial harvesting might wipe out native species, they flourish here, along with over 130 species of birds and a carpet of Oriental lotus blossoms, which covers a kettle pond come summer. The trail fee is $3 for adults and $2 for seniors and children under 16.

Close to the center of Falmouth (just follow Depot Rd. to the end) is the 650-acre **Beebe Woods** ★★, a treasure for hikers and dog walkers. From here, you can wend your way to the **Peterson Farm** ★★ (entrance off Woods Hole Rd.; take a right at the Quisset farm stand), purchased by the town of Falmouth in 1997. The 90-acre farm has paths through woods and fields, as well as a flock of sheep grazing in a meadow near historic farm buildings. Bluebird boxes (special birdhouses for bluebirds) line the path on the way to a quiet pond. There is no charge to walk in Beebe Woods.

Tiny but dazzling, the privately owned **Spohr Garden** ★★ on Fells Road, off Oyster Pond Road in Woods Hole, invites visitors to explore 6 magical acres beside Oyster Pond. In the spring, thousands of daffodils bloom, followed by rhododendrons and day lilies. Paths wind past a collection of nautical treasures, like huge anchors and millstones. Remarkably, this private garden is free and open to the public. Donations for garden maintenance are accepted.

Named for its round shape that sticks out into the harbor, **The Knob** ★★, 13 acres of trails at Quissett Harbor at the end of Quissett Road, provides a perfect short walk and lovely views of Buzzards Bay. There's very limited parking at this small, secluded harbor, so try it early or late in the day. The Knob is owned by the nonprofit group, Salt Pond Areas Bird Sanctuaries, and is free and open to the public.

The 2,250-acre **Waquoit Bay National Estuarine Research Reserve (WBN-ERR),** at 149 Waquoit Hwy. in East Falmouth (✆ 508/457-0495; www.waquoit bayreserve.org), maintains a 1-mile, self-guided nature trail. The reserve also offers a number of walks and interpretive programs, including the popular "Evenings on the Bluff," on Thursday nights at 6:30pm that is geared toward families. Inquire about WBNERR's cruise over to **Washburn Island** ★★★ on Saturdays in season by reservation. It takes several hours to explore all the wooded trails on the island. There are also several pristine beaches. The 12-passenger motorboat leaves at 9am and returns by 12:30pm. After the 20-minute boat trip to the island, naturalist-led guided walks are offered. The reserve also manages 11 primitive campsites on Washburn Island. Permits cost a mere $5 to $6 a night. Reservations are required in advance and can be made by calling ✆ 877/422-6762. (The campsites book up 6 months in advance for summer weekends, but you'll have better luck with a late spring or early fall booking.)

TENNIS   Among the courts open to the public are those at the **Falmouth High School,** 874 Gifford Rd., Falmouth Recreation Department; and at the **Lawrence School** on Lakeview Avenue, a few blocks from the center of town. Call the Falmouth Chamber of Commerce (✆ 508/548-8500) for information. Both are first-come, first-served. Among the commercial enterprises offering outdoor courts—clay, Har-Tru, and hard—are **Ballymeade Country Club** (see "Golf," above) and the **Falmouth Sports Center** (see "Fitness," above), which has six indoor courts in addition to three outside. Rates are $21 an hour per person for singles play.

WATERSPORTS   Falmouth is something of a sailboarding mecca, prized for its unflagging southwesterly winds. While Old Silver Beach in North Falmouth is the most popular spot for windsurfing, the sport is allowed there only prior to 9am and after 5pm. The Trunk River area on the west end of Falmouth's Surf Drive Beach and a portion of Chapoquoit Beach are the only public beaches where windsurfers are allowed during the day. Concessions rent windsurfing equipment at Surf Drive Beach.

SEA SCIENCE IN WOODS HOLE

Marine Biological Laboratory   The small Robert W. Pierce Visitors Center and Gift Shop offers visitors short on time a chance to gain some insight into the goings-on at this preeminent scientific facility, part of which is housed in an 1836 candle factory. Visitors can observe marine organisms and learn how they help scientists understand nature. The "Into The Lab" exhibit allows visitors to peer into a microscope, like the scientists on staff here. A guided tour requires a little more forethought—the MBL prefers that reservations be made a week in advance—but will definitely reward the curious. After a slide presentation, a retired scientist leads visitors through the holding tanks and then to the lab to observe actual research in progress. The MBL's area of inquiry is not limited to the aquatic but encompasses the "biological process common to all life forms"; some of what you see may have an immediate bearing on your own life or on those of your descendants.

100 Water St. (at MBL St., in the center of town), Woods Hole. ✆ 508/289-7623. Free admission. Visitors Center hours July–Aug Mon–Fri 10am–4pm, Sat and Sun 10am–3pm; call for off-season hours. Closed Jan. Tours by reservation (no children under 10) mid-June to Aug Mon–Fri 1, 2, and 3pm.

Woods Hole Science Aquarium ★ *Kids*   A little beat-up after 1¼ centuries of service and endless streams of eager schoolchildren, this aquarium—the first such institution in the country—may not be state of the art, but it's a treasure nonetheless. The displays, focusing on local waters, might make you think twice before taking a dip. Children show no hesitation, though, in getting up to their elbows in the "touch tanks"; adults are also welcome to dabble. A key exhibit that everyone should see concerns the effect of plastic trash on the marine environment. You might time your visit to coincide with the feeding of the two seals that live here. The fish fly at 11am and 4pm.

Albatross St. (off the western end of Water St.), Woods Hole. ✆ 508/495-2001. Donations accepted. Mid-June to early Sept daily 11am–4pm; mid-Sept to mid-June Mon–Fri 10am–4pm. You need a picture ID to enter.

Woods Hole Oceanographic Institution Exhibit Center and Gift Shop   This world-class research organization—locally referred to by its acronym, WHOI (pronounced *hooey*)—is dedicated to the study of marine science. And with some $80 million in annual funding at stake, there's serious science going on here. This is a small but interactive exhibit center. Kids might enjoy looking through microscopes at organisms or listening to sounds of marine animals on a computer. *Titanic* fans will enjoy the brief video, displays, and a life-size model of the submersible that discovered the wreck. You can climb into the model and flick switches, if you like. One-hour walking tours of WHOI are offered twice a day on weekdays in July and August, reservations required; call ✆ **508/289-2252.**

15 School St. (off Water St.), Woods Hole. ✆ 508/289-2663. $2 donation requested. Late May to early Sept Mon–Sat 10am–4:30pm, Sun noon–4:30pm; call for off-season hours. Closed Jan–Mar.

FALMOUTH HISTORICAL SIGHTS

The Falmouth Historical Society runs air-conditioned 1½-hour **trolley tours** of Falmouth's historic sites on select dates in summer and fall. The trolley runs every other Saturday from late June to mid-December, and tickets are $10 for adults and $8 for children. Stop by the Historical Society, 55–65 Palmer Ave., or the chamber of commerce, Academy Lane, for this year's schedule.

Falmouth Museums On The Green ★★   Knowledgeable volunteers will lead you through three buildings that contain fascinating vestiges of Falmouth's colorful history. Tours begin at the 1790 Julia Woods House, built by Revolutionary physician Dr. Francis Wicks; a simulacrum of his office, complete with terrifying tools, is not for the faint of heart. Next door, past an authentic colonial garden, is the mid-18th-century Conant House, which evolved from a half-Cape built to accommodate the town's minister; it now houses nautical collections, including intricate "sailor's valentines" made of shells, and whaling exhibits. A china hutch in the dining room displays romantic Staffordshire china. A special room chronicles the life of Katharine Lee Bates, Falmouth-born author of "America the Beautiful." Also on the grounds is the Dudley Hallett Barn, which contains vintage farm tools and the sleigh that Dr. Wicks used for house calls.

In the summer, the museum sponsors guided strolls, trolley tours, and afternoon teas. The free 90-minute guided strolls take place Tuesdays in July and August. Groups meet at 4pm at the Old Burying Ground at the intersection of Locust Street and Mill Road, a few blocks from the museum. Trolley tours take place every other Wednesday at 10am in July and August. The $10-per-person cost includes museum admission. Teas take place Thursdays mid-July through August from 1 to 3pm, weather permitting. The $10-per-person fee includes museum admission.

55–65 Palmer Ave. (at the Village Green). © 508/548-4857. www.FalmouthHistoricalSociety.org. Admission $5 adults, free for children under 13. June to mid-Sept Tues–Sat 10am–4pm; mid-Sept to Oct Sat –Sun 1–4pm. Open Nov–May by appointment.

Woods Hole Historical Museum ✿   Exhibits change at this small but charming museum, a local labor of love. The permanent 1895 diorama of the town should give you the former flavor of this combination seaport/scientific community and tourist destination. The neighboring barn shelters a Small Boat Museum including an Old Town canoe, a Cape Cod "knockabout," a Herreshoff 12½, and a fine example of a "spritsail" boat. There's also the reconstructed 1893 hobby workshop of a local doctor. To delve into town lore in more detail, reserve a place on one of the free walking tours offered Tuesdays at 4pm in July and August.

579 Woods Hole Rd. (on the eastern edge of town), Woods Hole. © 508/548-7270. Free admission. Donations welcome. Mid-June to mid-Sept Tues–Sat 10am–4pm; off season by appointment.

BASEBALL

Part of the elite-amateur **Cape Cod Baseball League** (© 508/432-6909; www.capecodbaseball.org), the Commodores play at Fuller Field, off Main Street, in July and August. Call the **Falmouth Chamber of Commerce** (© 508/ 548-8500) to check the schedule, or pick one up at the **Falmouth Recreation Center,** 790 E. Main St. (© 508/457-2567).

SHOPPING

Falmouth's spiffy Main Street has a number of good clothing, home goods, and gift stores. There are several good arts and crafts galleries in West Falmouth and Woods Hole.

ANTIQUES/COLLECTIBLES   On her way to the Martha's Vineyard ferry in Woods Hole, Jackie O. often stopped at the **Antiquarium,** at 204 Palmer Ave. It is the exquisite red-clapboard Greek Revival house with the red fence located next to the Steamship Parking lots (© 508/548-1755). This is a quirky place, open only when the flag is out, but inside are treasures. Mr. O. D. Garland carries a general mixture of American and European antiques, as well as decorative arts. **Chrisalis Country Home,** 550 Rte. 28A, West Falmouth (© 508/540-5884), a pleasantly packed shop, is owned by Dorothy Donlan. She operates an interior-design business from these digs—it ought to be booming, judging from her astute antiques selection and inspired pairings of old and new.

Village Barn Antiques, 606 Rte. 28A, West Falmouth (© **508/540-3215**), housed in a beautiful old barn, has a large selection of odds and ends.

ARTS & CRAFTS   The **Woods Hole Gallery,** 14 School St. (north of Water St.), Woods Hole (© **508/548-7594**), is far enough off the beaten path so you won't stumble onto it by accident, but collectors will want to call on Edith Bruce, an art restorer who operates a distinguished gallery out of her home. Landscapes—dunescapes, specifically—are a specialty. Closed mid-September to late June.

FASHION   Don't be too intimidated to browse in **Maxwell & Co.,** 200 Main St. (in the center of town), Falmouth (© **508/540-8752**), which may be the highest-end clothier on the Cape. Comfortable Italian fashions are displayed here in an elegant setting. Their end-of-summer sale in mid-August offers up to 70% off the prices of these exquisite goods.

The clothing at **Caline for Kids,** 149 Main St. (in the center of town), Falmouth (© **508/548-2533**), ranges from practical to elegant, and sometimes manages to be both. Sizes from newborn to 14 are available.

Europa, 628 Rte. 28A, West Falmouth (© **508/540-7814**), features interesting and stylish international clothes and gifts. They add up to a sophisticated look, liberated from cookie-cutter predictability. There's also a small but adorable selection of clothes for very young children.

FOOD & WINE   People drive from all over the region for the wine selection (and prices) at **Kappy's,** 21 Spring Bars Rd., off Route 28 (© **508/548-2600**), the Cape's largest liquor, beer, and wine store. "Pick your own" is the password at the long-established **Tony Andrews Farm and Produce Stand,** 398 Old Meeting House Rd. (about 1½ miles north of Rte. 28), East Falmouth (© **508/548-4717**), where it's strawberries early in the summer, and tomatoes, sweet corn, and more as the season progresses. Of course, you can just buy them here without picking, though the Puritans wouldn't have approved. **Coonamessett Farm,** 277 Hatchville Rd. (about 1 mile east of Sandwich Rd.), Hatchville (© **508/563-2560**), has a full farm stand of vegetables grown in the fields out back. You can pick your own vegetables, look at the farm animals (including two cute llamas), or rent a canoe for a paddle in the pond out back. A **vegetarian buffet dinner** is served Friday and Saturday nights in season (5–8pm; $13 adults, $6.95 children, free for ages 5 and under).

GIFTS   **Bojangles,** 239 Main St. (© **508/548-9888**), a high-end gift shop/women's clothing boutique, is a significant addition to Falmouth's Main Street shopping. Stop here for funky gifts and fine crafts, including exceptional hand-painted glassware.

WHERE TO STAY

For a basic motel with a great location, try the **Tides Motel** (© **508/548-3126**) at the west end of Grand Avenue in Falmouth Heights. The 1950s-style no-frills (no air-conditioning, no phone) motel sits on the beach at the head of Falmouth Harbor facing Vineyard Sound. Rates in season are $140 to $150 double, $195 suite. It's closed late October to mid-May.

The **Red Horse Inn** ★ (© **508/548-0053;** www.redhorseinn.com) is a family-friendly option just a short walk from Falmouth Harbor in Falmouth Heights. The 22 rooms are priced from $150 to $250 and kids will love the large outdoor pool.

EXPENSIVE

Coonamessett Inn ★★   A gracious inn built around the core of a 1796 homestead, the Coonamessett Inn is Falmouth's most traditional lodging choice.

The original inn was a few miles away and flanked the namesake river. Its future was in question until the late Josiah K. Lilly, a local resident, funded it with a trust designed to keep its body and soul intact. Set on 7 lushly landscaped acres overlooking a pond, it has the feel of a country club where all comers are welcome. Some of the rooms, decorated in reproduction antiques, can be a bit somber, so try to get one with good light. Most have a separate sitting room attached. On-site is a restaurant featuring a very comfortable tavern room as well as a more formal dining room. The extensive buffet brunch here on Sundays brings out people from all over town.

Jones Rd. and Gifford St. (about ½ mile north of Main St.), Falmouth, MA 02540. © 508/548-2300. Fax 508/540-9831. www.capecodrestaurants.org. 27 units, 1 cottage. Summer $150–$180 double, $175–$230 2-bedroom suite, $200–$260 cottage. Rates include continental breakfast. AE, MC, V. **Amenities:** 2 restaurants (1 fancy, 1 tavern with entertainment). *In room:* A/C, TV, coffeemaker, hair dryer.

Inn at West Falmouth ★★

One of the loveliest small inns on the Cape, this turn-of-the-20thcentury shingle-style house is set high on a wooded hill with distant views to Buzzards Bay. Though it suffered some hard knocks in its day, serving at one point as a children's camp, innkeeper Susan Moran has purged it of the last trace of institutionalism. Throughout the house you'll find spacious rooms lavished with custom linens and accented by a few judicious, unusual antiques. The large living room, decked with fresh flowers, has heaps of bestsellers begging to be borrowed. Feel free to enjoy a cocktail at the open bar. Mornings, after enjoying an elaborate continental breakfast buffet highlighted by fresh-baked pastries, you might carry off a tome to the small, sparkling heated pool set in the deck or wander the beautiful landscaped grounds. Chapoquoit Beach is about a 10-minute walk down a country lane. You are also within walking distance from the antiques shops and galleries of West Falmouth village. On blustery days, you can sink into one of the voluminous couches by the fireplace or retreat to your private marble whirlpool bath.

66 Frazar Rd. (off Rte. 28A), West Falmouth, MA 02574. © 508/540-7696. www.innatwestfalmouth.com. 7 units. Summer $250–$345 double. Rates include continental breakfast. AE, MC, V. **Amenities:** Small outdoor heated pool; clay tennis court; billiard room; masseuse on staff (fee). *In room:* AC, cable TV, hair dryer, iron.

Scallop Shell Inn ★★ *Finds*

This deluxe inn, located just steps from Falmouth Heights Beach, is one of Falmouth's best. Several rooms have wonderful views of Vineyard Sound and Martha's Vineyard. Guests are apt to lounge on the wide front porch during the day. The inn is also a short walk from a fun bar/restaurant, the British Beer Company. Several of the rooms have gas fireplaces and two- or three-person whirlpool tubs. In addition to air-conditioning and those brisk ocean breezes, the rooms have ceiling fans. All are thoughtfully appointed with extras like robes and high-quality toiletries. Two rooms have mahogany balconies, and several have private entrances; one of the rooms is accessible to travelers with disabilities. In the billiard and sitting room guests can enjoy a drink from the wet bar or sit by the fireplace. Guests also have free rein in the 24-hour guest kitchenette, which is stocked with hot and cold beverages and homemade treats. The four-course gourmet breakfast with a different entree every day could include crème brûlée French toast or lobster, asparagus, and Gruyère cheese omelets.

16 Massachusetts Ave., Falmouth Heights, MA 02540. © 800/249-4587 or 508/495-4900. Fax 508/495-4600. www.scallopshellinn.com. 7 units. Summer $225–$330 double. Rates include full breakfast. AE, DISC, MC, V. **Amenities:** Free laundry room. *In room:* A/C, TV/VCR, safe.

MODERATE

Inn on the Sound ★★ *(Finds)* The ambience here is as breezy as the setting, high on a bluff beside Falmouth's premier sunning beach, with a sweeping view of Vineyard Sound from the large front deck. Innkeeper Renee Ross is an interior decorator, and it shows: There's none of the usual frilly/cutesy stuff in these well-appointed guest rooms, most of which have ocean views, several with their own private decks. Many of the bathrooms have been renovated with large, luxurious tiled showers. The deluxe suite ideal for families has two bedrooms, living room, kitchenette and a private entrance. The focal point of the inn's living room is a handsome boulder hearth (nice for those nippy nights). Most guests enjoy having their breakfast, which features lots of home-baked goodies, served on the front deck.

313 Grand Ave., Falmouth Heights, MA 02540. ℂ 800/564-9668 or 508/457-9666. Fax 508/457-9631. www.inn onthesound.com. 7 units (5 tub/shower; 2 shower only). Summer $150–$295 double, $3,500 a week. Rates include continental breakfast. AE, DISC, MC, V. No children under 16. *In room:* TV, hair dryer, robes, no phone.

Nautilus Motor Inn ★ The Nautilus is a crescent-shaped motel poised above Woods Hole's picturesque Little Harbor. The two tiers of rooms have the standard motel look, but each room comes with a private balcony for taking in the view and/or sunning. An unusual restaurant used for private parties, The Dome, is right on the premises. An architectural landmark, this very sturdy geodesic dome was R. Buckminster Fuller's first and must have seemed grandly futuristic in 1953. The Martha's Vineyard ferry is a very short stroll away. Not so much a destination in and of itself, the Nautilus makes an ideal launching pad for a day trip to the Vineyard or an exploration of Woods Hole.

539 Woods Hole Rd., Woods Hole, MA 02543. ℂ 800/654-2333 or 508/548-1525. Fax 508/457-9674. www. nautilusinn.com. 54 units (all with tub/shower). Summer $145–$185 double. AE, DC, DISC, MC, V. Closed mid-Oct to mid-Apr. **Amenities:** Good-size outdoor pool with large deck; 2 tennis courts. *In room:* A/C, TV, dataport.

Sands of Time Motor Inn & Harbor House ★★ This property, which is across the street from the Woods Hole ferry terminal, consists of two buildings: a two-story motel in front of a shingled 1879 Victorian mansion. The motel rooms feature crisp, above-average decor, plus private porches overlooking the harbor. The rooms in the Harbor House are more lavish and romantic—some with four-posters, working fireplaces, wicker furnishings, and harbor views. There is a small heated pool on the grounds, and guests can use the tennis court at the motel property next door. All rooms are equipped with computer jacks.

549 Woods Hole Rd., Woods Hole, MA 02543. ℂ 800/841-0114 or 508/548-6300. Fax 508/457-0160. www. sandsoftime.com. 36 units (2 with shared bathroom). Summer $130–$200 double. Rates include continental breakfast. AE, DC, DISC, MC, V. Closed Nov–Mar. **Amenities:** Small heated pool; 2 tennis courts. *In room:* A/C, TV.

Village Green Inn An 1804 Federal house decked with Victorian trim, this B&B proudly presides over the historic Village Green. The ambience is comfy rather than stuffy. For room to really stretch out, opt for the sunny suite. It comes complete with desk and daybed for (respectively) tackling the homework you imprudently lugged along, or ditching it in favor of a novel and bonbons—provided you're still peckish after a breakfast of, say, caramelized French toast, plus a sweet afternoon snack on the geranium-bedecked porch. Two rooms have working fireplaces. The suite also has a mini-fridge. Loaner bikes are provided to explore the nearby Shining Sea Bicycle Path.

40 Main St. (at the Village Green), Falmouth, MA 02540. ℂ 800/237-1119 or 508/548-5621. Fax 508/457-5051. www.villagegreeninn.com. 5 units (2 tub/shower, 3 shower only). Summer $160–$175 double, $195–$225 suite. Rates include full breakfast. AE, MC, V. Closed Jan–Mar. No children under 12. **Amenities:** Loaner bikes. *In room:* A/C, TV, hair dryer, iron.

Wildflower Inn ★★   Though located on a busy stretch of road, this B&B is immaculately appointed inside, and its exterior with its colorful gardens consistently wins beautification awards from the town. The inn is full of welcoming touches like the row of red wooden rocking chairs lining the front porch. The rooms are creatively and individually decorated with summery items like wicker furnishings and country quilts. There's even a safari-style room with an iron canopy bed draped with decorative mosquito netting and accents of burlap, bamboo, and rattan. Two dormer rooms on the top floor come with whirlpool baths, and the attached apartment features a loft bedroom served by a spiral staircase. The five-course breakfast, served on the wraparound porch in summer, starts with a fruit compote and might include such treats as apple-pie French toast garnished with edible flowers. All rooms have hair dryers and robes, as well as beach chairs and beach towels. Loaner bikes are available, and the inn is across the street from the satellite parking lot for the Martha's Vineyard ferries, so you can easily hop a bus down to the terminal in Woods Hole.

167 Palmer Ave. (2 blocks north of Main St.), Falmouth, MA 02540. ℂ 800/294-5459 or 508/548-9524. Fax 508/548-9524. www.wildflower-inn.com. 5 units, 1 cottage (4 tub/shower; 2 shower only). Summer $185–$250 double, $275 cottage. Rates include full breakfast. AE, MC, V. *In room:* A/C, hair dryer, robes, no phone.

Woods Hole Passage   Innkeeper Deb Pruitt has put her stamp on this quaint B&B. The walls of the individual rooms and the great room remain boldly painted from the former owner's time, but the furniture reflects the new innkeeper's more down-to-earth persona. In season, you can dine outside on the slate porch overlooking the grounds, which include a croquet course, boccie, horseshoes, and a hammock for lazing. The two cathedral-ceiling loft rooms in the adjoining 18th-century barn are definitely the most comfortable and seem custom-made for honeymooning (or otherwise cocooning) couples. There are loaner bikes and an outdoor shower. A 15-minute walk brings you to Vineyard Sound.

186 Woods Hole Rd. (about 2 miles north of Woods Hole center), Woods Hole, MA 02540. ℂ **800/790-8976** or 508/548-9575. Fax 508/540-4771. www.woodsholepassage.com. 5 units. Summer $155–$165 double. Rates include full breakfast. AE, DC, DISC, MC, V. **Amenities:** Loaner bikes. *In room:* A/C, hair dryer, no phone.

INEXPENSIVE

Inn at One Main   Though a centenarian (built in 1892), this shingled house with Queen Anne flourishes has a crisp, youthful air. The bedrooms embody barefoot romance, rather than the Victorian brand. Lace, chintz, and wicker have been laid on lightly, leaving plenty of room to kick about. The Turret Room, with its big brass bed, is perhaps the most irresistible. Breakfasts would instantly convert a "Just coffee, please" morning grouch. Gingerbread pancakes, orange-pecan French toast, homemade scones—it's a good thing the Shining Sea Bicycle Path is right at hand.

1 Main St. (1 block northwest of the Village Green), Falmouth, MA 02540. ℂ **888/281-6246** or 508/540-7469. Fax 603/462-5680. www.innatonemain.com. 6 units. Summer $110–$150 double. Rates include full breakfast. AE, DISC, MC, V. *In room:* A/C, hair dryer, no phone.

WHERE TO DINE
EXPENSIVE

Fishmonger's Cafe ★★ NATURAL   A cherished carry-over from the early 1970s, this sunny, casual cafe attracts local young people and scientists, as well as Bermuda-shorted tourists, with an ever-changing array of imaginatively prepared dishes. Prices have risen substantially over the past couple of years, making dinner in this casual setting feel like a splurge. Chefs Anne Hunt and Harold Broadstock change the eclectic dinner menu every few days and have added some Thai entrees. Regulars sit at the counter to enjoy a bowl of the Fisherman's Stew while schmoozing with staff bustling about the open kitchen. Newcomers usually go for the tables by the window, where you can watch boats come and go from Eel Pond. The menu ranges widely (lunch could be a tempeh burger made with fermented soybeans, or ordinary beef), and longtime customers look to the blackboard for the latest innovations, which invariably include delectable desserts like pumpkin-pecan pie.

56 Water St. (at the Eel Pond drawbridge), Woods Hole. ℂ 508/540-5376. Main courses $15–$25. AE, MC, V. Mid-June to Oct Wed–Mon 7am–10pm; Tuesday noon–10pm; call for off-season hours. Closed mid-Dec to mid-Feb.

La Cucina Sul Mare ✸✸ ITALIAN   Locals and tourists alike line up outside this popular Main Street restaurant, craving its hearty Italian fare. The interior features cheerful murals and a tin ceiling, and large picture windows overlook Main Street. Chef/owner Mark Ciflone's signature dishes include classic Italian specialties like lasagna, braised lamb shanks, osso buco, lobster fra diavlo over linguine, zuppa de pesce, rigotoni a la vodka, chicken Parmesan, and veal piccata, among others. The desserts here are homemade and truly delicious.

237 Main St., Falmouth. ℂ 508/548-5600. Reservations required. Main courses $15–$25. AE, MC, V. Tues–Sun 11:30am–2pm and 5–10pm. Open year-round.

Phusion Grille ✸✸ NEW AMERICAN/ASIAN   This is one of Falmouth's best restaurants, combining excellent food, professional service, and a terrific location on Eel Pond in Woods Hole. The interior is all blond wood and Asian screens, but nothing blocks the views of the wraparound floor-to-ceiling windows. The chef/owner Bin Phu combines his classical training with imaginative innovations nightly. The menu changes nightly depending on the catch of the day, but keep an eye out for the bouillabaisse and the sauteéd sea scallops tossed with artichokes and a lobster sherry cream sauce. There's also a sushi bar. The dessert menu here is an all-chocolate affair, with scrumptious homemade items like Key lime pie with chocolate sauce and chocolate mousse.

71 Water St., Woods Hole. ℂ 508/547-3100. Reservations not accepted. Main courses $20–$27. AE, MC, V. Daily 11:30am–2pm and 5–10pm. Open year-round.

RooBar ✸✸ NEW AMERICAN   RooBar is the top restaurant in town for service, food and atmosphere. Owner Dana Heilman, who also owns RooBars in Hyannis and Chatham, has created an exciting bistro with handblown glass lamps over the bar and metal sconce sculptures on the walls; it's an arty and hip setting. An eclectic crowd fills the bar area, which has picture windows overlooking Falmouth's Main Street. The food is exceptionally yummy if pricey. Creative appetizers include Thai wontons with ginger chicken and a crispy tuna stick with a spicy dipper sauce. Good main course choices include the snapper pie, which is a braised snapper in a puff pastry; and coriander-crusted day boat cod with fried coconut polenta. Pizzas ($11–$15) from the wood-burning oven come with unusual toppings like scallop and prosciutto and beef satay. For dessert, skip the heavy Key lime pie and go for the crème brûlée. They don't take reservations, but if you call a half-hour ahead, you can put your name on the waiting list.

285 Main St. (at Cahoon Court), Falmouth. ℂ 508/548-8600. Reservations not accepted. Main courses $11–$26. AE, MC, V. Daily 5–10pm; call for off-season hours.

The Waterfront ✸✸ NEW AMERICAN   This upscale restaurant on pretty Eel Pond is in the same building as the down-and-dirty Cap'n Kidd (see below) and is serviced by the same kitchen. Unlike the Kidd, the Waterfront is open only for a few months in the summer. It offers expensive dinners served by a fresh-faced and professional staff. Sitting on the back deck overlooking Eel Pond is a very pleasant way to spend a summer evening. The cavernous room inside is also comfortable, with romantic lighting. The food is fairly standard for these parts: fresh fish, steaks, and chicken prepared with an attempt at a flourish. Good choices are Turbans of Sole stuffed with crab and topped with a rich lobster sauce. A lighter choice is Mediterranean Shrimp and Scallops sautéed with olive oil, garlic tomatoes, olives, asparagus, mushrooms, and capers over angel hair pasta. It's perhaps a tad pricey for what it is, but the atmosphere is top-notch.

77 Water St. (next to the Cap'n Kidd), Woods Hole. ✆ **508/548-8563**. Reservations accepted after 4pm. Main courses $19–$30. AE, MC, V. Mid-June to early Sept daily 5:30–10pm. Closed early Sept to mid-June.

MODERATE

The Cantina Mexican Bar and Grill ✪ MEXICAN   This is Falmouth's only Mexican restaurant, and it's a stylish and lively addition to the restaurant scene. In season there is often a long wait for a table because of the no reservations policy. There are usually seats available at the bar, if you don't mind the roar of the blender as it whips up frozen margaritas. The menu features traditional dishes such as burritos, fajitas, and tacos, made with meat, seafood, or vegetarian style. For dessert, there's fried ice cream or drunken plantains topped with vanilla ice cream.

327 Gifford St. (½ mile north of town). ✆ **508/548-9861**. Reservations not accepted. Main courses $7–$15. MC, V. Daily 5–10pm.

Chapoquoit Grill ✪✪ NEW AMERICAN   One of the few worthwhile dining spots in sleepy West Falmouth, this little roadside bistro has Californian aspirations: wood-grilled slabs of fish accompanied by trendy salsas, and crispy personal pizzas delivered straight from the brick oven. People drive here from miles around for the flavorful food. A no-reservations policy means long waits nightly in season and weekends year-round.

410 Rte. 28A, West Falmouth. ✆ **508/540-7794**. Reservations not accepted. Main courses $10–$18. MC, V. Daily 5–10pm.

The Flying Bridge ✪ AMERICAN/CONTINENTAL   Seafood, appropriately enough, predominates at this shipshape harborside mega-restaurant (capacity: nearly 600). With three bars tossed into the mix and live music upstairs on weekends, things can get a bit crazy; you'll find comparative peace and quiet—as well as tip-top nautical views—out on the deck. In addition to basic bar food (Buffalo chicken wings and the like), you'll find hefty hunks of protein and fish in many guises, from fish and chips—with optional malt vinegar—to appealing blackboard specials. This is a great place to bring the kids because they'll enjoy wandering onto the attached dock to watch the ducks in the harbor.

220 Scranton Ave. (about ½ mile south of Main St.). ✆ **508/548-2700**. www.capecodrestaurants.org. Reservations not accepted. Main courses $8–$20. AE, MC, V. Apr–Dec daily 11am–10pm; call for off-season hours.

Landfall ✪✪ AMERICAN   A terrific harbor setting, Cape Cod-y cuisine, and good service make this Woods Hole seafood restaurant stand out. This is the type of place where you'll see the owner busing tables on busy nights. Besides the usual fish and pasta dishes, there's "lite fare" like burgers and fish and chips for under $15. This is a great place to bring the kids; a children's menu comes with games and crayons. Or come for a drink at the half-dory bar to enjoy this massive wooden building constructed of salvage, both marine and terrestrial. The "ship's knees" on the ceiling are the ribs of an old schooner which broke up on the shores of Cuttyhunk Island; the big stained-glass window came from a mansion on nearby Penzance Point. A large bank of windows looks out onto the harbor, and the Martha's Vineyard ferry, when docking, appears to be making a beeline straight for your table.

Luscombe Ave. (½ block south of Water St.), Woods Hole. ☎ **508/548-1758.** Reservations recommended. Main courses $7–$26. AE, MC, V. Mid-May to Sept daily 11:30am–9pm; call for off-season hours. Closed late Nov to mid-Apr.

Pesci's ★★ NEW AMERICAN/ITALIAN   Despite the uninspiring location in a traffic-y commercial area, Pesci's is a jewel of a restaurant, offering attentive service and yummy food. Many come for the fancy thin-crust brick oven pizza, like the *gambaretto picante* with shrimp, garlic, and jalapeños. Specialties include the zuppa de pesce with scallops, shrimp, mussels, and littleneck clams. A wide range of pastas includes the delectable lobster scampi. While waiting for your meal, you can watch the chef perform his magic in the open kitchen or admire the colorful paintings on the walls.

100 Davis Straits (the continuation of Main St., ¼ mile east of town center). ☎ **508/495-5553.** Reservations recommended. Main courses $12–$26. MC, V. June–Aug daily 5–10pm; Sept–May Sun, Tues, and Wed 5–9pm, Thurs–Sat 5–10pm.

The Silver Lounge Restaurant *Value* *Kids* REGIONAL   In the middle of winter when many Cape restaurants are struggling to survive, this place has an hour's wait and a line out the door. It's long been a favorite with locals, and visitors often "discover" it while driving scenic Route 28A. Although it's a publike place with a large stone hearth, families come in droves because kids love to sit in the railroad caboose where there are just nine booths (come early if you want one). This is a meat-and-potatoes crowd, and the most popular menu item is the Black Diamond steak. This is the only place in the area that serves a full menu until 1am. An extensive sandwich menu (most under $6) is served all day. Weekends in summer, you might find the talented kids from the College Light Opera Company at the piano, entertaining the late-night dinner crowd with show tunes.

412 Rte. 28A, North Falmouth. ☎ **508/563-2410.** No reservations. Main courses $8–$18. AE, DISC, MC, V. Daily 11:30am–1am.

INEXPENSIVE

Betsy's Diner ★ *Finds* *Kids* AMERICAN   I once had the best piece of baked scrod ever at this vintage 1950s diner. It was breaded with corn flakes. This is hearty food like your mother used to make, if your mother was a variation of June Cleaver. The menu features turkey dinner, breakfast all day, and homemade soups. Some say the fried clams here are the best in town. Many people come for the large selection of scrumptious homemade pies, which may be the best on Cape Cod. Each red vinyl booth is equipped with its own jukebox with retro hits.

457 Main St. (in the center of town). ☎ **508/540-0060.** No reservations accepted. All items under $11. AE, MC, V. Mon–Sat 6am–9pm; Sun 6am–2pm; call for off-season hours.

The British Beer Company ★ PUB FARE/PIZZA   The view is great at this faux British pub across the street from Falmouth Heights beach. The food quality, though, is inconsistent. Stick with the fish and chips, and you'll be fine. The lobster bisque is also good and has won local awards. Of course, there is beer, 23 drafts available, like Guinness and John Courage, as well as bottled selections.

263 Grand Ave. (across from the beach), Falmouth Heights. ☎ **508/540-9600.** Reservations not accepted. All items under $15. AE, DC, DISC, MC, V. Mon–Sat 11:30am–10pm; Sun noon–10pm.

Cap'n Kidd ★★ *Finds* SEAFOOD   The semiofficial heart of Woods Hole, this well-worn pub really comes into its own once the tourist hordes subside. It's then that the year-round scientists and fishing crews can huddle around the fireplace, congregate on the glassed porch overlooking Eel Pond and order reasonably priced seafood, or belly up to the hand-carved mahogany bar (thought to date from the early 1800s) and drink to their heart's content. The notorious 17th-century pirate, who is rumored to have debarked in Woods Hole on his way back to England to be hanged, would probably get a warm reception were he to wander in today. Although the Kidd shares a kitchen with a fancier restaurant called The Waterfront, the fare here is pub grub and some seafood, with individual pizzas, burgers, and sandwiches the mainstays. Homemade clam chowder is thick as paste, with large chunks of potato and clam; stuffed quahogs are piled high, and french fries are the real deal, thickly sliced.

77 Water St. (west of the Eel Pond drawbridge), Woods Hole. ℂ 508/548-9206. Reservations not accepted. Main courses $12–$18. AE, MC, V. Daily 11:30am–3pm and 5–9pm.

The Clam Shack ★ *Kids* SEAFOOD   This classic clam shack sits at the head of Falmouth harbor and offers steaming plates of fried seafood that you carry to a picnic table inside, outside, or up on the roof deck with the best view in town. The food is basic clam-shack fare, but the fish is fresh and you can't beat the view.

227 Clinton Ave. (off Scranton Ave., about 1 mile south of Main St.). ℂ 508/540-7758. Reservations not accepted. Main courses $5–$15. No credit cards. Daily 11:30am–7:45pm. Closed early Sept to late May.

Peking Palace ★ CHINESE   Known as the best Chinese restaurant on the Cape, this restaurant has been infused with TLC at every turn. From the fringes of bamboo gracing the parking lot to the gleaming rosewood tables, no detail has been overlooked to create a cosseting, exotic environment. It's a wonder the staff finds the time, what with 300-plus items on the menu, spanning three regional Chinese cuisines (Cantonese, Mandarin, and Sichuan), as well as Polynesian. New additions this year are Japanese and Thai cuisine. Sip a fanciful drink to give yourself time to take in the menu, and be sure to solicit your server's opinion: That's how I encountered some heavenly spicy chilled squid.

452 Main St. (in the center of town). ℂ 508/540-8204. Main courses $5–$15. AE, MC, V. June–Aug daily 11:30am–midnight; Sept–May Sun–Thurs 11:30am–midnight, Fri–Sat 11:30am–midnight.

TAKEOUT & PICNIC FARE

Cape Cod Bagel Co., 419 Palmer Ave. (ℂ **508/548-8485**), carries the usual bagel sandwiches, soups, coffee, and other beverages, but the bagels here, made on the premises, are definitely the best in town. **Box Lunch,** 781 Main St. (ℂ **508/ 457-7657**), is one of a number of franchises on the Cape that carry the pita "roll-wiches." These are excellent sandwiches (over 50 selections) made fast, and they're perfect for picnics. In season, Thursday and Saturday from 8am to 2pm, there's a **Farmers Market** on Main Street in Peg Noonan Park with salad greens, homemade jams, breads, plants, and more. **Laureen's,** at 170 Main St. in the center of town (ℂ **508/540-9104**), is a sophisticated coffee bar/deli, ideal for a quick bite or sip. It specializes in vegetarian and Middle Eastern fare. Try one of the feta pizzas. Everything is available to go or you can eat here. Kitchen gear and gifts, including some great stuff for kids, round out the stock.

COFFEE

Coffee Obsession, 110 Palmer Ave. in the Queen's Buyway Shops (ℂ **508/ 540-2233**), is a hip coffee bar where everyone goes for a cuppa joe. You'll see slackers, suits, and surfers all lined up for the best coffee in town. A new branch of Coffee O., as it's known to locals, is opening on Water Street in Woods Hole in 2004. It will be equipped with Internet access and an area for children.

SWEETS
Locals know to get to **Pie in the Sky Dessert Café and Bake Shop,** 10 Water St., Woods Hole (© **508/540-5475**), by 9am for sticky buns, the best anywhere. Those bound for Martha's Vineyard stop at this small cafe for treats before hopping on the ferry.

Falmouth residents are the beneficiaries of a struggle for ice-cream bragging rights: **Ben & Bill's Chocolate Emporium** ⚢, at 209 Main St., in the center of town (© **508/548-7878**), draws crowds even in winter, late into the evening. They come for the homemade ice cream, not to mention the hand-dipped candies showcased in a wraparound display—a chocoholic's nightmare or dream come true, depending. Those who can trust themselves not to go hog-wild might enjoy watching the ice cream being made.

There's also **Smitty's Homemade Ice Cream** ⚢, at 326 E. Falmouth Hwy. (© **508/457-1060**) and 402 N. Falmouth Hwy. (© **508/564-7661**), whose proprietor, the cheerful blond Smitty, is an ice-cream man from central casting.

FALMOUTH AFTER DARK
DRINKS   Ever since the close of the famous nightclub The Casino-By-The-Sea in Falmouth Heights, those looking for a fun waterfront drinking establishment have frequented **The Boathouse** (© **508/548-7800**) at 88 Scranton Ave. on Falmouth Inner Harbor. The Boathouse features live bands in season, from classic rock to jazz, and dancing is popular here. Closed September to mid-May. Cover varies.

Grab a stool at **The British Beer Company** ⚢, 263 Grand Ave., Falmouth Heights (© **508/540-9600**), and choose from a revolving selection of over 18 drafts from the British Isles as you ponder views of the beach across the street. This place is packed in season.

God knows whom you'll meet in the rough-and-tumble old **Cap'n Kidd** ⚢, 77 Water St., in Woods Hole (© **508/548-9206**): maybe a lobsterwoman, maybe a Nobel Prize winner. Good grub, too—see "Where to Dine," above.

Everyone heads to **Liam Maguire's Irish Pub** ⚢, on 273 Main St. in Falmouth (© **508/548-0285**), for a taste of the Emerald Isle. Liam is the jolly backslapper with a touch of the blarney. Live music on weekends year-round, often by Liam himself. No cover.

Grumpy's, at 29 Locust St. (© **508/540-3930**), is a good old bar/shack with live music (rock, blues, and jazz) Thursday to Saturday nights. Cover is $2 to $10.

RooBar, 285 Main St., in Falmouth (© **508/548-8600**), draws a hip crowd by a great menu with lots of intriguing appetizers.

FILM   The Cape's only year-round art-house cinema is **Nickelodeon Cinemas,** 742 Rte. 151, East Falmouth (© **508/563-6510**). With six small screens, this is a great alternative to the usual mall movies.

PERFORMANCE   **The Woods Hole Folk Music Society** ⚢ (© **508/540-0320**) mounts biweekly concerts October through May (1st and 3rd Sun of each month), attracting a real grassroots crowd to Community Hall on Water Street, by the Eel Pond drawbridge. General admission is $8, discounts for members, seniors, and children.

The **Cape Cod Theatre Project** (© **508/457-4242**) is a playwrights' workshop open to the public. These staged play readings are performed for just a few weeks in July, usually at the Woods Hole Community Hall. In 1998, they premiered a Lanford Wilson play. The rest of the year the talent behind these productions is most likely strutting the boards in New York City. Call for a schedule. Suggested donation is $10.

Starting at about 7:30pm on Thursday evenings in July and August, the spirited volunteers of the **Falmouth Town Band** swing through big-band numbers as small fries (and some oldsters) dance about. Concerts are held at the Band Shell, on Scranton Avenue next to Falmouth Inner Harbor, and are free.

The top talent from college drama departments across the country form the **College Light Opera Company** ⚓ (✆ **508/548-0668**), which puts on a fast-paced summer repertory—a classic musical a week, from late June through August. So winning is the work of these 32 young actors and 17 musicians (some of them ultimately Broadway-bound) that the house is usually booked solid, so call well ahead or keep your fingers crossed for a scattering of singles. Its venue, the Highfield Theatre, on the Depot Avenue Extension off North Main Street in Falmouth, is a former horse barn and for the past half century has been a terrific straw-hat theater. Performances are held Tuesday to Saturday at 8:30pm; there's also a Thursday matinee at 2:30pm. Tickets are $22.

4 Mashpee

11 miles SE of Sagamore; 12 miles W of Hyannis

Mashpee is a study in contrasts and awash in controversy. This is the location of South Cape Beach State Park, a beautiful stretch of unspoiled coastline on Nantucket South, but the major portion of Mashpee's shoreline has been claimed by the New Seabury Resort development. Further housing developments are rapidly carving up the inland woods, leaving less and less room for the region's original residents, the Mashpee Wampanoags, whose nomadic ancestors began convening in summer camps by these shores millennia ago. In 1660, concerned by the natives' rapid disenfranchisement and heartened by their willingness to convert, missionary Richard Bourne got the Plymouth General Court to grant his "praying Indians" a 10,500-acre "plantation" in perpetuity. The provision proved far from perpetual, as settlers—and much later, developers—began chipping away at the holdings.

After lengthy litigation in the 1970s and early 1980s, the Mashpee Wampanoags—whose tribal roster now numbers about 1,000—were denied tribal status (unlike the Gay Head Wampanoags of Martha's Vineyard) and were stymied in their efforts to preserve the land. It was only in 1995, with the backing of Senators Edward Kennedy and John Kerry (both of whom summer on the Cape), that the sizable—5,871 acres—Mashpee National Wildlife Refuge was carved out of the disputed territory. Influential supporter Gerry Studds hailed the move as "a harbinger of things to come . . . Creation of this refuge ranks in significance with the Cape Cod National Seashore."

ESSENTIALS

GETTING THERE   After crossing the Sagamore Bridge, take Route 6 to Exit 2, and Route 130 south. Or fly into Hyannis (see "Getting There," in chapter 2).

VISITOR INFORMATION   Contact the **Mashpee Chamber of Commerce** at the Cape Cod Five Cent Savings Bank, Mashpee Commons, P.O. Box 1245, Mashpee, MA 02649 (✆ **800/423-6274** or 508/477-0792; fax 508/477-5541; www.mashpeechamber.com), or the **Cape Cod Chamber of Commerce** (see "Visitor Information" in the "Sandwich" section, earlier in this chapter).

BEACHES & RECREATIONAL PURSUITS

BEACHES   The small part of the shoreline not reserved for the New Seabury Resort is an undersung sleeper: **South Cape Beach** ★★★, off Great Oak Road (5 miles south of the Mashpee rotary). Mashpee is set amid the 450-acre South Cape Beach State Park (© **508/457-0495,** ext. 4). This lengthy stretch of beach has miles of hiking trails. Parking costs $7 per day.

BOATING   Cape Cod Kayak (www.capecodkayak.com) rents kayaks (free delivery) by the day or week and offers lessons and eco-tours on local waterways. Call for a schedule and more information, or see "Beaches & Recreational Pursuits" in the "Falmouth" section, earlier in this chapter.

If you'd rather explore on your own, you can rent a canoe in Falmouth (see the "Falmouth" section, earlier in this chapter) and paddle around the Mashpee River, Popponesset Bay, and Mashpee/Wakeby Pond.

FISHING   Mashpee/Wakeby Pond (boat landing off Rte. 130, Fisherman's Dr.) is considered one of the top-10 bass-fishing lakes in the country. Saltwater fishing licenses can be obtained at Sandwich, Falmouth, or Barnstable town halls. South Cape Beach in Mashpee (see "Beaches," above) is a primo spot for surf-casting.

GOLF   Though you have to question the wisdom of its placement amid delicate wetlands, the **New Seabury Resort** at 155 Rock Landing Rd. (© **508/477-9111**) is, from all reports, tops. In fact, the championship-level Blue Course has consistently ranked among the top-100 courses in the country. Relative slackers have recourse to the Green Course, a regulation par-70 course. Greens fees go up to $150 at the Blue Course and $125 at the Green Course in season.

NATURE TRAILS   The **Mashpee Conservation Commission** (© **508/539-1414,** ext. 540) sponsors free naturalist-guided nature tours throughout Mashpee from May through December. Call for a schedule. A shady peninsula jutting into the Cape's largest body of fresh water (the adjoining Wakeby/Mashpee Pond), the 135-acre **Lowell Holly Reservation** off South Sandwich Road in the northern corner of the township harbors some 500 holly trees and a number of magnificent centennial beeches. The stewards of this enchanted place, the **Trustees of the Reservation** (© **978/921-1944**), charge $6 per day for the 2-mile trail loop on summer weekends; weekday admission is free. **South Cape Beach State Park** (see "Beaches," above) also offers a network of sandy trails.

WATERSPORTS   The town of Mashpee offers swimming lessons at **Attaquin Park** at Mashpee/Wakeby Pond off Route 130, and also at South Cape Beach; call the **town leisure services department** (© **508/539-1400,** ext. 519) for details.

MUSEUMS

Wampanoag Indian Museum ★   Centuries of heartbreaking history are encapsulated in this unprepossessing museum, housed in a 1793 half-Cape built by a great-grandson of pioneer missionary Richard Bourne. Though the native population embraced the colonists' religion wholeheartedly, they never fully grasped the ethos of private property; thus over the years the land vouchsafed to them by the Plymouth court in 1660 was steadily whittled away—most egregiously, starting in the 1960s, when the ratio of undeveloped to developed land in Mashpee was roughly 80 to 20. The percentages have since been reversed, despite a long legal wrangle.

The museum sells copies of Russell M. Peters's tribal history, *The Wampanoags of Mashpee*—a must-read for anyone who hopes to understand the divided nature of this semirural/semisuburban region, much less the role that indigenous peoples played in ensuring the colonists' foothold in the wilderness. The story is far from over, and tourists who take the time to look beneath the surface will gain a deeper appreciation of an area still in flux.

Rte. 130 (opposite The Flume, on Lake Ave.). © 508/477-1536. Donation requested. Mon–Fri 9am–4pm or Sat by appointment.

FOR KIDS   The Cape Cod Children's Museum ✦, 577 Great Neck Rd. S. (© **508/539-8788;** www.capecodchildrensmuseum.pair.com), has a toddler castle and a 30-foot pirate ship, among other kid pleasers. It also sponsors many special events. The museum is open Monday through Saturday 10am to 5pm and Sunday noon to 5pm. Admission is $5 for those over 4, $4 for kids under 4 and seniors.

SHOPPING

Shopping in Mashpee is pretty much limited to the **Mashpee Commons,** at the Mashpee rotary, routes 151 and 28 (© **508/477-5400**). Designed to resemble an ideal New England village (right down to the sidewalk measurements, modeled on Woodstock, Vermont), Mashpee Commons is a gussied-up shopping complex with a facadelike feel: The been-here-forever look to which it aspires has never quite materialized, despite massive influxes of capital. This is where you'll find chains like **Gap, Talbots, Banana Republic,** and **Starbucks Coffee.** There's also **M. Brann** for retro accessories and the **Signature Gallery** for superb American crafts.

WHERE TO STAY

New Seabury Resort ✦✦ (Kids   One of the few full-bore "destination resorts" on the Cape, this 2,300-acre complex packing some 1,600 condos and a 3½-mile private beach on Vineyard Sound occupies more than half the town's shoreline—land formally granted to the Mashpee Wampanoags in 1660. Being the beneficiary of such a troubled legacy might make some uncomfortable, and you would also have to question the wisdom of positioning and maintaining golf courses in the midst of fragile wetlands. Still, the damage is mostly done, and vacationers not saddled with such concerns are sure to enjoy themselves here. The tastefully decorated condos are clustered into "villages" of varying personalities: Maushop, for instance, with its crushed-shell walkways and clambering roses, is meant to mimic Nantucket. The Popponessett Marketplace with restaurants and gift shops on the premises also sponsors concerts and other family events.

Great Neck S. Rd. (about 4 miles south of the Mashpee rotary), New Seabury, MA 02649. © 800/999-9033 or 508/477-9111. Fax 508/477-9790. www.newseabury.com. About 160 units (depending on rental pool). Summer $255–$260 1-bedroom villa, $355–$400 2-bedroom villa. AE, DC, MC, V. **Amenities:** 5 restaurants (including the Popponesset Inn, an upscale venue popular for weddings; and the congenial Raw Bar with fresh seafood); 2 outdoor pools; 2 18-hole golf courses; 16 all-weather tennis courts; health club; scheduled children's activities; bike trails (w/rentals); miniature golf. *In room:* TV.

WHERE TO DINE

Contrast ✦✦ ECLECTIC   Besides sporting the funkiest interior (all bright splashes of color), the dining spot has Mashpee's most creative and sophisticated menu, with Mexican and Asian influences. Bistro fare such as cod cakes with citrus rémoulade and chicken pot pie shares the menu with soy-marinated salmon with stir-fried spinach. The daring of palate will want to try the skate wing seared in brown butter with lemon, capers, and fried potatoes; it's tasty. There are also specialty pizzas like grilled shrimp with pine nuts and aioli.

"Deconstructed sushi" usually appears as an appetizer, and there's always a different preparation of Black Angus club steak. The bar here is top-notch, especially the comfortable niche in the corner with a couch and armchairs.

Market St. Mashpee Commons (at the intersection of routes 151 and 28). ℂ **508/477-1299.** Main courses $9–$28. AE, MC, V. Daily 11:30am–10pm.

The Flume ⭐ *(Finds)* REGIONAL   At this small, friendly restaurant set above a herring run, chef Earl Mills, who is also Chief Flying Eagle of the Wampanoag tribe, dishes out solid Yankee fare, from a classic clam chowder to fried smelts, pot roast, lobster Newburg, and a colonial-era Indian pudding spiced with molasses and ginger. Seasonal specialties include, in the spring, herring roe plucked right from the flume (a stream that fish climb to spawn), which runs right beside its namesake.

Lake Ave. (off Rte. 130, about 2½ miles north of the Mashpee rotary). ℂ **508/477-1456.** Main courses $9–$26. MC, V. Apr–Nov Tues–Sat 5–9pm; Sun 5–8pm. Closed Dec–Mar.

Sienna Italian Bar and Grill NORTHERN ITALIAN   This large, loud, and popular restaurant serves tasty Italian fare next to the movie theater in Mashpee Commons, an open air mall. Specialties include the brick oven pizzas and the creative pasta dishes. Some find the portions on the small size, but the quality is usually quite good.

Mashpee Commons. ℂ **508/477-5929.** Main courses $9–$26. MC, V. Mon–Sat 11:30–9pm; Sun noon–9pm.

The Mid Cape: Barnstable, Hyannis, Yarmouth & Dennis

If the Cape had a capital, Hyannis would be it. It's a sprawling concrete jungle where the Kennedy mystique of the 1960s led to heedless development that has nearly doubled the Cape's year-round population to over 200,000 and climbing. The summer population is about three times that, and you'd swear every single person had daily errands to run in Hyannis. That said, this overrun town still has plenty of pockets of charm. The waterfront area in particular, where the Islands ferries dock, has benefited greatly from an influx of civic pride and attention, and Main Street in Hyannis, long eclipsed by the mega-stores along Route 132, is once again a pleasant place to stroll.

The town of Barnstable, the seat of Cape Cod's Barnstable County government, is made up of eight villages: Hyannis, Hyannisport, Barnstable Village, West Barnstable, Osterville, Centerville, Cotuit, and Marstons Mills. Along the north side of the Cape on Route 6A (the Old King's Hwy.) are Barnstable Village, with a compact Main Street anchored by an imposing granite county courthouse, and West Barnstable, containing a handful of delightful specialty stores and views of acres of salt marsh leading out to Cape Cod Bay. Along the south coast (off Rte. 28) are Cotuit, Marstons Mills, Osterville, and Centerville, all with gracious residential sections. Osterville has a charming strollable Main Street, and Centerville has the best public beach, at Craigville.

While Barnstable is an ideal location for exploring the rest of the Cape and the Islands, there's also fun to be had nearby. If you are staying in the vicinity of Hyannis, you'll certainly want to head over to the north side of the Cape for a drive along the Old King's Highway, but you'll also want to stroll around Hyannis Harbor, stopping for lunch at Tugboat's or Baxter's, where seagulls will compete for a bite of your lobster roll. Main Street Hyannis has had its good and bad years; currently, things are looking good, so you'll find a number of interesting shops and galleries (see "Shopping," later in this chapter), as well as cafes and bars (see "Hyannis & Environs After Dark," later in this chapter).

Some of the finest seaside mansions on the Cape are in the old-money villages of Cotuit, Osterville, Centerville, and Hyannisport. To explore this "Gold Coast" by car, take some detours off Route 28, driving south toward Nantucket Sound. These winding country roads are also good for biking (see "Bicycling," below).

The towns of Yarmouth and Dennis straddle the Cape from north to south, with the northside villages along the historic Old King's Highway and the southside villages along commercialized and overdeveloped Route 28. That's not to say there aren't some very nice enclaves along the south shore. Some of the beaches along this stretch of Nantucket Sound (West Dennis Beach and Parker's River Beach in

South Yarmouth) are popular with families, but the villages themselves (Dennisport and South and West Yarmouth) have definitely seen better days. Developers in the last 30 years have gotten carried away. In stark contrast, Yarmouth Port and Dennis Village on the north side are perfect little time capsules, loaded with old-fashioned New England charm, an encyclopedic array of historic homes, and terrific small businesses.

1 Barnstable, Hyannis, Neighboring Villages & Environs ⭐⭐

15 miles E of Sagamore; 44 miles S of Provincetown

As the commercial center and transportation hub of the Cape, hyperdeveloped Hyannis—a mere "village"—grossly overshadows the actual seat of government in the bucolic village of Barnstable. The two locales couldn't be more dissimilar. As peaceful as Hyannis is hectic, the bay area along historic Route 6A unfolds in a blur of greenery and well-kept colonial houses. It's no wonder many visitors experience "post-Camelot letdown" the first time they venture southward to Hyannis. The downtown area, sapped by the strip development that proliferated at the edges of town after the Cape Cod Mall was built in 1970, is making a valiant comeback, with attractive banners and a pretty public park flanking the wharf where frequent ferries depart for the Islands. If you were to confine your visit to this one town, however, you'd get a warped view of the Cape. Along routes 132 and 28, you could be visiting Anywhere, USA: They're lined with the standard chain stores, restaurants, and hotels, and mired with maddening traffic.

Hyannis has more beds and better "rack rates" (in travel-industry jargon) than anywhere else on the Cape, but there's little rationale for staying right in town or along the highways—unless you happen to have missed the last ferry out. Even full resort facilities can't begin to compensate for the lack of local color, and the central location means little when the scenery is so dispiriting as to deter the most determined of walkers.

The best strategy is to stay somewhere peaceful near the edge of town, in one of the moneyed villages—Hyannisport, Osterville, Marstons Mills, and Cotuit—to the west, or in one of the bayside villages of Barnstable and West Barnstable due north, and just go into the "city" to sample the restaurants and nightlife. Hyannis and environs can offer plenty of both to suit every palate and personality.

ESSENTIALS

GETTING THERE   After crossing either the Bourne or Sagamore bridge, head east on Route 6 or 6A. The Sagamore Bridge will get you closer to your destination. Route 6A passes through Barnstable; Exit 6 (Rte. 132) off Route 6 leads to Hyannis.

You can fly into Hyannis, and there is good bus service from Boston and New York (see "Getting There" in chapter 2 for more information).

The **Sea Line** (© **800/352-7155**) makes a circuit of Barnstable, Mashpee, and Falmouth, Monday through Saturday, and the fare is a reasonable $1 to $4 (depending on the distance); children under 6 ride free. The **Hyannis Area Trolley** (© **800/352-7155** or 508/790-2613) covers two loops—the Route 132 malls and the Main Street/waterfront area—every half-hour from 10am to 9pm from late June to early September. Rates are 50¢ for adults, 25¢ for seniors, and free for children under 6.

VISITOR INFORMATION   For information, contact the **Hyannis Area Chamber of Commerce,** 1481 Rte. 132, Hyannis, MA 02601 (© **800/449-6647,** 877/492-6647, or 508/362-5230; fax 508/362-9499; www.hyannis.com), which is

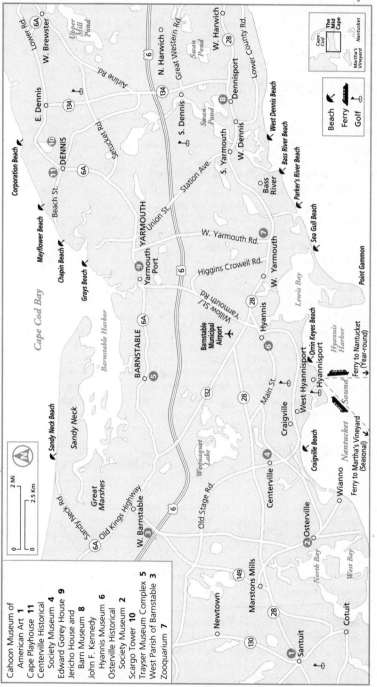

The Mid Cape

Cahoon Museum of
American Art **1**
Cape Playhouse **11**
Centerville Historical
Society Museum **4**
Edward Gorey House **9**
Jericho House and
Barn Museum **8**
John F. Kennedy
Hyannis Museum **6**
Osterville Historical
Society Museum **2**
Scargo Tower **10**
Trayser Museum Complex **5**
West Parish of Barnstable **3**
Zooquarium **7**

Beach
Ferry
Golf

Cape Cod Bay

Barnstable Harbor

Sandy Neck

Great Marshes

Corporation Beach
Mayflower Beach
Chapin Beach
Grays Beach
Sandy Neck Beach

W. Brewster
Upper Mill Pond
N. Harwich
W. Harwich
Swan Pond
Dennisport
West Dennis Beach
Bass River Beach
Parker's River Beach
Sea Gull Beach
Point Gammon

E. Dennis
DENNIS
YARMOUTH
Yarmouth Port
BARNSTABLE
Barnstable Municipal Airport

S. Dennis
Swan Pond
W. Dennis
S. Yarmouth
Bass River
W. Yarmouth

Lewis Bay

Hyannis
Orrin Keyes Beach
Hyannis Harbor
Ferry to Nantucket
(Year-round)

West Hyannisport
Hyannisport
Nantucket Sound

Craigville
Craigville Beach

Wequaquet Lake

Centerville
Osterville
Wianno

North Bay
West Bay

Marstons Mills
Newtown
Cotuit
Santuit

Lower Rd.
Airline Rd.
Seapuit Rd.
Beach St.
Station Ave.
Union St.
W. Yarmouth Rd.
Higgins Crowell Rd.
Willow St./
Yarmouth Rd.
Main St.
Old Stage Rd.
Old Kings Highway
Sandy Neck Rd.
Great Western Rd.
Lower County Rd.

6A
6
134
28
6A
7
9
5
8
10
11
6
32
28
149
28
30
6

2 Mi
2.5 Km

open Monday through Saturday 9am to 5pm, Sunday 10am to 2pm; or the **Cape Cod Chamber of Commerce,** routes 6 and 132, Hyannis, MA 02601 (© **888/ 332-2732** or 508/862-0700; fax 508/362-2156; www.capecodchamber.org), open year-round, mid-April to mid-November daily 9am to 5pm; mid-November to mid-April Monday through Saturday 10am to 4pm.

BEACHES & RECREATIONAL PURSUITS

BEACHES Barnstable's primary bay beach is Sandy Neck Beach, accessed through East Sandwich (see "Beaches & Recreational Pursuits" under "Sandwich" in chapter 4). Most of the Nantucket Sound beaches are fairly protected and thus not big in terms of surf. Beach parking costs $10 a day, usually payable at the lot; for a weeklong parking sticker ($40), visit the Recreation Department at 141 Basset Lane, at the **Kennedy Memorial Skating Rink** (© **508/790-6345**).

- **Craigville Beach** ☆☆☆, off Craigville Beach Road in Centerville: Once a magnet for Methodist "camp" meetings (conference centers still line the shore), this broad expanse of sand boasts lifeguards and restrooms. A destination for the bronzed and buffed, it's known as "Muscle Beach."
- **Orrin Keyes Beach** ☆☆ (also known as Sea Beach), at the end of Sea Street in Hyannis: This little beach at the end of a residential road is popular with families.
- **Kalmus Beach** ☆☆, off Gosnold Street in Hyannisport: This 800-foot spit of sand stretching toward the mouth of the harbor makes an ideal launching site for windsurfing enthusiasts, who sometimes seem to play chicken with the steady parade of ferries. The surf is tame, the slope shallow, and the conditions ideal for little kids. There are lifeguards, a snack bar, and restrooms to facilitate family outings.
- **Veterans Beach,** off Ocean Street in Hyannis: A small stretch of harborside sand adjoining the John F. Kennedy Memorial (a moving tribute from the town), this spot is not tops for swimming, unless you're very young and easily wowed. Parking is usually easy, though, and it's walkable from town. The snack bar, restrooms, and playground will see to a family's needs.

BICYCLING While there are no paved bike paths in Barnstable (the Rail Trail in Dennis is the closest), the winding roads in Marstons Mills and Osterville make for pleasant scenic rides. There's free public parking at the Marstons Mills millpond at the intersection of routes 28 and 149 or behind the stores in Osterville Center. From the intersection of routes 28 and 149, bear right on Route 149 where it turns into Main Street. Main Street soon intersects with Route 28; cross Route 28 (carefully), and then cruise down South County Road into Osterville. Several roads here afford wonderful bay views, not to mention views of some of the finest homes on Cape Cod. For the best views, bike to the ends of Bay Street, West Bay Road, and Eel River Road to Sea View Avenue. A leisurely bike ride through this area is perhaps the best way to see some of the most impressive seaside mansions on the Cape.

BOATING You can rent a kayak from Eastern Mountain Sports (see "Watersports," below) for $40 to $50 a day and paddle around **Scorton Creek, Sandy Neck,** and **Barnstable Harbor** on the north side of the Cape. On the south side of the Cape, paddlers enjoy the waters around **Great Island** in Osterville. In Centerville, you can navigate the **Centerville River.** For experienced paddlers, **Barnstable's Great Marsh**—one of the largest in New England—offers beautiful waterways out to Sandy Neck.

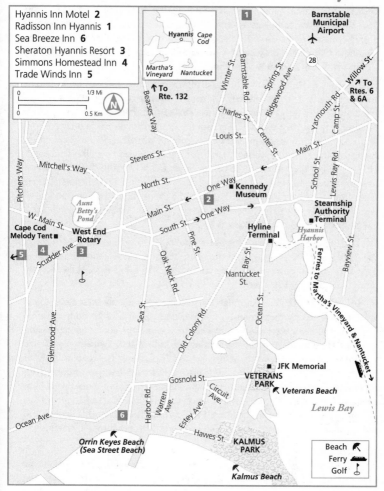

Hyannis Inn Motel **2**
Radisson Inn Hyannis **1**
Sea Breeze Inn **6**
Sheraton Hyannis Resort **3**
Simmons Homestead Inn **4**
Trade Winds Inn **5**

FISHING The township of Barnstable has 11 ponds for freshwater fishing; for information and permits, visit **Town Hall** at 367 Main St., Hyannis (📞 **508/790-6240**), or **Sports Port,** 149 W. Main St., Hyannis (📞 **508/775-3096**). Shell-fishing permits are available from the **Department of Natural Resources** at 1189 Phinneys Lane, Centerville (📞 **508/790-6272**). Surf-casting, sans license, is permitted on Sandy Neck (see "Beaches & Recreational Pursuits" under "Sandwich" in chapter 4).

Among the charter boats berthed in Barnstable Harbor is the *Drifter* (📞 **508/398-2061**), a 36-foot boat offering half- and full-day trips costing $440 to $590, depending on the length of the trip and the number of people. **Hy-Line Cruises** offers seasonal sonar-aided "bottom" or blues fishing from its Ocean Street dock in Hyannis (📞 **508/790-0696**). The cost for a half-day trip is $23 to $25 per person. **Helen H Deep-Sea Fishing** at 137 Pleasant St., Hyannis (📞 **508/790-0660**), offers year-round expeditions aboard a 100-foot boat with a heated cabin and full galley.

GOLF   Open year-round, the **Hyannis Golf Club,** Route 132 (© **508/ 362-2606**), offers a 46-station driving range, as well as an 18-hole champi- onship course. High-season greens fees are $50 to $76. Smaller, but scenic, the nine-hole **Cotuit High Ground Country Club** is at 31 Crockers Neck Rd., Cotuit (© **508/428-9863**). An 18-hole round costs $15.

HARBOR CRUISES   For a fun and informative introduction to the harbor and its residents, take a leisurely, 1- to 2-hour, narrated tour aboard one of Hy-Line Cruises' 1911 steamer replicas *Patience* or *Prudence.* There are five 1-hour family cruises a day in season, but for a real treat take the Sunday 3:15pm "Ice Cream Float," which includes a design-your-own Ben & Jerry's ice-cream sundae, or the Thursday 7:30pm "Jazz Boat," accompanied by a Dixieland band. Hy-Line Cruises depart from the Ocean Street Dock (© **508/790-0696;** www. hy-linecruises.com), and you should call for a reservation and schedule. Tickets range from $12 to $21 for adults and free to $15 for children 12 and under; 17 departures daily from late June to September; closed November to mid-April. Credit cards are accepted. Parking is $3 per car.

WATERSPORTS   **Eastern Mountain Sports,** 1513 Iyannough Rd./Rte. 132 (© **508/362-8690;** www.ems.com), offers rental kayaks—tents and sleeping bags, too—and sponsors free clinics and walks, like a full-moon hike. Kayaks rent for about $40–$50 a day.

WHALE-WATCHING   Although Provincetown is about an hour closer to the whales' preferred feeding grounds, it would take you at least an hour (possibly hours on a summer weekend) to drive all the way down-Cape. If your time and itinerary are limited, hop aboard **Hyannis Whale-Watch Cruises,** Barnstable Harbor (about ½ mile north of Rte. 6A on Mill Way), Barnstable (© **888/ 942-5392** or 508/362-6088; fax 508/362-9739), for a 4-hour voyage on a 100- foot high-speed cruiser. Naturalists provide the narration, and should you fail to spot a whale, your next trek is free. Tickets cost $29 for adults, $25 for seniors (62 and older), and $16 for children 4 to 12 from April through October; call for a schedule and off-season rates. No trips mid-October through March.

BASEBALL

The two locally based Cape Cod Baseball League elite amateur teams are the **Hyannis Mets** (who play at McKeon Field on Old Colony Blvd.) and the **Cotuit Kettleers** (Lowell Park). For a schedule, contact the **Hyannis Area Chamber of Commerce** (© **800/449-6647** or 508/362-5230) or the **Barnsta- ble Recreation Department** (© **508/790-6345**).

KID STUFF

The **Cape Cod Storyland** mini-golf course, in the middle of town at 70 Cen- ter St. (© **508/778-4339**), actually provides a bit of a local-history lesson, with traps that replicate notable sites on the Cape and Islands; adjoining the course is a little lagoon set up for refreshing bumper-boat rides. A round costs $7 for adults, $6 for children. There are also bumper boats on-site for $5 to $6. About a mile north, off Route 132, the **Cape Cod Potato Chips factory** on Breed's Hill Road at Independence Drive (© **508/775-7253**) offers free quickie tours that end with a tasting. Tours are held in July and August, Monday to Friday from 9am to 5pm. Call for off-season hours. On Wednesday mornings in sum- mer, the **Cape Cod Melody Tent** at the West End rotary (© **508/775-9100**) offers children's theater productions.

SHOPPING

Although Hyannis is undoubtedly the commercial center of the Cape, the stores you'll find there are fairly standard for the most part; you could probably find their ilk anywhere else in the country. It's in the wealthy enclaves west of Hyannis, and along the antiquated Old King's Highway (Rte. 6A) to the north, that you're likely to find the real gems.

ANTIQUES/COLLECTIBLES **The Farmhouse,** 1340 Main St. (about 1 mile south of Rte. 28), Osterville (© **508/420-2400**), Carolyn and Barry Crawford's 1742 farmhouse, is set up like an adult-scale dollhouse, and the "life-like" settings should lend decorative inspiration. Self-confident sorts will go wild in the barn; it's packed with intriguing architectural salvage.

Of the hundreds of antiques shops scattered through the region, perhaps a dozen qualify as destinations for well-schooled collectors. **Harden Studios,** 3264 Rte. 6A (in the center of town), Barnstable Village (© **508/362-7711**), is one. Owner Charles M. Harden used to supply to-the-trade-only dealers in the Boston Design Center. An architect by training, he renovated this antique house, built around 1720, to display his finds. Some items, such as primitive portraits and mourning embroidery, are all but extinct outside of museums. Other sturdy, serviceable pieces, such as colonial corner cabinets and slant-top desks, are competitively priced, as are the antique Oriental carpets underfoot. An adjoining barn gallery features nature-centered works by area artists, including Harden's son, an accomplished etcher.

Prince Jenkins Antiques, 975 Rte. 6A (at the intersection of Rte. 149), West Barnstable (no phone), is one spooky shop, the piled-high kind that captivates scavengers. Wend your way (carefully) around the narrow path still discernible amid the heaped-up inventory, and you'll come across case upon case of vintage jewelry and watches, paintings, tapestries, urns and jade carvings, musty 18th-century garb, a Pilgrim chair or two, and all sorts of oddments. The aged proprietor, Dr. Alfred King claims that the admittedly ancient-looking house next door belonged to Gov. William Bradford in 1626—a dubious boast, given that the town wasn't settled until 1639, and Bradford was awfully busy in Plymouth. But what would you expect from a man whose card reads "In Business Since 1773"? Closed mid-November to March.

ARTS & CRAFTS The intricate, infinitely variable patterns of Jacquard weaving not only prompted the Industrial Revolution but prefigured the computer chip. Today only one weaver in the United States creates Jacquard designs by hand, and that's Bob Black, who began his trade at age 14 and refined it at the Rhode Island School of Design. He works out of **The Blacks' Handweaving Shop,** 597 Rte. 6A (about ⅔ mile west of Rte. 149), West Barnstable (© **508/362-3955**), and specializes in custom coverlets on commission; the double-sided designs can be used as blankets, throws, even tapestries. Customers often ask for special motifs to be worked in, with the ultimate goal a one-of-a-kind, commemorative artifact. Bob's wife, Gabrielle, contributes colorful fashion accessories—hats, scarves, shawls, and even ties.

The caliber of the shows at the **Cape Cod Art Association,** 3480 Rte. 6A (about ⅓ mile west of Hyannis Rd.), Barnstable (© **508/362-2909**), may vary—this is, after all, a nonprofit community venture—but it's worth visiting just to see the sky-lit studios, designed by CCAA member Richard Sears Gallagher in 1972. Everyone raves about "Cape light," and here you'll see it used to optimal

Camelot on Cape Cod: The Kennedys in Hyannisport

It's been more than 40 years since those days of Camelot, when JFK was in the White House and America seemed rejuvenated by the Kennedy style, but the Kennedy sites on Cape Cod still attract record numbers of visitors every summer. In July 1999, when John Jr.'s plane crashed into Vineyard Sound, thousands visited the Kennedy Hyannis Museum to mourn the loss by viewing classic photos of the family in Hyannisport.

Images of Jack Kennedy sailing his jaunty *Wianno Senior* on Nantucket Sound off Hyannisport form part of this nation's collective memory. The vacationing JFK was all tousled hair, toothy grin, earthy charisma, and attractive joie de vivre. Remember Jackie sitting beside him, wearing a patterned silk scarf around her head and looking like she'd rather be in Newport, where no one had ever heard of touch football?

The Kennedys always knew how to have fun, and they had it in Hyannisport. And ever since Hyannisport became the summer White House, Cape Cod has been inextricably linked to the Kennedy clan. While the Kennedys spend time elsewhere—working in Washington or wintering in Palm Beach—when they go home, they go to Cape Cod. Generations of Kennedys have sailed these waters, sunned on these beaches, patronized local businesses, and generally had a high old time.

Meanwhile, much has changed since the early 1960s on Cape Cod, especially in the Mid Cape area. In those 40-plus years, the mall was built in Hyannis, and urban sprawl infested routes 132 and 28. Yet much, thankfully, remains the same. The Kennedy compound, with its large, gabled Dutch Colonial houses, still commands the end of Scudder Avenue in Hyannisport. Nearby is the private Hyannisport Golf Club, where Rose loved to play a short round on the foggy oceanfront course. The beaches here are still pristine.

To bask in the Kennedys' Cape Cod experience, visit the John F. Kennedy Hyannis Museum, 397 Main St., Hyannis (© **508/790-3077**).

advantage. If the setting fires up artistic yearnings, inquire about classes and workshops, which are held year-round.

Ex-Nantucketer Bob Marks fashions the only authentic Nantucket lightship baskets crafted off-island; and as aficionados know, they don't come cheap (a mere handbag typically runs in the thousands). The other handmade furnishings found at **Oak and Ivory,** 1112 Main St. (about 1 mile south of Rte. 28), Osterville (© **508/428-9425**), from woven throw rugs to pared-down neo-Shaker furniture, fit the country-chic mode at more approachable prices.

At 374 Main St. in Hyannis, **Red Fish, Blue Fish** (© **508/775-8700**) wins the funky-gallery award, hands down. Owner Jane Walsh makes jewelry in the front window, but inside this closetlike space, every inch is covered with something unusual and handmade. There is usually a teenager or two hanging out here.

Tao Water Art Gallery, 1989 Rte. 6A, West Barnstable (© **508/375-0428**), is a former garage converted into a very Zenlike space. It features paintings by Chinese artists as well as museum reproductions of Chinese antiques and jade.

Admission is $5 for adults, $2.50 for children 10 to 16 and seniors, and hours are from mid-February through December Monday to Saturday 9am to 4:30pm and Sunday and holidays from noon to 4:30pm. Last admission is at 3:30pm. The museum shows a documentary on Kennedy narrated by Walter Cronkite and contains several rooms' worth of photos of the Kennedys on Cape Cod. The candid shots included in this permanent display capture some of the quieter moments, as well as JFK's legendary charm. Most of us have seen some of these photos before, but here they are all blown up, mounted, and neatly labeled; if you get confused about lineage, consult the family tree on the wall at the end of the exhibit. The last 3 years of JFK's life were a bit chaotic (some 25,000 well-wishers thronged the roads when the senator and president-to-be returned from the 1960 Democratic Convention), but he continued to treasure the Cape as "the one place I can think and be alone."

Busloads of tourists visit the **Kennedy Memorial** just above Veterans Beach on Ocean Avenue; it's a moving tribute, beautifully maintained by the town, but crowds in season can be distracting. Finally, you may want to drive by the simple white clapboard church, St. Francis Xavier, on South Street; Rose attended Mass daily, and Caroline Kennedy and several other cousins got married here.

Spend your day in the Mid Cape recreating like a privileged Kennedy scion. Rent a Windsurfer at Kalmus Beach. Play a round of golf at the **Hyannis Golf Club** (© 508/362-2606), a public course on Route 132. **Four Seas Ice Cream** (© 508/775-1394), at 360 S. Main St. in Centerville, apparently a favorite of secret-service agents, is a must. For lodging right in Hyannisport, stay at **Simmons Homestead Inn,** 288 Scudder Ave., Hyannisport (© 800/637-1649 or 508/ 778-4999).

Rose Kennedy once told a reporter, "Our family would rather be in Hyannisport in the summer than anyplace else in the world." And yours?

Richard Kiusalas and Steven Whittlesey salvage antique lumber and turn it into cupboards, tables, and chairs, among other things; old windows are retrofitted as mirrors. Most of the stock at **West Barnstable Tables,** 2454 Meetinghouse Way (off Rte. 149 near the intersection of Rte. 6A), West Barnstable (© **508/362-2676**), looks freshly made, albeit with wood of unusually high quality. Pieces are priced accordingly: A dining room set—pine trestle table with six bow-back chairs—would run over $4,000. When the wood still bears interesting traces of its former life, it's turned into folk-art furniture. A cupboard made out of old painted red boards, secured with Model-T Ford hinges, for example, might fetch $3,600.

BOOKS & EPHEMERA   Named for the revolutionary printer who helped foment the War of Independence, **Isaiah Thomas Books & Prints,** 4632 Falmouth Rd. (Rte. 28, near Rte. 130), Cotuit (© **508/428-2752**), has a 60,000-volume collection, housed in an 1850 home. The shop is full of treasures, clustered by topic. Owner/expert James S. Visbeck is happy to show off his first editions, rare miniatures, and maps; you get the sense that sales are secondary to sheer bibliophilic pleasure. You can buy a 200-year-old map of your favorite Cape Cod village at **Maps of Antiquity,** 1022 Rte. 6A, West Barnstable (② **508/362-7169**).

FASHION **Europa,** 37 Barnstable Rd. (at North St., in the center of town), Hyannis (② **508/790-0877**), is a boutique where women can bone up on that world-traveler look, even if they've never been abroad. **Mark, Fore & Strike,** 21 Wianno Ave. (at Main St., in the center of town), Osterville (② **508/428-2270**), stocks preppie classics for both genders.

FOOD **Cape Cod Potato Chips,** Breed's Hill Road (at Independence Way, off Rte. 132), Hyannis (② **508/775-7253**), really are the world's best. Long a local favorite—they're chunkier than the norm—these snacks actually do originate here. Free factory tours are offered Monday to Friday from 9am to 5pm in July and August. Call for off-season hours.

HOME DECOR As a Nantucket innkeeper whiling away the winter, Claire Murray took up hooking rugs and turned her knack into an international business. At **Claire Murray,** 867 Main St. (in the center of town), Osterville (② **508/420-3562**), and at her new store at 770 Rte. 6A in West Barnstable (② **508/375-0331**), hobbyists can find all the fixings for various needle crafts, including kits, and advice as needed. Those of us with little time on our hands can just buy the finished goods, from sweaters and quilts to the signature folk-motif rugs.

Flowery pastels are the hallmark of **Joan Peters,** 885 Main St. (in the center of town), Osterville (② **508/428-3418**), favored by the Town & Country set. She designs a wide array of compatible fabrics and ceramics—right down to the bathroom sink, if need be—so that it's easy to achieve a pervasive, light-splashed look that doesn't look too overtly matched and mixed.

On Main Street in Hyannis, you'll find a world of wonderful kitchen products at **Nantucket Trading Company,** 354 Main St. (② **508/790-3933**).

SEAFOOD Besides Mill Way at Barnstable Harbor (see "Takeout & Take-Home Food," later in this chapter), the best place to buy fresh seafood in the vicinity of Hyannis is **Cape Fish & Lobster** at 406 W. Main St. in Centerville (② **508/771-1122**). This is where the top restaurateurs in Hyannis get their seafood. The prices are reasonable, and the catch is the freshest in town.

WHERE TO STAY
IN HYANNIS, HYANNISPORT & CRAIGVILLE

There are a variety of large, generic but convenient hotels and motels in Hyannis.

Right smack on Main Street within strolling distance of restaurants, shopping, and the ferries is the **Hyannis Inn Motel,** 473 Main St., Hyannis (② **800/922-8993** or 508/775-0255; www.hyannisinn.com). Summer rates are $110 to $127 double—a real value. During the Kennedy administration, this motel served as the press headquarters. It has an indoor pool, a breakfast restaurant (not included with room rates), and a cocktail lounge.

If you prefer more amenities, there's the **Sheraton Hyannis Resort** at the West End Circle just off Main Street (② **800/598-4559** or 508/775-7775; www.sheraton.com). Summer rates are $209 to $309 double. Out the back door is an 18-hole, par-3 executive golf course. There are also four tennis courts, an indoor and an outdoor pool, four restaurants, and a fitness center.

Another upscale alternative is the **Radisson Inn Hyannis,** 287 Iyannough Rd. (Rte. 28), Hyannis, just east of the airport rotary (© **800/333-3333** or 508/771-1700; www.radisson.com), which features a full health club (a branch of Gold's Gym) and a bistro/pizzeria. Summer rates are $179 to $199 double, $239 to $259 suite. You'll have to overlook the uninspiring location in strip-mall hell, but it's within spitting distance of the airport. Rooms are clean and comfortable, with attractive blonde-wood furniture and plush carpeting.

Expensive

Simmons Homestead Inn ★★ *Finds*   The first things passers-by notice are all the classic red sports cars: 50 at last count. A former ad exec and race-car driver, innkeeper Bill Putman likes to collect. He's made his sports car collection into a small museum open to the public called Toad Hall, after *The Wind in the Willows.* Inside the inn is his animal collection. The stuffed toys, sculptures, needlepoint, and wallpaper differentiate the rather traditional rooms in this rambling 1820s captain's manse. This is an inn where you'll find everyone around the hearth sipping complimentary wine (served at "6-ish") while they compare notes and nail down dinner plans. To help his guests plan their days and evenings, Putman has typed up extensive notes on day trips (including the Islands), bike routes (he supplies the bikes), and his own quirky restaurant reviews. Guests who prefer privacy may book the spiffily updated "servants' quarters," a spacious, airy wing with its own private deck. Rooms vary in size, but all are decorated with comfort and a sense of humor in mind. Four hammocks swing from trees in the shady backyard of this homey establishment.

288 Scudder Ave. (about ¼ mile west of the West End rotary), Hyannisport, MA 02647. © **800/637-1649** or 508/778-4999. Fax 508/790-1342. www.SimmonsHomesteadInn.com. 14 units. Summer $200–$260 double, $350 2-bedroom suite. Rates include full breakfast. AE, DISC, MC, V. Dogs welcome. **Amenities:** 6-person hot tub; loaner bikes; billiards parlor. *In room:* Hair dryer, iron, no phone.

Moderate

Sea Breeze Inn ★ *Kids*   Within whistling distance of the beach, this classic shingled beach house has been decked with the totems of small-town America: a picket fence, exuberant plantings, and even a wooden rocker built for two couples—or better yet, one. All this attention to the exterior is mirrored in the neat and cheerful interior. The coast used to be lined with superior guesthouses of this sort, and to find one still in its prime is a real treat. Also on the intensively gardened grounds are four cottages (a five-bedroom, a three-bedroom, and two one-bedrooms) that rent by the week, including one with a "honeymooners" double Jacuzzi.

270 Ocean Ave. (about 1 mile south of the West End rotary), Hyannis, MA 02601. © **508/771-7213.** Fax 508/ 862-0663. www.seabreezeinn.com. 14 units. Summer $100 double. Rates include continental breakfast. AE, DISC, MC, V. *In room:* A/C, TV.

Trade Winds Inn ★ *Finds* *Kids*   Many rooms in this attractive motel have patios and balconies with wonderful views of Craigville Beach, one of the Cape's most popular strips of sand. However, since it's hard to see the sand once the summer crowds hit, this property also has its own immaculate 500-foot private stretch of beach. Beach chairs and beach towels are provided. On cloudy days, guests may enjoy strolling to the Craigville Campground next door, a compound of 19th-century gingerbread-style cottages that still serves as a Methodist meeting camp preserve. The motel, which is on 6 acres, also abuts tiny Lake Elizabeth where young Jack and Ted Kennedy learned to sail.

780 Craigville Beach Rd. (across the street from Craigville Beach), Centerville, MA 02632. © **877/444-7966** or 508/775-0365. www.twicapecod.com. 46 units. Summer $199 double, $219–$229 suite. Rates include continental breakfast in season. AE, MC, V. Closed Nov–Apr. **Amenities:** Small bar; putting green. *In room:* A/C, TV.

IN BARNSTABLE & WEST BARNSTABLE
Moderate

The Acworth   Innkeeper Lisa Callahan knows that it's the small touches that make a stay memorable, and she has refreshed and redecorated this small B&B with TLC. Anyone looking to avoid the excess of Victorian furnishings in many B&Bs will delight in the simple, fresh, immaculate decor here. A couple of rooms have extra amenities like TVs, mini-fridges, and whirlpool baths. Two rooms in the carriage house have been combined into a romantic luxury suite with whirlpool bath, TV/VCR, working fireplace, air-conditioning, and mini-fridge. The three-course breakfasts include such favorites as cranberry pie, quiches, and stuffed French toast. The inn is close to Barnstable Village and popular Cape Cod Bay beaches, so the complimentary bikes may be all you need in the way of wheels.

4352 Rte. 6A (near the Yarmouth Port border), Cummaquid, MA 02637. © **800/362-6363** or 508/362-3330. Fax 508/375-0304. www.acworthinn.com. 5 units. Summer $145–$165 double, $195 suite. Rates include full breakfast. AE, DISC, MC, V. *In room:* A/C, hair dryer, iron, no phone.

Ashley Manor Inn   A lovely country inn along the Old King's Highway, this house is a much-modified 1699 colonial mansion that retains many of its original features, including a hearth with beehive oven (the perfect place to sip port on a blustery evening), built-in corner cupboards in the wainscoted dining room, and wide-board floors, many of them brightened with Nantucket-style splatter paint. The rooms, all but one of which boast a working fireplace, are spacious and inviting: true retreats. A deluxe room in its own wing has a separate entrance, whirlpool bath, glass-enclosed shower, canopy bed, and fireplace. All bathrooms are supplied with luxury towels of 100% Egyptian cotton. The 2-acre property itself is shielded from the road by an enormous privet hedge, and fragrant boxwood camouflages a Har-Tru tennis court. (You'll find loaner bikes beside it, ready to roll.) Romantics can sequester themselves in the flower-fringed gazebo. Breakfast on the brick patio is worth waking up for: You wouldn't want to miss the homemade granola, much less the main event—quiche, perhaps, or crepes.

3660 Rte. 6A (just east of Hyannis Rd.), Barnstable, MA 02630. © **888/535-2246** or 508/362-8044. Fax 508/362-9927. www.ashleymanor.net. 6 units. Summer $150–165 double, $200–$215 suite. Rates include full breakfast. AE, DISC, MC, V. **Amenities:** Har-Tru tennis court; loaner bikes. *In room:* A/C, dataport, coffeemaker, hair dryer.

Beechwood Inn ★★ *Finds*   Look for a butterscotch-colored 1853 Queen Anne Victorian all but enshrouded in weeping beech trees. Admirers of late-19th-century decor are in for a treat: The interior remains dark and rich, with a red-velvet parlor and tin ceilings in the dining room where innkeeper Debbie Traugot serves a three-course breakfast featuring home-baked delights such as applesauce pancakes and raspberry bread. Two of the upstairs bedrooms embody distinctive period styles: The Cottage Room contains furniture painted in an 1860s mode, and the Eastlake Room is modeled on the aesthetic precepts of William Morris that flourished in the 1880s. Each affords a distant view of the sparkling bay. All rooms have Sealy Posturepedic Plush mattresses. Rooms range from quite spacious (Lilac) to romantically snug (Garret); some have fireplaces and TVs/VCRs.

2839 Rte. 6A (about 1½ miles east of Rte. 132), Barnstable, MA 02630. © **800/609-6618** or 508/362-6618. Fax 508/362-0298. www.beechwoodinn.com. 6 units (4 tub/shower, 2 shower only). Summer $160–$180 double. Rates include full breakfast. AE, DISC, MC, V. *In room:* A/C, fridge, hair dryer, no phone.

Lamb and Lion Inn ★   This is an unusual property: part B&B, part motel. From the roadside, it's one of those charming old Cape Cod cottages (ca. 1740) along the Old King's Highway (where charming "Capes" are ubiquitous), set up on a knoll with a sloping lawn full of colorful flowers. Inside, it's a motel-like space with units encircling a pool and hot tub. The rooms are all individually decorated, and six rooms have kitchenettes. All rooms in the main inn building are air-conditioned. The multilevel barn suite, with three loft-type bedrooms, is a funky historic space (built in 1740), filled with rustic nooks and crannies.

2504 Main St. (Rte. 6A), Barnstable, MA 02630. © **800/909-6923** or 508/362-6823. Fax 508/362-0227. www.lambandlion.com. 10 units (6 tub/shower, 4 shower only). Summer $145–$250 double. Rates include continental breakfast. MC, V. Well-behaved pets allowed (40-lb. limit). **Amenities:** Pool; hot tub. *In room:* A/C, TV.

WHERE TO DINE
IN HYANNIS
Expensive

Alberto's Ristorante ★★ ITALIAN   Alberto's explores the full range of Italian cuisine, with a classicist's attention to components and composition. Owner/chef Felisberto Barreiro's most popular dishes are his treatments of lobster, rack of lamb, and beef tenderloin. Hand-cut pasta is also a specialty, including the ultra-rich seafood ravioli cloaked in saffron-cream sauce. Though the atmosphere is elegant, with sconces shedding a warm glow over well-spaced, linen-draped tables, it is not one of hushed reverence: People clearly come here to have a good time, and the friendly service and fabulous food ensure that they do. Locals who appreciate a bargain know to come between 3 and 6pm, when a full dinner, with soup, salad, and dessert, costs as little as $10 to $15. There's live jazz or piano music daily year-round.

360 Main St., Hyannis. © **508/778-1770**. Reservations recommended. Main courses $11–$27. AE, DC, DISC, MC, V. Mon–Sat 3–11pm; Sun noon–11pm.

The Black Cat ★ NEW AMERICAN   Conveniently located on Hyannis Harbor less than a block from the Hy-Line ferries, this is a fine place to catch a quick bite or full meal while you wait for your boat to come in. The menu is pretty basic—steak, pasta, and, of course, fish—but attention is paid to the details; the onion rings, for instance, are made fresh. The dining room, with its bar of gleaming mahogany and brass, will appeal to chilled travelers on a blustery day; in fine weather, you might prefer the porch. There's live jazz on the weekends in season.

165 Ocean St. (opposite the Ocean St. Dock), Hyannis. © **508/778-1233**. Reservations not accepted. Main courses $15–$29. AE, DC, DISC, MC, V. Apr–Oct daily 11:30am–10:30pm; call for off-season hours. Closed Jan.

The Paddock ★★ CONTINENTAL   In the almost 30 years that the Zartarian family has run this large, traditional restaurant, they have maintained a solid reputation in the community with consistently good food and service. The decor might be a little dated, but Grandma will love the Victorian motifs; better yet, you can dine on the plant-and-wicker–filled summer porch. The menu combines creative options with traditional choices (you can still order extra béarnaise sauce on the side). For appetizers, there's chicken liver pâté, but also polenta crab cakes with chipotle chile cream and sweet mango salsa. Main courses include filet mignon and sesame-encrusted yellowfin tuna served rare with Asian greens. The 300-bottle wine list has received awards from *Wine Spectator* for 16 years. There is free valet parking, and a pianist entertains nightly in the pub area. Because the Cape Cod Melody Tent is right next door, you'll need to go after 9pm to avoid the crowds if an act is playing.

West End rotary (at the intersection of W. Main St. and Main St.), Hyannis. ✆ **508/775-7677.** www.paddock capecod.com. Reservations recommended. Main courses lunch $7–$13, dinner $17–$28. AE, DC, DISC, MC, V. Apr to mid-Nov Mon–Sat 11:30am–2:30pm and 5–10pm, Sun noon–10pm. Closed mid-Nov to Mar.

Penguin SeaGrill & Steakhouse ★★ INTERNATIONAL   For years, this has been considered one of the top restaurants on the Cape. Chef/owner Bob Gold is one of those restless types who, having mastered one style of cuisine (Italian), can't wait to take on another. Hence the versatile menu, which bounces from Asian influences, like "Thai Jumpin' Squid," to mussels Portuguese-style. The top dishes here are seafood and steaks; pay attention to the specials and you can't go wrong. Large lobsters are served nightly; meats and fish are wood-grilled. The wine list is impressive, with many fine vintages in all price ranges. The setting is contemporary, with brick walls, mirrored accents, and mammoth carved fish. There's even entertainment Friday nights in season.

331 Main St. (in the center of town), Hyannis. ✆ **508/775-2023.** Reservations recommended. Main courses $15–$24. AE, DC, DISC, MC, V. June–Sept Tues–Thurs and Sun 5–10pm, Fri–Sat 5–11pm; closed Monday; call for off-season hours.

Ristorante Barolo ★★ NORTHERN ITALIAN   This is the best Italian restaurant in town. Part of a smart-looking brick office complex, this thoroughly up-to-date establishment does everything right, from offering extra-virgin olive oil in which to dunk its crusty bread to getting those pastas perfectly al dente. Appetizers perfect for sharing are *Polpette Gartinate alla Romana* (homemade meatballs in a tomato-and-basil sauce) and *Gamberi al Martini* (shrimp sautéed with fresh scallions and martini-wine sauce). Entrees include a number of tempting veal choices, like *Vitello alla Sorrentina* (Provimi-brand veal, mozzarella, and basil with plum-tomato sauce), as well as such favorites as *Linguine al Frutti di Mare,* with littlenecks, mussels, shrimp, and calamari. The desserts are brought in daily from Boston's famed North End.

1 Financial Place (297 North St., just off the West End rotary), Hyannis. ✆ **508/778-2878.** Reservations recommended. Main courses $10–$27. AE, DC, MC, V. June–Sept Sun–Thurs 4:30–10pm, Fri–Sat 4:30–11pm; call for off-season hours.

Roadhouse Café ★★ AMERICAN/NORTHERN ITALIAN   This is neither a roadhouse nor a cafe, but it is a solid entry in the Hyannis dining scene. The extensive menu is pretty much split between American standards such as steak (not to mention oysters Rockefeller or casino) and real Italian cooking, unstinting on the garlic. A less expensive, lighter-fare menu, including what some have called "the best burger in the world," is served in the snazzy bistro in back. Among the appetizers are such delicacies as beef carpaccio with fresh-shaved Parmesan, and vine-ripened tomatoes and buffalo mozzarella drizzled with balsamic vinaigrette. The vinaigrette also makes a tasty marinade for native swordfish headed for the grill. The signature dessert, a distinctly non-Italian cheesecake infused with Baileys Irish Cream, is a must-try. Music lovers know to come on Monday nights for the live jazz in the bistro (see "Hyannis & Environs After Dark," below).

488 South St. (off Main St., near the West End rotary), Hyannis. ✆ **508/775-2386.** Reservations recommended. Main courses $15–$26. AE, DC, DISC, MC, V. Daily 4pm–midnight.

Roo Bar ⚓ BISTRO   This stylish bistro is one of the few truly hip spots in Hyannis. You may want to sit at the bar and have a few appetizers like the chicken pot sticker (pan-seared wonton wrappers filled with an Asian chicken and vegetable stuffing with an orange marmalade dipping sauce) or a simple plate of oysters on the half shell. The most popular entree may be the seafood Provençale (jumbo shrimp and sea scallops sautéed with fresh tomatoes and basil in a white-wine garlic sauce and served over fresh angel-hair pasta), but there are a number of other lobster, fish, and steak dishes. There's also a selection of delicious gourmet pizzas (see "Hyannis & Environs After Dark," below).

586 Main St., Hyannis. ✆ **508/778-6515.** Main courses $9–$25. AE, DC, MC, V. Daily 5–10pm.

Moderate

Harry's ★ CAJUN   Seemingly transported from the French Quarter, this small restaurant/bar—park benches serve as booths—has added some Italian and French options to its menu, but it's the authentic Cajun cooking that keeps customers coming back: ribs, jambalaya, hoppin' John, red beans, and rice. On the weekends, get set for a heaping serving of R&B (see "Hyannis & Environs After Dark," below). This place hops until 1am. *A Hint:* Arrive for a late dinner around 8:30pm and you'll be all set with a great table once the music starts.

700 Main St. (near the West End rotary), Hyannis. ✆ **508/778-4188.** Reservations not accepted. Main courses $10–$19. MC, V. Daily 11:30am–10pm.

Tugboats ★ (Kids) AMERICAN   Yet another harborside perch for munching and ogling, but this one's especially appealing. The two spacious outdoor decks are angled just right to catch the sunset, with cocktail/frappés to match, or perhaps a bottle of Moët et Chandon. Forget fancy dining and chow down on blackened-swordfish bites (topping a Caesar salad, perhaps), lobster fritters, or the double-duty Steak Neptune, topped with scallops and shrimp. Among the "decadent desserts" is a Key lime pie purportedly lifted straight from Papa's of Key West.

21 Arlington St. (at the Hyannis Marina, off Willow St.), Hyannis. ✆ **508/775-6433.** Reservations not accepted. Main courses $11–$18. AE, DC, DISC, MC, V. Late May to Oct daily 11:30am–10:30pm; Apr to late May Tues–Sun 11:30am–10:30pm. Closed Nov–Mar.

Inexpensive

Baxter's Boat House ⚓ (Value) (Kids) SEAFOOD   A shingled shack on a jetty jutting out into the harbor, Baxter's has catered to the boating crowd since the mid-1950s with Cape classics such as fried clams and fish virtually any way you like it, from baked to blackened, served on paper plates at picnic tables. This is a good place to bring a brood of kids. If you sit out on the deck, be wary of swooping seagulls looking to spirit away your lunch.

177 Pleasant St. (near the Steamship Authority ferry), Hyannis. ✆ **508/775-7040.** Main courses $8–$14. AE, MC, V. Late May to early Sept Mon–Sat 11:30am–10pm, Sun 11:30am–9pm; hours may vary at the beginning and end of the season. Closed mid-Oct to April.

Collucci Brothers Diner DINER   In the tradition of great diners, this one has a tin ceiling, comfy booths, and a shiny counter. It also has sassy waitresses who pour really good coffee. Selections from the children's menu are under $4. Wash down a tuna melt with a root beer float or splurge on the roast turkey dinner. The diner is a block from Main Street and about a half mile from the Hy-Line ferry terminal with boats to Nantucket.

50 Sea St. (at the corner of South St.). ✆ **508/771-6896.** Reservations not accepted. All items under $10. AE, MC, V. Late May to Sept Mon–Sat 6am–3pm, Sun 6am–2pm.

Common Ground Cafe ★ *Value* AMERICAN Talk about an out-of-body experience: Step off tacky Main Street Hyannis into this New Age-y sandwich shop run by a commune. The barn-board walls and wide-board floors surround alcoves with private booths containing amorphous tree-stump tables. You can see straight up to the second-floor juice and smoothie bar, where they also sell some health and beauty products. But enough about atmosphere; this place makes the best iced tea on Cape Cod (the house blend is a mixture of mint teas and lemon). Everything is made from scratch here. The sandwiches and salads are, as you'd expect, wholesome and delicious. They also have some south-of-the-border choices: The burrito with turkey is a winner. If I understand correctly from their literature (available at the door), the "Common Ground" is love. Count me in.

420 Main St., Hyannis. © 508/778-8390. Most items under $6. AE, DC, DISC, MC, V. Mon–Thurs 10am–9pm; Fri 10am–3pm.

Coffee & Desserts

Hyannis does have an authentic French cafe. **La Petite France Cafe,** 349 Main St., in the center of town (© **508/771-4445**), owned by Lucien Degioanni of San Remy, serves scrumptious croissants, breads, and pastries, all baked on-site. For lunch, there are homemade soups and quiches, as well as popular sandwiches and salads. Closed January to March.

Vermont's favorite sons, **Ben & Jerry,** have one of their playful ice-cream parlors at 352 Main St., Hyannis (© **508/790-0910**).

A modest luncheonette may make an unlikely shrine, but since 1934, several generations of summer goers—including enthusiastic Kennedys—have fed their ice-cream cravings at **Four Seas,** 360 S. Main St., at Main Street, in the center of Centerville (© **508/775-1394**). Founder Richard Warren was into exotic flavors long before they became the norm. His specialties include rum-butter toffee, cantaloupe, and—at the height of the season—Cape Cod beach plum. Closed early September to late May.

Takeout & Picnic Fare

Another branch of the popular **Box Lunch** (© **508/790-5855**), serving pita "rollwiches," is right on Main Street (no. 357) in Hyannis. These are the best—and fastest—sandwiches in town.

IN BARNSTABLE VILLAGE, OSTERVILLE & COTUIT
Very Expensive

The Regatta of Cotuit at the Crocker House ★★★ NEW AMERICAN One of the best restaurants on Cape Cod, this year-round fine-dining restaurant serves elaborate cuisine in a suite of charmingly decorated Federal-era rooms. This 1790 Cape was once a stagecoach inn and some may find the atmosphere a wee bit stuffy, but the food and service are always top-notch. Nightly specials might include such hearty offerings as roasted buffalo tenderloin with blackberry Madeira sauce served with braised fresh greens and a Stilton sage bread pudding; or sautéed filet of halibut with a citrus beurre blanc, lobster mashed potatoes, and a marinated vegetable salad. The cuisine is exquisitely prepared and presented, fortified by herbs and vegetables plucked fresh from the kitchen garden, and the mood is invariably festive. For budget-minded gourmands, the Regatta menu also includes several less expensive "bistro" items, like chicken fricassee and grilled pork loin medallions. A pianist plays 5 to 7 nights a week, year-round.

4631 Rte. 28 (near the intersection of Rte. 130), Cotuit. © 508/428-5715. Reservations recommended. Main courses $26–$35; bistro menu $16–$17. AE, MC, V. Apr–Dec daily 5–10pm; Jan–Mar Wed–Sun 5–10pm.

Moderate

Dolphin Restaurant ★★ NEW AMERICAN   It looks like just another run-of-the-mill roadside eatery, so it's easy to miss from the road. Never mind the corny decor (pine paneling and clunky captains' chairs) or the little plate of crackers and cheese dip that greets you at the table, both carryovers from the restaurant's 1953 debut. The finesse is to be found in the menu, where amid the more typical fried fish you'll find such delicacies as Chilean sea bass with roasted corn salsa and lime vinaigrette, roast duck with mango glaze and toasted coconut, or arctic char with caramelized onions and citrus butter. It's a painless segue from there to the signature dessert: amaretto bread pudding.

3250 Rte. 6A (in the center of town), Barnstable. ✆ **508/362-6610**. Main courses $17–$23. AE, MC, V. May–Oct Mon–Sat 11:30am–3pm and 5–9:30pm, Sun 5–9:30pm.

Keepers Restaurant ★ NEW ENGLAND   You'll really feel like an insider as you wind your way through the fancy neighborhoods of Osterville to this small, casual restaurant set in the old Crosby boatyard. In the mid–19th century, the Crosby brothers invented a new kind of sailboat that came about "quick like a cat." You can still see wooden Crosby Cat sailboats in the boatyard, as well as million-dollar yachts. The menu offers local standards, like a lobster roll and baked cod. It's a cozy restaurant with only about 10 tables.

72 Crosby Circle (on the harbor at the Crosby Boat Yard), Osterville. ✆ **508/428-6719**. Main courses $12–$17. MC, V. June–Aug Wed–Sun 11:30am–2:30pm and 5–9:30pm; call for off-season hours. Closed Oct–Apr.

Mattakeese Wharf ★ SEAFOOD   This water-view fish house, with broad decks jutting out into the Barnstable harbor, gets packed in season; don't even bother on summer weekends. The outdoor seating fills up first, and no wonder, with Sandy Neck sunsets to marvel over and fish so fresh it could have flopped on deck. There's a Mediterranean subtext to the extensive menu. The bouillabaisse is worthy of the name, and the varied combinations of pasta, seafood, and sauce—from Alfredo to fra diavolo—invite return visits. There's live piano music most nights in season.

271 Mill Way (about ½ mile north of Rte. 6A), Barnstable. ✆ **508/362-4511**. Reservations recommended. Main courses $14–$28. AE, DC, DISC, MC, V. June–mid-Oct daily 11:30am–10pm; call for off-season hours. Closed mid-Oct to mid-Apr.

Takeout & Take-Home Food

Area residents like to think of **Mill Way** ★★, Mill Way Road, on Barnstable Harbor, about ⅓ mile north of Route 6A (✆ **508/362-2760**), a high-falutin' fish shack, as their own little secret. Certainly there are no outward signs to suggest that chef/co-owner Ralph Binder is a product of the prestigious Culinary Institute of America. You can order the usual Cape specialties, from chowder to fried clams to lobster, from the takeout window, but be sure to step inside to see what else is available—perhaps a pungent calamari salad, or seafood sausage, a delicately seasoned mélange of lobster, shrimp, and scallops. Closed mid-October through April.

HYANNIS & ENVIRONS AFTER DARK
LOW-KEY EVENINGS

Baxter's Boat House   This congenial little lounge, with map-topped tables and low-key blues piano, draws an attractive crowd, including the occasional vacationing celebrity. See "Where to Dine," above. 177 Pleasant St., Hyannis. ✆ **508/775-7040**. No cover.

Roadhouse Café   Duck into this dark-paneled bar, decorated like an English gentlemen's club in burgundy leather if you're looking for sophisticated entertainment and company. The bar stocks 48 boutique beers, in addition to all the usual hard, soft, and sweet liquors, and you won't go hoarse trying to converse over the soft jazz. The bistro area next to the bar has live jazz piano nightly. See "Where to Dine," above. Insiders know to show up Monday nights to hear local jazz great Dave McKenna. 488 South St, Hyannis. ℂ **508/775-2386.** No cover.

Roo Bar   This bistro feels very Manhattan, with ultra-cool servers, a long, sleek bar area, and lots of attitude. The food is good, too. See "Where to Dine," above. Trendy cigar smoking commences after 10pm. 586 Main St., Hyannis. ℂ **508/778-6515.** No cover.

LIVE & LOUD

Duval Street Station   Hyannis's only gay bar occupies an old train station. The lower level is a comfortable lounge, and upstairs there's a dance bar complete with light show and DJ mixes that spin from Latin rhythms to New Wave to "gay disco classics" of the '70s and '80s. 477 Yarmouth Rd. (about 1 mile northeast of Main St.), Hyannis. ℂ **508/771-7511.** Nominal cover charge Fri–Sat in season.

Harry's   There's hardly room to eat here, let alone rock out, but the cramped dance floor makes for instant camaraderie. The classic blues music heard here, like Rick Russell and the Cadillac Horns, really demands to be absorbed in such an intimate space. Live performance reigns nightly in season and about 5 nights a week year-round. 700 Main St. (see "Where to Dine," above), Hyannis. ℂ **508/778-4188.** Cover Thurs–Sat $3–$4.

Star City Grill   Acoustic acts and soft-rock bands, like John Poussette Dart, attract a 30-plus crowd. But the drinks range from silly (for example, Grape Crush) to serious (27-oz. margaritas), and both the setting and staff contrive to ensure a good time. Live music starts at 9:30pm Tuesdays through Sundays. 645 Rte. 132, Hyannis. ℂ **508/778-6767.** No cover.

Steamers Grill & Bar   Everyone's glowing with the day's exertions as they cram onto the deck to enjoy liberal libations, a lingering sunset, and, on weekends, live bands. Upstairs, there's a young, sporty crowd for the most part; and by 9pm on Friday and Saturday in season, it's packed. Entertainment tends to be acoustic guitar acts in a James Taylor mode. Downstairs, the Putter's Pub with its fuddy-duddy duffers' motif is more sedate. 235 Ocean St., Hyannis. ℂ **508/778-0818.** No cover.

PERFORMANCES, READINGS & LECTURES

The Barnstable Comedy Club   A local favorite since 1922, the oldest amateur theater group in the country (Kurt Vonnegut is an admiring ex-member) offers a mix of old chestnuts and original farces off season. Call for schedule. 3171 Rte. 6A (in the center of town), Barnstable. ℂ **508/362-6333.** Tickets $10–$12; students and seniors $8–$10.

The Cape Cod Melody Tent 🏆   Built as a summer theater in 1950, this billowy blue big-top proved even better suited to variety shows. A nonprofit venture since 1990 (proceeds fund other cultural initiatives Cape-wide), the Melody Tent has hosted the major performers of the past half century, from jazz greats to comedians, crooners to rockers. Every seat is a winner in this grand oval, only 20 banked aisles deep. Curtain 8pm nightly July to early September. There's also a children's theater program Wednesday mornings at 11am. Call for schedule. West End rotary, Hyannis. ℂ **508/775-9100.** Tickets $18–$45.

2 Yarmouth 🛧

19 miles E of Sandwich; 38 miles S of Provincetown

This cross section represents the Cape at its best—and worst. Yarmouth Port, on Cape Cod Bay, is an enchanting town, clustered with interesting shops and architectural pearls, whereas the sound-side "villages" of West to South Yarmouth are an object lesson in unbridled development run amuck. This section of Route 28 is a nightmarish gauntlet of tacky accommodations and "attractions." Yet even here, you'll find a few spots worthy of the name Cape Cod.

Legend has it that Leif Eriksson found the region very attractive indeed, and set up what was meant to be a permanent camp by the Bass River around A.D. 1000. No trace has yet been found—other than the puzzling "Bournedale stone," with its vaguely runic inscriptions, now housed at the Aptucxet Trading Post Museum in Bourne. Why Eriksson left—and whether, in fact, he came to Cape Cod at all, and not some similar spot—are mysteries still unanswered. We do know that Yarmouth, most likely named for an English port, was the second Cape town to incorporate, following closely on the heels of Sandwich; and that at the height of the shipping boom, Yarmouth Port boasted a "Captain's Row" of 50 fine houses, most of which remain showpieces to this day.

So, you've got the north shore for culture and refinement, and the south shore for kitsch. Take your pick, or ricochet, enjoying the best of both worlds.

ESSENTIALS

GETTING THERE   After crossing either the Bourne or Sagamore bridge, head east on Route 6 or 6A. The section of Route 6A north of Route 6's Exit 7 passes through the village of Yarmouth Port. The villages of West Yarmouth, Bass River, and South Yarmouth are located along Route 28, east of Hyannis; to reach them from Route 6, take Exit 7 south (Yarmouth Rd.) or Exit 8 south (Station St.); or fly into Hyannis (see "Getting There," in chapter 2).

If you need to get around the area without a car, the Yarmouth Easy Shuttle circles Route 28 from Hyannis's bus terminal; for details, contact the Yarmouth Area Chamber of Commerce (see below).

VISITOR INFORMATION   Contact the **Yarmouth Area Chamber of Commerce,** 657 Rte. 28, West Yarmouth, MA 02673 (© **800/732-1008** or 508/778-1008; fax 508/778-5114; www.yarmouthcapecod.com); or the **Cape Cod Chamber of Commerce** (see "Visitor Information" in the "Barnstable, Hyannis, Neighboring Villages & Environs" section, earlier in this chapter). The Yarmouth chamber is open Monday through Friday 9am to 5pm, Sunday 10am to 3pm, in season. Off season, the hours are Monday through Friday 9am to 5pm.

BEACHES & RECREATIONAL PURSUITS

BEACHES   Yarmouth boasts 11 saltwater and 2 pond beaches open to the public. The body-per-square-yard ratio can be pretty intense along the sound, but so is the social scene, so no one seems to mind. The beachside parking lots charge $10 a day and sell week-long stickers ($45).

• **Bass River Beach** 🛧, off South Shore Drive in Bass River (South Yarmouth): Located at the mouth of the largest tidal river on the eastern seaboard, this sound beach offers restroom facilities and a snack bar, plus a wheelchair-accessible fishing pier. The beaches along the south shore (Nantucket Sound) tend to be clean and sandy with comfortable water temps (kids will want to stay in all day), but they can also be crowded during peak times. You'll need a beach sticker to park here.

- **Grays Beach,** off Center Street in Yarmouth Port: This isn't much of a beach, but tame waters make this tiny spit of dark sand good for young children; it adjoins the Callery–Darling Conservation Area (see "Nature & Wildlife Areas," below). The Bass Hole boardwalk offers one of the most scenic walks mid-Cape. Parking is free here, and there's a picnic area with grills.
- **Parker's River Beach,** off South Shore Drive in Bass River: The usual amenities are available, like restrooms and a snack bar, plus a 20-foot gazebo for the sun-shy.
- **Seagull Beach** 🐾, off South Sea Avenue in West Yarmouth: Rolling dunes, a boardwalk, and all the necessary facilities, like restrooms and a snack bar, attract a young crowd. Bring bug spray, though: Greenhead flies get the munchies in July.

BICYCLING The **Cape Cod Rail Trail** 🐾🐾🐾 (© **508/896-3491**) is just a few miles away on Route 134 (near the entrance to Rte. 6) in South Dennis. Rent a bike at the trail head, and if you are feeling Olympian, bike all the way to Wellfleet (25 miles).

BOATING You can rent a canoe at **Cape Cod Waterways,** 16 Rte. 28, Dennisport (© **508/398-0080**), and paddle along the Bass River, which flows between South Yarmouth and West Dennis on the south side of the Cape. A full-day canoe or kayak rental costs $50 to $65.

FISHING Of the five fishing ponds in the Yarmouth area, Long Pond near South Yarmouth is known for its largemouth bass and pickerel; for details and a license (shellfishing is another option), visit **Town Hall** at 1146 Rte. 28 in South Yarmouth (© **508/398-2231**), or **Riverview Bait and Tackle** at 1273 Rte. 28 in South Yarmouth (© **508/394-1036**). Full-season licenses for Massachusetts residents cost $29, for out-of-staters, $39. You can cast for striped bass and bluefish off the pier at Bass River Beach (see "Beaches," above).

FITNESS The **Mid-Cape Racquet Club** (see "Tennis," below) doubles as a fitness center.

GOLF The township maintains two 18-hole courses: the seasonal **Bayberry Hills,** off West Yarmouth Road in West Yarmouth (© **508/394-5597**); and the **Bass River Golf Course,** off High Bank Road in South Yarmouth (© **508/398-9079**), founded in 1900 and open year-round. A round at either of these costs $53. Another 18-holer open to the public is the par-54 **Blue Rock Golf Course** off High Bank Road in South Yarmouth (© **508/398-9295**), open year-round, where a round costs $45.

NATURE & WILDLIFE AREAS For a pleasant stroll, follow the 2 miles of trails maintained by the **Historical Society of Old Yarmouth** on 53 acres. Park behind the post office and check in at the gatehouse, whose herb garden displays a "Wheel of Thyme." The in-season trail fee (50¢ adults, 25¢ children) includes a keyed trail guide: Look for—but do not pick—the endangered pink lady's slipper, a local orchid. Your path will cross the transplanted 1873 Kelley Chapel, said to have been built by a Quaker grandfather to comfort his daughter after the death of her child.

In Yarmouth Port, follow Centre Street about a mile north and bear northeast on Homers Dock Road; from here a 2.5-mile trail through the Callery–Darling Conservation Area leads to Grays Beach, where you can continue across the Bass Hole Boardwalk for a lovely view of the marsh.

TENNIS   There are four public courts at Flax Pond, off North Main Street in South Yarmouth; four more at Sandy Pond, on Buck Island Road off Higgins Crowell Road; plus 10 at Dennis–Yarmouth High School at Station Avenue in South Yarmouth. For details, contact the **Yarmouth Recreation Department** (*C* **508/398-2231,** ext. 284). **The Mid-Cape Racquet Club,** 193 Whites Path, South Yarmouth (*C* **508/394-3511**), has nine indoor courts ($18 per person, per hour), plus racquetball and squash courts (one each) and health-club facilities ($10 per day).

BASEBALL & SOCCER

The **Dennis–Yarmouth Red Sox,** part of the Cape Cod Baseball League, play at Dennis–Yarmouth Regional High School's Red Wilson Field off Station Avenue in South Yarmouth. For a schedule, contact the **Yarmouth Chamber of Commerce** (*C* **508/778-1008**), the **Yarmouth Recreation Department** (*C* **508/ 398-2231,** ext. 284), or the **League** (*C* **508/432-6909**).

The **Cape Cod Crusaders** soccer team takes on a dozen other Atlantic-coast teams mid-May to early August, also at the Dennis-Yarmouth Regional High School. For details, contact the **Yarmouth Chamber of Commerce** (*C* **508/ 778-1008**).

KID STUFF

Children tend to crave the "junk" we adults condemn, so they're likely to be enthralled by the rainy-day enticements of Route 28, which include trampolines, batting cages, pitch and putt, and bumper cars. Among the more enduringly appealing miniature-golf courses clamoring for attention is **Pirate's Cove,** at 728 Main St./Rte. 28, South Yarmouth (*C* **508/394-6200;** open daily 9am–10:30pm in season; closed Nov to mid-Apr), where the trap decor is strong on macabre humor.

ZooQuarium *★* *Kids*   This slightly scruffy wildlife museum has made great strides in recent years toward blending entertainment with education. It's a little easier to enjoy the seal and sea lion show once you've been assured that the stars do, in fact, like performing. They have been trained with positive reinforcement only and arrived with injuries that precluded their survival in the wild. The aquarium is arranged in realistic habitats, and the "zoo" consists primarily of indigenous fauna, both domesticated and wild (the pacing bobcat is liable to give you pause). Children will be entranced by the Zoorific theater (a live-animal education program) and the children's discovery center with hands-on activities. The new exhibit, "A Walk Through the Cape Cod Woods," features some of the little creatures that inhabit the woodland floor. In addition, a very creditable effort is made to convey the need for ecological preservation.

674 Rte. 28 (midway between West Yarmouth and Bass River), West Yarmouth. *C* 508/775-8883. www. zooquariumcapecod.net. Admission $9 adults, $6 children 2–9. MC, V. July to early Sept daily 9:30am–6pm; mid-Feb to June and Sept–Nov 9:30am–5pm. Closed Dec to mid-Feb.

SHOPPING

Driving Route 6A, the Old King's Highway, in Yarmouth Port, you'll pass a number of antiques stores and fine shops for the home. Unless you have children in tow, you may want to bypass Route 28 entirely and stay on the pretty north side of Yarmouth.

ANTIQUES/COLLECTIBLES   Check out **Town Crier Antiques,** 153 Rte. 6A (in the center of town), Yarmouth Port (*C* **508/362-3138**), for fun stuff including well-priced (if not museum-quality) quilts, glassware, and attendant paraphernalia. Closed November to mid-May.

BOOKS   The most colorful bookshop on the Cape (if not the whole East Coast) is **Parnassus Books,** 220 Rte. 6A (about ¼ mile east of the town center), Yarmouth Port (℃ **508/362-6420**). This jam-packed repository—housed in an 1858 Swedenborgian church—is the creation of Ben Muse, who has been collecting and selling vintage tomes since the 1960s. Relevant new stock, including the Cape-related reissues published by Parnassus Imprints, is offered alongside the older treasures. Don't expect much hand-holding on the part of the gruff proprietor. You'll earn his respect by knowing what you're looking for or, better yet, being willing to browse until it finds you. The outdoor racks, maintained on an honor system, are open 24 hours a day, for those who suffer from anbibliophobia—fear of lacking for reading material.

GIFTS/HOME DECOR   To emulate that Cape look—breezy chic—study the key ingredients artfully assembled at **Design Works,** 159 Rte. 6A (in the center of town), Yarmouth Port (℃ **508/362-9698**): stripped-pine antiques, crisp linens, and colorful majolica. There are also books and cards.

A darling little gift shop along Route 6A is **From Prothesia's Attic** (399 Route 6A, Yarmouth Port, ℃ 508/362-6951). It stocks a colorful and eclectic mix of handcrafted items and unusual gifts.

The design approach at **Peach Tree Designs,** 173 Rte. 6A (in the center of town), Yarmouth Port (℃ **508/362-8317**), is much more adventurous and eclectic. A bold hand is evident in the juxtaposition of disparate elements, from hunting prints to beribboned hats, model ships to hand-woven throws. The gift pickings are superlative as well—especially if you're shopping for yourself.

MUSEUMS

Captain Bangs Hallet House Museum ✷   Typical of the sumptuous tastes of the time, this 1840 Greek Revival house is named for the China Trade seafarer who lived here from 1863 to 1893. The Historical Society of Old Yarmouth, which oversees the property, has filled its beautifully proportioned rooms with the finest furnishings of the day, from Hitchcock chairs to a Hepplewhite sofa. The rustic kitchen in back belongs to the 1740 core around which this showy edifice was erected. Note the nearly 200-year-old weeping beech tree and the herb garden beyond, which lead to a scenic 2-mile walking trail (see "Nature & Wildlife Areas," above).

11 Strawberry Lane (off Rte. 6A, about ½ mile east of the town center; park behind the post office at 231 Rte. 6A), Yarmouth Port. ℃ 508/362-3021. www.hsoy.org. Admission $3 adults, 50¢ children 12 and under. June–Oct 15 Thurs–Sun tours at 1, 2, and 3pm. Groups by appointment. Closed Nov–May.

The Edward Gorey House ✷✷   The Cape's newest attraction is a museum devoted to the life and works of illustrator Edward Gorey, whose whimsically mischievous works may be most famous as the animated opening to the television series Mystery! on PBS. Gorey died in the spring of 2000, and his home on the Yarmouth Port Common off Route 6A (the Old King's Hwy.) has been converted into an intimate museum displaying original artworks, photographs and first editions from his career as an author, playwright, illustrator, and costume and set designer. Gorey's passion for animals is also a focus of the collection.

8 Strawberry Lane (off Rte. 6A, on the Common), Yarmouth Port. ℃ 508/362-3909. www.edwardgorey house.org. Admission $5 adults, $3 students and seniors, $2 children 6–12, free for children under 6. May–Sept Wed–Sat 10am–5pm, Sun noon–5pm; Oct–Apr Thurs–Sat 11am–4pm, Sun noon–4pm. Closed Feb.

Booked aisle seat.

Reserved room with a view.

With a queen – no, make that a king-size bed.

Plan your vacation

- flights, hotels, car rentals
- cruises & vacation packages
- destination guides
- fare alerts
- go to yahoo.com, click travel

Winslow Crocker House ★★ The only property on the Cape currently preserved by the prestigious Society for the Preservation of New England Antiquities, this house, built around 1780, deserves every honor. Not only is it a lovely example of the shingled Georgian style, it's packed with outstanding antiques—Jacobean to Chippendale—collected in the 1930s by Mary Thacher, a descendent of the town's first land grantee. Anthony Thacher and his family had a rougher crossing than most: Their ship foundered off Cape Ann in 1635 (near an island that now bears their name), and though their four children drowned, Thacher and his wife were able to make it to shore, clinging to the family cradle. You'll come across a 1690 replica in the parlor. Thacher's son, John, a colonel, built the house next door in around 1680, and—with the help of two successive wives—raised a total of 21 children. All the museum-worthy objects in the Winslow Crocker House would seem to have similar stories to tell. For antique lovers, as well as anyone interested in local lore, this is a valuable cache and a very worthwhile stop.

250 Rte. 6A (about ½ mile east of the town center), Yarmouth Port. © 508/362-4385. www.spnea.org. Admission $5 adults, $4 seniors, $2.50 children 6–12, free to Cape Cod residents and SPNEA members. June to mid-Oct Sat–Sun tours hourly 11am–5pm (last tour at 4pm). Closed mid-Oct to May.

WHERE TO STAY

So many hotels and motels line Route 28 and the shore in West and South Yarmouth that it may be hard to make sense of the choices. The following are some that offer clean rooms and cater to families looking for a reasonably priced beach vacation. All are within a few miles of the beach or right on the beach. For those staying on Route 28, the town runs frequent beach shuttles in season.

The Tidewater Motor Lodge, 135 Main St./Rte. 28, West Yarmouth (© **800/ 338-6322** or 508/775-6322; www.tidewaterml.com), is a short walk (½ mile) from a small beach on Lewis Bay, and a not-so-short walk (about a mile) from Hyannis's Main Street and the ferries to Nantucket. Summer rates are $120 to $136 double. One of the more attractive motels along this strip, it's a white clapboard double-decker motel with green shutters and doors. The Tidewater also has an indoor pool, an outdoor pool, and a breakfast restaurant.

All Seasons Motor Inn, 1199 Main St./Rte. 28, South Yarmouth (© **800/ 527-0359** or 508/394-7600; www.allseasons.com), is popular with families. Summer rates are $130 to $145 double. It has indoor and outdoor pools, a breakfast restaurant, and exercise and game rooms.

Ocean Mist ★, 97 S. Shore Dr., South Yarmouth (© **800/248-6478** or 508/ 398-2633; www.capecodtravel.com/oceanmist), is a large motel right on the beach. There's also an indoor pool, just in case it rains. Summer rates are $189 to $209 double, $249 suites. A good choice if you have kids.

VERY EXPENSIVE

Red Jacket ★★ 〈Kids〉 Of the huge resort motels lining Nantucket Sound in South Yarmouth, Red Jacket has the best location. It is the last hotel at the end of the road and borders Parker's River on the west, so sunsets are particularly fine. Families who want all the fixings will find them here, though the atmosphere can be a bit impersonal. Some of the activities include kayaking; paddleboat and sailboat rentals; catamaran cruises; daily summertime children's program of supervised sports and activities (which may take advantage of the playground); mini-golf; shuffleboard; horseshoes; badminton; and basketball and volleyball courts (one of each). All rooms have a balcony or private porch; you'll want one overlooking the private beach on Nantucket Sound or looking out towards Parker's River. Some rooms have Jacuzzis. Cottages rent only by the week in season.

1 S. Shore Dr. (P.O. Box 88), South Yarmouth, MA 02664. ℂ 800/672-0500 or 508/398-6941. Fax 508/398-1214. www.redjacketresorts.com. 150 units, 14 cottages. Summer $250–$395 double, $325–$550 cottages. Cottages weekly: $3,000–$5,500. MC, V. Closed Nov to mid-Apr. **Amenities:** Restaurant; bar/lounge; ice-cream shop; indoor and outdoor heated pools; putting green; tennis court; exercise room; whirlpool; sauna; full concierge service. *In room:* A/C, TV/VCR, fridge, hair dryer.

EXPENSIVE

Captain Farris House ★★ "Sumptuous" is the only way to describe this 1845 inn, improbably set amid a peaceful garden, a block off bustling Route 28. A skilled interior decorator has combined fine antiques and striking contemporary touches to lift this inn's interiors way above the average homey B&B decor. Some suites are apartment-size, containing sitting rooms equipped with a fireplace, and whirlpool-tub bathrooms bigger than the average bedroom. Next door, the 1825 Elisha Jenkins House contains an additional large suite with its own sun deck. Welcoming touches in rooms include chocolates, fresh flowers, and plush robes. Breakfast consists of three courses served in the formal dining room or the sunny courtyard. The central location puts the entire Cape, from Woods Hole to Provincetown, within a 45-minute drive, assuming you can tear yourself from this pampering environment.

308 Old Main St. (just west of the Bass River Bridge), Bass River, MA 02664-4530. ℂ 800/350-9477 or 508/760-2818. Fax 508/398-1262. www.captainfarris.com. 10 units (9 tub/shower; 1 shower only). Summer $140–$180 double, $185–$250 suite. Rates include full breakfast. AE, DISC, MC, V. *In room:* A/C, TV/VCR, dataport, hair dryer, iron.

The Inn at Cape Cod ★ Innkeepers Mary and Doug Heywood have been busy upgrading this captain's manse/stylish inn. You can't miss the building; it's the one that looks like a tall, thin Southern plantation manor with four towering Ionic columns. Upon entering the elegant foyer, with its grandly curving staircase, you are led into a comfortable common seating-and-breakfast area. Ceilings in the guest rooms are probably the highest you'll find in the area, and the rooms are furnished with well-chosen antiques and period reproductions. One room has a canopy bed, and one has a working fireplace. The two suites with sitting areas are spacious. My favorite is the very romantic front room with the sitting room and large private balcony overlooking the Old King's Highway. The inn is centrally located in Yarmouth Port village just off the Old King's Highway with several shops and restaurants within walking distance. Behind the inn are miles of wooded walking trails.

4 Summer St. (P.O. Box 96), Yarmouth Port, MA 02675. ℂ 800/850-7301 or 508/375-0590. www.innatcapecod.com. 10 units (2 tub/shower; 8 shower only). Summer $125–$160 double, $175–$195 suite. Rates include full breakfast. MC, V. No children under 8. *In room:* A/C, TV, beach towels, robes.

Liberty Hill Inn ★ John and Ann Cartwright run this top-notch B&B set high on a knoll in charming Yarmouth Port. This 1825 Greek Revival captain's house is just off Route 6A, the Old King's Highway, which, with its majestic captains' houses and century-old elm trees, hasn't changed much in the last 100 years. The Cartwrights have paid particular attention to the grounds, which are colorful with floral plantings. Rooms in the main house, with its narrow stairways, have colonial antiques and wicker furniture. The rooms vary and are larger than at most local B&Bs. Some are more formal and several are bathed in sunlight from the tall windows. Some have whirlpools and gas fireplaces. All but one has a television. The carriage house with four rooms is suitable for families with children. All rooms have extras like down pillows and all-natural soap products. The inn stands out for its scrumptious full breakfasts with such delectables as baked blueberry French toast and crab scramble, which guests can enjoy on the large front porch. One room is accessible for visitors with disabilities.

77 Main St. (Rte. 6A, 1 mile from the village center), Yarmouth Port, MA 02675. (C) **800/821-3977** or 508/362-3976. Fax 508/362-6485. www.libertyhillinn.com. 9 units. Summer $125–$210 double. Rates include full breakfast and afternoon refreshment. AE, MC, V. *In room:* A/C, hair dryer, iron, no phone.

One Center Street Inn ⭐   This historic home is run by a young couple with teenage children, and their fresh and up-to-date attitude makes this inn stand out. The inn's guest rooms are small, but comfortable and cheerfully decorated. Most have mini-fridges. The Thatcher Suite downstairs with two adjoining rooms that share a bathroom is perfect for families. Teens will enjoy the Playstation, available for guests. Most guests like to take their breakfast on the screened porch or outside on the patio next to the water garden. A helpful apres-beach touch is the outdoor shower with hot and cold water. Your innkeepers are techies, and the entire inn site has access to wireless Internet service. They also like to plan trips for their guests with custom-made maps. On-site is a coffee house, specializing in espresso drinks, that is open to the public.

One Center St. at Rte. 6A (in the center of town), Yarmouth Port, MA 02675. (C) **866/362-9951** or **508/362-9951**. Fax 508/362-9952. www.onecenterstreetinn.com. 5 units (1 tub/shower, 4 shower only). Summer $125–$155 double, $165–$175 suite. Rates include continental breakfast. AE, DC, DISC, MC, V. *In room:* A/C, TV/VCR, CD player, hair dryer, iron, no phone.

Wedgewood Inn ⭐⭐   This elegant 1812 Federal house sits atop its undulating lawn with unabashed pride. The first house in town to be designed by an architect, it still reigns supreme as the loveliest—one that happens to welcome strangers, though you won't feel like one for long. Innkeepers Gerrie and Milt Graham provide a warm welcome, complete with tea delivered to your room on request. In the main house, the four formal and spacious front rooms all have cherry-wood pencil-post beds, Oriental rugs, antique quilts, and wood-burning fireplaces, and the two downstairs rooms have private screened porches. All have ample bathrooms. The two romantic hideaways under the eaves are decorated in a cheerful country-casual style. The picturesque barn in back has been completely revamped to include three very private, spacious suites, with canopy beds, fireplaces, decks, and sparkling contemporary bathrooms. These new barn suites also include telephones and televisions cleverly tucked into painted cabinets.

83 Main St./Rte. 6A (in the center of town), Yarmouth Port, MA 02675. (C) **508/362-5157** or 508/362-9178. Fax 508/362-5851. 9 units. Summer $135–$225 double. Rates include full breakfast. AE, MC, V. No children under 10. *In room:* A/C.

WHERE TO DINE
EXPENSIVE

abbicci ⭐⭐⭐ MEDITERRANEAN   This sophisticated dining spot serves high-quality cuisine that is a cut above most of the New England-y fare you'll find around these parts. While the exterior is a modest mustard-colored 18th-century Cape, the stylish interior features mosaic floors and mural-covered walls in several cozy dining rooms. The knowledgeable and efficient waitstaff delivers delicious, artfully prepared, innovative dishes. In fact, the whole setup seems almost out of place in folksy Yarmouth Port. On the menu, you'll find seafood dishes, as well as veal, lamb, and, of course, pasta, all in a delicate Northern Italian style. A taste of the veal *nocciole* (with toasted hazelnuts and a splash of balsamic vinegar), and you'll be transported straight to Tuscany. For budget diners, there are early bird seatings at 5 and 5:30pm with three courses for $12 to $15. This small restaurant can get overburdened on summer weekends, so expect a wait even with a reservation.

43 Main St./Rte. 6A (near the Cummaquid border), Yarmouth Port. ℂ **508/362-3501**. Reservations recommended. Main courses $18–$28. AE, MC, V. Daily 11:30am–2:30pm and 5–10pm.

MODERATE

Inaho ★★ *Finds* JAPANESE What better application of the Cape's oceanic bounty than fresh-off-the-boat sushi? You can sit in awe at the sushi bar and watch chef/owner Yuji Watanabe perform his legerdemain, or enjoy the privacy afforded by a gleaming wooden booth. From the front, Inaho is a typical Cape Cod cottage, but park in the back so you can enter through the Japanese garden. The decor is minimalist with traditional shoji screens and crisp navy-and-white banners softened by tranquil music and service.

157 Main St./Rte. 6A (in the village center), Yarmouth Port. ℂ **508/362-5522**. Reservations recommended. Main courses $13–$23; sushi pieces and rolls $3–$7. MC, V. Tues–Sun 5–10pm; call for off-season hours.

Lobster Boat *Kids* SEAFOOD Just about every town seems to have one of these barnlike restaurants plastered with flotsam and serving the usual array of seafood in the usual manner, from deep-fried to boiled or broiled. True to its setting on Nantucket Sound, this tourist magnet advertises itself rather flamboyantly with a facade that features the hull of a ship grafted onto a shingled shack. Families tend to come in packs, and with waitstaff running around, the atmosphere can seem a bit frantic at times.

681 Rte. 28 (midway between West Yarmouth and Bass River), West Yarmouth. ℂ **508/775-0486**. Main courses $12–$22. AE, MC, V. May–Oct daily 3–9:30pm; call for off-season hours. Closed late Oct to mid-Apr.

Old Yarmouth Inn NEW ENGLAND If a traditional Cape Cod atmosphere is what you are looking for, you can't do much better than this. It's an old stagecoach inn, serving Yankee basics like prime rib and baked scrod. The food is fresh and hearty and the preparations are tasty. People are catching on that this is good food at reasonable prices, so it can be crowded on weekends in season. There's also a lighter fare menu. One of the most requested dishes is the deluxe lobster roll, with huge chunks of fresh lobster. The Sunday brunch, a combination buffet and a la carte meal, is popular.

223 Rte. 6A (in the center of Yarmouth Port), Yarmouth Port. ℂ **508/362-9962**. Reservations recommended. Main courses $14–$25. AE, DISC, DC, MC, V. June–Oct Tues–Sat 11:30am–2:30pm, Sun 10am–1pm; daily 4:30–8pm; call for off-season hours.

INEXPENSIVE

Jack's Out Back *Finds* *Kids* AMERICAN This is a neighborhood cafe as Dr. Seuss might have imagined it: hyperactive (okay, semi-crazed) and full of fun. Chef/owner Jack Braginton-Smith makes a point of dishing out good-natured insults along with the home-style grub, which you bus yourself from the open kitchen, thereby saving big bucks as well as time. This is a perfect place for impatient children, who'll find lots of familiar, approachable dishes on the handscrawled posters that serve as a communal menu.

161 Main St./Rte. 6A (behind Main St. buildings, in the center of town), Yarmouth Port. ℂ **508/362-6690**. Reservations not accepted. All items under $7. No credit cards. Daily 6:30am–2pm.

Pizzas by Evan ★ PIZZA This joint gets my vote as the best pizza on the Cape. The crust is crisp on the outside, doughy on the inside; the toppings are fresh and bountiful. There are also grinders, pasta, and salads. There are plenty of tables in this clean, if uninspiring, restaurant, but you may want to take your pizza pie down the road to Grays Beach and watch the sun set over the marsh.

559 Rte. 6A (1 mile from the village center), Yarmouth Port. ℂ 508/362-7977. Reservations not accepted. Most items under $10. MC, V. June–Sept daily 10am–10pm; Oct–May 10am–9pm.

3 Dennis ⊛

20 miles E of Sandwich; 36 miles S of Provincetown

If Dennis looks like a jigsaw puzzle piece snapped around Yarmouth, that's because it didn't break away until 1793, when the community adopted the name of Rev. Josiah Dennis, who had ministered to Yarmouth's "East Parish" for close to 4 decades. His 1736 home has been restored and now serves as a local-history museum.

In Dennis, as in Yarmouth, virtually all the good stuff—pretty drives, inviting shops, and restaurants with real personality—are in the north, along Route 6A. Route 28 is chockablock with more typical tourist attractions, RV parks, and family-oriented motels—some with fairly sophisticated facilities but nonetheless undistinguished enough not to warrant even a drive-by (the few exceptions are noted below). In budgeting your time, be sure to allocate the lion's share to Dennis Village and not its southern offshoots. It's as stimulating and unspoiled today as it was when it welcomed the Cape Playhouse, the country's oldest surviving straw-hat theater, during the anything-goes 1920s.

ESSENTIALS

GETTING THERE After crossing either the Bourne or Sagamore bridge, head east on Route 6 or 6A. The Sagamore Bridge will get you closer to your destination. Route 6A passes through the villages of Dennis and East Dennis (which can also be reached via northbound Rte. 134 from Rte. 6's Exit 9). Route 134 South leads to the village of South Dennis; if you follow Route 134 all the way to Route 28, the village of West Dennis will be a couple of miles to your west, and Dennisport a couple of miles east. Or fly into Hyannis (see "Getting There," in chapter 2).

The **Coach of Dennis Trolley** (ℂ 800/352-7155) operates daily from late June to early September. Passengers may board at official stops (Patriot Sq., Windmill Plaza, Dennisport beaches, and the intersection of routes 28 and 134) or flag down the driver from anywhere on the route. Fares are 25¢ to 50¢. This shuttle connects with the Harwich Beach Shuttle and the Yarmouth Easy Shuttle.

VISITOR INFORMATION Contact the **Dennis Chamber of Commerce,** 242 Swan River Rd., West Dennis, MA 02670 (ℂ 800/243-9920 or 508/398-3568; www.dennischamber.com), or the **Cape Cod Chamber of Commerce** (see "Visitor Information" in the "Barnstable, Hyannis, Neighboring Villages & Environs" section, earlier in this chapter). The Dennis chamber is open May to October Monday through Friday 9am to 5pm, Saturday and Sunday 9am to 4pm; November to April Monday through Friday 10am to 2pm.

BEACHES & RECREATIONAL PURSUITS

BEACHES Dennis harbors more than a dozen saltwater and two freshwater beaches open to nonresidents. The bay beaches are charming and a big hit with families, who prize the easygoing surf, so soft it won't bring toddlers to their knees. The beaches on the sound tend to attract wall-to-wall families, but the parking lots are usually not too crowded, since so many beachgoers stay within walking distance. The lots charge $10 per day; for a week-long permit ($40), visit **Town Hall** on Main Street in South Dennis (© **508/394-8300**).

- **Chapin Beach** ✯✯, off Route 6A in Dennis: This is a nice, long bay beach pocked with occasional boulders and surrounded by dunes. There is no lifeguard, but there are restrooms.
- **Corporation Beach** ✯✯, off Route 6A in Dennis: Before it filled in with sand, this bay beach—with wheelchair-accessible boardwalk, lifeguards, snack bar, restrooms, and a children's play area—was once a packet landing owned by a shipbuilding corporation comprised of area residents.
- **Mayflower Beach** ✯✯, off Route 6A in Dennis: This 1,200-foot bay beach has the necessary amenities, plus an accessible boardwalk. The tide pools attract lots of children.
- **Scargo Lake in Dennis:** This large kettle-hole pond (formed by a melting fragment of a glacier) has two pleasant beaches: Scargo Beach, accessible right off Route 6A; and Princess Beach, off Scargo Hill Road, where there are restrooms and a picnic area.
- **West Dennis Beach** ✯✯, off Route 28 in West Dennis: This long (½-mile) but narrow beach along the sound has lifeguards, a playground, a snack bar, restrooms, and a special kite-flying area. The eastern end is reserved for residents; the western end tends, in any case, to be less packed.

BICYCLING The 25-mile **Cape Cod Rail Trail** ✯✯✯ (© **508/896-3491**) starts—or, depending on your perspective, ends—here, on Route 134, a half mile south of Route 6's Exit 9. Once a Penn Central track, this 8-foot-wide paved bikeway extends all the way to Wellfleet (with a few on-road lapses), passing through woods, marshes, and dunes. Sustenance is never too far off-trail, and plenty of bike shops dot the course. At the trail head is **Bob's Bike Shop,** 430 Rte. 134, South Dennis (© **508/760-4723**), which rents bikes and in-line skates and does repairs. Rates are $10 for a couple of hours and up to $22 for the full day. Another paved bike path runs along Old Bass Road, 3½ miles north to Route 6A.

BOATING Located on the small and placid Swan River, **Cape Cod Waterways,** 16 Rte. 28, Dennisport (© **508/398-0080**), rents canoes, kayaks, and paddleboats for exploring 200-acre Swan Pond (less than a mile north) or Nantucket Sound (2 miles south). A full-day canoe or kayak rental costs $50.

Bass River Cruises, located at Bass River Bridge (at Rte. 28) in West Dennis (© **508/362-5555**), explores the Bass and Weir rivers the way Leif Eriksson might have—by boat. This one, a poky but stable custom mini-barge, the M/V *Starfish,* is motorized, so the whole circuit takes only 1½ hours. If some of the tales strike you as rather tall, there's still plenty of wildlife and prime real estate to ogle. Trips are offered mid-May through mid-October; tickets are $14 for adults and $7 for children ages 2 to 12. Call for the schedule.

FISHING Fishing is allowed in Fresh Pond and Scargo Lake, where the catch includes trout and smallmouth bass; for a license (shellfishing is also permitted), visit **Town Hall** on Main Street in South Dennis (© **508/394-8300**), or **Riverview Bait and Tackle** at 1273 Rte. 28 in South Yarmouth (© **508/394-1036**). Plenty of people drop a line off the Bass River Bridge along Route 28 in West Dennis. Several charter boats operate out of the Northside Marina in East Dennis's Sesuit Harbor, including the *Albatross* (© **508/385-3244**). Local deepwater charters include the *Tigger Two,* docked in the Sesuit Harbor (© **508/888-8372**), which charges $150 to $300 for a half-day charter.

FITNESS/JOGGING **David's Gym** at 50 Rte. 134 in South Dennis (© 508/ 394-7199) offers aerobics, weight training, and cardio equipment, plus Cybex equipment, Nautilus, and boxing. A day pass costs $12.

For joggers, and fitness freaks in general, the 1½-mile **Lifecourse trail,** located at Old Bass River and Access roads in South Dennis, features 20 exercise stations along its tree-shaded path.

GOLF The public is welcome to use two 18-hole championship courses: the hilly, par-71 **Dennis Highlands** on Old Bass River Road in Dennis (© 508/ 385-8347), and the even more challenging par-72 **Dennis Pines** on Golf Course Road in East Dennis (© 508/385-8347). Both are open year-round.

NATURE & WILDLIFE AREAS Behind the town hall parking lot on Main Street in South Dennis, a half-mile walk along the **Indian Lands Conservation Trail** leads to the Bass River, where blue herons and kingfishers often take shelter. Dirt roads off South Street in East Dennis, beyond the Quivet Cemetery, lead to Crow's Pasture, a patchwork of marshes and dunes bordering the bay; this circular trail is about a 2.5-mile round-trip.

TENNIS Public courts are located at the Dennis–Yarmouth Regional High School in South Yarmouth and at Wixon Middle School on Route 134 in South Dennis; for details, contact the **Dennis Recreation Department** (© 508/ 394-8300). Or you may be able to book time at the **Mashantum Tennis Club** off Nobscussett Road in Dennis Village (© 508/385-7043), which has clay courts for $10 per person. Also try **Sesuit Tennis Centre** at 1389 Rte. 6A in East Dennis (© 508/385-2200). At Sesuit, singles and doubles are $15 per person.

MUSEUMS

Cape Museum of Fine Arts ★★ Part of the prettily landscaped Cape Playhouse complex, this museum has done a great job of acquiring hundreds of works by representative area artists dating back to the turn of the 20th century. The main gallery has been recently renovated and expanded, and two galleries have been added to better display the collection and the revolving schedule of exhibits. There's also a new outdoor sculpture garden. Call ahead for a schedule of special shows, lectures, concerts, and classes.

60 Hope Lane (off Rte. 6A in the center of town). © 508/385-4477. www.cmfa.org. Admission $7 adults, free for children under 18. MC, V. Mon–Sat 10am–5pm; Sun noon–5pm; Wed 10am–1pm, free with a donation.

Jericho House and Barn Museum For a century and a half, this classic 1801 Cape house remained in the family of its builder, Capt. Theophilus Baker, and was the model for Richard Henry Dana's *Two Years Before the Mast.* Its mostly Federal furnishings embody the understated elegance of the era. Among the displays are mannequins outfitted in antique clothing. Out back is an 1810 barn housing assorted displays, from a miniature saltworks (the clearest possible depiction of one of the Cape's earliest and most lucrative industries) to an ingenious "driftwood zoo" improvised several decades ago by a playful summer resident. In August, the museum sponsors demonstrations of skills of the 1800s.

Trotting Park Rd. (at Old Main St., off Rte. 28 about ½ mile east of the Bass River Bridge), West Dennis. © 508/ 394-0260. Donations accepted. July–Aug Wed 2–4pm and Fri 10am–noon; also open by special request. Closed Sept–June.

Josiah Dennis Manse and Old West Schoolhouse *Kids* This compact 1736 saltbox housed Rev. Josiah Dennis, the town's first minister. Though not necessarily original, the furnishings are fascinating, as is a diorama of the Shiverick Shipyard, which was the source in the mid-1800s of the world's swiftest ships.

Costumed guides lead guests through a maritime room and a children's room. There is also a Native American exhibit. Don't miss the 1770 schoolhouse, where a comprehensive (if strict) approach to learning is beautifully preserved.

77 Nobscusset Rd. (north of Rte. 6A, about ½ mile west of the town center). ✆ 508/385-2232. Donations accepted. Late June to mid-Sept Tues 10am–noon and Thurs 2–4pm. Closed mid-Sept to late June.

Scargo Tower   All that remains of the grand Nobscusset Hotel, this 28-foot stone observatory looks out from its 160-foot perch over the entire Outer Cape, including the tightly furled tip that is Provincetown. In the foreground is Scargo Lake—the legacy, native legend has it, of either the giant god Maushop or perhaps a princess who bid her handmaidens to scoop it out with clamshells.

Scargo Hill Rd. (off Old Bass River Rd., south of Rte. 6A in the center of town). No phone. Free admission. Daily 6am–10pm.

BASEBALL
The Dennis–Yarmouth Red Sox, part of the Cape Cod Baseball League, play at Dennis–Yarmouth High School's Red Wilson Field off Station Avenue in South Yarmouth. For a schedule, contact the **Yarmouth Area Chamber of Commerce,** 657 Rte. 28, West Yarmouth, MA 02673 (✆ **508/778-1008**), the **Yarmouth Recreation Department** (✆ **508/398-2231,** ext. 284), or the **League** (✆ **508/432-6909**).

KID STUFF
If kids get sick of all the miscellaneous go-carts and mini-golf concessions on Route 28, they can take in a show. On Friday mornings in season, at 9:30 and 11:30am, the **Cape Playhouse** at 820 Rte. 6A in Dennis (✆ **508/385-3911**) hosts various visiting companies that mount children's theater geared toward kids 4 and up; at only $6 to $7, tickets go fast.

SHOPPING
You can pretty much ignore Route 28. There's a growing cluster of antiques shops in Dennisport, but the stock is flea-market level and requires more patience than most mere browsers—as opposed to avid collectors—may be able to muster. Save your time and money for the better shops along Route 6A, where you'll also find fine contemporary crafts.

ANTIQUES/COLLECTIBLES   More than 136 dealers stock the co-op **Antiques Center of Cape Cod,** 243 Rte. 6A (about 1 mile south of Dennis Village center), Dennis (✆ **508/385-6400**); it's the largest such enterprise on the Cape. You'll find all the usual "smalls" on the first floor; the big stuff—from blanket chests to copper bathtubs—beckons above.

   Eldred's, 1483 Rte. 6A (about ¼ mile west of Dennis Village center), East Dennis (✆ **508/385-3116**), where the gavel has been wielded for more than 40 years, is the Cape's most prestigious auction house. Specialties include Asian art, American and European paintings, marine art, and Americana. Call for a schedule.

   The premier place for antique wicker furniture on the Cape is **Leslie Curtis Antiques** at two locations in Dennis Village, 776 Main St./Rte. 6A and 838 Main St./Rte. 6A (✆ **508/385-2921**). Her wicker selection includes Victorian pieces and Bar Harbor wicker of the 1920s. She also specializes in French Quimper pottery and American 19th-century furniture.

ARTS & CRAFTS   The creations of **Ross Coppelman,** 1439 Rte. 6A (about ¼ mile west of the town center), East Dennis (✆ **508/385-7900**)—mostly fashioned of lustrous 22-karat gold—have an iconic drama to them: They seem to draw on the aesthetics of some grand, lost civilization.

Scargo Stoneware Pottery and Art Gallery, 30 Dr. Lord's Rd. S. (off Rte. 6A, about 1 mile east of the town center), Dennis (© **508/385-3894**), is a magical place. Harry Holl set up his glass-ceilinged studio here in 1952; today his work, and the output of his four grown daughters, fills a sylvan glade overlooking Scargo Lake. Much of it—such as the signature birdhouses shaped like fanciful castles—is meant to reside outside. The other wares deserve a place of honor on the dining-room table or perhaps over a mantle. Hand-painted tiles by Sarah Holl are particularly enchanting.

BOOKS Bookstore junkies (you know who you are) will love **Armchair Bookshop,** 619 Rte. 6A, Dennis Village (© **508/385-0900**), one of those quaint little bookshops that does everything right. This one seems to specialize (unofficially) in books about dogs, in tribute to the friendly golden retrievers in residence. But you'll find everything here, from bestsellers to books of local interest to children's books and more. There is also a large selection of cards and gift items. It's all very well-organized and a delight for browsers.

WHERE TO STAY
EXPENSIVE

Lighthouse Inn ★★ *Kids* Set on placid West Dennis Beach on Nantucket Sound, this popular resort has been welcoming families for over 60 years. In 1938, Everett Stone acquired a decommissioned 1855 lighthouse and built a charming inn and a 9-acre cottage colony around it. Today his grandsons run the show, pretty much as he envisioned it; the lighthouse has even been resuscitated. As they have for at least two generations, families gather at group tables in the summer-camp-scale dining room to plot their day over breakfast and recap over dinner. Many coordinate their vacations so that they can catch up with the same group of friends year after year. With a private beach, heated outdoor pool, tennis courts, and motley amusements such as miniature golf and shuffleboard right on the premises, there's plenty to do. The rooms aren't what you'd call fancy, but some have great Nantucket Sound views. Four rooms are fully accessible to travelers with disabilities.

The dining room—with state flags rippling from the rafters—is open to the general public and serves breakfast, lunch, and dinner. The prices are reasonable (entrees rarely exceed $17), and the menu isn't half as stuffy as you might expect: Lunch is served under umbrellas on the deck overlooking Nantucket Sound, a delightful setting in which to enjoy a club sandwich. Down the road, at the entrance to the complex, The Sand Bar, a classic bar with cabaret-style entertainment, serves as an on-site nightspot (see "The Dennises After Dark," below).

1 Lighthouse Inn Rd. (off Lower County Rd., ½ mile south of Rte. 28), West Dennis, MA 02670. © **508/398-2244**. Fax 508/398-5658. www.lighthouseinn.com. 44 units, 24 cottages (all with tub/shower). Summer $244–$298 double, $447–$650 2-bedroom cottage, $480–760 3-bedroom cottage. MC, V. Rates include full breakfast and all gratuities. Closed mid-Oct to mid-May. **Amenities:** 2 restaurants (large dining room, pool snack bar); bar with entertainment; outdoor heated pool with ample sunning deck, chairs, umbrellas, and pool house/changing rooms; outdoor tennis court; InnKids, a free supervised play program (ages 3–11) offered July–Aug; game room; shuffleboard; volleyball; mini-golf. *In room:* A/C, TV, fridge, hair dryer, iron, safe.

MODERATE

Corsair & Cross Rip Resort Motels ★ *Kids* Of the many family-oriented motels lining this part of Nantucket Sound, these two neighbors are among the nicest, with fresh contemporary decor, two beach-view pools, and their own chunk of sand. As a rainy-day backup, there's an indoor pool, a game room, and a toddler playroom equipped with toys. Some rooms have kitchenettes. All rooms have access to barbecue grills.

41 Chase Ave. (off Depot St., 1 mile southeast of Rte. 28), Dennisport, MA 02639. ✆ **800/201-1072** or 508/398-2279. Fax 508/760-6681. www.corsaircrossrip.com. 47 units (all with tub/shower). Summer $135–$265 double, $175–$295 efficiency. Special packages and family weekly rates available. AE, MC, V. Closed mid-Oct to Apr. **Amenities:** 2 outdoor pools, indoor pool; outdoor Jacuzzi; game room; toddler playroom and kids' playground; coin-op washers and dryers. *In room:* A/C, TV w/HBO, fax, dataport, fridge, coffeemaker, hair dryer, iron.

Isaiah Hall B&B Inn ★★   So keyed-in is this Greek Revival farmhouse to the doings at the nearby Cape Playhouse that you might as well be backstage. Many stars have stayed here over the past half century, and, if you're lucky, you'll find a few sharing the space. Your animated hostess, Marie Brophy, has been entertaining the entertainers for over 15 years. The "great room" in the carriage-house annex seems to foment late-night discussions, to be continued over home-baked breakfasts at the long plank table that dominates the 1857 country kitchen. Room styles range from 1940s knotty pine to spacious and spiffy. They are quaint, countrified, and spotlessly clean. Four have balconies or decks. Two of the rooms have mini-fridges, and one has a fireplace. The inn's location on a quiet side street in a residential neighborhood bodes well for a good night's sleep, but it's also just a short walk to restaurants, entertainment options, and Corporation Beach on Cape Cod Bay.

152 Whig St. (1 block northwest of the Cape Playhouse), Dennis, MA 02638. ✆ **800/736-0160** or 508/385-9928. Fax 508/385-5879. www.isaiahhallinn.com. 10 units (5 with tub/shower, 5 with shower only). Summer $110–$155 double, $185 suite. Rates include continental breakfast. AE, DISC, MC, V. Closed mid-Oct to late Apr. No children under age 7. *In room:* A/C, TV/VCR, dataport, hair dryer.

WHERE TO DINE
MODERATE

Gina's by the Sea ★★   ITALIAN   A landmark amid Dennis's "Little Italy" beach community since 1938, this intimate little restaurant has a few tricks up its sleeve, such as homemade ravioli stuffed with smoked mozzarella. Most of the fare here is the traditional Italian food of our youth, but nonetheless tasty: The ultra-garlicky shrimp scampi, for instance, needs no updating. Save room for Mrs. Riley's Chocolate Rum Cake, made daily by owner Larry Riley's mother; it's scrumptious. This popular place fills up fast, so if you want to eat before 8:30pm, arrive before 5:30pm. Take a sunset or moonlight walk on the beach (just over the dune) to round out the evening.

134 Taunton Ave. (about 1½ miles northwest of Rte. 6A; turn north across from the Public Market and follow the signs). ✆ **508/385-3213.** Reservations not accepted. Main courses $10–$23. AE, MC, V. June–late Aug daily 5–10pm; Apr–May and late Aug–Nov Thurs–Sun 5–10pm. Closed Dec–Mar.

Olde Inn at West Dennis ★ *Finds* NEW ENGLAND   You'd probably drive right by this Irish pub/roadhouse if we didn't tell you about it. A walk through the doors of this modest old Cape cottage is a step back in time. Large families of several generations sit at big round tables, and everyone seems to know one another. With wide wooden floorboards and a low beamed ceiling, it's very atmospheric. Later in the evenings, someone takes out a guitar or a fiddle and starts to play and everyone sings along. The food is about as traditional as it gets; nothing fancy here. Stick with the basics, like the baked scrod, prime rib, or roast chicken.

348 Main St. (Rte. 28), West Dennis. ✆ **508/760-2627.** Reservations not accepted. Main courses $10–$19. MC, V. June–Sept daily 4–9:30pm; call for off-season hours.

The Red Pheasant Inn ⭐⭐ CONTEMPORARY AMERICAN   An enduring Cape favorite since 1977, this handsome space—an 18th-century barn
turned chandlery—has managed not only to keep pace with trends but to
remain a front-runner. Favorites from chef/owner Bill Atwood include roast rack
of lamb, boneless roast duckling, and sole meunière. In the fall, expect game
specials like venison and ostrich. His signature cherrystone-and-scallop chowder
gets its zip from fresh-plucked thyme. Two massive brick fireplaces tend to
be the focal point in the off season, drawing in the weary—and delighted—
wanderer. In fine weather, you'll want to sit out in the garden room.

905 Main St. (about ½ mile east of the town center). © 508/385-2133. Reservations required. Main courses
$18–$30. DISC, MC, V. Apr–Dec daily 5–10pm; Jan–Mar Wed–Sun 5–10pm.

Scargo Cafe ⭐ INTERNATIONAL   A richly paneled captain's house given a
modernist reworking, this lively bistro—named for Dennis's scenic lake—deftly
spans old and new with a menu neatly split into "traditional" and "adventurous"
categories. Traditionalists will find surf and turf, and the popular grilled lamb
loins served with mint jelly (talk about traditional!); adventurous dishes include
the likes of "wildcat chicken" (a sauté of sausage, mushrooms, and raisins,
flambéed with apricot brandy). Lighter nibbles, such as burgers or "Scallop
Harpoon"—a bacon-wrapped skewerful, served over rice—are available throughout the day, a boon for beachgoers who tend to return ravenous. Serving food
until 11pm makes this the perfect (and only) place in the neighborhood to go
after a show at the Cape Playhouse across the street.

799 Main St./Rte. 6A (opposite the Cape Playhouse). © 508/385-8200. Reservations accepted for parties
of 6 or more. Main courses $14–$22. AE, DISC, MC, V. Mid-June to mid-Sept daily 11am–3pm and 4:30–11pm;
mid-Sept to mid-June 11am–10pm.

Swan River Seafood ⭐ SEAFOOD   Every town has its own version of the
"fish place with a fantastic view." Here the scenic vista is relatively low-key: a
marsh punctuated by an old windmill. The fish—from the adjoining market—
is snapping fresh and available deep-fried, as it is everywhere, but also smartly
broiled or sautéed. The difference here is that the fish is unloaded daily from 10
to 25 fishing boats and served that day or the next. Go for the assertive shark
steak *au poivre* (with black pepper) and such specialties as scrod San Sebastian,
fresh filets poached in a garlic-infused broth.

5 Lower County Rd. (at Swan Pond River, about ⅔ mile southeast of the town center), Dennisport. © 508/
394-4466. www.swanriverseafoods.com. Reservations for parties of 8 or more only. Main courses $13–$22.
AE, DISC, MC, V. June–Aug daily noon–9pm; call for off-season hours. Closed Oct to late May.

INEXPENSIVE

Bob Briggs' Wee Packet Restaurant and Bakery ⭐ *Finds* *Kids* SEAFOOD
It's been Bob Briggs's place since 1949; otherwise, the name that might leap to
mind would be "Mom's." This tiny joint serves all the requisite seafood staples,
fried and broiled, plus steak and chicken dishes. Five generations have been
known to commandeer a couple of Formica tables for a traditional summer feast
topped off by a timeless dessert such as blueberry shortcake.

79 Depot St. (at Lower County Rd., about ⅓ mile south of the town center), Dennisport. © 508/398-2181.
www.weepacket.com. Reservations not accepted. Main courses $6–$15. MC, V. Late June to late Sept daily
8am–8:30pm; early May to late June daily 11:30am–8:30pm. Closed late Sept to early May.

Captain Frosty's ⭐ *Kids* SEAFOOD   Here you won't find the typical, taste-
less, deep-fried seafood seemingly dipped in greasy cement. The breading is light
(thanks to healthy canola oil), and the fish itself is the finest available—fresh off

the local day boats and hooked rather than netted (the maritime equivalent of clear-cutting a forest). You won't find a more luscious lobster roll anywhere, and the clam-cake fritters seem to fly out the door.

219 Rte. 6A (about 1 mile west of the town center). © 508/385-8548. Most items under $15. No credit cards. June–Aug daily 11am–9pm; call for off-season hours. Closed late Sept to early Apr.

The Dog House ★ *Finds* HOT DOG STAND This just might be the ultimate hot dog stand, housed in a tiny peaked-roofed hut about a half mile from Nantucket Sound. Hot dogs, cheese dogs, and chili dogs with all the fixings are the specialty here, but there's also chili and hamburgers. For non-carnivores there's the Surf Burger (salmon). French fries are thickly cut, and onion rings are hand-battered. Fresh lemonade is on hand to wash it all down. There are 12 picnic tables in this pine glade.

189 Lower County Rd., Dennisport. © 508/398-7774. All items under $10. No credit cards. Mid-May to mid-Sept daily 11am–8:30pm; call for off-season hours. Closed mid-Oct to mid-May.

Marathon Seafood SEAFOOD Family-owned and -operated for over 15 years, this place holds its own among the Route 28 fast-food/clam-shack competition. You should order a heaping, steaming platter of fried fish, clams, scallops, or shrimp, or a combo served with french fries and onion rings. Wash it down with a chocolate milkshake. It's hard on the heart but easy on the wallet.

231 Rte. 28, West Dennis. © 508/394-3379. Main courses $7–$15. MC, V. June–Sept daily 11am–11pm; call for off-season hours. Closed Dec–Feb.

The Marshside ★ AMERICAN This is one of the Cape's best diners; the clean, well-run establishment overlooks a picturesque marsh and, in the distance, Sesuit Harbor. The relaxed atmosphere comes from a year-round waitstaff that knows what it's doing (a rarity on the Cape). The food is fresh, tasty, and cheap, be it a fried-fish platter, a cheeseburger with french fries, or a veggie melt. Save room for homemade desserts.

28 Bridge St. (at the junction of routes 134 and 6A), East Dennis. © 508/385-4010. Reservations not accepted. Main courses $7–$17. AE, DC, DISC, MC, V. Daily 7:30am–9pm. Open year-round.

A FARM STAND

Tobey Farm The remarkable thing about this farm stand is that it has been in the same family since 1681. The fresh-picked corn should go straight into the pot; a dried flower arrangement might make a nice memento. In October, Tobey Farm comes alive with Halloween treats like Hobgoblin hayrides at night and not-so-scary hayrides during the day on weekends. Call for a schedule.

352 Rte. 6A (about ½ mile west of the town center). © 508/385-2930.

SWEETS

Ice Cream Smuggler ★ A noteworthy stop on any Cape-wide ice-cream crusade, this cheerful parlor dispenses terrific custom homemade flavors, as well as seductive sundae concoctions and fudge-bottom pies.

716 Rte. 6A (in Dennis Village center). © 508/385-5307. July–Aug daily 11am–11pm; Apr–June and Sept to mid-Oct noon–9pm. Closed mid-Oct to Mar.

Sundae School ★ For a time-travel treat, visit this spacious barn retrofitted with a turn-of-the-20th-century marble soda fountain and other artifacts from the golden age of ice cream. Homemade flavors include Milky Way, Kahlúa Chip, and Grapenut. Local berries and real whipped cream make for especially tasty toppings.

381 Lower County Rd. (at Sea St., about ⅓ mile south of Rte. 28), Dennisport. © **508/394-9122.** Summer daily 11am–11pm, weekends only in spring and fall. Closed mid-Sept to mid-Apr.

Woolfie's Home Baking The families clustered along the southern shore have a friend in Terri Moretti, who gets up before dawn to bake fabulous megamuffins as well as strudel, Danish, and other tasty eye-openers.

279 Lower County Rd. (about ½ mile southwest of the town center), Dennisport. No phone. May–Sept daily 8am–2pm. Closed Oct–Apr.

THE DENNISES AFTER DARK
PERFORMANCES

The Cape Playhouse The oldest continuously active straw-hat theater in the country and still one of the best, this way-off-Broadway enterprise was the 1927 brainstorm of Raymond Moore, who'd spent a few summers as a playwright in Provincetown and quickly tired of the strictures of "little theater." Salvaging an 1838 meetinghouse, he plunked it amid a meadow and got his New York buddy, designer Cleon Throckmorton, to turn it into a proper theater. Even with a roof that leaked, it was an immediate success, and a parade of stars—both established and budding—have trod the boards in the decades since, from Ginger Rogers to Jane Fonda (her dad spent his salad days there, too, playing opposite Bette Davis in her stage debut), Humphrey Bogart to Tab Hunter. Not all of today's headliners are quite as impressive (many hail from the netherworld of TV reruns), but the theater can be counted on for a varied season of polished work. Performances are held mid-June to early September, Monday to Saturday at 8pm; matinees take place Wednesday to Thursday at 2pm. On Friday mornings, performances of children's theater are at 9:30 and 11:30am. 820 Rte. 6A (in the center of town). © **877/385-3911** or 508/385-3911. www.capeplayhouse.com. Tickets $25–$45; children's theater $6–$7.

DANCING & LIVE MUSIC

Christine's Restaurant The 300-seat showroom of this Lebanese/Italian restaurant draws some big acts nightly in season, and weekends off season, including local jazz great pianist Dave McKenna and all sorts of oldies bands; also on the roster are comedy acts and novelty acts, like a hypnotist. 581 Rte. 28 (about ¼ mile east of the town center). © **508/394-7333.** Cover varies.

The Sand Bar This homey cabana was built in 1949, the very year Dennis went "wet." Rock King, a combination boogie-woogie pianist and comedian, still rules the evening and wows the crowd. At the Lighthouse Inn (see "Where to Stay," above), West Dennis. © **508/398-2244.** Cover varies. Free admission for guests of the Lighthouse Inn.

A RETRO MOVIE THEATER

Cape Cinema In 1930, Raymond Moore—perceiving of motion pictures as a complement rather than a threat to live theater—added a movie house, modeled on Centerville's Congregational Church, to the Cape Playhouse complex. The interior decoration is an Art Deco surprise, with a Prometheus-themed ceiling mural and folding curtain designed by artist Rockwell Kent and Broadway set designer Jo Mielziner. Independent-film maven George Mansour, curator of the Harvard Film Archive, sees to the art-house programming. That, plus the setting and seating—black leather armchairs—may spoil you forever for what passes for cinemas today. Open early April to mid-November daily at 4:30, 7, and 9pm. From mid-November to early April, art-house films are shown in the small theater located in the complex. 36 Hope Lane (off Rte. 6A, in the center of town). © **508/385-2503** (recording) or 508/385-5644. www.capecinema.com.

6

The Lower Cape: Brewster, the Harwiches, Chatham & Orleans

The four towns on the Lower Cape are primarily family-oriented summer communities. The quaint village of Harwich Port was all set for an upscale overhaul when the recession struck in the early 1990s; faltering funds have left it in an agreeable limbo: not too fancy, but with a small-town feel. Here, the beach is a mere block off Main Street, so the eternal summertime verities of a barefoot stroll capped off by an ice-cream cone can still be easily observed. To get to Chatham at the Cape's elbow requires an intentional detour, which may have helped preserve that town as a charming and more upscale locale than some of the other towns along the Nantucket Sound. Chatham, with its Main Street a gamut of appealing shops and eateries, approaches an all-American, small-town ideal—complemented nicely by a scenic lighthouse and plentiful beaches nearby.

Occupying the easternmost portion of historic Route 6A, Brewster still enjoys much the same cachet that it boasted as a high roller in the maritime trade. But for a relatively recent incursion of condos and, of course, the cars, it looks much as it might have in the late 19th century; its general store still serves as a social center. For some reason—perhaps because excellence breeds competition—Brewster has spawned several fine restaurants in recent years and has become something of a magnet for gourmands.

As the gateway to the Outer Cape, where all roads merge, Orleans offers more variety in the way of shops and entertainment than some of its neighbors. Its nearby cousin, East Orleans, is on the upswing as a destination, offering a couple of fun restaurants and—best of all—a goodly chunk of magnificent, unspoiled Cape Cod National Seashore.

1 Brewster ★★

25 miles E of Sandwich; 31 miles S of Provincetown

One of the "youngest" of the Cape towns, Brewster—named for the Pilgrim leader William Brewster—dissociated itself from Harwich in 1803, the better to enjoy its newfound riches as a hotbed of the shipping industry. All along the winding curves of the Old King's Highway (now Rte. 6A), successful captains erected scores of proud houses—99 in all, according to the local lore. When Henry David Thoreau passed through in the mid-1850s, he remarked: "This town has more mates and masters of vessels than any other town in the country."

The Greek/Gothic Revival First Parish Church, built in 1834, embodies many of their stories. Among the more dramatic tales conjured by the gravestones in back is that of Capt. David Nickerson, who is said to have rescued an infant during the French Revolution—possibly the son of Louis XVI and Marie Antoinette. Whatever his origins, "René Rousseau" followed in his adoptive

The Lower Cape

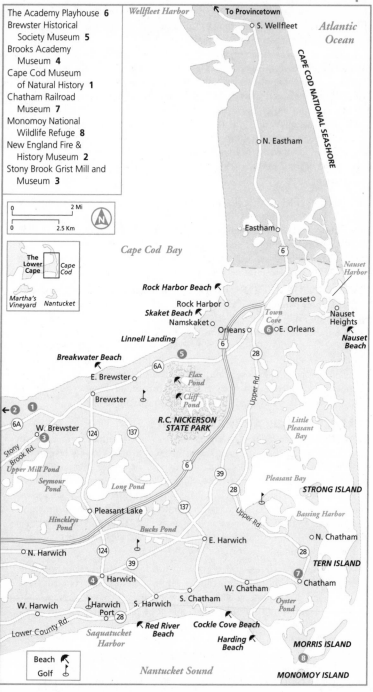

The Academy Playhouse **6**
Brewster Historical
  Society Museum **5**
Brooks Academy
  Museum **4**
Cape Cod Museum
  of Natural History **1**
Chatham Railroad
  Museum **7**
Monomoy National
  Wildlife Refuge **8**
New England Fire &
  History Museum **2**
Stony Brook Grist Mill and
  Museum **3**

0   2 Mi
0   2.5 Km

The Lower Cape   Cape Cod
Martha's Vineyard   Nantucket

Wellfleet Harbor

To Provincetown
S. Wellfleet

Atlantic Ocean

CAPE COD NATIONAL SEASHORE

N. Eastham

Eastham

Cape Cod Bay

Nauset Harbor

Rock Harbor Beach
Rock Harbor
Skaket Beach
Namskaket
Tonset
Nauset Heights

Linnell Landing

Orleans
Town Cove
E. Orleans
Nauset Beach

Breakwater Beach
E. Brewster

Brewster

Flax Pond
Cliff Pond

R.C. NICKERSON STATE PARK

6A
W. Brewster

Stony Brook Rd.
Upper Mill Pond
Seymour Pond

124   137

Long Pond

Little Pleasant Bay

Pleasant Bay

STRONG ISLAND

Hinckleys Pond

Pleasant Lake

Bassing Harbor

Bucks Pond
E. Harwich

Upper Rd.

N. Chatham

N. Harwich

124

39

Harwich

TERN ISLAND

Chatham

W. Harwich

Harwich Port
28

S. Harwich

S. Chatham

W. Chatham

Oyster Pond

MORRIS ISLAND

Lower County Rd.

Saquatucket Harbor

Red River Beach

Cockle Cove Beach

Harding Beach

MONOMOY ISLAND

Nantucket Sound

Beach
Golf

father's footsteps, ultimately drowning at sea. His name was incised on the back of Nickerson's headstone, according to the custom of the day. Nickerson's name also appears on a pew in the white clapboard church.

Brewster still gives the impression of setting itself apart. Mostly free of the commercial encroachments that have plagued the southern shore, this thriving community seems to go about its business as if nothing were amiss. It has even managed to absorb an intrusively huge development within its own borders, the 380-acre condo complex known as Ocean Edge, on what was once a huge private estate. The dust settled, the trees grew back, the buildings started to blend in, and it's life as usual, if a bit more closely packed. Brewster also welcomes the tens of thousands of transient campers and day-trippers who arrive each summer to enjoy the nearly 2,000 wooded acres of Nickerson State Park.

ESSENTIALS

GETTING THERE   After crossing either the Bourne or Sagamore bridge (see "Getting There" in chapter 2), head east on Route 6 or 6A. Crossing the Sagamore Bridge will get you closer to your destination. Route 6A on the north side of the Cape passes through the villages of West Brewster, Brewster, and East Brewster. You can also reach Brewster by taking Route 6's Exit 10 north, along Route 124. Or fly into Hyannis (see "Getting There," in chapter 2).

VISITOR INFORMATION   Contact the **Brewster Chamber of Commerce Visitor Center** behind Brewster Town Hall, 2198 Main St./Rte. 6A, Brewster (© **508/896-3500;** fax 508/896-1086; www.brewstercapecod.org); or the **Cape Cod Chamber of Commerce,** Routes 6 and 132, Hyannis, MA 02601 (© **888/ 332-2732** or 508/862-0700; fax 508/362-2156; www.capecodchamber.org). The Brewster Visitor Center is open from mid-June to early September daily from 9am to 3pm and is closed from mid-October to late April. The Cape Cod chamber of commerce visitor center is open year-round Monday to Saturday from 9am to 5pm and Sundays and holidays from 10am to 4pm.

BEACHES & RECREATIONAL PURSUITS

BEACHES   Brewster's eight lovely bay beaches have minimal facilities. When the tide is out, the "beach" enlarges to as much as 2 miles, leaving behind tide pools to splash in and explore, and vast stretches of rippled, reddish "garnet" sand. On a clear day, you can see the whole curve of the Cape, from Sandwich to Provincetown. That hulking wreck midway, incidentally, is the USS *James Longstreet,* pressed into service for target practice in 1943, and used for that purpose right up until 1970; it's now a popular dive site. You can purchase a beach parking sticker ($10 per day, $30 per week) at the **Visitor Center** behind Town Hall at 2198 Main St. (Rte. 6A; © **508/896-4511**).

- **Breakwater Beach** ★★, off Breakwater Road, Brewster: Only a brief walk from the center of town, this calm, shallow beach (the only one with restrooms) is ideal for young children. This was once a packet landing, where packet boats would unload tourists and load up produce—a system that saved a lot of travel time until the railroads came along.
- **Flax Pond** ★★ in Nickerson State Park (see "Nature & Wildlife Areas," below): This large freshwater pond, surrounded by pines, has a bathhouse and offers watersports rentals. The park contains two more ponds with beaches—Cliff and Little Cliff. Access and parking are free.
- **Linnells Landing Beach** ★, on Linnell Road in East Brewster: This is a ½-mile, wheelchair-accessible bay beach.

- **Paines Creek Beach** 🏖, off Paines Creek Road, West Brewster: With 1½ miles in which to stretch out, this bay beach has something to offer sun lovers and nature lovers alike. Your kids will love it if you arrive when the tide's coming in—the current will give an air mattress a nice little ride.

BICYCLING The **Cape Cod Rail Trail** ★★★ intersects with the 8-mile **Nickerson State Park** trail system at the park entrance, where there's plenty of free parking; you could follow the Rail Trail back to Dennis (about 12 miles) or onward toward Wellfleet (13 miles). **Idle Times** (© 508/255-8281) provides rentals within the park, in season. Another good place to jump in is Underpass Road about a half mile south of Route 6A. Here you'll find **Brewster Bicycle Rental,** 442 Underpass Rd. (© 508/896-8149); and Brewster Express, which makes sandwiches to go. Just up the hill is the well-equipped **Rail Trail Bike & Blade,** 302 Underpass Rd. (© 508/896-8200). All three shops offer free parking. Bicycle rentals start at around $13 for 4 hours and go up to about $20 for 24 hours.

BOATING You can rent a canoe at **Jack's Boat Rentals** (© 508/896-8556), located on Flax Pond within Nickerson State Park. Canoes cost $22 an hour and $7 for each additional half-hour. There are also kayaks, paddleboats, surf bikes, and Sunfish sailboats to rent. To check out other canoeing locations in Brewster, you can rent a boat by the day or the week from **Goose Hummock** 🏖 in Orleans (© 508/255-2620) and paddle around Paines Creek and Quivett Creek, as well as Upper and Lower Mill ponds. For 4 hours, canoes cost $25 and kayaks cost $25 to $35.

FISHING Brewster offers more ponds for fishing than any other town: 14 in all. Among the most popular are Cliff and Higgins ponds (within Nickerson State Park), which are regularly stocked. For a license, visit the town clerk at **Town Hall** at 2198 Rte. 6A (© 508/896-3701). Brewster lacks a deep harbor, so would-be deep-sea fishers will have to head to Barnstable or, better yet, Orleans.

GOLF Part of a large resort, the 18-hole championship **Ocean Edge Golf Course** at 832 Villages Dr. (© 508/896-5911) is the most challenging in Brewster, followed closely by **Captain's Golf Course** at 1000 Freemans Way (© 508/896-5100). In season, a round at the Ocean Edge course will run you about $80 (including mandatory cart).

NATURE & WILDLIFE AREAS Admission is free to the two trails maintained by the Cape Cod Museum of Natural History (see below). The **South Trail,** covering a .75-mile round-trip south of Route 6A, crosses a natural cranberry bog beside Paines Creek to reach a hardwood forest of beeches and tupelos; toward the end of the loop, you'll come upon a "glacial erratic," a huge boulder dropped by a receding glacier. Before heading out on the .25-mile **North Trail,** stop in at the museum for a free guide describing the local flora, including wild roses, cattails, and sumacs. Also accessible from the museum parking lot is the **John Wing Trail,** a 1.5-mile network traversing 140 acres of preservation land, including upland, salt marsh, and beach. (*Note:* This can be a soggy trip. Be sure to heed the posted warnings about high tides, especially in spring, or you might very well find yourself stranded.) Keep an eye out for marsh hawks and blue herons.

As it crosses Route 6A, Paines Creek Road becomes Run Hill Road. Follow it to the end to reach **Punkhorn Park Lands,** an undeveloped 800-acre tract popular with mountain bikers; it features several kettle ponds, a "quaking bog," and

45 miles of dirt paths composing three marked trails (you'll find trail guides at the trail heads).

Though short, the .25-mile jaunt around the **Stony Brook Grist Mill** (see below) is especially scenic. In spring, you can watch the alewives (freshwater herring) vaulting upstream to spawn, and in the summer, the millpond is surrounded and scented by honeysuckle. Also relatively small, at only 25 acres, the **Spruce Hill Conservation Area** behind the Brewster Historical Society Museum (see below) includes a 600-foot stretch of beach, reached by a former carriage road reportedly favored by Prohibition bootleggers.

Just east of the museum is the 1,955-acre **Nickerson State Park** at Route 6 and Crosby Lane (© **508/896-3491**), the legacy of a vast, self-sustaining private estate that once generated its own electricity (with a horse-powered plant) and attracted notable guests, such as President Grover Cleveland, with its own golf course and game preserve. Today it's a back-to-nature preserve encompassing 418 campsites (reservations pour in a year in advance, but some are held open for new arrivals willing to wait a day or two), eight kettle ponds, and 8 miles of bicycle paths. The rest is trees—some 88,000 evergreens, planted by the Civilian Conservation Corps. This is land that has been through a lot but, thanks to careful management, is bouncing back.

TENNIS   Five public courts are located behind the police station; for details, contact the **Brewster Recreation Department** (© **508/896-9430**).

WATERSPORTS   Various small sailboats, kayaks, canoes, and even aqua bikes (also known as sea cycles) are available seasonally at **Jack's Boat Rentals** (© **508/896-8556**), located on Flax Pond within Nickerson State Park (see above under Boating). Canoe or kayak rentals for a couple of hours cost $36.

BREWSTER HISTORIC SIGHTS & MUSEUMS

Brewster Historical Society Museum   This somewhat scattershot collection offers glimpses of Brewster's past. It includes a model of the town's first house (built in 1660), vestiges of an old post office and barber shop, and various relics of the China Trade—the import business that made the town's fortune.

3341 Rte. 6A (about 1 mile east of the town center). © **508/896-9521**. Donation requested. July–Aug Tues–Fri 1–4pm; call for off-season hours. Closed early Sept to May.

Brewster Ladies' Library   So inviting is the buttercup-yellow facade of this Victorian library, built in 1868, that curiosity will undoubtedly draw you inside. A major new addition has doubled the space and added meeting rooms, an auditorium, and a Brewster history room. The original pair of reading rooms remain, however, with facing fireplaces and comfy armchairs. The two young ladies who started up this enterprise in 1852 with a shelf full of books had the right idea. The library hosts special exhibits, lectures, and music programs.

1822 Rte. 6A (about ⅛ mile southwest of the Brewster Store). © **508/896-3913**. www.gis.net/~brewllib. Free admission. Tues–Wed 10am–8pm; Thurs 10am–6pm; Fri–Sat 10am–4pm. Closed Sun–Mon.

Cape Cod Museum of Natural History ★★★ *Kids*   Long before "ecology" had become a buzzword, noted naturalist writer John Hay helped found a museum that celebrates—and helps preserve—Cape Cod's unique landscape. Open since 1954, the museum was also prescient in presenting interactive exhibits. The display on whales, for instance, invites the viewer to press a button to hear eerie whale songs; the children's exhibits include an animal-puppet theater. All ages are invariably intrigued by the "live hive"—like an ant farm, only with busy bees. Four marine-room tanks (one 125-gal. tank and three 55-gal. tanks) contain freshwater and saltwater fish, turtles, frogs, crabs, lobsters, starfish, and a variety of mollusks. The bulk of the museum, naturally, is outdoors, where 85 acres invite exploration (see "Nature & Wildlife Areas," above). Visitors are encouraged to log their bird and animal sightings upon their return. The museum features an on-site archaeology lab on Wing Island, thought to have sheltered one of Brewster's first settlers—the Quaker John Wing, driven from Sandwich in the mid–17th century by religious persecution—and before him, summering native tribes dating back 10 millennia or more. A true force in fostering environmental appreciation, the museum sponsors all sorts of activities, like lectures, concerts, marsh cruises, bike tours, and "eco-treks"—including a sleepover on uninhabited Monomoy Island off Chatham. Other activities include evening astronomy cruises, seal cruises, and Pleasant Bay excursions. Call for a schedule.

869 Rte. 6A (about 2 miles west of the town center). © 800/479-3867 (eastern Mass. only), or 508/896-3867. www.ccmnh.org. Admission $7 adults, $6 seniors, $3.50 children 3–12. May–Sept Mon–Sat 9:30am–4:30pm, Sun 11am–4:30pm. Closed Oct–Apr and major holidays.

Harris-Black House and Higgins Farm Windmill   Most Cape towns can still boast a windmill or two, with a few of them even functioning, but this no-longer-working model is especially handsome. Built in 1795 in the "smock" style that can be traced back to colonial days, it boasts an unusual cap shaped like a boat's hull. A few steps away is a classic half-Cape house, built that same year, consisting of one square room, 16 feet to a side. Here, one of the poorer members of the community—a blacksmith who doubled as barber—lived simply, yet apparently happily, with his wife and 10 children.

785 Rte. 6A (about 2 miles west of the town center). © 508/896-9521. Free admission. July–Aug Tues–Thurs 1–4pm; call for off-season hours. Closed Nov–Apr.

New England Fire & History Museum ⋆ Kids   The gas-lit displays may come across as a little hokey (and murky), but little kids as well as grown-up fire-fighting aficionados will probably find the array of equipment pretty enthralling. More than 30 antique fire engines have found a home here, including an extraordinarily decorative 1837 French provincial rig from Philadelphia and a unique 1929 Mercedes Benz worth a cool million. Also on the grounds, and included with admission, is a smithy offering frequent demos and an old-fashioned apothecary shop.

1439 Main St./Rte. 6A (about 1 mile west of the town center). © 508/896-5711. Admission $7 adults, $6 seniors, free for children 5–12, $1 children under 5. Mid-May to Labor Day Mon–Fri 10am–4pm, Sat–Sun noon–4pm; Labor Day to mid-Oct Sat–Sun noon–4pm. Closed mid-Oct to mid-May.

Stony Brook Grist Mill and Museum ⋆ Kids   It may be hard to believe, but this rustic mill beside a stream was once one of the most active manufacturing communities in New England, cranking out cloth, boots, and ironwork for over a century, starting with the American Revolution. The one remaining structure was built in 1873, toward the end of West Brewster's commercial run, near the site of a 1663 water-powered mill, America's first. After decades of producing overalls and, later, ice cream (with ice dredged from the adjoining pond), the factory was bought by the town and fitted out as a corn mill, with period mill-stones. Volunteers now demonstrate and urge onlookers to get in on the action in the newly restored grist mill. A bag of corn meal costs $2. The second story serves as a repository for all sorts of Brewster memorabilia, including some ancient arrowheads. Recent archaeological excavations in this vicinity, sponsored by the Cape Cod Museum of Natural History, have unearthed artifacts dating back some 10,000 years. As you stroll about the millpond (see "Nature &

Wildlife Areas," above), be on the lookout—who knows what you'll stumble across?

830 Stony Brook Rd. (at the intersection of Satucket Rd.). ℂ **508/896-6745**. Free admission. July–Aug Sat–Sun 10am–2pm; call for off-season hours. Closed Sept–Apr.

BASEBALL

The Brewster Whitecaps of the **Cape Cod Baseball League** play at the Cape Cod Tech field off Route 6's Exit 11. For a schedule, contact the **Brewster Chamber of Commerce** (ℂ **508/255-7045**), the **Brewster Recreation Department** (ℂ **508/896-9430**), or the **League** (ℂ **508/432-6909**).

KID STUFF

For an educational experience that's also fun, take the kids to the **Cape Cod Museum of Natural History** 🏵🏵🏵 and the **Stony Brook Grist Mill** 🏵 (see above for both). Both have walking trails, and the museum has extensive exhibits geared toward children, including a number of interactive exhibits.

SHOPPING

ANTIQUES/COLLECTIBLES   Brewster's stretch of Route 6A offers the best antiquing on the entire Cape. Die-hards would do well to stop at every intriguing shop; you never know what you might find. There are several consistent standouts.

The artifacts gathered at **Kingsland Manor Antiques,** 440 Rte. 6A, about 1 mile east of the Dennis border (ℂ **800/486-2305** or 508/385-9741), tend to be on the flamboyant side (accent pieces rather than serviceable, retiring classics)—which makes browsing all the more fun.

Imagine a town dump full of treasures all meticulously arranged, and you'll get an idea of what's in store at **Diane Vetromile's Antiques** at 3884 Rte. 6A in Brewster (no phone). If the sign that reads ANTIQUES is out, it's open; if not, it's closed. This place is a tad kooky, but any junk aficionado will be thrilled by the pickings: hubcaps, wooden nails, iron rakes, wood shutters—the more peeled paint the better. Owner Diane Vetromile is herself a sculptor, who works with (surprise) found objects, and you'll find her work on view at Jacob Fanning Gallery and Farmhouse Antiques, both in Wellfleet.

ARTS & CRAFTS   Clayton Calderwood's **Clayworks,** 3820 Main St. (Rte. 6A), Brewster (ℂ **508/255-4937**), is always worth a stop, if only to marvel at the famous mammoth urns. There's also a world of functional ware here like bowls, pots, and lamps, in porcelain, stoneware, and terra cotta.

At **The Spectrum,** 369 Rte. 6A, about 1 mile east of the Dennis border (ℂ **800/221-2472** or 508/385-3322), you'll find the kind of crafts that gave crafts a good name: fun stuff, with a certain irony to it, but unmistakably chic. In 1966, two young RISD (Rhode Island School of Design) grads opened shop in a rural schoolhouse. Bob Libby and Addison Pratt now oversee six stores: three on the Cape and Islands (the other branches are in Hyannis and on Nantucket), and one each in Newport, Troy (Mich.), and Palm Beach. Their taste is top-of-the-line, as you'll see in a quick tour of this split-level, country-modern shop.

GIFTS/HOME DECOR   Though quite a bit spiffier than a "real" general store, **The Brewster Store,** 1935 Main St./Rte. 6A, in the center of town (ℂ **508/896-3744**), an 1866 survivor—fashioned from an 1852 Universalist church—is a fun place to shop for sundries and catch up on local gossip. The wares are mostly tourist-oriented these days but include some handy kitchen gear (cobalt glassware, for example) and beach paraphernalia. Give the kids a couple of dimes to feed the

Nickelodeon piano machine, and relax on a sunny church pew out front as you pore over the local paper.

You don't have to be a foodie—though it helps—to go gaga over the exhaustive collection of culinary paraphernalia, from esoteric instruments to foodstuffs, at **The Cook Shop,** 1091 Rte. 6A, about 1½ miles west of the town center (𝒞 **508/ 896-7698**). If you're stuck cooking up a practical yet unusual house gift, look no further.

SEAFOOD   Breakwater Fish and Lobster at 235 Underpass Rd. in Brewster (𝒞 **508/896-7080**) stocks the freshest fish in town and also sells smoked fish.

WHERE TO STAY
EXPENSIVE

Captain Freeman Inn ★★   Donna and Peter Amadeo are the owners of this mint-green 1866 Victorian, one of the best B&B's in the area. The "luxury rooms"—each complete with fireplace and private porch with two-person hot tub—incorporate every extra you could hope to encounter: a canopied, four-poster queen-size bed; a love seat facing the cable TV/VCR (she has a store's worth of tapes available for loan); telephone with answering machine; even a little fridge pre-stocked with cold soda. The plainer rooms are just as pretty—one nice feature of the porch-encircled house is that the second-story windows reach almost to the floor. Delectable yet healthy breakfasts—Edmondson, a culinary maven, hosts weekend cooking courses off-season—are served in the elegant parlor or on a screened porch overlooking the outdoor pool and a lush lawn set up for badminton and croquet. Breakwater Landing is a bucolic 5-minute walk away or just moments away if you avail yourself of a loaner bike. Bliss.

15 Breakwater Rd. (off Rte. 6A, in the town center), Brewster, MA 02631. 𝒞 **800/843-4664** or 508/896-7481. Fax 508/896-5618. www.captainfreemaninn.com. 12 units (all with tub/shower). Summer $180–$225 double. Rates include full breakfast and afternoon tea. MC, V. No children under age 10. **Amenities:** Outdoor pool; loaner bikes. *In room:* A/C, hair dryer.

MODERATE

Beechcroft Inn ★   Though it looks every inch the gracious summer home, this 1828 building, an inn since 1852, began as a meetinghouse. Subtract one steeple, relocate atop a little hillock crowned with magnificent beeches, and presto—a made-to-order country retreat. Innkeepers, Jan and Paul Campbell-White from England, have spruced up the place with English antiques and have turned two rooms into suites. Conveniently, there's a restaurant/tearoom on the premises: The Brewster Tea Pot serves lunch and an authentic afternoon tea.

1360 Rte. 6A (about 1 mile west of the town center), Brewster, MA 02631. 𝒞 **877/233-2446** or 508/896-9534. Fax 508/896-8812. www.beechcroftinn.com. 10 units. Summer $110–$175. Rates include full breakfast. AE, DISC, MC, V. Open year-round. **Amenities:** Restaurant (lunch and tea). *In room:* A/C, coffeemaker, hair dryer.

The Bramble Inn ★★ *Value*   Cliff and Ruth Manchester oversee this rambling mid-19th-century home, decorated in a breezy, country-casual manner. The inn building, constructed in 1861, houses one of the Cape's best restaurants (see "Where to Dine," below) on the first floor. The rooms are cozy, simple, and quaint, with antique touches like crocheted bedspreads. Cliff makes creative breakfasts, such as mixed-fruit Swedish pancakes, which are served outside in the courtyard garden. The inn is about a half mile from calm beaches on Cape Cod Bay.

2019 Rte. 6A (about ⅓ mile east of the town center), Brewster, MA 02631. 𝒞 **508/896-7644**. Fax 508/896-9332. www.brambleinn.com. 5 units (2 tub/shower, 3 shower only). Summer $138–$178 double. Rates include full breakfast. AE, DISC, MC, V. Closed Dec 31–Apr 1. **Amenities:** Restaurant. *In room:* A/C, TV, hair dryer, iron.

Candleberry Inn ⭐   Innkeepers Jeff and Cheryl Morse graciously welcome guests to their restored 18th-century Federal-style home. These spacious accommodations feature wide-board floors, wainscoting, and windows with original glass. The decor is country but not cutesy. Some rooms have working fireplaces and canopy beds. Extras include hair dryers and terry-cloth robes in every room as well as down pillows and featherbeds. Three rooms in the carriage house are decorated in a more contemporary style; two share an outside deck, one is a deluxe suite, and all have TVs. In season, the three-course full breakfast is frequently served on the sunny porch overlooking the 2 acres of landscaped grounds—which have colorful flower beds throughout. Guests love the view of Main Street from the "glider" rocking benches on the lawn.

1882 Main St./Rte. 6A, Brewster, MA 02631. © 800/573-4769 or 508/896-3300. Fax 508/896-4016. www. candleberryinn.com. 9 units (1 tub/shower, 8 shower only). Summer $125–$145 double, $215 suite. Rates include full breakfast. AE, DISC, MC, V. *In room:* A/C.

Isaiah Clark House ⭐ *Value*   Many mementos of bygone days are found throughout this expanded 1780 Cape cottage owned by Jan and Dale Melikan. Antique hardware and wide-board floors are original to the house. Many beds are canopied, but the most spectacular is the suspended canopy bed in the front room with its plaid curtains. Some rooms have telephones. For breakfast, keep your fingers crossed for the Belgian waffles with fresh fruit (the strawberries, blueberries, and raspberries are all picked locally) and whipped-cream toppings.

1187 Main St./Rte. 6A, Brewster, MA 02631. © 800/822-4001 or 508/896-2223. Fax 508/896-2138. www. isaiahclark.com. 7 units (all with tub/shower). Summer $140–$150 double. Rates include full breakfast. DISC, MC, V. *In room:* A/C, TV, no phone.

Michael's Cottages ⭐ *Value*   These cottages on an immaculately groomed compound are small yet centrally located. Across the street is Brewster's Drummer Boy park, which has a playground, historic windmill, and antique house. Brewster's summer band concerts are held there as well. The closest beach is Paines Creek, about 1 mile away. There are three one-bedroom cottages, one small two-bedroom cottage, one efficiency, and two B&B rooms. The cottages have screened porches, fireplaces, and microwaves. The two-bedroom cottage also has a dishwasher and washer/dryer. In July and August, rentals are available by the week only.

618 Main St./Rte. 6A, Brewster, MA 02631. © 800/399-2967 or 508/896-4025. Fax 508/896-3158. www. sunsol.com/michaels/. 7 units (2 tub/shower, 5 shower only). Summer $100–$150 double, weekly rates $750–$825 double, $1,350 2-bedroom. B&B rooms include continental breakfast. AE, DISC, MC, V. Open year-round. *In room:* A/C, TV, fridge, coffeemaker, hair dryer.

Ruddy Turnstone Bed & Breakfast ⭐⭐ *Finds*   Bird lovers will be particularly entranced by this cozy B&B; the salt marsh makes for frequent sightings. In fact, the upstairs suite and the common room of this lovely early 1880s home offer distant Cape Cod Bay and sweeping marsh views, for about the same price as other inns along this stretch without panoramic views. The house is beautifully situated up on a knoll and is furnished with antiques, Oriental rugs, and some canopy beds. The 1860s barn, moved here from Nantucket, houses two additional rooms. Your country breakfast served out on the screened porch or in the old keeping room might feature home-baked apple French toast. Innkeepers "Swanee" and Sally Swanson are the kind you look forward to seeing year after year.

463 Main St./Rte. 6A, Brewster, MA 02631. © 800/654-1995 or 508/385-9871. Fax 508/385-5696. www. theruddyturnstone.com. 5 units (4 tub/shower, 1 shower only). Summer $125–$195 double. Rates include full breakfast. DISC, MC, V. Closed Nov–Feb. *In room:* A/C, TV, hair dryer, no phone.

INEXPENSIVE

Old Sea Pines Inn ★★ (Value) (Kids)   This reasonably priced, large historic inn is a great spot for families, and hosts Michele and Steve Rowan have done their best to re-create the gracious ambience of days gone by. In the main house, the parlor, the expansive porch lined with rockers, and a handful of rather minuscule boarding-school-scale rooms on the second floor recall the inn's days as the Sea Pines School of Charm and Personality for Young Women. (These bargain rooms with shared bathrooms are the only ones in the house without air-conditioning, but at $75 per night in season, who cares?) This is one of the few places on the Cape where solo travelers can find a single room for substantially less than a double. There are two other buildings, one of which is fully wheelchair-accessible (another rarity among historic inns). Whereas the main house has an air of exuberance muted by gentility, the annex rooms are downright playful, with colorful accoutrements, including pink TVs. Steve does double duty as the breakfast chef and prepares good old-fashioned food. Sunday evenings from mid-June through mid-September, Old Sea Pines is the site of a dinner/theater performance by the Cape Cod Repertory Theatre (see "Brewster After Dark," below).

2553 Main St. (about 1 mile E of the town center), Brewster, MA 02631. © **508/896-6114.** Fax 508/896-7387. www.oldseapinesinn.com. 24 units, 5 with shared bathroom. Summer $95–$150 double, $135–$155 suite. Rates include full breakfast and afternoon tea. AE, DC, DISC, MC, V. Closed Jan–Mar. *In room:* TV, hair dryer, iron.

WHERE TO DINE
VERY EXPENSIVE

The Bramble Inn Restaurant ★★★ CONTINENTAL   Often named among the best restaurants on Cape Cod, there's an impromptu feel to this intimate restaurant, an enclave of five small rooms each imbued with its own personality, from sporting (the Tack Room) to best-Sunday-behavior (the Elegant Parlor). One-of-a-kind antique table settings add to the charm. Such niceties fade to mere backdrop, though, beside Ruth Manchester's extraordinary cuisine. A four-course (8- to 10-option) menu that evolves every few weeks gives her free rein to follow fresh enthusiasms, as well as seasonal delicacies. Any specifics are quickly history, but she has a solid grounding in Mediterranean cuisines and a gift for improvising exotic influences. Her assorted seafood curry (with lobster, cod, scallops, and shrimp in a light curry sauce with grilled banana, toasted almonds, coconut, and chutney) and her rack of lamb (with deep-fried beet-and-fontina polenta, pan-seared zucchini, and mustard port cream) have been written up in the *New York Times.*

2019 Main St. (about ⅓ mile east of Rte. 124). © **508/896-7644.** Reservations suggested. Fixed-price dinner $44–$59. AE, DISC, MC, V. June to early Sept daily 5:30–9pm; call for off-season hours. Closed Jan–Mar.

Chillingsworth ★★★ FRENCH   This longtime contender for the title of fanciest restaurant on the Cape now has two dining options: the formal dining room with jackets suggested for men and the more casual bistro. The fancy dining room boasts antique appointments reaching back several centuries and a six-course table d'hôte menu that will challenge the most shameless gourmands. Focus on the taste sensations, which are indeed sensational. Specialties include steamed lobster over spinach and fennel with sea beans and lobster-basil butter sauce; and seared and roasted boneless rib eye of veal with fresh morels, mushroom torte, and asparagus. Finish it off with warm chocolate cake with pistachio ice cream and chocolate drizzle. Or try the moderately priced, a la carte Bistro, which operates from a separate kitchen and serves lunch and dinner daily in season in the adjoining greenhouse

---

Kids Family-Friendly Hotels & Restaurants

The Barley Neck Inn Lodge in East Orleans (p. 170)   Tastefully rehabbed, this motel offers basic, low-priced rooms, a small pool, and a pair of superb, chic restaurants.

Binnacle Tavern in Orleans (p. 173)   Design-your-own pizzas are the draw at this often-raucous eatery, decorated with nautical salvage.

Chatham Bars Inn in Chatham (p. 158)   This luxury beachside resort offers well-heeled tots the best of everything, including organized play programs morning, noon, and night.

Old Sea Pines Inn in Brewster (p. 143)   Children will appreciate the traditional food and friendly, informal atmosphere of this former finishing school.

---

or under huge umbrellas on the shady lawn. There are also three deluxe inn rooms on the premises.

2449 Main St. (about 1 mile east of the town center). © **800/430-3640** or 508/896-3640. www.chillingsworth. com. Reservations suggested. Jacket advised for men in fine-dining section. Fixed-price meals $50–$68. Bistro $13–$24. AE, DC, MC, V. Mid-June to mid-Oct Tues–Sun noon–2pm and 6–9:30pm (bistro opens for dinner at 5:30pm), Mon 5:30–9:30pm (dinner in bistro only on Mon); call for off-season hours. Closed Dec–Apr.

MODERATE

The Brewster Fish House ★★ NEW AMERICAN   Spare and handsome as a Shaker refectory, this small restaurant bills itself "non-conforming" and delivers on the promise. The approach to seafood borders on genius: Consider, for instance, squid delectably tenderized in a marinade of soy and ginger; or silky-tender, walnut-crusted ocean catfish accompanied by kale sautéed in Marsala. These are but two examples of the daily specials devised to take advantage of the latest haul. Besides seafood, there are always beef dishes, as well as vegetarian dishes, on the menu. No wonder the place is packed. Better get there early (before 7pm) if you want to get in.

2208 Main St. (about ½ mile east of the town center). © **508/896-7867.** Reservations not accepted. Main courses $14–$26. MC, V. May–Aug Mon–Sat 11am–3pm and 5–9:30pm, Sun noon–3pm and 5–9:30pm; call for off-season hours. Closed mid-Dec to Apr.

INEXPENSIVE

Brewster Inn & Chowder House ★ ECLECTIC   To really get the gist of the expression "chow down," just observe the early-evening crowd happily doing so at this plain century-old restaurant known mostly by word of mouth. The draw is hearty, predictable staples—the homemade chowder; various fried, broiled, or baked fish—at prices geared to ordinary people rather than splurging tourists. Check the blackboard for interesting variations—maybe mussels steamed in cream and curry. If you like to indulge in a martini before your meal, this place makes the best ones in town. There's also a good old bar, The Woodshed (see "Brewster After Dark," below), out back.

1993 Rte. 6A (in the center of town). © **508/896-7771.** Main courses $12–$18. AE, DISC, MC, V. Late May to mid-Oct daily 11:30am–2:30pm, Sun–Thurs 5–9:30pm, Fri–Sat 5–10pm; call for off-season hours. Open year-round.

Cobie's ⟨★⟩ AMERICAN   Accessible to cars whizzing along Route 6A and within collapsing distance for cyclists exploring the Rail Trail, this picture-perfect clam shack has been dishing out exemplary fried clams, lobster rolls, foot-long hot dogs, black-and-white frappés, and all the other beloved staples of summer since 1948.

3260 Rte. 6A (about 2 miles east of Brewster center). ⟨𝒞⟩ **508/896-7021.** Most items under $15. No credit cards. Late May to early Sept daily 11am–9pm. Closed early Sept to late May.

SWEETS

How unusual to find a bake shop tucked away in a sweet little country gift shop. **Hopkins House Bakery,** 2727 Main St. (⟨𝒞⟩ **508/896-3450**), is an especially good one, with hermit cookies (molasses, raisins, and nuts) a standout. Heather Baxter also bakes breads and terrific muffins, including what she calls "the best corn muffin ever." Homemade fruit pies and sticky buns are also a specialty. Open Thursdays through Sundays July and August, weekends only in June and September. Closed October to May.

BREWSTER AFTER DARK

Performances at the **Cape Cod Repertory Theatre Company,** 3379 Rte. 6A, East Brewster, about 2½ miles east of Brewster center (⟨𝒞⟩ **508/896-1888**), are given Tuesday to Saturday at 8pm from early July to early September. In summer, this shoestring troupe tackles the Bard, as well as serious contemporary fare, at a 200-seat outdoor theater on the old Crosby estate (now state-owned and undergoing restoration). Tickets for outdoor performances are $16 for adults and $10 for those under 21. In season, they also put on a Broadway-musical dinner revue Sunday nights at the **Old Sea Pines Inn** ($45 fixed price; see "Where to Stay," above). Off season they perform at various locales. Call for off-season hours. Tickets cost $15 for adults and $8 for those under 22.

Hot local bands take the tiny stage seasonally at **The Woodshed,** at the Brewster Inn & Chowder House, 1993 Rte. 6A (⟨𝒞⟩ **508/896-7771**), a far cry from the glitzy discos on the southern shore. If your tastes run more to Raitt and Buffett than techno, you'll feel right at home in this dark, friendly dive. Cover charge $5.

2 Harwich ⟨★⟩

24 miles E of Sandwich; 32 miles S of Provincetown

Harwich Port, the village in the town of Harwich where most vacationers find themselves, is the quintessential sleepy seaside village, not too mucked up—as yet—by the creeping commercialization of Route 28. The town's main claim to fame is as the birthplace, in 1846, of commercial cranberry cultivation: The "bitter berry," as the Narragansetts called it, is now Massachusetts's leading agricultural product. The curious can find elucidating displays on this and other local distinctions at the Brooks Academy Museum in the inland town of Harwich. The incurious, or merely vacation-minded, can loll on the beach.

ESSENTIALS

GETTING THERE   After crossing either the Bourne or Sagamore bridge (see "Getting There," in chapter 2), head east on Route 6 and take Exit 10 south along Route 124. Harwich is located at the intersection of Route 39, where the two routes converge. Head southwest to Harwich Port and West Harwich, both located on Route 28. East Harwich (more easily reached from Rte. 6's Exit 11) is inland, a few miles northeast. Or fly into Hyannis (see "Getting There," in chapter 2).

VISITOR INFORMATION   Contact the **Harwich Chamber of Commerce,** Route 28, Harwich Port, MA 02646 (© **800/441-3199** or 508/432-1600; fax 508/430-2105; www.harwichcc.com), open late May to late September daily from 9am to 5pm; call for off-season hours. You can also contact the **Cape Cod Chamber of Commerce** (see "Visitor Information" in the "Brewster" section, earlier in this chapter).

BEACHES & RECREATIONAL PURSUITS

BEACHES   The Harwich coast is basically one continuous beach punctuated by the occasional harbor. Harwich Port is so close to the sound that it's a snap to walk the block or two to the water—provided you find a parking place in town (try the lot near the chamber of commerce booth in the center of town). Parking right at the beach is pretty much limited to residents and renters, who can obtain a weekly sticker for $25 at the **Community Center,** 100 Oak St., Harwich (© **508/432-7638**).

- **Bank Street Beach** ✷✷, at the end of Bank Street in Harwich Port: This is one of the few sound beaches in Harwich Port that has parking, but you will need a sticker. The sound beaches are generally warm and calm and very good beaches for swimming. This is a pretty (and popular) stretch where you'll see lots of families as well as the self-conscious college crowd.
- **Hinckleys Pond** ✷ and **Seymours Pond** ✷, west of Route 124 and right off the Rail Trail, and **Bucks Pond** ✷✷, off Depot Road at Route 39 northeast of Harwich: While Hinckleys and Bucks have limited parking, no parking sticker is required. At Seymours, however, you will need a sticker.
- **Red River Beach** ✷, off Uncle Venies Road south of Route 28 in South Harwich: This is the only sound beach in town offering parking for day-trippers (they still have to turn up early); the fee is $5 on weekdays or $10 weekends and holidays. Marked off with stone jetties, this narrow, 2,700-foot beach has full facilities.
- **Sand Pond** ✷, off Great Western Road near Depot Street: This beach honors the weekly beach sticker, as do the two parking lots at Long Pond (between routes 137 and 124).

BICYCLING   Transecting Harwich for about 5 miles, the Cape Cod Rail Trail skirts some pretty ponds in the western part before veering north and zigzagging toward Brewster along Route 124. For rentals and information, contact **Harwich Port Bike Co.,** 431 Rte. 28 (© **508/430-0200**); they can also provide in-line skates. A 24-hour bike rental costs $18.

BOATING   You can rent a canoe by the day or the week at **Goose Hummock** in Orleans (© **508/255-2620**) and paddle down the Herring River in West Harwich. Meandering from a reservoir south to the sound, the river is a natural herring run framed by a cattail marsh.

   Cape Sail, out of Saquatucket Harbor (© **508/896-2730**), offers sailing lessons as well as private charters.

FISHING   There are six ponds available for fishing in the Harwich area, as well as extensive shellfishing in season; for details and a license, visit **Town Hall** at 732 Main St. in Harwich (© **508/430-7516**). For supplies and instruction, visit **Fishing the Cape,** at the Harwich Commons, routes 137 and 39 (© **508/432-1200**); it's the official Cape headquarters for the **Orvis Saltwater Fly-Fishing**

School (℡ 800/235-9763). Trips for two and a half days cost $490. Several deep-sea fishing boats operate out of Saquatucket Harbor (off Rte. 28, about a half mile east of Harwich Port), including the 33-footer *Fish Tale* (℡ 508/432-3783), which charges $350 for 6 hours and $425 (includes lunch) for 8 hours. The 65-foot *Yankee* (℡ 508/432-2520) is a party boat out of Saquatucket Harbor offering two 4-hour trips per day Monday through Saturday and one trip on Sunday in season. Off season, there's one trip per day. Trips cost $27 adults and $25 for children 9 and under. The deep-sea party boat *Golden Eagle* (℡ 508/432-5611), offering two fishing trips a day, heads out from Wychmere Harbor. Rates for the *Golden Eagle* day trips are $26 for adults and $22 for children under 12.

GOLF   Both the championship 18-hole **Cranberry Valley Golf Course** at 183 Oak St. in Harwich (℡ 508/430-5234), which wends its way among cranberry bogs, and the nine-hole **Harwich Port Golf Club** on Forest and South streets in Harwich Port (℡ 508/432-0250), are open to the public. Cranberry Valley charges $60 for a round, and Harwich Port Golf Club charges $18 for nine holes.

NATURE & WILDLIFE AREAS   The largest preserve in Harwich is the 245-acre **Bells Neck Conservation Area** north of Route 28 near the Dennis border. It encompasses the Herring River, ideal for birding and canoeing (see "Boating," above).

TENNIS   Public courts are available on a first-come, first-served basis at the Cape Cod Technical High School on Route 124 and Brooks Park on Oak Street, about ¼ mile east of Harwich center off Route 29; for details, contact the **Harwich Recreation Department** (℡ 508/430-7553). Open late May through September, the **Wychmere Harbor Tennis Club** at 792 Main St. in Harwich Port (℡ 508/430-7012) comprises nine Har-Tru courts and two hard courts; lessons can be scheduled. Court time is a whopping $50 an hour.

HISTORICAL HARWICH

Brooks Academy Museum ⚐   Gathered in an 1844 Greek Revival academy that offered the country's first courses in navigation, the collections of the Harwich Historical Society are good for a rainy afternoon's worth of wonderment. On permanent display is an extensive exhibition chronicling the early days of the cranberry industry, when harvesting was a backbreaking chore performed on hands and knees with a wooden scoop, mostly by migrant workers. (It simplified matters enormously once someone figured out that the bogs could be flooded and threshed so that the berries bob to the surface.) Other holdings include Native American tools, paintings by local artist C. D. Cahoon, nautical items of historical interest, and extensive textiles, imaginatively presented. The complex also includes a Revolutionary powder house and—kids might get a kick of out this—a nicely restored 1872 outhouse.

80 Parallel St. (at the intersection of Sisson Rd. and Main St., about 1 mile north of Harwich Port center). ℡ 508/432-8089. www.capecodhistory.org. Donations accepted. Mid-June to mid-Sept Tues–Fri 1–4pm; mid-Sept to mid-Oct Wed–Fri 1–4pm. Closed mid-Oct to mid-June.

BASEBALL

The Harwich Mariners, part of the **Cape Cod Baseball League,** play at Whithouse Field behind the high school in Harwich. For a schedule, contact the **Harwich Chamber of Commerce** (℡ 508/432-1600), the **Harwich Recreation & Youth Department** (℡ 508/430-7553), or the **League** (℡ 508/432-6909).

KID STUFF

West Harwich gets some spillover from Dennis's overdevelopment, including such junior-tourist attractions as **Harbor Glen Miniature Golf** at 168 Rte. 28 (© **508/432-8240**), the **Trampoline Center** at 296 Rte. 28 (© **508/432-8717**), and **Bud's Go-Karts** at the intersection of routes 28 and 39 (© **508/432-4964**), which welcomes hot-rodders as young as 8, provided they meet the height requirement (54 in.). The go-karts are $5 per ride. All three are open until 11pm in summer. For free self-entertainment, visit **Castle in the Clouds,** a community-built playground behind the Harwich Elementary School on South Street in Harwich. Young culture mavens might want to take in a performance at the **Harwich Junior Theatre** at 105 Division St. in West Harwich (© **508/432-2002**), which has been satisfying summer customers since 1952; if you plan to stick around for a while, your youngsters could even take classes and possibly work their way onstage. Tickets cost $12 to $16.

SHOPPING

Route 28 harbors lots of mini-malls and shops, big on gifts (on the trite side) and unsensational art. With a few exceptions, save your power shopping for Chatham.

ANTIQUES/COLLECTIBLES **The Barn at Windsong,** 245 Bank St., a half mile north of Harwich Port center, midway between routes 28 and 39 (© **508/432-8281**), is the kind of archetypal shop antiquers crave: a lovely old barn in the country, packed with premium goods. Offerings include furniture, glass, china, and rugs. Closed November through April.

ARTS & CRAFTS **Cape Cod Cooperage,** 1150 Queen Anne Rd., at the intersection of Route 137 (© **508/432-0788**), is the oldest surviving barrel factory in the state (in fact, the only one), and is packed to the rafters with useful wooden goods, mostly made on-site. You might come away with a naif-painted chest or just a set of Shaker pegs, but you're unlikely to depart empty-handed.

Ron Kusins's designs range from the traditional (for example, a burnished porringer) to the contemporary (for example, sleek and shiny asymmetrical candlesticks). There's a style to suit every look, and you can watch this nearly extinct art in action at **Pewter Crafters of Cape Cod,** 791 Rte. 28, Harwichport (© **508/362-3407**).

BOOKS At **Wychmere Book & Coffee** at 587 Main St. (at the corner of Rte. 28 and Bank St.) in Harwich Port (© **508/432-7868**), you'll find a large selection and a friendly staff.

WHERE TO STAY

In addition to the more expensive choices listed below, there are several affiliated above-average motels in Harwich. **The Tern Inn,** 91 Chase St., West Harwich (© **800/432-3718** or 508/432-3714; www.theterninn.com), is in a quiet residential neighborhood. Summer rates are $119 to $159 double, and $725 to $850 per week for a cottage. The Tern has a small, unheated pool. Rooms do not have phones, but all have TVs, mini-fridges, and air-conditioning. Just 75 yards from a wide Nantucket Sound beach, **The Commodore Inn** ⚐, 30 Earle Rd., West Harwich (© **800/368-1180** or 508/432-1180; www.commodoreinn.com), has lovely rooms resembling upscale condos with cathedral ceilings and handsome, functional furniture. Rates are $175 to $225 double and include a full buffet breakfast in season. All rooms have microwave ovens and mini-fridges, as well as air-conditioning, TVs, and phones with dataports. Some have Jacuzzis and fireplaces. Closed mid-October to March. **Sandpiper Beach Inn** ★★, 16 Bank St., Harwich Port (© **800/433-2234** or 508/432-0485; www.sandpiperbeachinn.com), is plunked right on a lovely Nantucket Sound beach. All rooms have air-conditioning, phones, TVs, hair dryers, and fridges. Summer rates are $175 to $385 double, $350 to $365 for suites. Closed November to mid-April.

VERY EXPENSIVE

The Winstead Inn and Beach Resort ★★   This property is composed of two buildings set about a mile apart: the 14-room Beach House Inn on a private Nantucket Sound beach and a short walk from Harwich Port; and the newly converted 5-room Winstead Inn near Harwich center. The Beach House is an antiques-filled 1920s inn with shiplike, narrow hallways leading to immaculate, spacious rooms. The original rooms still boast their varnished pine paneling, as well as updated whirlpool baths; and the four glorious front rooms each feature a fireplace or deck as well, plus sweeping views of Nantucket Sound. In fact, all but two of the rooms here have a view of the beach. The Winstead, a handsome colonial-style building with a pool, has undergone a deluxe remodeling. Both inn buildings are within walking distance from shops and restaurants, so you don't have to contend with summer traffic. Those staying at the Winstead can take a free shuttle to the beach in a 1949 Pontiac Woody.

4 Braddock Lane, Harwich, MA 02646. © **800/870-4405** or 508/432-4444. Fax 508/432-9152. www.winstead inn.com. 19 units. Summer $225–$395 double. Rates include continental breakfast. MC, V. Open year-round. **Amenities:** Outdoor pool at Winstead property. *In room:* A/C, TV, fridge, hair dryer.

EXPENSIVE

The Augustus Snow House ★★   A local landmark for almost a century, you can't miss this Queen Anne Victorian with gabled dormers and wraparound veranda centrally located on Main Street. The house was precisely situated so that Captain Snow could look out the front door and see the ocean a block away at the end of Pilgrim Lane. Rooms are spacious, immaculate, and very comfortable, with interesting antique appointments throughout. All have fireplaces. Several of the bathrooms are particularly unique, some with claw-foot tubs, old sink tables, and restored antique toilets. A new suite in the carriage house has a private entrance, fireplace, Jacuzzi tub, and shower. The full breakfast features such delicacies as peach kuchen, baked pears with raspberry and cream sauce, and cinnamon apple quiche.

528 Main St. (in the center of town), Harwich Port, MA 02646. © **800/320-0528** or 508/430-0528. Fax 508/432-6638. www.augustussnow.com. 7 units. Summer $160–$210 double, $275–$395 suite. Rates include full breakfast. AE, DISC, MC, V. Open year-round. *In room:* A/C, TV, fridge, iron.

Dunscroft by the Sea ★   This gracious Colonial Revival home, which sits a block from town and 500 feet from the beach, is decorated in a feminine style with lots of pinks and hearts. Innkeepers Alyce and Wally Cunningham have enhanced the house and honeymoon suite (formerly the chauffeur's quarters) with extensive renovations in a Valentine-ish vein. Several of the rooms have Jacuzzis and TVs/VCRs, including the cottage suite, which also has a kitchenette and a working fireplace. Alyce hails from Virginia originally, and her Southern hospitality is particularly evident in the bountiful breakfast, which may feature Virginia fried apples or Caribbean French toast.

24 Pilgrim Rd. (south of Rte. 28 near the beach), Harwich Port, MA 02646. © **508/432-0810.** Fax 508/432-5134. www.dunscroftbythesea.com. 8 units, 1 cottage suite (6 tub/shower, 3 shower only). Summer $195–$295 double, $315–$350 cottage. Rates include full breakfast. AE, MC, V. No children under 12. *In room:* A/C, hair dryer, iron.

WHERE TO DINE
MODERATE

The Cape SeaGrille ★★ NEW AMERICAN Two ambitious chef/owners are the power behind the stove of this upscale enterprise occupying the pared-down, peach-toned shell of a beach house. The menu is under constant revision, the better to springboard off market finds, but among the keepers are a salmon carpaccio appetizer with grilled exotic mushrooms, lemon capers, and Dijon sauce; and a grilled medley entree starring lobster, shrimp, and bacon-wrapped swordfish. City sophisticates who insist on creativity and innovation will find this the most consistently rewarding source in town.

31 Sea St. (south of Rte. 28 in the center of town), Harwich Port. ✆ **508/432-4745.** Reservations recommended. Main courses $15–$26. AE, MC, V. June–Aug daily 5–10pm; call for off-season hours. Closed mid-Nov to mid-May.

L'Alouette ★ CLASSIC FRENCH There's no way to fake the seductive aromas of an authentic French restaurant. The secrets are all in the stock, and chef Jean Louis Bastres, formerly of Biarritz, makes his from scratch. He's a strict classicist (none of this nouvelle nonsense): Specialties at this auberge-style restaurant include such time-honored tests of prowess as bouillabaisse and chateaubriand.

787 Rte. 28 (about ½ mile east of the town center), Harwich Port. ✆ **508/430-0405.** Reservations recommended. Main courses $16–$28. AE, DISC, MC, V. May–Oct Tues–Sun 5–9pm (last reservation at 8:30pm); Nov–Dec and mid-Mar to Apr Wed–Sun 5–9pm. Closed Jan to mid-Mar.

INEXPENSIVE

Seafood Sam's SEAFOOD Strategically located within a big bounce of the Trampoline Center, this McDonald's-style clam shack—part of a Cape-wide chain—dishes out deep-fried seafood, fast.

302 Rte. 28 (about ½ mile east of the town center), Harwich Port. ✆ **508/432-1422.** www.seafoodsams.com. Most items under $12. DISC, MC, V. Mid-Feb to late Nov daily 11am–10pm. Closed late Nov to mid-Feb.

PICNIC FARE

Lambert's Farm Market ★ Don't be dissuaded by the size: Yes, it's a full-size grocery store, but seek out the deli/bakery to throw together a beach lunch, or shop for some trendy comestibles.

710 Main St. (Rte. 28, about ½ mile east of the town center), Harwich Port. ✆ **508/432-5415.**

SWEETS

Sundae School ★ ICE CREAM Another branch of the local chain (also in Dennis Port and East Orleans), this is homemade ice cream and a sure crowd pleaser with the kids. Real whipped cream and real cherries will keep the parents happy, too. Fresh fruit sundaes are a popular choice here, and everyone likes to admire the 1938 ice-cream truck.

606 Main St. (in the center of town), Harwich Port. ✆ **508/430-2444.** Closed mid-Oct to mid-May.

THE HARWICHES AFTER DARK

The Irish Pub ★ For years, this has been the premier Irish bar on the Cape. It feels authentic because it is. A variety of live entertainment (it could be Irish music, karaoke, or anything in between) Thursday to Saturday in season is usually rollicking good fun. 126 Main St. (Rte. 28), West Harwich. ✆ **508/432-8808.** Cover varies.

3 Chatham ★★★

32 miles E of Sandwich; 24 miles S of Provincetown

Sticking out like a sore elbow (and out of the way of much of the Cape's tourist flow), Chatham was one of the first spots to attract early explorers. Samuel de Champlain stopped by in 1606 but got into a tussle with the prior occupants over some copper cooking pots; he ended up leaving in a hurry. The first colonist to stick around was William Nickerson of Yarmouth, who befriended a local *sachem* (tribal leader) and built a house beside his wigwam in 1656. One prospered; the other—for obvious reasons—didn't. To this day, listings for Nickersons still occupy a half page in the Cape Cod phone book.

Chatham, along with Provincetown, is the only area on the Cape to support a commercial fishing fleet—against increasing odds. Overfishing has resulted in closely monitored limits to give the stock time to bounce back. Boats must now go out as far as 100 miles to catch their fill. Despite the difficulties, it's a way of life few locals would willingly relinquish. As in Provincetown, there's surprisingly little animosity between the hardworking residents and the summer vacationers at play, perhaps because it's clear that discerning tourist dollars are helping to preserve this lovely town for all.

ESSENTIALS

GETTING THERE   After crossing either the Sagamore bridge (see "Getting There" in chapter 2), head east on Route 6 and take Exit 11 south (Rte. 137) to Route 28. From this intersection, the village of South Chatham is about a half mile west, and West Chatham is about 1½ miles east. Chatham itself is about 2 miles farther east on Route 28.

To fly to Chatham, take a commercial flight into Hyannis (see "Getting There," in chapter 2).

VISITOR INFORMATION   Visit the **Cape Cod Chamber of Commerce** (see "Visitor Information" in the "Brewster" section, earlier in this chapter); or the **Chatham Chamber of Commerce,** 533 Main St., Chatham, MA 02633 (© **800/715-5567** or 508/945-5199; www.chathaminfo.com); or the new **Chatham Chamber booth** (no phone) at the intersection of routes 137 and 28. Hours for both the Chatham chamber and the booth are July and August Monday to Saturday 10am to 6pm, Sunday noon to 6pm; closed late October to April. Call for off-season hours.

A STROLL AROUND CHATHAM

Parking on Main Street can be a challenge at the height of summer, so pretend you're a turn-of-the-20th-century traveler and start out at the **Chatham Railroad Museum** ★ on 153 Depot St. (closed mid-Sept to mid-June), 1 block north of Main Street at the western end of town. You can't miss it: It's a gaudy 1887 Victorian station in the "Railroad Gothic" style, painted yellow with fanciful russet ornamentation. The building itself is full of railroading memorabilia, and the big exhibits—antique passenger cars—are out back.

If you've got children along, they'll surely want to stretch their legs (and imaginations) at the **Play-a-Round Park** ★★, opposite the Railroad Museum. Dreamed up by prominent playground designer Robert Leathers, it's a marvelous maze of tubes, rope ladders, slides, and swings. The only way you'll get going again is to promise to come back.

Head west to the end of Depot Street and right on Old Harbor Road, which, if followed past Main Street, becomes State Harbor Road. About a mile farther along, past Oyster Pond, you'll encounter the **Old Atwood House and Museums** ✿ at 347 Stage Harbor Rd. (© **508/945-2493;** www.chathamhistorical society.org; closed Oct to mid-June). The 1752 house itself shelters the odds and ends collected by the Chatham Historical Society over the past 7 decades; piece by piece, they tell the story of the town. The Society even managed to save an entire 1947 "fishing camp," a run-down cottage that looks as if the occupant just stepped out to check a line.

Heading back toward Main Street, bear right on Cross Street and look for **Chase Park and Bowling Green,** presided over by the Old Grist Mill, built in the late 18th century. You might actually try some lawn bowling along the lovingly tended greens before returning to Main Street, where the shops are too prolific and special to pass up. Then head eastward toward the shore, but be sure to duck into the **Mayo House** at 540 Main St. (© **508/945-4084**), a sweet little three-quarter Cape built in 1818. Entrance is free, and—if you've studiously avoided lengthy historical house tours so far—it can give you, in just a couple of minutes, a good sense of what life might have been like here in centuries past.

Main Street veers right when it reaches the shore. Continue along for about ¼ mile to view the **Chatham Light** ✶✶, an 1876 beacon not open to the public, but still in operation: Its light shines 15 miles out to sea. This is a good vantage point from which to marvel over the "break" that burst through Chatham's barrier beach in 1987. In the years since, the newly created island, South Beach, has already glommed onto the coastline, becoming a peninsula. This is one landscape that rarely stays put for long.

Retrace your steps northward along the shore. In about ¾ mile, you'll pass the grand **Chatham Bars Inn** ✶✶✶ at Shore Road and Seaview Street (© **800/527-4884** or 508/945-0096), which started out life as a private hunting lodge in 1914. Passersby are welcome to look around the lobby, restored to reflect its original Victorian splendor. Linger on the porch over coffee or a drink, if you like, before pressing on to the **Chatham Fish Pier,** about ⅛ mile farther along Shore Road (© **508/945-5177**). If you've timed your visit right (from noon on), the trawlers should just now be bringing in the catch of the day: You can observe the haul from an observation deck. Also have a look at *The Provider,* an intriguing outdoor sculpture by Woods Hole artist Sig Pursin.

Winding Down When you've had enough, or the insects insist that you head on home, go back to Main Street down Seaview Street, past the Chatham Seaside Links golf course. One long block later (about ½ mile), you're back in the center of town. You can relax and unwind at the **Chatham Wayside Inn** ✿ at 512 Main St. (© **508/945-5550**). Secure a table on the greenery-curtained patio and watch the world go by, as you fortify yourself with regionally inspired snacks and sweets on the large screened porch.

BEACHES & RECREATIONAL PURSUITS

BEACHES Chatham has an unusual array of beach styles, from the peaceful shores of the Nantucket Sound to the treacherous, shifting shoals along the Atlantic. For information on beach stickers ($10 per day, $50 per week), call the **Permit Department** on George Ryder Road in West Chatham (© **508/945-5180**).

- **Cockle Cove Beach, Ridgevale Beach,** and **Hardings Beach** ✶✶: Lined up along the sound, each at the end of its namesake road south of Route 28,

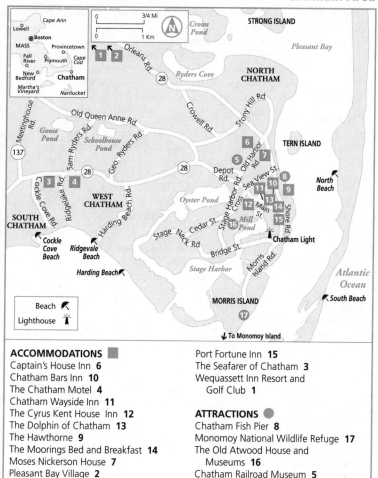

these family-pleasing beaches offer gentle surf suitable for all ages, as well as full facilities.

- **Forest Beach** 🏖: No longer an officially recognized town beach (there's no lifeguard), this sound landing near the Harwich border is still popular, especially among surfboarders.

- **Oyster Pond Beach,** off Route 28: Only a block from Chatham's Main Street, this sheltered saltwater pond (with restrooms) swarms with children.

- **Chatham Light Beach** 🏖🏖: Located directly below the lighthouse parking lot (where stopovers are limited to 30 minutes), this narrow stretch of sand is easy to get to: Just walk down the stairs. Currents here can be tricky and swift, though, so swimming is discouraged.

- **South Beach** 🏖🏖: A former island jutting out slightly to the south of the Chatham Light, this glorified sandbar can be equally dangerous, so heed posted warnings and content yourself with strolling or, at most, wading.

- **North Beach** ★★: Extending all the way south from Orleans, this 5-mile barrier beach is accessible from Chatham only by boat; if you don't have your own, you can take the **Beachcomber,** a water taxi, which leaves from Chatham fish pier. Call ✆ **508/945-5265** to schedule your trip. The round-trip costs $10 for adults, and $5 for children 12 and under. The water taxi makes the trip from 10am to 5pm daily in season. Inquire about other possible drop-off points if you'd like to beach around.

BICYCLING Though Chatham has no separate recreational paths per se, a demarcated bike/blading lane makes a scenic, 8-mile circuit of town, heading south onto "The Neck," east to the Chatham Light, up Shore Road all the way to North Chatham, and back to the center of town. A descriptive brochure prepared by the **Chatham Chamber of Commerce** (✆ **800/715-5567** or 508/945-5199) shows the suggested route, and there are lots of lightly trafficked detours worth taking. Rentals are available at **Bikes & Blades,** 195 Crowell Rd., Chatham (✆ **508/945-7600**). Rates are $15 per day for bikes, $20 per day for in-line skates (including pads).

BIRD-WATCHING In summer both the **Cape Cod Museum of Natural History** (✆ 508/896-3867) and the Wellfleet Bay Wildlife chapter of the **Audubon Society** (✆ 508/349-2615) offer bird-watching trips to the **Monomoy National Wildlife Refuge** ★★ on North Monomoy Island. On the Audubon Society tours of North Monomoy (2 hr.), after a 10-minute boat ride from Chatham, you'll embark on a guided tour, where you'll encounter a variety of species—from herring gulls and sandpipers to black-bellied plovers and willets. Tours cost around $35 adults, $25 children 12 and under and are recommended not just for avid bird-watchers, but for anyone who enjoys the outdoors. Reservations are required.

BOATING You can rent a kayak (see below) and paddle down the Oyster River, past Hardings Beach, and over to Morris Island. You can also explore Pleasant Bay and reach the inside shore of the Outer Beach.

NautiJane's Boat Rental at 337 Rte. 28 in Harwich Port (✆ **508/430-6893**) also offers lessons and rentals at the Wequasett Inn on Pleasant Bay and on Ridgevale Beach in Chatham (✆ 508/432-4993): Available craft include kayaks, Sunfish, surfbikes, and sailboats up to 22 feet. Kayaks rent for $25 per hour or $39 for 2 hours, Sailboats rent for $70 to $95 for a couple hours or $125 to $175 for half a day.

Seaworthy vessels, from surf- and sailboards to paddle craft and Sunfish, can be rented from **Monomoy Sail and Cycle** at 275 Rte. 28 in North Chatham (✆ **508/945-0811**). Kayaks and sailboards rent for $45 for 24 hours. This rental location is not on the beach, so you need a car roof rack to rent here.

Pleasant Bay, the Cape's largest bay, is the best place to play for those with sufficient experience; if the winds don't go your way, try Forest Beach on the South Chatham shore.

FISHING Chatham has five ponds and lakes that permit fishing; Goose Pond off Fisherman's Landing is among the top spots. For saltwater fishing sans boat, try the fishing bridge on Bridge Street at the southern end of Mill Pond. First, though, get a license at **Town Hall** at 549 Main St. in Chatham (✆ **508/945-5101**). If you hear the deep sea calling, sign on with the *Booby Hatch* (✆ 508/430-2312; www.capecodfishingcharters.com), a 33-foot sportfishing boat, or the 31-foot *Banshee* (✆ **508/945-0403**), both berthed in Stage Harbor. Sportfishing rates average around $500 to $600 for 8 hours. Shellfishing licenses are

available at the **Permit Department** on George Ryder Road in West Chatham
(© **508/945-5180**).

GOLF   Once part of the Chatham Bars Inn property and now owned by the
town, the scenic nine-hole, par-34 **Chatham Seaside Links** at 209 Seaview St.
in Chatham (© **508/945-4774**) isn't very challenging, but is fun for neophytes;
inquire about instruction. A nine-hole round costs $15.

NATURE & WILDLIFE AREAS   Heading southeast from the Hardings
Beach parking lot, the 2-mile, round-trip **Seaside Trail** offers beautiful parallel
panoramas of Nantucket Sound and Oyster Pond River; keep an eye out for
nesting pairs of horned lark. Access to 40-acre Morris Island, southwest of the
Chatham Light, is easy: You can walk or drive across and start right in on a
marked .75-mile trail. Heed the high tides, as advised, though—they can come
in surprisingly quickly, leaving you stranded.

The **Beachcomber** ✹✹ (© **508/945-5265**) runs **seal-watching cruises** out
of Stage Harbor from mid-May to mid-October daily in season and weekends
in the shoulder seasons. Parking is behind the former Main Street School on the
left before the rotary. The cruises cost $18 for adults, $16 for seniors, $12 for
children 3 to 15, and are free for children under 3.

Chatham's natural bonanza lies southward: The uninhabited **Monomoy
Islands** ✹✹, 2,750 acres of brush-covered sand favored by some 285 species of
migrating birds, is the perfect pit stop along the Atlantic Flyway. Harbor and
gray seals are catching on, too: Hundreds now carpet the coastline from late
November through May. If you go out during that time, you won't have any
trouble seeing them—they're practically unavoidable. Both the **Wellfleet Bay
Wildlife Sanctuary,** operated by the Audubon Society (© **508/349-2615**), and
Brewster's **Cape Cod Museum of Natural History** (© **508/896-3867**) offer
guided trips. The Audubon's 3-, 4-, or 7-hour trips take place April through
November, and they cost $30 to $60 per person. The boat to Monomoy leaves
from Chatham, and the trip includes a naturalist-guided nature hike. About a
dozen times each summer, the museum organizes sleepovers in the island's only
surviving structure—a clapboard "keeper's house" flanked by an 1849 lighthouse. The cost is $200 per person (dinner and breakfast provided), and the trip
lasts from 10am until return the next day at 1pm. Reservations should be made
at least a month prior, as there is only space for six people in the three rooms.
It's just you and the birds and seals and lots of deer, plus various other species
that are harder to spot.

TENNIS   Free public courts are located near the Railroad Museum on Depot
Street and at Chatham High School on Crowell Road; for details contact the
Chatham Recreation Department (© **508/945-5100**). In addition, you may
be able to rent one of the three courts at the **Chatham Bars Inn** on Shore Road
(© **508/945-6759**), which cost $30 an hour.

CHATHAM HISTORICAL SIGHTS

Chatham Railroad Museum ✹ *Kids*   Even if you're not a railroad fanatic, it's
worth visiting this beautiful 1887 depot to imagine the sights that would greet
a Victorian visitor. To begin, the building itself is a "Railroad Gothic" work of
wooden art, topped by a tapering turret. Inside you'll find volunteers dispensing
lore and explaining the many displays. The museum's major holding is lined up
in back: a "walk-through" 1918 New York caboose.

153 Depot Rd. (off Main St., 1 block north of the rotary). No phone. Donations accepted. Mid-June to mid-
Sept Tues–Sat 10am–4pm. Closed mid-Sept to mid-June.

Mayo House For a speedy version of the historical-house tour (these can get awfully drawn out), duck into this cheerful little yellow cottage, a three-quarter Cape that has stood its ground on Main Street since 1818. Ask all the questions you like—or just zip through, admiring the needlepoint handiwork of local lasses long gone, or the economy of movement required to subsist in one of the tiny dormered bedrooms.

540 Main St. (in the center of town). ℂ **508/945-4084.** Free admission. Mid-June to Sept Tues–Thurs 11am–4pm. Closed Oct to mid-June.

The Old Atwood House Museum ⭐ For further glimpses of Chatham's past, visit this gambrel-roofed 1752 homestead, divided (rather awkwardly) into assorted wings celebrating different phases and products of the local culture. The house harbors all sorts of odd collections, from seashells to the complete works of early-20th-century author Joseph C. Lincoln, a renowned Cape writer whose hokey books are avidly collected by locals. One room definitely worth a visit is the New Gallery, featuring admirably direct portraits of crusty sea-goers by local artist Frederick Stallknecht. His work, unfortunately, was always overshadowed by the oeuvre of his mother, Alice Stallknecht Wight, who executed pretend-primitive murals of villagers enacting religious scenes (a contemporary Christ-as-fisherman, for instance, celebrating the Last Supper). Her work occupies an adjoining barn; see if you think she deserves it. By far, the most enchanting exhibit on hand is an entire 1947 fishing "camp"—a one-room old boys' club salvaged, complete with shabby furnishings, from the onslaught of the winter storms that brought about the "break" of 1987.

347 Stage Harbor Rd. (about ⅔ mile south of Main St.). ℂ **508/945-2493.** www.atwoodhouse.org. Admission $3 adults, $1 students. Mid-June to Oct Tues–Fri 1–4pm, Sat 10am–1pm. Closed Oct to mid-June.

BASEBALL

The Chatham Athletics (or "A's"), part of the **Cape Cod Baseball League,** play at Veterans Field off Depot Street. For a schedule, contact the **Chatham Chamber of Commerce** (ℂ **800/715-5567** or 508/945-5199), the **Chatham Recreation Center** (ℂ **508/945-5175**), or the **League** (ℂ **508/432-6909**).

KID STUFF

The **Play-a-Round Park** ⭐⭐ on Depot Street (see "A Stroll Around Chatham," above) will suffice to keep kids entertained for hours on end. Treat them to lunch at the quirkily casual Breakaway Cafe at the Chatham airport (perhaps followed by a sightseeing flight?). The weekly **band concerts** ⭐⭐ (ℂ **508/945-5199**) at Kate Gould Park, held Friday nights in summer, are perfectly gauged for underage enjoyment: There's usually a bunny-hop at some point in the evening. Junior connoisseurs get a chance, once a year in late July, to enjoy some really fine music, when the Monomoy Chamber Ensemble puts on a free morning children's performance at the **Monomoy Theatre** (ℂ **508/945-1589**), and musicals there are always fun.

SHOPPING

Chatham's tree-shaded Main Street, lined with specialty stores, offers a terrific opportunity to shop and stroll. The goods tend to be on the conservative side, but every so often, you'll happen upon a hedonistic delight.

ARTS & CRAFTS Headed for such prestigious outlets as Neiman Marcus, the handblown glassworks of James Holmes originate at **Chatham Glass Company,** 758 Main St., just west of the Chatham rotary (ℂ **508/945-5547**), where you can literally look over their shoulders as the pieces take shape. Luscious colors are their hallmark; the intense hues, combined with a purity of form at once traditional and cutting-edge contemporary, add up to objects that demand to be coveted.

At **Chatham Pottery,** 2058 Rte. 28, east of the intersection with Route 137 (© **508/430-2191**), striking graphics characterize the collaborative work of Gill Wilson (potter) and Margaret Wilson-Grey (glazer). Their work consists primarily of blue block print–style designs set against off-white stoneware. The most popular design may be the etched pair of swimming fish, based on sketches over 100 years old. It's a look that's somewhat addictive. Luckily, it's available in everything from platters and bowls to lamps and tiles.

One of Chatham's oldest and most respected galleries is **Wynne/Falconer Gallery,** 492 Main St., Chatham (© **508/945-2867**), which started by showing just the work of Marguerite Falconer: oil paintings of Cape Cod scenes. The gallery has been expanded to include some of the more interesting fine crafts available in town. This is a good place to look for that one-of-a-kind gift.

BOOKS   **Yellow Umbrella Bookstore,** 501 Main St., in the center of town (© **508/945-0144**), offers both new and used books (from rare volumes to paperbacks perfect for a disposable beach read). This full-service, all-ages bookstore invites protracted browsing.

Cabbages and Kings Bookstore, 628 Main St., in the center of town (© **508/945-1603**), carries books, toys, and cards. They have frequent in-store author signings as well as special events held at the Chatham Bars Inn.

FASHION   Catering to fashionable parents and their kids, ages newborn well into the teens, **The Children's Shop,** 515 Main St., in the center of town (© **508/945-0234**), is the best children's clothing store in a 100-mile radius. While according a nod to doting grannies with such classics as hand-smocked party dresses, Ginny Nickerson also stays up-to-speed on what kids themselves prefer.

The flagship store of **Puritan Clothing Company** is at 573 Main St., Chatham (© **508/945-0326**). This venerable institution, with stores all over the Cape, has updated its clothing considerably in the last 10 years. You'll find a wide range of quality men's and women's wear, including Polo, Nautica, Eileen Fisher, and Teva, at good prices.

Another Cape Cod institution, the elite **Mark, Fore & Strike** at 482 Main St., Chatham (© **508/945-0568**), offers upscale and classic men's and women's sportswear. There's also a branch in Osterville.

GIFTS/HOME DECOR   For quintessentially Cape-y gifts, stop in the **Regatta Shop,** 483 Main St., Chatham (© **508/945-4999**). It's a colorful shop with popular regional gift items like Claire Murray rugs, boat models, Wedgwood china, and the intriguing weatherglass that supposedly predicts the weather.

WHERE TO STAY

Chatham's lodging choices tend to be more expensive than those of neighboring towns, because it's considered a chichi place to vacation. But for those allergic to fussy, fancy B&Bs and inns, Chatham has several good motel options.

Practically across the street from the Chatham Bars Inn, **The Hawthorne** ✖, 196 Shore Rd. (© **508/945-0372;** www.thehawthorne.com), is a very basic, no-frills motel with one of the best locations in town: right on the water, with striking views of Chatham Harbor, Pleasant Bay, and the Atlantic Ocean. An additional perk here is phone calls (local and long distance) and Internet access are free. Rates for the 26 rooms are $165 to $195 double. The more expensive rooms are efficiencies with kitchenettes. Closed mid-October to mid-May.

Chatham Seafarer, 2079 Rte. 28 (about ½ mile east of Rte. 137), West Chatham (℃ **800/786-2772** or 508/432-1739; www.chathamseafarer.com), is a lovely, personable, well-run motel on Route 28. Though it does not have a pool, it's only about a half mile from Ridgevale Beach. Rates are $125 to $145 double.

The least expensive option is **The Chatham Motel,** 1487 Main St./Rte. 28, Chatham (℃ **800/770-5545** or 508/945-2630; www.chathammotel.com), 1½ miles from Hardings Beach. Look for the shingled motel with yellow shutters. There's an outdoor pool, shuffleboard, and plenty of BBQ grills. Summer rates in the 32 rooms are $135–$185 double, $305 suites.

VERY EXPENSIVE

Chatham Bars Inn ★★★ *Kids*   Set majestically above the beach in Chatham and commanding views out to a barrier beach and the Atlantic Ocean beyond is the grand old Chatham Bars Inn. A private hunting lodge built for a Boston family in 1914, this curved and colonnaded brick building—surrounded by 26 shingled cottages on 25 acres—has regained its glory days with recent renovations. The large and cushy lobby clearly invites lingering, as the professional staff bustles around fluffing pillows and tending to guests' every whim. The best spot to take in the grandeur—as well as the sweeping ocean views—is the breezy veranda, from where you can order a drink (make mine an old-fashioned) and recline in an Adirondack chair. From here you can admire the inn's ¼-mile private beach. Most rooms have had tasteful makeovers within the last few years, and many have private balconies with views of the beach or the prettily landscaped grounds. Some rooms also have VCR players and DVD players; the inn has a small selection of movies available to borrow for free. Cottage rooms are cheery with painted furniture and Waverly fabrics. A boat launch to Nauset Beach, a barrier beach, is available for a fee of $8 for adults, $4 for children—as is tennis and golf at the adjacent nine-hole course. For on-line habitues, the Chatham Bars Inn offers unlimited high-speed Internet access free to all rooms.

The Inn has four restaurants, the **Main Dining Room, Chef's Table & Wine Cellar,** the **Tavern,** and the **Beach House Grill.** The main dining room is a ballroom-sized formal space with distant ocean views that is open daily in season. Dinners in the dining room consist of hearty traditional fare like roasted duckling or lobster with Newberg sauce. In the intimate Chef's Table & Wine Cellar, opened in Summer 2003, diners watch Master Chefs prepare seven-course meals in an open kitchen—complete with overhead plasma screens—while sipping wines from the 6,000-bottle cellar. See the website for the special events held here.

Shore Rd. (off Seaview St., about ½ mile northwest of the town center), Chatham, MA 02633. ℃ **800/527-4884** or 508/945-0096. Fax 508/945-5491. www.chathambarsinn.com. 205 units. Summer $320–$550 double, $550–$620 1-bedroom suite, $790–$1,600 2-bedroom suite. AE, DC, MC, V. **Amenities:** 4 restaurants (the formal Main Dining Room, Chef's Table & Wine Cellar, the Tavern, and the seasonal Beach House Grill located on the beach); outdoor heated pool; putting green (Seaside Links, a 9-hole course open to the public, adjoins the resort; guests play for an $18 fee); 3 all-weather tennis courts ($15 an hour); Wellness Center offering spa and massage services and fitness equipment; complimentary children's program for ages 3½ and up, available morning through night in summer; concierge; room service (7am–10pm in season, 7am–9pm off season); babysitting. *In room:* A/C, TV/VCR, dataport, hair dryer, iron.

Wequassett Inn Resort and Golf Club ★★★   For decades, this 22-acre resort set on Pleasant Bay has been the place to go for vacationing tennis and sailing enthusiasts. Now, with the 18-hole Cape Cod National Golf Club next door, it also appeals to the golfing crowd. Inn guests enjoy exclusive nonmember privileges to this challenging course. The restaurant on-site, 28 Atlantic, was recently revamped and is now one of the Cape's top dining spots (see below). Rooms are spread out in a half dozen buildings and are uniformly spacious and comfortable. Tucked amid the woods along the shore, 15 modest dwellings, built in the 1940s, harbor roomy quarters done up in an country style. They cost a bit more than the 56 more modern "villa" rooms because of their beachfront locations. All rooms have either a balcony or a patio, and rooms for guests with disabilities are available. The calm private bay beach just steps from the rooms is called Clam Point. Chatham's North Beach is a 15-minute ride via the inn's Power Skiff (cost $12 adults, $5 children). The resort staff offers instruction in tennis (there are two pros on-site) and sailing. Complimentary van service is offered to two public golf courses, Cranberry Valley in Harwich and Captain's Course in Brewster, in addition to the Cape Cod National Golf Club. Van service is also available to Chatham village for shopping; box lunches are available on request.

2173 Rte. 28 (about 5 miles northwest of Chatham center, on Pleasant Bay), Chatham, MA 02633. ✆ 800/ 225-7125 or 508/432-5400. Fax 508/432-5032. www.wequassett.com. 104 units. Summer $340–$665 double, $600–$1,100 suites. AE, DC, DISC, MC, V. Closed Dec–Mar. **Amenities:** 2 restaurants (28 Atlantic for fine dining and Outer Bar and Grille for casual fare, both open to the public); golf course next door ($105 a round plus $20 for a cart); pear-shaped heated outdoor pool; 4 all-weather Plexipave tennis courts (additional fee, $15 an hour per person) plus a pro shop; fitness room (with new machines and weights); rental bikes ($20 to $40 per day) and watersports equipment (sailboards, Sunfish, Daysailers, and Hobie Cats) for about $40 an hour; free horseshoes, basketball, and volleyball equipment; Children's Fun Club, $25 for half day, $45 for full day; concierge; room service (daily 7am–10pm); yoga and massage; secretarial and babysitting services available; yoga and pilates classes for $15. *In room:* A/C, TV, minibar, coffeemaker, hair dryer, iron.

EXPENSIVE

Captain's House Inn ★★★ *Finds*   This 1839 Greek Revival house—along with a cottage and a carriage house—set on 2 meticulously maintained acres is a shining example of its era and style. The hospitality and amenities here make this one of the top B&Bs on Cape Cod. The rooms, named for clipper ships, are richly furnished, with canopied four-posters, beamed ceilings, and brick hearths. The inn provides a wonderful array of extras, like robes, bottled water, newspapers, early morning coffee, and room service. Many rooms have mini-fridges and Jacuzzis. Breakfast is served at noncommunal tables (a thoughtful touch for those of us slow to rev up, sociability-wise), and the window-walled breakfast room is also the site of a traditional tea—presided over by innkeeper Jan McMasters, formerly of Bournemouth in Great Britain, who knows how to pour a proper cuppa. Light lunches can be enjoyed poolside for an extra charge. Be sure to book your room well in advance.

369–377 Old Harbor Rd. (about ½ mile north of the rotary), Chatham, MA 02633. ✆ 800/315-0728 or 508/ 945-0127. Fax 508/945-0866. www.captainshouseinn.com. 16 units (14 tub/shower, 2 shower only). Summer $235–$425 double. Rates include full breakfast and afternoon tea. AE, DISC, MC, V. **Amenities:** Outdoor heated pool; exercise room. *In room:* A/C, TV/VCR, dataport, coffeemaker, hair dryer, iron.

Chatham Wayside Inn ★★   Centrally located on Chatham's Main Street, this former stagecoach stop, dating from 1860, has undergone a thoroughly modern renovation. Don't expect any musty antique trappings: it's lush carpeting, a warehouse worth of Waverly fabrics, and polished reproduction furnishings, including four-posters. There's an outdoor heated pool in the back. The restaurant serves sophisticated New American fare, indoors and out, and the prize rooms boast patios or balconies overlooking the town bandstand. This is one of the few inns on the Cape with rooms and a restaurant fully accessible to travelers with disabilities.

512 Main St. (in the center of town), Chatham, MA 02633. ✆ 800/391-5734 or 508/945-5550. Fax 508/945-3407. www.waysideinn.com. 56 units. Summer $185–$295 double, $325–$375 suite; off-season packages available. DISC, MC, V. **Amenities:** Restaurant/bar; outdoor heated pool. *In room:* A/C, TV/VCR, hair dryer, iron.

Pleasant Bay Village ★★ Across the street from Pleasant Bay, a few minutes' walk from Pleasant Bay beach, this is one fancy motel (with prices set accordingly). Owner Howard Gamsey is a prodigious gardener: Over the past 25 years, he has transformed this property into a playful Zen paradise, where waterfalls (five) cascade through colorful rock gardens into a stone-edged pool dotted with lily pads and flashing koi. Actually, he has poured that kind of attention into the entire 6-acre complex. The rooms and cottages, done in restful pastels, are unusually pleasant. Many bathrooms feature marble countertops and stone floors. Howard is an art collector, and all rooms display wonderful pieces he has picked up at Wellfleet's finest galleries. The suites have fully-equipped kitchens, including microwave ovens, as well as two televisions, one with a VCR. The breakfast room (extra charge) features antique kilims, crewel curtains, and antique tables. In summer, you can order lunch from the grill without having to leave your place at the heated pool. Teens love the game room here, complete with pinball machines.

1191 Orleans Rd./Rte. 28 (about 3 miles north of Chatham center), Chatham Port, MA 02633. © 800/547-1011 or 508/945-1133. Fax 508/945-9701. www.pleasantbayvillage.com. 58 units. Summer $135–$275 double, $295–$455 1- or 2-bedroom suite (for 4 occupants). AE, MC, V. Closed Nov–Apr. **Amenities:** Restaurant (breakfast; July–Aug lunch by the pool and dinner); heated pool and 8-person hot tub. *In room:* A/C, TV, dataport, fridge, hair dryer, iron.

MODERATE

The Cyrus Kent House Inn ★ Built in 1877, when sea captains lived like modern-day software moguls, this tall Victorian beauty was lavished with the latest in fancy fixings, including marble fireplaces (in both the butterscotch-yellow parlor and the wainscoted dining room) and a heavy helping of decorative plasterwork. Rooms, with very high ceilings, have canopy beds and are elegantly decorated with antiques. Fireplaces grace each of the slightly more modern carriage-house suites, rendered light and airy by a lofty Palladian window on the top floor and, below, French doors that give onto the garden. You'll find an open hearth in the lovely country kitchen. In the morning, an elaborate continental breakfast (perhaps hot fruit compote, oatmeal brûlée, or baked French toast) is served at individual tables set with Limoges china and sterling silver. Innkeepers Sandra and Steve Goldman have worked hard on recent renovations, improvements, and landscaping.

63 Cross St. (1 block south of Main St. in the center of town), Chatham, MA 02633. © 800/338-5368 or tel/fax 508/945-6104. www.cyruskent.com. 10 units (6 tub/shower, 4 shower only). Summer $155–$195 double, $245 suite, $345 2-bedroom suite. Rates include continental breakfast. AE, DISC, MC, V. No children under 10. *In room:* A/C, TV/VCR, hair dryer.

The Dolphin of Chatham ★ *Value* With an 1805 main inn building, motel units, and several cottages, The Dolphin offers a wide range of lodging options in the heart of Chatham. Even on exquisitely groomed Main Street, this property's extensive and colorful gardens stand out. The main inn has seven individually decorated rooms with romantic touches like beamed ceilings, canopied beds, and lacy curtains. These rooms tend to be smaller than the motel rooms, which are in an adjacent building. There is also a honeymoon suite, which is housed in a whimsical windmill. Several rooms have Jacuzzis. The inn has a bar and restaurant, Martini's with a Twist, serving fixed price dinners. The best seats are on the screened porch from which guests can watch the world go by on Main Street. Lighthouse Beach is a pleasant stroll away.

352 Main St. (at the east end of Main St.), Chatham, MA 02633-2428. © 800/688-5900 or 508/945-0070. Fax 508/945-5945. www.dolphininn.com. 34 units, 3 cottages. Summer $169–$220 double, $230–$285 2-bedroom suite, $2,000 weekly cottages. Rates include continental breakfast. AE, DC, DISC, MC, V. Open year-round.

Amenities: Restaurant (Martini's serves dinner only); 2 bars (including pool bar for lunch and drinks); outdoor heated pool; 10-person hot tub. *In room:* A/C, TV, fax, fridge, coffeemaker, hair dryer, iron.

The Moorings Bed and Breakfast ★★
This is a charming, well-run property on the east end of Chatham's Main Street. Whether you end up in the main house, a Victorian beauty built by Adm. Charles H. Rockwell, or the individualized units in the carriage houses in the back, you'll enjoy a full breakfast in the gazebo surrounded by flower gardens. Several rooms in the carriage houses are spacious, with kitchenettes and private decks or courtyards. Some rooms have VCRs, irons, and mini-fridges. All are immaculate and quaintly decorated, joined by a central courtyard area and porches lined with rocking chairs. In addition, everything you need to enjoy Chatham's winding roads and beautiful beaches is provided: bikes, beach chairs, and umbrellas.

326 Main St. (at the east end of Main St.), Chatham, MA 02633. © **800/320-0848** or 508/945-0848. www. mooringscapecod.com. 15 units, 1 cottage (14 tub/shower; 2 shower only). Summer $148–$215 double, $230–$235 suite, $2,200 weekly cottage. Rates include full breakfast. DISC, MC, V. **Amenities:** Loaner bikes. *In room:* A/C, TV, hair dryer.

Moses Nickerson House ★ *Value*
Your host George "I am not Moses" Watts and his wife Linda run this gem of a B&B with a sense of humor mixed with gracious hospitality. A grand captain's home in the classicist style, this 1839 manse's every inch is devoted to stylish comfort. Whether you opt for a canopied bed with freshly scented linens or a ruggedly handsome, hunt club–style room, rest assured you'll be pampered—with a home-baked breakfast served in the garden-view solarium, and later a late-afternoon pick-me-up in the dazzling parlor, which is mostly white, with glints of vintage cranberry glass.

364 Old Harbor Rd. (about ½ mile north of Main St.), Chatham, MA 02633. © **800/628-6972** or 508/945-5859. Fax 508/945-7087. www.mosesnickersonhouse.com. 7 units (1 tub/shower; 6 shower only). Summer $149–$209 double. Rates include full breakfast and afternoon tea. AE, DISC, MC, V. *In room:* A/C, TV, dataport, hair dryer.

Port Fortune Inn ★
This classic shingled cottage is just a short stroll from Lighthouse Beach, and the prime beach-y location sets it apart. The cheerful name comes from explorer Samuel de Champlain, who named this area Port Fortune when he landed in Chatham in 1606. A couple of the spacious, traditionally decorated rooms have water views, and all have queen beds, some of them four-poster. Many rooms have fridges. Breakfast with an ocean view is served in the front building, which also has a few rooms upstairs that share the view.

201 Main St. (on the shore, near Chatham Light), Chatham, MA 02633. © **800/750-0792** or 508/945-0792. Fax 508/945-0792. www.portfortuneinn.com. 12 units (10 tub/shower; 2 shower only). Summer $155–$215 double, $265 suite. Rates include continental breakfast. AE, DISC, MC, V. No children under 12. *In room:* A/C, TV, dataport, hair dryer, iron.

WHERE TO DINE
EXPENSIVE
The Blue Coral ★ NEW AMERICAN
This new restaurant features "seaside cuisine" on an outdoor courtyard just off Main Street. Specialties include the three-pound lobster dinner with all the fixins', and sushi-grade blue fin tuna pan-seared with balsamic demi-glaze. One of the most popular dishes is the lobster ravioli served with a brandy cream sauce. There's live entertainment in the form of jazz and blues on Thursday through Sunday nights in season. This place gets a big crowd on clear nights, so come early or late.

483 Main Street, Chatham. © **508/348-0485**. Reservations accepted. $18–$40. AE, DISC, MC, V. 11:30am–2:30pm and 5–10pm. Closed late Sept to late June.

RooBar ★★ NEW AMERICAN   Like its sister restaurants in Hyannis and Falmouth, this new RooBar in Chatham has quickly become the place to see and be seen. Somehow the owners have turned a former Friendly's Restaurant into a sleek and stylish venue that features a garden patio area as well as a welcoming bar. The food and service here are top notch. The menu offers a wide range of options, from seafood specialties like seafood jambalaya or fine meat dishes, like herb-grilled Delmonico. You may also opt for a brick-oven pizza like the spicy prawn or the barbeque chicken. The only downside to this restaurant is it's not on Chatham's main drag with all the other shops and restaurants. It's a short drive (about a mile) away.

907 Main Street, Chatham. ✆ 508/945-9988. Reservations accepted. $17–$28. AE, MC, V. Daily 5–10pm. Open year-round.

28 Atlantic ★★★ NEW AMERICAN   A major renovation has turned this restaurant on the grounds of the Wequasett Inn resort into one of the top places to eat on Cape Cod. The elegant spacious dining room overlooks Pleasant Bay through immense floor-to-ceiling glass panels. Service is professional and stylish. And the food stands out as superb, from the *amuse bouche* (a little taste teaser) offered at the start of the meal, to the exceptional desserts served at the end. Menu items use local provender as much as possible, but there are also delicacies from around the world. You might start with the Cape lobster and roasted corn bisque with sherried Devonshire cream; move on to the composed salad of mache, melon, prosciutto, grapes, goat cheese mousse, and tawny port syrup; and then get to your main course, perhaps skillet-seared local bluefish with saffron smoked mussel risotto, wilted Swiss chard, and lobster oil. You're in for a treat here; it's all exquisite.

2173 Rte. 28 (at the Wequasett Inn, about 5 miles northwest of Chatham center, on Pleasant Bay). ✆ 508/430-3000. www.wequasett.com. Reservations recommended. Main courses $21–$44. AE, DC, DISC, MC, V. May–Nov daily 7am–10pm; call for off-season hours. Closed Dec–Mar.

MODERATE

Chatham Squire ★★ *Finds* AMERICAN   The Chatham Squire is the unofficial center of Chatham where generations of summer residents mix with the year-rounders: fishermen and landed gentry. The surprise is that this quintessential Cape Cod pub has the best clam chowder in these parts. It turns out the Squire gets their clams from the elite clam beds off Monomoy, cultivated in pristine water and considered the freshest around. The menu also features pasta (zebra ravioli is filled with lobster meat) and barbecued baby back ribs (with the Squire's secret sauce), among other dishes.

487 Main St. (in the center of town). ✆ 508/945-0945. Main courses $11–$23. AE, DISC, MC, V. Sun–Thurs 11:30am–10pm; Fri–Sat 11:30–10:30; call for off-season hours (Nov–Apr).

Chatham Wayside Inn ★ NEW AMERICAN   The Wayside's central location on Main Street makes it a good spot for a reasonably priced meal in Chatham. Diners have several seating choices depending on their mood (and the weather): the clubby tavern with gleaming wood tables surrounded by comfy Windsor chairs, the front room with cozy booths, or the large screened terrace, perfect during summer's dog days. More important, perhaps, is what's on the plate. Wayside specialties include crab cakes, or entrees like rack of lamb and pesto cod. For something a little different, try the chowder; it's prepared Portuguese-style with double-smoked bacon, fresh quahogs, and red bliss potatoes. Whether it's summer or winter, you'll want to end your meal with the apple-and-cranberry crisp; the secret is the oatmeal and brown-sugar crust. The Wayside is an even better choice at lunchtime, when the terrace is the perfect spot to watch Main Street's parade of shoppers.

512 Main St. (in the center of town). ℂ 508/945-5550. Main courses $16–$25. DISC, MC, V. May–Oct daily 8–11am, 11:30am–4pm, and 5–9pm; Nov–Apr Tues–Sun 8–11am, 11:30am–4pm, and 5–9pm. Closed Jan.

Christian's ✦ NEW AMERICAN   Upstairs in the bar area or outside deck are the best places to eat at this popular boîte owned by the Chatham Wayside Inn. The atmosphere in the downstairs dining room, which is only open in season, is definitely more staid. But the upstairs is British clubby, with leather couches, mahogany paneling, a piano bar, and a smattering of classic movie posters. The same cinematic-motif menu applies to both venues: Famous movie titles are accorded to such specialties as prawns sautéed in olive oil with garlic, shallots, spinach, and mushrooms over Florentine gnocchi—aka Forrest Gump. Upstairs in the bar or on the outside deck, you can also order small pizzas, burgers, and fries.

443 Main St. (in the center of town). ℂ 508/945-3362. Reservations accepted only between Memorial Day and Columbus Day for downstairs tables. Main courses $14–$30. DISC, MC, V. Late May to mid-Oct daily 5–10pm; call for off-season hours. Open year-round.

The Impudent Oyster ✦ INTERNATIONAL   All but hidden off the main drag, this perennially popular 1970s-era eatery—complete with decorative stained glass—continues to cook up fabulous fish in exotic guises, ranging from Mexican to Szechuan, but mostly Continental. The flavorful specialties of the house are the *sole picatta* (native sole with lemon, fresh herb, and caper butter sauce), the steak *au poivre*, and *the pesca fra diablo* (local littlenecks, lobster, and other seafood simmered in a spicy sauce over fettuccine). A tavern menu is served at the bar from 3 to 5pm with soup, salads, raw bar, chicken fingers, and burgers. There is also a children's menu. This place is very busy in the summer and if you don't make a reservation, you may be out of luck.

15 Chatham Bars Ave. (off Main St., in the center of town). ℂ 508/945-3545. Reservations recommended. Main courses $14–$20. AE, MC, V. Mon–Thurs 11:30am–3pm and 5–9:30pm; Fri–Sat 11:30am–3pm and 5–10pm; Sun noon–3pm and 5–9:30pm.

Vining's Bistro ✦✦ *Finds* FUSION   If you're looking for cutting-edge cuisine in a sophisticated setting, venture upstairs at Chatham's innocuous-looking mini-mal and into this ineffably cool cafe. The film-noirish wall murals suggest a certain bohemian abandon, but the food is up-to-the-minute and priced to suit young people. The menu offers compelling juxtapositions such as the warm lobster tacos with salsa fresca and crème fraîche, or the spit-roasted chicken suffused with achiote-lime marinade and sided with a salad of oranges and jicama. These creative choices are reason enough to return here.

595 Main St. (in the center of town). ℂ 508/945-5033. Reservations not accepted. Main courses $16–$24. AE, DC, MC, V. June to mid-Oct daily 5:30–9:45pm; call for off-season hours. Closed Jan–Mar.

INEXPENSIVE

Carmine's Pizza ✦ ITALIAN   A new-wave pizzeria that pays homage to the old ways with checkered tablecloths and soda-parlor chairs, this little eatery takes a bold approach to toppings—for example, pineapple, jalapeños, and pesto. A favorite is the Californian, with garlic, feta cheese, spinach, sautéed mushrooms and onions, plum tomato, artichoke, and Kalamata olives. Cool down with creamy gelato.

595 Main St. (in the center of town). ℂ 508/945-5300. Pizzas: $10–$19. MC, V. May–Sept daily 10am–11pm; call for off-season hours. Closed Jan–Mar.

A PIE SHOP

Marion's Pie Shop ⭐ *Finds*   Nearly a half-century's worth of summer visitors have come to depend on this bakery for dinner and dessert pies, from sea clam to lemon meringue. Load up on the fruit breads and sweet rolls, and you can pretend you're having a four-course B&B breakfast—on the beach.

2022 Rte. 28 (about ½ mile east of Rte. 137). ℂ **508/432-9439.** Mon–Sat 7am–6pm; Sun 7am–2pm.

FRESH SEAFOOD

Nickerson Fish & Lobster ⭐   The fish have to travel all of 50 yards from the boat, so you can imagine how fresh they are. And you don't need a kitchen to partake: They sell homemade *quahog* (giant clam) chowder and precooked frozen entrees to go.

Chatham Fish Pier, Shore Rd. ℂ **508/945-0145.** Daily 9am–6pm. Closed mid-Oct to late May.

SWEETS

Chatham Candy Manor ⭐ *Kids*   Normally, I cross the street to avoid this type of temptation, but Naomi Turner's hand-dipped chocolates (her mother opened the shop in the 1940s) are just too good to pass up. Surely there can't be anything too terribly harmful in an occasional "cranberry cordial" or chocolate-dipped strawberry, right? But once you start perusing the old-fashioned oak cases, it can be very hard to stop. Turtles, truffles, and the homemade fudge are tops. Children line up to watch them make candy canes here at Christmastime.

484 Main St. (in the center of town). ℂ **800/221-6497** or **508/945-0825.** June–Aug 9am–10pm; Sept–May 9am–6pm.

CHATHAM AFTER DARK

While most towns boast some comparable event, Chatham's free **band concerts**— 40 players strong—are arguably the best on the Cape and attract crowds in the thousands. This is small-town America at its most nostalgic, as the band, made up mostly of local folks, plays those standards of yesteryear that never go out of style. Held in Kate Gould Park (off Chatham Bars Ave., in the center of town) from July to early September, it kicks off at 8pm every Friday. Better come early to claim your square of lawn (it's already a checkerboard of blankets by late afternoon), and be prepared to sing—or dance—along. Call ℂ **508/945-5199** for information.

PERFORMANCE ARTS

Monomoy Theatre   Every summer since 1958, the Ohio University Players have commuted to this jewel box of a 1930s theater to put on a challenging play a week, from musicals to Shakespeare. In late July, they take a well-earned week off to cede the stage to the highly accomplished Monomoy Chamber Ensemble. Performances take place mid-June to August, Tuesday to Saturday at 8pm and Thursday matinee at 2. Closed September to mid-June. 776 Rte. 28 (about ¼ mile west of the rotary). ℂ **508/945-1589.** Tickets $15–$26.

BARS & LIVE MUSIC

The Chatham Squire   A great leveler, this local institution attracts patrons from all the social strata in town. CEOs, seafarers, and college students alike convene to kibitz over the roar of a jukebox or band (Fri–Sat off season) and their own hubbub. Good pub grub, too (see above). 487 Main St. (in the center of town). ℂ **508/945-0942.** No cover.

Upstairs at Christian's   Beloved of moneyed locals, this sporting piano bar has the air of a vintage frat house—it summons up young scions gracefully slumming it among scuffed leather couches and purloined movie posters. The live music is offered nightly in season and weekends year-round. Cinematically themed nibbles are always available to offset the generous movie-motif drinks. Piano music begins at 7pm. 443 Main St. (in the center of town). © **508/945-3362.** No cover.

4 Orleans ★★

31 miles E of Sandwich; 25 miles S of Provincetown

Orleans is where the *Narrow Land* (the early Algonquin name for the Cape) starts to get very narrow indeed: From here on up—or "down," in paradoxical local parlance—it's never more than a few miles wide from coast to coast, and in some spots it's as little as 1 mile. All three main roads (routes 6, 6A, and 28) converge here, too, so on summer weekends, it acts as a rather frustrating funnel.

But this is also where the oceanside beaches open up into a glorious expanse some 40 miles long, framed by dramatic dunes and blessed—from a swimmer's or boarder's perspective—with serious surf. The thousands of ship crews who crashed on these shoals over the past 4 centuries could hardly be expected to assume so sanguine a view. Shipwrecks may sound like the stuff of romance, but in these frigid waters, hitting a sandbar usually spelled a death sentence for all involved. So enamored were local inhabitants by the opportunity to salvage that some improved their odds by becoming *mooncussers*—praying for cloudy skies and luring ships toward shore by tying a lantern to the tail of a donkey, so as to simulate the listing of a ship at sea.

Such dark deeds seem very far removed from the Orleans of today, a sedate town that shadows Hyannis as a year-round center of commerce. Lacking the cohesiveness of smaller towns, and somewhat chopped up by the roadways coursing through, it's not the most ideal town to hang out in, despite some appealing restaurants and shops. The village of East Orleans, however, is fast emerging as a sweet little off-beach town with allure for both families and singles. About 2 miles east is seemingly endless (nearly 10 miles long) Nauset Beach, the southernmost stretch of the Cape Cod National Seashore preserve, and a magnet for the young and the buff.

ESSENTIALS

GETTING THERE After crossing the Sagamore bridge (see "Getting There" in chapter 2), head east on Route 6 or 6A, which converges with Route 28 in Orleans. Or fly into Hyannis (see "Getting There" in chapter 2).

VISITOR INFORMATION Contact the **Orleans Chamber of Commerce,** 44 Main St. (P.O. Box 153), Orleans, MA 02653 (© **800/865-1386** or 508/255-1386; www.capecod-orleans.com), open year-round Monday through Friday from 9am to 2pm; or the **Cape Cod Chamber of Commerce** (see "Visitor Information" in the "Brewster" section, earlier in this chapter). There's an **information booth** at the corner of Route 6A and Eldredge Parkway (© **508/240-2484**). Its hours are early June to mid-October, Monday through Saturday from 10am to 6pm and Sunday from 11am to 3pm. Closed mid-October to mid-May.

BEACHES & RECREATIONAL PURSUITS

BEACHES From here on up, on the eastern side you're dealing with the wild and whimsical Atlantic, which can be kittenish one day and tigerish the next. While storms may whip up surf you can actually take a board to, less confident swimmers should definitely wait a few days until the turmoil and riptides subside. In any case, current conditions are clearly posted at the entrance. Week-long parking permits ($40 for renters; $135 seasonal sticker for transients) may be obtained from **Town Hall** on School Road (② **508/240-3775**). Day-trippers who arrive early enough—better make that before 10am on weekends in July and August—can pay at the gate (② **508/240-3780**).

- **Nauset Beach** ⭐⭐⭐, in East Orleans (② **508/240-3780**): Stretching southward all the way past Chatham, this 10-mile-long barrier beach, which is part of the Cape Cod National Seashore but is managed by the town, has long been one of the Cape's gonzo beach scenes—good surf, big crowds, lots of young people. Full facilities, including a terrific snack bar complete with fried fish offerings, can be found within the 1,000-car parking lot; the in-season fee is $10 per car, which is also good for same-day parking at Skaket Beach (see below). Substantial waves make for good surfing in the special section reserved for that purpose, and boogie boards are ubiquitous. In July and August, there are concerts from 7 to 9pm in the gazebo.
- **Skaket Beach** ⭐, off Skaket Beach Road to the west of town (② **508/255-0572**): This peaceful bay beach is a better choice for families with young children. When the tide recedes (as much as a mile), little kids will enjoy splashing about in the tide pools left behind. Parking costs $10, and you'd better turn up early.
- **Pilgrim Lake** ⭐, off Monument Road about 1 mile south of Main Street: This small freshwater beach is covered by a lifeguard in season. You must have a beach parking sticker.
- **Crystal Lake** ⭐, off Monument Road about ¾ mile south of Main Street: Parking—if you can find a space—is free, but there are no facilities.

BICYCLING Orleans presents the one slight gap in the 25-mile off-road **Cape Cod Rail Trail** ⭐⭐⭐ (② **508/896-3491**): Just east of the Brewster border, the trail merges with town roads for about 1½ miles. The best way to avoid vehicular aggravation and fumes is to zigzag west to scenic Rock Harbor. Bike rentals are available at **Orleans Cycle** at 26 Main St. in the center of town (② **508/255-9115**), which charges $18 for a full day rental, and there are several good places (see "Takeout & Picnic Fare," later in this chapter) to grab some comestibles.

BOATING You can rent a canoe (see below) and paddle around Town Cove, Little Pleasant Bay (to Sampson Island, to Hog Island, and to Pochet Island), and the body of water called simply The River. Experienced paddlers can paddle through Pleasant Bay to the inside shore of the Outer Beach.

Arey's Pond Sailing School, off Route 28 in South Orleans (② **508/255-7900**), offers sailing lessons on Daysailers, Catboats, and Rhode 19s in season on Little Pleasant Bay. Individual lessons are $60 per hour; weekly group lessons are around $160 to $250. The **Goose Hummock Outdoor Center** at 15 Rte. 6A, south of the rotary (② **508/255-2620;** www.goose.com), rents out canoes, kayaks, and more, and the northern half of Pleasant Bay is the perfect place to use them; inquire about guided excursions. Canoe and kayak rentals are $55 per

---

Fun Fact **Rock Harbor**

Yes, those are trees in the middle of the harbor at Rock Harbor; and no, they are not live trees. For decades, dead trees have been erected in the harbor in order to mark the channel. At sunset, the row of narrow trees silhouetted against the horizon makes a pretty picture.

day or $175 per week. A 4-hour guided trip called the Nauset Marsh Tour is $55 per person.

FISHING Fishing is allowed in Baker Pond, Pilgrim Lake, and Crystal Lake; the third is a likely spot to reel in trout and perch. For details and a license, visit **Town Hall** at Post Office Square in the center of town (© **508/240-3700**, ext. 305) or **Goose Hummock** (see above). Surf-casting—no license needed—is permitted on Nauset Beach South, off Beach Road. **Rock Harbor** ★★, a former packet landing on the bay (about 1¼ miles northwest of the town center), shelters New England's largest sportfishing fleet: some 18 boats at last count. One call (© **800/287-1771** in MA, or 508/255-9757) will get you information on them all. Or go look them over. Rock Harbor charter prices range from $450 for 4 hours to $700 for 8 hours. Individual prices are also available ($115 per person for 4 hr.; $140 per person for 8 hr.).

FITNESS If you're here for a while and need a place to stay in shape on rainy days, check out **Willy's Gym, Fitness, and Wellness Center** at 21 Old Colony Way at Orleans Marketplace (© **508/255-6826**). The Cape's biggest (21,000 sq. ft.) exercise facility is air-conditioned and open year-round. Dozens of classes are offered weekly, from basic aerobics to tai chi and Indonesian martial arts. Willy's also provides child care. Day passes are $17.

HORSEBACK RIDING The small farm **Black Sand Stable** at 36 Bakers Pond Rd. (© **508/255-7185**) is one of the only places still offering horseback riding in the area. Trail rides through Nickerson State Park take 1 to 1½ hours and cost $50. Pony rides, hayrides, and carriage rides are also available.

ICE-SKATING Orleans boasts a massive municipal rink, the **Charles Moore Arena** on O'Connor Way, off Eldredge Park Way, about 1 mile southwest of town center (© **508/255-2971**). In season, it's open to the public Tuesday, Wednesday, and Thursday 2 to 4pm; Sunday 5 to 7pm. From September through March, it's open to the public Monday and Wednesday from 11am to 1pm, Thursday from 3:30 to 5pm, and Sunday from 2 to 4pm. Friday night is "Rock Nite" for party animals ages 9 through 14. The cost is $5 adults, $4 children 12 and under; skate rentals run $2.

NATURE & WILDLIFE AREAS Inland there's not much, but on the Atlantic shore is a biggie: **Nauset Beach.** Once you get past the swarms of people near the parking lot, you'll have about 9 miles of beach mostly to yourself. You'll see lots of birds (take a field guide) and perhaps some harbor seals off season.

TENNIS Hard-surface public courts are located at the Nauset Middle School in Eldredge Park on a first-come, first-served basis; for details, contact the **Orleans Recreation Department** (© **508/240-3785**).

WATERSPORTS The **Pump House Surf Co.** at 9 Cranberry Hwy./Rte. 6A (© **508/240-2226**) rents and sells wet suits, body boards, and surfboards, while providing up-to-date reports on where to find the best waves. **Nauset Sports** at Jeremiah Square, Route 6A at the rotary (© **508/255-4742**), also rents surfboards, boogie boards, skim boards, kayaks, and wet suits.

HISTORICAL MUSEUMS

French Transatlantic Cable Station Museum ★ This ordinary-looking house was, from 1890 to 1940, a nexus of intercontinental communications. Connected to France via a huge cable laid across the ocean floor, local operators bore the responsibility of relaying stock-market data, keeping tabs on World War

I troops, and receiving the joyous news of Lindbergh's 1927 crossing. Service was discontinued with the German invasion of France in 1940, and resumed briefly between 1952 and 1959, when newer, automated technologies rendered the facility obsolete. The exhibits, prepared with the assistance of the Smithsonian, are a bit technical for nonscientists, but there are docents on hand who will patiently fill in the blanks.

41 Rte. 28 (corner of Cove Rd., north of Main St.). ℭ **508/240-1735**. Free admission. July–Sept Mon–Sat 1–4pm; June Fri–Sun 1–4pm. Closed Oct–May.

Jonathan Young Windmill (Kids) The majestic old windmill in Cove Park (next to Town Cove) has been authentically restored and is open for guided tours in season. Though it is no longer grinding corn and barley, the mill's works are fully operable. Most mills on the Cape have been moved many times from town to town, and the Orleans mill has certainly seen more than its share of relocations. The mill was built in the early 1700s in South Orleans. In 1839, it was moved to Orleans center and then to Hyannisport. In 1983, it was moved back to Orleans and donated to the Orleans Historical Society. Some of the guides at the mill are actual millers, who give visitors an entertaining spiel about the millwrights (the men who built the mills and kept the gears in working order) and millers (who ground the corn) who have worked at this mill over the centuries.

Rte. 6A (just south of the rotary). ℭ **508/240-1329**. Free admission; donations accepted. Late June to Aug daily 11am–4pm; call for off-season hours.

Orleans Historical Society at The Meeting House Museum ★ Other towns may have fancier facilities to house their historical societies, but few have quite so colorful a history as Orleans—the only town on the Cape with a non-English, non-native name. Upon separating from Eastham in 1797, Orleans assumed the name of an honored guest: future king Louis-Philippe de Bourbon, duke of Orleans, who safely sat out the Revolution abroad, earning his living as a French tutor. Not that all remained quiet on these shores either: Orleans suffered British naval attacks during the War of 1812 and German submarine fire in 1918. You'll find a great many mementos in this 1833 Greek Revival church, along with assorted artifacts—from arrowheads to hand-hewn farm tools—and a thinly veiled terrorist threat, dated 1814, from a British captain offering to spare the town's saltworks in Rock Harbor for a paltry $1,000. The townspeople balked, a warship struck, and the home team triumphed in the Battle of Orleans. Though the displays are far from jazzy, a great many have interesting stories attached and could spark an urge to learn more. Head over to Rock Harbor to see a gold-medal, award-winning Coast Guard rescue boat. Shipwreck items from the wreck of the *Pendleton* tanker in 1952 were installed by the Historical Society as an additional exhibit.

3 River Rd. (at Main St., about 1 mile east of the town center). ℭ **508/240-1329**. Donation $2. July–Aug Thurs–Sat 10am–1pm; off season by appointment.

BASEBALL

The Orleans Cardinals, the easternmost team in the **Cape Cod Baseball League,** play at Eldredge Park (off Eldredge Park Way between routes 6A and 28). For a schedule, call the **Orleans Chamber of Commerce** (ℭ **800/865-1386** or 508/255-1386), the **Orleans Recreation Department** (ℭ **508/240-3785**), or the **League** (ℭ **508/432-6909**).

KID STUFF

The **Charles Moore Arena** (see "Ice-Skating," above) offers respite from a rainy day. Young skaters—and anxious parents—might be interested to know that the

Nauset Regional Middle School in Eldredge Park has its own **skateboard park,** with four ramps and a "fun box"; helmets are required.

SHOPPING

Though shops are somewhat scattered, Orleans is full of great finds for browsers and grazers.

ANTIQUES/COLLECTIBLES   Got an old house in need of illumination, or a new one in want of some style? You'll find some 400 vintage light fixtures at **Continuum Antiques,** 7 S. Orleans Rd., Route 28, south of the junction with Route 6A (© **508/255-8513**), from Victorian on down, along with a smattering of old advertising signs and venerable duck decoys.

Deborah Rita, proprietor of **Countryside Antiques,** 6 Lewis Rd., south of Main Street in the center of East Orleans (© **508/240-0525**), roams the world in search of stylish furnishings, mostly old, though age—and price—are evidently no object.

ARTS & CRAFTS   As a publicist, Helen Addison has forged friendships with some of the most interesting artists now working on the Cape. Her gallery, **Addison Art Gallery,** 43 Rte. 28, north of Main Street (© **508/255-6200**), represents such diverse artists as Lois Griffel of Provincetown, whose luminous oils and watercolors typify "Cape Cod Impressionism"; and Gary Gilmartin of Truro, a realist working in egg tempera and watercolor, who paints Cape-inspired subjects.

Stop by **Kemp Pottery,** 9 Cranberry Hwy./Rte. 6A, about ¼ mile south of the rotary (© **508/255-5853**), and check out Steve Kemp's turned and slab-built creations. From soup tureens to fanciful sculptures, they're remarkably colorful and one of a kind.

Tree's Place, Route 6A at the intersection of Route 28, Orleans (© **888/255-1330** or 508/255-1330), is considered the premier gallery for contemporary realist work in the region. There is also an extensive fine crafts, gift, and tile shop here.

BOOKS   In the Skaket Corners shopping center on Route 6A is a branch of the large retailer **Booksmith/Musicsmith** (© **508/255-4590**).

FASHION   Karol Richardson, 47 Main St., in the center of town (© **508/255-3944**), is a preview of Richardson's main showroom in Wellfleet; stop in to see the latest from this gifted ex-Londoner.

GIFTS   Birders will go batty over **Bird Watcher's General Store,** 36 Rte. 6A, south of the rotary (© **800/562-1512** or 508/255-6974). The brainchild of local aficionado Mike O'Connor, who'd like everyone to share his passion, it stocks virtually every bird-watching accessory under the sun, from basic binoculars to costly telescopes, modest birdhouses to birdbaths fit for a tiny Roman emperor. Recorded bird song trills through the rafters, and, in addition to CDs and field guides to take home, the store offers hundreds of bird-motif gifts, from mobiles to mugs.

The tasteful selections—tapes, books, jewelry, clothing, and more—found in **Oceana,** 1 Main St. Sq., north of Main Street, in the center of town (© **508/240-1414**), celebrate the myriad gifts of nature.

WHERE TO STAY
MODERATE

A Little Inn on Pleasant Bay ★★ *Finds*   What a welcoming, beautifully situated place! Set back from a winding road that follows the coast between Orleans and Chatham, A Little Inn on Pleasant Bay sits on a hill next to a cranberry bog and overlooks the water (Pleasant Bay, naturally). The sprawling grounds are a riot of colorful, creeping flowers. The four rooms in the peaceful main house, which dates to 1798, have been completely renovated in warm tiles, light woods, and subtle colors that reflect a sort of Zen–Pottery Barn aesthetic. An adjacent building, called the "Paddock," has three additional rooms. There is also a two-bedroom suite. Breakfast (served outside overlooking either the garden or the bay) is an extravagant affair; the spread of pastries, yogurt, muesli, cereals, fresh fruits, and assorted meats and cheeses feels vaguely European. Innkeepers Bernd and Sandra are happy to help with whale-watching reservations; both are also an excellent source for local restaurant recommendations. Pictures posted in the kitchen chronicle the "wildlife" spotted on the grounds—chief among them the resident Yorkie, Penny, who's a sucker for the love and attention guests routinely shower on her.

654 S. Orleans Rd., South Orleans, MA 02662. ℂ 888/332-3351 or **508/255-0780.** www.alittleinnonpleasant bay.com. 9 units. $185–$275 double; $1,000 per week suite. Extra person in room $20 per night. Rates include continental breakfast and evening sherry. AE, MC, V. No children under 10 accepted. *In room:* A/C, TV (in Paddock rooms), hair dryer, no phone.

The Barley Neck Inn Lodge ★ *Kids*   Owners Kathi and Joe Lewis are the owners of this motel as well as the restaurant and tavern next door (see below). Every room is a little different, but all boast fluffy designer comforters and stylish appointments. A new family suite has two bathrooms, two TVs, and three beds. Three newly renovated rooms have been decorated in a cottage style with wicker furniture. Six deluxe rooms have country decor and extra amenities like irons, coffeemakers, and hair dryers. The policy of adults only in the upstairs rooms means a quieter atmosphere. Nauset Beach, an ocean beach with heavy surf, is a mile down the road, and the motel provides beach-parking stickers. For those who prefer calmer swimming conditions, there's a pool on-site.

5 Beach Rd. (in the center of town), East Orleans, MA 02643. ℂ **800/281-7505** or 508/255-0212. Fax 508/255-3626. www.barleyneck.com. 17 units. Summer $129–$179 double. Rates include continental breakfast. AE, DC, MC, V. Open year-round. **Amenities:** 2 restaurants (tavern and more formal); outdoor pool. *In room:* A/C, TV, fridge.

The Cove ★   This well-camouflaged motel complex on busy Route 28 also fronts placid Town Cove, where guests are offered a free mini-cruise in season. The interiors are adequate, if not dazzling, and a small heated pool and restful gazebo overlook the waterfront. Some rooms have kitchenettes and balconies with cove views.

13 S. Orleans Rd. (Rte. 28, north of Main St.), Orleans, MA 02653. ℂ **800/343-2233** or 508/255-1203. Fax 508/255-7736. www.thecoveorleans.com. 47 units. Summer $119–$189 double, $179–$189 suite or efficiency. AE, DC, DISC, MC, V. Open year-round. **Amenities:** Small heated pool. *In room:* A/C, TV/VCR, fridge, coffeemaker, microwave, hair dryer.

High Nauset ★★   This humble B&B has an excellent location, just a stone's throw from Nauset Beach, and all of the rooms, which are on the second floor of the house, have large picture windows with ocean views. This is one of the very few B&Bs adjacent to the National Seashore, and it's a real treat to be so close to the famous "Great Beach." Rooms have ceiling fans to circulate the fresh ocean breezes. Continental breakfast served in the guest living room might feature homemade muffins and coffeecake.

227 Beach Rd., East Orleans, MA 02643. ℂ **508/255-1658.** www.highnauset.com. 4 units. Summer $159 double. Rates include continental breakfast. MC, V. Open year-round. No children under 12. *In room:* TV, no phone.

Nauset Knoll Motor Lodge ★★ *Value*   Overlooking Nauset Beach, one of Cape Cod's most popular beaches, this nothing-fancy motel with picture windows will suit beach lovers to a T. The simple, clean rooms are well maintained, and by staying here, you'll save on daily parking charges at Nauset Beach. The whole complex is owned by Uncle Sam and is under the supervision of the National Park Service.

237 Beach Rd. (at Nauset Beach, about 2 miles east of the town center), East Orleans, MA 02643. © **508/ 255-2364.** www.capecodtravel.com. 12 units (all with tub/shower). Summer $150 double. MC, V. Closed late Oct to early Apr. *In room:* TV, no phone.

The Orleans Inn ★   You can't miss this mansard-roofed beauty, perched right on the edge of Town Cove. Absolutely, get one of the rooms facing the water. Built in 1875, the inn has been lovingly restored and maintains its central place in the community. The simple rooms, some with twin beds or sleeper sofas, are cheerful with modern amenities and extra touches like a box of chocolates on the bureau. Downstairs is a bar and restaurant with wonderful views of the cove.

Rte. 6A (P.O. Box 188; just south of the Orleans rotary), Orleans, MA 02653. © **508/255-2222.** Fax 508/255-6722. www.orleansinn.com. 11 units. Summer $125–$250 double. Rates include continental breakfast. AE, DC, DISC, MC, V. **Amenities:** Restaurant/bar. *In room:* TV, fridge.

INEXPENSIVE

Nauset House Inn ★★ *Value*   Just a half mile from Nauset Beach, this reasonably priced country inn is a cozy setting for those seeking a quiet retreat. Several of the rooms in greenery-draped outbuildings feature such romantic extras as a sunken bath or private deck. The most romantic hideaway here, though, is a 1907 conservatory appended to the 1810 farmhouse inn. It's the perfect place to lounge as the rain pounds down, prompting the camellias to waft their heady perfume. Breakfast would seem relatively workaday, were it not for the setting— a pared-down, rustic refectory—and innkeeper Diane Johnson's memorable muffins and pastries.

143 Beach Rd., (P.O. Box 774; about 1 mile east of the town center), East Orleans, MA 02643. © **508/ 255-2195.** Fax 508/240-6276. www.nausethouseinn.com. 14 units, 6 with shared bathroom (4 tub/shower, 4 shower only). Summer $60 single, $75–$85, shared bathroom, $100–$160 double with private bathroom. Rates include full breakfast. DISC, MC, V. Closed Nov–Mar. No children under 12. *In room:* No phone.

The Parsonage Inn ★ *Value*   Blessed with charming British innkeepers, this 1770 full Cape—whose name describes its original function—offers the kind of unique, personalized experience especially prized by *"innies"* (the country-inn counterpart to foodies). Elizabeth Browne is an accomplished pianist who might, if the evening mood is right, take flight in a Chopin mazurka or Mozart sonata, as her husband, Ian, treats guests to a glass of wine. Rooms are prettily decorated, and several offer the convenience of mini-fridges. The most expensive room is quite a bargain with its separate entrance, pullout couch, and kitchenette, for little more than a standard room.

202 Main St. (P.O. Box 1501), East Orleans, MA 02643. © **888/422-8217** or 508/255-8217. Fax 508/255-8216. www.parsonageinn.com. 8 units (3 tub/shower, 5 shower only). Summer $115–$145 double. Rates include full breakfast. AE, MC, V. Closed Jan to mid-Feb. *In room:* A/C, TV, coffeemaker, hair dryer, iron, no phone.

WHERE TO DINE
EXPENSIVE

The Barley Neck Inn and Joe's Beach Road Bar and Grill ★★ FRENCH This 1857 captain's house with adjoining tavern is a favorite with locals. While the front room has a more traditional ambience, the tavern space features a huge fieldstone fireplace and World War II posters. With denim tablecloths and bandannas serving as napkins, the atmosphere is casual. The 28-foot mahogany bar is a popular meeting place. The menu varies from fancy dishes such as grilled Atlantic salmon filet with a red-pepper coulis and basil vinaigrette to Joe's pizza (with goat cheese, roasted peppers, and spinach) or high-falutin' fish and chips—beer-battered, with saffron aioli.

At The Barley Neck Inn, 5 Beach Rd. (about ½ mile east of the town center). ✆ **508/255-0212.** www.barley neck.com. Reservations accepted. Main courses $10–$25. AE, DC, MC, V. June to early Sept daily 5–10pm; call for off-season hours. Open year-round.

Captain Linnell House ★★ AMERICAN The plantation-like facade of this colonnaded 1854 mansion, modeled on a Marseilles villa, foreshadows the romantic ambience that awaits within. This is really an old-style New England restaurant with a traditional menu and dependable service, making this a reliable choice for fine dining, and, for some, the best restaurant in town. Chef/owner William Conway's lobster bisque, bolstered with bourbon, is the kind that lingers in memory. Ask to be seated in the garden room, where the pleasing view will enable you to accord the food the undivided focus it deserves. Better yet, be really smart and come early (before 6pm) to score free soup and dessert.

137 Skaket Beach Rd. (about 1 mile northwest of Rte. 6A). ✆ **508/255-3400.** www.linnell.com. Reservations recommended. Main courses $17–$27. AE, MC, V. Late May to Oct daily 5–9pm; call for off-season hours. Closed mid-Feb to Mar.

MODERATE

Academy Ocean Grille NEW AMERICAN Just the basics here, but it's fresh food prepared simply, and sometimes that's just what you want. Seafood specialties include flounder sautéed and topped with blue crab and a lemon thyme and lavender beurre blanc sauce; and local cod baked and served with a sweet beet and horseradish beurre blanc sauce. There's also veal, steak, and roast duck. On clear summer evenings, dinner is served outside on the trellised patio, which is quite lovely. The interior of the restaurant is on the bland side.

2 Academy Place (in the center of town). ✆ **508/240-1585.** Reservations recommended. Main courses $20–$30. AE, MC, V. Late June to mid-Sept daily 11:30am–2:30pm, 5:30–9:30pm; call for off-season hours. Closed Jan to mid-April.

The Lobster Claw Restaurant ★ SEAFOOD This family-owned and operated business has been serving up quality seafood for almost 30 years. There's plenty of room for everyone in this sprawling restaurant, where booths spill over with boisterous families, and the usual flotsam and jetsam hang artfully from the ceiling. Get the baked stuffed lobster here with all the fixings. There's a children's menu, as well as early-bird specials served daily from 4 to 5:30pm.

Rte. 6A (just south of the rotary), Orleans. ✆ **508/255-1800.** Main courses $10–$19. AE, DC, DISC, MC, V. Daily 11:30am–9pm. Closed Nov–Mar.

Mahoney's Atlantic Bar & Grill ★ NEW AMERICAN Seafood is the specialty at this casual bar/restaurant on Main Street. Dishes like tuna sashimi, grilled sea bass, and pan-seared lobster explain why you came to Cape Cod. The menu also offers poultry, meat, pasta, and vegetarian dishes. Sixteen wines are available by the glass for those who like to sample. Grab a booth and stay awhile. Thursday and Saturday nights in season, there's live jazz and blues with no cover.

28 Main St. (in the center of town). ✆ **508/255-5505.** www.mahoneysatlantic.com. Reservations recommended. Main courses $12–$21. AE, MC, V. May–Sept daily 5–10pm; Oct–April Tues–Sun 5–10pm.

INEXPENSIVE

Binnacle Tavern ⭐ *Kids* AMERICAN All sorts of strange nautical salvage adorn the barn-board walls of this popular pizzeria, where the pies—reputed to be the Cape's best—come with some very peculiar toppings (Thai pizza with chicken, ginger, cilantro, scallions, and peanut sauce, topped with mozzarella cheese!) for those so inclined. More conservative combos are available, along with traditional Italian fare. Kids love the funky atmosphere. The margaritas are marvelous here, and there are homemade desserts and espresso.

20 S. Orleans Rd./Rte. 28 (north of Main St.). ℃ 508/255-7901. Reservations not accepted. Most items under $12. AE, MC, V. Mid-May to mid-Oct daily 5–11:30pm; mid-Oct to mid-May Wed–Sun 5–11:30pm.

Cap't Cass Rock Harbor Seafood ⭐ SEAFOOD Most tourists figure that a silvered shack sporting this many salvaged lobster buoys has an inside track on the freshest of seafood. The supposition makes sense, but the stuff here is about par for the area and the preparations are plain. Nevertheless, it's fun to eat in a joint left untouched for decades as time—and dining fads—marched on.

117 Rock Harbor Rd. (on the harbor, about 1½ miles northwest of the town center). No phone. Most main courses under $12. No credit cards. Late June to mid-Oct Tues–Sun 11am–2pm and 5–9pm. Closed mid-Oct to late June.

Land Ho! ⭐⭐ AMERICAN A longtime hit with the locals (who call it, affectionately, "the Ho"), this rough-and-tumble pub attracts its share of knowledgeable tourists as well, drawn by the reasonable prices and relaxed feeling. The food may be nothing to write home about, but it's satisfying and easy on the budget. Light fare is served until midnight. Just being there (provided you can find the door; it's around back) will make you feel like an insider.

38 Main St. (at Rte. 6A, in the center of town). ℃ 508/255-5165. Reservations not accepted. Main courses $9–$22. AE, DISC, MC, V. Mon–Sat 11:30am–10pm; Sun noon–10pm. Open year-round.

The Yardarm ⭐ PUB GRUB This rough and rowdy joint serves the best chowder in town. It's a delectable seafood concoction that comes in three sizes: little predicament, big predicament, and huge dilemma. It's also available frozen in pint and half-pint sizes. Locals also flock to Prime Rib Night (Mon and Thurs), Mexican Night (Tues–Wed), and Steak Night (Fri–Sat). But you'll go to watch the colorful characters bellying up to the bar for a burger and a brew.

48 Rte. 28. (just east of Main St.). ℃ 508/255-4840. Most items under $15. AE, DC, MC, V. Daily 11:30am–3pm and 5:30–9pm. Open year-round.

TAKEOUT & PICNIC FARE

Fancy's Farm ⭐ Rarely are vegetables rendered so appealing. They're especially prime whether domestic or imported from halfway across the world. The charming barnlike setting helps, as do the extras—fresh breads, pastries, juices, sandwiches, and exotic salads and soups to go. This is a great place to stop on the way to Nauset Beach for picnic supplies.

199 Main St., East Orleans. ℃ 508/255-1949.

Nauset Fish & Lobster Pool ⭐ The area's premier spot for fresh seafood; the selection is extensive and bountiful.

Just south of the rotary on Rte. 6A in Orleans. ℃ 508/255-1019.

New York Bagels Longing for the real thing, a real mouth wrestler? These chewy rounds are authentic and tasty; add the customary accompaniments for a satisfying sandwich. Among the other "Noo Yawk" mainstays are knishes and potato pancakes—and, of course, chicken soup. While awaiting your order, you can study the decorative pastiche of nostalgic tchotchkes.

125 Rte. 6A (south of Main St.). ℭ **508/255-0255.**

Orleans Whole Food   The largest health-food store on the Cape, this bright and cheerful porch-fronted grocery offers all sorts of freshly made snacks and sandwiches to take out—or to tear into during an impromptu picnic in the adjoining garden.

46 Main St. (in the center of town). ℭ **508/255-6540.**

SWEETS

The Hot Chocolate Sparrow ★★   Success means a larger location for this coffeehouse-cum-bakery. Real fudge flavors the hot chocolate and all mocha derivatives thereof. Frozen hot chocolate and frozen mochas are summer specialties. It's a good place to stop in, casually check the posters announcing local happenings, then dive in for a remorseless pig-out. This place serves the best coffee and cappuccinos in town, too.

85 Rte. 6A (Lowell Sq.). ℭ **508/240-2230.** Open year-round.

Sundae School ★   A smaller branch of the local chain (also in Dennis Port and Harwich Port), this little ice-cream shop offers some mighty sophisticated flavors, drawing on fruits in season and even the liquor cabinet.

210 Main St., East Orleans. ℭ **508/255-5473.**

ORLEANS AFTER DARK

Joe's Beach Road Bar & Grille (ℭ **508/255-0212;** see "Where to Dine," above) is a big old barn of a bar that might as well be town hall: It's where you'll find all the locals exchanging juicy gossip and jokes. On Sunday evenings in season, the weekend warriors who survived in style can enjoy live "Jazz at Joe's." Other nights, Jim Turner, a blind piano player, entertains with show tunes and boogie-woogie. There's never a cover charge.

There's live music on weekends at the **Land Ho!** (ℭ **508/255-5165;** see "Where to Dine," above), the best pub in town, on Monday and Tuesday nights in season, and Thursday and Saturdays off season. There's usually no cover charge.

The Academy Playhouse, 120 Main St., about ¾ mile southeast of the town center (ℭ **508/255-1963**), makes a fine platform for local talent in the form of musicals and drama, recitals and poetry readings. The 162-seat arena-style stage is housed in the town's old town hall (built in 1873). Tickets are $14 to $16. Shows take place July through August Monday to Saturday at 8:30pm; call for off-season hours. A children's theater series runs from late June to early September on Saturday mornings. Cost is $16.

The Outer Cape: Eastham, Wellfleet, Truro & Provincetown

The rest of the Cape may have its civilized enticements, but it's only on the Outer Cape that the landscape and even the air feel really beachy. You can smell the seashore just over the horizon—in fact, you can smell it everywhere you go because you're never more than a mile or two away from sand and surf.

You won't find any high-rise hotels along the shoreline here. No tacky amusement arcades either. Just miles of pristine beaches and dune grass rippling in the wind. You'll also see the occasional cottage inhabited by some lucky soul who managed to get his or her hands on it (inevitably through some grandfather clause) before the coastline became the federally protected Cape Cod National Seashore in the early 1960s.

Henry David Thoreau witnessed virtually the same peaceful panorama when he roamed here in the 1850s. With luck and determination on the part of current inhabitants and visitors, the landscape will remain untouched. The Outer Cape, after all, is a place to play—in the sand, and in the delightful, nonconformist towns that sprouted up here, far from the censures of civilization.

While they share the majestic National Seashore, Outer Cape towns are quite diverse. Eastham, as the official gateway to the National Seashore, certainly gets its share of visitors, yet there is also a sleepy quality to this town, which used to have the distinction of being the turnip capital of the country. Grab a stool at a locals' joint like Flemings Donut Shop on Route 6 for a taste of old Cape Cod before there was ever any talk of a National Seashore.

Wellfleet, called the art-gallery town, is in my view one of the nicest towns on Cape Cod. The very strollable Main Street is lined with intriguing shops in historic buildings. Commercial Street, which leads to the harbor, has the art galleries, filled with work by mainly local artists inspired by this region. Wellfleet was for years one of the premier fishing villages on Cape Cod, and it still has the bustling and picturesque harbor to prove it. There are also freshwater ponds and National Seashore beaches; some of Cape Cod's finest swimming holes and most spectacular beaches line the coast of Wellfleet.

Tiny Truro is the least developed of the Cape's towns; it has the smallest population and the highest percentage of acres reserved for the National Seashore. The center of town is one of those blink-and-you-miss-it affairs, though the fact that Truro has four libraries should tell you something about the property owners here.

Provincetown is a former Portuguese fishing village turned into an internationally famous art and gay colony with a flamboyant nightlife. The main drag (so to speak) is Commercial Street, with the best shopping on Cape Cod. Families come for the strolling, museums, and whale-watching; sophisticates for the restaurants, cafes, and entertainment; and gays for the camaraderie. And the beaches? On a clear day, they say you can see Europe.

1 Eastham

35 miles E of Sandwich; 21 miles S of Provincetown

Despite its optimal location (the distance from bay to ocean is as little as 1 mile in spots), Eastham is one of the least pretentious locales on the Cape—and yet highly popular as the gateway to the magnificent Cape Cod National Seashore.

The downside—or upside, depending on how you look at it—is that there aren't many shops or attractions worth checking out. Even Eastham's colorful history, as the site of the Pilgrims' first encounter with hostile natives, has faded with time. One prominent vestige remains as a reminder of the days when, according to Cape historian Arthur Wilson Tarbell, Eastham served as "the granary of eastern Massachusetts": the mock 1680s windmill in the center of town. Also, those who take the trouble to track them down will find the graves of three "First Comers" in the Old Cove Burying Ground, near a condo complex across from Arnold's clam shack.

Most visitors won't bother, though—this is a place to kick back and let the sun, surf, and sand dictate your day.

ESSENTIALS

GETTING THERE   After crossing the Sagamore Bridge, head east on Route 6 or 6A to Orleans, and north on Route 6. Or fly into Hyannis or Provincetown (see "Getting There" in chapter 2).

VISITOR INFORMATION   An information booth run by the town of Eastham is located on Route 6 at Governor Prence Road (© 508/255-3444) and is open Memorial Day to late September daily from 9am to 7pm with reduced hours in the shoulder season. Call or write the **Eastham Chamber of Commerce** for an informational brochure: P.O. Box 1329, Eastham, MA 02642 (© 508/240-7211; www.easthamchamber.com). You may also contact the **Cape Cod Chamber of Commerce,** routes 6 and 132, Hyannis, MA 02601 (© 888/332-2732 or 508/ 862-0700; fax 508/362-2156; www.capecodchamber.org), open year-round Monday to Saturday from 9am to 5pm and Sunday and holidays from 10am to 4pm.

BEACHES & RECREATIONAL PURSUITS

BEACHES   From here on up, the Atlantic beaches are best reserved for strong swimmers: Waves are big (often taller than you), and the undertow can be treacherous. The flat, nearly placid bay beaches, on the other hand, are just right for families with young children. The sand slopes so gradually that you won't have to worry about them slipping in over their heads. When the tide recedes (twice daily), it leaves a mile-wide playground of rippled sand full of fascinating creatures, including horseshoe and hermit crabs.

- **Coast Guard & Nauset Light** ★★★, off Ocean View Drive: Connected to outlying parking lots by a free shuttle, these pristine National Seashore beaches have lifeguards and restrooms. In 1998, Coast Guard Beach was ranked the 18th best beach in the United States by a beach expert. Though National Seashore beaches can be chilly (this is the Atlantic Ocean, after all), the water is clean and clear. Similar to all National Seashore beaches, the vistas are lovely (just 30 miles of beach). At Coast Guard Beach, the old white Coast Guard building is scenically perched on a bluff. At Nauset Light Beach, the red striped lighthouse, having moved back from its oceanfront perch, looks over the parking lot. Parking is $10 per day, $30 per season.

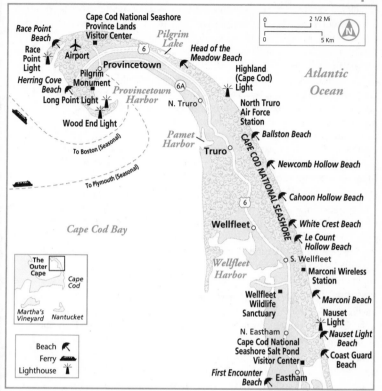

- **First Encounter, Campground, & Sunken Meadow** ★★: These town-operated bay beaches generally charge $10 a day; permits ($40 per week) can be obtained from the Highway Department on Old Orchard Road in North Eastham (☎ **508/240-5900**).
- **Great Pond & Wiley Park** ★: These two town-run freshwater beaches are also open to the public, on the same terms as the bay beaches.

BICYCLING   With plenty of free parking available at the **Cape Cod National Seashore's Salt Pond Visitor Center** ★★ (☎ **508/255-3421**), Eastham makes a convenient access point for the **Cape Cod Rail Trail** ★★ (☎ **508/896-3491**). Northward, it's about 5 wildflower-lined miles to Wellfleet, where the trail currently ends (further expansion is planned); Dennis is about 20 miles southwest. A 1½-mile spur trail, winding through locust and apple groves, links the visitor center with glorious Coast Guard Beach: It's for bikes only (no blades). Rentals are available at the **Little Capistrano Bike Shop** (☎ **508/255-6515**), on Salt Pond Road just west of Route 6. Bikes cost about $20 per day. The best trail-side eatery—fried clams, lobster, and the like—is **Arnold's** (☎ **508/255-2575**), located on Route 6 about 1 mile north of the visitor center.

BOATING   The best way to experience Nauset Marsh is by kayak or canoe. Rentals are available in neighboring towns: The closest source would be the **Goose Hummock Outdoor Center** at 15 Rte. 6A in Orleans (☎ **508/255-2620**).

Jack's Boat Rentals (© 508/349-9808) is located on Route 6 next to the Cumberland Farms in Wellfleet. Canoes rent for $40 a day. Jack's also rents kayaks, Sunfish sailboats, and *yakboards* (small kayaks). If you rent for 2 days, the third day is free. They have a seasonal outlet from mid-June to early September on **Wellfleet's Gull Pond** (© 508/349-7553). Kayak and canoe rentals at Gull Pond cost $20 for an hour and $12 for each additional hour. After 3 hours, the fourth hour is free. In addition to watercraft to go, Jack's is also the place for info about **Eric Gustavson's guided kayak tours** (© 508/349-1429), which include tours of Eastham's Herring River and Nauset Marsh. A 2½-hour trip costs $30. For information about other excellent naturalist-guided tours, inquire about trips sponsored by the **Cape Cod Museum of Natural History** (© 800/479-3867 or 508/896-3867) and by the **Wellfleet Bay Wildlife Sanctuary** (© 508/349-2615).

FISHING   Eastham has four ponds open to fishing; Herring Pond is stocked. Freshwater-fishing licenses (starting at $29 for residents of Massachusetts) can be purchased at **Goose Hummock,** Route 6A, Orleans (© 508/255-0455), or from the town clerk at Town Hall, Route 6 (© 508/240-5900). For a shellfishing license, visit the **Natural Resources Department** at 555 Old Orchard Rd. (© 508/240-5972). Surf-casting is permitted at Nauset Beach North (off Doane Rd.) and Nauset Light Beach (off Cable Rd.).

FITNESS   **Willy's Gym, Fitness and Wellness Center,** 4730 Rte. 6, North Eastham (© 508/255-6370), offers racquet sports, plus Nautilus and free weights, various classes, an Olympic pool, saunas, steam rooms, and whirlpools. Non-members pay $20 a day.

NATURE TRAILS   There are five self-guided nature trails with descriptive markers—for walkers only—within this portion of the Cape Cod National Seashore. The 1.5-mile **Fort Hill Trail** off Fort Hill Road (off Rte. 6, about 1 mile south of the town center) takes off from a free parking lot just past the **Captain Edward Penniman House** ✿, a fancy multicolored 1868 Second Empire manse maintained by rangers from the Cape Cod National Seashore. Seashore rangers lead occasional tours of the house's interior in season. For times, call the visitor center at © 508/255-3421. But the exterior far outshines the interior, and more interesting sights await outside. Check out the huge whale-jawbone gate before walking across the street to the trail. Following the trail markers, you'll pass "Indian Rock" (bearing the marks of untold generations who used it to sharpen their tools) and enjoy scenic vantage points overlooking the channel-carved marsh—keep an eye out for egrets and great blue herons— and out to sea. The Fort Hill Trail hooks up with the half-mile **Red Cedar Swamp Trail,** offering boardwalk views of an ecology otherwise inaccessible.

Three relatively short trails fan out from the Salt Pond Visitor Center. The most unusual is the .25-mile **Buttonbush Trail** ✿, specially adapted for the sight-impaired, with a guide rope and descriptive plaques in both oversize type and Braille. The **Doane Loop Trail** ✿, a .5-mile woodland circuit about 1 mile east of the visitor center, is graded to allow access to wheelchairs and strollers. The 1-mile **Nauset Marsh Trail** ✿ skirts Salt Pond to cross the marsh (via boardwalk) and open fields before returning by way of a recovering forest. Look both ways for bike crossings!

TENNIS   Five public courts are located at the **Nauset Regional High School** in North Eastham and can be used on a first-come, first-served basis; for details, contact the Nauset Regional High School (© 508/255-1505). **Willy's Gym,**

⌒ Tips Drive with Caution

There have been many serious accidents on Route 6 in Eastham, and as a result, the speed limit here declines rather abruptly from 55 to 40 mph. Eastham police are vigilant about enforcement.

4730 Rte. 6, North Eastham (© **508/255-6370**), offers six indoor courts at a fee of $20 per day.

TWO MUSEUMS

The 1869 Schoolhouse Museum   Run by the volunteers of the Eastham Historical Society, this former one-room schoolhouse—with separate entrances for boys and girls—encapsulates the town's accomplishments. Exhibits range from early Native American tools to mementos of author Henry Beston's year-long stay on Coast Guard Beach, which resulted in *The Outermost House,* as compelling a read today as it was back in 1928. And in case you were wondering—yes, that strange garden gate is in fact the washed-up jawbones of a rather large whale.

Nauset Rd. (off Rte. 6, opposite the Salt Pond Visitor Center). © 508/255-0788. Free admission. July–Aug Mon–Fri 1–4pm; Sat only in Sept 1–4pm. Closed Sept–June.

Salt Pond Visitor Center ⚜⚜   The Salt Pond Visitor Center is an ideal place to begin your exploration of the seashore, with exhibits and information about this unique environment. After all, since you're undoubtedly going to spend a fair amount of time on the beach, you might as well find out how it came to be, what other creatures you'll be sharing it with, and how not to harm it or them.

Occupying more than half the landmass north of Orleans and covering the entire 30-mile oceanfront, the 44,000-acre Cape Cod National Seashore is a free gift from legislators who had the foresight to set it aside as a sanctuary in 1961. Take advantage of the excellent educational exhibits and continuous film loops offered here; particularly fascinating is a video about the 1990 discovery of an 11,000-year-old campsite amid the storm-ravaged dunes of Coast Guard Beach, which was about 5 miles inland when these early settlers spent their summers here. After absorbing some of the local history, be sure to take time to venture out—on your own or with a ranger guide—to the surrounding trails (see "Nature Trails," above).

Note: The Salt Pond Visitor Center is scheduled to be closed through the spring of 2004. During the renovation, temporary facilities with limited exhibits are in place. If the visitor center is closed during your visit, you can still enjoy the trails around the center, as well as take advantage of ranger information and bathroom facilities. For more information about the Cape Cod National Seashore, journey up to Race Point in Provincetown, where another visitor center is tucked into the dunes.

Salt Pond Rd. (east of Rte. 6). © 508/255-3421. www.nps.gov/caco. Free admission. Late May to mid-Oct daily 9am–5pm; mid-Oct to late May daily 9am–4:30pm.

KID STUFF

No one will look askance if you let your kids try the **Buttonbush Trail** ⚜ (see "Nature Trails," above) in a blindfold: In fact, it's encouraged, not only as a good way to foster empathy for the blind but also to heighten multisensory awareness. You'll find more predictable pastimes, such as miniature golf, along Route 6, and, of course, at the beaches.

SHOPPING

Eastham has fewer businesses than its southern neighbors, but poking around in unexpected places can pay off.

ANTIQUES It would be easy to pass by **Collectors' World,** on Route 6 in Eastham, 1 mile north of the Salt Pond Visitor Center (© **508/255-3616**), without ever realizing there are prime pickings inside. Interesting items line every square inch of the shop, from nautical antiques and weather vanes to lamps, toys, furniture, and, of course, collectibles.

ARTS & CRAFTS **Sunken Meadows Basketworks and Pottery,** Sunken Meadow Road (off Aspinet Rd.), North Eastham (© **508/255-8962**), is a hidden gem tucked into the pines of North Eastham. Paulette Penney and her husband Hugh make stoneware-pinched pots, begging bowls, and wall pieces, as well as woven baskets and sculptures.

WHERE TO STAY
EXPENSIVE

The Whalewalk Inn ★★ *Finds* This is where you stay if you are looking for a deluxe B&B in the Outer Cape. Regularly hailed as one of the Cape's prettiest inns, this 1830s Greek Revival manse, run by Elaine and Kevin Conlin, fully deserves its reputation. Located in a quiet residential area just a few blocks off the Rail Trail, the inn is decorated in a tasteful, mostly pastel, palette. Eclectic furnishings cohabit harmoniously in the common rooms, where complimentary evening hors d'oeuvres are served. The rooms are spacious. A new six-room carriage house sports deluxe rooms with antique four-poster beds, fireplaces, and private decks, and several have whirlpool baths for two. Some of the suites have kitchenettes. Most of the rooms are outfitted with TVs, phones, and mini-fridges. Loaner bikes are available to explore the area.

220 Bridge Rd. (about ¾ mile west of the Orleans rotary), Eastham, MA 02642. © **800/440-1281** or 508/255-0617. Fax 508/240-0017. www.whalewalkinn.com. 16 units (11 tub/shower, 5 shower only). Summer $190–$325 double, $275–$325 suite. Rates include full breakfast. AE, DISC, MC, V. Closed Jan–Feb. **Amenities:** Loaner bikes. *In room:* A/C, TV, hair dryer, iron.

MODERATE

Over Look Inn ★ This 1869 Queen Anne Victorian, across the street from the Salt Pond Visitor Center and about a mile from Coast Guard Beach, is one of the few bed-and-breakfasts on Cape Cod with a billiard room. The house also contains such niceties from another era as a wood-paneled library and a cozy parlor. Some guest rooms have brass beds and claw-foot tubs. Most of the rooms have televisions. The carriage house in back has several larger rooms. Those planning to hike along the Rail Trail will appreciate the hearty Danish breakfasts.

3085 County Rd./Rte. 6 (opposite Salt Pond Visitor Center), Eastham, MA 02642. © **508/255-1886.** Fax 508/240-0345. www.overlookinn.com. 12 units (7 tub/shower, 5 shower only). Summer $145–$220 double. Rates include full breakfast and afternoon tea. AE, DISC, MC, V. Open year-round. *In room:* A/C, hair dryer.

The Penny House Whizzing past on Route 6, you'd scarcely suspect there's a peaceful inn tucked away behind a massive hedge. This neat, comfortable B&B, graced with the warmth of Australian innkeeper Margaret Keith, is clustered around a 1690 saltbox, now the setting for rather rich homemade breakfasts. The rooms vary widely in size and price. Many rooms have fireplaces; a couple have whirlpool tubs. Five deluxe rooms are equipped with bathrobes, phones, TVs, and mini-fridges. A communal TV in the cathedral-ceiling "gathering room" encourages socializing.

4885 Rte. 6, Eastham, MA 02651. ☏ **800/554-1751** or 508/255-6632. Fax 508/255-4893. www.pennyhouse inn.com. 12 units (8 tub/shower, 4 shower only). Summer $165–$315 double. Rates include full breakfast. AE, DISC, MC, V. *In room:* A/C, hair dryer.

INEXPENSIVE

Beach Plum Motor Lodge *Value*　Look for the riot of flowers that Gloria Moll tenderly cultivates each year around her tiny front-yard pool, which is just big enough for a cool dip and fragrant sunning. The rooms—in classic little cabins out back—are also smallish, but they're more than adequate for most people's needs and very generously priced, especially when you take into account the home-baked breakfast treats. After 20 years in business, Beach Plum's regulars may outnumber new guests, so make your reservations early.

2555 Rte. 6 (about ¼ mile north of the town center), Eastham, MA 02642. ☏ **508/255-7668.** 5 units (2 with shared bathroom, showers only). Summer $64–$68 double. Rates include continental breakfast. AE, MC, V. Closed Nov–Apr. **Amenities:** Small outdoor pool. *In room:* No phone.

Mid-Cape American Youth Hostel *Value*　Though nowhere near as picturesque as the Little America AYH-Hostel 14 miles north (see "Where to Stay" in section 3 of this chapter), this inland cluster of cabins makes a good stopover along the almost adjacent Rail Trail, and the bay is a quick glide away.

75 Goody Hallet Dr. (off Bridge Rd., about ½ mile west of the Orleans rotary), Eastham, MA 02642. ☏ **508/ 255-2785.** 50 beds. $22–24 for members, $25–$27 for non-members. $88–$99 private cabins. MC, V. Closed mid-Sept to mid-May. *In room:* No phone.

WHERE TO DINE
MODERATE

Eastham Lobster Pool *Kids* AMERICAN　For 3 decades, the scrape of metal chairs against the cement floor of this no-frills dining hall has been synonymous with seafood feasts. You can eye your potential entree—scrambling among a tankful of feisty lobsters—as you wait in line to gain admittance. (Smart diners know to show up in the early, early evening—as in, late afternoon.) Beyond the lobsters, all sorts of fish are available grilled, broiled, baked, fried, stuffed, or poached. As far back as the early 1980s, the specials were harbingers of New American panache, and they still pack some sophisticated surprises: champagne-shallot butter, perhaps, to top a halibut steak. The bluefish, always affordable, is fabulous. Some rather nice wines are available by the glass. The fish market area sports a 1,000-foot lobster tank; lobsters are available live or cooked to take home, as is the rest of the menu.

4380 Rte. 6 (in the center of town). ☏ **508/255-9706;** takeout ☏ 508/255-3314. www.lobsterpool.com. Reservations not accepted. Main courses $11–$28. AE, DC, DISC, MC, V. Early July to early Sept daily 11:30am–10pm; mid-Apr to early July and early Sept to mid-Oct Thurs–Mon 11:30am–2:30pm, daily 5–9:30pm. Closed mid-Oct to mid-Apr.

INEXPENSIVE

Arnold's AMERICAN　Offering a takeout window on the Rail Trail and a picnic grove for those who hate to waste vacation hours sitting indoors, this popular eatery dishes out all the usual seashore standards, from rich and crunchy fried clams (cognoscenti know to order whole clams, not strips) to foot-long chili dogs.

3580 Rte. 6 (about 1¼ miles north of the town center). ☏ **508/255-2575.** www.arnoldsrestaurant.com. Main courses $3–$24. No credit cards. Mid-June to mid-Sept daily 11:30am–9pm; late May to mid-June call for hours. Closed mid-Sept to late May.

TAKEOUT & PICNIC FARE

Box Lunch ★ (Finds This is yet another source of the popular, Cape-invented pita "rollwiches."

4205 Rte. 6, North Eastham. © 508/255-0799. May–Oct daily 7am–8pm; call for off-season hours. Closed Jan.

SWEETS

Ben & Jerry's Scoop Shop ★ (Kids This premium ice-cream parlor is just about all most Eastham residents need in the way of evening entertainment.

50 Brackett Rd. (at Rte. 6), North Eastham. © 508/255-2817. July–Aug 11am–11pm; call for off-season hours. Closed Nov–Apr.

The Chocolate Sparrow ★ (Finds Let the seductive aroma of simmering chocolate lead you to this source of hand-dipped delights.

4205 Rte. 6, North Eastham. © 508/240-0606. Daily 9:30am–5:30pm. Open year-round.

Hole-in-One Donut Shop Old-timers convene at the counter of this tiny shop (open daily 5am–noon) to ponder the state of the world. You can join in, or scurry home with your haul of hand-cut donuts and fresh-baked muffins and bagels.

4295 Rte. 6 (about ¼ mile south of the town center). © 508/255-9446. Daily 5am–noon. Open year-round.

EASTHAM AFTER DARK

The young crowd is now heading to the **Beach Break Grill and Lounge** at the Main Street Mercantile (Rte. 6) in North Eastham (© **508/240-3100**) for evening fun. There's an outdoor deck, raw bar, late-night menu, and frozen cocktails. Live bands play Thursday to Sunday in season. Cover $3 to $10.

Most Saturday nights in season (the schedule is somewhat erratic), the **First Encounter Coffee House,** Chapel in the Pines, 220 Samoset Rd. (off Rte. 6, ¼ mile west of town center), Eastham (© **508/255-5438**), a tiny 1899 church, hosts some very big names on the folk/rock circuit, such as Livingston Taylor and Patty Larkin. Tickets are $12; call for a schedule. Closed May and September.

The **Salt Pond Visitor Center,** on Salt Pond Road in Eastham (east of Rte. 6; © **508/255-3421**), puts on a varying schedule of entertainment (including concerts and guest presentations) in season. A nominal fee ($2–$3) may apply. Call for a schedule.

2 Wellfleet ★★★

42 miles NE of Sandwich; 14 miles S of Provincetown

Wedged between tame Eastham and wild Truro, Wellfleet—with the well-tended look of a classic New England village—is the golden mean, the perfect destination for artists, writers, off-duty psychiatrists, and other contemplative types who hope to find more in the landscape than mere quaintness or rusticity. Distinguished literati such as Edna St. Vincent Millay and Edmund Wilson put this rural village on the map in the 1920s, in the wake of Provincetown's bohemian heyday. In her brief and tumultuous tenure as Wilson's wife, Mary McCarthy pilloried the pretensions of the summer population in her novel, *A Charmed Life,* but had to concede that the region boasts a certain natural beauty: "steel-blue freshwater ponds and pine forests and mushrooms and white bluffs dropping to a strangely pebbled beach."

To this day, Wellfleet remains remarkably unspoiled. Once you depart from Route 6, commercialism is kept to a minimum, though the town boasts plenty of appealing shops—including a number of distinguished galleries—and a couple of excellent New American restaurants. It's hard to imagine any other community on the Cape supporting so sophisticated an undertaking as the Wellfleet Harbor Actors' Theatre, or hosting such a wholesome event as public square dancing on the adjacent Town Pier. And where else could you find, right next door to an outstanding nature preserve (the Wellfleet Bay Wildlife Sanctuary), a thriving drive-in movie theater?

ESSENTIALS

GETTING THERE   After crossing the Sagamore Bridge, head east on Route 6 or 6A to Orleans, and north on Route 6. Or fly into Provincetown or Hyannis (see "Getting There" in chapter 2).

VISITOR INFORMATION   Contact the **Wellfleet Chamber of Commerce,** off Route 6, Wellfleet, MA 02663 (© **508/349-2510;** fax 508/349-3740; www. wellfleetchamber.com), or the **Cape Cod Chamber of Commerce** (see "Visitor Information" in the "Eastham" section, earlier in this chapter). The Wellfleet information center is open mid-June to mid-September 9am–6pm daily. Call for off-season hours.

BEACHES & RECREATIONAL PURSUITS

BEACHES   Though the distinctions are far from hard and fast, Wellfleet's fabulous ocean beaches tend to sort themselves demographically: LeCount Hollow is popular with families, Newcomb Hollow with high-schoolers, White Crest with the college crowd (including surfers and off-hour hang gliders), and Cahoon Hollow with 30-somethings. Alas, only the latter two beaches permit parking by nonresidents ($15 per day). To enjoy the other two, as well as Burton Baker Beach on the harbor and Duck Harbor on the bay, plus three freshwater ponds, you'll have to walk or bike in, or see if you qualify for a sticker ($50 per week). Bring proof of residency to the seasonal Beach Sticker Booth on the Town Pier, or call the **Wellfleet Recreation Department** (© **508/349-9818**). Parking is free at all beaches and ponds after 4pm.

- **Marconi Beach** ★★, off Marconi Beach Road in South Wellfleet: A National Seashore property, this cliff-lined beach (with restrooms) charges an entry fee of $10 per day, or only $30 for the season. *Note:* The bluffs are so high that the beach lies in shadow by late afternoon.

- **Mayo Beach,** Kendrick Avenue (near the Town Pier): Right by the harbor, facing south, this warm, shallow bay beach (with restrooms) is hardly secluded but will please young waders and splashers. And the price is right; parking is free. You could grab a bite (and a paperback) at The Bookstore Restaurant across the street, which serves three meals a day and sells used books around back.

- **White Crest & Cahoon Hollow Beaches** ★★★, off Ocean View Drive in Wellfleet: These two town-run ocean beaches—big with surfers—are open to all. Both have snack bars and restrooms. Parking costs $15 per day.

BICYCLING   The end (to date) of the 25-mile (and growing) **Cape Cod Rail Trail** ★★★ (© **508/896-3491**), Wellfleet is also among its more desirable destinations: A country road off the bike path leads right to LeCount Hollow Beach. Located at the current terminus, the **Black Duck Sports Shop** at 1446 Rte. 6 in Wellfleet, at the corner of LeCount Hollow Road (© **508/349-9801**), stocks everything from rental bikes to boogie boards. Bikes rent for $20 a day. The deli at the adjoining **South Wellfleet General Store** (© **508/349-2335**) can see to your snacking needs.

Cape Cod National Seashore

No trip to Cape Cod would be complete without a visit to the Cape Cod National Seashore on the Outer Cape and an afternoon barefoot stroll along the **"The Great Beach,"** where you see exactly why the Cape attracts artists and poets. On August 7, 1961, Pres. John F. Kennedy signed a bill designating 27,000 acres in the 40 miles from Chatham to Provincetown as the Cape Cod National Seashore, a new national park. Unusual in a national park, the Seashore includes 500 private residences, the owners of which lease land from the park service. Convincing residents that a National Seashore would be a good thing for Cape Cod was an arduous task back then, and Provincetown still grapples with Seashore officials over town land issues.

The Seashore's claim to fame is its spectacular beaches—in reality, one long beach—with dunes 50 feet to 150 feet high. This is the Atlantic Ocean, so the surf is rough (and cold), but a number of the beaches have lifeguards. Seashore beaches include Coast Guard and Nauset Light Beaches in Eastham, Marconi Beach in Wellfleet, Head of the Meadow Beach in Truro, and Provincetown's Race Point and Herring Cove beaches. A $30 pass will get you into all of them for the season, or you can pay a daily rate of $10.

The Seashore also has a number of walking trails—all free, all picturesque, and all worth a trip. In Eastham, **Fort Hill** (off Rte. 6) has one of the best scenic views on Cape Cod and a popular boardwalk trail through a red maple swamp. The **Nauset Marsh Trail** is accessed from the Salt Pond Visitor Center on Route 6 in Eastham. **Great Island** on the bay side in Wellfleet is surely one of the finest places to have a picnic; you could spend the day hiking the trails. On **Pamet Trail** off North Pamet Road in Truro, hikers pass the decrepit old cranberry-bog building (restoration is in the works) on the way to a trail through the dunes.

BOATING **Jack's Boat Rentals,** located on Gull Pond off Gull Pond Road, about a half mile south of the Truro border (② 508/349-9808), rents out canoes, kayaks, sailboards, and Sunfish, as well as sea cycles and surf bikes. Gull Pond connects to Higgins Pond by way of a placid, narrow channel lined with red maples and choked with yellow water lilies. Needless to say, it's a great place to paddle. Renting a kayak or canoe at Gull Pond for a couple of hours costs about $32. If you'd like a canoe for a few days, you'll need to go to the Jack's Boat Rentals location on Route 6 in Wellfleet (next to the Cumberland Farms). There, a canoe rents for about $33 for 24 hours, and only $76 for 3 days. Rentals come with a roof rack if you need it. There are many wonderful places to canoe in Wellfleet. A trip from Wellfleet's Town Pier across the harbor to Great Island, for instance, will get you nowhere fast, beautifully.

In addition to watercraft to go, Jack's is also the place for information about **Eric Gustavson's guided kayak tours** (② 508/349-1429) of kettle ponds and tidal rivers from Chatham to Truro. The cost is $35 for a 2½-hour tour, $55 for a 4-hour tour, and $90 for a 6-hour tour that includes lunch. Eric also offers windsurfing lessons and rentals on Pleasant Bay and in Wellfleet ($40 an hour),

Don't try the old boardwalk trail over the bogs here; it has flooded and is no longer in use. The **Atlantic White Cedar Swamp Trail** is located at the Marconi Station site, **Small Swamp** and **Pilgrim Spring** trails are found at Pilgrim Heights Beach, and **Beech Forest Trail** is located at Race Point in Provincetown. The best bike path on Cape Cod is the Province Lands Trail, 5 swooping and invigorating miles, at Race Point Beach. If that's not enough in the way of sports, surf-casting is allowed from the ocean beaches—Race Point is a popular spot.

The Seashore also includes several historic buildings that tell their part of the region's history. At Race Point Beach in Provincetown, the **Old Harbor Lifesaving Station** serves as a museum of early lifesaving techniques. **Captain Edward Penniman's 1868 house** at Fort Hill in Eastham is a grandly ornate Second Empire home, and the 1730 **Atwood-Higgins House** in Wellfleet is a typical Cape-style home; both are open for tours. Five lighthouses dot the Seashore, including Highland Light in Truro and Nauset Light in Eastham, both recently moved back from precarious positions on the edges of dunes.

Most of the Seashore beaches have large parking lots, but you'll need to get there early (before 10am) on busy summer weekends. If the beach you want to go to is full, try the one next door—most of the beaches are 5 miles to 10 miles apart. Don't forget your beach umbrella; the sun exposure here can get intense.

Getting There: Take Route 6, the Mid-Cape Highway, to Eastham (about 50 miles). Pick up a map at the Salt Pond Visitor Center in Eastham. There is another visitor center at Race Point. Both centers have ranger activities, maps, gift shops, and restrooms. Seashore beaches are all off Route 6 and are clearly marked. Additional beaches along this stretch are run by individual towns, and you must have a sticker or pay a fee.

surfing lessons ($40 an hour), mountain-bike tours ($15 per person, per hour), and, for the most adventurous, kite surfing ($75 an hour). For information about other excellent naturalist-guided tours, inquire about trips sponsored by the **Cape Cod Museum of Natural History** (© 800/479-3867 or 508/896-3867) and the **Wellfleet Bay Wildlife Sanctuary** (© 508/349-2615).

The **Chequessett Yacht & Country Club** on Chequessett Neck Road in Wellfleet (© 508/349-0198) offers group sailing lessons. Call for rates. For experienced sailors, **Wellfleet Marine Corp.,** on the Town Pier (© 508/349-2233), rents 14- and 19-foot sailboats in season. The cost is $40 to $50 for the first hour, $12 to $15 for each additional hour, or $100 to $125 for the day. They also rent 14- to 16-foot motorboats for $40 to $70 for the first hour and $12 to $30 for each additional hour.

FISHING   For a license to fish at Long Pond, Great Pond, or Gull Pond (all stocked with trout and full of native perch, pickerel, and sunfish), visit **Town Hall** at 300 Main St. (© 508/349-0301). Massachusetts residents pay $14 for a 3-day pass or $29 for a season pass; nonresidents pay $25 for a 3-day pass or $39 for a season pass. Surf-casting, which doesn't require a license, is permitted at the town beaches. Shellfishing licenses—Wellfleet's oysters are world-famous—can be obtained from the **Shellfish Department** on the Town Pier off Kendrick Avenue (© **508/349-0300**). Shellfish licenses are $40 per season for residents, $125 per season for nonresidents. Also heading out from here, in season, is the 60-foot party fishing boat *Navigator* (© **508/349-6003**), which charges $25 for adults, $22 for seniors, and $17 for children for a 4-hour trip, gear and bait provided. There are three charter boats: the *Erin-H* (© **508/349-9663;** www.virtualcapecod.com/erinh), *Jac's Mate* (© **508/255-2978**), and *Snooper* (© **508/349-6113**). The charter boats all charge $450 for a half day and $575 for a full day.

GOLF   Hugging a pretty cove, the **Chequessett Yacht & Country Club** on Chequessett Neck Road (© **508/349-3704**) has one of the loveliest nine-hole courses on the Cape; nonmembers need to reserve at least 3 days ahead. Greens fees are $30 for nine holes, $44 for 18 holes.

NATURE & WILDLIFE AREAS   You'll find 6 miles of very scenic trails lined with lupines and bayberries—Goose Pond, Silver Spring, and Bay View—within the Wellfleet Bay Wildlife Sanctuary in South Wellfleet (see below). Right in town, the short, picturesque boardwalk known as Uncle Tim's Bridge, off East Commercial Street, crosses Duck Creek to access a tiny island crisscrossed by paths. The Cape Cod National Seashore maintains two spectacular self-guided trails. The 1.25-mile **Atlantic White Cedar Swamp Trail,** off the parking area for the Marconi Wireless Station (see below), shelters a rare stand of the lightweight species prized by Native Americans as wood for canoes; red maples are slowly crowding out the cedars, but meanwhile the tea-tinted, moss-choked swamp is a magical place, refreshingly cool even at the height of summer. A boardwalk will see you over the muck (these peat bogs are 7 ft. deep in places), but the return trip does entail a calf-testing half-mile trek through deep sand. Consider it a warm-up for magnificent **Great Island,** jutting 4 miles into the bay (off the western end of Chequessett Neck Rd.) to cup Wellfleet Harbor. Before attaching itself to the mainland in 1831, Great Island harbored a busy whaling post; a 1970 dig turned up the foundations of an early-18th-century tavern. These days the "island" is quite uninhabited and a true refuge for those strong enough to go the distance. Just be sure to cover up, wear sturdy shoes, bring water, and venture to Jeremy Point—the very tip—only if you're sure the tide is going out.

A spiffy, eco-friendly visitor center serves as both introduction and gateway to the **Wellfleet Bay Wildlife Sanctuary,** off Route 6, a couple hundred yards north of the Eastham border, in South Wellfleet (© **508/349-2615;** fax 508/349-2632; www.wellfleetbay.org), a 1,000-acre refuge maintained by the Massachusetts Audubon Society. Passive solar heat and composting toilets are just a few of the waste-cutting elements incorporated into the seemingly simple $1.6-million building, which nestles in its wooded site like well-camouflaged wildlife. You'll see plenty of the latter—especially lyrical red-winged blackbirds and circling osprey—as you follow 5 miles of looping trails through pine forests, salt marsh, and moors. To hone your observation skills, avail yourself of the naturalist-guided tours offered during the day and sometimes at night (see "Wellfleet After Dark," below): You'll see and learn much more. Also inquire about special workshops for children (some, like the Japanese "fish-printing" session, are truly ingenious), and about canoeing, birding, and seal-watching excursions. Seal-watching trips are $35 for adults, $30 for children for a 1½-hour tour by boat. Canoe trips for experienced paddlers (over age 12) are scheduled in season throughout the Lower Cape. The cost is $25 to $35. A listing of all Wellfleet Bay Wildlife Sanctuary events with dates and times is posted in the main building.

Trail use is free for Massachusetts Audubon Society members; the trail fee for non-members is $5 for adults and $3 for seniors and children. Trails are open July through August from 8am to 8pm, and September through June from 8am to dusk. The visitor center is open Memorial Day to Columbus Day daily from 8:30am to 5pm; during the off season, it's closed Monday.

Note: It's worth joining the Massachusetts Audubon Society just for the chance—afforded only to members—to camp out here.

TENNIS   Public courts are located at Mayo Beach on Kendrick Avenue near the harbor; for details and exact fees, contact the **Wellfleet Recreation Department** (© 508/349-0330). Also for a fee, book one of the five clay courts at the **Chequessett Yacht & Country Club** on Chequessett Neck Road (© 508/349-3704) or one of the eight at **Oliver's Clay Courts** at 2183 Rte. 6, about 1 mile south of town (© 508/349-3330). At Chequessett, 1 hour of singles play costs $18, doubles $20. Both settings are beautiful.

WATERSPORTS   Surfing is restricted to White Crest Beach, and sailboarding to Burton Baker Beach at Indian Neck during certain tide conditions; ask for a copy of the regulations at the Beach Sticker Booth on the Town Pier.

WELLFLEET HISTORICAL SIGHTS

Marconi Wireless Station   It's from this bleak spot that Italian inventor Guglielmo Marconi broadcast, via a complex of 210-foot cable towers, the world's first wireless communiqué: "Cordial greetings from President Theadore [sic] Roosevelt to King Edward VII in Poldhu, Wales." It was also here that news of the troubled *Titanic* first reached these shores. There's scarcely a trace left of this extraordinary feat of technology (the station was dismantled in 1920); still, the displays convey the leap of imagination that was required.

Marconi Site Rd. (off Rte. 6, about ¾ mile south of the town center). © 508/349-3785. www.nps.gov/caco. Free parking and admission. Open dawn–dusk.

Wellfleet Historical Society Museum   Every last bit of spare Wellfleet memorabilia seems to have been crammed into this old storefront. The volunteer curators have taken pains to arrange the surfeit of artifacts so that visitors can follow up on a particular interest—the United Fruit Company (now Chiquita Brands International, Inc.), say, which got its start here in 1870 when one of Lorenzo Dow Baker's swift clipper ships delivered a cargo of exotic bananas, or Marconi's mysterious transoceanic experiments. Even restless children are likely to find something of interest, particularly among the antique toys in the attic. Inquire about the lecture schedule: The museum hosts fascinating speakers and sponsors a chowder supper once a summer. Historical walking tours around town take 1¼ hours, cost $3, and leave at 10:30am.

266 Main St. (in the center of town). © 508/349-9157. Admission $1 adults, free for children under 12. Late June to early Sept Tues and Fri 10am–noon; Tues–Sat 1–4pm. Closed early Sept to late June.

KID STUFF

No conceivable nocturnal treat beats an outing to the Wellfleet Drive-In Theater—unless it's a double feature prefaced by a game of on-site mini-golf while you're waiting for the sky to darken. The restaurant on-site is the **Dairy Bar and Grill** (© 508/349-7007), which specializes in fried seafood and is open from 11:30am to 10pm daily in season. There's mini-golf next to the restaurant.

During the day, check out what's up at the Wellfleet Bay Wildlife Sanctuary (see "Beaches & Recreational Pursuits," above).

SHOPPING

Boasting over a dozen arts emporia, Wellfleet has begun hailing itself as "the art-gallery town." Though it may lag behind Provincetown in terms of quantity, the quality does achieve comparable heights. Crafts make a strong showing, too, as do contemporary women's clothing and eclectic home furnishings. There's just one drawback: Unlike Provincetown, which has something to offer virtually year-round, Wellfleet pretty much closes up come Columbus Day, so buy while the getting's good.

ANTIQUES/COLLECTIBLES   Wheeler-dealers should head for the **Wellfleet Flea Market,** 51 Rte. 6, north of the Eastham–Wellfleet border (✆ 800/696-3532 or 508/349-2520). A few days a week in summer and during the shoulder seasons, the parking lot of the Wellfleet Drive-In Theater "daylights" as an outdoor bazaar featuring as many as 300 booths. Though a great many vendors stock discount surplus, there are usually enough collectibles dealers on hand to warrant a browse through. An added bonus: Kids can kick loose in the little playground or grab a quick bite at the snack bar. Lookers are charged $1 to $2 per carload. Open weekends and Monday holidays, from mid-April through June, September, and October, from 8am to 4pm; Wednesdays, Thursdays, weekends, and Monday holidays in July and August from 8am to 4pm.

   Farmhouse Antiques, Route 6 at Village Lane, South Wellfleet (✆ 508/349-1708), is a large storehouse filled with an enormous variety of goods, including a wide array of furniture, stacks of books and ephemera, and the antique chandeliers that didn't fit in the Orleans shop, Continuum (Farmhouse is a dealer for Continuum's wares).

ARTS & CRAFTS   **Cherrystone Gallery,** 70 E. Commercial St., about ¼ mile south of East Main Street (✆ 508/349-3026), is slightly off the main arts drag and intentionally out of step, but this tiny gallery is probably more influential than all the others put together. It got a head start—opening in 1972, and showing such luminaries as Rauschenberg, Motherwell, and, more recently, Wellfleet resident Helen Miranda Wilson. Closed late September to mid-June.

   One of the more distinguished galleries in town, the smallish **Cove Gallery,** 15 Commercial St., by Duck Creek (✆ 508/349-2530)—with a waterside sculpture garden—carries the paintings and prints of many well-known artists, including Barry Moser and Leonard Baskin. John Grillo's work astounds every summer during his annual show, which recently featured boldly painted tango-themed paintings, watercolors, and prints. Alan Nyiri, whose dazzling color photographs are collected in the coffee-table book *Cape Cod,* shows regularly, as does Carla Golembe, whose lively Caribbean-influenced tableaux have graced several children's books. Closed mid-October through April.

   Crafts make a stronger stand than art at **Left Bank Gallery,** 25 Commercial St., by Duck Creek (✆ 508/349-9451). A 1933 American Legion Hall, it's an optimal display space. Whereas the paintings occupying the former auditorium sometimes verge on hackneyed, the "Potter's Room" overlooking the cove is packed with sturdy, handsome, useful vessels, along with compatible textiles. Also worth hunting out are the curious collages of Kim Victoria Kettler. The **Left Bank Small Works & Jewelry Gallery,** 3 W. Main St., in the center of town (✆ 508/349-7939), features the spillover from the Left Bank Gallery, and in some ways, it is superior. There's also an irresistible sampling of new-wave jewelry designs, collected from over 100 noted artisans across the nation and arrayed in clever thematic displays.

FASHION At **Hannah,** 234 Main St. (© **508/349-9884**), Susan Hannah, whose main store is in ultrahip Northampton, Massachusetts, shows her own private label in this nicely rehabbed house, along with other designers' works. The emphasis is on flowing lines and relaxed fabrics—slinky rayons, soft cotton jersey, and nubby linen. Closed mid-September to late May.

Slightly more citified is **Off Center,** 354 Main St. (© **508/349-3634**), where the clothes are neither traditional nor trendy, but right on, go-anywhere chic. Closed January through March.

Somewhat to the left of—and across the street from—its parent shop, Off Center, is **Eccentricity,** 361 Main St., in the center of town (© **508/349-7554**), which lives up to its name with dramatic antique kimonos and artifacts from Japan, India, and Africa. Closed January through March.

Karol Richardson, 11 W. Main St. (© **508/349-6378**), is owned and operated by its namesake, an alumna of the London College of Fashion and a refugee from the New York rag trade. She has a feel for sensual fabrics and a knack for fashions that, in her own words, are "wonderfully comfortable but sophisticated at the same time and very flattering to the less-than-perfect body." The lovely clothes that are seasonally displayed in this barn showroom, and slavered over by several generations, bear out the claim. Closed mid-October through April.

GIFTS **Jules Besch Stationers,** 15 Bank St. (© **508/349-1231**), specializes in stationery products, including papers, ribbon, gift cards, handmade journals and albums, desktop pen sets, guest books, and unusual gift items. This is an exquisite store in a mansard-roofed former bank building and is certainly worth a browse. Closed January through March.

WHERE TO STAY
MODERATE

Aunt Sukie's Bayside Bed & Breakfast ✿   Sue and Dan Hamar's house is perched on a bluff in an exclusive residential neighborhood overlooking Cape Cod Bay. Behind the house, a boardwalk path leads to a private bay beach. They also own a two-bedroom cottage located about a mile away in the pines that is available by the week and offers, among other features, a galley kitchen, washer/dryer, and barbecue. The main house was built in 1830 but has been modernized and added on to over the years. The Nickerson Suite is in the old part of the house and has wide-board wood floors and a fireplace. The Chequessett and Billingsgate rooms are more contemporary, as befits the addition completed in 1993. All rooms have sweeping bay views. There are beautiful gardens in front of the house, and in the back is a large deck where guests eat breakfast and can sunbathe during the day.

525 Chequessett Neck Rd., Wellfleet, MA 02667. © 800/420-9999 or 508/349-2804. www.auntsukies.com. 3 units (1 tub/shower; 2 shower only), 1 cottage. Summer $225, cottage $1,600 per week. Room rates include continental breakfast. MC, V. Closed mid-Oct to mid-May. *In room:* Fridge.

Even'tide ✿ *Kids*   Set back from the road in its own roomy compound, complete with playground, this motel on the main highway of the outer Cape feels more like a friendly village centered around a 60-foot, heated indoor pool—a godsend in inclement weather and a rarity in this part of the Cape. Four "apartments" have kitchenettes. There are seven cottages on the property with one, two, and three bedrooms. There's a barbecue and picnic area in the pines. The

Rail Trail goes right by the motel, and a 1-mile footpath through the woods leads to Marconi Beach.

650 Rte. 6 (about 1 mile north of the Eastham border), South Wellfleet, MA 02663. ℭ **800/368-0007** in MA only, or 508/349-3410. Fax 508/349-7804. www.eventidemotel.com. 40 units (39 tub/shower; 1 shower only). Summer $125–$205 double, $155–$200 efficiency, $950–$1,400 weekly for cottages. AE, DISC, MC, V. **Amenities:** Large heated indoor pool; playground; self-service laundromat. *In room:* A/C, TV, fridge, coffeemaker.

Surfside Cottages ★★ *(Kids)* This is where you want to be: smack dab on a spectacular beach with 50-foot dunes, within biking distance of Wellfleet Center, and a short drive from Provincetown for dinner. These cottages, fun and modern in a 1960s way, have one, two, or three bedrooms. All cottages have kitchens including microwaves, as well as fireplaces, barbecues, outdoor showers, and screened porches. Some have dishwashers and (most important) roof decks. From mid-May to mid-October, the cottages rent weekly. It's best to bring your own sheets and towels; renting a set costs $10 per person. Reserve early.

Ocean View Dr. (at LeCount Hollow Rd.; P.O. Box 937), South Wellfleet, MA 02663. ℭ/fax **508/349-3959.** www.surfsidevacation.com. 18 cottages (showers only). Summer $875–$1,575 weekly; off season $80–$130 per day. MC, V. Pets allowed off season. *In room:* Fridge, coffeemaker. Closed mid-Nov to early Apr.

INEXPENSIVE

The Inn at Duck Creeke *(Value)* This historic complex consists of four buildings set on 5 woodsy acres overlooking a tidal creek and salt marsh. Three lodging buildings include the main building, an 1880s captain's house with wide-board floors and charming but basic rooms, many with shared bathrooms; the carriage house with a few light and airy cabin-style rooms; and the 1715 salt-works building with smaller, cottage-type rooms with antique decor. In the main building, the shared bathrooms adjoin two rooms, so there's an intimacy here those in search of privacy might not desire. And if the adjoining room houses a family of four, it might be a rough night. All rooms have fans, and the third floor rooms in the main house have air-conditioning. The rooms in the carriage house and saltworks building are quieter and can be downright romantic. But there's definitely a no-frills quality to this lodging option—towels are thin, and so are walls. Even the continental breakfast is very basic: a buffet of tiny muffins on paper plates. A big plus is that there are two good restaurants (see "Where to Dine," below) on-site: Sweet Seasons, the more expensive, and the Duck Creeke Tavern, with a publike atmosphere and live entertainment in season.

70 Main St. (P.O. Box 364), Wellfleet, MA 02667. ℭ **508/349-9333.** Fax 508/349-0234. www.innatduckcreeke. com. 26 units (13 tub/shower; 5 shower only; 8 with shared bathroom). Summer $85–$90, double with shared bathroom, $90–$125 double with private bathroom. Rates include continental breakfast. AE, MC, V. Closed Nov–Apr. **Amenities:** 2 restaurants (seafood restaurant and tavern). *In room:* No phone.

WHERE TO DINE
EXPENSIVE

Aesop's Tables ★★ NEW AMERICAN This delightful restaurant—offbeat and avant-garde enough to stay interesting year after year—has it all: a handsome, historic setting; a relaxed and festive atmosphere; and utterly delectable food, reliably and artistically presented. Brian Dunne is the owner and host; he sets the mood and oversees the sourcing of the superb local provender, even growing some of the edible flowers and delicate greens that go into the Monet's Garden salad. The scallops and oysters come straight from the bay. Stella del Mer is pan-seared scallops in a citrus-saffron broth. The desserts are sacrosanct. Many followers simply could not get through the summer without enjoying at least one encounter with "Clementine's Citrus Tart," a rich pastry offset by a piquant mousse blending fruit and white chocolate.

316 Main St. (in the center of town). ☎ 508/349-6450. Reservations recommended. Main courses $16–$26. AE, MC, V. July–Aug daily 5:30–9:30pm; May, June, and Sept Thurs–Sun 5:30–9:30pm. Closed Oct–May.

Sweet Seasons Restaurant ✦ NEW AMERICAN   Chef-owner Judith Pihl's Mediterranean-influenced fare is still appealing after 20-plus years, as is this mullion-windowed dining room's peaceful pond view. Some of the dishes can be a bit heavy by contemporary standards, but there's usually a healthy alternative: Wellfleet littlenecks and mussels in a golden, aromatic tomato-and-cumin broth, for instance, as opposed to Russian oysters with smoked salmon, vodka, and sour cream. Specialties of the house include creamy sage-and-asparagus ravioli, swordfish with artichoke tapenade, and Seasons shrimp with feta and ouzo. Lighter fare is served in the adjoining Duck Creeke Tavern, with main courses costing $9 to $17.

At the Inn at Duck Creeke, 70 Main St. (about ¼ mile west of Rte. 6). ☎ 508/349-6535. Reservations recommended. Main courses $19–$26. AE, MC, V. July–Sept Tues–Sun 5:30–10pm. Closed Oct–June.

MODERATE

Finely JP's ✦ (Value) NEW AMERICAN   The passing motorist who happens upon this roadside eatery will feel like a clever explorer indeed, even if locals have long been in on the secret. Were it not for the venue—a rather nondescript wood-paneled box right by the busy roadway—chef-owner John Pontius could charge a lot more for his polished cuisine. You can feast on baked oysters Bienville (doused with wine and cream and topped with a mushroom-onion duxelle and grated Parmesan) and an improvised "Wellfleet paella," for very reasonable prices. Pass it on.

554 Rte. 6 (about 1 mile north of the Eastham border). ☎ 508/349-7500. Reservations not accepted. Main courses $13–$21. DISC, MC, V. July to early Sept daily 5–10pm; call for off-season hours. Closed mid-Dec to mid-Jan.

INEXPENSIVE

The Lighthouse (Kids) AMERICAN   Nothing special in and of itself, this bustling, nearly year-round institution on Main Street is an off-season haven for locals and a beacon to passing tourists year-round. Except on Thursday's Mexican Night, the menu is all-American normal, from the steak-and-eggs breakfast to the native seafood dinners. Appreciative patrons usually keep up a dull roar throughout the day, revving up to a deafening roar as the Bass and Guinness flow from the tap.

317 Main St. (in the center of town). ☎ 508/349-3681. Main courses $10–$25. DISC, MC, V. May–Oct daily 7am–10pm; call for off-season hours. Closed Mar.

Moby Dick's Restaurant ✦ (Kids) SEAFOOD   This is your typical clam shack, with the requisite netting and buoys hanging from the ceiling. Order your meal at the register, sit at a picnic table, and a cheerful college student brings it to you. During your meal, one of the owners, Todd or Mignon Barry, will usually come by to ask how you're doing. Fried fish, clams, scallops, and shrimp are all good here; try the Moby's Seafood Special—a heaping platter of all of the above, plus coleslaw and fries. Then there's the clambake special with lobster, steamers, and corn on the cob. The lobster bisque is quite popular. There's also a kids' menu. Portions are huge; bring the family and chow down.

Rte. 6, Wellfleet. ☎ 508/349-9795. www.mobydicksrestaurant.com. Reservations not accepted. Main courses $8–$20. MC, V. Mid-June to early Sept daily 11:30am–10pm; call for off-season hours. Closed mid-Oct to Apr.

TAKEOUT & PICNIC FARE

Box Lunch ⭐ With a porch usually hemmed in by bicycles, this is the original source of the Cape's signature "rollwiches": rolled pita sandwiches with unusual fillings.

50 Briar Lane (north of Main St. in the town center). ℂ 508/349-2178. Mid-June to mid-Sept daily 7am–7pm; mid-Sept to mid-June 7am–2:30pm.

Hatch's Fish & Produce Market *(Finds)* This former fishing shack is the unofficial heart of Wellfleet. You'll find the best of local bounty, from fresh-picked corn and fruit-juice Popsicles to steaming lobsters and home-smoked local mussels and pâté. Virtually no one passes through without picking up a little something, along with the latest talk of the town.

310 Main St. (behind Town Hall). ℂ 508/349-6734 for produce, or 508/349-2810 for fish market. Closed late Sept to May.

Mac's Seafood Market and Harbor Grill Restaurant ⭐ *(Finds)* *(Kids)* Located on the town pier, this takeout shack with picnic tables features fresh local seafood unloaded from the boats just steps away. Besides grilled fish dinners, there are homemade chowders, seafood salads, sushi, and a raw bar. Sit on the picnic tables overlooking the harbor or take your meal over to Mayo Beach next door.

Wellfleet Town Pier. ℂ 508/349-9611. MC, V. Daily 7:30am–10pm. Closed mid-Oct to late May.

SWEETS

The Chocolate Sparrow ⭐ This closet-size outlet of a local chocolatier is hard to pass by once you've happened upon it. There's also a room full of penny candy.

326 Main St. (in the center of town). ℂ 508/349-1333. Call for hours. Closed early Sept to late May.

A Nice Cream Stop *(Kids)* This is Wellfleet's premier premium ice-cream parlor, scooping Emack & Bolio's, a luscious Boston boutique brand.

326 Main St. (in the center of town). ℂ 508/349-2210. Mid-June to early Sept 11am–10pm. Closed mid-Sept to mid-June.

WELLFLEET AFTER DARK
CLUBS & WATERING HOLES

The Beachcomber ⭐ Arguably the best dance club on Cape Cod, the 'Comber—housed in an 1897 lifesaving station—is definitely the most scenic, and not just in terms of the barely legal-age clientele. It's right on Cahoon Hollow Beach—so close, in fact, that late beachgoers on summer weekends can count on a free concert: reggae, perhaps, or the homegrown Toots and the Maytalls. Other nights, you might run into blues, ska, or rock, and often some very big names playing mostly for the fun of it. For victims of late-night munchies, the Beachcomber serves food until midnight. Open late June to early September daily noon to 1am; call for off-season hours. Closed early September to late May. 1220 Old Cahoon Hollow Rd. (off Ocean View Dr. at Cahoon Hollow Beach). ℂ 508/349-6055. www.beachcomber.com. Cover varies.

Duck Creeke Tavern Live music featuring local talent—jazz, pop, folk, blues, and various hybrids—is on the bill Thursdays through Sundays in the summer. A good light fare menu is also available. Check out the bar itself, fashioned from old doors. Closed mid-October to late May. At the Inn at Duck Creeke, 70 Main St. (about ¼ mile west of Rte. 6). ℂ 508/349-7369. No cover.

Upstairs Bar at Aesop's Tables Locally spawned blues and jazz usually inhabit this cozy attic, where revelers can recline in comfy armchairs and velvet settees. A cafe menu from the superb restaurant downstairs (see "Where to Dine," above) can be enjoyed, along with the signature desserts and seductive "special finales," blending coffee or tea and select liqueurs. There is live music, along the lines of acoustic guitar, some weekends in the off season with no cover charge. Open July to August daily 5:30pm to 1am; call for off-season hours. Closed mid-October to mid-May. 316 Main St. (in the center of town). ✆ 508/349-6450. No cover.

FROM BELFRIES TO BATS & OTHER ENTERTAINMENT
The **First Congregational Church of the United Church of Christ,** 200 Main St., about ¼ mile west of Route 6 (✆ **508/349-6877**), hosts organ concerts Sundays at 8pm during July and August on its elaborate 1873 instrument. They're a good excuse to stop in and take a look around—the soaring 1850 Greek Revival church has the world's only bell tower ringing ship's time (an innovation introduced in 1952). Admission is free.

Wednesday nights in July and August, Wellfleet's workaday fishing pier (off Kendrick Ave.) resounds to the footfalls of avid amateur square dancers of every age. Call ✆ **508/349-0330** for more information.

How about a night hike or bat walk? Both are offered at the **Wellfleet Bay Wildlife Sanctuary** (✆ **508/349-2615;** see "Beaches & Recreational Pursuits," earlier in this chapter). Rates vary; call for schedule and reservations. Just don't take in any vampire movies at the drive-in beforehand.

The **Wellfleet Drive-In Theater,** 51 Rte. 6, just north of the Eastham border (✆ **800/696-3532** or 508/349-2520), clearly deserves National Landmark status: Built in 1957, it's the only drive-in left on Cape Cod and one of a scant half dozen surviving in the state. The rituals are unbending and every bit as endearing as ever: the playtime preceding the cartoons, the countdown plugging the allures of the snack bar, and finally, two full first-run features. The drive-in is open daily from late May through mid-September; show time is at dusk. Call for off-season hours. Admission is $7 for adults and $4 for seniors and children 5 to 11.

The principals behind the **Wellfleet Harbor Actors' Theatre,** 1 Kendrick Ave., near the Town Pier (✆ **508/349-6835**), aim to provoke—and usually succeed, even amid this very sophisticated, seen-it-all summer colony. Co-artistic directors Jeff Zinn and playwright Gip Hoppe go to great lengths to secure original work, some local and some by playwrights of considerable renown, with the result that the repertory rarely suffers a dull moment. Tickets are $21. Performances are given daily at 8pm from late May through October; call for a schedule.

3 Truro ✮✮

46 miles E of Sandwich; 10 miles S of Provincetown

Although Truro is one of those blink-and-you'll-miss-it towns, the location is great: a tranquil village between charming Wellfleet and rowdy Provincetown. With only 1,600 year-round residents (fewer than it boasted in 1840, when Pamet Harbor was a whaling and shipbuilding port), the town amounts to little more than a smattering of stores and public buildings, and lots of low-profile houses hidden away in the woods and dunes. As in Wellfleet, writers, artists, and vacationing therapists are drawn to the quiet and calm. Edward Hopper lived in contented isolation in a South Truro cottage for nearly 4 decades.

If you find yourself craving cultural stimulation or other kinds of excitement, Provincetown is only a 10-minute drive away (you'll know you're getting close when you spot the wall-to-wall tourist cabins lining the bay in North Truro). Here, the natives manage to entertain themselves pretty well with get-togethers at the Truro Center for the Arts or, more simply, among themselves. However much money may be circulating in this rusticated community (the answer is: a lot), inconspicuous consumption is the rule of the day. The culmination of the social season, tellingly enough, is the late-September "dump dance" held at Truro's recycling center.

ESSENTIALS

GETTING THERE　After crossing the Sagamore Bridge, head east on Route 6 or 6A to Orleans and north on Route 6. Or fly into Provincetown (see "Getting There" in chapter 2).

VISITOR INFORMATION　Contact the **Truro Chamber of Commerce,** Route 6A (at Head of the Meadow Rd.), Truro, MA 02666 (© **508/487-1288**) or the **Cape Cod Chamber of Commerce** (see "Visitor Information" in the "Eastham" section, earlier in this chapter). The Truro Chamber office is open 10am to 4pm in season.

BEACHES & RECREATIONAL PURSUITS

BEACHES　Parking at all of Truro's exquisite Atlantic beaches, except for one Cape Cod National Seashore access point, is reserved for residents and renters. To obtain a sticker ($20 for 1 week; $30 for 2 weeks), inquire at the beach-sticker office at 14 Truro Center Rd. behind the post office in Truro Center (© **508/487-3635**). Walkers and bikers are welcome to visit such natural wonders as Ballston Beach, where all you'll see is silky sand and grass-etched dunes. Parking is free at all beaches after 4pm.

- **Corn Hill Beach** 🐾🐾, off Corn Hill Road: Offering restrooms, this bay beach—near the hill where the Pilgrims found the seed corn that ensured their survival—is open to nonresidents for a parking fee of $10 per day.
- **Head of the Meadow** 🐾🐾🐾, off Head of the Meadow Road: Among the more remote National Seashore beaches, this spot (equipped with restrooms) is known for its excellent surf. A parking lot connected by a short boardwalk to the beach makes this beach more easily accessible than other National Seashore beaches. It is also connected by a short bike path to Pilgrim Heights (see "Bicycling," below). Parking costs $10 per day, or $30 per season.

BICYCLING　Although it has yet to be linked up to the Cape Cod Rail Trail, Truro does have a stunning 2-mile bike path of its own: the **Head of the Meadow Trail** 🐾, off the road of the same name (look for a right-hand turn about a half mile north of where routes 6 and 6A intersect). Part of the old 1850 road toward Provincetown—Thoreau traveled this same route—it skirts the bluffs, passing Pilgrim Heights (where the Pilgrims found their first drinking water) and ending at High Head Road. Being fairly flat as well as short, this stretch should suit youngsters and beginners. You can rent a bike in Provincetown or Wellfleet.

BOATING　The inlets of Pamet Harbor are great for canoeing and kayaking; when planning an excursion, study the tides so you won't be working against them. The closest rentals are in Wellfleet at **Jack's Boat Rentals** (© **508/349-9808**) on Route 6, next to the Cumberland Farms. Eric Gustavson (© **508/349-1429**) leads naturalist kayak tours along the Pamet River and other locations on the Outer Cape. You can get the schedule from Jack's Boat Rentals.

FISHING　Great Pond, Horseleech Pond, and Pilgrim Lake—flanked by parabolic dunes carved by the wind—are all fishable; for a freshwater fishing license, visit **Town Hall** on Town Hall Road (✆ **508/487-2702**). You can also call town hall for a shellfishing license. Surf-casting is permitted at Highland Light Beach, off Highland Road.

GOLF   North Truro boasts the most scenic—and historic—nine-hole course on the Cape. Created in 1892, the minimally groomed, Scottish-style **Highland Links** at 10 Lighthouse Rd., off South Highland Road (✆ **508/487-9201**), shares a lofty bluff with the 1853 Highland Light, where Thoreau used to stay during his Outer Cape expeditions. Greens fees at the federally owned, town-run Highland Links are reasonable ($16 for nine holes, $32 for 18 holes), considering the spectacular setting.

NATURE TRAILS   The Cape Cod National Seashore, comprising 70% of Truro's land, offers three self-guided nature trails. The .5-mile **Pamet Trail** ✿ off North Pamet Road leads you past an old cranberry-bog building and bogs that have reverted to marshland. Park in the lot to the left of the Little America youth hostel (see "Where to Stay," below) and walk back to the fire road entrance about 500 feet down North Pamet Road. The **Pilgrim Spring Trail** ✿ and **Small Swamp Trail** ✿ (each a .75-mile loop) head out from the National Seashore parking lot just east of Pilgrim Lake. Pilgrim Spring is where the parched colonists sipped their first fresh water in months. Small Swamp is named for Thomas Small, a rather overly optimistic 19th-century farmer who tried to cultivate fruit trees in soil more suited to salt hay. Both paths overlook Salt Meadow, a freshwater marsh favored by hawks and osprey.

TENNIS   Courts are available at the **Pamet Harbor Yacht and Tennis Club** on Depot Road (✆ **508/349-3772**). Hourly fees are $16 singles and $20 doubles.

A MUSEUM & AN ARTS CENTER

Highland House Museum and Highland Lighthouse   Built as a hotel in 1907, the Highland House is a perfect repository of the odds and ends collected by the Truro Historical Society: ship's models, harpoons, primitive toys, a pirate's chest, and so on. Be sure to visit the second floor, set up as if still occupied by 19th-century tourists. In 1996, Highland Lighthouse was moved back from its perilous perch above a rapidly eroding dune. Now the lighthouse is within 800 feet of the museum and is also operated by the Truro Historical Society. Seasonal lighthouse tours run May through October. There is a 51-inch height requirement so, unfortunately, little ones can't climb up the tower.

27 Highland Light Rd. (off S. Highland Rd., 2 miles north of the town center on Rte. 6). ✆ **508/487-1121**. Admission to both museum and lighthouse $5 adults, free for children under 12. Admission to museum or lighthouse $3; free for children under 12 at museum only. Museum June–Sept daily 10am–4:30pm. Last ticket sold at 3:30pm. Lighthouse May–Oct daily 10am–6pm. Closed Oct–May.

Truro Center for the Arts at Castle Hill   Send ahead for a brochure, and you could work some learning into your vacation. A great many celebrated writers and artists—from poet Alan Dugan to painter Edith Vonnegut—emerge from their summer hideaways to offer courses, lectures, and exhibits at this bustling little complex, an 1880s horse barn with windmill (now home to the administrative offices). The roster changes slightly from year to year, but you can rest assured that the stellar instructors will be at the top of their form in this stimulating environment. The center also offers lots of children's workshops for artists age 7 and up. Castle Hill Evenings, which are $5 lectures and readings, take place Tuesdays in July and August at 8pm at the Wellfleet Library.

10 Meetinghouse Rd. (at Castle Rd., about ¾ mile northwest of the town center). ✆ **508/349-7511**. www. castlehill.org. Admission varies. MC, V. Call for schedule. Closed Oct–May.

A GALLERY WITH A SENSE OF HUMOR

The Susan Baker Memorial Museum, 46 Shore Rd., Route 6A, ¼ mile north-west of Route 6 (© **508/487-2557**), showcases Ms. Baker's creative output, from fanciful/functional papier-mâché *objets* to brightly colored European land-scapes. Despite the place's name, Baker has not passed on; it seems that she her-self has exaggerated rumors of her death so as to rate her own museum without actually croaking. You might guess that she is definitely a character, as original as her work. Her main stock in trade—here, and at her Provincetown outlet—is humor displayed in various media, from artist's books to very atypical T-shirts (among the more popular of slogans in Provincetown: "Too Mean to Marry"). Call ahead October through May.

WHERE TO STAY

Days Cottages ★ *Value*   These are the famous tiny cottages you always see in local paintings and photos. Lined up along the bay beach in North Truro, these absolutely identical cottages—named after flowers—are all white clapboard with sea-foam green shutters. Although lacking frills, each has a living room, two small bedrooms, a kitchen, and a bathroom. The downside is that these accom-modations are somewhat rough: The bedrooms are minuscule, and in some of the cottages, the fireplace has about 10 years' worth of graffiti written on the brick chimney. There is also the noise of passing cars on this busy stretch of road to contend with. The upside is miles of bay beach for walking and swimming with views of Provincetown's quirky skyline in the distance. In season, beginning June 1, the cottages are rented only by the week, and they usually book up far in advance. Nevertheless, you may be able to squeeze in.

Rte. 6A. (a couple miles south of the Provincetown border), North Truro, MA 02652. © **508/487-1062**. Fax 508/487-5595. www.dayscottages.com. 23 cottages (all with shower only). Summer $920 weekly. No credit cards. Closed mid-Oct to Apr. *In room:* Fridge.

Hostelling International-Truro *Value*   By far the most scenic of the youth hostels on the Cape, this Hopperesque house on a lonely bluff a short stroll from Ballston Beach was once a Coast Guard station; these days, it winters as an envi-ronmental-studies center. During the all-too-short summer, it's a magnet for hikers, cyclists, and surfers.

111 N. Pamet Rd. (1¼ miles east of Rte. 6), Truro, MA 02666. © **508/349-3889**. 42 beds. $22–$24 members; $25–$27 non-members. MC, V. Closed early Sept to late June.

Kalmar Village ★★ *Value* *Kids*   Spiffier than many of the motels and cottages along this spit of sand between Pilgrim Lake and Pilgrim Beach, this 1940s com-plex resembles a miniaturized Edgartown, with little white cottages shuttered in black. There are picnic tables, grills, and daily maid service. Some cottages have air-conditioning. The clientele—mostly families—can splash the day away in the 60-foot freshwater pool or on the 400-foot private beach.

674 Shore Rd. (Rte. 6A, about ¼ mile south of the Provincetown border), North Truro, MA 02652. © **508/ 487-0585**. Fax 508/487-5827. www.kalmarvillage.com. 16 units, 40 cottages. Summer $135 double, $175 2-bedroom suite, $1,295–$1,495 cottages weekly. DISC, MC, V. Closed mid-Oct to late May. **Amenities:** Out-door pool; coin-op laundry. *In room:* TV, fridge.

Outer Reach Motel *Value*   This motel set high on a bluff on Route 6 (the Mid Cape Hwy.) is where you stay if you are looking for a cheap, no-frills motel room and you don't plan to spend much time there. Rooms are clean and surprisingly spacious, some with king beds. Many rooms have distant ocean views, and some have balconies and views of Provincetown. But the complex is a bit run down in places, and the staff is unusually surly (even by Cape Cod standards). In addition to the outdoor pool and tennis court, there's a basketball hoop and shuffleboard. The ocean is 1 mile east. The rooms are standard issue with large fans. There's a mediocre restaurant, Adrian's, within the complex. You're better off driving to Provincetown for dinner.

535 Rte. 6 (midway between North Truro center and the Provincetown border), North Truro, MA 02652. © 800/942-5388 or 508/487-9090. Fax 508/487-9007. www.outerreachresort.com. 58 units. Summer 119–$159 double. MC, V. Closed late Oct to mid-May. **Amenities:** Restaurant; outdoor pool; concrete tennis court. *In room:* TV, fridge, no phone.

A Vineyard in the Dunes *(Moments)*   This pastoral property just off Route 6 in Truro is one of the last working farms in the Outer Cape and the site of an honest-to-goodness vineyard. Horticulturist/innkeepers Kathy Gregrow and Judy Wimer of **Truro Vineyard of Cape Cod** (11 Shore Road/Rte. 6A, North Truro; © 508/487-6200) uncorked their first homegrown chardonnay and Cabernet Franc in the fall of 1996, the muscadet in 1997, the merlot in 1998. Inside the main house, the living room, with its exposed beams, is decorated with interesting oenological artifacts. Late May through October, free wine tastings are held daily from noon to 5pm. Guided tours of the property take place at 1 and 3pm.

11 Shore Rd. (Rte. 6A, 6½ miles south of town center), North Truro, MA 02652,. ©/fax 508/487-6200. 5 units. Summer $99 double, $129 suite. Rates include continental breakfast. MC, V. Closed mid-Sept to mid-May. *In room:* No phone.

WHERE TO DINE

Babe's Bakery and Restaurant ★ *(Finds)* DINER   Perched on a windswept hill in North Truro, this terrific diner serves very basic but consistently good meals. The pastries are homemade and baked on-site daily. Babe's is popular, so expect a half-hour wait in season (timing is everything; the earlier the better). Hearty lunch selections include a Reuben sandwich, bacon-and-cheese burger, or perhaps quiche Lorraine. There's also a selection of fresh salads and sandwiches.

Rte. 6A (about ¼ mile north of the North Truro center), North Truro. © 508/487-9473. Most items under $8. No credit cards. Mid-June to Sept daily 7:30am–noon. Closed Oct to mid-June.

Terra Luna ★ FUSION   People come from miles around to sample the outstanding breakfasts at this modest restaurant. The muffins and scones emerge fresh from the oven, and entrees such as the breakfast burrito or strawberry mascarpone-cheese pancakes call for a hearty appetite. You can start in again in the evening, on well-priced Pacific Rim and/or neo-Italian fare, such as penne prosciutto sautéed with garlic, black pepper, and a splash of vodka. Main courses include local seafood and lobster dishes, like lobster risotto with asparagus and saffron. There's even a creative children's menu here.

104 Shore Rd. (Rte. 6A), North Truro. © 508/487-1019. Reservations recommended. Main courses $14–$20. AE, MC, V. Late May to mid-Oct daily 8am–1pm and 5:30–10pm. Closed mid-Oct to late May.

SWEETS & TAKEOUT

Jams *(Finds)*   Seeing as this deli/bakery/grocery is basically the whole enchilada in terms of downtown Truro, and seasonal to boot, it's good that it's so delightful. It's full of tantalizing aromas: fresh, creative pizzas (from pesto to pupu); rotisserie fowl sizzling on the spit; or cookies straight from the oven. The pastry and deli selections deserve their own four-star restaurant, but they are all the more savory as part of a picnic.

14 Truro Center Rd. (off Rte. 6, in the center of town). © 508/349-1616. Call for hours. Closed early Sept to late May.

Paradice *Finds*   Hot, thirsty travelers will think they've died and gone to Hawaii when they happen upon "shave ice," a Pacific treat available here in 38 flavors, from Kahlúa to apple pie a la mode.

1 Depot Rd. (at Old County Rd., about ½ mile west of Rte. 6). ℂ 508/349-2499. Call for hours. Closed early Sept to June.

4 Provincetown ★★★

56 miles NE of Sandwich; 42 miles NE of Hyannis

You made it all the way to the end of the Cape: one of the most interesting, rewarding spots on the eastern seaboard. Explorer Bartholomew Gosnold surely felt much the same thrill in 1602, when he and his crew happened upon a "great stoare of codfysshes" here (it wasn't quite the gold they were seeking but valuable enough to warrant changing the peninsula's name). The Pilgrims, of course, were overjoyed when they slogged into the harbor 18 years later: Never mind that they'd landed several hundred miles off course—it was a miracle they'd made it round the treacherous Outer Cape at all. And Charles Hawthorne, the painter who "discovered" this near-derelict fishing town in the late 1890s and introduced it to the Greenwich Village intelligentsia, was besotted by this "jumble of color in the intense sunlight accentuated by the brilliant blue of the harbor."

He'd probably be aghast at the commercial circus his enthusiasm has wrought—though proud, perhaps, to find the Provincetown Art Association & Museum, which he helped found in 1914, still going strong. Although it's bound to experience the occasional off year or dull stretch, the town is wholeheartedly dedicated to creative expression, both visual and verbal, and right now, it's on a roll. Some would ascribe the inspiration to the quality of the light (and it is particularly lovely—soft and diffuse) or the solitude afforded by long, lonely winters. But the general atmosphere of open-mindedness plays at least as pivotal a role, allowing a very varied assortment of individuals to pull together in pushing the cultural envelope.

That same warm embrace of different lifestyles accounts for Provincetown's ascendancy as a gay and lesbian resort. During peak season, Provincetown's streets are a celebration of the individual's freedom to be as out as imagination allows. This isolated outpost has always been a magnet for the adventurous minded. In fact, the tightly knit Portuguese community mostly descends from fishermen and whaling crews who set out from the Azores in centuries past. You might think that a culture so bound by tradition and religion would look askance at a way of life so antithetical to their own, but "family values" enjoy a very broad definition here. Those who've settled in Provincetown (affectionately referred to as "P-town") know they've found a very special place, and in that, they have something precious in common.

ESSENTIALS

GETTING THERE   After crossing the Sagamore Bridge (see "Getting There" in chapter 2), head east on Route 6 or 6A to Orleans, then north on Route 6.

If you plan to spend your entire vacation in Provincetown, you don't need a car because everything is within walking or biking distance. And since parking is a hassle in this tiny town, consider leaving your car at home and taking a boat from Boston or Plymouth. Another advantage is that you'll get to skip the horrendous Sagamore Bridge traffic jams and arrive like the Pilgrims did.

Bay State Cruises (ℂ 617/748-1428; www.baystatecruises.com) makes round-trips from Boston, daily from late June through September.

Provincetown

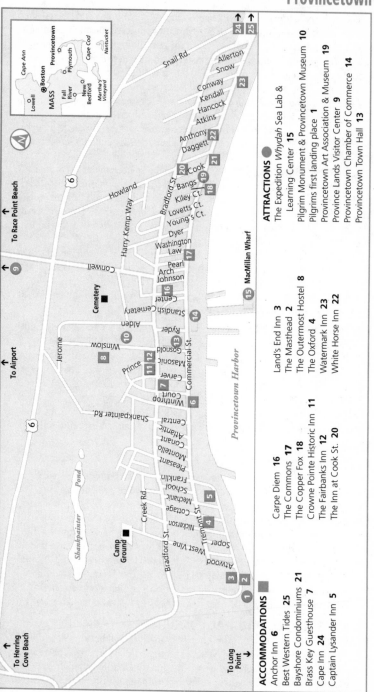

ACCOMMODATIONS ◾

Anchor Inn **6**
Best Western Tides **25**
Bayshore Condominiums **21**
Brass Key Guesthouse **7**
Cape Inn **24**
Captain Lysander Inn **5**

Carpe Diem **16**
The Commons **17**
The Copper Fox **18**
Crowne Pointe Historic Inn **11**
The Fairbanks Inn **12**
The Inn at Cook St. **20**

Land's End Inn **3**
The Masthead **2**
The Outermost Hostel **8**
The Oxford **4**
Watermark Inn **23**
White Horse Inn **22**

ATTRACTIONS ●

The Expedition *Whydah* Sea Lab &
  Learning Center **15**
Pilgrim Monument & Provincetown Museum **10**
Pilgrims first landing place **1**
Provincetown Art Association & Museum **19**
Province Lands Visitor Center **9**
Provincetown Chamber of Commerce **14**
Provincetown Town Hall **13**

The high-speed *Provincetown Express* boat takes 1½ hours and makes three round-trips daily from mid-May to late September. It leaves Boston's Commonwealth Pier at 8am, 1pm, and 5:30pm. On the return trip, it leaves Provincetown at 10am, 3pm, and 7:30pm. Tickets on the high-speed boat cost $35 one-way, $55 round-trip for adults. Seniors are $30 one-way and $50 round-trip. Children 4 to 11 are $20 one-way, $45 round-trip. Reservations are recommended.

The regular 3-hour boat, called *Provincetown II,* leaves Boston's Commonwealth Pier on Fridays, Saturdays and Sundays at 9:30am and arrives in Provincetown at 12:30pm. At 3:30pm, the boat leaves Provincetown, arriving in Boston at 6:30pm. On the slow boat, round-trip fare is $29 for adults, $19 for children 4 to 11, and $23 for seniors.

Capt. John Boats (℃ **508/747-2400;** www.provincetownferry.com) connects Plymouth and Provincetown daily mid-June through August; Tuesday, Wednesday, Saturday, and Sunday in September; and weekends only from late May to mid-June. The 1½-hour boat ride leaves Plymouth at 10am; it leaves Provincetown at 4:30pm. The adult round-trip fare is $30, seniors $25, children under 12 $20; bikes are $3 extra.

You can also fly into Provincetown (see "Getting There" in chapter 2). Cape Air (℃ **800/352-0714;** www.flycapeair.com) offers flights from Boston and from Nantucket in season. Both trips take about 25 minutes.

As far as getting around once you're settled, you can enjoy the vintage fleet of the **Mercedes Cab Company** (℃ **508/487-3333**).

VISITOR INFORMATION   Contact the **Provincetown Chamber of Commerce,** 307 Commercial St., Provincetown, MA 02657 (℃ **508/487-3424;** fax 508/487-8966; www.ptownchamber.com), open late May to mid-September daily from 9am to 5pm (call for off-season hours); the gay-oriented **Provincetown Business Guild,** 115 Bradford St., P.O. Box 421, Provincetown, MA 02657 (℃ **800/637-8696** or 508/487-2313; fax 508/487-1252; www.ptown.org), open Monday to Friday from 9am to noon and 12:30 to 2pm; or the **Cape Cod Chamber of Commerce** (see "Visitor Information" in the "Eastham" section, earlier in this chapter).

GETTING AROUND

Parking is at a premium in Provincetown. Illegally parked cars are ticketed (even on Sun), and repeat offenders will be towed. If your inn provides parking, you may want to keep your car there and get around on foot, bicycle, or shuttle. **Provincetown's Summer Shuttle** (℃ **508/487-8966**) loops through town daily every 20 minutes late June to mid-September from 7am to 12:30am, traveling all along Bradford Street, to Macmillan Wharf off Commercial Street, and all the way to North Truro. The beach loop travels to Herring Cove every 20 minutes from 9am to 7pm. Riders may flag down the bus at any intersection on Bradford Street. Service continues through October in Provincetown only, without the Truro stops. All rides cost $1 for adults, 50¢ for seniors and kids 6 to 17.

BEACHES & RECREATIONAL PURSUITS

BEACHES   With nine-tenths of its territory (basically, all but the "downtown" area) protected by the Cape Cod National Seashore (CCNS), Provincetown has miles of beaches. The 3-mile bay beach that lines the harbor, though certainly swimmable, is not all that inviting compared to the magnificent ocean beaches overseen by the National Seashore. The two official access areas (see below) tend to be crowded; however, you can always find a less densely populated stretch if you're willing to hike.

Note: Local beachgoer activists have been lobbying for "clothing-optional" beaches for years, but the rangers, fearful of voyeurs trampling the dune grass, are firmly opposed and routinely issue tickets, so stand forewarned (and fully clothed).

- **Herring Cove** ★★★ and **Race Point** ★★★: Both National Seashore beaches are spectacular, with long stretches of pristine sand, and they are very popular. Herring Cove, facing west, is known for its spectacular sunsets; observers often applaud. Race Point, on the ocean side, is rougher, and you might actually spot whales en route to Stellwagen Bank. Calmer Herring Cove is a haven for same-sex couples, who tend to sort themselves by gender. Parking costs $10 per day, $30 per season.
- **Long Point:** Trek out over the breakwater and beyond, or catch a water shuttle—$8 one-way, $12 round-trip, hourly in season or by demand off season—from Flyer's Boat Rental (see "Boating," below) or slip 2 on Macmillan Wharf to visit this very last spit of land, capped by an 1827 lighthouse. Locals call it "the end of the Earth." Shuttles run hourly in July and August.

BICYCLING North of town, nestled amid the Cape Cod National Seashore preserve, is one of the more spectacular bike paths in New England, the 7-mile **Province Lands Trail** ★★, a heady swirl of steep dunes (watch out for sand drifts on the path) anchored by wind-stunted scrub pines. With its free parking, the **Province Lands Visitor Center** ★ (℗ **508/487-1256**) is a good place to start: You can survey the landscape from the observation tower to try to get your bearings before setting off amid the dizzying maze. Follow signs to follow a spur path leading to one of the beaches, Race Point or Herring Cove. Bike rentals are offered seasonally by **Nelson's Bike Shop** at 43 Race Point Rd. (℗ **508/487-8849**). It's also an easy jaunt from town, where you'll find plenty of good bike shops—such as the centrally located **Ptown Bikes** at 42 Bradford St. (℗ **508/487-8735;** reserve several days in advance)—as well as all the picnic fixings you could possibly desire. Bike rentals cost $5 an hour or $20 a day.

BOATING In addition to operating a Long Point shuttle from its own dock (see "Beaches," above), **Flyer's Boat Rental** at 131 Commercial St. in the West End (℗ **508/487-0898**)—established in 1945—offers all sorts of craft, from kayaks ($25 half day; $40 full day) and dinghies to sailboats of varying sizes; they also give sailing lessons ($80 for 2 hr.). They offer a special fishing rate of $55 to rent a small boat with light tackle from 8am to 12:30pm.

FISHING Surf-casting is permitted at Herring Cove Beach (off Rte. 6) and Race Point Beach (near the Race Point Coast Guard Station); also, many people drop a hand-line or light tackle right off the West End breakwater. For low-cost deep-sea fishing via party boat, board the *Cee Jay* (℗ **800/675-6724** or 508/ 487-4330); it makes two 4-hour trips a day and costs $27 for adults and $17 for children. For serious sportfishing, sign on for the *Shady Lady II* (℗ **508/487-0182**). Both depart from MacMillan Wharf.

FITNESS For days when the weather forces your workouts indoors, the **Provincetown Gym** at 81 Shank Painter Rd. (℗ **508/487-2776**) has the usual equipment and promises a non-intimidating atmosphere. Day passes cost $12. The **Mussel Beach Health Club,** 35 Bradford St. (℗ **508/487-0001**), attracts a rather buff clientele. Day passes are $15. For postworkout pampering, book a massage or herbal wrap at the **West End Salon & Spa,** 155 Commercial St. (℗ **508/ 487-1872**).

NATURE TRAILS   Within the Province Lands (off Race Point Rd., ½ mile north of Rte. 6), the **Cape Cod National Seashore** maintains the 1-mile, self-guided **Beech Forest Trail** 🐾, a shaded path that circles a shallow freshwater pond blanketed with water lilies (also look for sunning turtles) before heading into the woods. You can see the shifting dunes (much of this terrain is soft sand) gradually encroaching on the forest.

A walk along the **West End breakwater** 🐾🐾 and out to the end of **Long Point,** about 5 miles round-trip, is for hearty hikers. Walking just to the end of the wide breakwater, located at the end of Commercial Street next to the Provincetown Inn, is quite popular. You'll see all ages maneuvering the layered boulders, which is about a 30-minute walk each way. If you want to continue to Long Point, the very tip of Cape Cod, it's about an hour and a half across soft sand to the end of the point. At low tide, the distance can be shortened by cutting across the salt flats. **Wood End Lighthouse** is directly across the spit of sand near the breakwater.

Whale-Watching

In 1975, 4 years after the U.S. government—fearing the species' extinction—called an official halt to whaling, fisherman Al Avellar noticed that they seemed to be making a comeback in the Stellwagen Bank feeding area, 8 miles off Provincetown. Together with marine biologist Charles "Stormy" Mayo of the Center for Coastal Studies, he came up with the notion of a new kind of hunt, spearheaded by tourists bearing cameras. An immediate success, their **Dolphin Fleet** 🐾🐾, on MacMillan Wharf (© **800/826-9300** or 508/349-1900), was widely copied up and down the coast. These are still the prime feeding grounds, however, which is why all the whale-watching fleets can confidently "guarantee" sightings—they offer a rain check should the cetaceans fail to surface.

Most cruises carry a naturalist (a very vague term) to provide running commentary: The *Dolphin*'s difference is that CCS scientists do research crucial to the whales' survival, and part of the proceeds goes to further their worthwhile efforts. Serious whale aficionados will want to try one of the day-long trips to the Great South Channel, where humpbacks and finbacks are likely to be found by the dozen.

Some tips for first-timers: Dress very warmly, in layers (it's cold out on the water), and definitely take along a windbreaker, waterproof if possible. The weather's capricious, and if you stand in the bow of the boat, the best viewing point, you can count on getting drenched. Veteran whale-watchers know to bring a spare set of dry clothes, as well as binoculars—although if the whales seem to be feeling friendly and frisky, as they often are, they'll play practically within reach. And last but not least, if you're prone to seasickness, you'd better bring along some motion-sickness pills: It can get pretty rough out there.

Tickets are $22 for adults, $20 for seniors, $19 for children 7 to 12, and free for children under 7. In season, there are nine 3½-hour trips daily. Call for a schedule and reservations (required). Closed late October through March.

Long Point Lighthouse is at the end of the point. Hikers determined to reach the end of Long Point will want to bring a hat, water, and sunscreen for this intense trek along the beach. The outside of the arm, where you look out on Cape Cod Bay, tends to be the more scenic route for contemplative hikers; the inside of the arm has views of Provincetown and Provincetown Harbor and a couple of shipwrecks. The Long Point Shuttle runs from MacMillan Wharf across to Long Point for about $12 round-trip. Service is continuous in season.

TENNIS Three public courts are located at Motta Memorial Field at the top of Winslow Street (near the Provincetown Monument); for details, contact the **Provincetown Recreation Department** (✆ 508/487-7097). Open mid-May to mid-October, the **Provincetown Tennis Club** at 186 Bradford St. (✆ **508/487-9574**) has seven courts—two asphalt, five clay—tucked amid tall trees. Court time is $25 to $30 an hour.

ORGANIZED TOURS

Art's Dune Tours ★★ In 1946, Art Costa started driving sightseers out to ogle the decrepit "dune shacks" where such transient luminaries as Eugene O'Neill, Jack Kerouac, and Jackson Pollock found their respective muses; in one such hovel, Tennessee Williams cooked up the steamy *A Streetcar Named Desire*. The park service wanted to raze these eyesores, but luckily saner heads prevailed: They're now National Historic Landmarks. The tours conducted by Art's son and others, via Chevy Suburban, typically take about 1 to 1½ hours and are filled with wonderful stories of local literati and other characters. Don't forget your camera for the views of this totally unique landscape. Additional tours offered include a sunset clambake dune tour ($66), a bar-be-que tour ($56) and a Race Point Lighthouse tour ($23 adults, $13 children 6 to 11), in which part of the proceeds is donated to the lighthouse foundation.

At the corner of Commercial and Standish sts. (in the center of town). ✆ 800/894-1951 or 508/487-1950. www.artsdunetours.com. Tickets $15 adults, $8 children 6–11. Sunset tours $20 adults, $10 children. Call for schedule and reservations.

Bay Lady II ★ In sightseeing aboard this 73-foot reproduction gaff-rigged Grand Banks schooner, you'll actually add to the scenery for on-lookers onshore. The sunset trip is especially spectacular.

MacMillan Wharf (in the center of town). ✆ 508/487-9308. www.sailcapecod.com. Tickets $12–$16 adults, $7 children under 12. MC, V. Mid-May to mid-Oct, 4 2-hr. sails daily; call for schedule and reservations. Closed mid-Oct to mid-May.

PROVINCETOWN MUSEUMS

The Expedition Whydah Sea Lab & Learning Center *Overrated* Though the subject matter here is fascinating, this site is a bit of a tourist trap. Cape Cod native Barry Clifford made headlines in 1984 when he tracked down the wreck of the 17th-century pirate ship *Whydah* (pronounced *Wid*-dah, like Yankee for "widow") 1,500 feet off the coast of Wellfleet, where it had lain undisturbed since 1717. Only 10% excavated to date, it has already yielded over 100,000 artifacts, including 10,000 gold and silver coins, plus its namesake bell, proving its authenticity. In this museum/lab, visitors can supposedly observe the reclamation work involving electrolytic reduction, though it's unusual to actually see scientists or scholars at work removing barnacles. Some of the loot, like a surprisingly small man's boot, is displayed in cases.

MacMillan Wharf (just past the whale-watching fleet). ✆ 508/487-8899. www.whydah.com. Admission $8 adults, $6 children 6–12. June–Sept daily 9:30am–9pm; Oct–Dec and Apr–May weekends only 10am–5pm. Closed Jan to mid-Apr.

Old Harbor Life-Saving Museum ⭐ One of 13 lifesaving stations mandated by Congress in the late 19th century, this shingled shelter with a lookout tower was part of a network responsible for saving some 100,000 lives. Before the U.S. Life-Saving Service was founded in 1872 (it became part of the Coast Guard in 1915, once the Cape Cod Canal was in place), shipwreck victims lucky enough to be washed ashore were still doomed unless they could find a "charity shed"—a hut supplied with firewood—maintained by the Massachusetts Humane Society. The six valiant "Surfmen" manning each lifesaving station took a more active approach, patrolling the beach at all hours, sending up flares at the first sign of a ship in distress and rowing out into the surf to save all they could. When the breakers were too high to breach, they'd use a Lyle gun to shoot a line to be secured to the ship's mast, and over this, one by one, the crew would be pulled to shore astride a "breeches buoy"—like a lifesaving ring fitted out with canvas BVDs. All the old equipment is on view at this museum, and Thursday evenings at 6pm in season, rangers re-enact a breeches-buoy rescue.

Race Point Beach (off Race Point Rd., about 2 miles northwest of the town center). ℂ 508/487-1256. Free admission; parking fee for Race Point is $10. July–Aug daily 1:30–3:30pm; call for off-season hours. Closed Nov–Apr.

Pilgrim Monument & Provincetown Museum ⭐⭐ You can't miss it: Anywhere you go in town, this granite tower looms, ever ready to restore your bearings. Climb up the 60 gradual ramps interspersed with 116 steps—a surprisingly easy lope—and you'll get a gargoyle's-eye view of the spiraling coast and, in the distance, Boston against a backdrop of New Hampshire's mountains. Definitely devote some time to the curious exhibits in the museum at the monument's foot, chronicling P-town's checkered past as both fishing port and arts nexus. Among the memorabilia, you'll find polar bears brought back from MacMillan's expeditions and early programs for the Provincetown Players. The museum now also houses the collection of the former Provincetown Heritage Museum, which includes a replica dune shack, furniture made by artist Peter Hunt, and paintings by Provincetown artists.

High Pole Hill Rd. (off Winslow St., north of Bradford St.). ℂ 508/487-1310. www.pilgrim-monument.org. Admission $7 adults, $3 children 4–12. July–Aug daily 9am–7pm; off season daily 9am–5pm. Last admission 45 min. before closing. Closed Dec–Mar.

Province Lands Visitor Center of the Cape Cod National Seashore ⭐ Though much smaller than the Salt Pond Visitor Center, this satellite also does a good job of explicating this special environment, where plant life must fight a fierce battle to maintain its hold amid shifting sands buffeted by salty winds. After perusing the exhibits, be sure to circle the observation deck for great views of the parabolic dunes. A variety of ranger-guided tours and programs is offered daily in July and August, and frequently during the shoulder seasons. Inquire about special events, such as family campfires (reservations required). There are also canoe programs ($15 adults; $9 children) and surf-casting programs ($12), both with equipment provided.

Race Point Rd. (about 1½ miles northwest of the town center). ℂ 508/487-1256. Free admission. Mid-Apr to late Nov daily 9am–5pm. Closed late Nov to mid-Apr.

Provincetown Art Association & Museum ⭐⭐ (Moments) This extraordinary cache of 20th-century American art began with five paintings donated by local artists, including Charles Hawthorne, the charismatic teacher who first "discovered" this picturesque outpost. Founded in 1914, only a year after New York's revolutionary Armory Show, the museum was the site of innumerable "space wars," as classicists and modernists vied for square footage; an uneasy truce was finally struck in 1927, when each camp was accorded its own show. In today's less competitive atmosphere, it's not unusual to see an acknowledged master sharing space with a less-skilled upstart. Juried members' shows usually accompany the in-depth retrospectives, so there are always new discoveries to be made. Nor is there a hard and firm wall between creators and onlookers. Fulfilling its charter to promote "social intercourse between artists and laymen," the museum sponsors a full schedule of concerts, lectures, readings, and classes, in such disciplines as dance, yoga, and life drawing.

460 Commercial St. (in the East End). © 508/487-1750. www.paam.org. Suggested donation $2 adults, $3 seniors and children under 12. July–Aug daily noon–5pm and 8–10pm; call for off-season hours. Open year-round.

KID STUFF

Kids love going out on whale-watching trips, where sightings are guaranteed. To really tire them out, climb the **Provincetown Monument.** Toddlers will also enjoy the story hour held Wednesday and Saturday at 10:30am at the homey and historic (1873) **Provincetown Public Library** (© 508/487-7094).

SHOPPING

If you want to stay one step ahead of the fashion-victims' pack, you have come to the right place. Many mavens visit off season just to stock up on markdowns that are still well ahead of the curve. Of the several dozen art galleries in town, quite a few (noted below) are reliably worthwhile. For the largest concentration of galleries, wander down to the east end of town. (For in-depth coverage of the local arts scene, look to *Provincetown Arts,* a glossy annual sold at the Provincetown Art Association & Museum shop.) In season, most of the galleries and even some of the shops open around 11am, then take a supper-time siesta from around 5 to 7pm, reopening and greeting visitors up to as late as 10 or 11pm. Shows usually open Friday evening, prompting a "stroll" tradition spanning the many receptions.

ANTIQUES/COLLECTIBLES

Remembrances of Things Past, 376 Commercial St. (© 508/487-9443), is a kitsch-fest with a jumble of 20th-century nostalgia ranging from Bakelite bangles to neon advertising art to vintage *True Confessions.*

At **Small Pleasures,** 359 Commercial St. (© 508/487-3712), proprietor Virginia McKenna (also known as "Ginny Jewels") stocks fine estate jewelry, ranging from romantic Victorian settings to sleek silver for the 1920s-era male.

ART GALLERIES

Showing the work of distinguished figures from Provincetown's past and current luminaries, **Albert Merola Gallery,** 424 Commercial St. in the East End (© 508/487-4424), is simply one of the best galleries in town. Each summer, such respected figures as Michael Mazur *(Dante's Inferno)* and Helen Miranda Wilson deliver their latest musings. Closed mid-October to March.

Berta Walker is a force to be reckoned with, having nurtured many top artists through her association with the Fine Arts Work Center, before opening her own gallery in 1990. At **Berta Walker Gallery,** 208 Bradford St. in the East End (© 508/487-6411), the historic holdings span Charles Hawthorne, Milton Avery, and Robert Motherwell. Whoever has Berta's current attention, such as figurative sculptor Romolo Del Deo, warrants watching. Closed late October to late May.

Founded in 1994 by artist and publishing scion Nick Lawrence, **DNA (Definitive New Art) Gallery,** 288 Bradford St. above the Provincetown Tennis Club in the East End (℡ **508/487-7700**), has risen to the top tier. It has attracted such talents as photographer Joel Meyerowitz, Provincetown's favorite portraitist, known for such tomes as *Cape Light;* sculptor Conrad Malicoat, whose free-form brick chimneys and hearths can be seen and admired about town; and painter Tabitha Vevers, who devises woman-centered shrines and "shields" out of goatskin vellum and gold leaf. Another contributor is local conceptualist/provocateur Jay Critchley. It's a very lively bunch, appropriately grouped under the rubric "definitive new art," and readings by cutting-edge authors add to the buzz. Closed mid-October to late May.

Julie Heller started collecting early P-town paintings as a child—and a tourist at that. She chose so incredibly well, her roster at **Julie Heller Gallery,** 2 Gosnold St. on the beach in the center of town (℡ **508/487-2169**), reads like a who's who of local art. Hawthorne, Avery, Hofmann, Lazzell, Hensche—all the big names from Provincetown's past are here, as well as some contemporary artists. Closed weekdays January to April. Open winter weekends by chance or appointment.

The work of Anne Packard and her daughters Cynthia and Leslie are displayed in **The Packard Gallery,** 418 Commercial St. in the East End (℡ **508/487-4690**), a majestic former church. Anne Packard's large canvases tend to depict emotive land and seascapes with the horizon as a focus. Cynthia's colorful figurative work has Fauvist elements, and Leslie's watercolors capture Provincetown landscapes. Closed mid-October to mid-June.

At **Rice/Polak Gallery,** 430 Commercial St. in the East End (℡ **508/487-1052**), you'll find art with a decorative bent, which is not to say that it will match anyone's sofa, only that it has a certain stylish snap. Several gallery artists have fun with dimensions—such as painter Tom Seghi with his mammoth pears, and sculptor Larry Calkins with his assemblages of undersized, antique-look dresses. Peter Plamondon's oil paintings capture still lifes with exquisite clarity. Closed December to April.

Schoolhouse Center for Art and Design, 494 Commercial St. in the East End (℡ **508/487-4800**), is an impressive setup with two galleries, studios, arts programs, and an events series. The Driskel Gallery features photography and fine objects, while the Silas-Kenyon Gallery shows contemporary fine arts.

William-Scott Gallery, 439 Commercial St. in the East End (℡ **508/487-4040**), can be counted on to showcase the work of local emerging artists, as well as several who seem to have made it. In the latter category is John Dowd. Still quite young, he's shaping up as Hopper's heir apparent (patrons include the Schiffenhaus brothers, who inherited the Hoppers' Truro house). Other selections, such as John DiMestico's Cape landscapes on paper, Dan Rupe's bold portraits in oil, and Will Klemm's lush and mysterious pastel landscapes, augur well for an influential future. Closed December to late May.

BOOKS

Now Voyager, 357 Commercial St. in the East End (℡ **508/487-0848**), offers both new and collectible gay and lesbian books and serves as an informal social center. There is also a large section of mystery and suspense books.

Provincetown Bookstore, 246 Commercial St. (℡ **508/487-0964**), has the most complete selection in town. You'll find all the bestsellers, as well as books about the region and local lore.

DISCOUNT SHOPPING

Marine Specialties, 235 Commercial St. in the center of town (© **508/487-1730**), is packed to the rafters with useful stuff, from discounted Doc Martens to cut-rate Swiss Army knives and all sorts of odd nautical surplus whose uses will suggest themselves to you eventually. Be sure to look up: Hanging from the ceiling are some real antiques, including several carillons' worth of ships' bells.

EROTICA

The dirtiest (and I don't mean dusty) store in Provincetown is **Shop Therapy,** 346 Commercial St. (© **508/487-9387**), a store with wild murals (or is it graffiti) that is filled with all manner of erotica. You'll want to wander in just for the sheer outrageousness of it all. Tall people beware; there's stuff hanging from the low ceiling that you might not want near your face.

FASHION

Giardelli/Antonelli Studio Showroom, 417 Commercial St. in the East End (© **508/487-3016**), is filled with Jerry Giardelli's unstructured clothing elements—shells, shifts, and palazzo pants—in vibrant colors and inviting textures. They demand to be mixed, matched, and perhaps offset by Diana Antonelli's statement jewelry.

Want to try on new identities? **Mad as a Hatter,** 360 Commercial St. (© **508/487-4063**), may be your best bet, with hats to suit every style and inclination, from folksy to downright diva-esque. Closed January to mid-February.

Moda Fina, 349 Commercial St. (© **508/487-6632**), specializes in women's clothing and accessories, including shoes and lingerie, and a variety of unique summer dresses.

Silk & Feathers, 377 Commercial St. in the East End (© **508/487-2057**), has seasonal styles, and the lingerie they sell is almost too pretty to cover up. Other indulgences include seaweed soaps and statement jewelry.

GIFTS/HOME DECOR

Christopher Pearson of **Pearson's Studio,** 214 Commercial St. in the East End (© **508/487-2851**), is the premier stained-glass maker in town; he's taught most of the others how it's done.

Ahoy Mate! A unique gift shop with a fun theme is **Peter's Royal Navy,** 120 Commercial St., (© **508/487-7141**), which features nautical antiques and accessories.

The colorful fabrics and ceramics will draw you in to **Provincia,** 140 Commercial St. (© **508/487-5603**) with mainly imports from Portugal.

A breath of fresh contemporary design, **Utilities,** 393 Commercial St. in the center of town (© **508/487-6800**), is a kitchenware/tabletop shop that features sleek and colorful essentials.

A study in beiges and blacks, **Wa,** 184 Commercial St. in the West End (© **508/487-6355**), is a minimalist shop—its name means "harmony" in Japanese—specializing in decorative home accessories that embrace a Zen aesthetic. This might mean a trickling stone fountain or Chinese calligraphy stones.

Profits on the gifts and books you buy at **The Whale and Dolphin Information Center & Shop,** 307 Commercial St. in the center of town (© **508/487-6115**), help support the cetacean research-and-rescue work carried out by the Center for Coastal Studies, a local non-profit organization. Identifying individual whales by their distinctive markings, center staffers have managed to compile the world's largest whale population database to date and have participated in many a dramatic disentanglement. To appreciate the depth of their dedication, go whale-watching with a center scientist aboard a Dolphin Fleet cruise (see "Whale-Watching," earlier in this chapter). Inquire about center-sponsored lectures, walks, and Elderhostel programs. Closed November to mid-April.

TOYS

Take advantage of the Cape's strong winds and wide-open beaches by shopping at **Outer Cape Kites,** 277A Commercial St. at Ryder Street Extension, near MacMillan Wharf (℃ **508/487-6133**). Closed mid-October to March.

WHERE TO STAY
VERY EXPENSIVE

Anchor Inn ★★ This waterfront property centrally located on Commercial Street recently underwent a multimillion-dollar face-lift. The rooms are exquisitely decorated with fine furniture and deluxe amenities. Each has a wet bar with sink and fridge, as well as luxury bathroom amenities, including a robe. Many of the rooms feature deluxe showers, whirlpool baths, and fireplaces. Sixteen rooms have waterfront balconies overlooking the harbor. Four rooms have separate entrances through private porches complete with wicker furniture. Some of the rooms, called "yacht cabins," are quite small but have fabulous views. Others are large suites with king-size beds, two-person whirlpool baths, and French doors leading to a private balcony. Breakfast is an elaborate affair that could include quiche or eggs Benedict.

175 Commercial St. (in the center of town), Provincetown, MA 02657. ℃ **800/858-2657** or 508/487-0432. Fax 508/487-6280. www.anchorinnbeachhouse.com. 23 units. Summer $255–$275 double, $375, suite. Rates Include continental breakfast. AE, MC, V. Closed Jan–Mar. *In room:* A/C, TV/VCR, dataport, fridge, hair dryer, CD player.

Brass Key Guesthouse ★★★ Brass Key Guesthouse, a compound of four buildings, is *the* place to stay in Provincetown. With Ritz-Carlton–style amenities and service in mind, Michael MacIntyre and Bob Anderson have created a paean to luxury. They are the kinds of innkeepers who think of everything: goose-down pillows, showers with wall jets, and gratis iced tea and lemonade delivered poolside in season. While all rooms share top-notch amenities like Bose radios, decorative styles vary according to the building. The original 1828 Federal-style Captain's House and the Gatehouse are decorated in a playful country style—a loft is filled with teddy bears, for instance—while rooms in the Victorian-era building are classically elegant, with materials like mahogany, walnut, and marble. In the center is the extensively landscaped multileveled patio area with outdoor heated pool and large (17-ft.) whirlpool. Most deluxe guest rooms have gas fireplaces and oversize whirlpool tubs. Fortunately, those bathrooms include phones, and some have TVs, so that you can be entertained while soaking. There are two wheelchair-accessible rooms. In high season, the clientele here is primarily gay men, though all are made to feel welcome.

67 Bradford St. (in the center of town), Provincetown, MA 02657. ℃ **800/842-9858** or 508/487-9005. Fax 508/487-9020. www.brasskey.com. 29 units, 4 cottages (9 tub/shower; 22 shower only; 2 with tub and shower). Summer $245–$445 double, $295–$445 cottage. Rates include continental breakfast and afternoon wine-and-cheese hour. AE, DISC, MC, V. Closed late Nov to early Apr. No children under 18. **Amenities:** Outdoor heated pool; 17-ft. hot tub. *In room:* A/C, TV/VCR, dataport, fridge, hair dryer, safe.

Crowne Pointe Historic Inn ★★ This newly restored property perched high on Bradford Street is a welcome addition to Provincetown's high-end lodging choices. The inn and grounds are exquisitely maintained with deluxe commons areas and attractive gardens. The staff is accommodating and professional.

Rooms are spacious and some of the deluxe rooms and suites have fireplaces, wet bars, and whirlpool spas. Buffet breakfast is served in the large living room, which has plenty of overstuffed couches to lounge around on while you plan your day.

82 Bradford St. (in the center of town), Provincetown, MA 02657. © 877/CROWNE1 or 508/487-6767. Fax 508/487-5554. www.crownepointe.com. 40 units. $195–$450, double. Rates include continental breakfast, afternoon tea, and wine and cheese hour. AE, MC, V. **Amenities:** Heated outdoor pool; 10-person outdoor spa. In-room: AC, TV/VCR, dataport, hair dryer, iron.

EXPENSIVE

Bayshore and Chandler House ★★ This cherished beachfront complex in the far east end of town continues to be a popular lodging choice. It's a short walk to the center of P-town, but being in the East End means quiet nights. A new property acquired by the innkeepers at 77 Commercial Street on the far west end of town has two additional one-bedroom units. All of the apartments have improvised charm, such as a few select antiques and salvaged architectural details. Rooms have private entrances and kitchenettes, including microwave ovens and dishwashers. Some have air-conditioning. The prize rooms at the east side property surround a flower-lined lawn, with pride of place going to a cathedral-ceiling loft right over the water; several more apartments, including a freestanding little house, can be found across the street. The bargain unit is in the "lower level" (read: basement) of this house; it's surprisingly quaint, but, as expected, dark. The decor is still not quite designer level, but the big plus is the opportunity to live among artworks by local P-town artists. From late June to early September, rooms are available on a weekly basis only.

493 Commercial St. (in the East End), Provincetown, MA 02657. ©/fax 508/487-9133. www.bayshorechandler. com. 25 units (20 tub/shower; 5 shower). Summer $1,200 weekly studio, $1,450–$1,950 weekly 1-bedroom, $1,650–$2,950 weekly 2-bedroom; shoulder season daily rates $110 studio, $140–$175 1-bedroom, $150–$275 2-bedroom. AE, DISC, MC, V. Dogs allowed with advance notice. Open year-round. In room: TV/VCR, fridge, coffeemaker, iron.

Best Western Tides Beachfront ★★ Kids Families will be delighted with this beachfront motel, located on a 6-acre parcel well removed both from Provincetown's bustle and North Truro's ticky-tacky congestion of motels. This surprise oasis, part of the Best Western chain, boasts every feature you might require, including a nice wide beach you can literally flop onto from the ground-level units. Most of the rooms overlook Provincetown's quirky skyline, as does the generously proportioned outdoor heated pool. Every inch of this complex has been groomed to the max, including the ultra-green grounds, the Wedgwood-blue breakfast room, and the spotless guest rooms decorated in a soothing palette of ivory and pale pastels. Because the hotel is set back from busy Route 6A, the only sound you'll hear at night is the mournful refrain of a foghorn.

837 Commercial St. (near the Truro border), Provincetown, MA 02657. © 800/528-1234 or 508/487-1045. Fax 508/487-1621. www.bwprovincetown.com. 64 units. Summer $159–$289 double, $299–$319 suite. AE, DC, DISC, MC, V. Closed late Oct to mid-May. **Amenities:** Outdoor heated pool; coin-op laundry. In-room: A/C, TV, dataport, fridge, coffeemaker, hair dryer, iron.

Land's End Inn ★★★ Finds Enjoying a prime 1-acre perch atop Gull Hill in the far West End of Commercial Street, this magical, whimsical 1907 bungalow is bursting with rare and often outlandish antiques. Some rooms would suit a 19th-century sheik, others your everyday hedonist. In other words, the place is unique in a way that will delight some guests and overwhelm others. There are three tower rooms that make use of the inn's soaring towers. The two-bedroom loft tower suite, entered through an armoire (very *Narnia*) must be one of the most unusual and spectacular lodging spaces on the Cape. From the spacious living room, climb the ironwork spiral stairway to the bedroom, where an immense stained-glass window serves as your headboard. Through the encircling clerestory windows, the Atlantic Ocean beckons. There's also a wonderful octagonal tower room with windows wrapping halfway around, bay-view decks on two sides, and a cobalt glass turret. Some of the other rooms are small, but they all positively drip with kitschy Victorian and Deco styles. Though the inn is predominantly gay, cosmopolitan visitors will feel welcome, regardless of gender or orientation. The inn is owned by Michael MacIntyre and Bob Anderson, the owners of the Brass Key, the town's top inn. While the inn's quirky qualities will remain, the inn has been freshened up with new beds, linens, and carpeting. The staff is top-notch here and the breakfast, an elaborate continental spread, features fresh fruits and homemade baked goods.

22 Commercial St. (in the West End), Provincetown, MA 02657. © **800/276-7088** or 508/487-0706. Fax 508/487-0755. www.landsendinn.com. 16 units. Summer $165–$195 double, $295–$495 tower rooms. Rates include continental breakfast and wine and cheese hour. AE, MC, V. Closed Nov–Apr. *In room:* A/C, no phone.

The Masthead ★★ *Kids* In its late-1950s heyday, glam types like Helena Rubenstein came to this funky resort on the beach at the far west end of Commercial Street to rough it. These days, it's one of the few places in town, other than the impersonal motels, that actively welcomes families, and the placid 450-foot private beach will delight young splashers. Many rooms are individually and creatively decorated, and all have coffeemakers with complimentary tea and coffee. In season, turndown service is provided with chocolates. The cottages are fun, some with net stair railings, wicker furniture, and hand-painted antique furniture by Peter Hunt, as well as full (if tiny) kitchens, which include microwave ovens. Two rooms are accessible to travelers with disabilities. In season, the cottage units rent weekly, but the rather generic motel units rent nightly. In some water-view rooms perched above the surf, with their 7-foot picture windows overlooking the bay and Long Point, you may feel like you're onboard a ship. The yachting crowd can take advantage of free deepwater moorings and launch service.

31–41 Commercial St. (in the West End), Provincetown, MA 02657. © **800/395-5095** or 508/487-0523. Fax 508/487-9251. www.themasthead.com. 21 units (3 tub/shower; 16 shower; 2 with shared bathroom), 4 cottages. Summer $86–$93 double with shared bathroom, $102–$249 double, $179–$235 efficiency, $265 2-bedroom apt, $1,750–$2,541 cottage weekly. AE, DC, DISC, MC, V. Open year-round. *In room:* A/C, TV, fridge, coffeemaker.

The Oxford ★ *Value* British innkeepers Stephen Mascilo and Trevor Pinker have restored and refurbished this 1853 house in the far West End, adding yet another posh address to the town. This is truly affordable elegance. All rooms have upscale amenities like down comforters, bathrobes, phones with voice mail and dataport, and radio/CD players. One downstairs room is quite large, with 8-foot windows overlooking the landscaped grounds. Rooms with shared bathrooms are smaller. The drawing room is especially cozy, with big down sofas and armchairs in front of a fireplace, above which a TV is cleverly hidden. An extensive continental breakfast is served in the morning, when the inn fills with the scrumptious aroma of home-baked breads and coffeecake. You may want to take your coffee outside on the veranda overlooking the courtyard's fountain and pond.

8 Cottage St. (in the West End), Provincetown, MA 02657. © **888/456-9103** or 508/487-9103. www.oxford guesthouse.com. 7 units (shower only; 2 with shared bathroom). Summer $150 double with shared bathroom, $200–$285 double with private bathroom. Rates include continental breakfast. AE, DC, DISC, MC, V. *In room:* A/C, TV/VCR, dataport, fridge, hair dryer, iron, CD player.

Watermark Inn ★★ *Kids* If you'd like to experience P-town without being stuck in the thick of it (the carnival atmosphere can get tiring at times), this contemporary inn at the peaceful edge of town is the perfect choice. Resident innkeeper/architect Kevin Shea carved this beachfront manor into 10 dazzling suites: The prize ones, on the top floor, have peaked picture windows and sweeping water views from their decks. All have kitchenettes that include dishwashers. Innkeeper/designer Judy Richland, Shea's wife, saw to the interior decoration—pastel handmade quilts brighten up clean, monochromatic rooms. From mid-May to mid-September, the suites rent only by the week. This inn is a favorite with families.

603 Commercial St. (in the East End), Provincetown, MA 02657. (C) 508/487-0165. Fax 508/487-2383. www.watermark-inn.com. 10 units. Summer $130–$270 suite, weekly rates $1,200–$2,440. AE, MC, V. Open year-round. *In room:* TV, fridge, coffeemaker.

MODERATE

Cape Inn ★ Formerly the Holiday Inn, this waterfront motel is a good choice for first-timers not quite sure what they're getting into. It's a no-surprises motel with a pool at the far eastern edge of town. Guests in waterfront rooms get a nice view of town, along with free movies in the restaurant/lounge shown on a 100-foot screen in season. During the movies, light fare and beverages are available. In season, dinner is served in the restaurant and there's also a poolside bar and grill. Though this motel is a bit of a hike from the town's center, an in-season town shuttle will whisk you down Commercial Street or to the beaches for a minimal cost.

698 Commercial St. (at Rte. 6A, in the East End), Provincetown, MA 02657. (C) 800/422-4224 or 508/487-1711. Fax 508/487-3929. www.capeinn.com. 78 units. Summer $119–$179 double. Rates include continental breakfast. AE, DC, DISC, MC, V. Closed Nov–Apr. Dogs allowed. **Amenities:** Restaurant; outdoor pool. *In room:* A/C, TV, dataport, fridge, coffeemaker, hair dryer, iron.

Carpe Diem ★★ Rainer and Jurgen, two young, urbane Germans, run this stylish lodging option, an 1884 house with mansard roof, whose devil-may-care theme is "seize the day." The location, a quiet side street right in the center of town, would suit most Provincetown habitués to a T. The rooms here are exquisitely decorated with European antiques and brightly painted walls and wallpapers. All rooms have down comforters and pillows, as well as bathrobes, and all but one has a mini-fridge. There are two deluxe garden suites with private entrances, Jacuzzis, and fireplaces. The cottage has a two-person whirlpool, a fireplace, a private patio, and a wet bar. The full breakfast prepared by the inn's French manager features homemade French-influenced pastries served at the family-size dining-room table. On clear days, sun worshippers prefer the patio where there's a six-person hot tub.

12 Johnson St. (in the center of town), Provincetown, MA 02657. (C) 800/487-0132 or 508/487-4242 (also fax). www.carpediemguesthouse.com. 14 units. Summer $140–$185 double, $225–$265 suites, $325 cottage. Rates include full breakfast and wine and cheese hour. AE, DISC, MC, V. Open year-round. **Amenities:** 6-person hot tub. *In room:* A/C, TV/VCR, dataport.

The Commons ★★ Right in the thick of town, but removed from the hurly-burly by a street-side bistro (see "Where to Dine," below) and peaceful brick patio, this venerable old guesthouse has received a stylish renovation at the hands of co-owners Carl Draper and Chuck Rigg, a Washington, D.C., interior designer whose colorful landscapes decorate the rooms. The parlor is comfortable; the bedrooms, with their marble-look bathrooms and (in most cases) bay views, are stylish and spacious. At the pinnacle is a beamed attic studio with its own deck overlooking MacMillan Wharf. All the delights of Provincetown are easily within reach, including—on-site—one of Provincetown's best up-and-coming restaurants.

386 Commercial St. (in the center of town), Provincetown, MA 02657. ✆ 800/487-0784 or 508/487-7800. Fax 508/487-6114. www.commonsghb.com. 14 units (3 tub/shower; 11 shower only). Summer $129–$159 double, $199 suite. Rates include continental breakfast. AE, MC, V. Closed Nov–Mar. Pets allowed. **Amenities:** Restaurant (bistro). *In room:* A/C, TV.

Copper Fox ★★ Cheerful innkeeper John Gagliardi owns this majestic house with a large wraparound porch, set well back from the road. The expansive lawn, unusual in Provincetown where space is at a premium, is dotted with urns and a birdbath. Built in 1856, the three-story, Federal-style captain's house is just a short walk from the galleries and restaurants of the East End. From the second floor deck, you have a perfect view of Provincetown harbor across the street. Several of the spacious rooms also have bay views. Two apartments have private entrances and kitchens. One has a private garden, and the other is large enough to accommodate six people comfortably (extra charge for more than two people). Bathrooms have been thoroughly modernized, but some have stylish clawfoot tubs and antique sinks.

448 Commercial St. (in the East End), Provincetown, MA 02657. ✆/fax **508/487-8583**. www.provincetown. com/copperfox. 7 units. Summer $140–$179 double, $195 apt. Rates include continental breakfast and afternoon tea. MC, V. Open year-round. *In room:* A/C, TV/VCR, no phone.

The Fairbanks Inn ★★ This B&B is on Bradford Street 1 block from Provincetown's main waterfront street, Commercial Street. Nevertheless, it is centrally located and beautifully maintained and managed. The main building is a colonial mansion (built in 1776), which looks its era without looking its age. It boasts gleaming wooden floors softened by rich Oriental rugs and romantic bedding—sleigh beds and four-posters. Two newer buildings on the grounds contain an apartment and an efficiency, which both sleep three people and have separate entrances. Those units all have fridges. Most of the rooms have fireplaces. A patio, porch, and rooftop sun deck lend themselves to pleasant socializing. The attention to detail throughout the inn makes this one of the top places to stay in town.

90 Bradford St. (near the center of town), Provincetown, MA 02657. ✆ 800/324-7265 or 508/487-0386. Fax 508/487-3540. www.fairbanksinn.com. 15 units (2 with shared bathroom). Summer $129–$189 double, $229–$269 efficiency. Rates include continental breakfast. AE, MC, V. Open year-round. *In room:* A/C, TV/VCR, hair dryer.

The Inn at Cook Street ★ *Value* This 1836 Greek Revival beauty on Bradford Street, 1 block from Provincetown's waterfront main street, positively exudes tasteful warmth, from its pale-yellow exterior trimmed with black shutters to its hidden garden complete with goldfish pool. All the handsomely appointed rooms are oriented to this oasis, with an assortment of private and shared decks. The suites have additional amenities like VCRs, hair dryers, mini-fridges, coffeemakers, and private entrances. The cottage room in a separate building has a VCR, mini-fridge, microwave, coffeemaker, and wet bar. The enthusiasm of innkeepers Paul Church and Dana Mitton is evident in every welcoming touch.

7 Cook St. (at Bradford St., in the East End), Provincetown, MA 02657. ✆ 888/COOK-655 or 508/487-3894. www.innatcookstreet.com. 6 units (5 tub/shower; 1 shower only). Summer $135 double, $155–$170 suite. Rates include continental breakfast. MC, V. *In room:* A/C, TV/VCR.

INEXPENSIVE

Captain Lysander Inn ⭐ _Value_   This 1840 Greek Revival captain's house has definite curb appeal: Set back from the street in the quiet West End, it's fronted by a flower-lined path leading to a sunny patio. The conservatively furnished rooms are quite nice for the price, and some have partial water views. Tall windows make these rooms light and airy; they're also spotlessly clean. Rooms with shared bathrooms share with just one other room. The whole gang can fit in either the apartment or the cottage, both of which sleep six and have TV/VCRs and kitchenettes.

96 Commercial St. (in the West End), Provincetown, MA 02657. ℭ **508/487-2253.** Fax 508/487-7579. 13 units (6 with shared bathroom), 1 cottage. Summer $105 double with shared bathroom, $115 double with private bathroom, efficiency $135 daily, $800 weekly, apt $200 daily, $1,200 weekly, cottage $250 daily, $1,400 weekly. Rates include continental breakfast except for apt and cottage. MC, V. Open year-round. _In room:_ No phone.

The Outermost Hostel _Value_   So what if these "European-style" dorms look more like an outtake from _The Grapes of Wrath_? Quite a deal for less than 20 bucks a night! And, unlike the strait-laced American Youth Hostels, they're curfew-free! For grungers (or misers) just looking for a place to crash, these bunks will fill the bill.

28 Winslow St. (off Bradford St., ⅛ mile northwest of the Provincetown Museum entrance), Provincetown, MA 02657. ℭ **508/487-4378.** 40 beds. Summer $19 per bed. No credit cards. Reservations advised on weekends. Registration daily 8–9:30am and 6–9:30pm at cabin no. 4. Closed Nov to mid-May. _In room:_ No phone.

White Horse Inn ⭐⭐ _Value_   Look for the house with the bright yellow door and oval window in the far East End of town. The rates are terrific, especially given the fact that this inn is the very embodiment of Provincetown's bohemian mystique. Frank Schaefer has been tinkering with this late-18th-century house since 1963; the rooms may be a bit austere, but each is enlivened by some of the 300 to 400 paintings he has collected over the decades. A number of his fellow artists helped him cobble together the studio apartments out of salvage: There's an aura of beatnik improv about them still. Guests over the past 35 years have embodied a range of low and high art: Cult filmmaker John Waters stayed here often, as did poet laureate Robert Pinsky.

500 Commercial St. (in the East End), Provincetown, MA 02657. ℭ **508/487-1790.** 24 units (10 with shared bathroom). Summer $60 single with shared bathroom, $70–$80 double, $125–$140 efficiency. No credit cards. _In room:_ No phone.

WHERE TO DINE
VERY EXPENSIVE

Chester ⭐⭐⭐ NEW AMERICAN   Look to this grandly columned Greek Revival house for sophisticated fine dining Provincetown-style. Chester specializes in local seafood, meats, and vegetables prepared simply yet with a flourish. The restaurant is named after the owners' Airedale terrier, whose regal profile serves as their logo. The candlelit dining room, painted a summery yellow, is decorated with brightly colored paintings by local artists. You'll want to sit at the comfy banquettes lining the edges of the room. As is to be expected, service is exceptional, the food is beautifully presented, and the portions are hearty. Appetizers like spinach and scallop risotto take advantage of local provender, as does the entree of Chatham cod with prosciutto and sage. Though I'm reluctant to order meat when I can see the ocean out the window, the braised leg of lamb with rosemary potato pancakes and French beans was a treat. The entire menu changes monthly. The inn's extensive and well-priced wine list has been rewarded by *Wine Spectator*. For dessert, look no further than the warm Scharffen Berger chocolate cake. There's also homemade ice cream. Terrace seating is available in season, with the last seating on the terrace at 8:15pm.

404 Commercial St. ℂ 508/487-8200. www.chesterrestaurant.com. Reservations recommended. Main courses $19–$34. AE, MC, V. Late June to mid-Sept daily 6–10pm; mid-Apr to late May Thurs–Mon; late May to late June and mid-Sept to Oct Thurs–Tues 6–10pm; call for off-season hours. Closed Jan to mid-Apr, except New Year's Eve.

The Dancing Lobster Cafe Trattoria ★★ MEDITERRANEAN This waterfront restaurant has a well-known chef and great location, but it's a tad pricey for the offerings. Chef/owner Nils "Pepe" Berg virtually grew up at the restaurant, Pepe's Wharf, run by his parents on this site for years, and now he has his own restaurant here. This is a popular place, and you should expect to wait a half-hour, even with a reservation. The mainstay here is seafood, but the menu also features Venetian specialties, among other special dishes. Start with the grilled-squid bruschetta, the saffrony Venetian fish soup, the crab ravioli, or perhaps the steamed mussels with a basil aioli. Main courses may include steak al "Pepe" with green and black peppercorns, brandy, demiglace, and cream; or Basque stew with littleneck clams, chicken, shrimp, linguica, squid, and mussels steamed with white beans. This is a particularly fine choice for lunch and extra-special lobster rolls, served on the outside terrace or on the second floor overlooking the beach.

373 Commercial St. (in the center of town). ℂ 508/487-0900. Reservations recommended. Main courses $17–$30. MC, V. July–Sept Tues–Sun 11:30am–5pm and 5:30–11pm; May–June and Oct 6–9pm. Closed Nov–Apr.

Martin House ★★★ CONTEMPORARY NEW ENGLAND/INTERNATIONAL Easily one of the most charming restaurants on the Cape, this snuggery of rustic rooms happens to contain one of the Cape's most forward-thinking kitchens. Co-owners Glen and Gary Martin conceived the inspired regional menu, and chef Alex Mazzocca creates it. The team favors regional delicacies, such as the Thai crab-and-shrimp soup with green curry and crispy rice noodles, or the local littlenecks that appear in a kafir-lime–tamarind broth with Asian noodles. Main courses might include local-lobster–stuffed squash blossoms with a warm porcini-saffron vinaigrette, or grilled rack of pork with mango salsa and cactus-pear demiglace on spicy masa. The peaceful, softly lit rooms make an optimal setting for exploring new tastes. In season, there's seating in the rose-covered garden terrace beside the small fountain. In season, breakfast is served in the garden on Saturdays and Sundays.

157 Commercial St. ℂ 508/487-1327. www.themartinhouse.com. Reservations recommended. Main courses $16–$33. AE, DC, DISC, MC, V. May–Oct daily 6–11pm, Sat–Sun 9am–12:30pm; Jan–May and Nov–Dec Thurs–Mon 6–10pm. Closed mid-Dec.

EXPENSIVE

Cafe Edwidge and Edwidge at Night ★ NEW AMERICAN/FUSION The tourist throngs generally walk right on by this second-story eatery, little suspecting what they're passing up. To start: superlative, healthy breakfasts featuring everything from tofu stir-fry to broiled sole with stir-fried vegetables. The cathedral-ceiling space, with hippie-era wooden booths and Deco accents, is a great place to greet the day. At night, it's commensurately romantic, with subdued lighting and the cuisine of chef Stephen Frappolli, who has been praised in the *New York Times*. Start your meal with the Maine crab cake with Creole-mustard dressing and cucumber slaw. Sake-and-plum-glazed Chilean sea bass served with wasabi mashed potatoes is another high point on the menu. Homemade desserts are exceptional here; you can't go wrong.

333 Commercial St. © 508/487-2008 or 508/487-4020 **(Edwidge at Night).** Reservations recommended. Main courses $19–$25. MC, V. Late May to Aug daily 8am–1pm and 6–11pm; Sept–Oct and early to late May daily 8am–1pm, Fri–Sun 6–10pm. Closed Nov–Apr.

Front Street ★★ MEDITERRANEAN FUSION/ITALIAN   For years, this restaurant has delivered consistently high-quality food and service, and locals consider it a favorite, even cherished, and dependable locale. Located in a below-ground space on Commercial Street in the center of town, this cozy restaurant feels most comfortable in the chilly days of spring and summer. The decor is very romantic with antique booths and low lighting. Chef Donna Aliperti is constantly improving her menu, inspired by trips to Italy and southern France. The fusion menu, available in season, has creative items like soft shell crabs with corn-studded risotto and Chinese five-spice grilled duckling. There is also a traditional Italian menu with pastas available every night.

230 Commercial St. © 508/487-9715. www.frontstreetrestaurant.com. Reservations recommended. Main courses $18–$25. DISC, MC, V. June–Sept daily 6–10pm; call for off-season hours.

The Mews & Cafe Mews ★★ INTERNATIONAL/AMERICAN FUSION Bank on fine food and suave service at this beachfront restaurant, an enduring favorite since 1961. Upstairs is the cafe with its century-old carved mahogany bar. The dining room downstairs sits right on the beach—and is practically of the beach, with its sand-toned walls warmed by toffee-colored Tiffany table lamps. The best soup in the region is the Mews' scrumptious summertime special, chilled cucumber miso bisque with curry shrimp timbale. Perennial pleasures include the Marsala-marinated portobello mushrooms and a mixed seafood carpaccio. Among the showier entrees is "captured scallops": prime Wellfleet specimens enclosed with a shrimp-and-crab mousse in a crisp wonton pouch and served atop a petite filet mignon with chipotle aioli. Desserts and coffees—you might take them upstairs in the cafe to the accompaniment of soft-jazz piano—are delectable. Awash in sea blues that blend with the view, Cafe Mews offers a lighter, less expensive menu and serves as an elegantly informal community clubhouse year-round.

429 Commercial St. © 508/487-1500. Reservations recommended. www.mews.com. Main courses $18–$29. AE, DC, DISC, MC, V. Mid-June to early Sept daily 6–10pm, Sun 11am–2:30pm; early Dec to mid-Feb daily 6–10pm. Open year-round.

The Red Inn ★★ NEW AMERICAN   New owners have turned this property at the far west end of Commercial Street into one of the toughest reservations to get in town. The dining room with its wrap-around floor-to-ceiling windows has some of the best beach views in town. The refined atmosphere makes this a favorite for special occasions, when your dinner might begin with a glass of champagne and end with a souffle. This is fine dining on the calorie-rich side, with entrees like grilled thick pork chops with tomatillo salso and pepper-crusted filet mignon with truffle mashed potatoes and Jack Daniel's sauce. There are always fresh fish and vegetarian main courses on the menu also.

15 Commercial St. © 508/487-7334. Reservations required. www.theredinn.com. Main courses $21–$38. AE, DC, DISC, MC, V. Mid-June to early Sept daily 5:30–10pm, Sat–Sun 10am–2:30pm; call for off-season hours.

MODERATE

Bubala's by the Bay ★ ECLECTIC   This trendy bistro—with a gaudy yellow paint job and Picasso-esque wall murals—promises "serious food at sensible prices." And that's what it delivers: from buttermilk waffles with real maple syrup to lobster tarragon salad to creative focaccia sandwiches to fajitas, Cajun calamari, and pad Thai. This is a big operation for Provincetown, and the huge outdoor patio facing Commercial Street means it's popular, particularly for breakfast. This is the only place on Cape Cod that serves ostrich. They're raised in Pennsylvania and served with a grilled pepper crust and a caramelized onion and balsamic glaze. In season, there's entertainment nightly from 10pm to 1am.

183 Commercial St. (in the West End). ⓒ 508/487-0773. Main courses $10–$21. AE, DISC, MC, V. Apr–Oct daily 8am–11pm. Closed late Oct–Apr.

Cafe Heaven ⭐ AMERICAN Prized for its leisurely country breakfasts (served till mid-afternoon, for reluctant risers), this modern storefront—adorned with big, bold paintings by acclaimed Wellfleet artist John Grillo—also turns out substantial sandwiches, such as avocado and goat cheese on a French baguette. The salads are appealing as well—especially the "special shrimp," lightly doused with dilled sour cream and tossed with tomatoes and grapes. For dinner, Café Heaven becomes a Thai restaurant. "No reservations" means long lines in July and August.

199 Commercial St. (in the center of town). ⓒ 508/487-9639. Reservations not accepted. Most items $11–$18. No credit cards. July–Aug daily 8am–3pm and 6:30–10pm; call for off-season hours. Closed Feb–May.

The Commons Bistro & Bar ⭐⭐ ECLECTIC/FRENCH BISTRO It's a toss-up: The sidewalk cafe provides an optimal opportunity for studying P-town's inimitable street life, whereas the plum-colored dining room inside affords a refuge adorned with the owners' extraordinary collection of Toulouse-Lautrec prints. Either way, you'll get to partake of tasty and creative fare. At lunchtime, overstuffed lobster club sandwich on country bread is unbeatable, and the smoked-chicken and avocado salad is the ultimate summertime refresher. The Commons boasts the only wood-fired oven in town to date, which comes in handy in preparing the popular gourmet pizzas with combos like spicy shrimp and artichoke. Dinner appetizers include shore favorites like crispy fried calamari, steamed mussels, and crab cakes. As a main course, you must try the paella with roasted chicken, chorizo, clams, mussels, and shrimp. The Commons also serves as an all-day coffee shop, serving cappuccinos and baked goods.

386 Commercial St. (see "Where to Stay," above). ⓒ 508/487-7800. www.commonsghb.com. Reservations recommended. Main courses $10–$26. AE, MC, V. Mid-June to mid-Sept daily 8am–3pm and 6–10:30pm; call for off-season hours. Closed Nov–Mar.

The Lobster Pot ⭐ SEAFOOD Snobbish foodies might turn their noses up at a venue so flagrantly Olde Cape Coddish, but for Provincetown regulars, no season seems complete without at least one pilgrimage. You may feel like a long-suffering pilgrim waiting to get in: The line, which starts near the aromatic, albeit frantic, kitchen, often snakes into the street. While waiting, check out the hand-painted bar stools, which provide an architectural history of Province-town. A lucky few will make it all the way to the outdoor deck; however, most tables, indoors and out, afford nice views of MacMillan Wharf. Spring for a jumbo lobster, by all means—boiled or broiled, sauced or simple. And definitely start off with the chowder, a perennial award-winner.

321 Commercial St. (in the center of town). ⓒ 508/487-0842. www.ptownlobster.com. Reservations not accepted. Main courses $15–$25. AE, DC, DISC, MC, V. Mid-June to mid-Sept daily 11:30am–10:30pm; mid-Apr to mid-June and mid-Sept to Dec 11:30am–9:30pm. Closed Jan–Mar.

Lorraine's ★★ MEXICAN/NEW AMERICAN Long heralded by year-rounders as a spot for creative food and a festive atmosphere, Lorraine's moved last year to a storefront locale on the far West End of Commercial Street. In its new smaller location, the restaurant continues its tradition of being one of the town's top dining spots. Even those who shy away from Mexican restaurants should try Lorraine's; chef/owner Lorraine Najar brings a certain daring to bear on the cuisine she learned at her grandmother's knee. Abandon all caution and begin with *chile relleno de queso,* which is fresh chile peppers stuffed with the chef's choice nightly, rolled in corn meal and corn flour, and lightly fried. Maryland soft-shell crabs are lightly dusted in flour with Chimayo chile power and pan-sautéed and served with a jalapeño aioli. For a main course, consider *viere verde*—sea scallops sautéed with tomatillos, flambéed in tequila, and cloaked in a green-chile sauce. For a treat, check out the extensive tequilla menu; shots are served with a wonderful tomato juice-based chaser.

133 Commercial St. (in the West End). ☎ 508/487-6074. Reservations suggested. Main courses $17–$26. DISC, MC, V. June–Sept daily 6–10pm; call for off-season hours. Closed mid-Dec to Mar.

Napi's ★★ INTERNATIONAL Restaurateur Napi Van Dereck can be credited with bringing P-town's restaurant scene up to speed—back in the early 1970s. His namesake restaurant still reflects that Zeitgeist, with its rococo-hippie carpentry, select outtakes from his sideline in antiques, and some rather outstanding art, including a crazy quilt of a brick wall by local sculptor Conrad Malicoat. The cuisine is a lot less granola than it was when it started out, or maybe we've just caught up—hearty peasant fare never really goes out of style. And these peasants really get around, culling dumplings from China, falafel from Syria, and, from Greece, shrimp feta flambéed with ouzo and Metaxa. The lower-priced tavern menu available on weeknights ranges from $5 to $11. Unusual in Provincetown, this restaurant has its own parking lot (around back).

7 Freeman St. (at Bradford St.). ☎ 800/571-6274 or 508/487-1145. Reservations recommended. Main courses $14–$26. DISC, MC, V. May to mid-Sept daily 5–10pm; late Sept–Apr daily 11:30am–4pm and 5–9pm.

INEXPENSIVE

Café Blasé ★ ECLECTIC Everyone wants to see and be seen under the tasseled pink-and-navy umbrellas at Blasé, an outdoor cafe in the center of town. This is where to go for cocktails before dinner. While the full dinner menu, served 5 to 10pm, has been expanded to include pastas, pizzas, and dinner specials like charbroiled steak, you can get better eats elsewhere. The most refreshing drink choices here are the sodas made from an assortment of esoteric European syrups (Richard Gere is said to have favored the orzata). The beers are pretty rarefied, too—everything from a microbrewed Vermont amber, courtesy of Catamount, to a pricey Belgian framboise. Service here tends to be casual, so don't be in a hurry.

328 Commercial St. (in the center of town). ☎ 508/487-9465. Reservations not accepted. Main courses $10–$22. AE, DISC, MC, V. Mid-May to late Sept daily 11:30am–midnight. Closed late Sept to mid-May.

Clem and Ursie's ★ *Finds* *Kids* SEAFOOD/BARBECUE This is a great choice for a big family dinner on picnic tables. Make it a shoreman's dinner or a clambake. The menu is heavy on fried seafood, as well as barbecue chicken, ribs, and seafood. There are also more elaborate choices like bouillabaisse, *fra diavolo* (fish and shellfish in a spicy tomato sauce), and Japanese udon (fish, shellfish, and vegetables in a dashi broth over noodles). There is also a full sushi bar on-site. On the children's menu, it's $5 for your choice of six entrees with french fries, drink, dessert, and a surprise. Takeout is popular here, as is the separate ice-cream section.

85 Shankpainter Rd. (off Bradford St., a few blocks south of town). © 508/487-2333. Main courses $6–$17. MC, V. Apr to mid-Oct daily 11am–10pm. Closed mid-Oct to Apr.

Mojo's ★ *(Kids)* SEAFOOD   This fried-seafood shack is known for its lightly breaded fried fish. French fries are hand cut daily. There are also hot dogs and hamburgers, subs, veggie burgers, burritos, pizza, and chicken tenders. Eat at one of the six picnic tables on the patio or take it to the beach.

5 Ryder St. Extension (near Fisherman's Wharf). © 508/487-3140. All items under $15. No credit cards. Early May to mid-Oct daily 11am–11pm; closed mid-Oct to early May.

Spiritus Pizza   A local landmark, Spiritus is an extravagant pizza parlor known for post-last-call cruising: It's open until 2am. The pizza's good, as are the fruit drinks, specialty coffees, and four brands of premium ice cream, from Emack & Bolio's to Coconut Joe's. For a peaceful morning repast—and perhaps a relaxed round of boccie—check out the little garden in back.

190 Commercial St. (in the center of town). © 508/487-2808. All items under $15. No credit cards. Apr–Oct daily 11:30am–2am. closed Nov–Mar.

ICE CREAM

Not only a good spot to satisfy any ice-cream cravings (how about a 20-scoop "Vermonster"?), **Ben & Jerry's** ★, 258 Commercial St., in the center of town (© 508/487-3360), is also handy for refueling midstroll with a fresh-fruit drink.

TAKEOUT & PICNIC FARE

Angel Foods, 467 Commercial St., in the East End (© 508/487-6666), is a gourmet takeout shop offering Italian specialties and other scrumptious prepared foods to go.

The rollwiches—pita bread packed with a wide range of fillings—at **Box Lunch,** 353 Commercial St., in the center of town (© 508/487-6026), are ideal for a strolling lunch.

One thing you absolutely have to do while in town is peruse the cases of pasties (meat pies) and pastries at **Provincetown Portuguese Bakery,** 299 Commercial St., in the center of town (© 508/487-1803). Point to a few and take your surprise package out on the pier for delectation. Though perhaps not the wisest course for the whale-watch–bound, it's the best way to sample the scrumptious international output of this beloved institution. Closed November to early April.

CYBERCAFE

To check your e-mail, surf online, or just hang out with techies, stop by **Cyber Cove,** an Internet lounge on the second floor of Whalers' Wharf on Commercial Street (© 508/487-7778).

PROVINCETOWN AFTER DARK

To order tickets for any of the shows at Provincetown's nightclubs and cabarets, call **In-Town Reservations** at (© 508/487-2234).

THE CLUB SCENE

The Atlantic House   The "A-house"—the nation's premier gay bar—also welcomes straights of both sexes, except in the leather-oriented Macho Bar upstairs. Late in the evening, there's usually plenty going on in the Big Room dance bar. In the little bar downstairs—warm up at the fireplace—check out the Tennessee Williams memorabilia, including a portrait au naturel; there's more across the street in a new restaurant called Grand Central. Open year-round. 6 Masonic Place (off Commercial St., 2 blocks west of town hall). © 508/487-3821. Cover for the Big Room $5–$10.

Boatslip Beach Club If you're wondering where all the beachgoers went, come late afternoon, it's a safe guess that a goodly number are attending the gay-lesbian tea dance held daily in season from 3:30 to 6:30pm on the Boatslip hotel's pool deck. Later in the evening, after a post-tea T-dance at the Pied (see below), they'll probably be back for some disco or two-stepping. Closed November to April. 161 Commercial St. © 508/487-1669. Cover varies. Cover $3–$10.

Club Euro Behind the second floor roof-top patio is a disco/club that has long been a contender for hottest nightclub in P-town. This is the current home of "Two Fags and a Drag" and the ever-popular all-star musical comedy drag revue "Big Boned Barbies," starring Kandi Kane. You'll see the two tall and svelte "Barbies" outside the club welcoming all comers. Daily 7pm to 1am. Closed October to May. 258 Commercial St. (beside Town Hall, 2nd floor). © 508/487-2505. Cover varies.

Crown & Anchor The specialty bars at the large complex span leather ("The Vault"), disco, comedy, drag shows, and cabaret. Facilities include a pool bar and game room. Call or check website for schedule. Closed November to April. 247 Commercial St. (in the center of town). © 508/487-1430. www.thecrownandanchor.net. Cover $5–$20.

Pied In season, a "parade" of gay revelers descends in early evening from the Boatslip to "the Pied," for its After Tea T-Dance from 5 to 10pm on the huge waterfront deck. The dance floor gets packed most summer evenings. The late-night wave (after 10pm) consists of a fair number of women, or fairly convincing simulacra thereof, and DJs turn up the heat for dance parties. For a glimpse of stars-in-the-making, check out "Putting on the Hits," a sampling of local talent held Tuesday nights at 10. Closed November to April. Call for a schedule. 193A Commercial St. (in the center of town). © 508/487-1527. www.thepied.com. Cover $5.

Post Office Café and Cabaret One of P-town's top clubs, the Post Office, despite its cramped space, can be depended on for amusing drag and comedy shows. In recent years, the B-Girlz (Hard Kora, Barbie-Q, and Belle Bottom) have been the featured act. Call for schedule. Closed November to April. 303 Commercial St. (in the center of town). © 508/487-3892. Cover $20.

Vixen This chic women's bar occupies the lower floors of a former hotel. On the roster are jazz, blues, and comedy acts. There are also pool tables. Call for schedule. Closed November to April. Pilgrim House, 336 Commercial St. (in the center of town). © 508/487-6424. Cover varies.

THE BAR SCENE

Cafe Mews This highly civilized venue, with its bay view and vintage mahogany bar, is one of the few nightspots in town to lend itself well to the art of conversation. The jazz piano enhances rather than intrudes. A light cafe menu, in addition to the dining room menu, is available. At The Mews (see "Where to Dine," above). © 508/487-1500.

Governor Bradford It's a good old bar, featuring pool tables, drag karaoke (summer nights at 9:30pm), and disco. Call for a schedule. 312 Commercial St. (in the center of town). © 508/487-2781. No cover.

PERFORMANCE, ETC.

Meetinghouse Theatre and Concert Hall   In season, this glorious space is given over to a wide range of performances, from plays to opera to cabaret. Upstairs is an acoustically superb concert hall with a restored 1929 Steinway concert grand piano. Downstairs is an intimate theater. The season is usually capped off by a series of concerts by the Flirtations, a gay a cappella ensemble. A highlight in-season is the Sunday at 5 Music Series with a variety of performers, costing $10. At the Unitarian-Universalist Meetinghouse, 236 Commercial St. (in the center of town). ℂ 508/487-9344. Ticket prices vary.

LOW-KEY EVENINGS

Fine Arts Work Center   Drawing on its roster of visiting artists and scholars, FAWC offers exceptional readings and talks (some serve as fund-raisers) year-round. Call for a schedule. 24 Pearl St. (off Bradford St. in the center of town). ℂ 508/487-9960. www.fawc.org. Most events free.

New Art Cinema   This small duplex theater shows the latest releases, usually a blockbuster pitted against an indie art film. Closed mid-September to mid-May. 214 Commercial St. (in the center of town). ℂ 508/487-9222. Tickets $8.

Provincetown Art Association & Museum   Concerts, lectures, and readings attract an intellectually inclined after-hours crowd. Call for a schedule. 460 Commercial St. (in the East End). ℂ 508/487-1750. Cover varies.

8

Nantucket

In his classic, *Moby Dick,* Herman Melville wrote, "Nantucket! Take out your map and look at it. See what a real corner of the world it occupies; how it stands there, away off shore . . .." More than 100 years later, this tiny island, 30 miles off the coast of Cape Cod, still counts its isolation as a defining characteristic. At only 3½ by 14 miles in size, Nantucket is smaller and more insular than Martha's Vineyard. But charm-wise, Nantucket stands alone—21st-century luxury and amenities wrapped in an elegant 19th-century package.

The island has long appealed to wealthy visitors, but the recent economic boom has tipped the scales in their favor. Locals shake their heads over the changing demographics. "If they can't get a reservation at a restaurant, they buy the restaurant," one islander said. Nevertheless, this is still a terrific spot for a family vacation or a romantic retreat. After all, window-shopping at the island's exclusive boutiques and soaking up the sunshine on the pristine beaches are both free activities!

The Nantucket we see today is the result of a dramatic boom and bust that took place in the 1800s. Once the whaling capital of the world, the Nantucket of Melville's time was a bustling international port whose wealth and sophistication belied its size. But the discovery of crude oil put an end to Nantucket's livelihood, and the island underwent a severe depression until the tourism industry revived it at the end of the 19th century. Stringent regulations preserved the 19th-century

character of Nantucket Town, and today 36% of the island (and counting) is maintained as conservation land.

Nantucket Island has one town, also called Nantucket, which hugs the yacht-filled harbor. This sophisticated burg features bountiful stores, quaint inns, cobblestone streets, interesting historic sites, and pristine beaches. Strolling ensures you won't miss the scores of shops and galleries housed in wharf shacks on the harbor. The rest of the island is mainly residential, but for a couple of notable villages. Siasconset (nicknamed 'Sconset), on the east side of the island, is a tranquil community with picturesque, rose-covered cottages and a handful of businesses, including a pricey French restaurant. Sunset aficionados head to Madaket, on the west coast of the island, for the evening spectacular.

The lay of the land on Nantucket is rolling moors, heathlands, cranberry bogs, and miles of exquisite public beaches. The vistas are honeymoon-romantic: an operating windmill, three lighthouses, and a skyline dotted with church steeples. Although July and August are still the most popular times to visit the island, Nantucket's tourist season has lengthened considerably by virtue of several popular festivals: Daffodil Festival in April, Nantucket Harvest Weekend in October, and the month-long Nantucket Noel, the granddaddy of all holiday celebrations in the region. Off season, visitors enjoy a more tranquil and certainly less expensive vacation. While the "Grey Lady's" infamous fog is liable to swallow you whole, frequent visitors learn to relish this moody, atmospheric touch.

1 Essentials

GETTING THERE

BY FERRY From Hyannis (South St. Dock), the **Steamship Authority** (© **508/477-8600** in Hyannis; © **508/228-3274** in Nantucket; www.steamship authority.com) operates year-round ferry service (including cars, passengers, and bicycles) to Steamship Wharf in Nantucket using both conventional and high-speed ferries. When planning to travel to the island with your car in summer, you must reserve *months in advance* to secure a spot on the conventional ferry since only six boats make the trip daily in season (three boats daily off season). Before you call, have alternative departure dates. Remember to arrive at least 1 hour before departure to avoid your space being released to standbys. If you arrive without a reservation and plan to wait in the standby line, there is no guarantee you will get to the island that day. There is a $10 processing fee for canceling reservations. No advance reservations are required for passengers traveling without cars.

Total trip time on the conventional ferry that carries cars is 2 hours and 15 minutes. A round-trip fare for a car costs a whopping $330 from mid-May to mid-October; $210 from mid-October to mid-May. (Do you get the impression they don't want you to bring a car?) Car rates do not include drivers or passengers; you must get tickets for each person going to the island. For passengers, a one-way ticket is $13 ($26 round-trip) for adults, $6.50 one-way ($13 round-trip) for children 5 to 12, and $10 extra round-trip for bikes. Remember that Steamship Authority parking costs $8 to $10 per day; you do not need to make parking reservations.

The Steamship Authority's fast ferry to Nantucket, *The Flying Cloud* (© **508/495-3278**), is for passengers only (no cars). It takes 1 hour and runs five to six times a day in season. It is cheaper than the Hy-Line ferry (see below), at $26 one-way ($52 round-trip) for adults, $20 one-way ($39 round-trip) for children 5 to 12. Parking costs $8 to $10 per day. Passenger reservations are highly recommended. No pets are allowed on *The Flying Cloud.*

Also from Hyannis, passenger ferries to Nantucket's Straight Wharf are operated by **Hy-Line Cruises,** Ocean Street Dock (© **888/778-1132** or

---

Tips Parking

You do not need a car on Nantucket, so plan to park your car in Hyannis before boarding the ferry to the island. For all **Hy-Line** ferry services, Ocean Street Dock (© **888/778-1132** or 508/778-2602) in July and August, it's a good idea to not only reserve tickets in advance, but also to reserve a parking spot ahead of time. The all-day parking fee is $15 in season. Travelers on **Steamship Authority** (© **508/477-8600**) vessels do not need a parking reservation. Be sure to arrive at least 1 hour before sailing time to allow for parking. Parking at the Steamship Authority lots is $8 to $10 per day. For both ferry services, overflow parking is now at the Cape Cod Community College parking lots just north of Route 6 on Route 132 (exit 6 off Rte. 6). Free shuttle buses take passengers to the ferry terminals, which are on opposite ends of Hyannis Harbor. In season, watch signs on Route 6 for up-to-the-minute ferry parking information.

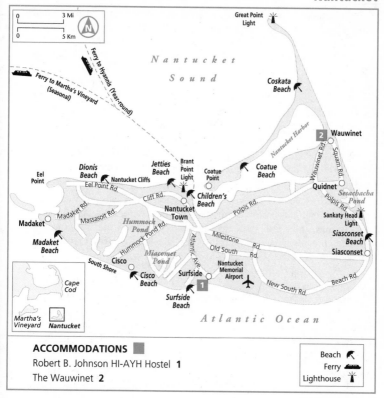

ACCOMMODATIONS ▪

Robert B. Johnson HI-AYH Hostel **1**
The Wauwinet **2**

Beach 🏖
Ferry ⛴
Lighthouse 🗼

508/778-2600; for high-speed ferry reservations, call ☏ **800/492-8082** or 508/778-0404; www.hy-linecruises.com). Hy-Line offers year-round service with its high-speed passenger catamaran, **_The Grey Lady,_** which makes five to six hourly trips per day. The cost of a one-way fare is $33 for adults ($58 round-trip), $25 for children 5 to 12 ($41 round-trip), and $5 extra for bicycles ($10 round-trip). This state-of-the-art vessel seats 260. It's best to make a reservation in advance.

From early May through October, Hy-Line's standard 1-hour-and-50-minute ferry service is also offered. Round-trip tickets are $27 for adults, $13.50 for children ages 5 to 12, and $10 extra for bikes. On busy holiday weekends, you may want to order tickets in advance; otherwise, be sure to buy your tickets at least half an hour before your boat leaves the dock.

Hy-Line's **MV _Great Point_** (less than a 2-hr. trip) has a first-class section with a private lounge, bathrooms, a bar, and a snack bar; a continental breakfast or afternoon cheese and crackers is also served onboard. One-way fare is $23 for adults and children ($46 round-trip). No pets are allowed on the _Great Point_ ferry in the first-class section.

Hy-Line's Around the Sound cruise is a 1-day round-trip excursion from Hyannis with stops in Nantucket and Martha's Vineyard that runs from early June to late September. The price is $41 for adults, $20 for children 5 to 12, and $15 extra for bikes.

Hy-Line runs three passenger-only ferries from Oak Bluffs in Martha's Vineyard to Nantucket from early June to mid-September (there is no car-ferry service between the islands). The trip time from Oak Bluffs is 2 hours and 15 minutes. The one-way fare is $14 for adults, $6.75 for children 5 to 12, and $5 extra for bikes.

From Harwich Port, you can avoid the summer crowds in Hyannis and board one of **Freedom Cruise Line**'s (702 Rte. 28 in Harwich Port, across from Brax Landing; ℂ **508/432-8999;** www.nantucketislandferry.com) passenger-only ferries to Nantucket. From mid-May to mid-October, boats leave from Saquatucket Harbor in Harwich Port and make three trips a day in season; the trip takes 1 hour and 30 minutes. A round-trip ticket is $46 for adults, $37 for children ages 2 to 11, $6 for children under 2, and $10 extra for bikes. Parking is free for day-trippers, $12 per night. Advance reservations are highly recommended.

BY AIR   You can also fly into **Nantucket Memorial Airport** (ℂ **508/325-5300**), which is about 3 miles south of Nantucket Road on Old South Road. The flight to Nantucket takes about 30 to 40 minutes from Boston, 15 minutes from Hyannis, and a little more than an hour from New York City airports.

Airlines providing service to Nantucket include: **Business Express/Delta Connection** (ℂ **800/221-1212**) from Boston (year-round) and New York (seasonally); **Cape Air/Nantucket Airlines** (ℂ **800/352-0714**) year-round from Hyannis ($79 round-trip), Boston (about $249 round-trip), Martha's Vineyard ($76 round-trip), and New Bedford ($139 round-trip); **Continental Express** (ℂ **800/525-0280**) from Newark, seasonally (about $723 round-trip); **Island Airlines** (ℂ **508/228-7575**) year-round from Hyannis ($79 round-trip); and **Colgan/US Airways Express** (ℂ **800/428-4322**) year-round from Boston ($316) and New York ($535 and up round-trip).

Island Airlines and Nantucket Airlines both offer year-round charter service to the island. Another charter company is **Ocean Wings** (ℂ **800/253-5039**).

GETTING AROUND

Nantucket is easily navigated on bike, moped, or foot, and also by shuttle bus or taxi. If you're staying outside of Nantucket Town, however, or if you simply prefer to explore by car, you might want to bring your own car or rent one when you arrive. Adventure-minded travelers may even want to rent a Jeep or other four-wheel-drive vehicle, which you can take out on the sand—a unique island experience—on certain sections of the coast (a permit is required—see "By Car and Jeep," below). Keep in mind that if you do opt to travel by car, in-town traffic can reach gridlock in the peak season, and parking can be a nightmare.

BY BIKE & MOPED   When I head to Nantucket for a few days, biking is my preferred mode of transportation. The island itself is relatively flat, and paved bike paths abound—they'll get you from Nantucket Town to Siasconset, Surfside, and Madaket. There are also many unpaved back roads to explore, which make mountain bikes a wise choice when pedaling around Nantucket.

A word of warning to bikers: One-way street signs apply to you, too! This law is enforced in Nantucket Town, and don't be surprised if a tanned but stern island policeman requests that you get off your bike and walk. Helmets are required for children under 12. Mopeds are also prevalent, but watch out for sand on the roads. Be aware that local rules and regulations are strictly enforced. Mopeds are not allowed on sidewalks or bike paths. You'll need a driver's license to rent a moped, and state law requires that you wear a helmet. The following shops rent bikes and scooters; all are within walking distance of the ferries:

Cook's Cycle Shop, Inc., 6 S. Beach St. (© **508/228-0800**); **Nantucket Bike Shops,** at Steamboat Wharf and Straight Wharf (© **508/228-1999**); and **Young's Bicycle Shop,** at Steamboat Wharf (© **508/228-1151**), which also does repairs. Bike rentals average $20 to $25 for 24 hours.

BY SHUTTLE BUS   From June through September, inexpensive shuttle buses, with bike racks and accessibility for those with disabilities, make a loop through Nantucket Town and to a few outlying spots; for routes and stops, contact the **Nantucket Regional Transit Authority** (© **508/228-7025**) or pick up a map and schedule at the visitor center on Federal Street or the chamber of commerce office on Main Street (see "Visitor Information," below). The shuttle permits you to bring your clean, dry dog along, too. The cost is $1–$2, and exact change is required. A 3-day pass can be purchased at the visitor center for $10.

Shuttle routes and fares are pretty simple. Downtown shuttle stops are located on the corner of Salem and Washington streets (for South and Miacomet loops), on Broad Street in front of the Foulger Museum (for Madaket loop and Beach Express), and on Washington Street at the corner of Main Street (for 'Sconset loops).

- **South Loop** services the Surfside Beach, Hooper Farm Road, and Pleasant Street areas; every 15 minutes from 7am to 11:30pm; $1.
- **Miacomet Loop** services the Fairgrounds Road, Bartlett Road, and Hummock Pond areas; every 30 minutes from 7am to 11:30pm; $1.
- **Madaket Route** services Madaket (from Broad St. downtown) via Cliff Road and New Lane; every 30 minutes from 7:30am to 11:30pm; $2 each way.
- **'Sconset Route 1** services 'Sconset via Polpis Road; every 30 minutes from 8:20am to 11pm; $2 each way.
- **'Sconset Route 2** services 'Sconset via Old South Road/Nobadeer Farm Road and Milestone Road; every 30 minutes from 7:40am to 10:30pm; $2 each way. This route makes a stop about ⅓ mile from the airport. If you don't have a lot of bags, this is the cheapest way to go.
- **Beach Express** services Surfside and Jetties Beach. The in-town stop is on Broad Street. $2 each way to Surfside; $1 each way to Jetties; every 30 minutes for Jetties Beach and every hour for Surfside Beach from 10:15am to 5:45pm.

BY CAR & JEEP   I recommend a car if you'll be here for more than a week or if you're staying outside Nantucket Town (or if you simply prefer to drive). However, there are no in-town parking lots; parking, although free, is limited to Nantucket's handful of narrow streets, which can be a problem in the busy summer months. Also, gas is much more expensive on Nantucket than it is on the mainland.

Four-wheel-drives are your best bet, since many beaches and nature areas are off sandy paths; be sure to reserve at least a month in advance if you're coming in summer. If you plan on doing any four-wheeling in the sand, you need to get an **Over-Sand Permit** ($100) from the Nantucket Police Department (© **508/228-1212**). To drive in the Coskata–Coatue nature area, you need a separate permit from the **Trustees of Reservations,** at the gatehouse (© **508/228-0006**), which costs about $125 for a season pass, or a $25 gate fee for a day-rental four-wheel drive that come with the Over-Sand Permit.

The following on-island rental agencies offer cars, Jeeps, and other four-wheel-drive vehicles: **Affordable Rentals of Nantucket,** 6 S. Beach Rd. (© **508/228-3501**); **Budget,** at the airport (© **800/527-0700** or 508/228-5666); **Hertz,** at the airport (© **800/654-3131** or 508/228-9421); **Nantucket Windmill Auto Rental,** at the airport (© **800/228-1227** or 508/228-1227); and **Young's 4x4**

& Car Rental, Steamboat Wharf (© **508/228-1151**). A standard car costs about $100 per day in season; a four-wheel-drive rental is about $185 per day (including an Over-Sand Permit).

BY TAXI   You'll find taxis (many are vans that can accommodate large groups or those traveling with bikes) waiting at the airport and at all ferry ports. During the busy summer months, I recommend reserving a taxi in advance to avoid a long wait upon arrival. Rates are flat fees, based on one person riding before 1am, with surcharges for additional passengers, bikes, and dogs. A taxi from the airport to Nantucket Town will cost about $9, plus $1 for each additional person. Reliable cab companies on the island include **A-1 Taxi** (© **508/228-3330**), **All Point Taxi** (© **508/228-5779**), **Bev's Taxi** (© **508/228-7874**), **Lisa's Taxi** (© **508/228-2223**) and **Val's Cab Service** (© **508/228-9410**).

VISITOR INFORMATION

For information contact the **Nantucket Island Chamber of Commerce** at 48 Main St., Nantucket, MA 02554 (© **508/228-1700;** www.nantucketchamber. org). When you arrive, you should also stop by the **Nantucket Visitors Service and Information Bureau** in Nantucket Town at 25 Federal St. (© **508/228-0925**), which is open daily from June to September, and Monday to Saturday from October to May. There are also information booths at Steamboat Wharf and Straight Wharf. Always check the island's newspaper, the *Inquirer & Mirror,* for information on current events and activities around town.

   Nantucket Accommodations, P.O. Box 217, Nantucket, MA 02554 (© **508/228-9559;** fax 508/325-7009; www.nantucketaccommodation.com), a 30-year-old private service, arranges advance reservations for inns, cottages, guesthouses, bed-and-breakfasts, and hotels. You can call until the day of arrival, and they will arrange a booking based on your preferences. A member of the chamber of commerce, Nantucket Accommodations has access to 95% of the island's lodging facilities, in addition to houses and cottages available to rent by the night or week (as opposed to most realtors, who will only handle rentals for 2 weeks or more). The charge for the service is $15—a fee assessed only when a reservation is made. The customer pays Nantucket Accommodations by any major credit card or check, and the service then pays the inn or hotel. Last-minute travelers should keep in mind that the **Nantucket Visitors Service and Information Bureau** (© **508/228-0925**), a daily referral service for available rooms rather than a booking service, always has the most updated list of accommodations availability and cancellations.

   Automated teller machines (ATMs) can be difficult to locate on Nantucket. **Nantucket Bank** (© **508/228-0580**) has five locations: 2 Orange St., 104 Pleasant St., Amelia Street, the Hub on Main Street, and the airport lobby, all open 24 hours. **Pacific National Bank** has four locations: A&P Supermarket (next to the wharves), the Stop & Shop (open 24 hr. seasonally), the Steamship Wharf Terminal, and Pacific National Bank lobby (open during bank hours only).

   In case of a **medical emergency,** the **Nantucket Cottage Hospital,** 57 Prospect St. (© **508/228-1200**), is open 24 hours.

2 Beaches & Recreational Pursuits

BEACHES   In distinct contrast to Martha's Vineyard, virtually all of Nantucket's 110-mile coastline is open to the public. Though the pressure to keep people out is sometimes intense (especially when four-wheel-drivers insist on their right to go anywhere, anytime), islanders are proud that they've managed to keep the shoreline in the public domain.

Each of the following areas tends to attract a different crowd.

- **Children's Beach** ★: This small beach is a protected cove just west of busy Steamship Wharf. Appealing to families, it has a park, a playground, restrooms, lifeguards, a snack bar (the beloved Downy Flake, famous for its homemade doughnuts), and even a bandstand for free weekend concerts.
- **Cisco Beach** ★★: About 4 miles from town, in the southwestern quadrant of the island (from Main St., turn onto Milk St., which becomes Hummock Pond Rd.), Cisco enjoys vigorous waves—great for the surfers who flock here, not so great for the waterfront homeowners. Restrooms and lifeguards are available.
- **Coatue** ★: This fishhook-shaped barrier beach, on the northeastern side of the island at Wauwinet, is Nantucket's outback, accessible only by four-wheel-drive vehicles, watercraft, or the very strong-legged. Swimming is strongly discouraged because of fierce tides.
- **Dionis Beach** ★★★: About 3 miles out of town (take the Madaket bike path to Eel Point Rd.) is Dionis, which enjoys the gentle sound surf and steep, picturesque bluffs. It's a great spot for swimming, picnicking, and shelling, and you'll find fewer children than at Jetties or Children's beaches. Stick to the established paths to prevent further erosion. Lifeguards patrol here, and restrooms are available.
- **Jetties Beach** ★★★: Located about a half mile west of Children's Beach on North Beach Street, Jetties is about a 20-minute walk, or an even shorter bike ride, shuttle bus ride, or drive, from town (there's a large parking lot, but it fills up early on summer weekends). It's another family favorite, for its mild waves, lifeguards, bathhouse, and restrooms. Facilities include the town tennis courts, volleyball nets, a skate park, and a playground; watersports equipment, and chairs are also available to rent. The Fourth of July fireworks are held here. Every August, Jetties hosts an intense sand-castle competition.
- **Madaket Beach** ★★★: Accessible by Madaket Road, the 6-mile bike path that runs parallel to it, and by shuttle bus, this westerly beach is narrow and subject to pounding surf and sometimes serious crosscurrents. Unless it's a fairly tame day, you might content yourself with wading. It's the best spot on the island for admiring the sunset. Facilities include restrooms, lifeguards, and mobile food service.
- **Siasconset ('Sconset) Beach** ★★: The eastern coast of 'Sconset is as pretty as the town itself and rarely, if ever, crowded, perhaps because of the water's strong sideways tow. You can reach it by car, by shuttle bus, or by a less scenic and somewhat hilly (at least for Nantucket) 7-mile bike path. Lifeguards are usually on duty, but the closest facilities (restrooms, grocery store, and cafe) are back in the center of the village.
- **Surfside Beach** ★★★: Three miles south of town via a popular bike/skate path, broad Surfside—equipped with lifeguards, restrooms, and a surprisingly accomplished little snack bar—is appropriately named and commensurately popular. It draws thousands of visitors a day in high season, from college students to families, but the free-parking lot can only fit about 60 cars—you do the math, or better yet, ride your bike or take the shuttle bus.

BICYCLING Several lovely, paved bike paths radiate from the center of town to outlying beaches. The **bike paths** run about 6¼ miles west to Madaket, 3½ miles south to Surfside, and 8¼ miles east to Siasconset. To avoid backtracking from Siasconset, continue north through the charming village, and return on the Polpis Road bike path. Strong riders could do a whole circuit of the island in a day, but most will be content to combine a single route with a few hours at a beach. You'll find picnic benches and water fountains at strategic points along all the paths.

On the way back to town, lighthouse enthusiasts will want to stop by Brant Point Light at the end of Easton Street. Located next to the Coast Guard station, this squat lighthouse is still used by boats maneuvering in and out of the harbor. It's a scenic spot to take a break and enjoy the view; you'll see ferries chugging by and immense yachts competing for prize berths along the wharves.

For a free map of the island's bike paths (it also lists Nantucket's bicycle rules), stop by **Young's Bicycle Shop,** at Steamboat Wharf (℃ **508/228-1151**). It's definitely the best place for bike rentals, from basic three-speeds to high-tech suspension models. In operation since 1931—check out the vintage vehicles on display—they also deliver door-to-door. See "Getting Around," above, for more bike-rental shops.

FISHING   For shellfishing, you'll need a permit from the **harbormaster's office** at 34 Washington St. (℃ **508/228-7261**). You'll see surf-casters all over the island (no permit is required); for a guided trip, try Mike Monte of **Surf & Fly Fishing Trips** (℃ **508/228-0529**), who charges $120 per person for a guided trip. Deep-sea charters heading out of Straight Wharf include Capt. Bob DeCosta's *The Albacore* (℃ **508/228-5074**), Capt. Josh Eldridge's *Monomoy* (℃ **508/228-6867**), and Capt. David Martin's *Flicka* (℃ **508/325-4000**). *Albacore* trips cost $650 for a half day and $1,300 for a full day for a boatload of six people. The *Monomoy* charges $650 for a half day and $1,200 for a full day. On the *Flicka*, 2½-hour trips for bluefish cost $350 for six people; 5-hour trips for bass cost $700.

FITNESS   **Nantucket Health Club** at 10 Youngs Way (℃ **508/228-4750**) offers all the usual equipment and classes. Non-members pay $20 a day.

GOLF   Two pretty nine-hole courses are open to the public: **Miacomet Golf Club,** 12 W. Miacomet Rd. (℃ **508/325-0333**), and the **Siasconset Golf Club,** off Milestone Road (℃ **508/257-6596**). You'll pay $26 for nine holes to $41 for 18 holes at Miacomet. New next year, Miacomet is increasing its course to 18 holes. At Siasconset, nine holes cost $22 and 18 holes cost $22 to $26.

NATURE TRAILS   Through preservationist foresight, about one-third of Nantucket's 42 square miles are protected from development. Contact the **Nantucket Conservation Foundation** at 118 Cliff Rd. (℃ **508/228-2884**) for a map of their holdings ($4), which include the 205-acre **Windswept Cranberry Bog** (off Polpis Rd.), where bogs are interspersed amid hardwood forests; and a portion of the 1,100-acre **Coskata–Coatue Wildlife Refuge,** comprising the barrier beaches beyond Wauwinet (see "Organized Tours," below). The **Maria Mitchell Association** (see "Museums & Historic Landmarks," below) sponsors guided birding and wildflower walks in season.

TENNIS   The town courts are located next to Jetties Beach, a short walk west of town; call the **Nantucket Park and Recreation Commission** (℃ **508/325-5334**) for information. The town courts cost $20 an hour for singles and $25 an hour for doubles. Nine clay courts are available for rent nearby at the **Brant Point Racquet Club,** on North Beach Street (℃ **508/228-3700**), for $34 an hour. Though it's not generally open to the public, the grand, turn-of-the-nineteenth-century **Siasconset Casino,** New Street, Siasconset (℃ **508/257-6585**), occasionally has courts available for rent from 1 to 3pm for $20–$25 an hour.

WATERSPORTS   **Nantucket Community Sailing** manages the concession at **Jetties Beach** (℃ **508/228-5358**), which offers lessons and rents out kayaks, sailboards, sailboats, and more. Rental rates for single kayaks are $25 per hour; windsurfers $20 to $25 per hour; and Sunfish $35 per hour. **Sea Nantucket,** on tiny Francis Street Beach off Washington Street (© 508/228-7499), also rents kayaks; it's a quick sprint across the harbor to beautiful Coatue. Single kayaks rent for $35 and tandems rent for $60 for 4½ hours. They also rent sailboats. **Nantucket Island Community Sailing** (© 508/228-6600) gives relatively low-cost private and group lessons from the Jetties pier for adults (16 and up) and children; a seasonal adult membership covering open-sail privileges costs $250 for 4 weeks. One 2-hour private lesson costs $100. Three 2-hour group lessons cost $165.

Gear for scuba-diving, fishing, and snorkeling are readily available at the souvenir shop **Sunken Ship** on South Water and Broad streets near Steamboat Wharf (© 508/228-9226). Fishing gear costs $20 per day; snorkeling gear costs $15 per day; and scuba-diving gear costs $60 per day. Scuba-diving lessons are $475.

3 Museums & Historic Landmarks

Hadwen House ★★   During Nantucket's most prosperous years, whaling merchant Joseph Starbuck built the "Three Bricks" (nos. 93, 95, and 97 Main St.) for his three sons. His daughter married successful businessman William Hadwen, owner of the candle factory that is now the Whaling Museum, and Hadwen built this grand Greek Revival home across the street from his brothers-in-law in 1845. Although locals (mostly Quakers) were scandalized by the opulence, the local outrage spurred Hadwen on, and he decided to make the home even grander than he had first intended. The home soon became a showplace for entertaining the Hadwens' many wealthy friends. Soon after, Hadwen built the matching home next door for his niece, and it is assumed that he enjoyed using its grand ballroom for his parties, too. The Historical Association has done a magnificent job of restoring the home and furnishing it with period furniture, fabrics, porcelains, wallpapers, and other decorative accessories thought to be original. The gardens are maintained in period style by the Nantucket Garden Club.

96 Main St. (at Pleasant St., a few blocks southwest of the town center). © 508/228-1894. www.nha.org. Admission included in Nantucket Historical Association's History Ticket ($15 adults, $8 children, $35 family). AE, MC, V. June–Sept Mon–Sat 10am–5pm, Sun noon–5pm; call for off-season hours. Closed Dec–Mar.

Jethro Coffin House ★★   Built around 1686, this saltbox is the oldest building left on the island. A National Historical Landmark, the brick design on its central chimney has earned it the nickname "The Horseshoe House." It was struck by lightning and severely damaged (in fact, nearly cut in two) in 1987, prompting a long-overdue restoration. Dimly lit by leaded-glass diamond-pane windows, it's filled with period furniture such as lathed ladder-back chairs and a clever trundle bed on wooden wheels. Nantucket Historical Association docents will fill you in on all the related lore.

Sunset Hill Rd. (off W. Chester Rd., about ½ mile northwest of the town center). © 508/228-1894. www. nha.org. Admission included in Nantucket Historical Association's History Ticket ($15 adults, $8 children, $35 families). AE, MC, V. Late May to mid-Oct Mon–Sat 10am–5pm, Sun noon–5pm. Closed mid-Oct to late May.

The Maria Mitchell Association ★★ *Kids*   This is a group of six buildings organized and maintained in honor of distinguished astronomer and Nantucket native Maria Mitchell (1818–89). The science center consists of astronomical observatories, with a lecture series, children's science seminars, and stellar observation opportunities (when the sky is clear) from the **Loines Observatory** at 59 Milk St. Extension (© 508/228-8690) and from the **Vestal Street Observatory**

at 3 Vestal St. (© **508/228-9273**). The Vestal Street Observatory is open June to September on Saturday at 11am for a 1-hour tour. The Loines Observatory is open July and August Monday, Wednesday, and Friday at 9pm; September to June it's open Friday at 8pm.

The **Hinchman House Natural Science Museum** (© **508/228-0898**) at 7 Milk St. houses a visitor center and offers evening lectures, bird-watching, wildflower and nature walks, and discovery classes for children and adults. The **Mitchell House** (© **508/228-2896**) at 1 Vestal St., the astronomer's birthplace, features a children's history series and adult-artisan seminars, and it has wildflower and herb gardens. The **Science Library** (© **508/228-9219**) is at 2 Vestal St., and the tiny, child-oriented **aquarium** (© **508/228-5387**) is at 28 Washington St.

4 Vestal St. (at Milk St., about ½ mile southwest of the town center). © 508/228-9198. www.mmo.org. Admission to each site: $4 adults, $3 children. Museum pass (for birthplace, aquarium, science museum, and Vestal Street Observatory) $10 adults, $7 children ages 6–14. MC, V. Early June to late Aug Tues–Sat 10am–4pm; call for off-season hours.

Nantucket Life-Saving Museum ★★ *(Finds)*

Housed in a replica of the Nantucket Life-Saving Station (the original serves as the island's youth hostel), the museum has loads of interesting exhibits, including historic photos and newspaper clippings, as well as one of the last remaining Massachusetts Humane Society surf boats and its horse-drawn carriage.

158 Polpis Rd. (2½ miles east of town) © 508/228-1885. Admission $5 adults, $2 children. Mid-June to mid-Oct daily 9:30am–4pm.

Whaling Museum ★★★ *(Kids)*

Housed in a former spermaceti-candle factory (candles used to be made from a waxy fluid extracted from sperm whales), this museum is a must-visit, if not for the awe-inspiring skeleton of a 43-foot finback whale (stranded in the 1960s), then for the exceptional collections of scrimshaw and nautical art. (Check out the action painting, *Ship Spermo of Nantucket in a Heavy Thunder-Squall on the Coast of California 1876*, executed by a captain who survived the storm.) A wall-size map depicts the round-the-world meanderings of the *Alpha*, accompanied by related journal entries. The admission price includes daily lectures on the brief and colorful history of the industry, like the beachside "whalebecue" feasts that natives and settlers once enjoyed. Pursued to its logical conclusion, this booming business unfortunately led to the near-extinction of some extraordinary species, but that story must await its own museum; this one is full of the glories of the hunt. Don't miss the gift shop on the way out.

Note: The Whaling Museum is scheduled to close for a one-year renovation from fall 2003 to fall 2004. Visitors can see some of the Whaling Museum exhibits at the Friends Meeting House at 7 Fair St., an 1838 former Quaker school, during the renovations. Call the Nantucket Historical Association at © **508/228-1894** for updates.

13 Broad St. (in the center of town). © 508/228-1894. www.nha.org. Admission $10 adults, $6 children 5–14. Admission is also included in the Nantucket Historical Association's History Ticket ($15 adults, $8 children, $35 families). AE, MC, V. Apr–Nov Mon–Sat 10am–5pm, Sun noon–5pm. Closed Dec–Mar.

4 Organized Tours

Christina ★★ *(Value)*

Built in 1926, the *Christina* is a classic solid-mahogany catboat. The boat makes seven 1½-hour trips daily in season, and the sunset trips tend to sell out a day or two in advance. Price-wise, a sail around the harbor on the *Christina* is probably the best entertainment bargain on Nantucket. Bring your own drinks and picnic supplies.

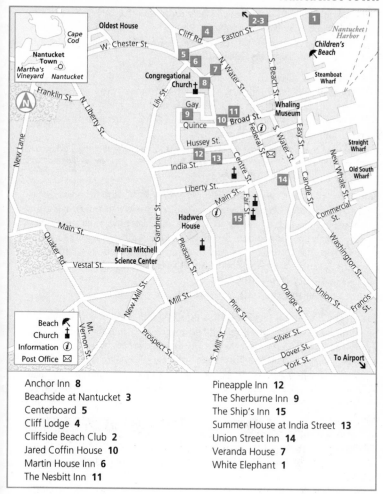

Anchor Inn **8**
Beachside at Nantucket **3**
Centerboard **5**
Cliff Lodge **4**
Cliffside Beach Club **2**
Jared Coffin House **10**
Martin House Inn **6**
The Nesbitt Inn **11**

Pineapple Inn **12**
The Sherburne Inn **9**
The Ship's Inn **15**
Summer House at India Street **13**
Union Street Inn **14**
Veranda House **7**
White Elephant **1**

Slip 1016, Straight Wharf. ✆ **508/325-4000**. Day sails $25 per person; sunset sails $35 per person. Reservations recommended. Closed Nov–Apr.

Coskata–Coatue Wildlife Refuge Natural History Tour ★★★ *Kids* The Trustees of the Reservations, a private statewide conservation organization that oversees the bulk of the Coskata–Coatue Wildlife Refuge, offers a 3-hour naturalist-guided tour twice a day. The trip is over sand dunes via Ford Expedition out to the **Great Point Lighthouse,** a partly solar-powered replica of the 1818 original. Those interested can also tour the inside of the lighthouse. During the trip through this rare habitat, you might spot snowy egrets, ospreys, terns, and oystercatchers. Call to make a reservation and meet the group at the Wauwinet Inn parking lot.

✆ **508/228-6799**. $30 adults, $15 children 15 and under. Call for reservations. Mid-May to mid-Oct daily 9:30am and 1:30pm. Closed mid-Oct to mid-May.

Endeavor Sailing Excursions ★★ The *Endeavor* is a spirited 31-foot replica Friendship sloop, ideal for jaunts across the harbor into Nantucket

Sound. Skipper James Genthner will gladly drop you off at one the beaches for a bit of sunbathing or beachcombing.

Slip 15, Straight Wharf. © **508/228-5585**. www.endeavorsailing.com. Reservations recommended. Rates $25–$35 for a 1½-hr. sail (highest rates July–Aug). Closed Nov–Apr.

Gail's Tours ★★ *Value* If you want to get some dirt on the island's colorful residents, Gail Nickerson Johnson—a seventh-generation native whose mother started a tour business back in the 1940s—has the inside track, and the charm, to keep a captive van-load rapt throughout a 1½-hour circuit of island highlights, including lots of celebrity info.

Departs from the Nantucket Information Bureau at 25 Federal St., and from pre-arranged pickup sites. © **508/257-6557**. Reservations required. Rates $15 adults, free for children 3 and under. July–Aug departures at 10am, 1pm, and 3pm; call for off-season hours.

Nantucket Harbor Cruises ★★ *Kids* The *Anna W. II*, a lobster-boat-turned-pleasure-barge, offers lobstering demos in summer (passengers sometimes get to take home the proceeds). Capt. Bruce Cowan also takes groups out just to view the lovely shoreline. In addition, he offers the Marine Life Discovery Cruise, a 1½-hour trip that costs $27 per person. In season, a 1-hour ice-cream cruise leaves at 1:30 and 3:30pm daily and costs $17 per person. Sunset cruises which last 1¼ hours cost $25 per person.

Slip 11, Straight Wharf. © **508/228-1444**. Call for reservations. MC, V. Closed mid-Oct to June.

Nantucket Historical Association Guided Walking Tours ★ Stroll along downtown's cobblestone streets on this Historical Society tour that spotlights the history and architecture of Nantucket. The tours are led by Nantucket Historical Society docents trained in Nantucket history.

Sign up for tour at the Whaling Museum. © **508/228-1894**. www.nha.org. Admission included with Historical Association's History Ticket (adults $15, children $8, family $35). AE, MC, V. Apr–Nov Mon–Sat 10:15am and 2:15pm. Closed Dec–Mar.

5 Kid Stuff

The **Nantucket Park and Recreation Commission** (© **508/228-7213**) organizes various free and low-cost activities for kids, like tennis clinics, a concert series, and tie-dye workshops (bring your own T-shirt). The **Artists' Association of Nantucket** (© **508/325-5251**) sponsors a variety of classes for children in different media, and the **Nantucket Island School of Design and the Arts** (© **508/228-9248**) offers all sorts of summer courses. The **Nantucket Atheneum** (© **508/228-1110**) holds readings in its spiffy new children's wing. The **Nantucket Historical Association** (© **508/228-1894**) sponsors **Living History for Children,** 2-hour adventures for ages 6 to 10, which include grinding flour at the Old Mill, baking bread at the Oldest House, and trying your hand at knots and sailors' valentines. The cost is $25.

The **Actor's Theatre of Nantucket** at the Methodist Church, 2 Centre St. (© **508/228-6325**), puts on theatrical performances for children by children from late July to mid-August, Tuesday to Saturday at 5pm; tickets are $6 to $12. Little kids might like to get their hands on (and into) the touch tanks at the modest little **Maria Mitchell Aquarium** at 28 Washington St. (© **508/228-5387**), which overlooks the harbor from whence the creatures came; the cost is only $1. It's open June through September Tuesday to Saturday from 10am to 4pm. For a real seafaring adventure, consider embarking on a treasure hunt aboard the *Endeavor* (© **508/228-5585**).

6 Shopping

Nantucket shopping is so phenomenal you'll be tempted to rent a U-Haul. It's as if all the best big-city buyers, from Bendel's to Brooks Brothers, got together and gathered their favorite stuff. True, some tourist dreck has managed to drift in, but most of what you'll find for sale is as high in quality as it is in price—everything from $6 boxes of chocolate-covered dried cranberries to $900 cashmere sweaters.

ANTIQUES/COLLECTIBLES   Most tourists aren't looking to return home with a new living-room set, but **Lynda Willauer Antiques,** at 2 India St., between Federal and Centre streets (© 508/228-3631), has such an exquisite selection of American, French, and English furniture that it's worth stopping by just to gawk. All pieces are painstakingly tagged as to provenance and state of repair, and most are quite pricey. The shop also stocks paintings, Chinese export porcelain, Staffordshire china, samplers, ship wool works, majolica, and brass and tortoise-shell boxes.

An island fixture since 1971, **Tonkin of Nantucket,** 33 Main St. (© 508/228-9697), specializes in English and French antiques. Antiques hounds will be in heaven browsing through the 9,000 square feet of showrooms, featuring such finery as silver, china, marine paintings, ship models, fireplace equipment, Quimper, and majolica.

ART & CRAFTS   **The Artists' Association of Nantucket** has the widest selection of work by locals, and the gallery at 19 Washington St. (© 508/228-0294) is impressive. It's open by appointment only February and March.

The celebrated sculptor **David L. Hostetler** exhibits his work in one of the little galleries along Old South Wharf, 2 Old South Wharf (© 508/228-5152). Private viewing appointments are also available in his large showroom. His work in various media appears as spiritual icons expressed in the female form.

Exquisite art glass pieces, as well as ceramics, jewelry, and basketry, can be found at **Dane Gallery,** 28 Centre St. (© 508/228-7779), where owners Robert and Jayne Dane show top-quality work. You'll be amazed at the colors and shapes of the glassware.

You'll definitely want to poke your head in **Sailor's Valentine** in the Macy Warehouse on lower Main Street (© 508/228-2011), which houses an international collection of contemporary fine art, sculpture, folk art, and "outsider art." There are also new versions of the namesake craft, a boxed design of colorful shells, which 19th-century sailors used to bring back from the Caribbean for their sweethearts at home.

BOOKS   At **Mitchell's Book Corner,** 54 Main St. (© 508/228-1080), Mimi Beman handpicks her stock, with an astute sampling of general-interest books and an entire room dedicated to regional and maritime titles.

Nantucket Bookworks, 25 Broad St. (© 508/228-4000), is a charming bookstore, strong on customer service and with a central location.

FASHION   Martha's Vineyard may have spawned "Black Dog" fever, but this island boasts the inimitable "Nantucket reds"—cotton clothing that starts out tomato-red and washes out to salmon-pink. The fashion originated at **Murray's Toggery Shop,** 62 Main St. (© 800/368-2134 or 508/228-0437). Legend has it that the original duds were colored with an inferior dye that washed out almost immediately. However, customers so liked the thick cottons and instant aged look that the proprietor was forced to search high and low for more of the same fabric.

Roland Hussey Macy, founder of Macy's, got his start here in the 1830s—his shop shows no signs of fading (no pun intended)—although today's management also manages to keep up with current trends. There's a bargain outlet on New Street.

Preppy patterns and bright colors are back! You'll find **Lilly Pulitzer's** latest, including sensational minidresses, at 5 S. Water St. (© **508/228-0569**).

GIFTS/HOME DECOR A casual counterpart to its Madison Avenue boutique, **Erica Wilson Needle Works,** 25–27 Main St. (© **508/228-9881**), features the designs of its namesake, an islander since 1958 and author of more than two dozen books on needlepoint. The shop offers hands-on guidance for hundreds of grateful adepts, as well as kits and handiwork of other noteworthy designers.

The also eponymous **Claire Murray,** 11 S. Water St. (© **508/228-1913**), is famous for its elaborate hand-hooked rugs. As a New York transplant running a Nantucket B&B in the late 1970s, Murray took up the traditional art of hooking rugs to see her through the slow season. She now runs a retail company grossing millions a year and is so busy creating new collections that she has hundreds of "hookers" (probably an old profession, but not the oldest) working for her around the world. Do-it-yourself kits ($100–$500) are sold in the shop here for about two-thirds the price of the finished rugs and come with complimentary lessons.

Resembling an old-fashioned pharmacy, **The Fragrance Bar,** 5 Centre St. (© **800/223-8660** or 508/325-4740), is run by a colorful fellow who goes by the solo sobriquet of Harpo. A self-professed "nose," he has assembled some 400 essential oils with which he can duplicate designer scents or customize blends. Uncut by alcohol (unlike their commercial counterparts), these perfumes linger on the skin and do not cause associated problems such as allergies and headaches. Harpo won't discuss his clientele but admits to creating a custom scent for a certain recording megastar who also goes by a single name, starting with an "M."

Centrally located **Nantucket Looms,** 16 Main St. (© **508/228-1908**), is an elegant shop featuring beautifully textured woven items as well as fine furniture and gifts.

Although certain influences are evident (from Queen Anne to Shaker), the hand-fashioned furniture at **Stephen Swift,** 34 Main St. (© **508/228-0255**), is far too individualized to pass as reproduction. Such is its classicism, though, that Swift's work would blend into the most traditional of homes, or just as easily adapt to a modern setting. Among his signature pieces are wavy-backed Windsor chairs and benches (as sturdy as the original but more comfortable) and delicate, pared-down four-poster beds.

JEWELRY Visit **The Golden Basket,** 44 Main St. (© **800/582-8205** or 508/228-4344), where the widely copied, miniaturized jewelry versions of Nantucket's trademark lightship baskets were introduced. Artisan Glenaan Elliot Robbins's rendition is still the finest. The baskets, complete with gold penny, represent a small portion of the inventory, all of which is exquisite.

SEAFOOD **Sayle's Seafood,** Washington Street Extension (© **508/228-4599**), sells fresh seafood from Nantucket waters and a new menu of takeout seafood platters. This is a great place to get a huge, steaming plate of fried clams to go.

TOYS **The Toy Boat,** Straight Wharf no. 41 (© **508/228-4552**), is keen on creative toys that are also educational. In addition to the top commercial lines, owner Loren Brock stocks lots of locally crafted, hand-carved playthings, such as "rainbow fleet" sailboats, part of the Harbor Series that includes docks, lighthouses, boats, and everything your child needs to create his or her own Nantucket Harbor. There are also stackable lighthouse puzzles replicating Nantucket's beams.

7 Where to Stay

Most visitors to Nantucket will wish to stay in the center of town. There's no need for a car here; in fact, parking can be a real problem in season. Everything is within walking distance, including beaches, restaurants, and the finest shopping in the region. Unless otherwise stated, hotels are open year-round.

VERY EXPENSIVE

Cliffside Beach Club ★★★ *(finds)* Right on the beach and within walking distance (about 1 mile) of town, this is the premier lodging on the island. It may not be as fancy as some, but there's a sublime beachy-ness to the whole setup, from the simply decorated rooms; the cheerful, youthful staff; the sea of antique wicker in the clubhouse; and of course, the blue, yellow, and green umbrellas lined up on the beach. All rooms have such luxuries as French milled soaps, thick towels, and exceptional linens. Turndown service is provided. Guests receive an umbrella, chairs, and beach towels. A very good continental breakfast is served in the large clubhouse room, its beamed ceilings draped with colorful quilts. Lucky guests on the Fourth of July get a front-row seat for the fireworks staged at Jetties Beach nearby.

46 Jefferson Ave. (about 1 mile from town center), Nantucket, MA 02554. © **800/932-9645** or 508/228-0618. Fax 508/325-4735. www.cliffsidebeach.com. 25 units, 1 cottage. Summer $380–$605 double, $695–$1,385 suite, $705 apt; $895 cottage. Rates include continental breakfast. AE. Closed mid-Oct to late May. **Amenities:** Restaurant (The Galley, an elegant French bistro); exercise facility (Cybex equipment and a trainer on staff); indoor hydrotherapy spa; steam saunas; concierge; climate-controlled massage room; babysitting. *In room:* A/C, TV/VCR, fridge, coffeemaker, hair dryer.

Nantucket Whaler Guesthouse ★★ This lodging option, an 1850s Greek Revival sea captain's house, is unique in that all of the rooms are suites with their own entrance and kitchen facilities. Compared to other B&Bs on the island, this one has a particularly private feel, almost like having your own apartment. Many of the rooms have decks or patios. The entire building has been recently restored and all rooms are comfortably outfitted with cottage-y furnishings including overstuffed couches and stacks of games and books. Those guests who would prefer not to whip up their own breakfast and want to eat in can order up a continental breakfast basket that costs $21 for two people.

8 N. Water St. (in the center of town), Nantucket, MA 02554. © **800/462-6882** or 508/228-6597. Fax 508/228-6291. www.nantucketwhaler.com. 12 units (8 tub/shower; 4 shower only). Summer $300–$400 double, $575 2 bedrooms. AE, DC, MC, V. Closed mid-Dec to mid-Mar. No children under age 12. *In room:* A/C, TV/VCR, dataport, hair dryer, iron, CD player.

Vanessa Noel Hotel (VNH) ★ This is Nantucket's trendiest inn: think Ian Schraeger–style wrapped in a historic package. Vanessa Noel, a shoe designer whose shoe store is on the first floor, has decorated the eight rooms in this historic building with boutique hotel features like Philippe Starck fixtures, queen-size feather beds with custom Frette linens, Bulgari toiletries, robes, slippers, 15-inch flat screen plasma televisions, and minibars stocked with the hotel's bottled water. Most of the rooms are tiny, though there are two including a fun attic space that are comfortably spacious. The Vanno Bar, a caviar and Champagne bar on the first floor, has novelties like leopard-print calfskin banquettes, two swings, and food imported from Caviarteria, the New York City caviar emporium.

5 Chestnut St. (in the center of town), Nantucket, MA 02554. © **508/228-5300.** Fax 508/228-8995. www. vanno.com. 8 units. Summer $340–$480 double. AE, DISC, MC, V. Open year-round. *In-room:* AC, TV, minibar, hair dryer.

The Wauwinet ✦✦✦ This ultradeluxe beachfront retreat, the most luxurious lodging choice on the island, is Nantucket's only Relais & Châteaux property. The inn is at the tip of a wildlife sanctuary and is nestled between the Atlantic Ocean and Nantucket Bay. With 25 rooms in the main building (which started out as a restaurant in 1850) and 10 more in five modest-looking shingled cottages, the complex can only hold about 80 decorously spoiled guests, outnumbered by 100 staffers. Each of the lovely rooms—all provided with a cozy nook from which to gaze out across the water—has a unique decorating scheme, with pine armoires, plenty of wicker, exquisite Audubon prints, handsome fabrics, and a lovely array of antique accessories. Extras include Egyptian cotton bathrobes and bottled water. Additional perks include a personalized set of engraved note cards. (Don't tell them I told you; it's supposed to be a surprise.) All rooms have CD players and VCRs, and if you order up a video from the extensive (400 videos) library, it is delivered on a tray by a steward with a couple of boxes of complimentary hot pop-corn. The staff goes to great lengths to please, ferrying you into town, for instance, in a 1946 "Woody," (12 trips daily) or dispatching you on a 21-foot launch across the bay to your own private strip of beach in season. There are also free guided nature tours on weekdays in season.

120 Wauwinet Rd. (P.O. Box 2580), about 8 miles east of Nantucket center, Nantucket, MA 02554. ✆ 800/426-8718 or 508/228-0145. Fax 508/325-0657. www.wauwinet.com. 25 units, 10 cottages (all with tub/shower). Summer $450–$800 double, $800–$1,500 cottage. Rates include full breakfast and afternoon wine and cheese. AE, DC, MC, V. Closed Nov to mid-May. **Amenities:** Fine-dining restaurant; 2 clay tennis courts with pro shop and teaching pro; croquet lawn; row boats, sail boats, sea kayaks, and mountain bikes on loan; concierge; room service (8am–9pm). *In room:* A/C, TV/VCR, hair dryer, iron, CD player.

White Elephant ✦✦✦ This luxury property, right on the harbor, is the ulti-mate in-town lodging and has been newly renovated by the owners of The Wauwinet (see above). Rooms (distributed among one building and 12 cottages) are big and airy (the most spacious rooms on Nantucket), with country-chic decor and most with harbor views. In-room amenities include DVD players. About half the rooms have working fireplaces. Guests can borrow from an exten-sive tape collection of new and old movies. The hotel has pleasant commons rooms including a cozy library with a large fireplace. The hotel's location wel-comes "sail-in" guests. The same company owns Breakers, a 25-room hotel next door that offers a less bustling atmosphere.

50 Easton St. (P.O. Box 1139), Nantucket, MA 02554. ✆ 800/445-6574 or 508/228-2500. Fax 508/325-1195. www.whiteelephanthotel.com. 52 units, 11 cottages (61 tub/shower, 2 shower only). Summer $350–$630 double, $440–$1,400 cottage. Rates include full breakfast. AE, DC, DISC, MC, V. Closed Nov–Mar. **Amenities:** Restaurant (lobster and steakhouse serving lunch and dinner daily plus an afternoon raw bar); exercise room; concierge; business lounge; full room service; fee-based laundry service; dry cleaning. *In room:* A/C, TV/VCR, dataport, fridge, hair dryer, iron, safe.

EXPENSIVE

Beachside at Nantucket ✦ No ordinary motel, the Beachside's 90 air-conditioned bedrooms and lobby have been lavished with Provençal prints and handsome rattan and wicker furniture; the patios and decks overlooking the cen-tral courtyard with its heated pool have been prettified with French doors and latticework. If you prefer the laissez-faire lifestyle of a motel to the sometimes constricting rituals of a B&B, you might find this the ideal base.

30 N. Beach St. (about ¾ mile west of the town center), Nantucket, MA 02554. ✆ 800/322-4433 or 508/228-2241. Fax 508/228-8901. www.thebeachside.com. 90 units (all with tub/shower). Summer $245–$290 double, $535 suite. Rates include continental breakfast. AE, DC, DISC, MC, V. Closed late Oct to late Apr. **Amenities:** Heated outdoor pool. *In room:* A/C, TV, fridge, hair dryer.

Centerboard ★★ Nantucket actually has very little in Victorian housing: The island was just too poor (and underpopulated) to build much in those days. The few to be found tend to get dolled up like this updated 1886 home, replete with parquet floors, Oriental rugs, lavish fabrics, plush feather mattresses, and lace-trimmed linens. The overall look is light, airy, and less cluttered than the original Victorian look. Of the inn's seven bedrooms, the first-floor suite is perhaps the most romantic, with a green-marble Jacuzzi and a private living room with fireplace. Other rooms and bathrooms are small, but all have bathrobes and mini-fridges.

8 Chester St. (in the center of town), Nantucket, MA 02554. ✆ **508/228-9696.** Fax 508/325-4798. www. centerboard.com. 7 units. Summer $225–$235 double, $325–$425 suite. Rates include continental breakfast. AE, MC, V. Closed Nov–Apr. *In room:* A/C, TV, fridge, hair dryer.

Harbor House Village ★★ (Kids) This resort has undergone a multimillion-dollar freshening-up. The main building, the 35-room historic Harbor House, was originally built 130 years ago, but there are few vestiges from the days of yore. The property is now one of Nantucket's most full-service lodging options. It is located just a short walk from the center of Nantucket Town, as well as Children's Beach, Jetties Beach, and Brant Point Lighthouse. The rooms are decorated with pine and wicker furniture and feature new mattresses and bedding. Some are spacious and have balconies. The Hearth Bar offers live entertainment some nights in season and doubles as a sports bar in the fall. The resort's restaurant, Harbor Wok, which is open in July and August, is the island's only gourmet Chinese food restaurant. Lunch is available poolside.

South Beach St., Nantucket, MA 02554. ✆ **866/325-9300** or 508/228-1500. Fax 508/228-7639. www.harbor housevillage.com. 104 units. Summer $370–$410 double. AE, DC, DISC, MC, V. Closed early Dec to mid-Apr. **Amenities:** 2 restaurants (a seasonal Chinese restaurant and a breakfast cafe); bar/lounge (featuring Monday Night Football on the large screen TV in the fall); outdoor heated pool (in season); free children's program in summer; concierge; babysitting; laundry service; dry cleaning; free shuttle from Steamship Authority ferry. *In room:* A/C, TV, dataport, hair dryer, iron, VCR or fridge available on request.

Jared Coffin House ★★ (Kids) This grand brick manse was built in 1845 to the specs of the social-climbing Mrs. Coffin, who abandoned Nantucket for the big city after 2 years and left the house to boarders. Lovingly renovated to its original splendor by the Nantucket Historical Trust, it is the social center of town, as well as a mecca for visitors. Accommodations range from well-priced singles (rare in these parts) to spacious doubles. Rooms in the neighboring annex houses are equally grand. Most have air-conditioning. The concierge, Mrs. K., can't do enough to help, and she refuses tips! The central location does have a drawback: The front rooms can be quite noisy. Twenty-minute waits for breakfast are not unusual because locals come, too. It's the best breakfast in town, though it is not included in the room rate. It's a good idea to call down ahead and put your name on the list.

29 Broad St. (at Centre St.), Nantucket, MA 02554. ✆ **800/248-2405** or 508/228-2400. Fax 508/228-8549. www.jaredcoffinhouse.com. 60 units (52 tub/shower; 8 shower only). Summer $290–$375 double. AE, DC, DISC, MC, V. Open year-round. **Amenities:** 2 restaurants (family and tavern); concierge. *In room:* TV, dataport, fridge, coffeemaker, hair dryer, iron.

The Pineapple Inn ★★ This newly renovated historic inn has quickly become one of the premier places to stay on the island. The graceful Quaker entrance of the 1838 home bespeaks the hospitality to come from veteran innkeepers Bob and Caroline Taylor. Rooms are spacious and decorated in a colonial style with fine reproductions and antiques, including handmade Oriental rugs, marble bathrooms, and many four-poster canopy beds. There are five large king bedrooms with beds of tiger maple. The smaller, less expensive rooms are on the third floor. All rooms are equipped with such extras as goose-down comforters, voice mail, and cable. The continental breakfast here is extra deluxe with fresh baked goods, espresso, cappuccino, and freshly squeezed orange juice among the offerings. The garden patio with climbing roses is a fine place to enjoy an afternoon cocktail and contemplate dinner plans.

10 Hussey St. (in the center of town), Nantucket, MA 02554. ℂ 508/228-9992. Fax 508/325-6051. www.pineappleinn.com. 12 units (8 tub/shower; 4 shower only). Summer $195–$325 double. Rates include continental breakfast. AE, MC, V. Closed early Dec to mid-Apr. No children under age 8. *In room:* A/C, TV, dataport, hair dryer, iron.

Sherburne Inn ⭐

You'd never guess from the gracious foyer of this 1835 house that it was once the headquarters of the Atlantic Silk Company, a short-lived 19th-century enterprise. Now it's an elegant and comfortable inn offering quiet comforts in the heart of Nantucket village. Innkeepers Dale Hamilton and Susan Gasparich, who bought the inn in 1994, are transplants from Pittsburgh who are active in a number of island organizations. Rooms vary in size, with smaller rooms a good value at lower rates. Ask for one on the sunny side of the house. Susan's recipes for baked goods like butterscotch coffee cake have been featured in *Gourmet* magazine.

10 Gay St. (in the center of town), Nantucket, MA 02554. ℂ 888/577-4425 or 508/228-4425. Fax 508/228-8114. www.sherburneinn.com. 8 units (2 tub/shower; 6 shower only). Summer $175–$295 double. Rates include continental breakfast. AE, DISC, MC, V. Open year-round. No children under 6. *In room:* A/C, TV/VCR, hair dryer.

Summer House at India Street ⭐

The Summer House management now owns three properties: the very expensive cottages overlooking the beach in Siasconset, an inn on Fair Street, and this property on India Street. The India Street property is the most centrally located and is a handsome historic house, fully renovated with all new furnishings and top-notch amenities. Rooms are equipped with robes and deluxe toiletries. Guests have access to complimentary jitney service to the Summer House beachfront property in 'Sconset and use of the pool there.

31 India St. (in the center of town), Nantucket, MA 02554. ℂ 508/257-4577. Fax 508/257-4590. www.thesummerhouse.com. 10 units. Summer $200–$250 double. Rates include continental breakfast. AE, MC, V. Closed Jan–Apr. *In room:* A/C, TV, hair dryer.

Union Street Inn ⭐⭐ *Finds*

Sophisticated innkeepers Deborah and Ken Withrow have a terrific location for their historic 1770s property, just steps from Main Street yet in a quiet, residential section. Ken's experience in big hotels shows in the amenities and full concierge service offered here. The Withrows have completely restored the inn, highlighting its period charms and updating all amenities. Many rooms have canopied or four-poster beds; half have working wood-burning fireplaces. All rooms are decorated with antique furniture and fixtures, some with toile wallpaper and Oriental rugs. The comfortable beds are made up with Egyptian cotton linens. Bathrooms are equipped with pique-woven bathrobes and large terry bath towels. Unlike many Nantucket inns that are forbidden by zoning laws to serve a full breakfast, this inn's location allows a superb complete breakfast on the garden patio. If you are hanging around in the afternoon, there are usually home-baked cookies or other goodies to sample as well.

7 Union St. (in the center of town), Nantucket, MA 02554. ℂ 800/225-5116 or 508/228-9222. Fax 508/325-0848. www.unioninn.com. 12 units (1 with tub/shower; 11 shower only). Summer $195–$365 double, $395 suite. Rates include full breakfast. AE, MC, V. Closed Jan–Mar. *In room:* A/C, TV, hair dryer, CD player, no phone.

MODERATE

Anchor Inn ★ *Value*   Innkeepers Ann and Charles Balas have a historic gem in this 1806 sea captain's home located next to the Old North Church. This year they have added a new property, 72 Centre Street, three doors down, to the inn. Authentic details can be found throughout both houses, in the antique hardware and paneling, wide-board floors, and period furnishings. All rooms are equipped with air-conditioning (in season) and voice mail. The five rooms in the 72 Centre Street house are a particularly good value; they are smaller and less expensive. Guests enjoy a continental breakfast with home-baked muffins at individual tables on the enclosed porch.

66 Centre St. (P.O. Box 387, in the center of town), Nantucket, MA 02554. (☎ **508/228-0072**. www.anchor-inn.net. 16 units (2 tub/shower, 9 shower only). Summer $185–$225 double. Rates include continental breakfast. AE, MC, V. Closed Jan–Feb. *In room:* A/C, TV, hair dryer.

Cliff Lodge ★★ *Finds*   Debby and John Bennett have freshened up this charming 1771 whaling captain's house with their own countrified style. It's located about a block from the center of town and has sunny, cheerful interiors featuring colorful quilts and splatter-painted floors. Rooms range from a first-floor beauty with king-size bed, paneled walls, and fireplace to the tiny third-floor rooms tucked into the eaves. All are spotlessly clean and blessed with quality beds and linens. The spacious apartment in the rear of the house is a sunny delight. The continental breakfast of home-baked breads and muffins on the garden patio is congenial. Chat with Debby for a wealth of island info and the latest goings-on, then climb up to the widow's walk for a bird's-eye view of the town and harbor.

9 Cliff Rd. (a few blocks from the center of town), Nantucket, MA 02554. (☎ **508/228-9480**. Fax 508/228-6308. www.nantucket.net/lodging/clifflodge. 12 units. Summer $135 single, $170–$265 double; $425 apt. Rates include continental breakfast. MC, V. Open year-round. No children under 12. *In room:* A/C, TV.

Martin House Inn ★★ *Value*   This is one of the lower-priced B&Bs in town but also one of the most stylish, with a formal parlor, dining rooms, and a spacious side porch, complete with hammock. This historic 1803 mariner's home is kept in shipshape; this is a well-run property. The four garret single rooms with a shared bathroom are a bargain. Higher-priced rooms have four-posters and working fireplaces. The extensive continental breakfast, served at the long dining room table, includes Martin's famous granola, as well as home-baked breads, muffins, and fresh fruits.

61 Centre St. (between Broad and Chester sts.; a couple blocks from town center), Nantucket, MA 02554. (☎ **508/228-0678**. Fax 508/325-4798. 13 units (4 tub/shower, 5 shower only; 4 with shared bathroom). Summer $95 single, $175–$245 double, $260–$320 suites. Rates include continental breakfast. AE, MC, V. Open year-round. *In room:* No phone.

The Ship's Inn ★ *Value*   This pretty, historic inn is on a quiet side street, just slightly removed—3 blocks—from Nantucket's center. Rooms are comfortable, spacious, and charming, and offer a good variety of bed arrangements like single rooms and twin beds. The restaurant downstairs holds its own (see "Where to Dine," below).

13 Fair St. (a few blocks from town center) Nantucket, MA 02554. (☎ **888/872-4052** or 508/228-0040. Fax 508/228-6524. www.nantucket.net/lodging/shipsinn. 12 units, 2 with shared bathroom. Summer $110 single with shared bathroom, $235 double. Rates include continental breakfast. AE, DISC, MC, V. Closed late Oct to mid-May. **Amenities:** Fine-dining restaurant located in the basement. *In room:* A/C, TV, fridge, hair dryer, iron.

The Veranda House ★★ *Finds*   Everyone is talking about the renovation and opening of this classic guesthouse, formerly known as the Overlook Hotel, that has been in the same family for generations. The younger generation has taken over and given the inn a stylish facelift. The inn is located in a quiet neighborhood, a short walk from the center of town. It is perched on a hill, so rooms on the third floor have distant harbor views. Wrap-around porches surround the inn and serve as the communal area for enjoying the sunshine or meeting fellow guests. Inn rooms are on the small side but smartly decorated with antique photos in sophisticated frames. It's a minimalist look but it works. Some of the more deluxe rooms have private balconies. All rooms have extras like robes; beds are made with frette linens and goose-down comforters. On the top floor, there are seven rooms that share a bathroom. Breakfast, which features hot delicacies like quiches and frittatas, is served with great hospitality on the ample front porch. The entire inn property is covered by a wireless Internet service.

Three Step Lane (a few blocks from town center), Nantucket, MA 02554. ☎ 508/228-0695. Fax 508/374-0406. www.theverandahouse.com 20 units, 7 with shared bathroom. Summer $155 double with shared bathroom, $195–$250 double, $320–$350 2-bedroom suite. Rates include continental breakfast. AE, MC, V. Closed mid-Oct to late May. *In room:* A/C, hair dryer.

The Woodbox Inn ★ *Value*   Built in 1709, this is Nantucket's oldest inn and it's an atmospheric place. Located in a residential section of the historic district, the inn is a short walk to Main Street. The well-known restaurant on-site serves breakfast and dinner and is famous for popovers. Your innkeeper Dexter Tutien, whose family has run the inn for 50 years, can fill you in on all the island lore and help you choose activities. The rooms, decorated with period antiques and reproductions, and canopy beds, range from cozy to spacious. Some rooms have refrigerators and phones. There are also one- and two-bedroom suites with working fireplaces. The Woodbox is a popular spot for breakfast, but the morning meal is not included in the room rates.

29 Fair St. (a few blocks from town center), Nantucket, MA 02554. ☎ 508/228-0587. Fax 508/228-7527. www.woodbox.com. 9 units. Summer $180–$210 double, $210 1-room suite, $310 2-room suite. (Unusual in the area, a 10% "service" fee is added to your bill here, in addition to tax.) No credit cards. Closed early Jan to late Mar. **Amenities:** Fine-dining restaurant serving breakfast and dinner. *In room:* Fridge.

INEXPENSIVE

The Nesbitt Inn *Value*   This Victorian-style inn in the center of town has been run by the same family for 95 years. It's quite old-fashioned and a bargain for Nantucket. All rooms have sinks and share bathrooms, which are in the hall. There's a friendly, family atmosphere to the inn, and beloved innkeepers Dolly and Nobby Noblit are salt-of-the-earth Nantucketers, who will cheerfully fill you in on island lore.

21 Broad St., P.O. Box 1019, Nantucket, MA 02554. ☎ 508/228-0156 or 508/228-2446. 15 units (13 with shared bathroom). Summer $75 single; $85–$125 double, $1,200 weekly apt. Rates include continental breakfast. MC, V. Closed mid-Dec to Mar. *In room:* No phone.

Robert B. Johnson HI-AYH Hostel *Value*   This youth hostel enjoys an almost perfect location. Set right beside Surfside Beach, the former "Star of the Sea" is an authentic 1873 lifesaving station, Nantucket's first. Where seven Surfmen once stood ready to save shipwrecked sailors, 49 backpackers now enjoy gender-segregated bunk rooms; the women's quarters, upstairs, still contains a climb-up lookout post. The usual hostel lockout (10am–5pm) and curfew (11pm) rules prevail.

31 Western Ave. (on Surfside Beach, about 3 miles south of Nantucket Town), Surfside, MA 02554. ☎ 508/228-0433. Fax 508/228-5672. 49 beds. $19 for members, $22 for non-members. MC, V. Closed mid-Oct to mid-Apr.

8 Where to Dine

Nantucket is filled with outrageously priced restaurants, in which star chefs create dazzling meals served in high style. Obviously, you don't need this kind of treatment every night, but you'll probably want to try at least one deluxe place. Many of the best restaurants serve terrific lunches at half the price of their dinners. Thankfully, there are also a number of cafes scattered around town that serve reasonably priced lunches and dinners. Nantucket also has two old-fashioned drugstore soda fountains, **Nantucket Pharmacy** and **Island Pharmacy** serving breakfast and lunch right next to each other on upper Main Street. If you dine in town, you may enjoy an evening stroll afterwards, since many stores stay open late.

VERY EXPENSIVE

Brant Point Grill ★★ NEW AMERICAN   Recent renovations to the entire White Elephant complex on the harbor have converted this pretty dining room into a lobster, steak, and chops house. Many of the signature dishes, like the cedar planked Atlantic salmon and rotisserie of prime rib, are prepared on the Fire Cone grill, a 21st-century interpretation of a Native American technique that cooks food by radiant heat and imparts it with a smoky mesquite flavor. If you can't sit on the terrace, try to snag a seat near one of the windows where you can watch the twilight fade over the harbor. The candlelight and white, airy dining room make for a perfectly romantic setting. Dinner at this establishment is an expensive proposition. However, the raw bar is open July through Labor Day from 4 to 7pm for light snacks, and a limited all-day menu is served noon to 11pm. You may want to consider having lunch here, a perfect idea for a rainy day, when prices are more reasonable.

At the White Elephant Hotel (Easton and Willard sts.). ✆ **508/325-1320.** Reservations strongly recommended. Collared shirt and long pants requested for gentlemen. Main courses $23–$39. AE, DISC, MC, V. Mid-Apr to early Dec daily noon–2:30pm and 6–10pm. Closed Nov–Mar.

Chanticleer Inn ★★★ FRENCH   A contender for the priciest restaurant on the Cape and Islands, this rose-covered, cottage-turned-French-auberge has fans who don't begrudge a penny, and who insist they'd have to cross an ocean to savor the likes of the classic cuisine that has been served here since the mid-1970s. Just to highlight a few glamorous options on the fixed-price menu: *gateau de grenouilles aux pommes de terre* (a frogs' legs cake in a potato crust); *tournedos de lotte marinée au gingembre, sauce au rhum, croquettes d'ail* (a gingered monkfish scaloppini with a lemon-rum sauce and sweet garlic fritters); and *pain perdu, glace au chocolat blanc, coulis d'abricots secs* (a very classy bread pudding with white-chocolate ice cream and apricot sauce). The restaurant's stellar wine cellar is stocked with 38,000 bottles. Unfortunately, this kind of luxury comes with beaucoup d'attitude, so whether you are royalty or hoi polloi, prepare to be snubbed.

9 New St., Siasconset. ✆ **508/257-6231** or 508/257-9756. Reservations recommended. Jacket preferred for men. Main courses $42–$45. AE, DC, MC, V. Mid-May to mid-Oct Wed–Sun noon–2:30pm and 6:30–9:30pm. Closed mid-Oct to mid-May.

Club Car ★★★ CONTINENTAL   For decades one of the top restaurants on Nantucket, this posh venue is popular with locals, many of whom particularly enjoy beef-Wellington night on autumn Sundays. Executive chef Michael Shannon is chummy with Julia Child, and the menu has classic French influences. Interesting offerings include a first course of Japanese octopus in the style of Bangkok (with mixed hot peppers, tiparos fish sauce, mint, cilantro, lime, and tomato concassee) and an entree of roast rack of lamb Club Car (with fresh herbs, honey-mustard glaze, and minted Madeira sauce). Some nights, seven-course tasting menus are available for $65 per person. The lounge area is within an antique first-class car from the old Nantucket railroad; you'll want to have a drink while cuddled in the red leather banquettes before or after dinner. Lunch at the Club Car is a great deal for those on a budget; all that atmosphere and hearty food arrive without the soaring prices.

1 Main St. ℂ **508/228-1101.** Reservations recommended. Main courses $32–$38. MC, V. July–Aug daily 11am–3pm and 6–10pm; call for off-season hours. Closed Jan–Apr.

The Galley on Cliffside Beach ★★★ NEW AMERICAN   Offering the best setting of any restaurant on the island, located about a mile from town on the property of Cliffside Beach Club (see earlier in this chapter), this restaurant is set on a private beach near Jetties Beach. The Galley offers a particularly chic yet beachy fine-dining experience, as fragrant ocean breezes perfume the air and guests relax on white wicker chairs. Given the setting, it's no surprise that the Galley specializes in seafood, caught locally by island fishermen. Produce comes from the restaurant's own organic garden. The menu changes often, but note-worthy menu options include the restaurant's signature New England clam chowder with smoked bacon, or the shrimp tempura served with Asian slaw. As a main course, there might be a luscious lobster risotto, native halibut with forest mushroom strudel, or Black Angus filet, or simply a 2-pound lobster with all the fixings. Desserts are made on-site by one of the island's finest pastry chefs. The Galley is also a good choice for lunch, when you can enjoy this delicious gourmet food at lower prices.

54 Jefferson Ave., Nantucket. ℂ **508/228-9641.** Reservations suggested. Main courses $29–$39. AE, MC, V. Open daily noon–2pm and 5–10pm. Closed Oct to late May.

The Pearl ★★ NEW AMERICAN   It's Miami Beach on Nantucket at the newest and swankiest fine-dining establishment on the island. The contemporary look here features bluish lighting and large fish tanks; it's definitely a different look for Nantucket. There are numerous stylish touches: appetizers and desserts served in martini glasses; local seafood prepared in innovative ways; an extensive champagne list. It's all very festive. Skip the *grande deluxe plateau de mer;* it's not a lot of shellfish for a lot of money. But do choose the wild mushroom galette with white truffle cream. As a main course, look no further than the pan-roasted striped bass with citrus tomato infusion and local lobster.

12 Federal St. ℂ **508/228-9701.** Reservations recommended. Main courses $28–$40. AE, MC, V. Mid-May to mid-Oct daily 6–10pm; call for off-season hours. Closed Jan–Mar.

Straight Wharf ★★ NEW AMERICAN   This is fine and very expensive dining on the waterfront in the center of town. Make your reservation for 8pm on the outside deck, so you can watch the sun set over the harbor. Straight Wharf has long been known for its creative cuisine, and it's also the place where the island's top chefs hang out after their shifts. As befits a harborside restaurant, the focus is seafood here. In addition to the regular menu, a "summer grill" menu served in the bar area is more reasonably priced. On the regular menu, you'll find fancy appetizers like seared beef carpaccio with white truffle oil, and main courses like native lobster *a la nage,* which is prepared with a champagne sauce. On the summer grill menu, you'll find simpler fare like Nantucket clam chowder and Maine crab cake BLT. Devoted regulars at Straight Wharf, of which there are many, swear by the smoked bluefish pâté served with herb focaccia.

Straight Wharf. ⓒ **508/228-4499.** Reservations recommended. Main courses $31–$38; summer grill menu $16–$22. AE, MC, V. July–Aug Tues–Sun 6–9:30pm; call for off-season hours. Closed late Sept to late May.

The Summer House ★★ *Finds* NEW AMERICAN   The classic Nantucket atmosphere, 'Sconset-style, distinguishes this fine-dining experience from others on the island: wicker and wrought-iron, roses and honeysuckle. A pianist plays nightly—often Gershwin standards. The pounding Atlantic Ocean is just over the bluff. Service is wonderful, and the food is excellent, though expensive. Specialties of the house include fresh, locally caught seafood with island vegetables delicately prepared and stylishly presented. Tempting appetizers include the grilled portobello mushrooms served with a pungent Stilton-basil terrine, and the house-smoked salmon frisée with avocado salsa. The distinctive main courses are roast saddle of lamb with rosemary caponatina port and feta mashed potatoes; the unusual and tasty lobster cutlets with coconut-jasmine risotto timbale and mint-tomato relish; and the grilled rib eye with wild mushrooms, foie gras, and Cabernet. Desserts are bountiful. Order the blueberry pie if it's in season. Lunch is served in season by the pool, weather permitting.

17 Ocean Ave., Siasconset. ⓒ **508/257-9976.** Reservations recommended. Main courses $33–$39. AE, MC, V. July–Aug daily 11:30am–3pm (weather permitting) and 6–11pm; mid-May to June and Sept to mid-Oct Wed–Sun 6–11pm. Closed mid-Oct to Apr.

Topper's at The Wauwinet ★★★ REGIONAL/NEW AMERICAN   This 1850 restaurant—part of a secluded resort—is a tastefully subdued knockout, with wicker armchairs, splashes of chintz, and a two-tailed mermaid to oversee a chill-chasing fire. Try to sit at one of the cozy banquettes if you can. The menu features the finest regional cuisine: Lobster is a major event (it's often sautéed with champagne beurre blanc), and be on the lookout for unusual delicacies such as *arctic char.* Those are Gruyère-and-chive biscuits in the breadbasket, and you must try one. Other recommendable house specialties include the lobster and crab cakes appetizer and the roasted Muscovy duck breast. Desserts are fanciful and fabulous: Consider the toasted brioche with poached pears and caramel sauce. The Wauwinet runs a complimentary launch service from mid-June to mid-September to the restaurant for lunch and dinner; it leaves from Straight Wharf at 11am and 5pm, takes 1 hour, and also makes the return trip.

120 Wauwinet Rd. (off Squam Rd.), Wauwinet. ⓒ **508/228-8768.** Reservations required for dinner and the launch ride over. Jacket requested for men. Main courses $34–$56. AE, DC, MC, V. May–Oct Mon–Sat noon–2pm and 6–10pm, Sun 11:30am–2pm and 6–10pm. Closed Nov–Apr.

EXPENSIVE

American Seasons ★★ REGIONAL AMERICAN   This romantic little restaurant has a great theme: Choose your region (New England, Pacific Coast, Wild West, or Down South) and select creative offerings. You can mix or match your appetizers and main courses. For instance, begin with the Louisiana crawfish risotto with fire-roasted onion and fried parsnips in a sweet corn purée from Down South; then from the Pacific Coast, an aged beef sirloin with caramelized shallot and Yukon potato hash served with an Oregon blue-cheese salad with white-truffle oil and fried onions. Owner Michael L. Getter is having fun here, and you will, too.

80 Centre St. (2 blocks from the center of town). ⓒ **508/228-7111.** Reservations recommended. Main courses $24–$30. AE, MC, V. Daily Apr–Nov 6–9pm. Closed early Dec to mid-Apr.

Boarding House ★★ NEW AMERICAN   This centrally located fine-dining restaurant doubles as one of the most popular bars in town. It is in the same building as The Pearl (see above) and owned by the same couple, hostess Angela Raynor and chef Seth Raynor. You can dine in the romantic lower-level dining room or upstairs in the hopping bar area. But on clear summer nights, you'll want to get one of the tables outside on the patio. The menu has definite Asian and Mediterranean influences in dishes like the seared yellowfin tuna with sesame sushi rice cake and wasabi aioli. One of the best soups on Nantucket is the luxe double lobster chowder with fresh corn and truffle mousseline. But the signature dish is the classic gilled lobster tails with grilled asparagus, mashed potatoes, and champagne beurre blanc. The award-winning wine list offers a range of prices.

12 Federal St. ℂ 508/228-9622. Reservations recommended. Main courses $26–$36. AE, MC, V. July–Aug daily 6–10pm; call for off-season hours. Open year-round.

Company of the Cauldron ★★★ CONTINENTAL   With its intimate candlelit dining room where, several nights a week in season, a classical harpist plays, this is one of the island's most romantic restaurants. Chef/owner Al Kovalencik offers one intricate and distinct three- to four-course fixed-price meal each night, so would-be patrons must check the menu out front or telephone and then choose which evening's menu is most appealing. Dietary preferences, like vegetarianism, can be accommodated if you call ahead. The menu, with classic American and Continental influences, changes nightly, and portions are generous. Don't miss the soft-shell crab appetizer in season. The main course could be seafood, a special swordfish preparation for instance, or a meat dish, like rack of lamb or beef Wellington.

5 India St. (between Federal and Centre sts.) ℂ 508/228-4016. www.companyofthecauldron.com. Reservations required. Fixed-price dinner $50. MC, V. Early July to early Sept Tues–Sun, 2 seatings 6:45 and 8:45pm; call for off-season hours. Closed mid-Oct to mid-May, except Thanksgiving weekend and the first 2 weeks of Dec.

DeMarco ★★ NORTHERN ITALIAN   This frame house carved into a cafe/bar and loft is the place on the island to get the best Northern Italian food. A forward-thinking menu and attentive service ensure a superior meal, which might include *antipasto di salmone* (house-smoked salmon rollantini, lemon-herb cream cheese, cucumber-and-endive salad with chive vinaigrette) and the delicate *capellini con scampi* (capellini with rock shrimp, tomato, black olives, capers, and hot pepper).

9 India St. (between Federal and Centre sts.). ℂ 508/228-1836. Reservations recommended. Main courses $18–$32. AE, MC, V. Mid-June to Sept daily 6–10pm; call for off-season hours. Closed mid-Oct to mid-May.

Òran Mór ★★★ *Finds* INTERNATIONAL   Renowned chef Peter Wallace runs this second-floor waterfront venue, which has quickly become the premier restaurant on the island. The unusual name is Gaelic and means "great song"; it's the name of Wallace's favorite single-malt Scotch. Climb the stairs of this historic building, and prepare yourself for a somewhat extravagant dining experience. The menu changes nightly, and there are always surprising and unusual choices. Appetizer standouts are the lobster risotto and the Thai littleneck clam hot pot with somen noodles. Intriguing entrees include grilled buffalo tenderloin and sautéed gray sole with sauce puttanesca. There are always local seafood specials. Some say the grilled breast of duck with savory tapioca and local nectar jus is the best duck dish on the island. An excellent sommelier is on hand to assist wine lovers. On Sundays during the off season, a scrumptious brunch is served.

2 S. Beach St. (in the center of town). ℂ 508/228-8655. Reservations recommended. Main courses $22–$34. AE, MC, V. July–Aug daily 6–10pm; Sept–June Thurs–Sat and Mon–Tues 6–9pm, Sun noon–9pm. Open year-round.

Ropewalk ✦ SEAFOOD This open-air restaurant on the harbor is Nantucket's only outdoor raw bar, and it's where the yachting crowd hangs out after a day on the boat. While the food is a bit overpriced, the location is prime. The raw bar, serving littlenecks, oysters, and shrimp, is open daily from 3 to 10pm and it attracts a crowd. This is a good place to enjoy a light meal or appetizers, such as fried calamari, crab cakes, or fried oysters. The dinner menu includes grilled swordfish with ratatouille and grilled breast of chicken with roasted garlic and rosemary jus.

1 Straight Wharf. ☎ 508/228-8886. No reservations. Main courses $23–$33. MC, V. Apr to mid-Dec daily 11am–10pm. Closed mid-Oct to Apr.

Ship's Inn Restaurant ✦✦ NEW AMERICAN This intimate restaurant in the brick-walled basement of a 12-room inn is one of the island's most romantic dining options. The restaurant is a short walk from Main Street down a quiet side street. The interior, with its candle-lit alcoves, is a cozy hideaway. The waitstaff here is professional and entertaining, a real treat. The menu features a variety of fresh fish, meat, and pasta dishes including several lighter options made without butter or cream. The lengthy wine list, which has a number of well-priced options has won awards. A flavorful starter here is the Roquefort and walnut terrine with Asian pear. As a main course, popular dishes include the pan-roasted Muscovy duck breast and the grilled yellowtail flounder. For a festive dessert, there's always the Grand Marnier souffle.

13 Fair St. ☎ 508/228-0040. Reservations recommended. Main courses $28–$38. AE, DISC, MC, V. July–Sept Wed–Mon 5–10pm; call for off-season hours. Closed Nov–Apr.

21 Federal ✦✦ NEW AMERICAN With 4 years of *Wine Spectator* awards to its credit, 21 Federal features about 11 carefully selected wines available by the glass each night. Chef Russell Jaehnig seems to get better and more refined every year. Don't fill up on the cheddar-cheese bread sticks: There's a lot of good food to come. For melt-in-your-mouth pleasure, try the appetizer of tuna tartare with wasabi crackers and cilantro aioli. Order a side of mashed potatoes if they don't come with your entree—not that you'll need more food; portions are generous. The fish entrees are the most popular here, although you might opt for the fine breast of duck accompanied by pecan wild rice and shiitake mushrooms. I prefer the pan-crisped salmon with champagne cabbage and beet-butter sauce, which has been a staple of the menu for years. Desserts are tantalizing and sinful.

21 Federal St. (in the center of town). ☎ 508/228-2121. Reservations recommended. Main courses $27–$37. AE, MC, V. Apr to mid-Dec daily 6–9:30pm. Closed mid-Dec to Mar.

MODERATE

Black Eyed Susan's ✦✦ *Finds* ETHNIC ECLECTIC This is supremely exciting food in a funky bistro atmosphere. The place is small, popular with locals, and packed. Reservations are accepted for the 6pm seating only, and they go fast. Others must line up outside the restaurant (the line starts forming around 5:30pm), and the hostess will assign you a time to dine. If you don't mind sitting at the counter, you'll have a better choice. Inside, it may seem a bit too cozy, but that's all part of the charm. The menu is in constant flux, as chef Jeff Worster's mood and influences change every 3 weeks. I always enjoy the spicy Thai fish cake when that is on the menu, and also the tandoori chicken with green mango chutney. There's usually a Southwestern touch like the Dos Equis beer–battered catfish quesadilla with mango slaw, hoppin' johns, and jalapeño. You'll mop up the sauce with the delectable organic sourdough bread. There's no liquor license, but you can BYOB. The corking fee is $1 per person.

10 India St. (in the center of town). ✆ **508/325-0308.** Reservations accepted for 6pm seating only. Main courses $15–$25. No credit cards. Apr–Oct daily 7am–1pm, Mon–Sat 6–10pm; call for off-season hours. Closed Nov–Mar.

Bluefin ✦✦ ASIAN/INTERNATIONAL   This new restaurant, an intimate and romantic spot a short walk from the center of town, offers great prices and tasty food, including sushi and tapas. The melt-in-your-mouth crispy crab rangoons come with the perfect hot-and-sour sauce, and shrimp lo-mein is served with wok-crisp vegetables. The lobster ravioli served with sweet basil cream is the ultimate in wretched excess. There's an extensive sushi menu, with six pieces costing $5 to $7. Keep in mind, there is a bar scene here, too, so if you are sitting near the bar area, it can be loud.

15 South Beach St. ✆ **508/228-2033.** Main courses $9–$16. AE, MC, V. June–Aug daily 5:30–10pm; call for off-season hours. Open year-round.

Centre Street Bistro ✦✦ NEW AMERICAN   This tiny fine-dining restaurant in the center of Nantucket town is owned and operated by Ruth and Tim Pitts, who are considered top chefs on the island. The dining room only has about eight tables and a few bar seats, though in the summer there is extra seating on the front patio. This cozy place features wonderful, creative cuisine at reasonable prices, especially compared to other island fine-dining restaurants. The menu is in constant flux, but recent high points included the warm goat cheese tart to start, and the Long Island duck breast with pumpkin and butternut squash risotto as a main course. If the sautéed Nantucket Bay scallops are on the menu, you won't want to miss whatever clever preparations the Pitts have dreamed up. One dish featured these world-famous local scallops with wontons and a citrus soy and spice glaze.

29 Centre St. ✆ 508/228-8470. No reservations. Main courses $16–$20. No credit cards. Wed–Sun noon–2:30pm and 6–10pm. Open year-round.

Eat, Fire, Spring ✦✦ NEW AMERICAN   Nantucket's newest restaurant, a hip outdoor cafe located past the galleries at the end of Old South Wharf, is getting rave revues. This is a casual place, the perfect spot to enjoy a leisurely lunch on a sunny day, or a light dinner on a sultry night. Many of the tables are outside under a canopy, a perfect people-watching location. The atmosphere here is given a stylish edge by the addition of unique hand-blown glassware, used for fixtures and table settings. The eclectic menu features standards like blackened tuna, for instance, or steak tips, but prepared with unique sauces and sides. There's live music nightly in season.

12 Old South Wharf. ✆ 508/228-5756. Reservations not accepted. Main courses $18–$25. AE, MC, V. Late June to early Sept noon–3pm and 6–9pm; call for off-season hours. Closed early Sept to early June.

Le Languedoc Cafe ✦✦ NEW AMERICAN   This is Nantucket's most authentic French cafe. The atmosphere in this historic building is wonderful and the prices are reasonable. There's also an expensive dining room upstairs, but locals prefer the casual bistro atmosphere downstairs and out on the terrace. There's a clubby feel here as diners come and go, greeting each other and enjoying themselves. Soups are superb, as are the Angus-steak burgers with garlic french fries. More elaborate dishes include the roasted tenderloin of pork stuffed with figs and pancetta; berlotti bean stew; and the napoleon of grilled tuna, tapenade, and roasted vegetables with pesto sauce.

24 Broad St. ✆ **508/228-2552.** www.lelanguedoc.com. Reservations not accepted for cafe; reservations recommended for dining room. Main courses $9–$19. AE, MC, V. June–Sept daily 5:30–9:30pm, Tues–Sun noon–2pm; call for off-season hours. Closed mid-Dec to Apr.

Nantucket Lobster Trap ✦ SEAFOOD   When only a bowl of chowder and a giant lobster roll will do, bring the whole family to this quintessential clam shack where the big game is usually on the TV behind the bar. Seating is on large picnic tables, and lobsters and other shellfish come straight from local waters. The mussels and clams served here are from local waters, as are the world-renowned Nantucket bay scallops. The prices are kept relatively affordable here. There's also a kids' menu.

23 Vestry St. ✆ **508/228-4200.** Reservations for parties of 6 or more only. Main courses $12–$30. AE, MC, V. June–Sept daily 5–10:30pm; call for off-season hours. Closed late Oct to early May.

INEXPENSIVE

Arno's ✦ *Kids* ECLECTIC   A storefront facing the passing parade of Main Street, this institution packs surprising style between its bare-brick walls (Molly Dee's mostly monochrome paintings, like vintage photographs, are especially nice). The internationally influenced menu yields tasty, bountiful platters for breakfast, lunch, and dinner. Specialties include grilled sirloin steaks and fresh grilled fish. Generous servings of specialty pasta dishes like shrimp and scallop scampi Florentine are featured nightly.

41 Main St. ✆ **508/228-7001.** Reservations recommended. Main courses $15–$23. AE, DC, DISC, MC, V. Apr–Dec daily 8am–2pm and 5–9:30pm. Closed Jan–Mar.

The Brotherhood of Thieves ✦ PUB   This classic whaling bar housed in the basement of an early-19th-century brick building in the center of town is a Nantucket institution. In July and August, tourists line up for a table in the dark tavern to chow on burgers and hand-cut curly fries. The specialty drink menu here is longer than the food menu and includes such playful concoctions as the "Dirty Girl Scout" and a wide selection of coffee and liquor drinks. In the fall and winter, locals enjoy the decently priced dinner offerings like chicken teriyaki and fried Cajun shrimp while sitting beside the cozy brick hearth.

23 Broad St. No phone. Reservations not accepted. Main courses $9–$18. No credit cards. Mid-May to mid-Oct Mon–Sat 11:30am–12:30am, Sun noon–12:30am; mid-Oct to mid-May Mon–Sat 11:30am–10:30pm, Sun noon–10pm. Closed Feb.

Cap'n Tobey's Chowder House ✦ SEAFOOD   This convenient eatery close to the harbor has recently undergone a redesign and an updating of the menu. The specialty here is seafood, obtained on a daily basis from local fishermen. Diners can choose between halibut, yellow-fin tuna, and haddock, and have it grilled, baked, or blackened. The raw bar features oysters, littlenecks, and shrimp. There is also a less-expensive fried fish menu, a good choice for families. Upstairs, called Off Shore at Cap'n Tobey's, there's live music in season.

20 Straight Wharf. ✆ **508/228-0836.** Reservations accepted. Main courses $9–$30. AE, MC, V. Late June to Sept daily 11:30am–10pm; call for off-season hours. Closed Jan–Apr.

The Even Keel Café ✦ AMERICAN   This low-key cafe in the heart of town serves breakfast, lunch and dinner both indoors and outside on the patio in the back. Unlike much of Nantucket's dining scene, you'll find reasonable prices and non-exotic fare here, like burgers and sandwiches. There are always vegetarian choices as well as meat and fish dishes, everything from a cheese burger to grilled salmon to veal osso buco. There's also a kids' menu, as well as high-speed Internet access. This place has lots of off-season dining deals, like half-price weekday breakfasts and two for one dinners. On Sundays, they serve a hearty brunch. There is no alcohol for sale here but you can B.Y.O.B.

40 Main St. ✆ **508/228-1979.** Reservations not accepted. Main courses $10–$25. AE, MC, V. July–Aug daily 7am–10pm; call for off-season hours. Open year-round.

Fog Island Cafe ★★ NEW AMERICAN You'll be wowed by the creative breakfasts and lunches at this sassy cafe; they're reasonably priced, with super-fresh ingredients. Homemade soups and salads are healthy and yummy. The dinner menu, served June through August only, features fresh seafood, pasta dishes, and a vegetarian alternative among the specialties. This local joint's cookbook is for sale on-site.

7 S. Water St. ☎ 508/228-1818. Reservations accepted. Main courses at dinner $10–$20. MC, V. July–Aug Mon–Sat 7am–9:30pm, Sun 7am–1pm; call for off-season hours. Open year-round.

TAKEOUT & PICNIC FARE

Bartlett's Ocean View Farm ★★ You can get fresh-picked produce (in season, the tomatoes are incomparable) right in town from Bartlett's traveling market, or head out to this seventh-generation farm where, in June, you might get to pick your own strawberries. They also sell sandwiches, quiches, pastries, pies, and more.

33 Bartlett Farm Rd. ☎ 508/228-9403. www.bartlettsoceanviewfarm.com. MC, V. Apr–Dec 9am–6pm. Truck parked on Main St. in season.

Henry's Sandwich Shop ★ Andrew Fee's classic sandwich shop, which opened in 1969, is set a block away from Steamboat Wharf, where the ferries dock. They bake their own sub rolls from scratch every morning, as well as their own chocolate chip cookies. Bring the family for a cheap and easy lunch.

Steamboat Wharf. ☎ 508/228-0123. July–Aug 8am–8pm; call for off-season hours. Closed Nov–May.

Nantucket Gourmet Besides an enticing array of kitchen items, Jonathan and Patty Stone have set up a deli full of scrumptious sandwiches, fixin's, and salads to take out.

4 India St. ☎ 508/228-4353. Daily 10am–5pm. Open year-round.

Provisions ★ Before you bike out of town to the beach, stop by this gourmet sandwich shop for picnic staples including salads, soups, and muffins.

3 Harbor Sq., Straight Wharf. ☎ 508/228-3258. Apr to early Nov daily 8am–6pm. Closed early Nov to Mar.

Something Natural ★★ A local institution and a terrific value, Something Natural turns out gigantic sandwiches, with fresh ingredients piled atop fabulous bread. Plan on sharing, so you'll have room for their addictive chocolate-chip cookies. It's a great place to stock up for a day at the beach, or you can eat your lunch at picnic tables on the grounds.

50 Cliff Rd. ☎ 508/228-0504. Apr to mid-Oct 7am–5:30pm. Closed mid-Oct to Mar.

Sushi by Yoshi ★★ This tiny place is Nantucket's best source of great sushi. The incredibly fresh local fish is artfully presented by chef Yoshihisa Mabuchi, who also dishes up such healthy, affordable staples as miso or *udon* (noodle) soup. This is a busy place; in season, allow an hour for takeout.

2 E. Chestnut St. ☎ 508/228-1801. May to mid-Oct daily 11:30am–10pm; mid-Oct to Apr Thurs–Sat 11:30am–10pm, Sun–Wed 5–10pm.

SWEETS

The Juice Bar ★★ This humble hole-in-the-wall scoops up some of the best homemade ice cream and frozen yogurt around, complemented by superb homemade hot fudge. Waffle cones are homemade, too. And, yes, you can also get juice—from refreshing lime rickeys to healthful carrot cocktails.

12 Broad St. ☎ 508/228-5799. June–Aug daily 10am–11:30pm; Apr–May and Sept to mid-Dec 11am–9pm. Closed mid-Oct to mid-Apr.

Nantucket's Music Scene

If body boarding, bike riding, and windsurfing coupled with sun and salt air haven't taken their toll, several nightspots offer live music and dancing, while others cater to those content with toe tapping. The Grey Lady can kick up her heels after dark.

Conveniently located in town, **Rose & Crown,** 23 S. Water St. (© 508/228-2595; closed Jan–Mar), has live music Thursday to Saturday ($3–$5 cover) with bands whose repertoires range from reggae to R&B, Motown to rock. The rest of the week is divided among karaoke, DJs spinning dance tunes, and the Full Monty Night, where audience members are coaxed into dancing behind a shadow box. With the ambience of an off-campus beer hall, Rose & Crown attracts a decidedly postgraduate crowd that's anywhere from 25 to 50 in age.

A car or a taxi ride is necessary to visit the two other large, live-band venues, The Muse and The Chicken Box. **The Muse,** 44 Atlantic Ave., about 1½ miles south of the town center (© 508/228-6873), is where you'll find college-age kids and the island's summer employees wolfing down pizza and subs, downing beer and exotic shots, and dancing to local and regional rock bands plus a scattering of name acts (George Clinton, Burning Spear, 10,000 Maniacs, and Maceo Parker are among recent headliners). The cover charge varies from $3 to the steep $50 required to lure George Clinton and his P-Funk All-Stars over from the mainland. Pool tables round out this 20-year-old club, which is open 365 days a year— there's a drastic upward shift in its demographics during the winter.

Pipe-smoking owner "Cap'n Seaweed" will tell you that **The Chicken Box,** 12 Dave St. (© 508/228-9717), has been jumping since the mid-1970s, and if you want to work up a sweat on the dance floor, the Box is a good bet most any night. Beer, shots, mixed drinks, and pool tables draw a crowd slightly older than Muse's. The cover charge runs from $4 to $15, and ska bands, a staple of what might be called New England Beach Music, are a favorite, along with reggae, funk, and rock. NRBQ and The Dirty Dozen Brass band have both dropped anchor here.

At the end of the day (when else?), it comes down to which of these three clubs has booked the best band on a given night. Check the *Inquirer & Mirror's* Music Beat column to find out.

You'll find folk, blues, and low-key acoustic performers at **The Brotherhood of Thieves,** 23 Broad St.; no phone, no cover; closed February.

Piano bars are numerous, including the **Club Car,** 1 Main St. (© 508/228-1101); **The RopeWalk,** 1 Straight Wharf (© 508/228-8886); **The Regatta,** at the White Elephant, Easton and Willard streets (© 508/228-5500; closed Oct–Apr); and **The Summer House,** 17 Ocean Ave., Siasconset (© 508/257-9976). The latter, a fine restaurant on the east end of the island, fills whatever need there is on Nantucket for the Manhattan martini bar experience, complete with fabulous people. The RopeWalk is where the rich and famous yachting crowd meets for drinks, and it's a major social scene in July and August. In addition, it's one of the only outdoor raw bars on the island.

9 Nantucket After Dark

Nantucket usually has an attractive crowd of bar hoppers making the scene around town. The best part is, everything is within walking distance, so you don't have to worry about driving back to your inn. You'll find good singles scenes at the **Boarding House, 21 Federal,** or the **Club Car.** Live music comes in many guises on Nantucket, and there are a number of good itinerant performers who play at different venues. For instance, the talented P. J. Moody sings all your favorite James Taylor, Cat Stevens, and Van Morrison tunes; he can be found at the **Jared Coffin House's Tap Room, The Hearth Bar at the Harbor House,** or the **White Elephant.** Meanwhile, it may be Reggae Night at **The Chicken Box,** when the median age of this rocking venue rises by a decade or two.

THEATER

Actors' Theatre of Nantucket   Drawing on considerable local talent of all ages, this shoe-box theater assays thought-provoking plays as readily as summery farces. Shows are mid-May to mid-September Monday to Saturday at 8:30pm; call for off-season hours. A children's production (tickets $12 for adults, $6 for children) is held mid-July to mid-August Tuesday to Saturday at 5pm. Closed November to April. Methodist Church, 2 Centre St. ℂ **508/228-6325.** Tickets $12–$20.

MOVIES

Nantucket has two first-run movie theaters: **Dreamland Theatre,** 19 S. Water St. (ℂ **508/228-5356**), and **Gaslight Theatre,** 1 N. Union St. (ℂ **508/228-4435**). The **Siasconset Casino,** 10 New St., Siasconset (ℂ **508/257-6661**), also shows films in season.

NANTUCKET LITERATI

Nantucket Atheneum   Continuing a 160-year tradition, the Nantucket Atheneum offers readings and lectures for general edification year-round, with such local literati as David Halberstam, Frank Conroy, and Nathaniel Philbrick filling in for the likes of Henry David Thoreau and Herman Melville. The summer events are often followed by a charming garden reception. Call for a schedule. Lower India St. ℂ **508/228-1110.** www.nantucketatheneum.org. Free admission.

9

Martha's Vineyard

Martha's Vineyard is a picturesque New England island with captains' houses and lighthouses, white picket fences and ice-cream shops, an authentic fishing village and a Native American community, miles of pristine beaches and rolling farmland. Unfortunately, it has been discovered, in a big way. If you can survive the hassles of getting to the island, and the crowds and traffic once you arrive, you may just have the perfect vacation. Better yet, visit the island off season, in May or October, when the weather is often mild and the crowds have cleared out.

When the former First Family, the Clintons, chose to vacation on the island several years in a row, it only increased the worldwide fascination with this popular place. In fact, the island is loaded with celebrities, but you are unlikely to see them, as they prefer private house parties. But don't come to this island for the celebrities; it's considered impolite to gawk and, like jaded New Yorkers, the locals barely seem to notice the stars in their midst.

Instead, visit the Vineyard to bicycle the shaded paths hugging the coastline. Admire the regal sea captains' houses in Edgartown, and stop by the Edgartown Scrimshaw Gallery for a memento of the sea. Stroll down Circuit Avenue in Oak Bluffs with a Mad Martha's ice-cream cone and then ride the Flying Horses Carousel, said to be the oldest working carousel in the country. Don't miss the cheerful "gingerbread" cottages behind Circuit Avenue, where the echoes of 19th-century revival

meetings still ring out from the imposing Tabernacle. Marvel at the red-clay cliffs of Gay Head, now known as Aquinnah, a National Historic Landmark and home to the Wampanoag Tribe. Travel the country roads of West Tisbury and Chilmark, stopping at Allen Farm for sweaters made from the wool of their flock of over 200 sheep. Buy bread at the Scottish Bakehouse in North Tisbury and a lobster roll in the fishing village of Menemsha. There is no dearth of terrific vacation activities on the island.

Unlike much of New England, Martha's Vineyard has long been a melting pot in which locals, homeowners, and summer people coexist in an almost effortless comfort, united in their disapproval of traffic, their criticism of the Steamship Authority, and their protective attitude toward the island. The roots of Martha's Vineyard's diversity go back more than 100 years. In the late 19th century, Oak Bluffs, with its religious roots, was one of the first spots where African Americans of means went on vacation. Today this community includes such notable celebrities as film director Spike Lee and Washington power broker Vernon Jordan. In the tiny town of Aquinnah, the Wampanoags are the only Native American tribe in the region to have official status in Washington, D.C. And 12th-generation Vineyarders farm the land in Chilmark and rub shoulders at Cronig's Market with posh Yankees from Edgartown.

There's always a lot of "hurry up and wait" involved in ferry travel, so allowing yourself just a weekend on

---

Fun Fact **Going Native on Martha's Vineyard**

Down-island: If you must buy a Black Dog T-shirt, wait until you get home to wear it. Don't loiter at the Charlotte Inn. Have cocktails on the porch of the Harbor View Hotel. In Oak Bluffs, don't ask when Illumination Night is (it's a secret). Experience Edgartown on a snowy winter weekend or in spring when the lilacs are in bloom. Up-island: When in doubt, don't wear shoes. Sail a boat to a remote beach for a picnic. Don't view the rolling farmlands from a tour bus. By all means, bike. Canoe. Rent a cottage for a week or two. Don't be a day-tripper.

---

the Vineyard may be less than you need. If you're traveling from New York, take an extra day off, allowing a minimum of 3 days for this trip. Four days will feel more comfortable. One great way to shorten the journey from New York is to take the ferry from Rhode Island or New Bedford and avoid Cape traffic.

From Boston, a couple of days is fine (the drive from Boston to Woods Hole takes 1½ hr. with no traffic), but beware of summer weekend bottlenecks (never aim for the last ferry). You really don't need to bring a car to get around this small island, but if you absolutely must be accompanied by four wheels, you'll need a car reservation for the ferry (see "Getting There," below, for details).

Try to savor the 45-minute ferry ride to and from this pastoral place. The Vineyard's pace is decidedly laid-back, and your biggest chore should be to try to blend in with the prevalent ultracool attitude. The six towns on Martha's Vineyard have distinct identities, but they can be divided into "down-island," referring to Vineyard Haven (officially called Tisbury), Edgartown, and Oak Bluffs; and "up-island," encompassing the towns of West Tisbury, Chilmark, and Gay Head.

1 Essentials

GETTING THERE

BY FERRY   Most visitors take the ferry service connecting the Vineyard and the mainland. If you're traveling via car or bus, you will most likely catch the ferry from Woods Hole in the town of Falmouth on Cape Cod; however, boats do run from Falmouth Inner Harbor, Hyannis, New Bedford, Rhode Island, and Nantucket. On weekends in season, the Steamship Authority ferries make over 25 trips a day to Martha's Vineyard from Woods Hole (two other companies provide an additional 12 passenger ferries a day from Falmouth Inner Harbor). Schedules are available from the **Martha's Vineyard Chamber of Commerce** (*C* **508/693-0085;** fax 508/693-7589; www.mvy.com) or the Steamship Authority (see below).

The state-run **Steamship Authority** (www.steamshipauthority.com) runs the show in Woods Hole (*C* **508/477-8600** Apr 4–Sept 7 daily 7am–9pm, and reduced hours the rest of the year; or 508/693-9130 daily 8am–5pm) and operates every day, year-round (weather permitting). It maintains the only ferries to Martha's Vineyard that accommodate cars, in addition to passengers, and makes about 25 crossings a day in season. The large ferries make the 45-minute trip to Vineyard Haven throughout the year; some boats go to Oak Bluffs from late May to late October (call for seasonal schedules). During the summer, you'll need a

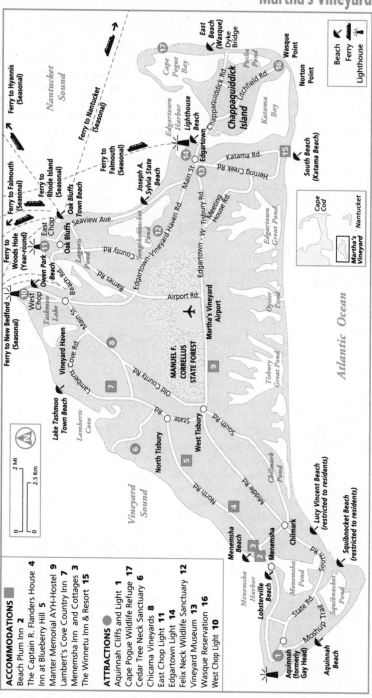

Martha's Vineyard

Beach ↖ **Ferry** ⛴ **Lighthouse** ☀

Vineyard Sound

Nantucket Sound

Atlantic Ocean

Ferry to New Bedford (Seasonal)

Ferry to Woods Hole (Year-round)

Ferry to Falmouth (Seasonal)

Ferry to Rhode Island (Seasonal)

Ferry to Falmouth (Seasonal)

Ferry to Nantucket (Seasonal)

Ferry to Hyannis (Seasonal)

West Chop

East Chop

Vineyard Haven

Oak Bluffs

Owen Park Beach

Town Beach

Joseph A. Sylvia State Beach

Edgartown

Edgartown Harbor Beach

Edgartown Lighthouse

Cape Pogue Bay

East Beach (Wasque)

Dyke Bridge

Chappaquiddick Island

Wasque Point

Norton Point

Katama Bay

South Beach (Katama Beach)

Herring Creek Rd.

Katama Rd.

Main St.

Edgartown-W. Tisbury Rd.

Chappaquiddick Rd.

Litchfield Rd.

Meeting House Rd.

Oyster Pond

Edgartown Great Pond

Tisbury Great Pond

Chilmark Pond

Airport Rd.

Martha's Vineyard Airport

MANUEL F. CORRELLUS STATE FOREST

South Rd.

Middle Rd.

North Rd.

State Rd.

Old County Rd.

West Tisbury

North Tisbury

Chilmark

Menemsha

Menemsha Beach

Menemsha Harbor

Lobsterville Beach

Menemsha Pond

Lucy Vincent Beach (restricted to residents)

Squibnocket Beach (restricted to residents)

Squibnocket Pond

Moshup Trail

Aquinnah (formerly Gay Head)

Aquinnah Beach

State Rd.

South Rd.

Lambert's Cove Rd.

Lambert's Cove

Cedar Tree Neck

Lake Tashmoo Town Beach

Tashmoo Lake

Main St.

Beach Rd.

Seaview Ave.

Lagoon Pond

Barnes Rd.

Edgartown-Vineyard Haven Rd.

Country Rd.

Sengekontacket Pond

Cape Cod

Martha's Vineyard

Nantucket

0 — 2 Mi
0 — 2.5 Km

N

reservation to bring your car to the island, and you must reserve *months in advance* to secure a spot. If you plan to bring your car over to the island, plan to get to the Woods Hole terminal at least 30 minutes before your scheduled departure.

Many people prefer to leave their cars on the mainland, take the ferry (often with their bikes), and then rent a car, Jeep, or bicycle on the island. You can park your car at the Woods Hole lots (always full in the summer) or at one of the many lots in Falmouth and Bourne that absorb the overflow of cars during the summer months; parking is $10 per day. Plan to arrive at the parking lots in Falmouth at least an hour before sailing time to allow for parking, taking the free shuttle bus to the ferry terminal, and buying your ferry ticket. Free shuttle buses (some equipped for bikes) run regularly from the outlying lots to the Woods Hole ferry terminal.

The cost of a round-trip passenger ticket on the ferry to Martha's Vineyard is $11 for adults and $5.50 for children 5 to 12 (kids under 5 ride free). If you bring your bike along, it's an extra $6 round-trip, year-round. You do not need a reservation on the ferry if you're traveling without a car, and no reservations are needed for parking. The cost of a round-trip car passage from mid-May to mid-October is $110; in the off season it drops to $68. Car rates do not include drivers or passengers; you must buy tickets for each person going to the island.

Once you are aboard the ferry, you have won the right to feel relieved and relaxed. Now your vacation can begin. Ferries are equipped with bathrooms and snack bars. Your fellow passengers will be a gaggle of kids, dogs, and happy-looking travelers.

From Falmouth, you can board the *Island Queen* at Falmouth Inner Harbor (© **508/548-4800;** www.islandqueen.com) for a 35-minute cruise to Oak

Reservations-Only Policy for Car Passage to Martha's Vineyard

Vehicle reservations are required to bring your car to Martha's Vineyard on Friday, Saturday, Sunday, and Monday from mid-June to mid-September. During these times, standby is in effect only on Tuesday, Wednesday, and Thursday. Vehicle reservations are also required to bring your car to Martha's Vineyard on Memorial Day weekend. Technically, vehicle reservations can be made up to 1 hour in advance of ferry departure, but ferries in season are almost always full with cars, and you cannot depend on a cancellation during the summer months. Also be aware that your space may be forfeited if you have not checked into the ferry terminal 30 minutes prior to sailing time. Reservations may be changed to another date and time with at least 24 hours' notice; otherwise, you will have to pay for an additional ticket for your vehicle.

If you arrive without a reservation on a day that allows standby in the summer, come early and be prepared to wait in the standby line for hours. The Steamship Authority guarantees your passage if you're in line by 2pm on designated standby days only. For up-to-date **Steamship Authority** information, check out their website (www. steamshipauthority.com).

Bluffs (passengers only). The boat runs from late May to mid-October; round-trip fare is $10 for adults, $5 for children under 13, and an extra $6 for bikes. There are seven crossings a day in season (eight on Fri and Sun), and no reservations are needed. Parking will run you $10 or $12 a day. Credit cards are not accepted.

The **Falmouth–Edgartown Ferry Service,** 278 Scranton Ave. (℃ **508/548-9400;** www.falmouthferry.com), operates a 1-hour passenger ferry, called the *Pied Piper,* from Falmouth Harbor to Edgartown. The boat runs from late May to mid-October, and reservations are required. In season, there are five crossings a day (six on Fri). Round-trip fares are $30 for adults and $24 for children under 12. Bicycles are $8 round-trip. Parking is $14 per day.

From Hyannis, you can take the **Hy-Line,** Ocean Street Dock (℃ **508/778-2600;** www.hy-linecruises.com), to Oak Bluffs, early June through late September. They run three trips a day, and trip time is about 1 hour and 45 minutes; round-trip costs $27 for adults and $14 for children 5 to 12 ($10 extra for bikes). From June through September, Hy-Line also operates a 1-day cruise, called **Around the Sound,** with stops on the Vineyard and Nantucket ($40 adults; $20 children 5–12).

From Nantucket, Hy-Line runs three passenger-only ferries to Oak Bluffs on Martha's Vineyard from early June to mid-September (there is no car-ferry service between the islands). The trip time is 2 hours and 15 minutes. The one-way fare is $14 for adults, $6.75 for children 5 to 12, and $5 extra for bikes.

From New Bedford, Massachusetts, the *Schamonchi,* Billy Woods Wharf (℃ **508/997-1688;** www.mvferry.com), which is run by the Steamship Authority, takes island-goers to Vineyard Haven from mid-May to mid-September. Trip time is about 1½ hours. A round-trip ticket is $20 for adults, $10 for children under 12, and $5 extra for bikes. Parking is $8 per calendar day. No reservations are needed.

In the summer of 2004, the *Schamonchi* may be replaced by a fast ferry that will make the trip to Martha's Vineyard in 45 minutes to an hour. While schedule and ferry specifics have not yet been announced, a round-trip ticket on the new ferry would cost about $40. Contact the Steamship Authority for details (℃ **508/477-8600;** www.steamshipauthority.com).

Traveling to Martha's Vineyard from New Bedford is a great way to avoid Cape traffic and enjoy a scenic ocean cruise.

From **North Kingstown, Rhode Island,** to Oak Bluffs, the new company Vineyard Fast Ferry runs its high-speed catamaran, *Millennium,* two to three round-trips daily from mid-June through October. The trip takes 90 minutes. The ferry leaves from Quonset Point, about ten minutes from Route I-95, 15 minutes from T.F. Green Airport in Providence, and 20 minutes from the Amtrak station in Kingston. There is dockside parking. Rates are $24 one-way, $48 round-trip for adults; $18 one-way, $36 round-trip for children; and $4 one-way, $8 round-trip for bikes. Parking next to the ferry port is $8 per day. Reservations can be made by calling ℃ **401/295-4040** or visiting their website www.vineyardfastferry.com.

BY AIR   You can fly into **Martha's Vineyard Airport,** also known as Dukes County Airport (℃ **508/693-7022**), in West Tisbury, about 5 miles outside Edgartown.

Airlines serving the Vineyard include **Cape Air/Nantucket Airlines** (℃ **800/352-0714** or 508/771-6944), which connects the island year-round with

Boston (trip time 34 min.; hourly shuttle service in summer about $240 round-trip), Hyannis (trip time 20 min., cost $80), Nantucket (15 min., $89), and New Bedford (20 min., $83); and **US Airways** (© 800/428-4322), which flies from Boston for about $215 round-trip and also has seasonal weekend service from La Guardia (trip time 1¼ hr.), which costs approximately $400 round-trip.

The only company offering year-round charter service is **Direct Flight** (© 508/693-6688). **Westchester Air** (© 800/759-2929) runs some charters from White Plains, New York.

BY BUS   **Bonanza Bus Lines** (© 888/751-8800 or 508/548-7588; www.bonanzabus.com) connects the Woods Hole ferry port with Boston (from the new South Station), New York City, and Providence, Rhode Island. The trip from South Station in Boston takes about 1 hour and 35 minutes and costs about $17 one-way, $30 round-trip; from Boston's Logan Airport, the cost is $22 one-way, $40 round-trip; from New York, the bus trip to Woods Hole takes about 6 hours and costs approximately $52 one-way or $93 round-trip.

BY LIMO   **King's Coach** (© 800/235-5669 or 508/563-5669) will pick you up at Boston's Logan Airport and take you to meet your ferry in Woods Hole (or anywhere else in the Upper Cape area). The trip takes about 90 minutes depending on traffic and costs about $125 one-way plus a gratuity for a carload or a vanload of people. You'll need to book the service a couple of days in advance. **Falmouth Taxi** (© 508/548-3100) also runs limo service from Boston and the airport.

GETTING AROUND

The down-island towns of Vineyard Haven, Oak Bluffs, and Edgartown are fairly compact, and if your inn is located in the heart of one of these small towns, you will be within walking distance of shopping, beaches, and attractions in town. Frequent shuttle buses can whisk you to the other down-island towns and beaches in 5 to 15 minutes. To explore the up-island towns, you will need to bike; it's possible to tour the entire island—60-some odd miles—in 1 day. In season, you can also take the shuttle bus up-island. Otherwise, you will have to take a cab.

BY BICYCLE & MOPED   You shouldn't leave without exploring the Vineyard on two wheels, even if only for a couple of hours. There's a little of everything for cyclists, from paved paths to hilly country roads (see "Beaches & Recreational Pursuits," below, for details on where to ride), and you don't have to be an expert rider to enjoy yourself. Plus, biking is a relatively hassle-free way to get around the island.

Mopeds are also a way to navigate Vineyard roads, but remember that some roads tend to be narrow and rough—the number of accidents involving mopeds seems to rise every year, and many islanders are opposed to these vehicles. The renting of mopeds is banned in Edgartown. You'll need a driver's license to rent a moped. If you rent one, be aware they are considered quite dangerous on the island's busy, narrow, winding and sandy roads. Also, there is a lot of negative feeling about mopeds from islanders.

Bike-, scooter-, and moped-rental shops are clustered throughout all three down-island towns. Bike rentals cost about $15 to $30 a day (the higher prices are for suspension mountain bikes), scooters and mopeds $46 to $85. For bike rentals in Vineyard Haven, try **Strictly Bikes,** Union Street (© 508/693-0782); or **Martha's Bike Rentals,** Lagoon Pond Road (© 508/693-6593). For mopeds, try **Adventure/Thrifty Rentals,** Beach Road (© 508/693-1959). In

Oak Bluffs, there's **Anderson's,** Circuit Avenue Extension (✆ 508/693-9346), which rents bikes only; **DeBettencourt's Bike Shop,** 31 Circuit Ave. Extension (✆ 508/693-0011), which is across from the Island Queen ferry landing; and **Sun 'n' Fun,** Lake Avenue (✆ 508/693-5457). In Edgartown, you'll find bike rentals only at **R. W. Cutler Bike,** 1 Main St. (✆ 508/627-4052); **Edgartown Bicycles,** 190 Upper Main St. (✆ 508/627-9008); and **Wheel Happy,** 204 Upper Main St. and 8 S. Water St. (✆ 508/627-5928).

BY CAR If you're coming to the Vineyard for a few days and you're going to stick to the down-island towns, it's best to leave your car at home, since traffic and parking on the island can be brutal in summer. Also, it's easy to take the shuttle buses (see below) from town to town, or you can simply bike your way around. If you're staying for a longer period of time or you want to do some exploring up-island, you should bring your car or rent one on the island—my favorite way to tour the Vineyard is by Jeep. Keep in mind that car-rental rates can soar during peak season, and gas is much more expensive on the island. Off-road driving on the beaches is a major topic of debate on the Vineyard, and the most popular spots may be closed for nesting piping plovers at the height of the season. If you plan to do some off-road exploration, check with the chamber of commerce to see if the trails are open to vehicles before you rent. To drive off-road at Cape Pogue or Cape Wasque on Chappaquiddick, you'll need to purchase a permit from the **Trustees of Reservations** (✆ 508/627-7260); the cost is $140 for the car and $3 per person. Keep in mind, if you drive a rental car off-road without permission from the rental company, you could be subjected to a $500 fine.

There are representatives of the national car-rental chains at the airport and in Vineyard Haven and Oak Bluffs. Local agencies also operate out of all three port towns, and many of them also rent Jeeps, mopeds, and bikes. The national chains include **Budget** (✆ 800/527-0700 or 508/693-1911), **Hertz** (✆ 800/654-3131), and **Thrifty** (✆ 800/874-4389).

In Vineyard Haven, you'll find **Adventure Rentals,** Beach Road (✆ 508/693-1959), where a Jeep will run you about $140 per day in season and a regular car costs about $68 per day. In Edgartown, try **AAA Island Rentals,** 141 Main St. (✆ 508/627-6800; also at Five Corners in Vineyard Haven, ✆ 508/696-5300). Another recommendable island company that operates out of the airport is **All Island Rent-a-Car** (✆ 508/693-6868).

BY SHUTTLE BUS & TROLLEY In season, shuttle buses certainly run often enough to make them a practical means of getting around. Two different types of shuttle bus make the rounds, and they provide the cheapest, quickest and easiest way to get around the island during the busy summer season. Connecting Vineyard Haven (across from the ferry terminal), Oak Bluffs (near the Civil War statue in Ocean Park), and Edgartown (Church St., near the Old Whaling Church), the Island Transport yellow school buses cost about $1.50 to $4, depending on distance. They run daily from April through October. From late June to early September, they run more frequently from 6am to midnight every 15 minutes or half-hour. Hours are reduced in spring and fall. From late June through August, buses go out to Aquinnah (via the airport, West Tisbury, and Chilmark), leaving every couple of hours from down-island towns and looping about every hour through up-island towns. For information and a schedule, call **Island Transport** (✆ 508/693-0058).

The **Martha's Vineyard Regional Transit Authority** (✆ 508/693-9440; www.vineyardtransit.com) operates shuttle buses daily from mid-May to mid-October (white buses with a purple COME RIDE WITH US logo) on about a dozen routes around the island. The Edgartown Downtown Shuttle and the South Beach buses circle throughout town or out to South Beach every 20 minutes in season. They also stop at the free parking lots just north of the town center—this is a great way to avoid circling the streets in search of a vacant spot on busy weekends. A one-way trip in town is just $1; a trip to South Beach (leaving from Edgartown's Church St. visitor center) is also $1.

BY TAXI   Upon arrival, you'll find taxis at all ferry terminals and at the airport, and there are permanent taxi stands in Oak Bluffs (at the Flying Horses Carousel) and Edgartown (next to the Town Wharf). Most taxi outfits operate cars as well as vans for larger groups and travelers with bikes. Cab companies on the island include **Adam Cab** (📞 **800/281-4462** or 508/693-3332), **Accurate Cab** (📞 **888/ 557-9798** or 508/627-9798; the only 24-hr. service), **All Island Taxi** (📞 **800/693- TAXI** or 508/693-2929), and **Marlene's Taxi** (📞 **508/693-0037**). Rates from town to town in summer are generally flat fees based on where you're headed and the number of passengers on board. A trip from Vineyard Haven to Edgartown would probably cost around $15 for two people. Late-night revelers should keep in mind that rates double after midnight until 7am.

THE CHAPPAQUIDDICK FERRY   The **On-Time ferry** (📞 **508/627-9427**) runs the 5-minute trip from Memorial Wharf on Dock Street in Edgartown to Chappaquiddick Island from June to mid-October daily, every 5 minutes from 7am to midnight. Passengers, bikes, mopeds, dogs, and cars (three at a time) are all welcome. The one-way cost is $2 per person, $8 for one car/one driver, $5 for one bike/one person, and $5 for one moped or motorcycle/one person.

VISITOR INFORMATION

Contact the **Martha's Vineyard Chamber of Commerce** at Beach Road, Vineyard Haven, MA 02568 (📞 **508/693-0085;** fax 508/693-7589) or visit their website at **www.mvy.com**. Their office is just 2 blocks up from the ferry terminal in Vineyard Haven and is open Monday to Friday 9am to 5pm year-round plus weekends in season. There are also information booths at the ferry terminal in Vineyard Haven, across from the Flying Horses Carousel in Oak Bluffs, and on Church Street in Edgartown. You'll want to poke your head into these offices to pick up free maps, tourist handbooks, and flyers on tours and events or to get answers to any questions you might have. Most inns also have tourist handbooks and maps available for guests.

Always check the two local newspapers, the *Vineyard Gazette* (www. mvgazette.com) and the *Martha's Vineyard Times* (www.mvtimes.com), for information on current events.

In case of an **emergency,** call 📞 **911** and/or head for the **Martha's Vineyard Hospital,** Linton Lane, Oak Bluffs (📞 **508/693-0410**), which has a 24-hour emergency room.

2 A Stroll Around Edgartown

A good way to acclimate yourself to the pace and flavor of the Vineyard is to walk the streets of Edgartown. This walk starts at the Dr. Daniel Fisher House and meanders along for about a mile; depending on how long you linger at each stop, it should take about 2 to 3 hours.

If you're driving, park at the free lots at the edge of town (you'll see signs on the roads from Vineyard Haven and West Tisbury), and bike or take the shuttle bus (it only costs 50¢) to the Edgartown Visitor Center on Church Street.

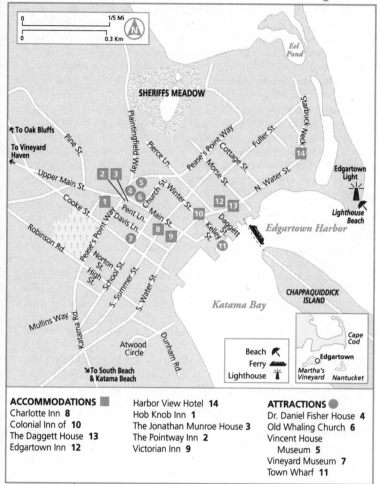

Edgartown

0   1/5 Mi
0   0.3 Km

SHERIFFS MEADOW

Eel Pond

← To Oak Bluffs

To Vineyard Haven ←

Pine St.

Upper Main St.

Cooke St.

Robinson Rd.

Plantingfield Way

Pierce Ln.

Pease's Point Way

Church St.

Winter St.

Main St.

Pent Ln.

Davis Ln.

Pease's Point Way

Norton St.

High St.

School St.

S. Summer St.

S. Water St.

Mullins Way

Katama Rd.

Dunham Rd.

Atwood Circle

↘ To South Beach & Katama Beach

Morse St.

Cottage St.

Fuller St.

Starbuck Neck

N. Water St.

Daggett St.

Kelley St.

Edgartown Light

Lighthouse Beach

Edgartown Harbor

CHAPPAQUIDDICK ISLAND

Katama Bay

Beach
Ferry
Lighthouse

Cape Cod
Edgartown
Martha's Vineyard
Nantucket

ACCOMMODATIONS
Charlotte Inn **8**
Colonial Inn of **10**
The Daggett House **13**
Edgartown Inn **12**

Harbor View Hotel **14**
Hob Knob Inn **1**
The Jonathan Munroe House **3**
The Pointway Inn **2**
Victorian Inn **9**

ATTRACTIONS ●
Dr. Daniel Fisher House **4**
Old Whaling Church **6**
Vincent House
Museum **5**
Vineyard Museum **7**
Town Wharf **11**

Around the corner are three local landmarks: the Dr. Daniel Fisher House, Vincent House Museum, and Old Whaling Church.

The **Dr. Daniel Fisher House,** 99 Main St. (© **508/627-8017**), is a prime example of Edgartown's trademark Greek Revival opulence. A key player in the 19th-century whaling trade, Dr. Fisher amassed a fortune sufficient to found the Martha's Vineyard National Bank. Built in 1840, his prosperous and proud mansion boasts such classical elements as colonnaded porticos, as well as a delicate roof walk. The only way to view the interior (now headquarters for the Martha's Vineyard Preservation Trust) is with a guided **Vineyard Historic Walking Tour** (© **508/627-8619**). This tour originates next door at the **Vincent House Museum,** off Main Street between Planting Field Way and Church Street. The transplanted 1672 full Cape is considered the oldest surviving dwelling on the island. Plexiglas-covered cutaways permit a view of traditional building techniques, and three rooms have been refurbished to encapsulate the decorative styles of 3 centuries, from bare-bones colonial to elegant Federal. The tour also takes in the neighboring **Old Whaling Church,** 89 Main St., a magnificent 1843 Greek Revival edifice designed by local architect Frederick Baylies Jr., and built as a whaling boat would have been, out of massive pine beams. With its 27-foot windows and 92-foot tower (a landmark easily spotted from the sea), this is a building that knows its place in the community (central). Maintained by the Preservation Trust and still supporting a Methodist parish, the building is now primarily used as a performance site.

Continuing down Main Street and turning right onto School Street, you'll pass another Baylies monument, the 1839 **Baptist Church,** which, having lost its spire, was converted into a private home with a rather grand, column-fronted facade. Two blocks farther, on your left, is the **Vineyard Museum,** 59 School St. (© **508/627-4441**), a fascinating complex assembled by the Dukes County Historical Society. An absorbing display of island history, this cluster of buildings contains exhibits of early Native American crafts; an entire 1765 house; an extraordinary array of maritime art, from whalers' logs to WPA-era studies by Thomas Hart Benton; a carriage house to catch odds and ends; and the Gay Head Light Tower's decommissioned Fresnel lens.

Give yourself enough time to explore the museum's curiosities before heading south 1 block on Cooke Street. Cater-cornered across South Summer Street, you'll spot the first of Baylies's impressive endeavors, the 1828 **Federated Church.** One block left are the offices of the *Vineyard Gazette,* 34 S. Summer St. (© **508/627-4311**). Operating out of a 1760 house, this exemplary small-town newspaper has been going strong since 1846; its 14,000 subscribers span the globe. If you are wandering by on a Thursday afternoon, you might catch a press run in progress.

Now, head down Main Street toward the water, stopping in at any of the inviting shops along the way. Veer left on Dock Street to reach the **Old Sculpin Gallery,** 58 Dock St. (© **508/627-4881;** open late June to mid-Sept). The output of the Martha's Vineyard Art Association displayed here tends to be amateurish, but you might happen upon a find. The real draw is the stark old building itself, which started out as a granary (part of Dr. Fisher's vast holdings) and spent the better part of the 20th century as a boat-building shop. Keep an eye out for vintage beauties when you cross the street to survey the harbor from the deck at Town Wharf. It's from here that the tiny On-Time ferry makes its 5-minute crossing to **Chappaquiddick Island,** hauling three cars at a time and a great many more sightseers—not that there's much to see on the other side. Just so you don't waste time tracking it down, the infamous **Dyke Bridge,** scene of the Kennedy/Kopechne debacle, has been dismantled and, at long last, replaced. However, the island does offer great stretches of conservation land that will reward the hearty hiker or mountain biker.

Mere strollers might want to remain in town to admire the many formidable captains' homes lining **North Water Street,** some of which have been converted into inns. Each has a tale to tell. The 1750 **Daggett House** (no. 59), for instance, expanded upon a 1660 tavern, and the original beehive oven is flanked by a secret passageway. Nathaniel Hawthorne holed up at the **Edgartown Inn** (no. 56) for nearly a year in 1789 while writing *Twice Told Tales*—and, it is rumored, romancing a local maiden who inspired *The Scarlet Letter.* On your way back to Main Street, you'll pass the **Gardner–Colby Gallery** (no. 27), filled with beautiful island-inspired paintings.

WINDING DOWN   After all that walking, you may need a refreshment. **The Newes from America,** at The Kelley House, 23 Kelley St. (just off N. Water St.;

© **508/627-4397**), is a classic old-world tavern with specialty beers and the best French onion soup on the island.

3 Beaches & Recreational Pursuits

BEACHES   Most down-island beaches in Vineyard Haven, Oak Bluffs, and Edgartown are open to the public and just a walk or a short bike ride from town. In season, shuttle buses make stops at **State Beach** between Oak Buffs and Edgartown. Most of the Vineyard's magnificent up-island shoreline, alas, is privately owned or restricted to residents, and thus off-limits to transient visitors. Renters in up-island communities, however, can obtain a beach sticker (around $35–$50 for a season sticker) for those private beaches by applying with a lease at the relevant **town hall:** West Tisbury, *©* **508/696-0147;** Chilmark, *©* **508/645-2115** or 508/645-2100; or Aquinnah, *©* **508/645-2300.** Also, many up-island inns offer the perk of temporary passes to residents-only beaches such as Lucy Vincent Beach (see below). In addition to the public beaches listed below, you might also track down a few hidden coves by requesting a map of conservation properties from the **Martha's Vineyard Land Bank** (*©* **508/627-7141**). Below is a list of visitor-friendly beaches.

- **Aquinnah Beach** ★★★ (Moshup Beach), off Moshup Trail: Parking costs $15 a day (in season) at this peaceful half-mile beach just east (Atlantic side) of the colorful cliffs. Go early, since the lot is small and a bit of a hike from the beach. I suggest that all but one person get off at the wooden boardwalk along the road with towels, toys, lunches, and so on, while the remaining person heads back up to park. In season, you can also take the shuttle buses from down-island to the parking lot at the Gay Head cliffs and walk to the beach. Although it is against the law, nudists tend to gravitate here. Remember that climbing the cliffs or stealing clay for a souvenir here is against the law for environmental reasons: The cliffs are suffering from rapid erosion. Restrooms are near the parking lot.

- **East Beach** ★★, Wasque (pronounced *Way*-squee) Reservation, Chappaquiddick: Relatively few people bother biking or hiking (or four-wheel driving) this far, so this beach remains one of the Vineyard's best-kept secrets (and an ideal spot for bird-watching). You should be able to find all the privacy you crave. If you're staying in Edgartown, the Chappy ferry is probably minutes by bike from your inn. Biking on Chappaquiddick is one of the great Vineyard experiences, but the roads can be sandy and are best suited for a mountain bike. You may have to dismount during the 5-mile ride to Wasque. Because of its exposure on the east shore of the island, the surf here is rough. Pack a picnic and make this an afternoon adventure. Sorry, no facilities. The area is owned by the Trustees of Reservations. It costs $160 for non-members to drive a four-wheel-drive vehicle out to the beach. Most people park their car near the Dike Bridge and walk the couple hundred yards out to the beach. Admission is $3 per person.

- **Joseph A. Sylvia State Beach** ★★★, midway between Oak Bluffs and Edgartown: Stretching a mile and flanked by a paved bike path, this placid beach has views of Cape Cod and Nantucket Sound and is prized for its gentle and (relatively) warm waves, which make it perfect for swimming. The wooden drawbridge is a local landmark, and visitors and islanders alike have been jumping off it for years. Be aware that State Beach is one of the Vineyard's most popular; come midsummer, it's packed. The shuttle bus stops here, and roadside parking is also available—but it fills up fast, so stake your claim early. Located on the eastern shore of the island, this is a Nantucket Sound beach, so waters are shallow and rarely rough. There are no restrooms, and only the Edgartown end of the beach, known as Bend-in-the-Road Beach, has lifeguards.

- **Lake Tashmoo Town Beach** ⍟, off Herring Creek Road, Vineyard Haven: The only spot on the island where lake meets ocean, this tiny strip of sand is good for swimming and surf-casting but is somewhat marred by limited parking and often brackish waters. Nonetheless, this is a popular spot, as beachgoers enjoy a choice between the Vineyard Sound beach with mild surf or the placid lake beach. Bikers will have no problem reaching this beach from Vineyard Haven; otherwise, you have to use a car to get to this beach.

- **Lighthouse Beach** ⍟, off North Water Street, Edgartown: Even though tiny, unattended, lacking parking, and often seaweed-strewn, the beach is very scenic and a perfect place to watch the boats drifting in and out of the harbor. **Fuller Beach** nearby is popular with a college crowd. No lifeguards or restrooms. Both these beaches are within walking distance of the center of Edgartown.

- **Lobsterville Beach** ⍟⍟, at the end of Lobsterville Road in Gay Head (restricted): This 2-mile beauty on Menemsha Pond boasts calm, shallow waters, which are ideal for children. It's also a prime spot for birding—just past the dunes are nesting areas for terns and gulls. Surf-casters tend to gravitate here, too. The only drawback is that parking is for residents only. This is a great beach for bikers to hit on their way back from Gay Head and before taking the bike ferry over to Menemsha.

- **Lucy Vincent Beach** ⍟⍟⍟ (restricted to residents), off South Road, Chilmark: It's a shame that the island's most secluded and breathtaking beach is restricted to Chilmark town residents and guests only (don't forget that many up-island inns offer guest passes). Lined with red and brown clay cliffs, this wide stretch of sand and pounding surf is a virtual oasis. If you want to let it all hang out, head left down the beach.

- **Menemsha Beach** ⍟⍟, next to Dutchers Dock in Menemsha Harbor: Despite its rough surface, this small but well-trafficked strand, with lifeguards and restrooms, is popular with families. In season, it's virtually wall-to-wall colorful umbrellas and beach toys. Nearby food vendors in Menemsha—selling everything from ice cream and hot dogs to steamers and shrimp cocktails—are a plus here. *Tip:* This beach is the ideal place to watch a sunset. Get a lobster dinner to go at the famous **Home Port restaurant** right next to the beach in Menemsha (see "The Quintessential Lobster Dinner," later in this chapter), grab a blanket and a bottle of wine, and picnic here for a spectacular evening. If you are staying at an up-island inn, Menemsha is a fun bike ride downhill. Energetic bikers can make it from down-island towns; plan to make it part of an entire day of scenic biking. Otherwise, you'll need a car to get here.

- **Oak Bluffs Town Beach,** Seaview Avenue: This sandy strip extends from both sides of the ferry wharf, which makes it a convenient place to linger while you wait for the next boat. This is an in-town beach, within walking distance for visitors staying in Oak Bluffs. The surf is consistently calm and the sand smooth, so it's also ideal for families with small children. Public restrooms are available at the ferry dock, but there are no lifeguards.

- **Owen Park Beach,** off Main Street in Vineyard Haven: A tiny strip of harborside beach adjoining a town green with swings and a bandstand will suffice for young children, who, by the way, get lifeguard supervision. There are no restrooms, but this is an in-town beach, which is probably a quick walk from your Vineyard Haven inn.

- **South Beach** ★★★ (Katama Beach), about 4 miles south of Edgartown on Katama Road: If you have time for only one trip to the beach and you can't get up-island, go with this popular, 3-mile barrier strand that boasts heavy wave action (check with lifeguards for swimming conditions), sweeping dunes, and, most important, relatively ample parking space. It's also accessible by bike path or shuttle. Lifeguards patrol some sections of the beach, and there are sparsely scattered toilet facilities. The rough surf here is popular with surfers. *Tip:* Families tend to head to the left, college kids to the right.

- **Wasque Beach** ★★, Wasque Reservation, Chappaquiddick: Surprisingly easy to get to (via the On-Time ferry and a bike or car), this half-mile-long beach has all the amenities—lifeguards, parking, restrooms—without the crowds. Wasque Beach is a Trustees of Reservations property, and if you are not a member of this land-preservation organization, you must pay at the gatehouse (© **508/627-7260;** $160 per car for non-members and $3 per person) for access in season.

BICYCLING　What's unique about biking on Martha's Vineyard is that you'll find not only the smooth, well-maintained paths indigenous to the Cape, but also long stretches of virtually untrafficked roads that, while rough in spots, traverse breathtaking country landscapes with sweeping ocean views. Serious cyclists will want to do a 1-day **circle-the-island tour** through the up-island towns and out to Aquinnah, stopping in Menemsha before heading back down-island. You'll pass through all six Vineyard towns and some unique off-the-beaten-track businesses.

For much of the trek, you'll travel country roads, so beware of sandy shoulders and blind curves. Avoid tour buses by taking routes outlined below, such as the Moshup Trail to Aquinnah or the triangle of paved bike paths between the down-island towns. These bike paths, roughly 8 miles to a side, link the down-island towns of Oak Bluffs, Edgartown, and Vineyard Haven (the sound portion along Beach Rd., flanked by water on both sides, is especially scenic). From Edgartown, you can also follow the bike path to South Beach (also known as Katama Beach). The bike paths are accessible off Edgartown–West Tisbury Road in Oak Bluffs, West Tisbury, and Edgartown.

The up-island roads leading to West Tisbury, Chilmark, Menemsha, and Aquinnah are a cyclist's paradise, with sprawling, unspoiled pastureland, old farmhouses, and brilliant sea views reminiscent of Ireland's countryside. But keep in mind that the terrain is often hilly, and the roads are narrow and a little rough around the edges. Try **South Road** from the town of West Tisbury to Chilmark Center (about 5 miles). En route, you'll pass stone walls rolling over moors, clumps of pine and wildflowers, verdant marshes and tide pools, and, every once in a while, an old Vineyard farmhouse. About halfway, you'll notice the road becoming hillier as you approach a summit, **Abel's Hill,** home to the **Chilmark Cemetery,** where comedian John Belushi is buried. A mile farther, don't miss the view of **Allen Farm,** an operating sheep farm amongst picturesque pastureland. **Middle Road** is another lovely ride with a country feel and will also get you from West Tisbury to Chilmark (it's usually less trafficked, too).

My favorite up-island route is the 6-mile stretch from Chilmark Center out to Aquinnah via **State Road** and **Moshup Trail** ★. The ocean views along this route are spectacular. Don't miss the **Quitsa Pond Lookout,** about 2 miles down State Road, which provides a panoramic vista of Nashaquitsa and Menemsha ponds, beyond which you can see Menemsha, the Vineyard Sound, and the Elizabeth Islands—it's an amazing place to watch the sunset on a clear evening. A bit farther, just over the Aquinnah town line, is the Aquinnah spring, a roadside iron pipe where you can refill your water bottle with the freshest and coldest water on the island. At the fork after the spring, turn left on Moshup Trail—in fact, a regular road—and follow the coast, which offers gorgeous views of the water and the sweeping sand dunes. You'll soon wind up in Aquinnah, where you can explore the red-clay cliffs and pristine beaches. On the return trip, you can take the handy bike ferry ($7 round-trip) from Aquinnah to Menemsha. It runs daily in summer and weekends in May.

A word about Aquinnah: Almost every visitor to the Vineyard finds his or her way to the cliffs, and with all the tour buses lined up in the huge parking lot and the rows of tacky concession stands and gift shops, this can seem like a rather outrageous tourist trap. You're right; it's not the Grand Canyon. But the observation deck, with its view of the colorful cliffs, the adorable brick lighthouse, and the Elizabeth Islands beyond, will make you glad you bothered. Instead of rushing away, stop for a cool drink and a clam roll at the snack bar with the deck overlooking the ocean.

The adventurous **mountain biker** will want to head to the trails in the **Manuel F. Correllus State Forest** (© 508/693-2540), a vast spread of scrub oak and pine smack-dab in the middle of the island that also boasts paved paths and hiking and horseback-riding trails. For those seeking an escape from the multitudes, the trails are so extensive that even during peak summer season it is possible to not see another soul for hours. On most of the conservation land on the Vineyard, however, mountain biking is prohibited for environmental reasons.

Bike-rental operations are ubiquitous near the ferry landings in Vineyard Haven and Oak Bluffs, and there are also a few outfits in Edgartown. For information on bike-rental shops, see "Getting Around," earlier in this chapter.

A very good outfit out of Boston called **Bike Riders** (© 800/473-7040; www. bikeriderstours.com) runs 6-day island-hopping tours of Martha's Vineyard and Nantucket. The cost is $1,395 per person plus $60 if you borrow one of their bikes. It's a perfect way to experience both islands.

The chamber of commerce has a great bike map available at its office on Beach Road in Vineyard Haven (see "Visitor Information," above).

BIRD-WATCHING **Felix Neck Wildlife Sanctuary,** Edgartown–Vineyard Haven Road, Edgartown (© 508/627-4850), is an easy 2-mile bike ride from Edgartown. A Massachusetts Audubon Property, it has a complete visitor center staffed by naturalists who lead bird-watching walks, among other activities. You'll see osprey nests on your right on the way to the center. Pick up a trail map at the center before heading out. Several of the trails pass Sengekontacket Pond, and the orange trail leads to Waterfowl Pond, which has an observation blind with bird-sighting information. While managed by the conservation group Sheriff's Meadow Foundation, the 300-acre **Cedar Tree Neck Sanctuary** ✶✶✶ (State Rd., follow to Indian Hill Rd. to Obed Daggett Rd. and follow signs), Tisbury (see "Nature Trails," below), was acquired with the assistance of Massachusetts Audubon. There are several trails, but you'll eventually arrive out on a picturesque bluff overlooking Vineyard Sound and the Elizabeth Islands. Check out the map posted at the parking lot for an overview of the property. The range of terrain here—ponds, fields, woods, and bog—provides diverse opportunities for sightings. **Wasque Reservation** ✶✶✶ **on Chappaquiddick,** Martha's Vineyard (see "Nature Trails," below), a sanctuary owned by the Trustees of Reservations and located on the easternmost reaches of the island, can be accessed by bike or four-wheel-drive vehicle (see "Getting Around," earlier in this chapter). The hundreds of untouched acres here draw flocks of nesting shorebirds, including egrets, herons, terns, and plovers.

FISHING   For shellfishing, you'll need to get information and a permit from the appropriate town hall (for the telephone numbers, see "Beaches," above). Popular spots for surf-casting include **Wasque Point** (Wasque Reservation) on Chappaquiddick (see "Nature Trails," below). The party boat *Skipper* (© 508/693-1238) offers half-day trips out of Oak Bluffs harbor in season. The cost is $35 for adults and $25 for children 12 and under. Deep-sea excursions can be arranged aboard **Big Eye Charters** (© 508/627-3649) out of Edgartown, and **Summer's Lease** (© 508/693-2880) out of Oak Bluffs. Up-island, there are **North Shore Charters** (© 508/645-2993; www.bassnblue.com) and **Flashy Lady Fishing Charters** (© 508/645-2462; www.flashyladycharters.com) out of Menemsha, locus of the island's commercial fishing fleet (you may recognize this weathered port from *Jaws*). Flashy Lady guarantees striped bass catches; their motto is "you don't catch, you don't pay." Charter costs are about $425 for a half day for five people and $750 for a full day.

IGFA (International Game Fish Association) world-record holder Capt. Leslie S. Smith operates **Backlash Charters** (© 508/627-5894), specializing in light tackle and fly-fishing, out of Edgartown. Cooper Gilkes III, proprietor of **Coop's Bait & Tackle** at 147 W. Tisbury Rd. in Edgartown (© 508/627-3909), which offers rentals as well as supplies, is another acknowledged authority. He's available as an instructor or charter guide and is even amenable to sharing hard-won pointers on local hot spots.

FITNESS   Gym addicts can get their workout fix at the **Health Club at the Mansion House Inn** on Main Street in Vineyard Haven (© 508/693-7400), which accepts visitors for a $15 fee.

GOLF   The nine-hole **Mink Meadows Golf Course** off Franklin Street in Vineyard Haven (© 508/693-0600), despite occupying a top-dollar chunk of real estate, is open to the general public. There is also the semiprivate, championship-level 18-hole **Farm Neck Golf Club** off Farm Neck Road in Oak Bluffs (© 508/693-3057). The Cafe at Farm Neck serves a wonderful lunch overlooking their manicured greens. In season, greens fees at Mink Meadows are $46 for nine holes and $66 (including cart) for 18 holes. In season, greens fees at Farm Neck are $135 (including cart) for 18 holes.

ICE-SKATING   The **Martha's Vineyard Ice Arena** on Edgartown–Vineyard Haven Road, Oak Bluffs (© 508/693-4438), offers public skating for $4 from mid-July to mid-April; call for details.

IN-LINE SKATING   In-line skaters are everywhere on the island's paved paths. You'll find rentals at **Sports Haven,** 5 Beach St., Vineyard Haven (© 508/696-0456). Rates are about $15 to $20 per day, including pads.

NATURE TRAILS   About a fifth of the Vineyard's landmass has been set aside for conservation, and it's all accessible to energetic bikers and hikers. The **West Chop Woods,** off Franklin Street in Vineyard Haven, comprise 85 acres with marked walking trails. Midway between Vineyard Haven and Edgartown, the **Felix Neck Wildlife Sanctuary** (see "Bird-Watching," above) includes a 6-mile network of trails over varying terrain, from woodland to beach. Accessible by ferry from Edgartown, quiet Chappaquiddick is home to two sizable preserves.

The **Cape Pogue Wildlife Refuge** ★★★ and **Wasque Reservation** ★★★ (gatehouse ℂ **508/627-7260**), covering much of the island's eastern barrier beach, have 709 acres that draw flocks of nesting or resting shorebirds. Also on the island, 3 miles east on Dyke Road, is another Trustees of Reservations property, the distinctly poetic and alluring **Mytoi**, a 14-acre Japanese garden that is an oasis of textures and flora and fauna.

The 633-acre **Long Point Wildlife Refuge** ★★★ off Waldron's Bottom Road in West Tisbury (gatehouse ℂ **508/693-7392**) offers heath and dunes, freshwater ponds, a popular family-oriented beach, and interpretive nature walks for children. In season, the Trustees of Reservations charge a $9 parking fee, plus $3 per adult over age 16. The 4,000-acre **Manuel F. Correllus Vineyard State Forest** occupies a sizable, if not especially scenic, chunk mid-island; it's riddled with mountain-bike paths and riding trails. This sanctuary was created in 1908 to try to save the endangered heath hen, a species now extinct. In season, there are free interpretive and birding walks.

Up-island, along the sound, the **Menemsha Hills Reservation** off North Road in Chilmark (ℂ **508/693-7662**) encompasses 210 acres of rocks and bluffs, with steep paths, lovely views, and even a public beach. The **Cedar Tree Neck Sanctuary**, off Indian Hill Road southwest of Vineyard Haven (ℂ **508/ 693-5207**), offers some 300 forested acres that end in a stony beach (alas, swimming and sunbathing are prohibited). It's still a refreshing retreat.

Some remarkable botanical surprises can be found at the 20-acre **Polly Hill Arboretum**, 8809 State Rd., West Tisbury (ℂ **508/693-9426**). Legendary horticulturist Polly Hill has developed this property over the past 40 years and allows the public to wander the grounds Thursday to Tuesday from 7am until 7pm. This is a magical place, particularly mid-June to July when the Dogwood Allee is in bloom. Wanderers will pass old stone walls on the way to The Tunnel of Love, an arbor of pleached hornbeam. There are also witch hazels, camellias, magnolias, and rhododendrons. To get there from Vineyard Haven, go south on State Road, bearing left at the junction of North Road. The arboretum entrance is about a half mile down, on the right. There is a requested donation of $5 for adults.

TENNIS Public courts typically charge a small fee and can be reserved in person a day in advance. You'll find clay courts on **Church Street** in Vineyard Haven; non-clay in Oak Bluffs' **Niantic Park,** West Tisbury's **grammar school** on Old County Road, and the **Chilmark Community Center** on South Road. Three public courts—plus a basketball court, roller-hockey rink, softball field, and children's playground—are located at the **Edgartown Recreation Area** on Robinson Road. You can also book a court (1 day in advance only) at two semi-private clubs in Oak Bluffs: the **Farm Neck Tennis Club** (ℂ **508/693-9728**) and the **Island Country Club** on Beach Road (ℂ **508/693-6574**). In season, expect to pay around $20 to $24 per hour for court time at these clubs.

WATERSPORTS **Wind's Up,** 199 Beach Rd., Vineyard Haven (ℂ **508/693-4252**), rents out canoes, kayaks, and various sailing craft, including windsurfers, and offers instruction on-site, on a placid pond; it also rents surfboards and boogie boards. Canoes and kayaks rent for $20 per hour; $45 to $50 for a half day; and $50 to $65 for a full day. Rank beginners may enjoy towing privileges at **M. V. Parasail** at pier 44 off Beach Road in Vineyard Haven (ℂ **508/693-8476**), where you'll be airborne by parachute. The thrill costs $90 for one ride for one person; $160 for a tandem ride; or $250 for three rides.

4 Museums & Historic Landmarks

Cottage Museum ✪ Oak Bluffs' famous "Camp Meeting Grounds," a 34-acre circle with more than 300 multicolored, elaborately trimmed carpenter's Gothic cottages, looks very much the way it might have more than a hundred years ago. These adorable little houses, loosely modeled on the revivalists' canvas tents that inspired them, have been handed down through the generations. Unless you happen to know a lucky camper, your best chance of getting inside one is to visit this homey little museum, which embodies the late-19th-century *Zeitgeist* and displays representative artifacts: bulky black bathing costumes and a melodeon used for informal hymnal sing-alongs.

The compact architecture is at once practical and symbolic. The Gothic-arched French doors off the peak-roofed second-story bedroom, for instance, lead to a tiny balcony used for keeping tabs on community doings. The daily schedule was, in fact, rather hectic. In 1867, when this cottage was built, campers typically attended three lengthy prayer services daily. Today's denizens tend to blend in with the visiting tourists, though opportunities for worship remain at the 1878 Trinity Methodist Church within the park or, just outside, on Samoset Avenue, at the non-sectarian 1870 Union Chapel, a magnificent octagonal structure with superb acoustics (posted signs give the lineup of guest preachers and musicians).

At the very center of the Camp Meeting Grounds is the striking **Trinity Park Tabernacle** ✪✪. Built in 1879, the open-sided chapel is the largest wrought-iron structure in the country. Thousands can be accommodated on its long wooden benches, which are usually filled to capacity for the Sunday-morning services in summer, as well as for community sings (Wed in July and Aug) and occasional concerts (see "Martha's Vineyard After Dark," later in this chapter). Give yourself plenty of time to wander this peaceful enclave, where spirituality is tempered with harmless frivolity.

1 Trinity Park (within the Camp Meeting Grounds), Oak Bluffs. ✆ 508/693-7784. Admission $1.50 (donation). Mid-June to Sept Mon–Sat 10am–4pm. Closed Oct to mid-June.

Flying Horses Carousel ✪✪ *Kids* You don't have to be a kid to enjoy the colorful mounts adorning what is considered to be the oldest working carousel in the country. Built in 1876 at Coney Island, this National Historic Landmark maintained by the Martha's Vineyard Preservation Trust predates the era of horses that "gallop." Lacking the necessary gears, these merely glide smoothly in place to the joyful strains of a calliope. The challenge lies in going for the brass ring that entitles the lucky winner to a free ride. Some regulars, adults included, have grown rather adept—you'll see them scoop up several in a single pass. In between rides, take a moment to admire the intricate hand-carving and real horsehair manes, and gaze into the horses' glass eyes for a surprise: tiny animal charms glinting within.

33 Circuit Ave. (at Lake Ave.), Oak Bluffs. ✆ 508/693-9481. Tickets $1 per ride, or $8 for 10. Late May to early Sept daily 10am–10pm; call for off-season hours. Closed mid-Oct to mid-Apr.

The Martha's Vineyard Historical Society ✪ All of Martha's Vineyard's colorful history is captured here, in a compound of historic buildings. To acclimate yourself chronologically, start with the precolonial artifacts—from arrowheads to colorful Gay Head clay pottery—displayed in the 1845 **Captain Francis Pease House;** there's also an oral history exhibit, a gift shop, and a gallery to showcase local students' work.

Menemsha: A New England Fishing Village

For an authentic slice of the Vineyard, leave the hordes down-island and take the winding roads up-island to picturesque Menemsha, one of the few remaining fishing villages in New England. Shuttle buses make the trip a few times daily, or you can take the bike ferry from Aquinnah—a spectacularly scenic but exhausting bike ride. It seems appropriate to approach Menemsha from its colorful harbor, alongside the commercial fishing fleet, the sportfishing vessels, and the pleasure boats. You can spend the afternoon strolling the wharves at leisure and watching the fishermen unload their catches—lobsters, tuna, and swordfish. Or simply wander over to the town beach, a colorful mélange of umbrellas, plastic buckets, and splashing youngsters. The water here can be quite cold, but after all that biking, you'll appreciate it.

For charter fishing trips operating out of Menemsha, call **North Shore Charters** (© 508/645-2993) and **Flashy Lady Charters** (© 508/645-2462).

For a wonderful boat ride around Menemsha Harbor, take Hugh Taylor's catamaran *Arabella* (© 508/645-3511). A sunset cruise before dinner at the Home Port (see below) will be a most perfect evening.

There are several charming clothing, crafts, and antiques shops in the village, as well as a fried-fish shack—**The Bite** ★★ (© 508/645-9239)—which some have dubbed the best restaurant on Martha's Vineyard. Or if you prefer, have a celebrity-monikered sandwich (I like the Art Buchwald) at the **Menemsha Deli** (© 508/645-9902). Two family-owned fish markets within yards of each other enjoy a healthy competition. **Larsen's** (© 508/645-2680) has picnic tables for on-site eating; **Poole's Fish Market** (© 508/645-2282) is strictly takeout. Order cooked lobsters early in the day to have them ready to pick up for your evening picnic.

At dinnertime, you might prefer to eat at the casual **Home Port** ★★ (© 508/645-2679), perhaps the most famous restaurant on the Vineyard; it has perfect sunset views. Places to stay in Menemsha with ocean views include the **Menemsha Inn and Cottages** ★★ (© 508/645-2521), a serene compound; and the **Beach Plum Inn** ★ (© 508/645-9454), an antique farmhouse with a full-service restaurant.

The **Gale Huntington Reference Library** houses rare documentation of the island's history, from genealogical records to whaling-ship logs. The recorded history of Martha's Vineyard (the name has been attributed, variously, to a Dutch seaman named Martin Wyngaard, and to the daughter and/or mother-in-law of early explorer Bartholomew Gosnold) begins in 1642 with the arrival of missionary Thomas Mayhew Jr., whose father bought the whole chain of islands, from Nantucket through the Elizabeths, for £40, as a speculative venture. Mayhew Jr. had loftier goals in mind, and it is a tribute to his methodology that long after he was lost at sea in 1657, the Wampanoags whom he had converted to Christianity continued to mourn him (a stone monument to his memory still survives by the roadside opposite the airport). In his relatively brief sojourn on-island, Mayhew helped to found what would become, in 1671, Edgartown (named for the British heir apparent). The library's holdings on this

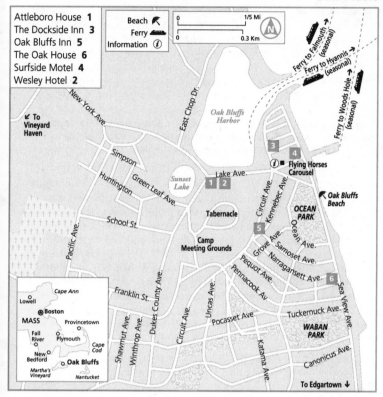

Attleboro House **1**
The Dockside Inn **3**
Oak Bluffs Inn **5**
The Oak House **6**
Surfside Motel **4**
Wesley Hotel **2**

Beach
Ferry
Information

1/5 Mi
0.3 Km

Ferry to Falmouth (seasonal)
Ferry to Hyannis (seasonal)
Ferry to Woods Hole (seasonal)

New York Ave.

To Vineyard Haven

Simpson

Huntington

Green Leaf Ave.

East Chop Dr.

Oak Bluffs Harbor

Sunset Lake

Lake Ave.

Flying Horses Carousel

Oak Bluffs Beach

OCEAN PARK

Circuit Ave.

Kennebec Ave.

Ocean Ave.

School St.

Pacific Ave.

Tabernacle

Camp Meeting Grounds

Grove Ave.

Samoset Ave.

Narragansett Ave.

Pequot Ave.

Pennacook Av.

Franklin St.

Dukes County Ave.

Uncas Ave.

Pocasset Ave.

Tuckernuck Ave.

Sea View Ave.

Cape Ann
Lowell
Boston
MASS
Provincetown
Fall River
Plymouth
Cape Cod
New Bedford
Oak Bluffs
Martha's Vineyard
Nantucket

Shawmut Ave.

Winthrop Ave.

Circuit Ave.

Katama Ave.

Canonicus Ave.

WABAN PARK

To Edgartown ↓

epoch are extensive, and some extraordinary memorabilia, including scrimshaw and portraiture, are on view in the adjoining **Francis Foster Maritime Gallery.** Outside, a reproduction "tryworks" shows the means by which whale blubber was reduced to precious oil.

To get a sense of daily life during the era when the waters of the East Coast were the equivalent of a modern highway, visit the **Thomas Cooke House,** a shipwright-built colonial, built in 1765, where the Customs collector lived and worked. A few of the house's 10 rooms are decorated as they might have been at the height of the maritime trade; others are devoted to special exhibits on other fascinating aspects of island history, such as the revivalist fever that enveloped Oak Bluffs. Further curiosities are stored in the nearby Carriage Shed. Among the vintage 19th-century vehicles are a painted peddler's cart, a whaling boat, a hearse, and a fire engine, and the odds and ends include some touching mementos of early tourism.

The Fresnel lens on display outside the museum was lifted from the Gay Head Lighthouse in 1952, after nearly a century of service. Though it no longer serves to warn ships of dangerous shoals (that light is automated now), it still lights up the night every evening in summer, just for show.

59 School St. (corner of Cooke St., 2 blocks southwest of Main St.), Edgartown. (C) 508/627-4441. www.marthas vineyardhistory.org. Admission in season $7 adults, $4 children 6–15. Mid-June to mid-Oct Tues–Sat 10am–5pm; mid-Oct to late Dec and mid-Mar to mid-June Wed–Fri 1–4pm, Sat 10am–4pm; early Jan to mid-Mar Wed–Fri by appointment, Sat 10am–4pm.

5 Organized Tours

Arabella ⭐ Hugh Taylor (James's brother) alternates with a couple of other captains in taking the helm of his swift 50-foot catamaran for daily trips to Cuttyhunk Island, and sunset cruises around the Aquinnah cliffs; you can book the whole boat, if you like, for a private charter. Zipping along at 15 knots, the boat provides a great way to see lovely coves and vistas otherwise denied the ordinary tourist.

Menemsha Harbor (at North Rd.), Menemsha. ℂ **508/645-3511.** Evening sunset sail $50 adults; day sail to Cuttyhunk Island $60 adults, $30 children under 12. Departures mid-June to mid-Sept daily 10:30am and 6pm (or 2 hr. before sunset). Reservations required. Closed mid-Sept to mid-June.

Ghosts, Gossip and Downright Scandal Walking Tours ⭐⭐ Laced with local lore and often led by the entertaining local historian Liz Villard, this 75-minute walking tour of Edgartown by the Vineyard History Tours organization gives a fun look at town history. Other tours provide access to the interiors of the 1672 Vincent House (the island's oldest surviving dwelling), the 1840 Dr. Daniel Fisher House (an elegant Greek Revival mansion), and the splendid Old Whaling Church, a town showpiece built in 1843. There are also a variety of other van and walking tours, including "A-Whaling We Will Go," in Edgartown and "Cottages, Campgrounds, and Flying Horses" in Oak Bluffs (which includes admission to the Cottage Museum and a ride on the Flying Horses).

From the Vincent House Museum, behind 99 Main St., Edgartown. ℂ **508/627-8619.** Also from the Cottage Museum, 1 Trinity Park, Oak Bluffs, and at the Steamship Authority kiosk in Vineyard Haven. $7–$10 adults, free for children 12 and under. June–Sept Mon–Sat noon–3pm; call for off-season hours. Closed Nov–Apr.

Trustees of Reservations Natural History Tours ⭐⭐⭐ The Trustees, a statewide land conservation group, offers several fascinating 2½-hour tours by safari vehicle or canoe around this idyllic nature preserve. The Natural History canoe tour on Poucha Pond and Cape Poge Bay is designed for all levels. It costs $35 for adults and $15 for children. There's also a tour of the Cape Poge lighthouse at 10am, noon, and 2pm. The cost is $20 for adults and $12 for children. The trustees also offer 2-hour kayak tours around Long Point for $35 for adults and $18 for children. Call ℂ 508/693-7392 for details.

Cape Pogue, Chappaquiddick Island. ℂ **508/627-3599.** www.thetrustees.org. In season, Mon–Fri 8:30am and 3pm. Call for reservations. Meet at Mytoi on Chappaquiddick. Closed mid-Oct to May.

6 Kid Stuff

A must for tots to preteens is the unique **Flying Horses Carousel** in the center of Oak Bluffs (see above). For an atmospheric mini-golf course, visit **Island Cove Mini Golf,** on State Road outside Vineyard Haven (ℂ **508/693-2611**), a family-friendly setup with a snack bar serving Mad Martha's ice cream, an island favorite. Island Cove is closed October through March. On weekends, from 10am to 3pm, children might enjoy visiting the **World of Reptiles** off Edgartown–Vineyard Haven Road on Bachelder Avenue, Edgartown (ℂ **508/627-5634**), where they'll meet various snakes, including a 21-foot python; turtles; and even an alligator. There's also a new bird park. Admission is $4. Call for hours. World of Reptiles is closed October through March. Nearby, the **Felix Neck Wildlife Sanctuary** (see "Beaches & Recreational Pursuits," earlier in this chapter) (ℂ **508/627-4850**), on Edgartown–Vineyard Haven Road, is always a popular destination with its exhibit room and self-guided trails. On Sundays in season, there are natural history talks and activities geared to children. Pony-cart

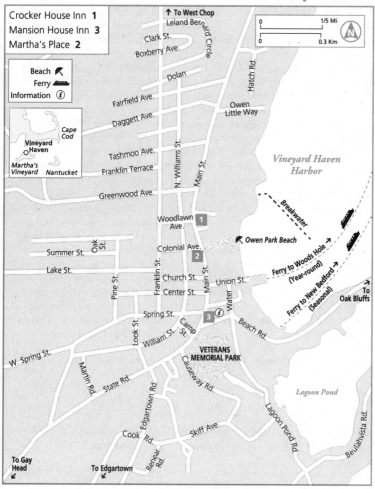

Vineyard Haven

Crocker House Inn 1
Mansion House Inn 3
Martha's Place 2

Beach
Ferry
Information ⓘ

Cape Cod
Vineyard Haven
Martha's Vineyard
Nantucket

↑ To West Chop
Leland Bernard Circle
Clark St.
Boxberry Ave.
Dolan
Fairfield Ave.
Daggett Ave.
Tashmoo Ave.
Franklin Terrace
Greenwood Ave.
Hatch Rd.
Owen Little Way
N. Williams St.
Main St.

Vineyard Haven Harbor

Breakwater

Woodlawn Ave. **1**
Colonial Ave. **2**
Summer St.
Oak St.
Lake St.
Pine St.
Franklin St.
Church St.
Center St.
Main St.
Union St.
Water St.

↖ Owen Park Beach

Ferry to Woods Hole (Year-round) →
Ferry to New Bedford (Seasonal)
→ To Oak Bluffs

Spring St.
Look St.
William St.
Camp St.
3 ⓘ
Beach Rd.
W. Spring St.
Martin Rd.
State Rd.

VETERANS MEMORIAL PARK

Causeway Rd.

Lagoon Pond

Lagoon Pond Rd.
Beulahvista Rd.

Edgartown Rd.
Cook Rd.
Renear Rd.
Skiff Ave.

To Gay Head ↙
To Edgartown ↙

---

rides ($1.50) are offered summer afternoons at the **Nip 'n' Tuck Farm** on State Road in West Tisbury (✆ 508/693-1449). Many families plan their vacations around the **Agricultural Society Annual Livestock Show and Fair** (✆ 508/693-9549) in West Tisbury in mid-August. It's an old-fashioned country fair with animals, food, and entertainment. An island event that your kids will always remember is **Illumination Night** in Oak Bluffs, when all the cottages in the campground are lit up with Japanese lanterns. The exact date is a secret, but it's usually a Wednesday evening at 7:30pm in mid-August.

7 Shopping

ANTIQUES/COLLECTIBLES For the most exquisite Asian furniture, lamps, porcelains, and jewelry, visit **All Things Oriental** at 123 Beach Rd. in Vineyard Haven (✆ 508/693-8375). The treasures here are handpicked in China by owner Shirley Seaton.

ARTS & CRAFTS Stop by **C. B. Stark Jewelers,** 53A Main St., Vineyard Haven (✆ **508/693-2284**), and 27 N. Water St., Edgartown (✆ **508/627-1260**), where proprietor Cheryl Stark started fashioning island-motif charms back in 1966.

No visit to Edgartown would be complete without a peek at the wares of scrimshander Thomas J. DeMont Jr., at **Edgartown Scrimshaw Gallery** at 43 Main St. (✆ **508/627-9439**). In addition to DeMont's work, the shop carries the work of a number of the country's top scrimshaw artists. All the scrimshaw in the gallery is hand-carved using ancient mammoth ivory or antique fossil ivory.

In the center of Edgartown, stop in at **Gardner Colby Gallery** on 27 N. Water St. (✆ **888/969-9500** or 508/627-6002), a soothing and sophisticated art showroom filled with Vineyard-inspired paintings by such popular artists as Robert Cardinal, whose landscapes often feature haunting purple skies; and Ovid Osborn Ward, who paints graphically realistic portrayals of Vineyard motifs.

The **Chilmark Pottery,** off State Road (about 4 miles southwest of Vineyard Haven), West Tisbury (✆ **508/693-6476**), features tableware fashioned to suit its setting. Geoffrey Borr takes his palette from the sea and sky and produces highly serviceable stoneware with clean lines and a long life span. Summer pottery classes are available.

The **Field Gallery,** State Road (in the center of town), West Tisbury (✆ **508/ 693-5595**), set in a rural pasture, is where Marc Chagall meets Henry Moore and where Tom Maley's playful figures have enchanted locals and passersby for decades. You'll also find paintings by Albert Alcalay and drawings and cartoons by Jules Feiffer. The Sunday-evening openings are high points of the summer social season. Closed mid-October to mid-May.

Don't miss the **Granary Gallery at the Red Barn,** Old County Road (off Edgartown–West Tisbury Rd., about ¼ mile north of the intersection), West Tisbury (✆ **800/472-6279** or 508/693-0455), which displays astounding prints by the late longtime summerer Alfred Eisenstaedt, dazzling color photos by local luminary Alison Shaw, and a changing roster of fine artists—some just emerging, some long since "discovered." A fine selection of country and provincial antiques is also sold here. Open April to December, and by appointment only January through March.

Another unique local artisans' venue is **Martha's Vineyard Glass Works,** State Road, North Tisbury (✆ **508/693-6026**). World-renowned master glass blowers sometimes lend a hand at this handsome rural studio/shop just for the fun of it. The three resident artists—Andrew Magdanz, Susan Shapiro, and Mark Weiner—are no slouches themselves, having shown nationwide to considerable acclaim. Their output is decidedly avant-garde and may not suit all tastes, but it's an eye-opening array and all the more fascinating once you've witnessed a work in progress.

Etherington Fine Art (✆ **508/693-9696**), 19 Main St., Vineyard Haven, features estimable work like Vineyard- and Venice-inspired paintings by Rez Williams, nature collages by Lucy Mitchell, pastels and oils by Wolf Kahn, and the colorful iconographic sculptures by Sam Milstein that grace the front yard. Gallery owner Mary Etherington's selection is a giant step up from the usual seascapes and lighthouses offered by other Vineyard galleries. Big-name museum people like Thomas Hoving and Agnes Gund stop here when on the island.

BOOKS **Edgartown Books,** Main Street (in the center of town), Edgartown (✆ **508/627-8463**), has a lively presentation of timely titles highlighting local endeavors; inquire about readings and signings. Closed January to March.

Bunch of Grapes, 44 Main St. (in the center of town), Vineyard Haven (✆ **800/693-0221** or 508/693-2291), offering the island's broadest selection (some 40,000 tomes), is a year-round institution and a browser's haven.

FASHION   The Great Put On, Dock Street (in the center of town), Edgartown (✆ **508/627-5495**), dates back to 1969, but always keeps up with the latest styles, including lines by Vivienne Tam, Moschino, and BCBG.

Treading a comfortable middle ground between functional and fashionable, the varied women's and men's labels at **LeRoux,** 89 Main St. (in the center of town), Vineyard Haven (✆ **508/693-6463**), include some nationally known names, such as Patagonia, Columbia Sportswear, and Tommy Bahama. It also carries Woodland Waders, an island-made line of sturdy woolen outerwear—everyday clothes for both sexes that are neither staid nor trendy.

GIFTS/HOME DECOR   The owners of **Bramhall & Dunn,** 23 Main St., Vineyard Haven (✆ **508/693-6437**), have a great eye for the kind of chunky, eclectic extras that lend character to country homes. Expect to find the requisite rag rugs, rustic pottery, a smattering of English country antiques, bed linens, and a large selection of sweaters.

My favorite place for gifts in Oak Bluffs is **Craftworks,** 149 Circuit Ave. (✆ **508/693-7463**), which is filled to the rafters with whimsical, colorful contemporary American crafts, some by local artisans.

Carly Simon owns a shop called **Midnight Farm,** 18 Water-Cromwell Lane, Vineyard Haven (✆ **508/693-1997**), named after her popular children's book. This home store offers a world of high-end, carefully selected, and imaginative gift items starting with soaps and candles and including children's clothes and toys, rugs, furniture, books, clothes, and glassware.

Paper Tiger, 29 Main St., Vineyard Haven (✆ **508/693-8970**), is an old-fashioned stationery store with wonderful papers and envelopes, and the best selection of cards anywhere.

A handsome shop on upper Circuit Avenue (no. 73) is **Argonauta** (✆ **508/696-0097**), which carries hand-painted vintage furniture, country pine, wicker, topiary, and artwork. **Third World Trading Co.,** 52 Circuit Ave., Oak Bluffs (✆ **508/693-5550**), features well-priced clothing, accessories, and home accents gathered from around the globe.

SEAFOOD   Feel like whipping up your own lobster feast? For the freshest and biggest crustaceans on the island, head to **The Net Result,** 79 Beach Rd., Vineyard Haven (✆ **800/394-6071** or 508/693-6071). Run by the Larsen family, you'll find everything from shrimp, scallops, and swordfish to bluefish and tuna. Their spreadable seafood salad makes a perfect hors d'oeuvre. If you're feeling sorry for your friends back home, the Larsens will ship fresh lobsters, quahogs, and other aquatic delicacies anywhere in the United States overnight. If you're up-island, stop by **Poole's Fish Market** or **Larsen's Fish Market,** both right on the docks at Menemsha Harbor.

WINE   With a name like Martha's Vineyard, you probably expected to find wild grapes here, which in fact have always grown on the island. But who knew whether fussy French vinifera would take? California transplants George and Catherine Mathiesen had high hopes when they started cultivating three backwoods acres in 1971, and their faith has been borne out in **Chicama Vineyards,** Stoney Hill Road (off State Rd., about 3 miles southwest of Vineyard Haven), West Tisbury (✆ **508/693-0309**), a highly successful winery yielding some 100,000 bottles a year. The dozen-plus varieties not only are palatable drinking wines, but also lend themselves beautifully to such gourmet uses as jellies, jams, and flavored oils and vinegars, all prepared and sold on the premises. Visitors are always welcome for a tasting, and in high season, they're treated to an entertaining 20-minute tour of the production line.

8 Where to Stay

When deciding where to stay on Martha's Vineyard, you'll need to consider the type of vacation you prefer. The down-island towns of Vineyard Haven, Oak Bluffs, and Edgartown provide shops, restaurants, beaches, and harbors within walking distance, and frequent shuttles to get you all over the island. But all three can be overly crowded on busy summer weekends. Vineyard Haven is the gateway for most of the ferry traffic; Oak Bluffs is a raucous town with most of the Vineyard's bars and nightclubs; and many visitors make a beeline to Edgartown's manicured Main Street. Up-island inns provide more peace and quiet, but you'll probably need a car to get around, including going to the beach. Nevertheless, there are some wonderful places to stay on the Vineyard, and all of the following choices have something special to offer.

EDGARTOWN
VERY EXPENSIVE

Charlotte Inn ★★★   Ask anyone to recommend the best inn on the island, and this is the name you're most likely to hear—not just because it's the most expensive, but because it's easily the most refined. Owners Gery and Paula Conover have been tirelessly fine-tuning this cluster of 18th- and 19th-century houses (five in all, counting the Carriage House, a replica) since 1971. Linked by formal gardens, each house has a distinctive look and feel, though the predominant mode is English country, with fascinating antiques, hunting prints, and quirky decorative accents. All but one room have televisions, and some have VCRs. Bathrooms are luxurious, and some are enormous (bigger than most hotel rooms). In the elegant 1860 Main House, the common rooms double as the Edgartown Art Gallery and feature Ray Ellis's wonderful oil paintings. This is one of only two Relais & Châteaux properties on the Cape and Islands— a world-class distinction that designates excellence in hospitality. On-site is L'étoile, the island's best fine-dining restaurant (see below).

27 S. Summer St. (in the center of town), Edgartown, MA 02539. ✆ 508/627-4751. Fax 508/627-4652. 25 units (all with tub/shower). Summer $295–$550 double, $695–$850 suite. Rates include continental breakfast; full breakfast offered for extra charge ($15). AE, MC, V. Open year-round. No children under 14. **Amenities:** L'étoile, the island's best fine-dining restaurant (see below). *In room:* A/C, TV, hair dryer.

Harbor View Hotel ★★   Grander than grand on the outside but hotel-standard on the inside, this shingle-style complex started out as two Gilded Age hotels, ultimately joined by a 300-foot veranda. Treated to a massive centennial makeover in 1991, it now boasts modern amenities and a lobby that's right out of an Adirondack lodge. Front rooms overlook little Lighthouse Beach; in back, there's a large pool surrounded by newer annexes, where some rooms and suites have kitchenettes. The hotel is located just far enough from "downtown" to avoid the traffic hassles, but it's close enough for a pleasant walk past impressive captain's houses. The hotel has two restaurants open to the public: the very good Coach House, which is open for three meals daily, and the Carlos Fuentes Clubhouse, a bar area where lunch is served.

131 N. Water St. (about ½ mile northwest of Main St.), Edgartown, MA 02539. ✆ 800/225-6005 or 508/627-7000. Fax 508/627-8417. www.harbor-view.com. 124 units (all with tub/shower). Summer $330–$600 double,

$490–$675 1 bedroom suite, $725–$850 2 bedroom suite, $900 3 bedroom suite. AE, DC, MC, V. Open year-round. **Amenities:** 2 restaurants (fine dining serving 3 meals daily, more casual bar open daily for lunch and dinner; you can ask to be served by the pool); heated outdoor pool; 2 tennis courts; concierge; room service (seasonal only: breakfast, lunch, and dinner); babysitting; same-day laundry service. *In room:* A/C, TV, fridge, hair dryer, iron, safe.

Hob Knob Inn ★★★ Owner Maggie White has reinvented this 19th-century Gothic Revival inn as an exquisite destination now vying for top honors as one of the Vineyard's best places to stay. Her style is peppy/preppy, with crisp floral fabrics and striped patterns creating a clean and comfortable look. Sure it's meticulously decorated, but nothing is overdone or overstuffed. All rooms are equipped with bathrobes and fine toiletries. Maggie and her attentive staff will pack a splendid picnic basket or plan a charter fishing trip on Maggie's 27-foot Boston Whaler. The full farm breakfast is a delight and is served at beautifully appointed individual tables in the sunny, brightly painted dining rooms. Bovine lovers will enjoy the agrarian theme, a decorative touch throughout the inn.

128 Main St. (on upper Main St., in the center of town), Edgartown, MA 02539. ℂ **800/696-2723** or 508/627-9510. Fax 508/627-4560. www.hobknob.com. 20 units, 4-bedroom cottage. Summer $270–$425 double. Rates include full breakfast and afternoon tea. AE, MC, V. Open year-round. **Amenities:** Exercise room; rental bikes ($20 per day); room service; massage (extra charge). *In room:* A/C, TV, hair dryer.

The Winnetu Inn & Resort ★★ One of the island's newest lodging options, this large luxury hotel sits on 11 acres overlooking South Beach in Katama. Guests can walk down a 250-yard path to get to the private beach. A 3-mile bike path links the inn to Edgartown, but the inn also runs a shuttle service that can pick up inn guests at the Edgartown ferry. Most rooms are two- and three-bedroom suites with kitchenettes, and there is one deluxe cottage with a four-person hot tub and a roof deck. Some have ocean views and conveniences like a washer/dryer. Many have private decks or patios. The rooms are decorated in a cozy beach-house style. The inn offers a number of amenities at an extra charge, including rental of beach cabanas, bicycle delivery service, grocery delivery service, and Wednesday evening family-style clam bakes in season. There are also children's programs. With outdoor Ping-Pong, foosball, the pool, and the putting green, there are many on-site amusements for kids. For active guests, the inn staff arranges "island adventure day trips" that include fishing, kayaking, and beach-buggy rides for an extra charge. The inn's fine-dining restaurant, Opus, is top-notch (see later in this chapter). There's also a general store on-site for snacks and sundries. In high season, late June to early September, there is a 3-night minimum stay during the week and a 4-night minimum on weekends. Several wheelchair-accessible rooms are available.

South Beach, Edgartown, MA 02539. ℂ **978/443-1733** (reservations line), or 508/627-4747. www.winnetu. com. 48 units. Summer $275 double, $475–$1,140 suite. AE, MC, V. Closed Dec to mid-Apr. **Amenities:** Fine-dining restaurant; outdoor heated pool; putting green; tennis courts with pro (6 Har-Tru, 4 all-weather); fitness room; children's program (late June to early Sept complimentary 9am–noon; fee in evenings for 3-year-olds through pre-teens); concierge; laundry facilities. *In room:* A/C, TV/VCR, microwave, fridge, coffeemaker, iron.

EXPENSIVE

Colonial Inn of Martha's Vineyard ★★ *Kids* This four-story 1911 inn in the center of Edgartown has been transformed into a fine modern hotel, and recent extensive renovations have elevated it to what can accurately be described as "affordable luxury." Its lobby serves as a conduit to the Nevins Square shops beyond, and there are also two fine restaurants on the premises. The 43 rooms, decorated in soothing, contemporary tones (with pine furniture, crisp fabrics, hardwood floors, beadboard wainscoting, and four-poster beds), offer all you could want in the way of conveniences. Guests whose rooms lack harbor views can wander onto one of the four common harbor-view decks to have a cocktail and enjoy the scenery. Suites have VCRs (complimentary videos) and kitchenettes. Many rooms have gas fireplaces. Be sure to visit the roof deck, ideally around sunset or, if you're up for it, sunrise over the water. Two rooms are accessible to guests with disabilities.

38 N. Water St., Edgartown, MA 02539. (© 800/627-4701 or 508/627-4711. Fax 508/627-5904. www.colonial innmvy.com. 43 units (42 tub/shower; 1 shower only). Summer $215–$415 double, $370–395 suite or efficiency. Rates include continental breakfast. AE, MC, V. Closed Dec–Mar. Pets allowed in designated rooms for $30 per day. **Amenities:** 2 restaurants; spa; fitness room; shopping arcade. *In room:* A/C, TV, dataport, hair dryer, iron.

The Daggett House ★★   What could be more Vineyard-y? Stay in the island's first tavern (the owner was fined for selling strong liquor), smack-dab on Edgartown Harbor and serving a hearty lunch and the best breakfast in town (for an extra charge). Actually, the property includes four buildings and one cottage, and the rooms vary greatly depending on the building. The main inn building has the most historical and charming accommodations (including a resident ghost; check out the photo on the way downstairs to the breakfast room). Request the secret staircase room, one of the many with a harbor view. The Captain Warren House across the street is home to, among other rooms, the dreaded "cozy fulls," which are tiny rooms (one is in a bay window). The newest acquisition is the Thomas House, a historic building on nearby Simpsons Lane whose rooms have been completely gutted and renovated. The cottage rooms are perhaps the nicest, located right on the harbor. Nine junior suites and full suites come equipped with kitchenettes with fridges and coffeemakers. Tea, lemonade, and homemade cookies are served in the parlor each afternoon in season.

59 N. Water St., Edgartown, MA 02539. (© 800/946-3400 or 508/627-4600. Fax 508/627-4611. www.the daggetthouse.com. 31 units (29 tub/shower, 2 shower only). Summer $155–$295 double, $395–$595 suite. Rates include continental breakfast off season. AE, DISC, MC, V. Open year-round. **Amenities:** Restaurant (breakfast only). *In room:* A/C, TV, hair dryer, iron.

The Jonathan Munroe House ★★ *(Finds)*   With its graceful wraparound, colonnaded front porch, the Jonathan Munroe House stands out from the other inns and captain's homes on this stretch of upper Main Street. Inside, the formal parlor has been transformed into a comfortable gathering room with European flair. Guest rooms are immaculate, antiques-filled, and dotted with clever details. Many rooms have fireplaces and baths with whirlpool jets. All have sitting areas, perfect for curling up with a bestseller (provided) or matching wits over a game of chess (also provided). Other thoughtful touches in the rooms include sherry, terrycloth robes, and Bose radios. At breakfast, don't miss the homemade waffles and pancakes, served on the sunny porch. Wine and cheese are served in the evening. Request the garden cottage, with its flowering window boxes, if you are in a honeymooning mood.

100 Main St., Edgartown, MA 02539. (© 877/468-6763 or 508/627-5536. Fax 508/627-5536. 7 units, 1 cottage (5 tub/shower, 2 shower only, 1 tub and shower). Summer $190–$250 double, $300 cottage. Rates include full breakfast and wine and cheese hour. AE, MC, V. Open year-round. No children under 12. *In room:* A/C, hair dryer.

The Point Way Inn ★★   This lovely inn has recently undergone a multimillion-dollar freshening up, and it's just as pretty as it could be. While some of the rooms are on the small side, they are cheerfully decorated in a contemporary style with cozy bedding and amenities. All rooms have robes, and some have VCRs. In the sunlit breakfast room with individual tables, guests are served hearty morning meals that sometimes include crepes, stuffed French toast, or quiche. In the afternoons, there are homemade cookies, and in the evenings, wine and cheese. The garden room is an especially cozy first-floor room with a separate entrance. In two units, you are allowed to bring a well-behaved pooch for a $50 surcharge. An unusual feature here is a complimentary guest car available for exploring the island.

104 Main St. (at Pease's Point Way), Edgartown, MA 02539. © 888/711-6633 or 508/627-8633. Fax 508/627-3338. www.pointway.com. 13 units (8 tub/shower, 5 shower only). Summer $250–$425 double, $400–$600 suite. Rates include full breakfast. AE, DISC, MC, V. Closed Jan to mid-Feb. *In room:* A/C, TV, hair dryer, no phone.

Victorian Inn ★★ Do you ever long to stay at a quaint, reasonably priced inn that is bigger than a B&B but smaller than a Marriott? In the center of Edgartown, the Victorian Inn is a freshened-up version of those old-style hotels that used to exist in the center of every New England town. There are enough rooms here so you don't feel like you are trespassing in someone's home, yet there's a personal touch. With three floors of long, graceful corridors, the Victorian could serve as a stage set for a 1930s romance. Several rooms have canopy beds and a balcony with a harbor view. Each year innkeepers Stephen and Karen Caliri improve and refine the inn, and they are always quick to dispense helpful advice with good humor.

24 S. Water St. (in the center of town), Edgartown, MA 02539. © 508/627-4784. www.thevic.com. 14 units (2 tub/shower, 12 shower only). Summer $165–$385 double. Rates include full breakfast and afternoon tea. MC, V. Open year-round. Dogs welcome Nov–Mar. *In room:* A/C, TV, hair dryer, no phone.

MODERATE

Edgartown Inn ★ *Value* This centrally located historic inn offers perhaps the best value on the island. Nathaniel Hawthorne holed up here for nearly a year, and Daniel Webster also spent time here. The lovely 1798 Federal manse is a showplace even here on captains' row. Rooms are no-frills but pleasantly traditional; some have TVs. Breakfast, which is open to the public, is available in the dining room for an extra charge of $5.50 to $8.50. Some rooms in the front of the house have harbor views and two have private balconies. Modernists may prefer the two cathedral-ceilinged quarters in the annex out back, which offer lovely light and a sense of seclusion. Service is excellent; be sure to say hello to Henry King, who has been on the staff for over 50 years.

56 N. Water St., Edgartown, MA 02539. © 508/627-4794. Fax 508/627-9420. www.edgartowninn.com. 20 units, 4 with shared bathroom. Summer $110 shared bathroom, $155–$250 double. No credit cards. Closed Nov–Mar. Children 8 years and older. *In room:* A/C, no phone.

OAK BLUFFS

If you're looking for a basic motel with a central location, you'll want to stay at **Surfside Motel** across from the ferry dock on Oak Bluffs Avenue in Oak Bluffs (© 800/537-3007 or 508/693-2500). Summer rates are $150 to $220 double; $250 to $300 for suites. Rooms are equipped with air-conditioning, TVs, mini-fridges, and phones. Open year-round. Well-behaved pets allowed.

EXPENSIVE

The Oak House ★★ *Finds* An 1872 Queen Anne bayfront beauty, this one-time home of former Massachusetts governor William Claflin has preserved all the luxury and leisure of the Victorian age. Innkeeper Betsi Convery-Luce trained at Johnson & Wales; her pastries (served at breakfast and tea) are sublime. The rooms toward the back are quieter, but those in front have Nantucket Sound views. The common rooms are furnished in an opulent Victorian mode, as are the 10 bedrooms (two are suites). This inn is very service-oriented, and requests for feather beds, down pillows, or non-allergenic pillows are accommodated. Anyone intent on decompressing is sure to benefit from this immersion into another era—the one that invented the leisure class.

75 Seaview Ave. (on the sound), Oak Bluffs, MA 02557. © **800/245-5979** or 508/693-4187. Fax 508/696-7385. www.vineyardinns.com. 10 units (1 tub/shower; 9 shower only). Summer $195–$250 double, $310–$315 suite. Rates include continental breakfast and afternoon tea. AE, DISC, MC, V. Closed late Oct to early May. *In room:* A/C, TV.

MODERATE

The Dockside Inn ★ *Kids*   Set close to the harbor, the Dockside is perfectly located for exploring the town of Oak Bluffs and is geared toward families. The welcoming exterior, with its colonnaded porch and balconies, duplicates the inns of yesteryear. Once inside, the whimsical Victorian touches will transport you immediately into the spirit of this rollicking town. Most of the standard-size rooms have either a garden or harbor view; they're decorated cheerfully in pinks and greens. Suites have kitchenettes, and some have private decks. Location, charm, and flair mean this is a popular place, so book early. There are two wheelchair-accessible rooms.

9 Circuit Ave. Extension (Box 1206), Oak Bluffs, MA 02557. © **800/245-5979** or 508/693-2966. Fax 508/696-7293. www.vineyardinns.com. 22 units. Summer $165–$210 double, $270–$360 suite. Rates include continental breakfast. AE, DISC, MC, V. Closed late Oct to early Apr. *In room:* A/C, TV, hair dryer, iron.

The Oak Bluffs Inn ★   This homey Victorian inn has a fun location at the top of Circuit Avenue, Oak Bluff's main drag that is crowded with restaurants, ice-cream parlors, clubs, and shops. The inn stands out with its whimsical, colorful Victorian paint scheme and its prominent cupola, from which guests can enjoy a 360-degree view of Oak Bluffs, including the beach and harbor a few blocks away. It's a 2-minute stroll from the inn to all the Oak Bluffs attractions, like the ginger bread cottages, the tabernacle, the Flying Horses Carousel, the waterfront park, and the ferries. With its large veranda, the inn has a particularly welcoming appearance. As is typical in a house of this vintage, some of the rooms are a tad on the small side, but others are spacious and even have comfortable seating areas. All rooms have ceiling fans.

64 Circuit Ave. (at the corner of Pequot Ave.), Oak Bluffs, MA 02557. © **800/955-6235** or 508/693-7171. Fax 508/693-8787. www.oakbluffsinn.com. 9 units. Summer $195–$255 double. Rates include continental breakfast. AE, MC, V. Closed Nov to Apr. *In room:* A/C, hair dryer, no phone.

Wesley Hotel ★ *Value*   Formerly one of the grand hotels of Martha's Vineyard, this imposing 1879 property, right on the harbor, is now a solid entry in the good-value category, especially with its low off-season rates. It occupies a terrific location in Oak Bluffs, across the street from the harbor, in the center of the action. The only drawback here can be the noise from revelers on the boats in the harbor or traffic on busy Lake Avenue. There are still remnants from the hotel's years of grandeur—the rockers that line the spacious wraparound porch; and the lobby with its old photographs, dark-stained oak trim, old-fashioned registration desk, and Victorian reproductions. Most of the rooms are fairly compact and basic, though some are roomy with harbor views. Many have easy access to the wraparound decks on all three floors of the inn. The Wesley Arms, behind the main building, contains 33 air-conditioned rooms with private bathrooms, accessible by elevator. Eight suites and executive suites contain kitchenettes. Five rooms are equipped for travelers with disabilities. *Note:* Reserve early to specify harbor views, which do not cost more than regular rooms. This is also one of the few Vineyard hotels that does not require a minimum stay in-season.

70 Lake Ave. (on the harbor), Oak Bluffs, MA 02557. ℂ 800/638-9027 or 508/693-6611. Fax 508/693-5389. www.wesleyhotel.com. 95 units (all with shower only). Summer $195–$215 double, $275 suite. AE, DC, MC, V. Closed late Oct to Apr. *In room:* A/C, TV, no phone.

INEXPENSIVE

Attleboro House *Value*   As old-fashioned as the afghans that proprietor Estelle Reagan crochets for every bed, this harborside guesthouse—serving Camp Meeting visitors since 1874—epitomizes the simple, timeless joys of summer. None of the 11 rooms is graced with a private bathroom, but the rates are so retro that you may not mind. What was good enough for 19th-century tourists more than suffices today.

42 Lake Ave. (on the harbor), Oak Bluffs, MA 02557. ℂ 508/693-4346. 11 units, all with shared bathroom. Summer $95–$115 double, $135–$175 suite. AE, DISC, MC, V. Closed Oct–May.

VINEYARD HAVEN (TISBURY)
VERY EXPENSIVE

The Mansion House Inn ★★ *Finds*   After a fire burned down the 200-year old Tisbury Inn several years ago, the owners decided to rebuild, making this one of the island's most full-service inns. The building, occupying a prominent corner location in Vineyard Haven, is now a community hub, with a restaurant, health club, and shops. The three-story hotel is comfortable with generous amenities. The rooms range in size from cozy to spacious, and prices vary accordingly. Many have kitchenettes, plasma-screen televisions, and extra-large bathtubs. Some have harbor views. All the rooms are equipped with high-speed Internet service. The lobby is abuzz with people bustling to and fro or just lounging on the ample chairs, planning activities. One of the most unique features of the inn is the 75-foot mineral spring (no chlorine) swimming pool in the health club in the inn's basement. There is still a lot of history here among the thoroughly modern amenities; for instance, an antique oak bar with elaborate carvings, saved from the old Island House, serves as the inn's bar. A full gourmet breakfast is served buffet-style at Zephrus, the hotel's restaurant. Zephrus is open to the public for lunch and dinner, and it also supplies room service for guests until late in the evening. There are wonderful panoramic views of Vineyard Haven and the harbor from the roof deck.

9 Main St., Vineyard Haven, MA 02568. ℂ 800/332-4112 or 508/693-2200. Fax 508/693-4095; www. mvmansionhouse.com. 32 units. $229–$439 double; $269–$649 suite. Rates include full buffet breakfast. AE, MC, V. Open year-round. **Amenities:** Restaurant (Zephrus, a fine-dining New American–style restaurant); health club; spa w/75-ft. pool. *In room:* AC, TV, fridge.

Martha's Place ★★   Martha's Place is exceptional for its elegance in the heart of this bustling port town; it's across the street from Owen Park, a harbor beach, and 1 block from the center of Vineyard Haven. Owners Richard Alcott and Martin Hicks lovingly restored and refurbished this stately Greek Revival home and surrounded it with rosebushes. Swags and jabots line the windows; every knob has a tassel, every fabric a trim. If you enjoy admiring a neoclassical armoire or an antique bed draped in blue velvet, Martha's is the place for you. Rooms are spacious and feature antique beds with excellent mattresses, Egyptian cotton linens, and down comforters. Rooms are also equipped with robes. The bathrooms here are quite luxurious: Ever seen one with a fireplace? Most rooms have harbor views. One is accessible to guests with disabilities. Breakfast is served at the large dining room table set with china and silver, or you may have breakfast in bed, if you prefer. For relaxing, nothing beats the 8-person hot tub. Mountain bikes are available for exploring the island, and the innkeepers also run a luxury-boat charter business that guests can book for a fee.

114 Main St. (across from Owen Park, in the center of town), Vineyard Haven, MA 02568. © 508/693-0253. Fax 508/693-1890. www.marthasplace.com. 6 units. Summer $225–$450 double. Rates include continental breakfast. AE, DISC, MC, V. *In room:* A/C, TV, dataport, hair dryer.

EXPENSIVE

Crocker House Inn ⭐ Jynell and Jeff Kristal have renovated this 1920s home near the harbor into a comfortable and casually elegant place to stay. Rooms are particularly light and airy here; they've all been completely redone with new linens, beds, and furniture with a country flavor. The third-floor suite includes a deck, mini-fridge, and two-person Jacuzzi. Jynell has Marriott experience, and it shows in the room details and service-oriented hospitality. Jeff bakes the blueberry muffins in the morning, and guests rave about his chocolate chip cookies set out with iced tea and lemonade in the afternoon.

12 Crocker Ave./P.O. Box 1658 (off Main St.), Vineyard Haven, MA 02568. © 800/772-0206 or 508/693-1151. Fax 508/693-1123. www.crockerhouseinn.com. 8 units. Summer $215–$285 double, $375–$385 suite. Rates include continental breakfast. AE, MC, V. Open year-round. No children under 12. *In room:* A/C, TV, hair dryer, iron.

CHILMARK (INCLUDING MENEMSHA), WEST TISBURY & AQUINNAH
VERY EXPENSIVE

Beach Plum Inn ⭐⭐ *Finds* This family-owned country inn, recently renovated, is set on 8 lush acres, with a lawn sloping gracefully down to Vineyard Sound. It's a beautiful secluded property, tucked away in Menemsha, yet within walking distance of the harbor. There's a croquet course and Nova Grass tennis court on the grounds, plus bikes to take exploring (extra charge). Rooms are in the main inn and in four cottages, which contain six additional rooms. The room decor is predominantly cottage-y, though some rooms lean towards elegance. Some have canopied beds and are quite romantic. Linens are 275 count and above; towels are Egyptian cotton. Five of the rooms have a whirlpool bath. All but one room have decks or patios, some with views of Menemsha Harbor. One room is wheelchair accessible. Inn guests get beach passes to the private up-island beaches. The inn's restaurant is one of the best fine-dining spots on the island (see "Where to Dine," below).

Beach Plum Lane (off North Rd., ½ mile northeast of the harbor), Menemsha, MA 02552. © 877/645-7398 or 508/645-9454. Fax 508/645-2801. www.beachpluminn.com. 11 units (all with tub/shower). Summer $250–$400 double or cottage. Rates include full breakfast in season; continental off season. AE, DC, DISC, MC, V. Closed Jan–Apr. **Amenities:** Restaurant (fine-dining); private beach passes; tennis court; croquet court; babysitting and in-room massage by arrangement; laundry service for a charge. *In room:* A/C, TV, dataport, fridge, hair dryer, iron.

The Inn at Blueberry Hill ⭐ This bucolic property, a former 300-year-old farm, is set on 56 acres in the up-island town of Chilmark. Book a room at this inn if you want a secluded vacation in the country, far away from the tourism crowds in Edgartown and Oak Bluffs. The comfortable rooms and suites are spread out in six traditional-style buildings. The overall feeling of the sunny rooms is serenity. They feature white cotton linens, ceiling fans, and hand-painted furniture. There are many thoughtful extras provided, like terry-cloth robes, penlight flashlights (for evening strolls), and coolers for the beach. Many rooms have private balconies or porches. Though the property is ancient, the inn feels very up-to-date. It includes exercise and spa services, as well as a lap pool and a tennis court. Also on site is Theo's, an attractive fine-dining restaurant. The restaurant is BYOB, as Chilmark is a dry town. The inn is surrounded by 2,000 acres of conservation land with a network of nature trails. Guests are given passes and offered shuttle service to the private beaches, Lucy Vincent and Squibnocket, which are about four miles away. Children over 12 are welcome at the inn.

74 North Rd., Chilmark. © **800/356-3322** or 508/645-3322. Fax 508/645-3799. www.blueberryinn.com. 25 units. Summer $240–$285 double, $325–765 suites and cottage. Rates include continental breakfast. AE, MC, V. Closed Nov–April. **Amenities:** Restaurant (New American fine-dining); 25-yd. lap pool; tennis court; exercise room; spa (facials, body treatments for extra charge); Jacuzzi; massage (extra charge); private beach passes. *In room:* A/C, TV (available on request), hair dryer.

EXPENSIVE

Lambert's Cove Country Inn ⭐   A dedicated horticulturist created this haven in the 1920s, expanding on a 1790 farmstead. You can see the old adzed beams in some of the upstairs bedrooms. Among his more prized additions is the Greenhouse Room, a bedroom with its own conservatory. You'll find an all-weather tennis court on the grounds, and the namesake beach 1 mile away. The inn's restaurant is known for skillfully prepared New American dinners prepared by one of the island's best chefs. Set far off the main road and surrounded by apple trees and lilacs, this secluded estate suggests an age when time was measured in generations. There's no better place to relax.

Lambert's Cove Rd. (off State Rd., about 3 miles west of Vineyard Haven), West Tisbury, MA 02568. © **508/ 693-2298.** Fax 508/693-7890. www.lambertscoveinn.com. 15 units. Summer $185–$250 double. Rates include full breakfast. AE, MC, V. Open year-round. **Amenities:** Restaurant (New American cuisine by one of the island's best chefs, dinner only); tennis court; private beach passes. *In room:* A/C, no phone.

Menemsha Inn and Cottages ⭐⭐   There's an almost Quaker-like plainness to this weathered waterside compound set in the pines near Menemsha Harbor, though many of the rooms are quite inviting. Mostly it's a place to revel in the outdoors (on 11 seaside acres) without distractions. The property is about a half-mile walk through a wooded path to the beach at Menemsha Harbor. The late *Life* photographer Alfred Eisenstaedt summered here for 4 decades, and the interior aesthetics would please any artist. There's no restaurant—just a restful breakfast room. Cottages have hair dryers, TVs, VCRs, dataports, outdoor showers, barbecue grills, and kitchenettes. The most luxurious suites are located in the Carriage House, which has a spacious common room with a fieldstone fireplace. The suites are equipped with hair dryers, ceiling fans, and mini-fridges. All rooms have private decks; most have water views. Guests have access to complimentary passes and shuttle bus service to the Lucy Vincent and Squibnocket private beaches.

Off North Rd. (about ½ mile northeast of the harbor), Menemsha, MA 02552. © **508/645-2521.** Fax 508/ 645-9500. www.menemshainn.com. 15 units, 12 cottages. Summer $225–$290 double, $25 2-bedroom suite, $2,100–$2,900 cottages weekly. Rates include continental breakfast for rooms and suites. MC, V. Closed Dec to mid-Apr. **Amenities:** Tennis court; fitness room (step machine, treadmill, exercise bike, and free weights); beach passes. *In room:* TV.

MODERATE

The Captain R. Flanders House ⭐ *(Finds)*   Set amid 60 acres of rolling meadows crisscrossed by stone walls, this late-18th-century farmhouse, built by a whaling captain, has remained much the same for 2 centuries. The living room, with its broad-plank floors, is full of astonishing antiques, but there's none of that "for show" feel that's prevalent in more self-conscious B&Bs. This is a working farm, so there's no time for posing (even if it was featured in Martha Stewart's *Wedding*

Book). Two new countrified cottages overlooking the pond have living rooms but not kitchenettes. After fortifying yourself with homemade muffins, island-made honey, and jam at breakfast, you are free to fritter the day away. The owners will provide you with a coveted pass to nearby Lucy Vincent Beach, or perhaps you'd prefer a long country walk.

North Rd. (about ½ mile northeast of Menemsha), Chilmark, MA 02535. © 508/645-3123. www.captain flanders.com. 5 units, 3 with shared bathroom; 2 cottages. Summer $80 single with shared bathroom, $175 double with shared bathroom, $195 double with private bathroom, $275 cottage. Rates include continental breakfast. AE, MC, V. Closed Nov to early May. **Amenities:** Private beach and shuttle bus passes. *In room:* No phone.

INEXPENSIVE

Hostelling International Martha's Vineyard   The first "purpose-built" youth hostel in the United States, this homey cedar-shake saltbox set at the edge of a vast state forest is still a front-runner. It hums with wholesome energy, from the huge group kitchen with recycling bins and two communal fridges to the five sex-segregated dorms containing 78 beds. The hallways are plastered with notices of local attractions (some stores offer discounts to hostelers), and the check-in desk also serves as a tourist information booth. Outside, there's a volleyball court and a sheltered bike rack. By bike, the hostel is a little more than 7 miles from the Vineyard Haven ferry terminal; shuttle buses also make the rounds in summer. You'll have no trouble at all finding enjoyable ways to spend the 10am-to-5pm lockout; just don't forget the 11pm curfew.

525 Edgartown–West Tisbury Rd. (about 1 mile east of the town center), West Tisbury, MA 02575. © 508/ 693-2665. Fax 508/693-2699. www.capecodhostels.org. 76 beds, 1 family room. $19 for members, $22 for non-members. MC, V. Closed mid-Oct to Mar. *In room:* No phone.

9 Where to Dine

Restaurants tend to be expensive on the Vineyard, but the stiff competition has produced a bevy of places that offer excellent service, evocative settings, and creative cuisine. *A note on spirits:* Outside Oak Bluffs and Edgartown, all of Martha's Vineyard is "dry," including Vineyard Haven, so bring your own bottle; some restaurants charge a small fee for uncorking. **Great Harbour Gourmet & Spirits,** 40 Main St., Edgartown (© **508/627-4390**), has a very good wine selection. There's also **Jim's Package Store** on Circuit Avenue Extension in Oak Bluffs (© **508/693-0236**).

EDGARTOWN
VERY EXPENSIVE

L'étoile ★★★ CONTEMPORARY FRENCH   Every signal (including the price) tells you that this is going to be one very special meal. After passing through a pair of ormolu-laden sitting rooms, you come upon a conservatory— a wonderfully summery room—sparkling with the light of antique brass sconces and fresh with the scent of potted citrus trees. Everything is perfection, from the table settings (gold-rimmed Villeroy & Boch) to a nouvelle-cuisine menu that varies seasonally but is always exquisite. Chef Michael Brisson, who came up through the kitchen of Boston's famed L'Espalier, is determined to dazzle, and he does, with an ever-evolving seven-course menu of delicacies flown in from the four corners of the earth. Sevruga usually makes an appearance—perhaps as a garnish for chilled leek soup. An étouffée of lobster with lobster, cognac, and chervil sauce might come with littlenecks, bay scallops, and roasted corn fritters; or roasted pheasant breast in a cider, apple-brandy, and thyme sauce may be accompanied by apple, sun-dried cherry, and mascarpone-filled wild-rice crepes.

At the Charlotte Inn, 27 S. Summer St. (off Main St.). © **508/627-5187.** Reservations required. Collared shirts requested for men. Fixed-price menu $78; Chef's Tasting Menu $120. AE, MC, V. July–Aug seatings daily from 6:30–9:30pm; May, June, Sept and Oct Tues–Sun 6:30–9:45pm; mid-Feb to Apr and Nov–Dec Thurs–Sat 6:30–9:45pm. Closed Jan to mid-Feb.

Opus ★★ NEW AMERICAN   This elegant restaurant on the second floor of the new Winnetu Resort in Katama is quickly making a name for itself as a wonderful place for dinner. Diners can watch the sun set as they enjoy fine cuisine and professional service in a comfortable setting. On Saturday nights in season, a harpist serenades diners. Menu selections utilize local produce and seafood. You might begin with a luscious sliced butter pear and goat cheese mille-feuille. Another favorite is the Hudson Valley foie gras trio. For a main course, you might have the roast Hill Farm chicken breast with morels, English peas, and garlic-potato puree. There is usually a creative lobster dish on the menu, as well as vegetarian options and grill selections. Homemade desserts like the caramelized apple charlotte are inspired. There is also a children's menu. From 3 to 5:30pm, a raw bar and light bar menu is served. On a sunny summer afternoon, this would be a perfect place to enjoy cocktails on the second floor deck of the restaurant.

At the Winnetu Inn and Resort, Katama © **508/627-3663.** Reservations required. Main courses $24–$37. AE, MC, V. July–Aug daily 5:30–9:30pm; call for off-season hours. Closed Dec to mid-Apr.

EXPENSIVE

Alchemy ★★ FRENCH BISTRO   Chef/owners Scott Caskey and Michael Presnol have a spiffy new restaurant that's a little slice of Paris on Edgartown's Main Street. Such esoteric choices as oyster brie soup and Burgundy Vintners salad share the bill with escargot-and-chanterelle fricassee and *lapin moutarde spatzle* (yes, that's rabbit). As befits a true bistro, there's a large selection of cocktails, liqueurs, and wines. In addition to lunch and dinner, a bar menu is served from 2:30 to 11pm. This choice isn't for everyone, but sophisticated diners will enjoy the Continental flair.

71 Main St. (in the center of town). © **508/627-9999.** Reservations accepted. Main courses $22–$33. AE, MC, V. Apr–Nov daily noon–2:30pm and 5:30–10pm; call for off-season hours. Open year-round.

Atria ★★ NEW AMERICAN   This fine-dining restaurant set in an 18th-century sea captain's house on Upper Main Street in Edgartown gets rave reviews for its gourmet cuisine and high-caliber service. Pronounced with the emphasis on the second syllable (ah-*tre*-ah), the name refers to the brightest of three stars forming the Southern Triangle constellation. You can sit in the elegant dining room, the rose-covered wraparound porch, or the brick cellar bar downstairs for more casual dining. Chef/owner Christian Thornton's menu offers a variety of creative dishes with influences from around the country and around the world, with stops in the Mediterranean, Middle East, and Asia. It features organic island-grown produce, off-the-boat seafood, local shellfish, and aged prime meats. Popular starters include miso soup with steamed crab dumplings or Thai lemongrass mussels. Unusual main courses include wok fried Martha's Vineyard lobster or cracklin' pork shank with southern collard greens. There is live entertainment in the bar, along the lines of acoustic guitar, on weekends.

137 Main St. (a short walk from the center of town). © **508/627-5850.** www.atriamv.com. Reservations recommended. Main courses $22–$36. AE, MC, V. June–Sept daily 5:30–10pm; call for off-season hours. Open year-round.

The Coach House ★★ NEW AMERICAN   This is a terrific place to have a drink or to dine, with its exquisite view of Edgartown Harbor and the lighthouse. The long and elegant bar is particularly smashing. The menu is simple but stylish.

To start, there's soft-shell crab with arugula and teardrop tomatoes. As a main course, try the caramelized sea scallops with a salad of Asian pear and apple. Service is excellent; these are trained waiters, not your usual college surfer dudes. At the end of your meal, you may want to sit on the rockers on the Harbor View Hotel's wraparound porch and watch the lights twinkling in the harbor.

At the Harbor View Hotel (see "Where to Stay" above), 131 N. Water St. ℰ **508/627-7000**. Reservations recommended. Main courses $18–$35. AE, MC, V. Mon–Sat 7–11am and noon–2pm; Sun 8am–2pm; daily 6–10pm; call for off-season hours. Open year-round.

Lattanzi's ★★ NORTHERN ITALIAN   Some say Al Lattanzi cooks the best veal chops on Martha's Vineyard. Lattanzi's would be the ideal place to eat in the dead of winter, by the glow of the paneled living room's handsome fireplace. Service is exceptional, and the wine list has a wide range of well-priced bottles. Back to the veal chop. You have two choices: *Piccolo Fiorentina*, which is hickory-grilled veal porterhouse chop with black peppercorns and lemon, or *Lombatina di Vitello al Porcini*, which pairs the chop with porcini-mushroom cream. If it's July, get the striped-bass special; from local waters, it's luscious. Lattanzi also owns the very good **brick-oven pizza joint** next door (ℰ **508/627-9084**).

19 Church St. (Old Post Office Sq., off Main St. in the center of town). ℰ **508/627-8854**. Reservations recommended. Main courses $22–$38. DC, DISC, MC, V. June–Sept daily 6–10pm; call for off-season hours. Open year-round.

MODERATE

Among the Flowers Cafe ★★ *Value* AMERICAN   Everything's fresh and appealing at this small outdoor cafe near the dock. Sit under the awning, and you'll just catch a glimpse of the harbor. The breakfasts are the best around, and all the crepes, waffles, and eggs are also available at lunch. The comfort-food dinners (chicken and black pepper sauté over pasta; butter-and-crumb-crusted baked haddock with a sautéed lobster-and-shallot-butter cream) are among the most affordable options in this pricey town. There's almost always a wait, not just because it's so picturesque, but because the food is homey, hearty, and kind on the wallet.

The Quintessential Lobster Dinner

When the basics—a lobster and a sunset—are what you crave, head to the **Home Port** on North Road in Menemsha (ℰ **508/645-2679**), a favorite of locals and visitors alike. At first glance, prices for the lobster dinners may seem a bit high, but note that they include an appetizer of your choice (go with the stuffed quahog), salad, amazing fresh-baked breads, a nonalcoholic beverage (remember, it's BYOB in these parts), and dessert. The decor is on the simple side, but who really cares? It's the riveting harbor views that have drawn fans to this family-friendly place for over 60 years. Locals not keen on summer crowds prefer to order their lobster dinners for pickup (less than half price) at the restaurant door, then head down to Menemsha Beach for a private sunset supper. Reservations are required. Fixed-price platters range from $25 to $45, and MasterCard and Visa are accepted. The Home Port is open mid-June to Labor Day daily at 5pm with last reservations at 9pm. It's closed mid-September to mid-May. Call for off-season hours.

Mayhew Lane. ℂ **508/627-3233.** Main courses $10–$18. AE, DC, DISC, MC, V. July–Aug daily 8am–10pm; May–June and Sept–Oct daily 8am–4pm. Closed Nov–Apr.

Chesca's ★★ (Finds) ITALIAN This modern-decor restaurant at the Colonial Inn is a solid entry, with yummy food at reasonable prices. You're sure to find favorites like paella (with roasted lobster and other choice seafood), risotto (with roasted vegetables), and ravioli (with portobello mushrooms and asparagus). Smaller appetites can fill up on homemade soup and salad.

At the Colonial Inn, 38 N. Water St. ℂ **508/627-1234.** Reservations accepted for parties with 6 or more only. Main courses $13–$32. AE, MC, V. Late June to early Sept daily 5:30–10pm; call for off-season hours. Closed Nov–Mar.

Seafood Shanty ★ (Finds) SEAFOOD This casual restaurant overlooking Edgartown Harbor features outdoor dining and cheerful service by college kids. This is a great place for lunch with a water view. Good lunch choices are the lobster roll or the cold poached salmon. For dinner, options include a classic bouillabaisse seafood stew or a prime-rib plate. There is also a children's menu. The restaurant has a convenient walk-up counter in a shack on Dock Street in front of the restaurant where virtually the entire menu is available to go.

31 Dock St., Edgartown ℂ **508/627-8622.** Reservations recommended. Lunch $9–$17; Dinner $17–$35. AE, MC, V. June–Aug daily 11:30–3pm and 5–10pm; call for off-season hours. Closed Nov–April.

INEXPENSIVE

Main Street Diner (Kids) AMERICAN It's a little kitschy-cute, what with cartoon wallpaper decorated with vintage doodads, but tony Edgartown could use a place geared to folks not out to bust the budget. Kids and adults alike will enjoy this ersatz diner, where the food, as well as the trimmings, hearken back to the 1950s. A one-egg breakfast with home fries and a buttermilk biscuit will set you back only $2; the burgers and sandwiches (including a classic open-face hot turkey with gravy, potatoes, and cranberry sauce) less than $6. Grab a grilled cheese or BLT, and wash it down with a cherry Coke.

Old Post Office Sq. (off Main St. in the center of town). ℂ **508/627-9337.** Most items under $15. AE, MC, V. Daily 7am–8pm year-round.

The Newes from America ★★ (Finds) PUB GRUB The food is better than average at this subterranean tavern, built in 1742. The decor may be more Edwardian than colonial, but those who come to quaff don't seem to care. Locals love the French onion soup. Beers are a specialty here. Try a rack of five esoteric brews, or let your choice of food—from a wood-smoked oyster "Island Poor Boy" sandwich with linguica relish to an 18-ounce porterhouse steak—dictate your draft; the menu comes handily annotated with recommendations. Don't miss their seasoned fries, accompanied by a savory Southwestern dipping sauce.

At The Kelley House, 23 Kelley St. ℂ **508/627-4397.** Main courses $7–$10. AE, MC, V. Daily 11:30am–11pm. Open year-round.

OAK BLUFFS
EXPENSIVE

Park Corner Bistro ★★★ (Finds) NEW AMERICAN This superb restaurant in the center of Oak Bluffs is an intimate and cozy bistro that has a definite European aura. With just ten tables, it's a romantic space for casual fine dining. Owner Josh Aronie and his partner chef Jesse Martin serve up creative offerings, and locals and visitors have been keeping the place packed all summer. Favorite appetizers are the beet salad and the Parmesan gnocchi, which is sautéed with chanterelle and black trumpet mushrooms. The best main courses are the Australian lamb loin with sweet corn flan and champagne corn emulsion; and the black Angus steak with arugula, Yukon Gold whipped potatoes, and Vidalia onion compote. For dessert, don't miss the warm fruit cobbler with vanilla ice cream. A jazz trio performs here several nights a week.

20H Kennebec Ave. (off Circuit Ave., across from the OB Post Office). ℂ 508/696-9922. Reservations suggested. Main courses $25–$37. AE, MC, V. July–Aug daily 9am–3pm and 6–10pm; call for off-season hours. Open year-round.

Sweet Life Cafe ★★★ FRENCH/AMERICAN Locals are crazy about this pearl of a restaurant, set in a restored Victorian house on upper Circuit Avenue and run by chef/owner Jackson Kenworth. In season, the most popular seating is outside in the gaily lit garden. Fresh island produce is featured, with seafood specials an enticing draw. The menu changes often, and everything is terrific. Expect yummy soups like vegetable white-bean pistou; and main courses like roast lamb loin with ratatouille. If the roasted lobster with potato-Parmesan risotto, roasted yellow beets, and smoked-salmon chive fondue is offered, order it. There are also always vegetarian entrees on the menu.

63 Circuit Ave. ℂ 508/696-0200. Reservations recommended. Main courses $18–$35. AE, DISC, MC, V. Mid-May to Aug daily 5:30–10pm; Apr to mid-May and Sept to Nov Thurs–Mon 5:30–9:30pm. Closed Dec to mid-May.

Tsunami ★★ *Finds* ASIAN/INTERNATIONAL For something a little different in fine dining, look for the bright red, two-story cottage on Oak Bluffs Harbor. When you climb the stairs and enter the second-floor dining room of this small restaurant, you'll feel like you've discovered something very special indeed. It's a picture-perfect view of Oak Bluffs Harbor in a spare room with Asian accents. But people also come to Tsunami for the food. There are wonderful pad Thai and tuna sashimi appetizers to start with. While the restaurant specializes in seafood, it also offers pheasant, duck, pork, and filet mignon. The chef's specialty is the seared tuna with mango mint mashed potatoes served with mixed vegetables and onion soy relish. There is also a sushi menu. The downstairs bar with its cozy sitting area has become quite a summer hangout in the evenings.

6 Circuit Ave. Extension, Oak Bluffs Harbor. ℂ 508/696-8900. Reservations accepted. Main courses $15–$29. AE, MC, V. June–Aug daily 12:30–4pm and 5:30–10:30pm; call for off-season hours. Closed mid-Oct to mid-May.

MODERATE

Lola's Southern Seafood ★ SOUTHERN This sultry New Orleans–style restaurant drips with atmosphere: crystal chandeliers; intricate wrought-iron, arched doorways; and starched linens in an ochre palette. Specialties include the chicken-and-seafood jambalaya, and the rib-eye steak spiced either "from heaven or hell." Meals are served family-style, with large helpings of side dishes. There's live entertainment nightly in season, while Sunday brunch also features live music. Off season, there's live music Friday and Saturday nights. A less-expensive pub menu is served in the bar with its mural of island personalities.

At the Island Inn, Beach Rd. ℂ 508/693-5007. www.lolassouthernseafood.com. Reservations accepted only for 5 or more. Main courses $20–$36. DC, MC, V. Sun 10am–2pm; daily 5–11pm. Open year-round.

Zapotec ★ *Value* MEXICAN/SOUTHWESTERN Look for the chile-pepper lights entwining the porch of this clapboard cottage: They're a beacon leading to tasty regional Mexican cuisine, from mussels Oaxaca (with chipotle peppers, cilantro, lime, and cream) to crab cakes Tulúm (mixed with grilled peppers and cilantro, served with dual salsas), plus the standard chicken and beef burritos. There are also tasty fish tacos, topped with a creamy yogurt dressing. A small children's menu is available. A good mole is hard to find this far north; here you can accompany it with Mexico's unbeatable beers (including several rarely spotted north of the border), refreshing sangria, or perhaps a handpicked, well-priced wine.

14 Kennebec Ave. (in the center of town). ✆ 508/693-6800. www.zapotecrestaurant.com. Reservations not accepted. Main courses $12–$20. AE, MC, V. May–Oct daily noon–3pm and 5–10pm. Closed Nov–Apr.

INEXPENSIVE

Coup de Ville ✪ SEAFOOD   Of the several open-air harborfront choices in Oak Bluffs, this one has the best service and food. This outdoor fried-seafood shack serves up tasty beer-battered shrimp, grilled swordfish, lobster salad, and "world-famous" chicken wings. Wing connoisseurs can choose from mild to suicide to three-mile island, as well as Cajun, mango, and Maryland style, among others. It's a fun place to people-watch on sunny summer days as boaters cruise around the harbor.

Dockside Market Place, Oak Bluffs Harbor. ✆ 508/693-3420. Most items $9–$20. MC, V. June–Aug daily 11am–10pm; call for off-season hours. Closed mid-Oct to Apr.

SWEETS

Hilliard's Kitch-in-Vue   Not even Candyland can match this pastel-painted cottage, where tantalizing renditions of white, milk, and dark chocolate are whipped up daily.

51 Circuit Ave. (in the center of town). ✆ 508/693-2191.

Mad Martha's ✪   Vineyarders are mad for this locally-made ice cream, which comes in two dozen enticing flavors. You could opt for a restrained mango sorbet, which isn't to say you shouldn't go for a hot-fudge sundae.

117 Circuit Ave. (in the center of town). ✆ 508/693-9151. Branches at 8 Union St., Vineyard Haven ✆ 508/693-9674; and 7 N. Water St., Edgartown ✆ 508/627-8761. Closed Oct–Apr.

Murdick's Fudge   Since 1887, the Murdick family has been serving up homemade fudge, brittle, clusters, and bark. Bring the kids and watch the candy-makers in progress.

5 Circuit Ave. and 21 N. Water St., Edgartown. ✆ 888/553-8343 or 508/627-8047. Summer Mon–Fri 10am–5pm, Sun–Sat 10am–8pm.

VINEYARD HAVEN (TISBURY)
EXPENSIVE

Black Dog Tavern ✪ NEW AMERICAN   How does a humble harbor shack come to be a national icon? Location helps. So do cool T-shirts. Soon after *Shenandoah* captain Robert Douglas decided, in 1971, that this hardworking port could use a good restaurant, influential vacationers, stuck waiting for the ferry, began to wander into this saltbox to tide themselves over with a bit of "blackout cake" or peanut-butter pie. The rest is history, as smart marketing moves extrapolated on word of mouth. The smartest of these moves was the invention of the signature "Martha's Vineyard whitefoot," a black Lab whose stalwart profile now adorns everything from baby's overalls to doggy bandannas, golf balls, and needlepoint kits. Originally the symbol signaled Vineyard ties to fellow insiders; now it merely bespeaks an acquaintance with mail-order catalogs.

Still, tourists love this rough-hewn tavern, and it's not just hype that keeps them happy. The food is home-cooking good—heavy on the seafood, of course, (including grilled swordfish with banana, basil, and lime; and bluefish with mustard-soufflé sauce)—and the blackout cake has lost none of its appeal. Though the lines grow ever longer (there can be a wait to get on the wait list!), nothing much has changed at this beloved spot. Eggs Galveston for breakfast at the Black Dog Tavern is still one of the ultimate Vineyard experiences—go early, when it first opens, and sit on the porch, where the views are perfect.

Beach St. Extension (on the harbor), Vineyard Haven. (C) **508/693-9223.** Reservations not accepted. Main courses $14–$27. AE, MC, V. June to early Sept daily 7–11am, noon–4pm, and 5–9pm; call for off-season hours. Open year-round.

Le Grenier ★★ FRENCH   If Paris is the heart of France, Lyons is its belly—and that's where chef-owner Jean Dupon grew up on his *Maman*'s hearty cuisine (she now helps out here, cooking lunch). Dupon has the Continental moves down, as evidenced by such classics as steak au poivre, calves' brains Grenobloise with beurre noir and capers, and lobster Normande flambéed with Calvados, apples, and cream. Despite the fact that Le Grenier means (and, in fact, is housed in) an attic, the restaurant is quite romantic, especially when aglow with hurricane lamps. Remember: You must BYOB here.

96 Main St. (in the center of town), Vineyard Haven. (C) **508/693-4906.** Reservations suggested. Main courses $22–$32. AE, DC, DISC, MC, V. Daily 5:30–9:30pm. Open year-round.

Zephrus at the Mansion House Inn ★★ INTERNATIONAL   This hip restaurant at the Mansion House Inn in the center of Vineyard Haven is a great place to go for casual fine-dining. Seating is at the sidewalk cafe on Main Street or inside by the hearth in view of the open kitchen. Food is creative at this high-energy venue, and portions are generous. For starters you might try the snow crab cakes or the spicy mussels. Main-course winners are pan-roasted pork tenderloin served with sweet 'tater tots; and shrimp and farfalle pasta. Though the menu is in constant flux, there is always a good vegetarian choice like the delicious vegetable risotto with truffle vinaigrette. Since the restaurant is in BYOB Vineyard Haven, you'll want to bring your favorite wine to complement this winning cuisine. The corkage fee is $5 per table.

9 Main St., Vineyard Haven (C) **508/693-3416.** www.zephrus.com. Reservations recommended. Main courses $20–$28. AE, DC, DISC, MC, V. July–Aug daily 11:30–3pm and 5:30–9pm; call for off-season hours. Open year-round.

TAKEOUT & PICNIC FARE

Black Dog Bakery ★   In need of a snack at 5am? That's when the doors to this fabled bakery open; from mid-morning on, it's elbow room only. The selection of freshly baked breads, muffins, and desserts can't be beat. Don't forget homemade doggie biscuits for your pooch.

Water St. (near the harbor), Vineyard Haven. (C) **508/693-4786.** Summer 5:30am–8pm; winter 5:30am–5pm.

CHILMARK (INCLUDING MENEMSHA) & WEST TISBURY
VERY EXPENSIVE

The Beach Plum Inn Restaurant ★★★ INTERNATIONAL   This jewel of a restaurant is located in an inn that sits on a bluff overlooking the fishing village of Menemsha. Extensive renovations and attention to quality have made this one of the island's top dining venues. Guests can dine inside in the spare, but elegant, dining room, or outside on the new tiled patio. Either way, diners enjoy sunset views of the harbor. Chef James McDonough's most popular dishes include hazelnut-encrusted halibut with Marsala wine beurre-blanc sauce; and Alaskan king salmon, grilled over Peruvian blue mashed potatoes with a morel mushroom sauce and crab-meat tambale. The most winning appetizer is the blackened lobster tips, served with mango cream sauce and house-cured gravlax with homemade wild rice and corn pancakes. For dessert, you'll flip for the chocolate quadruple-layer cake made with white and dark chocolate mousse and Chambord. In the spring and fall, there is usually an ethereal souffle on the menu, either Grand Marnier or chocolate.

At the Beach Plum Inn, 50 Beach Plum Lane (off North Rd.), Menemsha. ℂ 508/645-9454. www.beachplum inn.com. Reservations required. Main courses $32–$40, 4-course fixed-price menu $68; off-season only fixed-priced menu $50. AE, MC, V. Mid-June to early Sept daily seatings from 5:30–6:45pm and 8–9:30pm; call for off-season hours. Closed Dec–Apr.

Ice House Restaurant ★★ NEW AMERICAN   A pricey but popular up-island restaurant, the Ice House is earning raves for the creative menu. It's also a trendy venue, a place where island-insiders who wouldn't be caught dead in the down-island towns, go to see and be seen. From the outside, it looks like a modest roadhouse, but the inside is stylishly decorated with the work of island artists. The chef combines unusual ingredients with island produce, meats, and locally-caught fish. His specialty appetizer is a golden-fried tomato with a lobster salad and avocado. As a main course, look no further than the pan-roasted halibut with sweet corn and fava bean succotash. West Tisbury is a "dry" town so you must BYOB.

688 State Rd., West Tisbury. ℂ **508/645-9329.** Reservations recommended. Main courses $25–$36. AE, MC, V. July–Aug Mon–Sat 6–10pm, Sun 11am–2pm and 6–10pm; call for off-season hours. Closed Jan–March.

MODERATE

The Bite ★★ *Finds* SEAFOOD   It's usually places like The Bite that you crave when you think of New England. This is your quintessential "chowdah" and clam shack, flanked by picnic tables. Run by two sisters using their grandmother's recipes, The Bite makes superlative chowder, potato salad, fried fish, and so forth. The food comes in graduated containers, with a jumbo portion of shrimp topping out at around $26.

Basin Rd. (off North Rd., about ¼ mile northeast of the harbor), Menemsha. ℂ **508/645-9239.** Main courses $18–$30. No credit cards. July–Aug daily 11am–8pm; call for off-season hours. Closed late Sept–Apr.

TAKEOUT & PICNIC FARE

Alley's General Store *Finds*   That endangered rarity, a true New England general store, Alley's—in business since 1858—nearly foundered in the profit-mad 1980s. Luckily the Martha's Vineyard Preservation Trust interceded to give it a new lease on life, along with a much-needed structural overhaul. The stock is still the same, though: basically, everything you could possibly need, from scrub brushes to fresh-made salsa. Best of all, the no-longer-sagging front porch still supports a popular bank of benches, along with a blizzard of bulletin-board notices. For a local's-eye view of noteworthy activities and events, this is the first place to check.

State Rd. (in the center of town), West Tisbury. ℂ **508/693-0088.** Summer Mon–Sat 7am–7pm, Sun 8am–6pm; winter Mon–Sat 7am–6pm, Sun 8am–5pm.

West Tisbury Farmer's Market *Finds*   This seasonal outdoor market, open Wednesday from 2:30 to 5:30pm and Saturday from 9am to noon, is among the biggest and best in New England, and certainly the most rarefied, with local celebrities loading up on prize produce and snacking on pesto bread and other international goodies. The fun starts in June and runs for 18 Saturdays and 10 Wednesdays.

Old Agricultural Hall, West Tisbury. ℂ **508/693-3638.**

10 Martha's Vineyard After Dark

The Vineyard has an active summer social life. TV journalism and pop-culture firmament types such as Diane Sawyer, Mike Wallace, Walter Cronkite, Carly Simon, and Art Buchwald may be busy attending private dinner parties, but they are apt to join the rest of us later at a nightspot. While the number-one club on the island is the Hot Tin Roof at the airport, there are plenty of other places within walking distance in the down-island towns. Hit Oak Bluffs for the rowdiest bar scene and best nighttime street life. In Edgartown, you may have to hop around before you find the evening's most happening spot; for instance, you could happen upon an impromptu performance by Vineyard Sound, a grooving all-male a cappella group. In addition, there are interesting cultural offerings almost every night in summer, so check local papers for details.

PUBS, BARS, DANCE CLUBS & LIVE MUSIC

Atlantic Connection   Disco lives! As do karaoke and comedy, on occasion. Locals such as Spike Lee and Ted Danson seem to love the hodgepodge. The unofficial house band, Entrain, has begun to attract a wide following (both on the island and on the mainland) with their funky, reggae-laced rock. A favorite act here is the Boogies, who play '70s disco. There's entertainment nightly in season. Open June to early September 9pm to 1am; call for off-season hours and a schedule. 19 Circuit Ave. (in the center of town), Oak Bluffs. ℂ **508/693-7129.** Cover free–$25; most nights $5–$10.

David Ryans   People have been known to dance on the tables at this boisterous bar. You can hear the music blaring from Main Street. The bartender decides the canned tunes, from Sinatra to Smashing Pumpkins. There's a martini bar upstairs. Open June to September daily 11:30am to 1am; call for off-season hours. 11 N. Water St., Edgartown. ℂ **508/627-4100.** No cover.

The Lampost/Rare Duck   Young and loud are the watchwords at this pair of clubs; the larger features live bands or DJs and a dance floor, the smaller (down in the basement), acoustic acts. This is where the young folk go, and the performers could be playing blues, reggae, R&B, or '80s. Call for a schedule. Closed November to March. 111 Circuit Ave. (in the center of town), Oak Bluffs. ℂ **508/696-9352.** Cover $1–$5.

Lola's   With a new large dance floor for the over-30 set, Lola's always has a hip and fun-loving crowd. There's live music 7 nights a week from June to Labor Day. Off season, bands play on Thursday, Friday, and Saturday nights. Call for a schedule. Open year-round. At the Island Inn, Beach Rd., Oak Bluffs. ℂ **508/693-5007.** No cover.

Offshore Ale Company *Finds*   In 1602, the first barley in the New World was grown on Martha's Vineyard. A few years ago, the Vineyard's first and only brewpub opened, featuring eight locally made beers on tap ($2.75–$5). It's an attractively rustic place, with high ceilings, oak booths lining the walls, and peanut shells strewn on the floor. There's a raw bar, and late-night munchies are served till 10pm, featuring pizza and hamburgers, among other offerings. Local acoustic performers entertain 6 nights a week in season. Open June to September daily noon to midnight; call for off-season hours. 30 Kennebec Ave., Oak Bluffs. ℂ **508/693-2626.** Cover $5.

The Ritz Cafe   Locals and visitors alike flock to this down-and-dirty hole-in-the-wall that features live music every night in season and on weekends year-round. The crowd, a boozing, brawling lot, enjoy the pool tables in the back. Call for a schedule. 1 Circuit Ave. (in the center of town), Oak Bluffs. ℭ **508/693-9851**. Cover $2–$3.

LOW-KEY EVENINGS

Old Whaling Church   This magnificent 1843 Greek Revival church functions primarily as a 500-seat performing-arts center offering lectures and symposiums, films, plays, and concerts. Such Vineyard luminaries as the actress Patricia Neal have taken their place at the pulpit, not to mention Livingston Taylor and Andre Previn, whose annual gigs always sell out. It's also the Edgartown United Methodist Church, with a 9am service on Sundays. Call for a schedule. 89 Main St. (in the center of town), Edgartown. ℭ **508/627-4442**. Ticket prices vary.

THEATER & DANCE

The Vineyard Playhouse   In an intimate (112-seat) black-box theater, carved out of an 1833 church-turned-Masonic lodge, Equity professionals put on a rich season of favorites and challenging new work, followed, on summer weekends, by musical or comedic cabaret in the gallery/lounge. Children's theater selections are performed on Saturdays at 10am. Townspeople often get involved in the outdoor Shakespeare production, a 3-week run starting in mid-July at the Tashmoo Overlook Amphitheatre about 1 mile west of town, where tickets for the 5pm performances Tuesday to Sunday run only $5 to $10. MasterCard and Visa are accepted. Open June to September Tuesday to Saturday at 8pm, Sunday at 7pm; call for off-season hours. 24 Church St. (in the center of town), Vineyard Haven. ℭ **508/696-6300** or 508/693-6450. www.vineyardplayhouse.org. Tickets $15–$30.

The Yard   For over 25 years, The Yard has been presenting modern dance performances on Martha's Vineyard. The choreographer residency program here is nationally recognized, and there are classes open to the public. Open late May to late September. Performances start at 8:30pm. A Colony for the Performing Arts (off Middle Rd. near Beetlebung Corner), Chilmark. ℭ **508/645-9662**. Tickets $12 adults, $9 students.

MOVIES

The **Entertainment Cinemas** at 65 Main St. (ℭ **508/627-8008**) in Edgartown has two screens. Call ℭ **508/627-5900** or check local newspapers. There are also three vintage Art Deco movie theaters: **Capawok,** Main Street, Vineyard Haven; **Island Theater,** at the bottom of Circuit Avenue, Oak Bluffs; and **The Strand,** Oak Bluffs Avenue Extension, Oak Bluffs. Call ℭ **508/627-6689** for movie times.

ONLY ON THE VINEYARD

Gay Head Lighthouse   Though generally closed to the public, this 1856 lighthouse opens its doors on summer-weekend evenings to afford an awe-inspiring view of the sunset over the Devil's Bridge shoals. The light has been automated since 1952 (the original lens lights up the night sky in Edgartown), but the experience continues to be romantic. Tour time varies nightly. It begins an hour and a half before sunset and ends a half-hour past sunset. Open late June to late September Friday to Sunday 7 to 9pm. Off State Rd., Aquinnah. ℭ **508/645-2211**. Admission $2 adults, free for children under 12.

Trinity Park Tabernacle   Designed by architect J. W. Hoyt of Springfield, Massachusetts, and built in 1879 for just over $7,000, this open-air church, now on the National Register of Historic Places, is the largest wrought-iron-and-wood structure in America. Its conical crown is ringed with a geometric pattern of amber, carmine, and midnight-blue stained glass. Old-fashioned community sings take place Wednesday at 8pm, and concerts are scheduled irregularly on weekends. James Taylor and Bonnie Raitt have regaled the faithful here, but usually the acts are more homespun. Open July to August Wednesday at 8pm and occasional weekend evenings. Call for a schedule. Trinity Park (within the Camp Meeting Grounds), Oak Bluffs. ℂ 508/693-0525. Free admission and $20 community tours.

Index

See also Accommodations and Restaurant indexes, below.

ACCOMMODATIONS

Frommer's
Portable Guides
Complete Guides for the
Short-Term Traveler

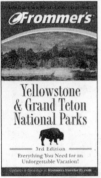

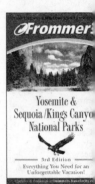

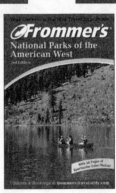

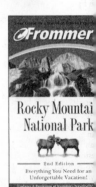

FROMMER'S® MEMORABLE WALKS

Chicago
London

New York
Paris

San Francisco

FROMMER'S® WITH KIDS GUIDES

Chicago
Las Vegas
New York City

Ottawa
San Francisco
Toronto

Vancouver
Washington, D.C.

SUZY GERSHMAN'S BORN TO SHOP GUIDES

Born to Shop: France
Born to Shop: Hong Kong,
  Shanghai & Beijing

Born to Shop: Italy
Born to Shop: London

Born to Shop: New York
Born to Shop: Paris

FROMMER'S® IRREVERENT GUIDES

Amsterdam
Boston
Chicago
Las Vegas
London

Los Angeles
Manhattan
New Orleans
Paris
Rome

San Francisco
Seattle & Portland
Vancouver
Walt Disney World®
Washington, D.C.

FROMMER'S® BEST-LOVED DRIVING TOURS

Britain
California
Florida
France

Germany
Ireland
Italy
New England

Northern Italy
Scotland
Spain
Tuscany & Umbria

HANGING OUT™ GUIDES

Hanging Out in England
Hanging Out in Europe

Hanging Out in France
Hanging Out in Ireland

Hanging Out in Italy
Hanging Out in Spain

THE UNOFFICIAL GUIDES®

Bed & Breakfasts and Country
  Inns in:
  California
  Great Lakes States
  Mid-Atlantic
  New England
  Northwest
  Rockies
  Southeast
  Southwest
Best RV & Tent Campgrounds in:
  California & the West
  Florida & the Southeast
  Great Lakes States
  Mid-Atlantic
  Northeast
  Northwest & Central Plains

Southwest & South Central
  Plains
  U.S.A.
Beyond Disney
Branson, Missouri
California with Kids
Central Italy
Chicago
Cruises
Disneyland®
Florida with Kids
Golf Vacations in the Eastern U.S.
Great Smoky & Blue Ridge Region
Inside Disney
Hawaii
Las Vegas
London
Maui

Mexio's Best Beach Resorts
Mid-Atlantic with Kids
Mini Las Vegas
Mini-Mickey
New England & New York with
  Kids
New Orleans
New York City
Paris
San Francisco
Skiing & Snowboarding in the
Southeast with Kids
Walt Disney World®
Walt Disney World® for
  Grown-ups
Walt Disney World® with Kids
Washington, D.C.
World's Best Diving Vacations

SPECIAL-INTEREST TITLES

Frommer's Adventure Guide to Australia &
  New Zealand
Frommer's Adventure Guide to Central America
Frommer's Adventure Guide to India & Pakistan
Frommer's Adventure Guide to South America
Frommer's Adventure Guide to Southeast Asia
Frommer's Adventure Guide to Southern Africa
Frommer's Britain's Best Bed & Breakfasts and
  Country Inns
Frommer's Caribbean Hideaways
Frommer's Exploring America by RV
Frommer's Fly Safe, Fly Smart

Frommer's France's Best Bed & Breakfasts and
  Country Inns
Frommer's Gay & Lesbian Europe
Frommer's Italy's Best Bed & Breakfasts and
  Country Inns
Frommer's Road Atlas Britain
Frommer's Road Atlas Europe
Frommer's Road Atlas France
The New York Times' Guide to Unforgettable
  Weekends
Places Rated Almanac
Retirement Places Rated
Rome Past & Present